PERILOUS MEMORIES

PERILOUS MEMORIES

The Asia-Pacific War(s)

EDITED BY T. FUJITANI,

GEOFFREY M. WHITE,

AND LISA YONEYAMA

Duke University Press Durham and London 2001

© 2001 Duke University Press
All rights reserved
Printed in the United States of
America on acid-free paper ∞
Typeset in Quadraat by Keystone
Typesetting, Inc.
Library of Congress Cataloging-in-
Publication Data appear on the last
printed page of this book.
This book is made possible in part
by a subvention from the Japan
Foundation.

CONTENTS

≡ Acknowledgments

Perilous Memories: The Asia-Pacific War(s) was first conceived as an international conference in 1995, the year commemorated as the fiftieth anniversary of the end of World War II. The conference was enabled by generous funding and institutional support from the Japan Foundation and the East-West Center. We would like to thank the East-West Center staff and students for their assistance throughout. At the conference, we also benefited from the attendance of four discussants, Chungmoo Choi, Susan Jeffords, Masao Miyoshi, and Shu-mei Shih, all of whom offered invaluable comments. Many of their insights were taken up and developed in the papers and in our introduction. We also would like to thank the participants of the concurrent evening symposium on Public History and War Memory, chaired by Patricia Masters with Tom Crouch, Daniel Martinez, Qinglin Shen, and Seiko Takana, all of whom added immeasurably to our discussions. We are grateful to Amy Parry for her assistance in editing Chen Yingzhen's chapter and to Andrew Morris for checking the Chinese romanization. We would like to thank artist Sam Adelbai, designer Amy Ruth Buchanan, Karen Neso, and Tina Rehaber for their work.

Chinese, Japanese, and Korean terms and proper nouns are transliterated following the pinyin, modified Hepburn, and McCune-Reischauer styles, respectively. The only exceptions are when there are other conventionally used romanizations, such as "Park Chun Hee."

Introduction

T. FUJITANI, GEOFFREY M. WHITE,

AND LISA YONEYAMA

Remembering and Dismembering the Asia-Pacific War(s)

Over the past several years we have been witnessing the massive production and reproduction of memories of the last military conflict to have been named a world war. This unmaking and remaking of war memories has taken place on a global scale, accelerating with the most recent spurt of fifty-year commemoratives: of the Rape of Nanjing, Kristallnacht, the Pearl Harbor attack, Japanese American internment, D-Day, firebombings, the liberation of Nazi death camps, the dropping of the atomic bombs, V-J Day, and the liberation of Korea and other former colonies from Japanese rule, to recall only some of the most widely reported. Not only professional historians but other agents of cultural production, both official and unofficial—government agencies, filmmakers, artists, journalists, writers, curators and custodians of museums and war memorials, and so on—have contributed to a historically unparalleled period of memory making on the subject of the Second World War.

One of the most obvious observations about this flurry of memory activities is that memory production concerning imagined collectivities is never simply about the politically disinterested recovery of a pure and undiluted past. Memories of the war do not loom up before those who remember in a natural, mechanical, or predictable fashion. There is no one-to-one correspondence between a discrete experience and a particular memory, for even experience itself might come to us through mediation.[1] Experience and memory, in other words, are always already mediated and this mediation in turn is always shaped by relations of power.

Memory work continually figures and refigures the past as a method for present purposes, particularly within contemporary social and cultural struggles. The politicized dimension of memory production is perhaps most acute when what is remembered involves violence, mass destruction, sexual atrocities, and oppression—all of which become especially salient in remembering war. Our intention in calling this book *Perilous Memories* is to highlight the dangers, that is to say the urgent and intense political stakes, involved in remembering wars even when they are considerably removed from the historical moments recalled. The range of current, unresolved issues that have provoked legal and political reexamination of war memories continues to expand, including trials and deportations of war criminals, disputes over money from Jewish families in Swiss banks, review of war medals issued to American minorities, and compensation for a wide range of victims, including those women forced into government-sponsored sexual enslavement and the survivors of Nazi death camps.

Although the works collected here do not always agree on the use of concepts such as memory, amnesia, repression, or trauma in discussing the production of knowledge about shared pasts, all focus on the predicament of historical representations of the cataclysmic events of the mid–twentieth century in the Asia-Pacific. All are concerned with pasts in which people (and governments) continue to have significant interests. In this regard, all are about the politics of remembering—about the structures of power and desire that variously sustain, erase, and transform memories of past events. Of course, given the enormous conflicts, costs, and trauma of war, it is not surprising that so much of the writing on collective memory has focused precisely on the politics and poetics of war memory, with innumerable major works in English alone on World War I, World War II, and especially the Holocaust.[2]

Memory of war, like war itself, is spawned through conflict at all levels: personal, social, national, and international. The papers presented here discuss memories related to the Asia-Pacific War that are recalcitrant and menacing, that continue to be unsettling, or that are in some cases forlorn and endangered. Some papers take up heretofore marginalized memories whose silence has been fundamental to the dominant order of historical knowledge; others try to recuperate disappearing memories that are in danger of becoming forever irretrievable. Many of the papers attempt to interject memories that unsettle and challenge established epistemological boundaries and categories. Still others introduce absent memories whose presence we sense only through their haunting images and fragments. Yet, memory deployed as an interdisciplinary method—a method, at base, of cultural and political analysis—has invited new kinds of questions regarding what we believed we fully knew about the wars fought in the Asia and Pacific region over fifty years ago, as well as about the means presently used to recall and understand them. Thus, the papers in this volume address the dual meanings of "perilous memories," both as precarious or endangered memories in need of recuperation and as memories that continue to generate a sense of danger for various peoples throughout the Asia-Pacific region.

We focus on the Asia-Pacific region not because we believe it should be privileged over any other part of the globe that became embroiled in the Second World War, but because we are interested in investigating, in some manageable way, the particularities of what is already a vast area. Whereas a comparative strategy examining European and Pacific war memory would be illuminating, it would also force a more superficial treatment of the Asia-Pacific War that, for Euro-American audiences, has remained largely overshadowed by interest in the war in Europe and the events of the Holocaust. Indeed, when asked to comment on the recent literature on "collective memory," Michael Schudson observed, "There are two kinds of studies of collective memory, those that examine the Holocaust and all the others."[3] In his monumental attempt at a "global history of World War II," Gerhard Weinberg achieves his aim by restricting his view to military planners and policymakers.[4] In the present work, we take a more limited view, focusing on the politically and culturally constituted memories that enable us to open up consideration of the multiplicity of experiences and remembrances that have often been systematically silenced by global, national, and masculinist narratives of the major warring powers.

The heterogeneity of the Asia-Pacific War(s), as well as memories of them, were and are directly related to the multiplicity of forces that have left their peculiar marks on individuals and peoples of the region. As Arif Dirlik's contribution to this volume very effectively points out, within the Asia-Pacific region different peoples remember the war through different temporalities and with various urgent political issues brought into sharpest focus. In this sense, he argues, we should consider that the Asia-Pacific War was in fact many wars, that for most people in the region who were caught up in the world war, their own local wars were of utmost significance. For most Chinese, for example, the Second World War has been above all the Anti-Japanese Resistance War, whose beginnings by no means coincided with the start of the world war as viewed from Europe or the United States and whose ending cannot be precisely dated at 1945. Such a remembering would begin at least with the September 1931 Japanese invasion of northeastern China and include Japan's establishment of the puppet state of Manchukuo in 1932, as well as the beginning of full-scale hostilities in July 1937. Indeed, some in China took the memory of the Sino-Japanese conflict back even further, commemorating 1995 less as a fifty-year milestone than as the centennial of the Sino-Japanese War of 1894–1895. This insight certainly applies to every part of the incredibly vast Asia-Pacific region, where memories of the world war are not seamless and untroubled but rather multiple, contradictory, unsettled, and unsettling. Differential positionings under imperialism, colonialism, nationalism, decolonization, neocolonialism, racism, gender discrimination and sexual brutality, class contradictions, and so on are inextricably entangled in the constitution of memory.

To be sure, our strategy of examining localized, marginalized, and often silenced memories is subject to being misunderstood. In this regard, it is worth mentioning an exchange that occurred in the planning stages of the conference. On reading our proposal, a political scientist at a major U.S. university worried that by focusing on marginalized memories we would miss the opportunity to understand the war's primary perpetrators, possibly even distracting attention from their means and motives, opening the door for endless historical revisionism. As he put it, "I'm all for the broadening of the scope but not at the cost of getting rid of the metanarratives that constituted and legitimated the major protagonists of the war . . . the latter give us a glimpse of why people of the major warring nations engaged in these activities."[5] The great preponderance of writing on the war in both Europe and the Pacific has focused precisely on the major military powers. Libraries are full of military and diplomatic histories focusing on the war's political leaders, military planners, and policymakers. Our project begins with the observation that the majority of people in the Asia-Pacific region were not "people of the major warring nations" that played commanding roles in designing or implementing the course of the war, even though they might have been deeply implicated in the war's outcome.

More important than the brute facts of the hegemony of the Allied war epic is the more subtle observation that the marginalized memories of war with which we concern ourselves do not occupy a separate or alternative space of remembrance. To the contrary, their marginality or silence is linked necessarily to the centrality, volume, visibility, and audibility of more dominant stories. And in some cases, the dominant stories obtain the force they do in popular imagination precisely because of their ability to simplify and transform troublesome or dissonant memories. Whereas our political scientist colleague worries that "the more the victims speak, the less I understand the perpetrators," we submit that the voices of victims and victimizers are necessarily intertwined. To understand how victimization can occur requires, at the least, a thorough archaeology of the cultural means through which some segments of society are disavowed and become voiceless—before, during, and after war(s).

Our project in critical remembering can be thought of as having two related dimensions. On the one hand, we have sought to denaturalize and dismember those memories that have become dominant and often officialized over the past half century or so. Along with the nationalist framework for remembering, which we will discuss in more detail in the next section, the papers interrogate the technologies by which the great global powers of the twentieth century—whether in the West or in Asia—have managed to produce a forgetfulness about themselves as imperial and colonial powers. Similarly, several authors challenge the patriarchal and racist modes of remembering that have long structured memory making. On the other hand, the papers are attentive to the exigency of recuperating those very memories that have been distorted, disavowed, or effaced by the effects of power. By not only focusing on the process whereby such memories are produced, distributed, and consumed, but by identifying what has been removed from our historical memory, they expose the dialectics between dominant historical knowledge and the subjugated and marginalized. The papers show us, in other words, that it is both important and possible to move beyond a strictly deconstructive mode, to intervene positively in the recovery and reinterpretation of events, experiences, and sentiments that have been pushed to the margins of the past.

The possibility of critical re-membering is intimately related to changes in the global and national conditions within which knowledge about the past is currently being reconstituted. The cumulative effects of the long process of decolonization that continues throughout Asia, the Pacific, and the rest of the globe further decenter the imperial powers' dominant memories and call attention to the forgetfulness produced by dominant narratives. The end of the cold war has likewise made it much less possible to imagine the earth as split neatly along a single axis formed by the incommensurability of two utopian, ideological visions. The void left by the collapse of the cold war order has in fact opened up possibilities for more diverse, localized, and contradictory narratives and memories about the past to emerge and compete in the various public spheres. In addition, transnational capitalism—contradictory in its dependency on both the continuation of imagined national boundaries and the restless dismantling of national controls of the movement of capital and workers—is no less involved in weakening national frameworks for remembering. Similarly, the effects throughout the world of feminist critiques, minority discourses, and other practices subsumed broadly under the banner of multiculturalism carry with them the potential for challenging the totalizing narratives that would posit taken-for-granted collectivities, such as nation-states, as seamless and unproblematic wholes.

Yet at the same time, these new opportunities for remembering in more diverse and critical ways are imperiled by a variety of factors. The powerful discourses of national, ethnic, and racial unity, the linear and teleological narratives of anticolonial struggles and emancipation, patriarchal and masculinist nostalgia for community and sexual ownership, and the conditions of transnational capitalism are only some of the forces that threaten to obscure and domesticate unsettling memories at the century's end.

Nationalism, Decolonization, and the Discourse of Liberation

In the memory wars that have taken place since 1945, some memories have occupied a dominant position over others. The most frequently cited written histories of the war, especially those that aim for a comprehensive view, generally achieve their breadth by limiting their temporal scope to the period 1941–1945 and by rendering their account in the framework of a binary clash between Japan and the United States and its allies. So, for example, when historian John Costello introduces his book *The Pacific War*, he states that his objective is to "span in a single narrative the century and a half of history that brought the United States, Great Britain, and the other Allied powers to the fatal collision with Japan on December 7, 1941."[6] Indeed, chapter 1 begins with President Roosevelt receiving news of the Pearl Harbor attack. The "century and a half" leading up to this event is then summarized in about seventy pages of text (of a seven-hundred-page volume) presented as context for the bombing.

In the United States the dominant mode of remembering the Asia-Pacific War(s) has been precisely as the singular war that the United States fought against the Japanese. This binary logic is neatly diagrammed in a mural of battle maps at the Punchbowl Cemetery in Honolulu (the National Memorial Cemetery of the Pacific), where the Second World War (in the singular) in this "theater" is depicted as a military struggle between two peoples, the Japanese and the Americans.[7] Arrows mark the movements of two national military forces, the Japanese and the Americans. In the mural's narrative, the war has a discrete beginning, the "Day of Infamy," and an unambiguous conclusion, namely, Japan's unconditional surrender on board the *Missouri*.[8]

This visual representation crystallizes dominant U.S. narratives of the war that construct the Pacific War as a military clash in which a uniform United States and a unified Japan were the only significant historical subjects. All other lands and peoples are simply background or, more precisely, battlefields for the clashes of the great powers. The multiple temporalities of those who peopled this region, constituted in great part by their differential experiences of waves of imperialism and colonialism, are completely effaced by the simple, celebratory, and teleological narrative that moves from the "sneak attack" on Pearl Harbor to V-J Day.

The history of the Punchbowl Cemetery illustrates this temporal dissonance well. Given the cemetery's location in a crater that was once a sacred site for native Hawaiian religious practice, the dominant narrative depicted there is literally built on top of an alternative indigenous temporality. As local proponents of Hawaiian sovereignty reexamine the history of American settlement that includes a century of massive population decline and a U.S. military–backed overthrow of the Hawaiian monarchy in 1893, the Pearl Harbor attack acquires new significance in relation to a longer history of colonization and militarization.[9] Remembering this alternative temporality connects the Japanese attack on Pearl Harbor with historical processes that led U.S. naval expeditions to survey Pearl Harbor even while Hawaiian monarchs still reigned, and ultimately to make it home to the largest naval base in the Pacific.

In other parts of the Asia-Pacific region as well, dominant narratives have tended to nationalize memories of the war. In Japan, for example, ever since the Tokyo War Crimes Trial, the most conventional mode of remembering the Asia-Pacific War has been to see it as a moment of historical aberration along the path of an otherwise successful modernization process. In this story line the Japanese people, including even the emperor, are imagined to have been a singular and uniform collectivity that was victimized by the military elite—the theory of the military's takeover of Japan from the 1930s to 1945—until they recovered their political agency in the wake of defeat. Though we would argue that there has been nowhere near the degree of managed consensus about the war that has ruled in the United States (and that, indeed, beginning with the American occupation of Japan in 1945, Japanese and American war memories have been mutually constitutive), it is nevertheless true that in postwar Japan the dominant modes of remembering have produced a national victimology, with almost the entire population, including the emperor, equally figured as victims of military misdeeds.

Yet this nationalization process is neither consistent nor always normative. In China, as Daqing Yang's paper in this volume points out, memories of the Nanjing Massacre have only at different historical moments come to the surface as a national experience. And Christine Choy and Nancy Tong's remarkable documentary *In the Name of the Emperor* also suggests that the Nanjing Massacre need not necessarily be recollected as a uniform experience for the people of Nanjing, let alone China. Many of the city's wealthy had the means to flee, while the poorer received the brunt of Japanese brutality. Undoubtedly, the nation-state has dominated narratives about modern politics; as a result, the relevance and importance of national rememberings cannot be overemphasized. In fact, it is precisely because of the widespread dominance of nationalist paradigms of remembrance that we wish to chart in this volume some of the means through which national modes of representation succeed in systematically marginalizing or silencing dissonant memories.

Critiquing nationalist discourse is a tricky task when dealing with situations where the national voice seemingly provides the only means through which people marginalized in the global order can make themselves visible and heard collectively. But feminist scholarship has warned that even in such contexts there are great dangers in uncritically accepting the masculinized premises of nationalism. During our conference, Hyun-Sook Kim shared her observations of the ways in which the patriarchal ideology of South Korean nationalism has long prohibited the history of the former "comfort women" from becoming widely known. Patriarchally constituted nationalist discourse, with its presumptions about "proper" sexuality and gender roles, has tended to register the violation of Korean women's bodies as a site of national "shame," in which men were unable to protect "their" women. Moreover, this discourse assumes that women must remain chaste, loyal to their men, and reproductively active.[10] Chungmoo Choi's essay in this volume takes these feminist critiques further and argues that the language of masculinist nationalism and anticolonial discourse, far from assisting in the healing process, has instead deepened the wounds of these victims of unspeakable sexual violence. Choi furthermore encourages us to explore beyond gendered nationalist discourse for diverse representational and linguistic forms that might allow these women to speak the unspeakable and, in so doing, restore their subjectivity and dignity.[11]

National memories of war are neither static nor bounded but are connected in complex ways with transnational and global forces of all kinds. In many regions, war anniversaries and ceremonies are typically organized and conducted in conjunction with former colonial powers such as Australia, Britain, and the United States. The fact that such practices usually omit any participation by Japan has resulted in a ghostly disparity—noted by Anthony Reid for Indonesia and Diana Wong (in this volume) for Singapore and Malaysia—between the decisive historical impact of the period of Japanese occupation and its absence in public memory.[12] Reconstructed alliances between the citizens of postcolonial states and former colonizing powers have worked, in the postwar era, both to homogenize the citizenry of individual postcolonial states as a single actor in narratives of global war and to overwrite stories of colonial resistance or cooperation with the Japanese. Dissonant memories such as Indian recollections of the independence leader Chandra Bose, who allied himself with Germany and Japan to lead three divisions of Indian troops against the British in Southeast Asia, have emerged, problematically, only decades after the war as a focus for national acts of public remembrance.

Each of the cases taken up in this volume demonstrates that the processes that nationalize war memories entail dialogic tensions among multiple, often competing voices within and across national boundaries. As Lisa Yoneyama's paper on the Smithsonian Enola Gay controversy and Geoffrey White's paper on the Pearl Harbor films reveal, even the most patriotic efforts by U.S. veterans to repudiate alien elements and to produce a pristine collective memory of the nation's heroic past cannot be accomplished without citing (and warping) struggles over historical memories found elsewhere in the world. Furthermore, almost any significant axis of interpellation and identification—such as nationality, gender, class, sexuality, or race—provides a critical matrix along which the forms of remembering and forgetting become unevenly differentiated. A particularly common theme in national histories of war is the relation between national and ethnic identifications, with national narratives often subsuming or subordinating existing conflicts. At the same time, minority discourses of remembrance may themselves take a variety of forms, from those that contest nationalism to the identitarian and hyperpatriotic, as discussed by George Lipsitz and T. Fujitani in their essays on memory in the United States.

When dominant national histories of war transform and submerge more localized memories, they often do so specifically through narratives of unity across ethnic lines. For example, the most widely circulated representations of Pearl Harbor, such as the War Department film *December 7th*, give prominent attention to the multiple ethnic identities of citizen soldiers and sailors who are remembered as having sacrificed their lives for the nation (not surprisingly, omitting reference to the internment of Japanese Americans).[13] Of course, in a national arena where ethnic equality is not a policy goal—as in Fiji, where an indigenous regime put in power by three military coups has disenfranchised Fiji's Indian population—the fact of differential war service may be a factor in rationalizing subordinate citizenship rights.[14]

Throughout most of Asia and the Pacific, nationalized memories of the war are intricately enmeshed in narratives of decolonization and liberation. Histories of the Asia-Pacific War(s) are also histories of colonization, decolonization, and nation formation, and they have served to construct newly imagined national identities, usually with the promise of liberation from past oppression and domination. By the end of the nineteenth century, the entire Pacific Island region (one third of the surface of the earth) had been carved up by Western colonial powers. Only the tiny island kingdom of Tonga retained an indigenous polity. The written history of the island region is largely a history of political conflict and negotiation among the European powers of Britain, France, and Germany and the United States. With the defeat of Germany in World War I, Japan entered the realm of Pacific empire building by taking control of Germany's possessions in Micronesia. These possessions stretched all the way from Saipan to the Marshall Islands, with the exception of Guam, which remained under U.S. administration.

Whereas World War I unsettled colonial arrangements by redistributing the colonial possessions of Germany, it did not disturb the colonial order itself. In contrast, the war years of 1941–1945 typically mark the beginning of the end of the colonial order that took shape during the nineteenth century. For most places in the Pacific, the disruptive effects of invasion and counterinvasion irreversibly subverted complacent relations of subordination between European or Japanese regimes and native populations. Once large numbers of people had witnessed the collapse and evacuation of colonial governments or, in some cases, served in or alongside American, Australian, or Japanese military organizations, the existing configurations of power could no longer be maintained or reinstated.[15]

In the Pacific Islands, war narratives emphasizing the participation of Islanders in Allied military and labor units work to transform images of Islanders from colonized natives to competent citizens of newly formed nation-states. Lamont Lindstrom (in this volume) finds evidence for this renarrativization of identity in war photos and captions depicting local contributions to the war effort.[16] As the process of decolonization in Asia and the Pacific moved forward after the war, new nations and national elites began fashioning images of emergent national identities according to global discourses of modernization and development. In previously isolated areas that were built up as staging points during military campaigns, the sudden expansion of economic infrastructure that came with newly constructed military bases fueled postwar visions of modernity. Especially for rural communities on the colonial fringe, roads, airfields, wharfs, and buildings built by foreign military powers still today iconically link war memory with present-day ambitions for economic development.

The war brought a confusing array of new possibilities for imagining cultural identities and political futures. The rapid and often violent displacement of one external power by another created extended periods of uncertainty in which the identity of local populations as colonial subjects was rendered meaningless in some areas and more intense and dangerous in others. In Papua New Guinea, scores were summarily tried and executed by both sides for cooperation with the enemy.[17]

The new forms of political imagination fostered by wartime uncertainties were in most cases quickly domesticated as the war ended and colonial regimes reestablished themselves. In many former colonies, narratives of native loyalty and bravery have been featured prominently in books, exhibits, and memorials and on ceremonial occasions, serving to authenticate military histories of liberation and to silence other, dissonant stories that tell of struggle against colonial regimes during and after the war—stories that do not align easily with the binary epic of Japan versus America.

In some places, local populations split according to prewar divisions and then faced each other across Allied-Japanese battle lines. In areas where people could avoid being pressed into labor or military service, communities often tried to avoid the occupying forces and adopt a wait-and-see attitude (unless acts of brutality compelled a choice). Just what "loyalty" meant in the liminal political situation of the war is unclear, with many communities rendering aid to both sides when needed. Many Pacific Islanders who encountered Americans came to view them more as liberators from British rule than from Japanese occupation. In the Solomon Islands, a major anticolonial movement spread rapidly after the war, led by men whose desire for independence had been fueled by their experience on American bases between 1942 and 1945.[18] Yet these sentiments are almost entirely absent from public representations of war in books, films, and memorial practices. Just as wartime propaganda lauded the bravery of native soldiers and laborers, postwar memory making has constructed images of the loyal native as a model for colonial and national subjectivity. Despite the importance of the anticolonial struggle and its wartime roots for Solomon Islands national history, official ceremonies marking the fiftieth anniversary of the war there made no reference to it, focusing only on the American-Japanese conflict and the supporting role played by native scouts.[19]

In the islands of Micronesia, the Asia-Pacific War(s) mark one more in a long series of colonial transitions that have included Spain, Germany, Japan, and the United States.[20] With the exception of Guam, which the United States obtained in 1898 at the same time it took control of Hawai'i and the Philippines, the Micronesian islands of the north Pacific came under Japanese control following World War I. As Japan began to militarize these islands during the 1930s, Micronesians were taught Japanese language and culture, signifying their inclusion in the outer circles of the Japanese empire.[21] Lingering evidence of that historical moment may be heard in the voices of war-generation Micronesians who speak Japanese, recall popular Japanese songs from the 1930s and, in some cases, make representations to the Japanese government for compensation as former imperial subjects.[22]

Despite the inevitable dissonance experienced by people forced to adapt to successive colonial regimes, narratives of liberation telling of American forces driving Japan from their militarized strongholds in the region have given collective memories of war in Micronesia remarkable coherence. As discussed by Vicente Diaz for Guam, the liberation trope is especially pronounced there because of the particularly harsh occupation that was imposed due to Guam's prewar American identity. However, as they did in the Marshall Islands and elsewhere in Micronesia, when the Americans returned to liberate Guam, they stayed. The annual celebration of Liberation Day in Guam not only honors and recalls the events of 1944; it does so by mobilizing an impressive array of military equipment, personnel, and ceremonial regalia that powerfully index the continuing presence of the U.S. military, owner of about one-third of the island's land base. As is the case for many memorial and anniversary events throughout the region, Guam's annual Liberation Day has been a public reminder of the strategic interests that underlie today's political relations. Guam's bases, for example, were active staging points during the Vietnam War and, as recently as September 1996, provided the takeoff point for U.S. bombers attacking Iraq following attacks on its Kurdish population. For some, "liberation" has come to signify occupation by yet another power that prioritizes its global ambitions over local interests.

On the eastern edge of Micronesia, the Marshall Islands present another history of remilitarization in the cold war context. The scene of fierce battles between U.S. and Japanese forces in 1944, the Marshall Islands became the site of America's nuclear testing in the 1950s, and Kwajalein atoll was developed as a missile-tracking facility and test range. In the eyes of the people of Enewetak, "The war that began in 1939 has never ended; it has only moved from place to place."[23] Located in the remote central area of the Pacific, the Marshall Islands have witnessed some of the most awesome weaponry of the twentieth century and have borne the consequences in the form of environmental hazards, dislocation, medical problems, and long court battles. In Bikini atoll, where the legacy of nuclear fallout settled on the coral surface has an unforgiving "memory" of about ten thousand years, individuals hoping to regain a remembered lifeway prior to evacuation struggle for ways to engineer a $200 million cleanup with only about half those funds received through compensation payments.

The cunning with which new oppressions or occupations came in the name of liberation can also be seen through the memory wars that have taken place in what were Japan's older colonial possessions. In these places, dominant memories of Japanese colonialism, the war, and the immediate postwar years have competed with popular memories that threaten to disrupt postwar regimes. In Okinawa, for example, the U.S. military presented itself not only as the conquering military force, but as the new defender of freedom and democracy for Okinawa and Japan, and indeed, for the entire world. As emphasized throughout the Occupation and formalized in the San Francisco Peace Treaty and the U.S.-Japan Security Treaty (both going into effect in 1952), the United States liberated Okinawa and the rest of Japan from Japanese military rule while derogating to itself the sole prerogative of maintaining a military presence. As General Douglas MacArthur, Supreme Commander for the Allied Powers, stated in no uncertain terms in 1946, the Japanese would welcome the military to Okinawa because the nation had been demilitarized and had no other means to defend its security.[24]

Yet, as became widely known through media reports on the September 1995 rape of a twelve-year-old schoolgirl by three U.S. servicemen, the Okinawan people have paid dearly for their supposed freedom and for Japan's apparent security. Not only did Okinawa remain under de facto U.S. rule until 1972 in an agreement entered into by the Japanese government (in other words, by the defeated colonial power) and the United States, it remains Japan's poorest prefecture even as it bears the disproportionate weight of Japan's U.S. military presence. During the cold war years, through inducements, physical coercion, and often at gunpoint, the U.S. military took Okinawan farmers off their land and built bases and runways. Furthermore, reversion to Japanese sovereignty in 1972, yet another "liberation," this time from U.S. rule, did not relieve Okinawans of their burdens. Today the overwhelming brunt of the U.S. military presence in Japan is felt by the people of Okinawa, where over twenty-nine thousand U.S. troops and their more than twenty-two thousand dependents are based. U.S. bases occupy some 20 percent of Okinawa Island and almost 11 percent of Okinawa Prefecture; 75 percent of all U.S. military facilities are located in Okinawa Prefecture, which is only 1 percent of Japan's total land area. Moreover, the recent rape case is only the most outrageous recent incident in a long history of U.S. physical and sexual violence against local residents.[25]

It should be noted that sexual assaults against local women by U.S. military personnel are not random and isolated incidents. Rather, they are direct outcomes of the political, economic, military, and sexual complex that has long enabled and sustained U.S. hegemony within the Pacific and Asia region.[26] In this complex, the dominant culture of U.S. militarized masculinity requires and underwrites a desire to dominate, possess, and destroy the "feminine"—in other words, precisely those elements that are subordinated and repudiated in constituting soldierly subjects.[27] Given the United States' political and economic dominance in the region, military personnel stationed there perceive the local population as a subordinated people; local women, signifying both the subordinated and the repudiated in the ideology of U.S. military masculinity, become the logical targets toward which soldiers invest their desires for destruction and domination. This militarized male sexuality, moreover, is assumed to be uncontrollable and not to be excessively punished. Immediately after the 1995 rape incident, Admiral John Macke was forced to resign for a controversial public statement in which he remarked, "For the money [the perpetrators] rented the van, they could have had a girl."

Thus, for many engaged in oppositional memory work in Okinawa—such as one of our contributors, the historian and activist Ishihara Masaie—the re-cuperation of popular memories about the Asia-Pacific War(s) has been coupled with a critique of the official memory making and forgetfulness that were engineered through a collaboration of cold war conservatives in both the United States and Japan. As Ishihara's essay makes clear, oppositional memory work in Okinawa is thus directed not only against Japanese imperialism and the sacrifices that Okinawans made in the name of the emperor and empire, but also against postwar U.S. imperialism that has used Okinawa for many of its military operations. Memory work in this context thus challenges the simple imperialist/nonimperialist dichotomy that would position Japan as the former imperial and colonial power and the United States as the liberator of East Asia.

In Taiwan, memories of the Asia-Pacific War(s)' ending and liberation from Japanese colonial rule collide with memories of different events. For many, including one of our contributors, Chen Yingzhen, who spent many years in prison for criticizing the Guomindang (GMD) government, liberation from Japanese rule brought with it oppression by another antidemocratic regime. In Chen's paper, these and other contradictions emerge through the life histories of several Taiwanese men who served in the Japanese imperial military forces. Through them we are given a vivid sense of the tragic ways in which former colonial subjects in Taiwan were caught up in and victimized by the postlibera-tion struggles and collaborations among the leaders of China, Japan, the United States, and the GMD government. No postwar power had a vested interest in reviving the memories of these men, who in 1945 suddenly found themselves positioned as members of both a liberated people and the defeated Japanese Imperial Army.

In the Taiwanese context, the most salient postwar event that has served to anchor a countermemory against the narrative of liberation from Japanese rule has been the February 28 Incident. This incident, an uprising that was followed by ruthless suppression and violence, was the culmination of a mass movement against the corrupt and repressive GMD regime. Death estimates vary widely, but thousands and perhaps tens of thousands of protesters and sympathizers were hunted down and massacred, setting the stage for a long reign of terror led by Jiang Jieshi's son Jiang Jingguo.[28] Thus, for many in Taiwan, the fifty-year anniversary that is at least as worthy of recognition as that which occurred in 1995 is that which took place in February 1997. For them, the date memorializes yet another stage in the succession of colonialisms in Taiwan, a history that, depending on one's politics, might be taken back to the Dutch conquest in the seventeenth century, the Chinese settlement (1661–1895), Japanese Occupation, or the establishment of the U.S.-backed Nationalist regime. In this connection, it might also be noted that the position of subalterneity and the particular colonialism remembered in the case of Taiwan is especially complicated in that there is not only a divide between the Nationalist "mainlanders" and Taiwanese, but also among different "aboriginal" and "native" Taiwanese peoples of various ethnicities. Chen concludes that in addition to catalyzing resistance to the postwar Taiwanese governments, oppositional memories in Taiwan have also lent themselves to a critique of Japanese and U.S. imperialism.

Similar contradictions between the discourse of liberation and the realities of new oppressions can be traced in the lives of Japan's former Korean colonial subjects. The approximately two million Japanese subjects from Korea who were residing in Japan shortly after the war were suddenly denationalized (that is, they were summarily deprived of their status as Japanese nationals), regardless of whether they wished to remain in Japan or not. For those hundreds of thousands who chose to or had no choice but to remain in Japan, liberation from Japanese colonial rule resulted in a new but familiar disprivileged status whereby they were required to either disavow all signs of their ethnic and cultural difference in order to naturalize, or to face discrimination in employment and everyday living simply by virtue of their being Koreans unwilling to comply with the extreme demands of the "administrative guidance" that has customarily been given to those who wish to acquire citizenship.[29]

As Utsumi Aiko points out in her essay, Korean soldiers in the Japanese Imperial Army, like their Taiwanese counterparts, were treated as nonnationals and hence became ineligible for benefits given to Japanese military personnel. Yet at the same time, many Koreans and Taiwanese faced charges as members of the Japanese wartime military, and some were executed for their crimes. For them, colonial liberation was the precursor to their death as subjects of the Japanese empire.[30]

For the people of Japan's former colony, it has been argued, "liberation" was a false promise that soon after the war resulted in partition and subordination to the postwar superpowers. As Bruce Cumings boldly argued in his pioneering *Origins of the Korean War*, liberation from Japanese rule was a prelude to U.S. domination in South Korea.[31] Therefore, as Chungmoo Choi, one of our contributors, once described the situation, Korea's postcoloniality was deferred. And in such products of popular culture as *madang guk* (people's theater), it is possible to see an attempt to recuperate dangerous memories out of the past— for example, concerning the United States' role in partition and complicity in the Kwanju Massacre—that might dislodge the dominance of the image of the United States as Korea's Liberator.[32]

Throughout the Asia-Pacific region, then, nationalism, decolonization, and discourses of liberation have been inextricably intertwined, and one of our central tasks throughout this volume is to demonstrate, with some degree of detail and concreteness, the particular interests involved in remembering the Asia-Pacific War(s) and their aftermaths. More often than not, what has been called decolonization or postcoloniality has meant the inauguration of new or the continuation of familiar relationships of subordination, whether among nations or between dominant and subaltern groups within nations. Perhaps it goes without saying that we make no claims to be comprehensive; there are admittedly huge gaps in our narratives and an infinite number of other stories that need to be told. We offer simply a beginning and a way of conceptualizing the politics of memory in the Asia-Pacific region.

Memory as Method

The problem of memory allows us to acknowledge that the past is not a stable object that exists divorced from our own time and location, waiting to be interpreted. Our knowledge about the past is always already mediated through narratives such as historical writings, memoirs, and textbooks, through dreams, through images on film, photographs, and paintings, through material objects such as memorial icons, and through ritual practices such as commemorative ceremonies and memorial services. Sometimes memory is negotiated through its very absence. As Maurice Halbwachs argued in *Social Frameworks of Memory* more than a half century ago, institutions such as families, local communities, academic institutions, and nation-states are the contexts within which we make sense of the past.[33] During the past decade, we have seen an increasing number of works that foreground practices of remembering and forgetting in analyzing social, cultural, and political issues. This volume reflects a number of disciplinary perspectives on problems of memory, particularly those prevalent in history, anthropology, literature, and communication studies. Unlike more individual or psychological approaches, however, the works included here grapple with memory as social, public, and collective. In this respect, these studies are motivated by a common theoretical interest in the strategic role of representational practices in making collective remembering possible, especially the institutionalized means of language, texts, film, and popular cultural media that underwrite the formation and reformation of sociopolitical realities.

The concept of "collective memory" has raised the conventional binaries of individual/collective, private/public, and past/present for some time. The long history in intellectual thought of dichotomizing the individual and society has impoverished our ability to theorize spaces of mediation in which knowledge of the past emerges in communicative practice and interaction.[34] The current spate of work on collective memory signals interdisciplinary and even postdisciplinary interest in such spaces. The broadening of "memory" as a key word in methodologies used to investigate representations of the past is both useful and problematic: useful in facilitating interdisciplinary discussion, and problematic in generating multiple and at times conflicting uses of terminology. In this thicket of choices, we do not attempt to impose a single orthodoxy. Instead, these essays articulate and exploit different styles of interpretation and analysis, including tensions between academic discourses and political critique.

Historians have pursued the problematic of collective memory through an interest in histories of collective remembering, especially the commemorative practices favored by national tradition as a means of ritually constructing images of community rooted in the past.[35] Contemporary historians increasingly find that histories of nations are also histories of nations engaged in acts of remembering (and forgetting)—a mapping of the ways nations think about themselves through time. A number of major works have appeared that pursue this tack in analyzing histories of nationalism in particular states. Perhaps the most extensive is the recently translated work of Pierre Nora and his associates, prompted initially by an interest in official commemorations of the French Revolution as they worked to reproduce a coherent and nostalgic vision of French nationalism.[36] We would also mention Fujitani's work on Japanese national ceremony, and Michael Kammen's and John Bodnar's histories of American patriotism, plotted through its changing institutions of myth production.[37]

The historical turn toward practices of remembrance, commemoration, and myth making pushes what is customarily seen as the historian's concern with events into the anthropologist's arena of culture.[38] At the same time as historians edge toward culture, anthropologists increasingly historicize their work to rescue it from essentializing conceptions of culture as timeless and bounded tradition. And, as once localized studies now range over more complex sites of national and transnational cultural production, earlier approaches to "collective memory" in the form of mythology, religion, and ritual are being applied to issues of national memory and historical consciousness.[39]

As the past becomes valorized as a locus for imagining and feeling national identity, history is often transmuted into tradition, a set of apparently timeless symbols and ritual acts that function as markers of shared (national) identity. As the past becomes an object of veneration, to be reawakened in moments of memorialization, it more easily takes on the properties of shared essence, to be guarded and reproduced as sacred memory. This we take to be one of the key insights of the literature on the "invention of tradition," a literature that has spawned innumerable studies of contemporary constructions of tradition as objectified political symbol. Here the authenticating power of remembered tradition and history has a double edge, a cultural means for propagating hegemonic powers of the state and/or dominant groups on the one hand, and a strategic device for recuperating the voice of marginalized groups on the other. The duality here poses both ethical and political dilemmas for the analyst concerned to anticipate the consequences of reanalyzing or recontextualizing the historical discourse of others.

"I was not there, and yet I was there." During our conference, Vicente Diaz described his relationship to Chamorro memories of war atrocities in this manner. As a child, Diaz often dreamt about the nightmarish past as if the trauma were his own. Acts of remembering link the rememberer, his dreams, and the past experience of Chamorro people. Despite his absence during the original historical moment, his memory mediates his own subjectivity and the ghastly incident survived by the community. Such acts of personal insight and social recuperation add a wider social dimension to the psychoanalytic notion of "dream work." Dreamlike remembering constitutes Diaz's "experience" of the past. Though in a different context, Marita Sturken's discussion in this volume of Tajiri's film *History and Memory* also eloquently demonstrates the dialectical interplay that links acts of memory, past experience, and official history. In the realm Sturken calls "cultural memory," we find an extremely fluid movement among personal remembering (and amnesia) and collective memory and history, also mediated, in this case, by recuperative efforts to narrativize inchoate images. Not only is memory constituted through various mediations, but it enables social and cultural practices of representation.

If, as Joan Scott has warned, the term "experience" has come to form a foundationalist concept, and if the word "history" connotes a fully narrativized, developmental story with a given closure and unity, "memory" intimates a fragmentary, less self-evident, repressed dimension of knowledge about the past. Utsumi Aiko's essay in this volume discusses the absence of memory in postwar Japan about the Korean and other colonial soldiers who were drafted into the Japanese military prior to 1945. Her shocking realization of the total lack of such a memory is what compelled her to excavate information about these Korean men.

During the conference, Ishihara Masaie shared a similar anecdote illustrating the often precarious nature of memory. Growing up in Okinawa, he had been constantly exposed in his everyday interactions to the sight of people bearing deep physical scars on their bodies. Yet the pervasive silence in postwar Okinawa about the horrors of the war prevented Ishihara and others from making any meaningful association between what they saw and the Battle of Okinawa. It was this gap between the common sight of scars etched onto survivors' bodies and positive historical knowledge, or more precisely, the lack thereof, that drove Ishihara and others in their decades-long efforts to fill the memory void. His essay demonstrates that one way to achieve this is through intense interactions between researchers and survivors, and through the reconstruction of memory into a meticulously personalized narrative form.

These are instances of unsettling memories that find troubled expression in the institutionalized forms of representation of a particular historical moment. Here we see the critical role of narrative and other representational forms in the interplay of the personal and the public, constituting a dialectic that always underlies transactions in collective memory. As recent research on posttraumatic disorders, multiple personality conditions, and so forth is showing, disruptions and dislocations of memory are inevitably linked to disturbances in the moral and political conditions for remembering as a social act.[40]

One of the profound developments in the production of collective memories, especially in remembering wars of the twentieth century, is the emergence of new and more powerful means of representation that project words and images to wider and more diverse audiences. In this volume, we can only touch on the implications of these developments, but we wish to underscore their significance for our interest in historical shifts in modes of memory making through time. In particular, the availability and use of specific technologies of representation may have diverse, even contradictory implications for imperiled local memories of war. On the one hand, access to new technologies of video, television, and the Internet makes possible global circulation of information in ways that enable the formation of new and sympathetic publics. Anyone interested in information on the Nanjing Massacre may, for example, access one or more Web sites for photographic and documentary information on the history of that event. On the other hand, processes of economic globalization also facilitate the reproduction of dominant national discourses, thus further crowding out marginal or dissonant memories.

For the postwar generation(s), especially Americans, World War II is known largely through popular books, magazines, and Hollywood films, if it is known at all.[41] Just as cultural historians of the Vietnam War have noted the critical role of television in the formation of American conceptions of that war, so have these popular cultural media shaped much of America's understanding of World War II as "the good war." Whereas the U.S. War Department and the Japanese bureaucracy carefully managed representation of wartime events during the war itself, much of the managed imagery produced then has since entered ordinary circles of cultural production.[42] The forces of economic globalization then carry these popular forms worldwide. And because it is the culture industries of the major industrial powers that dominate the shape and direction of these cultural flows, their constructions of the war are increasingly influential across national boundaries. Add to this the direct influence of official government agencies, such as the U.S. Department of Defense World War II 50th

Anniversary Committee, in orchestrating memorial events in all the major theaters of combat, and it is apparent that the structures of economic and political influence of today exert systematic influence on public acts of collective remembering.

Of course, differential access to means of representation and its consequences for the shape of public memory is not a new phenomenon. The same economic and material disparities that separated colonizers from colonized have also determined whose histories circulate most widely—through technologies of print, radio, film, and other means. Indeed, in the Pacific Islands, where only a small proportion of the population is literate, very few indigenous authors have contributed to the voluminous archives and libraries on the Pacific War. The cultural force of any given technology is further amplified through institutions such as schools, libraries, museums, and government offices that in fact use them to reproduce histories of war according to the constraints and expectations of established publics. Institutions such as these are precisely organized to make efficient use of technologies of representation for purposes of storing and reproducing cultural memory. Not only do such institutions have resources to devote to the production of histories in multiple media, but the sheer fact of presentation in such spaces heightens their perceived truth value. The conflict that erupted at the Smithsonian Air and Space Museum over its planned fiftieth-anniversary exhibit on the atomic bombings reveals the degree of political force that may be mobilized to police representations in institutions defined as guardians of national heritage.[43]

This approach to the past does not mean that all attempts to recover what are deemed to be original experiences should always be rejected out of hand. To do so in a consistent and a priori fashion would be to totally disregard the implications of doing so in diverse and complex local situations. It could also lead to the facile denial of the truthfulness of victims' claims for recompense. In fact, several essays in this volume engage in precisely this mode of recuperative memory work, and they question the view that knowledge of the past is simply constructed. They reflect on the ways in which certain cultural practices are empowered by the assumption that the community's historical experiences, personal trajectories, traditions, and so forth can somehow be reliably recovered and shared. Furthermore, it should not be thought that we disavow the notion of facticity altogether, as some detractors of critical discourse studies often seem eager to claim of writers in this field. Instead, we are interested in exploring the processes through which past events acquire truthfulness and power by virtue of being represented, shared, debated, suppressed, and negotiated. By conceiving of memory in this way, we begin to see the complex and fluid relationships between what are identified as facts and their meanings, between historical knowledge and the structures of power and desire within which they are enmeshed.

Memory in Peril

Walter Benjamin once wrote, "The tradition of the oppressed teaches us that the 'state of emergency' in which we live is not the exception but the rule."[44] This piece of Benjaminian wisdom warns us that there is a risk involved in constituting the Second World War as our object of investigation. Focusing on a conspicuous, explosive, and temporally bounded moment of violence in history—understanding it as an extra-ordinary crisis—may inadvertently obscure the less immediately evident yet equally insidious acts of violence and brutality that occur constantly in the everyday lives of people throughout the world. The contributors to this volume deal with a wide range of ongoing issues that demonstrate how structures of violence associated with the war(s) have been reproduced through postwar political arrangements as well as by the discursive conditions of knowledge. These issues include the structural dependency of the Asia-Pacific nations generated by the cold war policies of the United States and Japan, the lingering effects of nuclear testing and the continuing threats posed by nuclear arsenals, the patriarchal complicity among national leaders in the postwar years that silenced the claims of women sexually enslaved by the Japanese military and government, the seemingly unending cases of military sexual assault against women in Okinawa, and the inability of survivors of Hiroshima and Nagasaki now living in Korea to receive substantial relief. Our task of critically remembering the Asia-Pacific War(s) is in large part to remind ourselves that the "state of emergency" did not conclude with the cease-fire or with formal decolonization. Instead, it has persisted into the present, even as most people of the dominant powers imagine that the world was made safe by the war's ending.

The "state of emergency" also continues for those who demand respect for diversity and pluralism. If a particular way of remembering became dominant through the homogenization and naturalization of knowledge about the past, examinations of diverse, localized, and situated memories may constitute "critical" memories that challenge and unsettle historical common sense. A number of papers presented in this volume aim to resuscitate the contradictory memories that cannot be entirely subsumed under the overarching narrative of any single collectivity. Yet critical narratives, memories, and discourses of the local and diverse, we need to be reminded, are in constant jeopardy. Stories recuperated about the past are ceaselessly appropriated by transnational corporatism, tourism, multicultural nationalism, and many other forces, ultimately domesticating their unsettling qualities and endorsing only the ideas of pluralism that produce an illusion of harmonious diversity.[45] Transnational capitalism not only licenses a diversity of memories that cannot be readily subsumed into national narratives, it also threatens to replace them with a newly strengthened and unidimensional regime of temporality that has as its single telos the victory of capitalism. For example, the emergence of Japan as a major investor, aid donor, and trade partner throughout the Asia-Pacific region has begun to unsettle anti-Japanese war memories. The rise of Japanese tourism and investment in Guam, Palau, and other parts of Micronesia is transforming oppositional narratives that have generally contrasted harsh Japanese occupiers with kind and generous American liberators.[46] In Hawai'i, criticisms of representations of the Pearl Harbor attack during the fiftieth anniversary in 1991 stemmed in part from American veterans' suspicions that government and business interests were revising history so as not to offend Japanese tourists and investors.[47] Similar effects of economic globalization on national memories of war have been noted for the development of war sites in Vietnam, to be marketed primarily to returning American servicemen.

In a quite different manner, the culture of late capitalism, as Morio Watanabe's fascinating contribution warns, threatens to transport memory fragments through time and space to create simulated realities that efface the weightiness of Japanese atrocities and postwar responsibilities. No fewer than 150 "what if" novels, he notes, have rewritten the Second World War and pervade contemporary Japanese popular culture, creating hyperrealities that are in some important ways, to use Jean Baudrillard's well-known phrase, "more real than the real itself." Hyperrealities, Watanabe cautions, have more than entertainment value, for their effects cannot be separated from such phenomena as the Aum Shinrikyō cult and its 1995 sarin gas attack. If the cold war's collapse has been in part responsible for enabling the recuperation of long-suppressed critical memories, it does not dictate the means or purpose of such re-membering, which can take a variety of forms, including simulated fantasies that function more to displace moral responsibility than to recover it.

Critical memories are also constantly imperiled by the reactionary responses of conservative political forces, especially those seeking to preserve various kinds of nationalist nostalgia. For example, despite the Japanese government's pro forma apologies for its past aggression and invasions,[48] there is seemingly no end to the pronouncements of prominent, old guard politicians within the Liberal Democratic Party who would deny the truthfulness of war atrocities. As Daqing Yang's contribution shows, there is a long history of such denials in Japan. Typically, in September 1996 former speaker of the Lower House Yoshio Sakurauchi stated publicly his doubts that the Nanjing Massacre had even occurred. Apparently believing that his memories of hearsay were sufficient evidence, he recalled, "I was fighting in China and was in a hospital in Nanjing [at the time], but did not hear anything about a massacre from the local people." That Sakurauchi's denial of the Nanjing Massacre was prompted in large part in reaction against the newly threatening recovery of critical memories is suggested by the fact that in 1982 Sakurauchi himself had actually supported revision of euphemistic textbooks.[49]

The so-called Liberal History Study Group (Jiyūshugi Shikan Kenkyūkai), established in 1995 by historian Fujioka Nobukatsu, has recently been at the forefront of attempts to recleanse national memories. Utilizing the mainstream mass print media and aiming for institutionalization of their historical view, supporters of this study group have referred to historical knowledge that is critical of the national past as the "masochistic view of history" (*jigyaku shikan*) and have captured a huge following.[50] Such reactions to critical outlooks have gained visibility and force, especially in the wake of government officials' and cabinet members' admissions of remorse and apologies for past military and colonial atrocities. More recently, in his best-selling comic book, *Sensōron*, Kobayashi Yoshinori charges that the Japanese people have been "brainwashed" by those critical of the national past, and urges them to sympathize with their forefathers rather than censure them for going to war.[51] This appeal for sympathy was also the theme of the movie *Pride*, which attempted to turn the war criminal Tōjō Hideki into a lovable grandfather figure.

As is well-known by now, a similar attack against what are deemed to be "unpatriotic" historical accounts occurred in the United States when Congress intervened in the *Enola Gay* commemorative exhibit at the Smithsonian Air and Space Museum, as well as in the conservative demand for revisions of U.S. history textbook standards that would have included a critical appraisal of the national past.[52]

Finally, we submit that our project of critical war remembering is part of a broader intellectual intervention in the human and social sciences that reaches far beyond the issue of the Asia-Pacific War(s). We hope that this volume can be read as one attempt to join in the battles between those who would claim the authority of the conventional languages and categories that have dominated our understanding of the world, and those both within and outside academia who wish to question, destabilize, and diversify familiar orders of knowledge. In fact, at a relatively early stage in the planning of our conference, we unexpectedly received strong indications of just how disconcerting and threatening our project seemed to those who see themselves as guardians of knowledge, and who have influence on funding decisions.

In response to our application for conference funding, we received several polemical reviews from the National Endowment for the Humanities (NEH). Although several supportive commentators recommended funding and noted the unique qualities of our proposal, the negative evaluation prevailed and our application was denied. One particularly hostile reviewer stated that the "program lacked diversity and balance among points of view." He or she explained, for example, that we did not include in our list of participants anyone who had "actually participated in the Second World War and who himself or herself has 'war memories' however faulty at this late date they may be." Clearly, this reviewer was unable to comprehend our understanding of the complex relationship between experience and memory, and had also missed the fact that several participants had indeed lived during the war years. Toyonaga Keisaburō, for example, is an atomic bomb victim who is now at the forefront of a local movement to provide compensation for Koreans victimized by the bomb, the war, and Japanese colonialism. This reviewer was oblivious to such an oversight, and it is likely that what he or she really desired was the inclusion of defenders of American nationalism and militarism. The reviewer criticized us for not including any "military historians," praised their scholarly contributions, and further instructed us to devote some time to reading their works. Noting none of the irony in instructing us on such matters, he or she charged that we were "didacticists" and would be better off educating ourselves in military history. Overall, the reviewer maintained that we were completely biased, and that we had "a very specific 'politically correct' agenda." The gist of this particular review and the animosity that several others expressed is captured very well in the following quote: "This [politically correct] agenda is revealed to me by the use of such terminology as 'atomic holocaust,' a term which I find a perversion of the Holocaust itself, 'American imperialism' etc. Self-flagellation and endless apologia may be one way to examine the Second World War in the Pacific. However, this proposed conference is totally imbalanced as it stands in favor of such a faddish view." In short, we and our participants were guilty of having "multicultural, gender-sensitive etc. 'commitments,'" and were not representative enough of American scholarship. Still another review mentioned that although the fears of this reviewer were probably exaggerated, "bias is dangerously threatening throughout."

These remarks should not be regarded as directed simply against our attempted intervention and our rather modest funding request. Instead, the level of enmity expressed here is indicative of the general degree of animosity that prevails against works that seek intellectual and cultural diversity and that endeavor to decenter the United States and Europe. In a perverted and caricaturing manner, these reviewers' comments actually captured our agenda quite accurately. As in the case of the Smithsonian controversy, they betrayed the attitudes still prevalent in the United States, both within and outside academia, toward the history and memory of the Second World War, and that continue to be played out in the so-called culture wars.

At the same time, the fruitful exchanges at the conference of international scholars and activists from various parts of Asia and the Pacific made it quite evident that such a reactionary position can no longer be effectively sustained. We were constantly reminded that our project would not have been possible without, and was in fact nourished by the persistence and proliferation of critical scholarly works in the humanities and social sciences throughout the region. Furthermore, such scholarly endeavors have been and continue to be in large part enabled by activist-intellectuals who have extended their practices beyond the academic ivory tower. Even within the conference itself, the activist orientation and discourse of such participants as Ishihara Masaie, Chen Ying-zhen, Utsumi Aiko, and Toyonaga Keisaburō reminded us of the critical role that such people have had throughout the postwar years. Ishihara, for example, had been part of a movement in Okinawa in which local scholars and activists took over tour buses during the early 1970s, proclaiming that their land was not just a tourist site, but that the people and the land continued to carry the scars of war and domination by both Japan and the United States. Chen spent many years in prison for his powerful critiques of the repressive government in Taiwan. Utsumi, though not initially a professional historian, was a pioneer in collecting oral histories of colonial experiences and making these known to a wide audience. Finally, Toyonaga, a former high school teacher and vice principal, took early retirement to devote all his time to grassroots political and intellectual work.

These writers' contributions may strike the reader as somewhat different from many of the others: they tend to be fairly confident about the transparency and stability of the "historical facts." As Shumei Shih, one of our conference commentators, incisively pointed out, their writings are more direct, less concerned about relating their work to the emerging academic discourses. In contrast, she noted, elaborate theories of resistance, as in Homi Bhabha's influential work, seem often to lose the immediacy and concreteness that resistance requires. No doubt, the immediate political exigencies of their work and the audiences to which their writings are usually directed—for example, to gain compensation or recognition for particular groups of people in societies that recognize the legitimacy of what are considered to be facts—are conditions that have figured in their discourse. Yet we have not felt compelled to homogenize the discourse employed in the various essays. For the conference participants, the recognizable dissonance in approaches and writings styles served to make us all aware of the limits as well as the possibilities of the intellectual and political effects of our work. Hopefully, this volume can attest to the depth, vigor, and potency of such ongoing critical practices and debates, while opening up new problematics in need of further investigation.

Notes

1 Joan W. Scott, "The Evidence of Experience," *Critical Inquiry* 17, no. 4 (summer 1991): 778.

2 On World War I, see Paul Fussell, *The Great War and Modern Memory* (Oxford: Oxford University Press, 1975); George L. Mosse, *Fallen Soldiers: Reshaping the Memory of the World Wars* (New York: Oxford University Press, 1980); Jay Winter, *Sites of Memory, Sites of Mourning: The Great War in European Cultural History* (New York: Cambridge University Press, 1995). On World War II, see Michael C. C. Adams, *The Best War Ever: America and World War II* (Baltimore: Johns Hopkins University Press, 1994); Ian Buruma, *The Wages of Guilt: Memories of War in Germany and Japan* (New York: Farrar, Straus and Giroux, 1994); Norma Field, *In the Realm of a Dying Emperor: Japan at Century's End* (1991; New York: Vintage Books, 1993); Paul Fussell, *Wartime: Understanding and Behavior in the Second World War* (New York: Oxford University Press, 1989); Laura Hein and Mark Selden, eds., *Living with the Bomb: American and Japanese Cultural Conflicts in the Nuclear Age* (New York: M.E. Sharpe, 1997); Michael J. Hogan, *Hiroshima in History and Memory* (Cambridge, England: Cambridge University Press, 1996). On the Holocaust, see Lawrence Langer, *Holocaust Testimonies: The Ruins of Memory* (New Haven: Yale University Press, 1991); James E. Young, *The Texture of Memory: Holocaust Memorials and Meaning* (New Haven: Yale University Press, 1993), among many others.

3 Cited in "Breakthrough Books," *Lingua Franca* (March–April 1995): 16.

4 Gerhard L. Weinberg, *A World at Arms: A Global History of World War II* (Cambridge, England: Cambridge University Press, 1994), 1178.

5 Faxed letter, 26 September 1994.

6 John Costello, *The Pacific War* (New York: Quill, 1982), v.

7 Kathy E. Ferguson and Phyllis Turnbull, "Narratives of History, Nature, and Death at the National Memorial Cemetery of the Pacific," *Frontiers* 16, nos. 2–3 (1996): 1–23.

8 Indeed, in postwar America the two most widely read sources about the opening and closing events of the war are two books that share the same highly circumscribed temporality, describing these events in terms of personal narratives of experiences during the course of a single day: Walter Lord's *Day of Infamy* (New York: Holt, 1957) and John Hersey's *Hiroshima* (New York: Knopf, 1946).

9 Poka Laenui, *Hawaiian Sovereignty and Pearl Harbor History* (Honolulu: East-West Center, 1992).

10 Hyun Sook Kim, "Women and the Nation: The Cultural Construction of the Colonized Body/Sexuality," abstract submitted for The Politics of Remembering the Asia Pacific War conference, 7–9 September 1995, East-West Center, Honolulu, Hawai'i. Kim has elaborated her views on this problem of masculinist protectionist discourse in South Korea in her "History and Memory: The 'Comfort Women' Controversy," in *The Comfort Women: Colonialism, War and Sex*, ed. Chungmoo Choi, special issue of *positions* 5, no. 1 (spring 1997): 73–106. The latter volume is the most comprehensive critical introduction to discourses on the "comfort women."

11 For important works that link the historical concern with the Japanese enslavement of women to militarism, nationalism, and women's sexual labor in contemporary South Korea, see Elaine H. Kim and Chungmoo Choi, eds., *Dangerous Women: Gender and Korean Nationalism* (New York: Routledge, 1998).

12 Anthony Reid, "Remembering and Forgetting the War in Indonesia," paper given at conference on Memory and the Second World War in International Comparative Perspective (Amsterdam, 1995).

13 Geoffrey White and Jane Yi, "*December 7th*: Race and Nation in Wartime Documentary," in *Classic Whiteness: Race and the Hollywood Studio System*, ed. Daniel Bernardi (Minneapolis: University of Minnesota Press, in press).

14 See John Kelly, "Diaspora and World War, Blood and Nation in Fiji and Hawai'i," *Public Culture* 7, no. 3 (1995): 475–97; and Brij Lal, "For King and Country: A Talk on the Pacific War in Fiji," in *Remembering the Pacific War*, ed. G. M. White, Honolulu, University of Hawai'i Center for Pacific Islands Studies Occasional Paper No. 36, 1991, 7–26.

15 See Geoffrey M. White and Lamont Lindstrom, eds., *The Pacific Theater: Island Representations of World War II* (Honolulu: University of Hawai'i Press, 1989).

16 When Solomon Islands gained its independence in 1978, the U.S. Information Agency presented the country with a film titled *Passage to Independence* that highlighted the bonds forged between Solomon Islanders and Americans during the war. Using stories such as the sinking of John F. Kennedy's famed PT-109 and his rescue by Solomon Islands scouts, the film recalls wartime experiences to frame the contemporary relationship between America and an independent Solomon Islands.

17 Hank Nelson, "Taim Bilong Pait: The Impact of the Second World War on Papua New Guinea," in *Southeast Asia under Japanese Occupation*, ed. A. W. McCoy (New Haven: Yale University Southeast Asia Studies, 1980), 144–66.

18 Jonathan Fifi'i, "World War II and the Origins of Maasina Rule," in *The Big Death: Solomon Islanders Remember World War II*, ed. G. M. White et al. (Suva, Fiji: Institute of Pacific Studies, 1988), 216–26.

19 Experiences such as those of the movement leaders, or of others such as George Bogese, a prominent Solomon Islander who sided with the Japanese largely out of anti-British sentiments (and who was imprisoned for seven years) are absent from public memory. See Geoffrey M. White, "Remembering Guadalcanal: National Identity and Transnational Memory-Making," *Public Culture* 7 (1995): 529–55.

20 Lin Poyer, Suzanne Falgout, and Laurence M. Carucci, *The Typhoon of War: Micronesian Experiences of the Pacific War* (Honolulu: University of Hawai'i Press, 2000).

21 Mark R. Peattie, *Nan'yo: The Rise and Fall of the Japanese in Micronesia, 1885–1945* (Honolulu: University of Hawai'i Press, 1988).

22 Wakako Higuchi, "War Reparations in Micronesia and Japan's Responsibility," unpublished paper, Micronesian Area Research Program, University of Guam, 1994.

23 Laurence M. Carucci, "The Source of the Force in Marshallese Cosmology," in *The Pacific Theater: Island Representations of World War II*, ed. G. M. White and Lamont Lindstrom (Honolulu: University of Hawai'i Press, 1989), 76.

24 Kinjō Seitoku and Takara Kurayoshi, *Iha Fuyu* (Tokyo: Shimizu Shoin, 1972).

25 Chalmers Johnson, " 'Go-banken-sama, GO HOME!' ", *The Bulletin of the Atomic Scientists* (July–August, 1996): 22–29. For lists of the more serious violent crimes committed against Okinawan residents by U.S. military personnel, as well as U.S. military accidents

leading to local civilian deaths or injuries, see Okinawa Heiwa Nettowāku, ed., *Shin aruku/miru/kangaeru Okinawa* (Walking/seeing/thinking Okinawa: New edition) (Naha, Okinawa: Okinawa Jiji Shuppan, 1997), 75, 103. Besides purposeful crimes, these "accidents" have been frequent and often large in scale. For example, in 1959 seventeen children were killed and one hundred suffered injuries when a U.S. plane crashed into an elementary school. In 1965 a small trailer fell from a plane engaged in bombing practice, killing an eleven-year-old girl in Yomitan Village. The United States paid $4,700 in compensation for her death.

26 The structural relationship between the U.S. military presence in South Korea, the Philippines, and Okinawa and local women sex workers in these places is analyzed in Saundra Pollock Sturdevant and Brenda Stoltfus, eds., *Let the Good Times Roll: Prostitution and the U.S. Military in Asia* (New York: The New Press, 1992).

27 Susan Jeffords, *The Remasculinization of America: Gender and the Vietnam War* (Bloomington: Indiana University Press, 1989). In *The Morning After: Sexual Politics at the End of the Cold War* (Berkeley: University of California Press, 1993), Cynthia Enloe discusses the importance of analyzing diverse and historically specific "military masculinities."

28 Ping-hui Liao, "Rewriting Taiwanese National History: The February 28 Incident as Spectacle," *Public Culture* 5 (1993): 281–96.

29 For useful overviews of the history of Korean residents in Japan, see Sŏ Kyŏng-shik, *Kōminka seisaku kara shimon ōnatsu made: zainichi Chōsenjin no "Shōwashi"* (From the imperial subjectification policy to fingerprinting: A "Shōwa history" of Korean residents in Japan) (Tokyo: Iwanami Shoten, 1989), and Kang Chae-ŏn and Kim Tong-hun, *Zainichi Kankoku/Chōsenjin: rekishi to tenbō* (South and North Korean residents in Japan: History and prospects) (Tokyo: Rōdō Keizaisha, 1989).

30 See also Utsumi's pathbreaking book on Koreans tried as war criminals, *Chōsenjin BCkyū senpan no kiroku* (A record of Korean B and C class war criminals) (Tokyo: Keisō Shobō, 1982).

31 Bruce Cumings, *The Origins of the Korean War* (Princeton, NJ: Princeton University Press, 1981).

32 Chungmoo Choi, "The Discourse of Decolonization and Popular Memory: South Korea," *positions* 1, no. 1 (spring 1993): 77–102.

33 Lewis A. Coser, ed., *Maurice Halbwachs on Collective Memory* (Chicago: University of Chicago Press, 1992).

34 Recent writings in the Vygotskian tradition of cultural psychology, approaching cognition as socially mediated activity, represent a significant countertrend to this dichotomization. See, e.g., Jerome Bruner, *Acts of Meaning* (Cambridge, MA: Harvard University Press, 1990), and James V. Wertsch, Pablo del Rio, and Amelia Alvarez, eds., *Sociocultural Studies of Mind* (New York: Cambridge University Press, 1995).

35 See John R. Gillis, ed., *Commemorations: The Politics of National Identity* (Princeton, N.J.: Princeton University Press, 1994), and Eric Hobsbawm and Terence Ranger, eds., *The Invention of Tradition* (Cambridge, England: Cambridge University Press, 1983).

36 Pierre Nora, "Between Memory and History: *Les Lieux de Mémoire*," *Representations* 26 (spring 1989): 7–25.

37 T. Fujitani, *Splendid Monarchy: Power and Pageantry in Modern Japan* (Berkeley: University of California Press, 1996); John Bodnar, *Remaking America: Public Memory, Commemoration, and Patriotism in the Twentieth Century* (Princeton, NJ: Princeton University Press, 1992); and

Michael Kammen, *The Mystic Chords of Memory: The Transformation of Tradition in American Culture* (New York: Knopf, 1991).

38 So, for example, Bodnar's interest in tensions between "official" and "vernacular" memory raises issues of meaning and voice that are central to the analysis of public culture generally. See Bodnar, *Remaking America*.

39 Jonathan Boyarin, *Storm from Paradise: The Politics of Jewish Memory* (Minneapolis: University of Minnesota Press, 1992), 161; Richard Handler, *Nationalism and the Politics of Culture in Quebec* (Madison: University of Wisconsin Press, 1988); White, "Remembering Guadalcanal"; Lisa Yoneyama, *Hiroshima Traces: Time, Space and the Dialectics of Memory* (Berkeley: University of California Press, 1999); and Ted Swedenburg, *Memories of Revolt: The 1936–1993 Rebellion and the Palestinian National Past* (Minneapolis: University of Minnesota Press, 1995).

40 Paul Antze and Michael Lambek, eds., *Tense Past: Cultural Essays in Trauma and Memory* (New York: Routledge, 1996).

41 Jeanine Basinger, *The World War II Combat Film* (New York: Columbia University Press, 1986); Clayton R. Koppes and Gregory D. Black, *Hollywood Goes to War: How Politics, Profits and Propaganda Shaped World War II Movies* (Berkeley: University of California Press, 1987).

42 George H. Roeder Jr., *The Censored War: American Visual Experience during World War II* (New Haven: Yale University Press, 1993); Gregory J. Kasza, *The State and the Mass Media in Japan, 1918–1945* (Berkeley: University of California Press, 1988).

43 Edward T. Linenthal and Tom Engelhardt, eds., *History Wars: The "Enola Gay" and Other Battles for the American Past* (New York: Henry Holt, 1996).

44 Walter Benjamin, "Theses on the Philosophy of History," in *Illuminations*, ed. Hannah Arendt, trans. Harry Zohn (New York: Schocken Books, 1969), 257.

45 See Eric Gable, Richard Handler, and Anna Lawson, "On the Uses of Relativism: Fact, Conjecture, and Black and White Histories at Colonial Williamsburg," *American Ethnologist* 19, no. 4 (1992): 791–805.

46 Karen L. Nero, "Time of Famine, Time of Transformation: Hell in the Pacific, Palau," in *The Pacific Theater: Island Representations of World War II*, ed. G. M. White and L. Lindstrom (Honolulu: University of Hawai'i Press, 1989), 117–47.

47 Elizabeth Diller and Ricardo Scofidio, *Back to the Front: Tourisms of War* (Princeton, NJ: Princeton Architectural Press, 1994).

48 Norma Field, "War and Apology: Japan, Asia, the Fiftieth, and After," *positions* 5, no. 1 (spring 1997): 1–49.

49 *San Jose Mercury News*, 19 September 1996.

50 Fujioka's representative work is *Ojoku no kingendaishi: ima kokufuku no toki* (A disgraceful modern and contemporary history: Now is the time to overcome it) (Tokyo: Tokuma Shoten, 1996), but he and his group have produced a deluge of similar publications.

51 Kobayashi Yoshinori, *Sensōron* (On war) (Tokyo: Gentōsha, 1998).

52 Gary B. Nash, Charlotte Crabtree, and Ross E. Dunn, *History on Trial: Culture Wars and the Teaching of the Past* (New York: Knopf, 1997).

I $\equiv$ MEMORY FRAGMENTS, MEMORY IMAGES

Absent Images of Memory: Remembering

and Reenacting the Japanese Internment

MARITA STURKEN

What would the construction of history be without the occasion of the anniversary? Time is marked in increments, each signaling a collective and institutional desire to fix history in place, declare it stable, coherent, and resolved. Some anniversaries speak louder than others, and the fiftieth anniversary of an event speaks perhaps most dramatically of all: fifty years, representing half a century, a time when, unlike the hundredth anniversary, many participants are still alive, reflecting on the meaning of their lives. In the context of the historical anniversary, the conflict between the desire for history as a means of closure and memory as a means for personal and cultural catharsis is revealed.

In the years 1994 and 1995, the unfolding of history was heavily marked, and memories were called on, retold, and dramatically reenacted. The fiftieth anniversaries of the end of World War II in Europe, the end of the Asia-Pacific War, and the bombing of Hiroshima and Nagasaki occasioned a broad array of memory rituals and acts of remembrance—of atonements for war activities and defiant reiterations of wartime rhetoric, each with conflicting agendas. In the reconsideration of the war's meaning, memories were conjured to justify arguments both for and against the war's actions; they were both subsumed within and entangled with official narratives of history.

The tension between memory and history is an active process that moves both ways: from memory to history as well as from history to memory. Thus, whereas the memories of survivors can become part of the texts of history, historical narratives can often reshape personal memories. The process of history making is highly complex, one that takes place in the United States through a variety of cultural arenas, including the media, Hollywood narrative films, and museums in addition to the academy. This means that memories, artifacts, images, and events often get marked as *historical* without the aid of historians. Rather than positing memory and history as oppositional, as they are often described, I consider them to be entangled, each pulling forms from the other. However, it is often politically important to mark when distinctions can be made between them.

When personal memories are deployed in the context of marking the anniversary of historical events, they are presented as either the embodied evidence of history or as evidence of history's failures. Survivors return to the sites of their war experience; they place their bodies within the discourse of remembering to either affirm history's narratives or to declare them incomplete, incapable of conjuring their experience. They represent a very particular form of embodied memory. History functions much more smoothly in the absence of survivors, and survivors are often dissenting voices to history's narratives, but history making also accords to them a very particular authority as authentic experience.

At the same time, the tension of history and memory problematizes this very question of experience. The original experiences of memory are irretrievable; we cannot ever "know" them except through memory remains. Memories are narratives that are told and retold, reenacted and reimaged. Memory is ontologically fluid and memories constantly subject to rescripting and fantasy. This does not mean that we cannot address issues of authenticity and accuracy in memory, but that we must foreground memory's relationship to desire and its political nature. Indeed, what memories tell us, more than anything, is about the stakes held by individuals and institutions in what the past means.

In this essay, I address the question of personal memory, history, and cultural memory in the context of the anniversary of the Asia-Pacific War by examining a historical event that has spoken its presence through its absent representation: the internment of mainland Japanese Americans in camps during the war. I have chosen to write this as a form of dialogue with the videotape *History and Memory* by the American videomaker Rea Tajiri.[1] Tajiri's reconstruction of her family's memories of the internment camps speaks in compelling ways about the role of the camera image in the production of history and memory, and remembering in the absence of memory. Through Tajiri's work, I examine what it means in the tangle of history and memory to render the internment visible. (All of the illustrations in this essay are taken from *History and Memory*.)

The Image As History

In the intersecting arenas of personal memory, cultural memory, and history, in which shared memories and memory objects can move from one realm to another, shifting meaning and context, the camera image—photograph, film, and video/television—plays a very particular role. Images have profound capacities to create, trouble, and interfere with our memories, as individuals and as a nation. Hollywood narrative film images often reenact and subsume documentary images, which can in turn subsume personal memories and images. For instance, for many World War II veterans, Hollywood World War II movies have *become* their memories, subsuming their personal images into a general script. The relationship of the camera image to memory and history, moreover, is one of contradiction. On one hand, camera images can embody and create memories; on the other hand, they have the capacity, through the power of their presence, to obliterate other, unphotographed memories. As technologies of memory, they actively produce both memory and forgetting.

Forgetting can be produced through the absence of images. Many horrific events of twentieth-century history, such as the Holocaust, were relentlessly and copiously documented in camera images. Yet, other traumatic events, such as the genocide of Cambodians under the Pol Pot regime in the late 1970s and the mass murders in Rwanda in the 1990s, have gone relatively undocumented, producing few photographic images to capture the global public's attention. Yet, forgetting can also be produced through the presence of images. A single-image icon can screen out other images of a historical event. For instance, the iconic image of the mushroom cloud of the atom bomb obliterates the less well-known images of the bomb's destruction.

Hence, memory acquires cultural and historical meaning when it is articulated through the processes of representation. Andreas Huyssen writes: "Rather than leading us to some authentic origin or giving us verifiable access to the real, memory, even and especially in its belatedness, is itself based on representation. The past is not simply there in memory, but it must be articulated to become memory. The fissure that opens up between experiencing an event and remembering it in representation is unavoidable. Rather than lamenting or ignoring it, this split should be understood as a powerful stimulant for cultural and artistic creativity."[2] Huyssen suggests that the tension that arises in the cultural mediation of memory is the source of artistic engagement with the past. I would push his point further to argue that it is precisely the instability of memory that provides for its importance in pointing to the meaning of the past. Camera images are a major factor in this traversing of memories among the realms of personal memory, cultural memory, and history.

For Americans, the Asia-Pacific War produced several image icons, most notably the raising by U.S. soldiers of the American flag at Iwo Jima (its iconic status as a photographic image further established by its rendering in the

Marine Corps Memorial in Arlington, Virginia) and the image of the mushroom cloud from the atomic blast rising over Hiroshima.[3] Other images are generic: men running as boats smoke and sink at Pearl Harbor, American soldiers in the trenches in tropical locations, and Japanese planes crashing into the sea. The sources of these images of history are many, as likely to be the screen images of *Thirty Seconds over Tokyo* (1944), *Guadalcanal Diary* (1943), *Sands of Iwo Jima* (1949), or *From Here to Eternity* (1953) as documentary footage. These images are components in the national narrative of the war, in which the United States is a triumphant and moral nation; as such, they screen out more disruptive images. Other images, such as the photographs and film footage of Hiroshima immediately after the bomb, were held in government archives until their cultural meanings were considerably muted.[4]

Absent Images of Memory

Yet, there are also events of World War II that did not produce image icons. The forced internment of mainland Japanese American citizens after the bombing of Pearl Harbor in 1941 is an event for which history provides images primarily through their absence. Indeed, the government attempted through censorship to control the representation of the internment: it produced propaganda films depicting the camps as a benevolent exercise in civil obedience. The federal government prohibited cameras in the camps, thus attempting to prevent any significant production of counterimages. This limited cultural representation of the camps was compounded by the protracted silence of many of the former internees.

In many ways, the historical narrative of the internment remains relatively intact. Despite the payment of reparations, despite the semblance of a national atonement, the internment continues to be narrativized as a regrettable step that appeared necessary in its time—not as bad as what other countries did. Even though the term "concentration camps" was used by government officials and Presidents Roosevelt and Truman, the image of prison camps where people were peaceably assembled screens out the image of prison camps where people became ill and died and where resisters were shot. The historical claim of the internment as benevolent remains fixed through its alliance with the claim of the use of the atomic bomb as inevitable, an act that was appropriate in its time. To question one of these narratives would be to question them all, hence they remain fundamentally unexamined.

As a historical event marked by silences and strategic forgetting, the internment of Japanese Americans produces memory in several ways: in its survivors, in the artifacts in which they imbue their memories, and in its "absent pres-

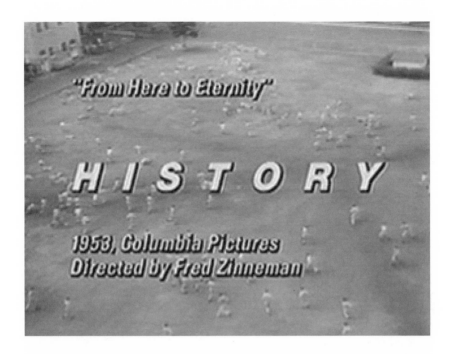

"From Here to Eternity"

HISTORY

1953, Columbia Pictures
Directed by Fred Zinneman

ence." Objects of memory haunt the remembering of the internment. It was an event for which the creation and destruction of memory objects were very particular. Although Japanese families in the American territory of Hawai'i were not interned en masse because of their importance to the local war economy, they were harassed and detained. Many destroyed their memory objects—photographs, letters, Japanese books and clothing—in an attempt to obliterate their ethnic status through destroying its evidence.[5] On the mainland, Japanese Americans were able to take very few possessions with them to the internment camps.[6] At the exhibition *America's Concentration Camps*, shown at the Japanese American National Museum in Los Angeles in 1995, maps, letters, and photographs were used to conjure the experience of the camps. There, amid the vitrines, sat a group of trunks and suitcases that were neatly packed and left at the Panama Hotel in Seattle but had never been claimed after the war—objects that had become, for many reasons, irretrievable.

The story that Rea Tajiri tells in *History and Memory* is marked by meanings found in objects of memory and the presence and absence of camera images. Tajiri is compelled by the gaps in her mother's memory, by her own sense of incompleteness, and by the absent presence of the camps in national memory to counter the historical images of her parents' families' internment. While her father served in the 442nd Regiment, their house was literally moved away, never to be seen again. She re-creates an image of her mother filling a canteen at a faucet in the desert, an image she has always carried, for which she wants to find a story. She states:

> There are things which have happened in the world while there were cameras watching, things we have images for. There are other things which have happened while there were no cameras watching, which we restage in front of cameras to have images of.
>
> There are things which have happened for which the only images that exist are in the minds of observers, present at the time, while there are things which have happened for which there have been no observers, except the spirits of the dead.

What are the traces of events for which there have been no camera images? Tajiri imagines the spirit of her grandfather watching an argument between her parents about the "unexplained nightmares that their daughter has been having on the twentieth anniversary of the bombing of Pearl Harbor." He is the witness of the absent image, one that she then re-creates.

Counterimages and Absent Presence

Despite government attempts to control all representations of the camps, counterimages were nevertheless produced. Artwork produced by camp internees such as Estelle Ishigo, Henry Sugimoto, George Matsusaburo Hibi, and Chiura Obata, among others, has been widely exhibited, and photographers such as Ansel Adams, and Toyo Miyatake photographed Manzanar.[7] The photographs taken by photographers hired by the War Relocation Authority (WRA), which included well-known photographer Dorothea Lange, were, like the famous Farm Security Administration photographs of the Depression era, government-sponsored images that transcended their original intent. These are moving images of internees being evacuated, of children wearing large identification tags and staring in disbelief at the camera, of families assembled in cramped quarters. Yet, these images are, for the most part, absent from the litany of World War II images that constitute its iconic history.

That the internment produced no singular-image icons cannot be attributed simply to the prohibition of cameras and the government's desire to render the event a kind of invisibility. The more relevant question is why photographs by Adams, Lange, Miyatake, and others are absent from the image-history canon of the war. It could be argued that the internment produced an image both too disruptive and too domestic to conform to the war's narratives. These were not aggressive enemies who were easily demonized; they were profoundly ordinary, too close for comfort to an image of hard-working Americans. These were

people who responded for the most part without resistance, who turned the desert into gardens. They also served in the army in terms that can be read as a determination to both prove national loyalty and counter racist stereotypes. As T. Fujitani writes, the military feats of the Nisei soldiers were subsumed into narratives of American nationalism.[8] This did not allow for their relatives to be easily demonized in simple terms.

Ironically, while the government and the media attempted at the time to depict the Japanese as sinister and untrustworthy, it also went to great lengths to distinguish other Asians and Asian Americans, such as the Chinese, in positive terms.[9] This allowed for the generic notion of Asian American to be troubled. At the same time, government propaganda films aimed to show how well the Japanese were being treated and depicted the camps as a kind of summer camp, with craft classes and group activities. This image of hyper-domesticity served to feminize the camps and emasculate the Japanese men in them, which may account in part for the hypermasculine discourse of the Nisei soldiers. The government films served to erase the elements of political activity and resistance that existed in the camps. Hence, the government's production of images of its "benevolent" treatment of the Nisei and Issei in these films was in part contingent on its producing images of them as model and obedient citizens. The home movies taken from cameras smuggled into the camps are in contrast to the evenly lit, clean images of government propaganda films. Yet, in their jerky movements and recordings of moments of shyness, daily routines, and snow-covered landscapes, they show not resistance and barbed wire but a profound ordinariness, an unexpected everydayness.[10] Indeed, their primary focus appears to be snow, as many internees were from the West Coast and had never seen it before.

Whereas the image of Iwo Jima achieved iconic status through its depiction of standard tropes of heroism and sacrifice, and the image of the atomic blast succeeds as pure spectacle, the internment of the Japanese Americans ultimately can find no such traditional narratives—of conflict, resistance, or brutal injustice. Its images are overwhelmed by their sense of the ordinary and the domestic, outside of the discourse of war.

Although the history of the Asia-Pacific War exists now in cultural memory more through the images of films such as *Bataan* (1943), *Sands of Iwo Jima*, and *Gung Ho!* (1944), the internment for the most part has not been subjected to the codes of jingoistic cinematic revisionism. It was recently retold in the 1990 film *Come See the Paradise*, in which the camps function primarily as a backdrop for an interracial romance. This film's more radical elements (for example, its depiction of racism) are undercut by its privileging of the story of its white male protagonist, played by Dennis Quaid, whose character allows white viewers to feel atoned through their identification with his apparent transcendence of racism. Unlike the battles of the war or the struggles at home of white, middle-class American families, which could be narrativized in the traditional clichés of nationalism, the internment has resisted certain kinds of direct cultural representation.

In *History and Memory*, Tajiri notes that the 1954 film *Bad Day at Black Rock*, directed by John Sturges, perhaps most powerfully reenacts the absent presence of the Japanese American internment. In the film, John Macreedy (Spencer Tracy) comes to Black Rock, a desolate desert town east of the Sierra Mountains, in a place strikingly similar to the Manzanar camp. He is looking for Komoko, a Japanese farmer, whose son died while saving his life during the war in Italy. Confronted by hostile and ultimately murderous cowboys, Macreedy learns that Komoko discovered water in the dry desert and, like the internees, made it blossom. Brutally murdered the day after Pearl Harbor, he is a figure whose death is a secret that haunts the town.[11]

Bad Day at Black Rock tells its story through presenting absence. Komoko is never seen in the film, but his death exposes the brutal reality of the all-American western town: lawless, self-loathing, fearful in its core. Macreedy, as the emblem of American justice, must stand in for him. Indeed, the film is less about Komoko than about the discovery by the jaded and cynical veteran that his life still has purpose, in this case to uphold the law in a lawless town.

Bad Day at Black Rock is also a film about postwar masculinity and the end of the American West. This end is signaled by the capacity of a Japanese American to be both better at farming the land (Komoko finds water where Reno Smith, his murderer, could not) and at being a war hero (Komoko's son is awarded a medal by the government). The cowboys in Black Rock, former icons of the American West (and played, not incidentally, by several major Hollywood stars, including Robert Ryan, Ernest Borgnine, Lee Marvin, and Walter Brennan), never went to war. Indeed, Smith's anger at being turned away by the draft the day after Pearl Harbor is presented in the film as instigating his rage to kill Komoko. The film thus portrays the cowboys as emblems of masculine hypocrisy and hollow bravado. This image of a morally bankrupt America is redeemed only by Macreedy, the wounded veteran with a sense of justice, a man who went to war and who suffered. (In a strange plot twist, though he has lost the use of one arm, he defends himself through the martial arts of judo and karate!) There is only one woman in this town, an ill-fated sister of one of the men, played by Ann Francis; otherwise, it is populated by men with nothing to do. They represent the end of a myth of the American West as the province of the white, male cowboy. Smith says to Macreedy: "Somebody's always looking for something in this part of the West. To the historians, it's the old West. To the book writers, it's the Wild West. To the businessman, it's the undeveloped West. . . . But, to us, this place is our West, and I wish they would leave us alone."

When the cowboys plot to kill Macreedy as he discovers too much, it is cowardice that compels them. He represents memory; they think they can obliterate it but it is already haunting them and festering within them. Indeed, when, in concession to standard Hollywood narrative form, law and order is restored at the end of the film, it remains unconvincing precisely because of the film's radical and effective portrayal of Black Rock as emblematic of the worst of America: racist, misogynist, brutal, and unrepentant.

Ironically, *Bad Day at Black Rock* succeeds in evoking the cultural implications of the Japanese internment and American racial conflict through their absence. The internment camps haunt national memory the way Komoko's death haunts Black Rock, speaking in their absence. It indicates precisely the underlying question raised by the internment: how this demonstration of racial hatred demands an investigation of the nature of the myth of what it means to be an American. In their attempt to murder the Other, the cowboys of Black Rock expose the fragility of the myth of the American West that provides them with meaning. In the end, they have nothing.

The Reenactment of Memory

The remembering of the internment camps and the demand for reparations have come primarily through the interventions of Sansei, the children of the Nisei who were imprisoned. Unlike their parents, they are a generation that grew up outside of the camps, with a conviction of their rights to redress and memory. In *History and Memory*, Tajiri represents those Sansei who, haunted by both the silence of their parents and the sense of a memory they cannot quite narrativize, choose to tell their own stories. She states: "I began searching for a history, my own history, because I had known all along that the stories I had heard were not true and parts had been left out. I remember having this feeling growing up that I was haunted by something, that I was living within a family full of ghosts. There was this place that they knew about. I had never been there, yet I had a memory of it. I could remember a time of great sadness before I was born. We had been moved, uprooted. We had lived with a lot of pain. I had no idea where these memories came from yet I knew the place." Tajiri offers testimony of her mother's embodied memory, yet she feels that this memory was born within her. She recounts these events with a collective "we." It is *already* her memory, demanding representation. This is an image that disrupts the concept of memory's dying with survivors, a different kind of embodied memory.

What is this kind of memory that is passed through generations, that is already within the child? Marianne Hirsch has used the term "postmemory" to describe the memories of the children of survivors, whose lives are dominated by the memories of events that preceded their birth. She writes:

> Postmemory is distinguished from memory by generational distance and from history by deep personal connection. Postmemory is a powerful and very particular form of memory precisely because its connection to its object or source is mediated not through recollection but through an imaginative investment and creation. . . . Postmemory characterizes the experience of those who grow up dominated by narratives that preceded their birth, whose own belated stories are evacuated by the stories of the previous generation shaped by traumatic events that can be neither understood nor recreated. . . . Photographs in their enduring "umbilical" connection to life are precisely the medium connecting first- and second-generation remembrance, memory and postmemory.[12]

Tajiri uses images to reenact the experience of the camps as a means to reconcile her memory of an event that she did not experience, to counter her mother's strategic forgetting. She wants to fill in the memory gaps with new images and to rework the images of the past in order to re-remember for her mother. Imagining her mother filling a canteen in the desert, she recreates that image. "For years," she states, "I have been living with this picture without the story. . . . Now I could forgive my mother for her loss of memory and could make this image for her." When her mother cannot remember how her family was transported to the camps, only that at the end they took a train in which the widows were closed, Tajiri goes back to film the landscape for her.

She is thus deliberately reconstructing and reenacting memories and their absence, showing her mother what she could not see, and actively participating in shifting personal memory into the realm of cultural memory. It ultimately matters little how close her reconstructions are to her mother's originary experience. This is her memory; she has claimed it. Indeed, her reinterpretation of her mother's experience and her intervention into the fragile text of memory allows for its resurgence and provides for a kind of closure. Like many other children of survivors of the internment camps, Tajiri's experience of history had been one of untold stories. She knows that her mother had kept a small carved wooden bird on her dresser, which Tajiri was not allowed to touch, but she doesn't know why. Later, she finds an image of her grandmother in the National Archives with the notation "Bird Carving Class." A memory object reinscribed, its cryptic meaning found, ironically, amidst the images of government propaganda. These carved and painted birds are primary memory artifacts of the camps, where crafts classes were clearly perceived as a means of keeping

Parker Station 1988
PARKER

Where my mother's train pulled in
in 1942

internees busy. They speak to the incongruities of the camps, the attempts to produce a camplike atmosphere in a prison, the production of paradoxical artifacts of memory.

The reenactment of Tajiri's videotape can be seen in the larger context of historical reenactment that has emerged in this fiftieth anniversary. History has been consistently reenacted in rituals such as the replaying of Civil War battles in the South, and is redramatized in docudramas and narrative films, but anniversaries form particular occasions for reenactment. On the fiftieth anniversary of World War II, seventy-year-old veterans parachuted into the fields of Normandy and were allowed through the marking of history to replay their experiences; these, perhaps, were the moments in which their lives held the most meaning. In Asia, peace marches crossed bridges once fought over, and in Japan, contradictory statements of the war reenacted its rhetoric. Endless documentary films replayed the war on television, and television movies and Hollywood films reenacted and rescripted its destruction in narratives of heroism and individual sacrifice.

It would be easy to dismiss these kinds of popular rituals as superficial, as forms of atonement that let the guilty feel cleansed, or as inaccurate attempts to rewrite history as a smooth and untroubled text. However, this is too simple a dismissal. In fact, cultural memory is always being rescripted, just as personal memories are constantly recrafted and rethought. Renarrativization is essential to memory. The reenactment of docudramas and anniversary rituals can be read not simply as history and memory's reinscription, but rather as indicators of the fluid realm of memory itself.

Memorializing the Internment

I argue that, despite the occasional public mentions of the camps, they remained absent in the national anniversary markings of the war. This raises the question of the meaning of national atonement: What does it mean for a nation to apologize? In Japan, the initial refusal to apologize for the war spoke much more loudly than the belated apology itself. Can we really say that, in the case of the United States, an apology and the payment of $20,000 to survivors was a gesture that absolved the act? Doesn't this allow for the placement of a very small price on the loss generated by the camps? In addition, if the mere mention of the camps by an American president or former president constitutes atonement, as is often noted in the media, then the price to assuage guilt is small indeed.

History and Memory raises the question of how the camps should be remembered in national discourse. Tajiri's videotape is one of several works made by Sansei and children of survivors and, as such, it constitutes a deliberate effort to move personal memory into cultural memory, and to deploy memory through postmemory. It speaks both to the continuity of memories and to the crucial role of survivors in speaking within history.

Yet, what is the appropriate memory here? What kind of memorial is demanded? Can a memorial properly memorialize the event? Each of the camp sites has a variety of memorial elements and Manzanar was declared a historic site in 1992. Yet these are deliberately isolated places. Since 1995, a barracks from the Heart Mountain internment camp has been a part of the permanent exhibition of the Japanese American National Museum. Spare and incongruous, it demands attention precisely because it has been moved from its site in a desolate part of Wyoming where it was designed not to be seen. The museum has organized reunions of camp survivors and gathered information on the stories of survivors. However, given its location in Little Tokyo in Los Angeles, its intervention into national discourse remains limited.

The most powerful kinds of memorials demand forms of reenactment in the sense that they force viewers to participate rather than to find a comfortable distance. The Vietnam Veterans Memorial in Washington, D.C., entices viewers to touch names and read the letters left by its walls. The Holocaust Museum gives viewers an identity card in an attempt to have them follow the exhibit as a participant. In Berlin, artists Renata Stih and Frieder Schnock created a series of signs that they posted in a formerly Jewish neighborhood that catalogues, calmly and relentlessly, the orders created by the German government to gradually curtail the lives of German Jews—"Jews Are Forbidden to Grow Vegetables," "Jews Are Forbidden to Buy Milk," "Jews Are Forbidden to Go Swimming," until, as Jane Kramer writes, Jews were forbidden to do anything but die.[13] The signs function as an ongoing memorial, a daily reminder of the normalization of death, of cultural memory as the everyday.

What, then, does the internment demand as a memory representation? What challenge does it pose to the complicity of memory and forgetting? What would it mean for Americans to remember the names Manzanar, Poston, Tule Lake, Topaz, Minidoka, Heart Mountain, Jerome, Gila River, Amache, and Rohwer in the way that they know the names Auschwitz, Dachau, and Buchenwald? To begin to memorialize the camps would mean to open up the question of what constitutes American nationalism and identity. To properly memorialize the camps and their survivors means to rethink the myth of America's actions in World War II that remains so resolutely intact.

Like the atomic bomb destruction of Hiroshima and Nagasaki, the internment of American citizens because of their race is an event that disrupts the compelling narrative of the United States as the triumphant country of World War II. This narrative of a moral nation forms the central image of American nationalism in the second half of the twentieth century; it is the primary element of what Lauren Berlant has termed the "national symbolic," the process by which individuals are transformed into "subjects of a collectively-held history."[14] Full acknowledgment of the memory of the camps would require a refiguring of the definition of the national meaning of "America," an acknowledgment that winning the war profoundly hampered discourse on the question of national myth for decades, a questioning that had been active prior to the war. In rethinking this history, it is therefore necessary for us to consider the weight of this myth of American war morality on subsequent historical events, not simply the cold war and U.S. imperialism, but the postwar ideology of what constitutes an American.

When internees left the camps, they were often provided with instructions on how to integrate back into America: ways to "successfully relocate." These guides read like instructions for status as model minorities: Don't stand out, don't congregate with other Japanese in public, speak English, be reliable and hardworking, remember the fate of others is in your hands. Ironically, one could argue that the internment succeeded in further Americanizing the Japanese Americans, precisely because as the Issei lost their economic power through the loss of business and property, they lost familial power over their offspring, and tightly knit communities were broken apart and dispersed after

the war. At the same time, new communities were formed as internees from different regions were placed together. In punishing the Japanese Americans as aliens, the camps ultimately worked to assimilate them.

This is the question that memorializing the camps poses. Perhaps it is only by understanding what kind of Americanness Japanese Americans constitute rather than problematize that we can begin to trouble the image of America produced by the war.

Notes

All illustrations are stills from Rea Tajiri's *History and Memory* and are reprinted courtesy of Electronic Arts Intermix. This essay is an extended version of a paper that was presented at the "Politics of Remembering the Asia-Pacific War," East-West Center, Honolulu, in September 1995. Thanks to Lisa Yoneyama, Tak Fujitani, and Geoff White for inviting me to the conference and for feedback on an earlier version of this article. It was originally published in *positions* 5, no. 3 (winter 1997).

1 *History and Memory*, produced and directed by Rea Tajiri, 33 min., 1991, videocassette. Distributed by Electronic Arts Intermix, New York.
2 Andreas Huyssen, *Twilight Memories* (New York: Routledge, 1995), 2–3.
3 The Pulitzer Prize–winning photograph taken by photojournalist Joe Rosenthal was the model for the Marine Corps Memorial. Of the six men in the photograph, three survived the war and posed for sculptor Felix W. de Weldon. Ironically, the famous Rosenthal

photograph was, in fact, not a photograph of the actual event of the initial flag raising, but of the replacement of the small original flag with a larger one. See Marvin Heiferman, "One Nation, Chiseled in Pictures," in "Lee Friedlander: American Monuments," *The Archive* 25 (1989): 10; the National Park Service brochure "The United States Marine Corps War Memorial"; and Karal Ann Marling and John Wetenhall, *Iwo Jima: Monuments, Memories, and the American Hero* (Cambridge, MA: Harvard University Press, 1991).

4 See Eric Barnouw, "Hiroshima-Nagasaki, August 1945," in *Transmission*, eds. Peter D'Agostino and David Tafler (Thousand Oaks, CA: Sage, 1995).

5 Gary Okihiro, *Cane Fires: The Anti-Japanese Movement in Hawai'i, 1865–1945* (Philadelphia: Temple University Press, 1991), 229–30.

6 Ronald Takaki, *Strangers from a Different Shore: A History of Asian Americans* (New York: Penguin, 1989), 393.

7 See, for instance, Peter Wright and John Armor, *Manzanar* (New York: Times Books, 1988); Ansel Adams, *Born Free and Equal* (New York: U.S. Camera, 1944); and Karin M. Higa, ed., *The View from Within: Japanese American Art from the Internment Camps, 1942–1945* (Seattle: University of Washington Press, 1992).

8 T. Fujitani, "*Go for Broke*, the Movie: Japanese American Soldiers in U.S. National, Military, and Racial Discourses," in this volume.

9 For instance, *Time* magazine explained how to distinguish Chinese from Japanese in an array of racist stereotypes: "The Chinese expression is likely to be more placid, kindly, open; the Japanese more positive, dogmatic, arrogant. Japanese are hesitant, nervous in conversation, laugh loudly at the wrong time. Japanese walk stiffly erect, hard heeled. Chinese, more relaxed, have an easy gait, sometimes shuffle" (quoted in Takaki, *Stranger from a Different Shore*, 370).

10 These are compiled in Robert Nakamura's film *Something Strong Within* (Los Angeles, Japanese American National Museum, 1994). Some cameras were smuggled in with the help of sympathetic camp employees; this was the case for Dave Tatsuno, who made *Topaz 1942–1945*. Toward the end of the camps, restrictions on cameras were enforced less strongly and some of the home movies were taken more openly.

11 The film here probably refers to several incidents in which Asian Americans were murdered the day after Pearl Harbor. In one still unsolved case, a Chinese-American man was decapitated in Tacoma, Washington, on 8 December 1941. See *Unfinished Business: The Japanese American Internment Cases*, produced and directed by Steven Okazaki, 58 min., Mouchette Films, San Francisco, 1984.

12 Marianne Hirsch, *Family Frames: Photography, Narrative, and Postmemory* (Cambridge, MA: Harvard University Press, 1997), 22–23.

13 Jane Kramer, "Letter from Germany: The Politics of Memory," *New Yorker* (14 August 1995): 65.

14 Lauren Berlant, *The Anatomy of National Fantasy* (Chicago: University of Chicago Press, 1991), 20.

The Malleable and the Contested:

The Nanjing Massacre in Postwar China and Japan

DAQING YANG

Over sixty years after the Japanese troops stormed into Nanjing and committed one of the worst atrocities in the Asian-Pacific War, what later became known as the Nanjing Massacre is stirring up intense emotions in China and Japan today, casting a long shadow over their bilateral relations.[1] According to a poll conducted by a Chinese newspaper in early 1997, when asked what they associated with Japan, nearly 84 percent of some one hundred thousand Chinese surveyed chose the Nanjing Massacre more than any other answer.[2] The infamous 1937 Japanese atrocity has been featured in numerous publications as well as a number of screen and television productions in the People's Republic, while each year hundreds of thousands of Chinese visit the Memorial Hall of the Victims in the Nanjing Massacre by Japanese Invaders. Across the sea in neighboring Japan, the so-called Debate over the Nanjing Massacre has been going on for nearly three decades and sees no sign of abating. Producing a seemingly endless stream of books and articles, the subject has apparently made careers for many a self-styled historian, but has also cost at least one politician his cabinet post for openly dismissing it as a Chinese fabrication. The often heated and acrimonious battle is not only carried out in print, but also fought in courtrooms as well as in the streets. When Japanese activists organized screenings of a 1997 Chinese film on the Nanjing Massacre, right-wing groups mounted protests and harassment with their sound trucks; in one case, an angry youth burst on stage and slashed the movie screen. By all standards, the Nanjing Massacre has become one of the most potent symbols of East Asia's "unmastered past," as interest in the subject seems to have transcended a particular historical event and taken on a life of its own.

If this indeed amounts to "a social phenomenon," as one Japanese historian once wryly put it, it is a relatively recent one.[3] With few exceptions, the flood of

Japanese publications on the subject have come out since the early 1970s. In fact, the country's leading liberal daily newspaper, *Asahi shinbun*, hardly ever mentioned the 1937 event throughout the 1950s and 1960s.[4] The same characterization is also largely true for China. The memorial complex in Nanjing was not built until the mid-1980s, nearly half a century after the victims perished. Moreover, although the Nanjing Massacre evokes strong emotions in both countries, it has been the subject of intense disagreement in Japan, whereas the Chinese have appeared to be speaking in unison. The Nanjing Massacre thus presents students of collective memories with a number of questions: Why has the Nanjing Massacre received so much attention in recent decades, in sharp contrast to its relative obscurity during the 1950s and 1960s? What factors have influenced the way this event has been remembered in China and Japan? In particular, what roles have historians played? What issues are at stake in the ongoing debate? This paper addresses these questions by examining the major shifts in the public representations of the Nanjing Massacre in postwar China and Japan, and in doing so, it seeks to shed light on how public history, collective memory, and politics became intertwined in both countries.[5]

An Atrocity Forgotten?

If the extensive media coverage is a recent phenomenon, how was the Nanjing Massacre remembered previously? Before we set out to examine its postwar representation, it is necessary to keep in mind how the event came to be known in the first place.

Compared to other wartime Japanese atrocities in China, the Nanjing Massacre was relatively well-known from early on, in large part due to the presence of a number of Westerners in the fallen Chinese capital. A few days after the city fell on 13 December 1937, the world learned of the atrocities in Nanjing in the pages of the *Chicago Daily News* and the *New York Times*. Public interest had already been heightened because of the Panay and Ladybird incidents, when American and British gunboats were attacked by the Japanese near Nanjing. In several dispatches sent from Shanghai, correspondents Archibald Steele and F. Tilman Durdin, who left Nanjing three days after the Japanese takeover, reported "wholesale atrocities and vandalism" by the Japanese Army.[6] Although some of the reports also criticized the Chinese defense, they gave horrific accounts of Japanese excesses, such as mass executions of captives as well as random murders of civilians. In the meantime, a few foreigners who remained in the city and organized refugee relief provided more detailed descriptions in letters to their friends in Shanghai of the rampant looting, raping, and slaughtering by Japanese soldiers. *Manchester Guardian* reporter H. J. Timperley reproduced some of these correspondences in his book, *What War Means: Japanese Terror in China*, published simultaneously in London and New York in 1938.[7] Although these Western accounts did not specify their magnitude, the Japanese atrocities in the fallen Chinese capital sent a shock wave around the Western world more than a year before Europe was plunged into another major war.[8]

Chinese reports of Japanese brutalities in Nanjing appeared in newspapers and magazines in unoccupied areas a few weeks later, as those who had escaped from the fallen capital recounted their experience and Western accounts were translated into Chinese.[9] Their extensive coverage would help harden the Chinese will to fight and gain international sympathy for China. In his preface to the Chinese translation of Timperley's Book, Guo Morou, a well-known writer with intimate knowledge of Japan, condemned the "unprecedented atrocities" as the crime of the "barbaric Japanese military that abused civilization" and appealed to international justice.[10] Some Chinese were troubled by the published photographs showing apparently docile Chinese victims of murder and rape in Nanjing. One writer questioned why those Chinese appeared simply to be "pitiful lambs" to be slaughtered and humiliated.[11] Such mixed reactions among the Chinese population are understandable in view of the fact that Japanese atrocities in the Nanjing area were by no means an exception, and the Chinese would have to endure their bitter struggle for almost another eight years.

In Japan, the fall of China's capital was celebrated with massive parades all over the country. Because of strict government censorship during the war, few Japanese had any extensive knowledge of the horror that went on in Nanjing. Perhaps even fewer would be disturbed by what they did know. Although the killing of Chinese soldiers in Nanjing and elsewhere was widely reported during the war, such events were considered Japan's military victories. Japan's prize-winning writer Ishikawa Tatsuzō made references to brutalities against Chinese civilians in the Nanjing area in his fiction, *The Living Soldiers*. The April 1938 issue of the monthly journal *Chūō Kōron*, which published an already sanitized version of his novel, was immediately withdrawn by the police and the author was given a four-month prison sentence.[12] Combined with the censorship was a vigorous propaganda campaign conducted by the government to portray Nanjing in peace and prosperity under Japan's benevolent occupation. It was only after the end of the war, therefore, that the Japanese public was confronted with the atrocities of their compatriots in Nanjing.[13] In 1946, the American Occupation authorities launched a program on national radio under the title "The Truth Box" as part of the effort to bring the "truths" to the

Japanese people. Deploying a first-person narrative, the episode on the "Rape of Nanjing" stated that some twenty thousand women and children were slaughtered in Nanjing by "our Japanese troops," and that streets were soaked in blood and covered with corpses for weeks. The unrestrained Japanese soldiers were said to have killed noncombatants, looted, and committed unspeakable atrocities in the city.[14]

These various earlier accounts notwithstanding, it was the war crimes trials in the early postwar years that placed the Nanjing Massacre on the scales of history. Immediately following Japan's surrender in August 1945, the Chinese Nationalist government launched investigations into the Japanese atrocities in Nanjing. In collaboration with the Supreme Command of the Allied Powers (SCAP) in Japan, it produced a large body of evidence on the alleged massacre in Nanjing. Among these were accounts by Chinese survivors and foreign eyewitnesses, in addition to contemporary newspaper reports, damage surveys conducted by an American professor, and burial records of Chinese charity organizations in Nanjing. In 1947 four Japanese Army officers received the death penalty at the military tribunal in Nanjing. Lieutenant General Tani Hisao, who commanded one of the Japanese divisions in the battle of Nanjing, was accused of organizing massacres and participating in atrocities against the Chinese. Three others were junior officers who had been featured in the wartime Japanese publications as heroes for killing hundreds of Chinese with their Japanese swords. Much better known was the international military tribunal in Tokyo, which found General Matsui Iwane, Commander of Japan's Central China Expedition Force, which took Nanjing in 1937, guilty for failing to stop the atrocities in the city. Matsui was hanged on this account together with six other Class-A Japanese war criminals. As to the extent of the Japanese atrocities, the military tribunals in Nanjing and Tokyo agreed on the estimates of about twenty thousand cases of rape and one third of all buildings in the city damaged, but reached somewhat different conclusions on the death toll. The Tokyo trial put it at over 200,000, but the figure of around 100,000 was also given in Matsui's verdict. The Nanjing trial claimed in the verdict that more than 300,000 Chinese had been massacred by the Japanese troops, although the prosecution cited the figure as high as 430,000.[15] With these trials, the Nanjing Massacre secured a prominent place in the histories of China and Japan.

Significantly, these trials brought together the narratives of victims, bystanders, and perpetrators for the first time. The cross-examinations resolved their differences, however. The accused Japanese challenged the verdicts in both trials, but to no avail. Representations of the Nanjing Massacre were to remain divergent after these trials, although they would not come into conflict with each other again until two decades later. In the meantime, the Nanjing Massacre would continue to take on new meanings in both China and Japan under different political conditions.

The founding of the People's Republic of China in 1949 and the outbreak of the Korean War the following year drastically altered the political framework within which the Nanjing Massacre was to be remembered. The Nationalist government that had fought the Japanese troops in Nanjing in 1937 was driven to Taiwan; it also signed a peace treaty with Japan that renounced the rights to war reparations. By excluding Beijing from the peace settlement with Japan and by encouraging Japan to remilitarize, the United States now appeared to be in close collusion with its own former enemy and posed a direct threat to the new government in China. The Nanjing Massacre, in this context, came to be invested with very different meanings. For the first time after the trials, survivors were interviewed in Nanjing. When the national monthly Xinhua Yuebao in 1951 published an article on the massacre, which it termed the "first great wartime Japanese atrocity in China," the author seemed more interested in revealing "the American crimes" during the Japanese atrocities in Nanjing. The article charged that a dozen or so Americans who remained in Nanjing "not only responded well to the imperialist policies of the U.S. Government, but also protected their companies, churches, schools and residences, with the blood and bones of the Chinese people." The International Safety Zone Committee, the article maintained, was made up of imperialists and fascists, and served as the vanguard for the invading Japanese troops. More specifically, the article called attention to the "faithful collusion" between the Japanese and the Americans, quoting one Chinese survivor as saying, "The American devils called out the names [of the Chinese] and the Japanese devils carried out the execution." The journal's editor accentuated the "present significance" of such a historical event by printing along the photographs of Japanese atrocities such banners as "Remembering the Nanjing Massacre. Resolutely Stop American Imperialists' Remilitarization of Japan!"[16] The use of history as an object lesson to serve the present could not have been more blatant.

This was not the only lesson that history could offer, however. As China continued its internal struggles to weed out domestic enemies, class conflict rather than national struggle became the officially sanctioned lens through which to view the country's past. The history of pre-1949 China, seen this way, was above all the history of the ruling classes, consisting of landlords and capitalists and represented by the Nationalist government, exploiting the masses and collaborating with foreign imperialists. Although exhibits of Japan's wartime atrocities, especially those in north and northeastern China, continued to exist, new museums were set up all over China during the 1960s to portray the brutality of China's own "reactionary classes." In Nanjing, annual commemorations were devoted to the revolutionary martyrs who had been executed in Yuhuatai by the Nationalist government. (Ironically, this is the same site where the four Japanese officers charged with the atrocities in Nanjing were executed, a coincidence conveniently ignored in later Chinese writings.) Under such conditions, the Nanjing Massacre of 1937 all but disappeared from the public. This relative obscurity might even have suited the survivors, who were either too ashamed to speak about their sufferings and humiliation, or too afraid to acknowledge their association with the Nationalist regime in defending its capital in 1937.

Interestingly, those who felt safe enough to reminisce semi-openly about the events leading to the Nanjing Massacre were the former Nationalist generals who had been captured and reeducated by the Communist regime after 1949. In a history journal issued for "internal circulation" in 1960, they recounted their participation in the defense of Nanjing and invariably condemned Chiang Kai-shek's "capitulation policy" as a major cause of the heavy loss of Chinese lives.[17] After all, the official history of China's War of Resistance claimed that the war was fought by the Chinese people under the Communist leadership, not the Nationalist government headed by Chiang Kai-shek. The domestic arch rival, widely accused of corruption and incompetence, seemed to be held no less responsible for the great catastrophe in Nanjing than the Japanese invaders.

Shortly after the recollections of these former Nationalist generals, Mei Ru'ao, the former Chinese justice at the Tokyo trial, recounted his own connections to the Nanjing Massacre in the same journal, although with quite a different message. Citing recently published works on the Nazi brutalities in Europe as well as a massive Japanese study of the devastation of the atomic bombs, Mei urged his fellow Chinese to make a "comprehensive and scientific study" of the Nanjing Massacre, which he called "second only to the Nazi atrocities in World War II."[18] What he did not anticipate, as his son revealed in 1997, was later being accused of stirring up national hatred against the Japanese people and his interest in the Nanjing Massacre equated with a hidden admiration of Japanese military prowess.[19]

Mei could not have foreseen how the memory of the Nanjing Massacre would be affected by China's policy toward Japan. Indeed, the early 1960s saw some drastic twists in Sino-Japanese relations. The deterioration in the wake of the 1958 Nagasaki Flag Incident and especially the 1960 renewal of the U.S.-Japan Security Treaty, perhaps more than sheer coincidence, may explain the fact that historians at Nanjing University were preparing the first comprehensive study in China around the same time Mei made his plea. In 1960, the faculty and students of the History Department interviewed many survivors of the atrocity and completed an eight-chapter manuscript two years later. Based on newly compiled statistics of massacre, rape, pillage, and property destruction in Nanjing, the new study essentially confirmed the verdicts reached at the Nanjing trial. That historians in the People's Republic of China put their seal of approval on the verdicts reached by the Nationalist regime is significant. Also noteworthy is that the plan for publication did not materialize, perhaps due to the improvement of the Sino-Japanese relations after the signing of the L-T memorandum in 1962. This study nonetheless served as the basis for future works and thus had important implications. Moreover, the History Department would provide the municipal Foreign Affairs Department with their findings in 1965, with all the statistical computations and photographs, to be used in the reception of interested Japanese visitors. Historians at Nanjing University also held briefings and photograph exhibitions for visiting Japanese delegations and facilitated Japanese scholars with these research materials. In this way, the rediscovered lesson of history would reach a Japanese audience as well.[20]

Before 1970, however, contact between Japan and mainland China was severely limited as the two countries remained without diplomatic relations or a formal conclusion of the state of war. Japan seemed preoccupied with healing its own war wounds, although the Japanese atrocities in Nanjing were not entirely forgotten there either. The incident was detailed in many school textbooks until the late 1950s and openly acknowledged by the educated.[21] The Nanjing Massacre was the subject of a novella by prize-winning writer Hotta Yoshie between 1953 and 1955. Even Mishima Yukio, later known for his dramatic samurai-style suicide but already a well-known writer by then, published a short story in 1955 about a former army officer responsible for killing tens of thousands of Chinese in Nanjing. By growing 580 peonies in his private garden after the war, the officer sought to "make a secret document of his wicked deed": killing 580 Chinese women with his own hands.[22] Though repentance was absent, acknowledgment was not.

Though far from being a news event in the mass media, the Nanjing Massacre began to resurface in popular magazines in the mid-1950s as part of war reminiscences. Here the opinions seemed divided, suggesting a brewing conflict. Whereas some of these recollections confirmed the atrocities in Nanjing in general, several former officers strove to emphasize Japan's innocence. For example, a writer who had been attached to one of the Japanese units in Nanjing offered a detailed account of the execution of tens of thousands of Chinese captives under the order of the high command; another newspaper reporter who followed the Japanese troops into Nanjing gave a similar story.[23] On the other hand, an officer who fought in Nanjing disputed the postwar Chinese estimate of 430,000 victims as completely false. Hata Shunroku, who had been a Field Marshall and Commander-in-Chief of the Japanese Army in China after 1938, admitted that some instances of atrocities did happen, but he considered most of the evidence presented at the Tokyo trial to be fabrications. Similarly, a junior officer serving in the military police in China after 1939 dismissed the evidence at the Tokyo trial as "seventy percent false," that massacring 430,000 Chinese civilians would have been an impossible task for only 8,000 Japanese soldiers in Nanjing.[24] Despite their differences, what these reminiscences had in common was their attribution of such behavior primarily to the conditions of war. This was the decade of the boom in war accounts, and public interest in war reminiscences seemed strong enough to allow for even conflicting stories. In the end, most such personal reminiscences were sketchy at best and amounted to nothing more than small ripples in the stream of postwar memory, without causing serious disturbance.[25]

The ascendance of conservative politics after the creation of the Liberal Democratic Party (LDP) in 1955, however, would gradually affect the public discourse on the war. As the ruling LDP tightened their control over the content of school education, references to Japan's wartime atrocities, including the Nanjing Massacre, were branded left-wing propaganda and gradually disappeared from school textbooks beginning in the late 1950s.[26] In 1957, Kishi Nobusuke, a wartime cabinet member and designated Class-A war criminal, became prime minister. The much celebrated era of "high economic growth" of the 1960s warranted a more positive self-image. In 1963, well-known writer Hayashi Fusao published *An Affirmation of the Great East Asia War*, a major attack on the Tokyo war crimes trial that extended the boundaries of acceptable rhetoric on the war in postwar Japan.[27] The conservative turn in history education soon set off a counteroffensive from progressive historians, whose influence had been steadily on the wane since the Occupation. In 1965, historian and educator Ienaga Saburō began his famous legal battle against the Ministry of Education, which had demanded numerous revisions from his history textbooks.[28] Although the Nanjing Massacre was not directly involved, Japanese conduct in the war became a matter of higher political stakes in this context than in the preceding decade.

While the conservative view of the war was gaining wider acceptance, the 1960s saw the increase in "nongovernmental exchanges" between Japan and China. The image of China still remained largely unfavorable in Japanese opinion polls throughout the decade, especially during the Cultural Revolution, but was steadily improving.[29] The number of Japanese visiting China increased considerably after 1962, reaching an all-time high in 1965.[30] A few of these visitors returned with renewed memories of Japanese wartime atrocities. In

1965, for instance, a group of Japanese veterans visiting the "war-ravaged areas" were briefed by Chinese officials in Nanjing on the Japanese massacre in 1937. Upon returning to Japan, they published their report in a newspaper devoted to promoting Sino-Japanese friendship.[31] After visiting Nanjing in 1967, Niijima Atsuyoshi, a professor of Chinese literature at Waseda University, wrote about the Nanjing Massacre in Japanese magazines and later organized perhaps the first public symposium on the subject at the University of Tokyo.[32] Not all Japanese visitors, to be sure, were persuaded by their Chinese hosts on the issue of the Japanese atrocities. Ōya Sōichi, a well-known commentator who had been in Nanjing as a newspaper reporter immediately after its fall in 1937, led an investigation group to China at the onset of the Cultural Revolution in 1966. At a briefing with Chinese officials in Nanjing, Ōya raised doubts over the figure of 300,000 killed and one third of buildings burned. However, he remained largely silent on the subject to his death in 1970.[33]

Among those Japanese visitors to Nanjing during the mid-1960s, Hora Tomio was to play a prominent role in the later debate. A professor of Japanese history at Waseda University, Hora also visited China in 1966. His 1967 book, *Puzzles in Modern Military History*, devoted over a third of its space to "the Nanjing Incident." The event had first caught his attention back in December 1937, when, taking note of the discrepancies in the numbers of Chinese captives and corpses reported in the press, Hora reached the conclusion that many captives must have been massacred by the Japanese soldiers. Thirty years later, he was greatly disturbed by the justifications of the "Greater East Asia War" in Japan and began to study the Japanese atrocities in Nanjing "in order to provide material for introspection, to renew the feeling of apology to the Chinese people, and to clarify the truth about the Nanjing Incident, which resulted from the erroneous national leadership by the military clique."[34] Making extensive use of the transcripts of the Tokyo trial, contemporary reports by Westerners in China, and reminiscences published in Japan after the war, Hora offered the first systematic examination of the Japanese massacre of disarmed Chinese soldiers as well as other atrocities against Chinese civilians. Although he considered the figure of 430,000 victims not credible, Hora basically agreed with the Chinese verdict of 300,000 as close to the actual number. In conclusion, he held high-ranking Japanese officers responsible for the massacre and charged that the entire Japanese military system was to blame for the atrocities in Nanjing.[35]

Perhaps by sheer coincidence, the first major revisionist account of the Nanjing Massacre also made it to print in Japan around this time. Written by the chief of staff of the Sixth Division that fought in Nanjing, the author sought to clear the name of the condemned divisional commander by arguing that the alleged atrocities were committed by other units. Significantly, the book was prefaced by Araki Sadao, a former Japanese Army minister who had been tried as a Class-A war criminal.[36] These two highly specialized works did not set off an immediate dispute, although they would lay down some of the familiar themes. It was not until after 1971, when the "taboo in the mass media" in Japan on the Nanjing Massacre was finally broken, that the great debate would begin.

Out of Oblivion

The credit for the demolition of this taboo goes to Honda Katsuichi, a journalist with the country's leading liberal newspaper, *Asahi shinbun*. Already known for his prize-winning reporting of the Vietnam War, Honda, who was born in 1931, questioned the Japanese knowledge of the war with China in the postwar period. He reasoned that stories of Hiroshima and Nagasaki, like the My Lai massacre in Vietnam, had all been well-known, but no systematic study of the Japanese wartime atrocities in China had ever been attempted. The absence of Chinese perspectives seemed to Honda to explain why many Japanese found it difficult to understand China's concern over the revival of militarism in Japan. During the summer of 1971, Honda embarked on a forty-day trip in China, visiting sites of Japanese atrocities and collecting eyewitness accounts and other evidence. After returning to Japan, he serialized his reports in *Asahi shinbun* and its weekly magazines, which were later compiled into a popular book, *The Journey in China*.[37] In these reports, Honda confronted the Japanese public with the Chinese experience of war for the first time in postwar Japan. Through the voices of Chinese victims, he recounted Japanese atrocities in many areas of China, including Nanjing. In a total of ten installments on the Nanjing Massacre, Honda described Japanese atrocities against Chinese civilians, mentioning, among them, Japanese officers engaging in "killing contests." Honda quoted from Chinese sources the death toll of 300,000 but also added different estimates such as those given at the Tokyo trial by the Nationalist government as well as the figures cited in Hora's study.[38] Honda's reports, published by Japan's premier newspaper, seized national attention.

The timing could not have been more critical. In fact, several Japanese magazines had published stories on the Nanjing Massacre a few months before Honda's series appeared. Certainly, America's war conduct in Vietnam loomed large in the background as the issue of Japan's military role was widely debated in Japan. The sudden flurry of these publications in 1971, however, was more indicative of the drastic changes in Japan's relations with China. Following U.S. President Richard Nixon's visit to Beijing, normalizing of relations with China became a national priority in Japan. In less than a year, Japan's Prime Minister Tanaka Kakuei would make a historic visit to China, which established diplomatic relations between the two countries. Opinion polls showed that the number of Japanese who liked China was climbing as rapidly as those who disliked China was declining.[39] A government report issued in early 1972 noted that war responsibility became a top issue in public discussions on China.[40] Riding the tide, historian Hora expanded the chapter in his 1967 book into the first scholarly monograph on the subject, appropriately entitled *The Nanjing Incident*.[41] The wartime Japanese translation of Timperley's book was reissued by a publisher in Japan, with a new preface by Niijima Atsuyoshi. By then, the Nanjing Incident had finally emerged from oblivion in postwar Japan.

It was not long before Honda's popular reports were openly challenged. A few months after Honda's series started, the April 1972 issue of *Shokun!*, a monthly "opinion journal" published by the well-known literary magazine *Bungei shunjū*, carried an article entitled "The Illusion of the Nanjing Massacre." Specifically, it questioned the truthfulness of the notorious "killing contest," an incident that was first reported in the Japanese press in 1937 and subsequently cited in Timperley's book. The author of the piece, writing under the name Suzuki Akira, claimed the entire story to be simply a fabrication by the wartime Japanese press to trump up war fever at home. He discredited much of the evidence used by Hora and Honda, both of whom mentioned the case, and stressed the scarcity of primary sources that confirmed the massacre in Nanjing. In subsequent articles published in the same journal, Suzuki probed the event further by interviewing many Japanese veterans, although he did make a trip to Taiwan to meet the former Chinese judge at the Nanjing trial. In contrast to Honda, Suzuki consciously framed his study from the position of the accused, and to prove that the Japanese were not as brutal as portrayed in Honda's reports, Suzuki highlighted the frequent massacres going on in modern China. Finally, he charged that Japanese journalists in the 1970s were turning the Nanjing Incident into another illusion, just as those in the late 1930s lacked the courage to confront the truth.[42]

Although, near the end, Suzuki did admit that tens of thousands of Chinese soldiers and civilians became victims in Nanjing, he stressed that "because the way it came to be known was influenced by politics from the beginning, facts were buried and nobody knows the truth of the [Nanjing] incident even today."[43] Relentless in casting doubt over some aspects of the event as covered in the press, Suzuki's articles created the impression that the entire Nanjing Massacre was a mere illusion concocted by the war crimes trials and journalists. Soon published in book form bearing the same title, *The Illusion of the Nanjing Massacre*, these articles won him a prize from *Bungei shunjū* in the category of nonfiction named after the late Ōya Sōichi. Literary celebrities who served as referees praised the work as an "admirable" and "courageous" challenge to shallow and irresponsible journalism, although one referee wished the book had "confronted the issue in a more frontal manner."[44] Consequently, "Nanjing Massacre as an illusion" became a convenient shorthand that summarized the skepticism or denial that had been harbored in many quarters in Japan.

The parameter of debate was thus set. To Suzuki's support came Yamamoto Shichihei, a commentator who had published an essay in *Shokun!* under the pseudonym Isaiah Ben-Dasan, arguing against making apologies to China over the war. In a series of articles, Yamamoto emphasized the fact that he knew the war firsthand from his two years in the army and disputed the physical possibility of a massacre by the Japanese troops in Nanjing.[45] Both Hora and Honda fought back and engaged Yamamoto in a few rounds of open letter debates.[46] Honda soon followed with another book on Japanese atrocities in China, complete with photographs of Chinese victims and survivors.[47] Hora also published a series of critiques in a history journal and pointedly named his subsequent rebuttal *The Great Nanjing Massacre: Repudiation of the "Illusionization."*[48] In addition to his own works, Hora published two volumes of documents on the Nanjing Massacre, including parts of transcripts of the Tokyo war crimes trial as well as contemporary Western reports of the incident.[49] Although some doubts about the media coverage of Nanjing were planted, the Nanjing Massacre in its entirety was far from disproved. Apart from Suzuki's book, no comprehensive study of the incident challenged Hora's work. In fact, following Ienaga's temporary victory against the Ministry of Education in a Tokyo lower court in 1970, government examination was somewhat relaxed and references to the Nanjing Massacre reappeared in several high school history textbooks after 1974.[50] In his memoir published in 1975, Matsumoto Shigeharu, a veteran journalist who had visited Nanjing and supported Timperley's 1938 publication, acknowledged the contributions of both Hora and Suzuki. Even if the truth of the incident remained unclear, Matsumoto wrote, he was above all saddened by the inhuman behavior of the Japanese troops more than the number of victims. At the same time, he quoted from fellow Japanese correspondents who had been in Nanjing that "it is inconceivable that the atrocities were an organized act" and "those massacred outside the battle probably numbered between 10,000 and 20,000."[51] Although the public debate soon ran out of steam, the battle lines over the Nanjing Massacre had already been drawn in Japan and have not shifted much since. In hindsight, the exchanges in the early 1970s seem a rehearsal for the later decades.

Sino-Japanese friendship seemed to be the dominant theme in China during the decade following the normalization of diplomatic relations in 1972. With Japan's official admission to "having caused trouble in China," the Chinese leaders renounced the right to war reparations. As China embarked on the ambitious program of the Four Modernizations, the importance of Japan's economic assistance appeared greater than ever. Even the revival of Japanese militarism, a perennial concern for China since the early 1950s, now became less threatening to the Chinese leadership, which sought to bring Japan into a strategic alliance against hegemonism, a euphemism for the Soviet expansion. "Although a handful of elements dreaming of the revival of Japanese militarism still exist in Japan," a *People's Daily* editorial confidently pointed out in 1975 on the occasion of the thirtieth anniversary of the end of the war, "we believe that the Japanese people would never allow the history of Japan and Asia to go backward."[52] Following the signing of the Treaty of Peace and Friendship in 1978, Japan's recent aggression receded further to what *Beijing Review* termed "a brief period in the current of over two thousand years of bilateral exchanges." Although the Chinese weekly acknowledged that "during the half century since the end of the 19th century, wars took place between the two countries, and the Chinese people endured great calamity," it was quick to point out that "the Japanese people also suffered damage."[53] By and large, China was only beginning to open up to the outside world. The few Chinese who were aware of this round of debate over the Nanjing Massacre in Japan largely kept it to themselves. When a revised version of the 1962 Nanjing University study was printed for "internal reference" in the late 1970s, its authors noted that "while most of the Japanese works adhere to the truth, uphold the historical facts, and condemn the atrocities of Japanese militarism from the standpoint of justice, a few Japanese from a reactionary position attempt to erase this historical fact."[54] Specifically, they added a chapter attacking Suzuki. Real concerns they might have been, but they were far from interrupting the friendship between the two countries.

The Great Debate in Japan

In late June 1982, all major Japanese newspapers carried headlines claiming that the Ministry of Education had demanded revisions in high school textbooks. The most controversial point in the textbook revision was the change from "shinryaku" (invade and plunder) to "shinkō" (enter and assault), or even to the neutral "shinshutsu" (advance into), in the description of pre-1945 Japanese activities on the Asian continent. Within days the news event escalated into a diplomatic crisis, as the governments of China and Korea filed formal protests against the alleged Japanese attempts to recant the recognition of their past aggression. In the face of strong protests from neighboring countries, the Japanese government expressed regret and its willingness to "study the matter seriously."[55]

The revised texts about the Nanjing Massacre also came under fire. One textbook, for example, had originally described the event in following words:

> When Nanjing was occupied the Japanese troops killed large numbers of Chinese soldiers and civilians, and engaged in assaulting, looting and burning, and were charged with the Nanjing Massacre by the world opinion. The number of Chinese victims allegedly reached 200,000.[56]

After the government-demanded revision, it reads:

> In the confusion when Nanjing was taken, the Japanese troops killed large numbers of Chinese soldiers and civilians, and were charged by the world with the Nanjing Massacre.[57]

Another prerevision text tells that "the Japanese troops that occupied Nanjing massacred a large number of noncombatants and received international condemnation." The revised text added an explanation:

> Meeting strong resistance from the Chinese forces, the Japanese troops suffered heavy losses. Aroused by this the Japanese troops massacred large numbers of Chinese soldiers and civilians when Nanjing was taken, and received international criticism.[58]

Although the dispute here often was over nothing more than a few lines in the textbooks and sometimes the footnotes, about which high school students could probably not care less, it seemed quite obvious that the Ministry of Education was trying to minimize wartime Japanese atrocities such as those in Nanjing. Such suspicion became confirmed when a member of the government Textbook Examination Council was quoted as calling it "unfair to describe the Nanjing Massacre in three to five lines while mentioning Soviet or American atrocities against the Japanese [during the war] in only one line or two." The government examiner further suggested that it was blasphemy to the Japanese troops to emphasize their atrocities.[59]

Although the initial newspaper stories were not entirely accurate—the revisions had been made in the previous year—the textbook fiasco quickly brought issues related to the past war once again to the forefront of national attention in Japan. Ienaga Saburō filed another lawsuit against the Ministry of Education for its improper demands in the textbook revisions. One of the three cases in Ienaga's suit concerned the Nanjing Massacre, which Ienaga described briefly in a footnote in his 1980 textbook. The government examiner demanded that it be rewritten to emphasize the confusion in Nanjing so as not to give the impression that it was an organized atrocity.[60]

The largely moribund debate over the Nanjing Massacre in Japan soon became galvanized in the wake of the textbook controversy. Only a few months later, Hora Tomio published *The Definitive Edition of the Great Nanjing Massacre.* Although the title was not exactly his own choice, as he later explained, the book represented his renewed effort to revise and fortify his earlier conclusions. Journalist Honda Katsuichi went on another visit to China and conducted interviews along the route of the 1937 Japanese attack from the Shanghai area. His *Road to Nanjing,* serialized in the *Asahi Journal* in 1984, told of more stories of atrocities by Japanese troops even before they approached Nanjing. At the initiatives of Honda and Hora, a Nanjing Incident Investigation and Research Group (*Nankin Jiken Chōsa Kenkyūkai*) was founded in the same year. Counting professional historians, attorneys, and schoolteachers among its members, the group meets regularly in monthly discussions and has organized team visits to Nanjing for research. Their studies have resulted in a steady stream of publications on the Nanjing Massacre, including translations of Chinese- and English-language materials.[61]

Also alarmed by the textbook fiasco, some Japanese became indignant at what they saw as foreign interference in Japan's internal affairs as well as the Japanese government's capitulation vis-à-vis China. Tanaka Masaaki, a self-proclaimed disciple under General Matsui during the war and a long-time advocate against the so-called Tokyo trial view of history, emerged as a leading voice. When the textbooks restored their original texts on the Nanjing Massacre in 1984, Tanaka and six others filed a suit against the Ministry of Education at the Tokyo District Court on behalf of "affected schoolchildren and their parents." They demanded 2 million yen as compensation for their "mental suffering" as a result of the Ministry's poor judgments.[62] In an effort to exonerate Matsui and to discredit the Tokyo trial, Tanaka published *Fabrication of the "Nanjing Massacre,"* which was largely based on Matsui's wartime diary. A number of well-known writers, such as Sophia University professor Watanabe Shōichi and University of Tokyo professor Kobori Keichirō, openly praised his work. In a glowing preface to the book, Watanabe recalled that he never heard of the massacre in Nanjing during the war, and further suggested that those who still believed in the massacre after Tanaka's book should simply be labeled "Reds."[63] The conservative daily newspaper *Sankei shinbun* requested former participants in the battle of Nanjing to write Tanaka and offer their corroborating testimonies.

By now the debate over the Nanjing Massacre was in full swing and certainly was not lacking in dramatic moments. A popular history journal discovered at the end of 1985 that in the newly published Matsui wartime diary there were as many as nine hundred errors. Although some of them were minor mistakes, others were obviously intentional alterations to deny the existence of the Japanese atrocities in Nanjing.[64] The great irony, however, was that the author of these distortions was no other than Tanaka Masaaki, himself, an adamant critic of falsification. Most people were shocked at such blatant alterations of important primary materials. Tanaka had discredited himself in the eyes of many.[65]

Fortunately for historians and the public alike, not everyone falsified documents. Important Japanese sources on the event began to be unearthed. In 1984, excerpts of General Nakajima Kesago's wartime diary were published "as it was" in a history magazine. Nakajima commanded the Sixth Division that took Nanjing and then served briefly as the garrison commander in the city. Among other things, his diary made references to "the policy generally not to take captives" as well as a search for large trenches in which to execute and bury seven or eight thousand men. At one point, he claimed to have watched a Japanese sword master decapitating two Chinese captives.[66] This was one of the most significant pieces of evidence of the organized nature of atrocities in Nanjing, recorded by a high-ranking Japanese commander on the scene. Meanwhile, many former enlisted men began to speak out about their wartime behavior and to publish recollections that confirmed the atrocities in Nanjing.[67]

Equally dramatic was the reversal made by a major veterans group on the issue of the Nanjing Massacre. In the wake of the textbook controversy, Kaikōsha, the fraternity association of the prewar army cadet school graduates, sent an urgent request to its eighteen thousand members for eyewitness accounts that could disprove the "so-called Nanjing Massacre."[68] At the center of this effort was Unemoto Masami, a participant in the battle of Nanjing himself and a postwar instructor at Japan's National Defense University. A firm believer in the innocence of the Japanese Army, Unemoto received over one hundred replies and edited them into an eleven-part series in the association's journal under the title "Battle History of Nanjing Based on Testimonies." Contrary to Kaikōsha's expectation, however, a number of its members offered testimonies that confirmed the existence of the atrocity. Among them was a former officer under Matsui, who estimated that some 120,000 captives were killed outside the city under orders of a staff officer. Although he later modified the figure to "no less than tens of thousands," his testimony alone would seem to abort the entire effort to deny the atrocity. Confronted with other compelling evidence, Unemoto estimated between three thousand and six thousand Chinese were illegally killed by the Japanese troops in Nanjing. In the concluding part of the series, Katokawa Kōtarō, an editor of Kaikōsha's journal, admitted that "there was no excuse for such massive illegal executions" and stated that "as someone related to the former Japanese Army, I have to apologize deeply to the Chinese people."[69] Although this statement was welcomed by many in Japan, including some of the Kaikōsha's own members, it also met with strong opposition from many others. Tanaka Masaaki, for one, sought to frustrate the planned publication of the complete testimony, questioning the wisdom of a veteran organization like Kaikōsha to publish anything that would tarnish the reputation of the Imperial Army.[70] The editorial board largely stood by Katokawa's position, and a few years later published a two-volume history that included many valuable military records though without the apology.[71]

To be sure, the verbal exchange has not always been so polite, and sarcasm has been commonplace. In such a highly politicized and polarized debate, there seems to be little room for dispassionate scholarship, as it becomes questionable if one can maintain an appearance of impartiality. The historian Hata Ikuhiko, for instance, claims to be taking a middle position in the debate. His important study of the Nanjing Massacre, published in paperback in 1986, made extensive use of many previously untapped military records as well as reminiscences of Japanese soldiers. Hata offered institutional and psychological explanations of the widespread Japanese atrocities in Nanjing and concluded that General Matsui was ultimately responsible for the behavior of his subordinates. Making the distinction between war casualties and illegal atrocities, Hata came to an estimate of 40,000 Chinese victims, while expecting a slight increase as new evidence might appear.[72]

By the late 1980s, those who insisted on a complete denial of the organized massacre in Nanjing were certainly losing ground. It had become apparent that the Japanese atrocities not only took place in Nanjing in 1937 but were far more than random acts of the rank and file. New evidence on the subject continued to be discovered. A factory worker named Ono Kenji, for one, for years devoted himself to unearthing records among former soldiers in his hometown in Fukushima Prefecture. After many failed attempts, Ono's effort paid off when he secured several valuable diaries by veterans. These diaries, published under pseudonyms, provide vivid descriptions of brutal killings of Chinese prisoners and civilians by ordinary Japanese soldiers.[73] Scholars also searched for new sources outside Japan. Kasahara Tokushi, a university professor and a member of the Nanjing Incident study group, for example, used previously untapped missionary records in the United States in his recent book on the horrors inside the Nanjing Refugee Zone.[74] Both Honda and Kasahara took the witness stand on behalf of Ienaga in his textbook trial. In October 1993, the Tokyo Higher Court ruled in Ienaga's favor on the issue of the Nanjing Massacre, considering the government demands for revision inappropriate. The Ministry of Education accepted its defeat by choosing not to appeal the verdict.[75]

Although there is some truth to the complaint that the debate produced more superficial comments and repetitions than concrete results, the publicity given to the Nanjing Massacre in Japan has contributed to the growing public awareness of issues of wartime atrocities, such as those committed by Unit 731, and wartime sex slaves known as "comfort women." As a result of the untiring efforts of many Japanese citizens determined to expose Japan's war crimes and thereby seek reconciliation with other Asian peoples, the Nanjing Massacre and other aspects of Japanese aggression have entered some Japanese memorials on the war. As early as 1978, the painters Maruki Iri and Maruki Toshi, well-known for their "Hiroshima murals" depicting the victims of the atomic bombs, created a four-by-eight-foot painting entitled The Nanjing Massacre. More recently, they joined overseas Chinese artists in exhibitions on the subject.[76] For more than ten years, a number of Japanese citizen groups have been visiting Nanjing to plant trees and to help repair the city's famed walls as gestures of repentance and reconciliation.[77] Japanese make up the overwhelming majority (170,000) of the some 200,000 foreign visitors to the Nanjing Massacre Memorial in Nanjing.[78] One Japanese artist even created a replica of the relief in the memorial back in Japan, using recycled aluminum cans. Within Japan, they have conducted symposia, exhibitions, and rallies to raise public awareness of Japan's past aggression in Asia. With the help of Japanese supporters, several survivors of the Nanjing Massacre have filed a lawsuit against the Japanese government, demanding compensation for their sufferings.[79] Even some politicians tried to deal with the matter. As if to address this serious issue in their bilateral relations, Japan's Prime Minister Hashimoto Ryūtarō considered paying a visit to Nanjing during his state visit to China in 1997, which would have been the first for any Japanese prime minister after the war. However, he dropped the idea, allegedly because of opposition from hard-liners within his own party (and perhaps from right-wing groups as well).[80] A year later, Nonaka Kōmu, LDP secretary-general, made an unprecedented visit to the Nanjing Massacre memorial.

However, such developments have also invited virulent backlash in recent years. A succession of politicians continued to call the Nanjing Massacre a Chinese fabrication. Although almost all of them ended up resigning from the cabinet, grassroots conservative efforts seemed to make some inroads in ending what was considered distorted views of modern Japan influenced by the Tokyo war crimes trial. Since the mid-1990s, the conservative voice found its leading spokesman in Fujioka Nobukatsu, a University of Tokyo education professor. His Society for Liberal Views of History has attracted considerable support from businesspeople and intellectuals. Higashinakano Osamichi, a university professor of European intellectual history, made himself a specialist on the Nanjing Massacre by dismissing contemporary reports as wartime propaganda. True, the initial heat in the wake of the textbook fiasco has somewhat died down, in part due to the discovery of new evidence and research and also because other issues related to the war, such as the "comfort women," came to claim center stage in recent years. The publication of Iris Chang's book in 1997, with its numerous factual errors, handed the conservatives a much needed opportunity to blame the Nanjing Massacre on the conspiracy of a second-generation Chinese American journalist.

Now that a complete denial of the massacre no longer seems possible, although such denial has by no means disappeared completely, the focus of contention has shifted to the issue of numbers of Chinese victims and other factual details. Whereas the objectives of Fujioka and his supporters are clearly political, their approach has given the impression of being empirical. To Fujioka and others, the Chinese estimate of 300,000 victims in Nanjing is a gross exaggeration, and as such, the Nanjing Massacre stands as a prime symbol of the injustice of the Tokyo war crimes trial. Even some well-respected historians have also found it difficult to acknowledge the "great massacre" as long as the Chinese estimate of 300,000 stands. In addition to relentless attacks on the Chinese version of the story, former Japanese soldiers who have confessed their crimes were also condemned as liars because of discrepancies in their accounts. In 1994, former members of Azuma Shirō's platoon filed a libel suit against him as well as his publisher, accusing them of fabricating an episode of atrocities in his published diary. Eighty-year-old Azuma lost the case two years later, when the court ruled his description could not be substantiated by "objective evidence."[81] In 1996, the target was the new Nagasaki Atomic Bomb Museum, where the curator included a brief reference to the Nanjing Massacre in a section on Japan's aggression in Asia. A massive protest spearheaded by nationalist groups mobilized some eighty sound trucks to Nagasaki and eventually forced the removal of photographs of Chinese victims of the Nanjing Massacre from the exhibit.[82] Similar attacks were mounted in a number of other localities throughout Japan.

Beneath these arguments over factual details, even greater division persists over the meaning of the entire war in prewar Japan. A telling example was the failure of the majority of Japan's Diet to support even an ambiguously worded resolution on the fiftieth anniversary of the end of the war.[83] While historians like Hora, Kasahara, and others have emphasized the nature of the prewar Japanese sociopolitical system as the basic cause of what happened in Nanjing, a number of writers have suggested, explicitly or otherwise, that Japanese atrocities in Nanjing pale in comparison with other mass killings in modern China and elsewhere. Fujioka and his supporters brand those Japanese who stress Japan's wartime atrocities as "masochistic" or "Japanese who are anti-Japanese." Their views are striking a chord with a significant number of Japanese who feel threatened by an assertive China.[84] Even if future evidence can narrow the difference in statistics and correct factual details, however, interpretations of the Nanjing Massacre are likely to remain divided. The contest over the history of the Japanese wartime behavior in Asia is unlikely to see closure soon.

A National Symbol for China

Only a few years after the Sino-Japanese friendship reached new symbolic heights with the 1978 Treaty of Peace and Friendship, the 1980s began to see Japan's relations with China and other Asian neighbors increasingly coming under the shadow of historical issues such as war and colonialism. The 1982 textbook fiasco in Japan provided a catalyst in this trend. Prime Minister Nakasone's visit to the Yasukuni Shrine in 1985, the break of the 1 percent ceiling of defense spending, and another controversy over a textbook in 1986, all raised the specter of a revival of Japanese militarism. Chinese leaders became alarmed and, justifiably or not, increasingly came to view other undesirable developments in Japan and in their bilateral relations with Japan through this lens.[85] When in 1988 a Japanese film company deleted the scene of Japanese atrocities in China from Bertolucci's film, The Last Emperor, for instance, Chinese newspapers immediately condemned it as an effort to "erase and whitewash history."[86] For a number of years, Japanese politicians themselves appeared to be lending credence to this view by making repeated statements denying Japan's aggression in Asia or wartime atrocities, culminating in Justice Minister Nagano Shigeto's categorical denial in 1994 of the Nanjing Massacre as a "fabrication."

When reports of the Japanese textbook revision first reached China in mid-1982, the Nanjing Massacre along with other Japanese wartime atrocities, surfaced in the Chinese press almost overnight. The mid-August commemoration of the anniversary of Japan's surrender in that year took a decidedly negative tone, as major Chinese newspapers carried articles under such titles as "How Can History Be Distorted? Records of the Japanese Massacre in Nanjing." Survivors of the 1937 massacre once again recounted their hellish experience, this time in the press and on television. On 12 August, the "Exhibition of Criminal Evidence of the Japanese Massacre in Nanjing" was opened to the public in Nanjing.[87] To counter what it perceived as renewed efforts to revive militarism in Japan, the Chinese government began a concerted effort at all levels aimed at preserving and strengthening the memories of Japanese wartime aggression in China.

The fortieth anniversary of the Japanese surrender—15 August 1985—saw the completion of the Memorial for the Compatriot Victims in the Nanjing Massacre by the Japanese Invading Troops. The construction of this 25,000-square-meter memorial complex, which began in late 1983 at the site of an alleged massacre in southwest Nanjing, was a direct response to the textbook revision

Figure 1. The abstract and the exact: a monument stands near the entrance to the memorial compound. Its three columns with five rings together represent three hundred thousand, the official Chinese estimate of the Chinese victims in Nanjing. The nearby column specifics the duration of the Nanjing Massacre.

Figure 2. The concrete and the grotesque: a blood-stained bayonet blade, an oversized Chinese victim agonizing half-buried, the broken city gate of Nanjing. *Calamity upon the Ancient City*, as the new sculpture is known, now makes up the altar of commemoration.

Figure 3. Heroic victims? These masculinized Chinese men and women are shown to have no fear facing their executioners.

in Japan the previous year. In addition to the numerous photographs and written accounts depicting Japanese brutality, on display in large glass showcases in a special room are human skeletons reportedly unearthed in the process of the construction. Inscribed on the front wall in Chinese, English, and Japanese is "VICTIMS 300,000"—the official Chinese estimate of those killed by the Japanese. Although the project started as a local initiative and received funding largely from the local government, the name of the building was in the handwriting of the country's paramount leader, Deng Xiaoping, making this undertaking an unmistakably national commemoration. Meanwhile, smaller but no less conspicuous monuments commemorating the massacre victims mushroomed at over a dozen sites of Japanese brutalities throughout the city. The inscriptions, often written by well-known local calligraphers, offer a vivid lesson in patriotism. Designated a "Site for Patriotic Education" for the city's schoolchildren and youths, the Nanjing Massacre Memorial seems to have become a great success. During the first decade after it opened, four million people have visited.[88] In 1997, the Memorial completed a new phase of expansion. New sculptures and monuments now form the center of public ceremony, with a much bigger space. Names of several hundred victims who had been identified have been engraved on a section of the wall, now referred to as the "crying wall." The indoor exhibits were also overhauled. An interior design firm in Shanghai was hired to create an atmosphere of sadness by accentuating the black color. Thus, although memorials and history museums are hardly new institutions in China, new techniques, some borrowed from abroad, were consciously adopted to enhance the ceremonial and emotional impact of commemorations.[89]

Apart from direct government projects, Chinese artists have joined the effort to make the Nanjing Massacre part of the country's collective memory. In 1985, Zhou Erfu, one of China's veteran novelists, published *The Fall of Nanjing*, a literary work he conceived at the time of the textbook controversy. Praised as "a monumental work depicting the great war of resistance," this historical novel describes in vivid language the defense of Nanjing as well as the Japanese atrocities.[90] A younger writer working for the Army authored a nonfiction work entitled *The Great Nanjing Massacre*, making extensive use of interviews with survivors. Written in the first person, the book was highly successful and has been translated into English and Japanese in China.[91] Two film studios in Fujian and Nanjing joined efforts in 1988 to bring the Nanjing Massacre to the screen for the first time, releasing *Evidence of the Massacre in Blood*. The film, based on the true experience of two Chinese who had found and hidden incriminating photographs taken by the Japanese themselves in Nanjing, was regarded by Chinese veterans of the Nanjing battle as "historically accurate and full of national sentiment."[92] Incidentally, those two Chinese were relocated in China and their story aired in a television documentary. In 1997, Wu Ziniu, a well-known film director, made yet another feature movie about the Nanjing Massacre, this time not just for the domestic audience but for those outside China as well. Mass media in particular thus helps popularize the images of the Japanese brutalities in Nanjing.

Considerable attention has been paid to new documentation. A citywide survey in the 1980s turned up 1,756 eyewitnesses to the atrocities, among whom 176 had escaped with scars still visible on their bodies, 514 had relatives killed, and 44 women were raped by Japanese soldiers.[93] Several of these survivors appeared on national and local television regularly to recount their harrowing experience, producing a dramatic effect especially on the younger generation. Many of their testimonies were published with reprints of contemporary Chinese reports and translations of English materials. In 1994, surveys of conditions in Nanjing, conducted by Japan's South Manchurian Railway Company in early 1938, were discovered. Although the same material had been reprinted in a Japanese documentary collection two years before, its publication in China coincided with Nagano's denial of the Nanjing Massacre and caused quite a sensation.[94]

As Chinese historians were once again called on to perform their duties, detailed studies of the massacre began to appear in academic journals in the early 1980s and, by the end of the decade, several major works on the Nanjing Massacre were completed. Most of them made use of the verdicts of both the Nanjing and Tokyo trials, which hitherto had been seldom touched in China. Gao Xingzu, a history professor at Nanjing University who coauthored its 1962 study, published the first scholarly book on the subject in China in 1985, using Chinese, English, and Japanese sources.[95] Gao also participated in a major collaborative project that resulted in the publication of three volumes on the Nanjing Massacre, consisting of a "draft history" and two volumes of archival and other historical materials published for the first time.[96]

Almost all of the Chinese studies emphasize the atrocity as a logical manifestation of the Japanese militarist-expansionist tradition. One writer called the Nanjing Massacre "nothing but a major display and act of Japanese militarist bushido spirit during the early stage of war."[97] "Japanese militarism, should bear the sole responsibility," concluded another Chinese writer, "but the Japanese people had no share of it, as they were victimized."[98] The clear distinction between Japanese people and Japanese militarism has been consistent, if contrived, in Chinese representation of the war. For instance, both above-mentioned films about the massacre made sure they included "good Japanese." Despite differences in style and emphasis, most of these writers reached the same conclusion, that "the textbook revision was a clear signal that a few people were attempting to revive Japanese militarism." They also shared the conviction that historians in the two countries "should join hands in educating themselves and the younger generation with true history, and in drawing lessons from it, in order to pass on the friendly relations between the two peoples to future generations."[99]

Alarm over the right-wing revisionism of the war in general and the Nanjing Massacre in particular was by no means limited to the People's Republic. A number of scholars in Taiwan, most notably Li Yunhan and Li Enhan, began addressing the issue in the 1980s, with no less vigor.[100] Two volumes in the *Documents of the Revolution* series, published by the official Committee on Guomindang History, were devoted to the Nanjing Massacre.[101] As trade and cultural exchange between Taiwan and mainland China increased in the past decade, many books and articles on the Nanjing Massacre authored by mainland Chinese were reprinted or published in Taiwan.[102] Of the over one hundred thousand overseas Chinese who have visited the Nanjing Massacre Memorial in Nanjing, many have come from Taiwan. More recently, such cross-straits collaboration was the hallmark of the 1995 feature film *The Rape of Nanjing*. Financed by a Taiwanese businessman and featuring a well-known actor from Taiwan, this independently produced film was aimed at the Chinese population worldwide. Perhaps not by coincidence, apart from portraying the heroic defense of Nanjing by Nationalist soldiers, the film included a fictional character—a Taiwanese serving in the Imperial Japanese Army. Indignant at the widespread Japanese brutality against Chinese civilians, he attempts to rescue a Chinese victim but ends up being killed by Japanese soldiers.[103] In this sense, Japan's wartime atrocities in China produced a new kind of "united front" of Chinese on both sides of the Taiwan Strait.

In contrast to China's portrayal of the Nanjing Massacre before the 1980s, international sympathy for China during the war has become a major theme. The discovery in 1996 of the diary of John Rabe, who headed the Nanjing International Safety Zone Committee, also created a sensation in China as in the West. In an unprecedented move, representatives from two Nanjing-based publishers were immediately dispatched to Germany and, after intense negotiation, purchased the Chinese-language rights for a significant sum. A full Chinese translation of Rabe's diary was published in less than a year, even ahead of its German editions, and has become something of a best-seller in China. In the meantime, Rabe's tombstone has been brought from Germany to rest on the grounds of the Memorial in Nanjing.[104] Likewise, artifacts belonging to American missionaries who stayed in Nanjing were also sought by the Memorial. The Nanjing Massacre Memorial itself has received some two hundred thousand visitors from foreign countries in its first decade, a fact its officials are now eager to emphasize. In 1998, the Memorial published in Chinese a collection of testimonies on the Nanjing Massacre by both Westerners and Japanese.[105]

These efforts at fortifying the collective memory of the Nanjing Massacre through visual images and verbal descriptions have produced a cumulative and remarkable effect in raising public awareness in China. Chinese historians who study the Nanjing Massacre, however, still face a task even more formidable than that of their counterparts in Japan. One overseas Chinese writer admitted in the late 1980s that "the Japanese have produced more works [on the Nanjing Massacre] that are systematic and persuasive, while the Chinese publications use more emotional language but lack detailed analysis and comment."[106] Frequent factual errors, unnecessary additions or exaggerations in the Chinese works, he emphasized, only provide the pretext for an opponent to dismiss their entire validity. This is still a sound reminder, although historical works on the Nanjing Massacre are making some limited progress.

In 1997, a group of Chinese historians and archivists in Nanjing published the most comprehensive history so far of the Nanjing Massacre. They differ little from the earlier conclusions on key issues. In their explanations of the Japanese atrocities, these Chinese authors still believe that the massacre was planned by the Japanese high command, including General Matsui Iwane, before the attack on Nanjing began. Regarding the scope of the atrocity in Nanjing, the aforementioned history still puts the total death toll of soldiers and civilians at over 300,000.[107] Sun Zaiwei, the lead author and editor of the book, however, made the important point that the exact death toll may be open to discussion "as long as one respects and recognizes the historical fact that the invading Japanese troops wantonly slaughtered the Chinese people on a large scale."[108] In a more recent article, Sun suggested distinguishing between Chinese soldiers who died in action and those who died afterwards. This is an unprecedented move, as the Chinese so far have viewed the entire conflict as the result of Japanese aggression and therefore such distinction as unnecessary.[109] Though these may be small steps, they nonetheless indicate that Chinese historians are beginning to take the initiative.

Writing history in the People's Republic of China used to be a hazardous profession.[110] Although official control has relaxed considerably for most areas of historical research and Chinese historians enjoy greater freedom than just a decade before, the state has not given up its role as the custodian of national historical memories. Requests for interviews with massacre survivors have to be approved by the local government, and it is only recently that survivors as well as researchers of the Nanjing Massacre are allowed to travel to Japan to participate in symposia and other activities. Privately organized commemorative activities not sponsored by the government, such as seminars held by overseas Chinese as well as the above-mentioned independently produced feature film in 1995, can encounter obstacles from the government.[111] Issues such as Japan's past aggression in China have always been placed in the larger context of the government's diplomatic maneuvers with Japan; at the same time, the collective memory of the country's past century is intimately linked to the government's legitimacy at home. As Lucian Pye has pointed out, the Chinese people face "unbearable pains for their recent history."[112] As the state faces an increasingly restive population, which in recent years has manifested itself in anti-Japanese demonstrations (a much-honored tradition going back to the early twentieth century) and demands for reparations from Japan, it is not clear how much autonomy the state still has.[113] It is obvious that where writing the history of the Nanjing Massacre in China is concerned, there is a lot more at stake than the oft-quoted dictum of "seeking truth from facts."

A Clash of Memories?

Collective memories of the Nanjing Massacre have never been unproblematic; instead, they have always been at variance with each other, even though the conflict therein remained dormant and did not erupt into the open until two decades ago.

The descriptions at the beginning of this paper suggest that the representation of the Nanjing Massacre functions rather differently in these two countries. The degree of unanimity with which the Chinese publicly remember the Nanjing Massacre today may seem a natural reflection of the widely shared views of Japanese militarism, but in fact, it has also been carefully cultivated by the state. Memories of Japanese aggression in general and of the Nanjing Massacre in particular play an increasingly important unifying role in the emerging Chinese self-perception, and as such are reinforced by government-sponsored news media and education and academic research. What is important and yet ignored by many (particularly in China) is that these memories have not been static, but rather have metamorphosed over time in postwar history. Just as the interpretations of the Nationalist defense in 1937 have changed considerably in China, the current Chinese evaluation of Westerners in the Nanjing Refugee Zone is sharply different from just two decades ago, the repeated admonition that "historical facts cannot be altered" notwithstanding. It goes without saying that these changes were made possible by the profound shifts in China's domestic and international politics.

In contrast, as a society with greater freedom of expression, Japan has seen the Nanjing Massacre becoming a divisive issue. Contestants on both sides of the debate have viewed it as a focal point of two diametrically opposed views on Japan's past war as well as a testing ground for attitudes toward present Sino-Japanese relations. Some would stress the aggressive and brutal nature of Japan's war as well as of prewar Japanese society; others would like to see the Tokyo trial denounced unequivocally and pride in Japan restored. The former would emphasize the importance of understanding Chinese sentiments and atoning for Japanese crimes; the latter would call such actions capitulation to foreign pressure and betrayal. In this sense, the debate over the Nanjing Massacre is a microcosm of the clashes between larger ideological undercurrents in postwar Japan in terms of evaluating the past and making choices for the future. Just as important is the fact that such issues are fiercely contested within Japan, which shows that the nation-state need not be the only boundary where collective memory is demarcated.

The changing postwar political milieux, domestic and international, have profoundly influenced the way the Nanjing Massacre has been remembered in Japan and China. It is too simplistic, however, to reduce the debate to merely a political or ideological battle, because it also raises important questions about how memory works and how histories are to be made.

At a fundamental level, the debate over the Nanjing Massacre can be seen as a contest between the memories of the victim and those of the perpetrator. Although such memories have been constantly recreated by latter-day politicians, historians, artists, and others, those who directly experienced the event carry much weight in each country. It is true that some perpetrators have confessed to their crime and, in doing so, have acknowledged the claims of the victims. It is also true that victims do not have an exclusive claim to authenticity. In this sense, such a conflict cannot be resolved by simply flattening it to the level of empirical facts, but instead must be approached with a better understanding of how individual memory is created and passed on.[114] With the passing of the generation of survivors, eyewitnesses, and perpetrators, the already tenuous link between past events and present understanding by way of direct experience will erode even further. This holds as much potential for dispassionate common understanding as for intensified differences.

The debate over the Nanjing Massacre is not about the difference between China and Japan. In fact, the mechanisms of remembering the Nanjing Massacre in both societies share some similarities. Neither country is prepared to leave such an important matter solely to historians to work out, and patriotism has been evoked in both China and Japan when the issue of the Nanjing Massacre is discussed. The media, in different ways, contributed to the heightened awareness of the Nanjing Massacre in both countries. Despite the resistance on the part of some Japanese to identify themselves with the Japanese state, the national framework seems to dominate the historiography in both countries. Moreover, the debate has been dominated and fueled by the prevailing views in both countries that there is one truth about the Nanjing Massacre that can be documented. Even a cursory look through Chinese and Japanese publications shows an unusually frequent use of the terms "truth" and "facts," and leaves the impression that "distortion" and "fabrication" have become most effective weapons to delegitimize one's opponent. They seem to share the strong belief not only that the past is knowable, but that such knowledge has important implications for the present. As I have argued elsewhere,[115] the Nanjing Massacre poses great challenges to historians, in fact, to anyone trying to make sense of a traumatic event in the recent past. Historians, who consider investigating the past and finding meaning for the present and future to be their professional mission, are by no means the only custodians of collective memories of the Nanjing Massacre. The debate should serve as a vivid reminder of our potential and capability as well as our limits and fallibility.

Notes

An earlier version of this paper was published as "A Sino-Japanese Controversy: The Nanjing Atrocity as History," *Sino-Japanese Studies* 3, no. 1 (November 1990): 14–35. The author is grateful to the many individuals who have generously shared their ideas and materials with me over the years, in particular my two fellow panelists at the 1997 AAS, Mark Eykolt, Takashi Yoshida, and our discussant, Joshua Fogel. I also thank Takashi Fujitani for offering extensive comments on an earlier draft. All translations are mine unless otherwise noted.

1 Although intense emotions over the Nanjing Massacre can be found outside these two countries, this paper is limited to China and Japan. To this day, there is still no agreement on the nomenclature describing the event. The choice of terminology often reflects discrepant representations and can therefore have important implications. Generally speaking, "the Rape of Nanjing" has been used primarily in the West. Since the end of the war, the Chinese have always referred to it as *Nanjing datusha*, which they have translated as the Nanjing Massacre. In Japan, *dai gyakusatsu* (great massacre) or *gyakusatsu* (massacre) tends to confirm the magnitude of an atrocity, as do *dai zangyaku* (great atrocity) and *Nankin atoroshitisu* (the Nanjing atrocities). *Nankin jiken* (Nanjing incident) clearly lacks these connotations, but it is occasionally used interchangeably with other terms. Throughout this essay, I use "Nanjing Massacre" to refer to the Japanese atrocities in the Nanjing area in the winter of 1937–1938; I add the term "great" whenever it appears in the original translation to indicate the nuance of the language.

2 The next highest choices given were "Japanese aggressors and the War of Resistance" (81.3 percent), cherry blossoms, *bushidō*, and Mount Fuji (all around 50 percent). See *Asahi shinbun*, 17 February 1997 (evening). All subsequent citations of this newspaper are from the national morning edition unless otherwise indicated.

3 Hata Ikuhiko, "Ronsō shi kara mita Nankin gyakusatsu jiken" (The Nanjing Massacre Incident as seen from the history of the controversy), *Seiron* 198 (February 1989): 234–35. Professor Hata is also a protagonist in this debate.

4 A search for references to the Japanese atrocities in Nanjing between 1948 and 1970 in the *Asahi shinbun* table of contents database turns up not a single hit. The result for 1945–1948 was thirteen. See *Asahi shinbun midashi dēta bēsu* (Tokyo: Asahi shinbunsha, 1995).

5 A number of authors have commented on the memories of the Nanjing Massacre among overseas Chinese after the publication of Iris Chang's bestseller, *The Rape of Nanjing: The Forgotten Holocaust of World War II* (New York: Basic Books, 1997). See, for example, James Dao, "New Interest in Japan's War Atrocities, but Why Now?" *New York Times*, 14 December 1997.

6 For F. Tillman Durdin's reports, see *New York Times*, 18 December 1937; 9 January 1938.

7 In the United States, it was published as *Japanese Terror in China* (New York: Modern Age Books, 1938).

8 One of the better-known contemporary accounts in English is Edgar Snow, *The Battle for Asia* (New York: Random House, 1941). The Japanese government issued a confidential translation of this book during the war.

9 Some of the Chinese accounts have been reprinted in Committee for the Compilation of Sources on the "Nanjing Massacre" and the Library of Nanjing, compilers, *Qin-Hua Rijun Nanjing datusha shiliao* (Source materials relating to the horrible massacre committed by the Japanese troops in Nanjing in December 1937) (Nanjing: Jiangsu Guji Chubanshe, 1985). The English rendition is original.

10 See Guo Moruo, preface to *Wairen mudu zhong zhi Rijun baoxing* (Atrocities of the Japanese troops as witnessed by foreigners), by H. J. Timperley (Hankou: Guomin Chubanshe, 1938).

11 See, for example, Liu Liangmo, "Kuai ba gaoyang bianchen tie de duiwu" (Let's quickly turn lambs into troops of iron), *Kangzhan sanri kan* 58 (29 June 1938): 5–6.

12 For a complete version with deleted passages restored, see Ishikawa Tatsuzō, "Ikiteiru heitai" (The living soldiers), *Chūō Kōron (Rinji Zōkan) Gekidō no Shōwa bungaku* (November 1997): 274–350.

13 For discussion of Japanese press coverage of this issue, see Takeshi Toshida, "Battle over History: The Nanjing Massacre in Postwar Japan," in *The Nanjing Massacre in History and Historiography*, ed. Joshua A. Fogel (Berkeley: University of California Press, 2000), 72–73.

14 SCAP Minkan Jōhō Kyōikubu, *Shinsō hako: Taiheiyō sensō no seiji, gaikō, rikukaisen no shinsō* (The truth box: The truths about the politics, diplomacy, and land and battles of the Pacific War) (Tokyo: Kozumo Shuppansha, 1946), 151–52.

15 Records of the Tokyo trial can be found in John Pritchard and Sonia Magbanua Zaide, compilers, *The Tokyo War Crimes Trial*, 27 vols. (New York: Garland, 1987). Hirota Kōki, Japan's foreign minister at the time of the incident, was also found guilty on account of the atrocities in Nanjing in addition to other alleged crimes. The complete records of the Nanjing trial have not yet been published, although some of its documents are included in Committee for the Compilation of Sources on the "Nanjing Massacre" et al., compilers,

Qin-Hua Rijun Nanjing datusha dang'an (Archival documents relating to the horrible massacre by the Japanese troops in Nanjing in December 1937) (Nanjing: Jiangsu Guji Chubanshe, 1987), 589–622. The English rendition is original.

16 See "Zhuiyi Rikou Nanjing datusha" (Recollections of the Great Nanjing Massacre committed by the Japanese invaders), *Xinhua yuebao* 3 (1951): 988–91. A similar accusation can be found in Guo Shijie, *Rikou qin-Hua baoxing* (Atrocities of the Japanese invasion of China) (Beijing: Lianhe Chubanshe, 1951). It is true that John Rabe, the chairman of the committee, was a Nazi Party member, but he frequently used his swastika armband to fend off Japanese soldiers. It is also true that committee members, believing the Japanese promise not to do harm, told Chinese soldiers hiding in the Safety Zone to surrender to the Japanese Army, an action they later regretted. The accusations of "fascism" and "collusion," however, greatly transcended interpretative possibilities offered by all the available evidence.

17 See the recollection of former Nationalist General Du Yuming and others in *Wenshi ziliao xuanji* 12 (December 1960).

18 Mei Ru'ao, "Guanyu Gu Shoufu, Songjing Shigeng he Nanjing datusha shijian" (On Tani Hisao, Matsui Iwane, and the Great Nanjing Massacre Incident), *Wenshi ziliao xuanji* 22 (1961): 16–36.

19 This has to be understood in the context that the Chinese defense of Nanjing ended in utter failure.

20 See the preface and epilogue to Nanjing Daxue Lishishi, *Riben diguozhuyi zai Nanjing de datusha* (The Great Nanjing Massacre of the Japanese imperialism) (Nanjing: "For internal distribution," 1979).

21 Tawara Yoshifumi, "Kyōkasho no 'Nankin jiken' kijutsu wa dō kawatta ka" (How did the textbook coverage of the "Nanjing Incident" change?), paper distributed at an international symposium on the sixtieth anniversary of the Nanjing Massacre, 13 December 1998, Tokyo. For a general survey of the coverage of war in postwar Japanese textbooks, see Tawara, *Kenshō 15-nen sensō to chū, kō rekishi kyōkasho* (An examination of the Fifteen Years' War in middle and high school history textbooks) (Tokyo: Gakushū no Tomosha, 1994).

22 For an analysis of this piece, see Irmela Hijiya-Kirschnereit, " 'Nanking' in Japanese Literature," *DIJ Newsletter* (October 1997): 1. For a long version in Japanese, see her "Hana to gyakusatsu: Nankin jiken to Mishima Yukio no 'botan' " (Flowers and the massacre: The Nanjing Incident and "Peonies" by Mishima Yukio), *Gunzō* 52, no. 8 (August 1997): 154–59.

23 Hata Kensuke, "Horyo no chi ni mamireta Byakko Butai" (The White Tiger Unit besmeared in captives' blood), *Nihon Shūhō*, 25 February 1957, 13–15; Imai Masatake, "Nankin jōnai no tairyō satsujin" (Massive killings inside Nanjing City), *Tokushū bungei shunjū*, 5 December 1956, 154–58; Shimada Katsumi, "Nankin kōryakusen to gyakusatsu jiken" (The attack on Nanjing and the massacre incident), *Tokushū jinbutsu ōrai*, June 1956, 106–11.

24 Hata Shunroku, "Nankin no gyakusatsu wa tashikani okonawareta ka" (Did the atrocities in Nanjing really happen?) *Maru*, Special issue on the military history of the "Great Army" (15 December 1956): 166–68; Miyazaki Kiyotaka, *Gunpō kaigi* (Military courts) (Tokyo: Fuji Shobō, 1953), 263–64. In fact, the Japanese troops in Nanjing were nearly ten times that number.

25 For a perceptive analysis of the postwar "boom in war stories" in Japan, see Yoshida

Yutaka, *Nihonjin no sensō kan: Sengoshi no naka no hen'yō* (Japanese views of the war: Transformations in postwar history) (Tokyo: Iwanami Shoten, 1995), esp. 85–100. One popular book that detailed Japan's wartime atrocities in northern China raised considerable objections in some quarters, however, so the publisher decided against releasing a new edition. See Joint Committee of Returnees from China, compilers, *Sankō* (Three all's) (Tokyo: Kōbunsha, 1957). The title refers to "Kill all, loot all, burn all," a phrase used to describe Japanese antiguerrilla tactics in northern China. It was written by a group of Japanese veterans who were released from China.

26 Tawara Yoshifumi, "Nankin daigyakusatsu to rekishi kyōkasho mondai," 2.

27 For a discussion of these developments, see Peter Duus, "Japan's Wartime Empire: Problems and Issues," in *The Japanese Wartime Empire, 1931–1945*, ed. Peter Duus et al. (Princeton, NJ: Princeton University Press, 1996), xli.

28 National Joint Committee in Support of the Textbook Trials, compilers, *Ienaga Kyōkasho saiban jūnenshi* (A ten-year history of the Ienaga textbook trials) (Tokyo: Sōtosha, 1977).

29 NHK Broadcasting Public Opinion Research Institute, *Zusetsu sengo yoron shi* (An illustrated history of postwar public opinion), 2d ed. (Tokyo: Nihon Hōsō Shuppan Kyōkai, 1982), 180–81.

30 For annual numbers of Japanese visitors to China between 1949 and 1969, see the China Institute, compilers, *Chūgoku nenkan 1970* (China yearbook 1970) (Tokyo: Taishūdō, 1970), 302.

31 See, for example, *Nit-Chū yūkō shinbun*, 15 August 1966.

32 Niijima Atsuyoshi, "Rittai kōsei Nankin daigyakusatsu" (The Great Nanjing Massacre in three dimensions), *Shinhyō* (May 1971): 48–57.

33 See "Ōya kōsatsu kumi no Chūkyō hōkoku" (A report on Communist China by the Ōya Investigation Group), *Sandē Mainichi* (Special issue) (22 October 1966): 77–79. See also Hora Tomio, *Nankin jiken* (The Nanjing Incident) (Tokyo: Shin Jinbutsu Ōraisha, 1972), 157–58, 193.

34 Hora Tomio, *Kindai senshi no nazo* (Puzzles in modern military history) (Tokyo: Jinbutsu Ōraisha, 1967), 170–71.

35 Ibid., 141.

36 Shimono Ikkaku and Gotō Kōsaku, *Nankin sakusen no shinsō: (Kumamoto) Dai-6-shidan senki* (The truth about the Nanjing battle: Battle records of the Sixth Division) (Tokyo: Tokyo Jōhōsha, 1966).

37 Honda Katsuichi, *Chūgoku no tabi* (The journey in China) (Tokyo: Asahi Shinbunsha, 1971); the Chinese translation is *Zhongguo zhi xing* (Hong Kong: Sihai Chubanshe, 1972).

38 Ibid., 288.

39 The former finally surpassed the latter for the first time between July and September 1972, around the time Tanaka announced his visit to Beijing. See NHK Broadcasting Public Opinion Research Institute, *Zusetsu sengō yoron shi*, 180–81.

40 Cited in Yoshida, *Nihonjin no sensō kan*, 133.

41 Hora Tomio, *Nankin jiken* (The Nanjing Incident) (Tokyo: Shin Jinbutsu Ōraisha, 1972).

42 Suzuki Akira, "*Nankin daigyakusatsu*" *no maboroshi* (The illusion of the "Great Nanjing Massacre") (Tokyo: Bungei Shunjūsha, 1973). In fact, as the historian Hata Ikuhiko later pointed out, the two officers might have included the Chinese captives they decapitated, as alleged in a source in 1971. See Hata Ikuhiko, *Nankin jiken: "Gyakusatsu" no kōzō* (The Nanjing Incident: Structure of the "Massacre") (Tokyo: Chūō Kōronsha, 1986), 49–50.

43 Suzuki, "*Nankin daigyakusatsu*" *no maboroshi*, 268.

44 "Ōya Sōichi shō senhyō" (Selection of the Ōya Sōichi Prize), *Bungei shunjū* 51, no. 7 (May 1973): 220–23.

45 Yamamoto's essays were published as *Watashi no naka no Nihongun* (The Japanese army that I knew) (1975; Tokyo: Bungei Shunjūsha, 1983).

46 For the text of these letters, see Honda Katsuichi, *Korosu gawa no ronri* (The logic of the killers) (Tokyo: Suzusawa Shoten, 1972): 113–306.

47 Honda Katsuichi, *Chūgoku no Nihon gun* (The Japanese army in China) (Tokyo: Sōjusha, 1972).

48 Hora Tomio, *Nankin daigyakusatsu: "Maboroshi"-ka kōsaku hihan* (The Nanjing Massacre: Repudiation of the "illusionization") (Tokyo: Gendaishi Shuppankai, 1975).

49 Hora Tomio, compiler, *Nit-Chū sensō shi shiryō 8 & 9: Nankin jiken* (Sources of the history of the Sino-Japanese War 8 and 9: The Nanjing Incident II), 2 vols. (Tokyo: Kawade Shoten, 1973).

50 Tawara Yoshifumi, "Nankin daigyakusatsu to rekishi kyōkasho mondai," 3.

51 Matsumoto Shigeharu, *Shanhai jidai* (The Shanghai era) (Tokyo: Chūō Kōronsha, 1975), 3: 249–53. In a later interview, however, Matsumoto reiterated that the Nanjing Massacre did happen. "Tsuini Nankin senryō, sono jitsuzō" (Finally the occupation of Nanjing and its real image), *Ekonomisuto* (21 May 1985): 82–87.

52 *Renmin ribao*, 3 September 1975.

53 *Pekin shūhō*, 22 August 1978.

54 Nanjing University History Department, *Riben diguozhuyi zai Nanjing de datusha* (The Great Nanjing Massacre of the Japanese imperialism) (Nanjing: For "internal publication," 1979), 2.

55 For an English-language overview of the controversy, see Chalmers Johnson, "The Patterns of Japanese Relations with China, 1952–1982," *Pacific Affairs* 59 (fall 1986): 402–20.

56 *Shūkan asahi*, 13 August 1982, 20.

57 Ibid.

58 Ibid.

59 Ibid., 18.

60 Ienaga Saburō, "*Misshitsu*" *kentei no kiroku* (Records of authorization behind "closed doors") (Tokyo: Meicho Kankōsha, 1993), 95–102; Kimijima Kazuhiko and Inoue Hisashi, "Nankin daigyakusatsu hyōka ni kansuru saikin no dōkō" (Recent developments concerning the evaluations of the Great Nanjing Massacre) *Rekishi hyōron* 433 (April 1986): 29.

61 Hora Tomio et al., eds., *Nankin jiken o kangaeru* (Reflections on the Nanjing Incident) (Tokyo: Ōtsuki Shoten, 1987); Hora Tomio et al., eds., *Nankin jiken no genba e* (To the scene of the Nanjing Incident) (Tokyo: Asahi Shinbunsha, 1988); Fujiwara Akira, *Nankin dai gyakusatsu* (The Great Nanjing Massacre) (Tokyo: Iwanami Shoten, 1985); Honda Katsuichi, *Nankin e no michi* (The road to Nanjing) (Tokyo: Asahi Shinbunsha, 1987); Yoshida Yutaka, *Tennō no guntai to Nankin jiken* (The emperor's army and the Nanjing Incident) (Tokyo: Aoki Shoten, 1986).

62 Hata Ikuhiko, "Ronsō shi kara mita Nankin gyakusatsu jiken," 240–41.

63 Tanaka Masaaki, "'Nankin daigyakusatsu kinenkan' ni monomōsu" (Objections to the "Memorial Hall to the Great Nanjing Massacre"), *Seiron* 160 (December 1985): 105. See also Tanaka, *Nankin jiken no sōkatsu* (A summary of the Nanjing Incident) (Tokyo: Kenkosha, 1987).

64 Itakura Yoshiaki, "Matsui Iwane taishō 'jinchū nikki' no kaizan no ayashi" (Suspicions of tampering with the "field diary" of German Matsui Iwane), *Rekishi to jinbutsu* 15 (winter 1985): 318–31; Tanaka Masaaki, *Matsui Iwane taishō no jinchū nisshi* (The field diary of General Matsui Iwane) (Tokyo: Fuyō Shobō, 1985).

65 Itakura, however, was not pleased to see this incident become the ammunition for the contending "massacre faction." A month later he wrote in *Bungei shunjū*, this time not so much criticizing Tanaka as attacking Hora and Honda. He argued that even without alteration, the diary would disprove the massacre, as Matsui did not mention massive executions of captives. Moreover, Itakura accused Hora and Honda of distortion and inconsistency in their own recent works and concluded that they were of the same stock as Tanaka. Itakura Yoshiaki, "Matsui Iwane nikki no kaizan ni tsuite" (On tampering with the diary of Matsui Iwane), *Bungei shunjū* (January 1986): 192–94.

66 Kimura Kuninori, "Kaisetsu: Nakajima Kesago chūjō to Nankin jiken" (An explanation of Lieutenant General Nakajima Kesago and the Nanjing Incident), *Zōkan rekishi to jinbutsu* (1984): 260–61.

67 Examples include Sone Kazuo, *Shiki Nankin gyakusatsu* (A personal account of the Nanjing Massacre) (Tokyo: Sairyūsha, 1984); Yamamoto Takeshi, *Ichi heishi no jūgun kiroku* (A record of one soldier's time at the front) (Tokyo: Yasuda Shoten, 1985); Azuma Shirō, *Waga Nankin puratūn* (Our Nanjing platoon) (Tokyo: Aoki Shoten, 1987).

68 "Iwayuru 'Nankin jiken' ni kansuru jōhō teikyō no onegai" (A request for information concerning the so-called "Nanjing Incident") *Kaikō* 395 (November 1983): 35–37.

69 Katokawa Kōtarō, "Shōgen ni yoru Nankin senshi: Sono sōkatsu teki kōsatsu" (The history of the battle of Nanjing: An overall examination) *Kaikō* 411 (March 1985): 9–18.

70 Hata Ikuhiko, "Ronsō shi kara mita Nankin gyakusatsu jiken," 242–43; Ishijima Noriyuki, "Nankin jiken o meguru aratana ronsōten" (New issues of contention concerning the Nanjing Incident), reprinted in *Chūgoku kankei ronsetsu shiryō* (Collected essays on China) (1986), part 4, 2: 188; and Kimijima and Inoue, "Nankin daigyakusatsu hyōka ni kansuru saikin no dōkō," 30–38.

71 Kaikōsha, *Nankin senshi* (A history of the Nanjing battle), 2 vols. (Tokyo: Kaikōsha, 1989). A third volume consisting of documents was added in 1993.

72 Hata Ikuhiko, *Nankin jiken*. In his more recent writings, however, Hata seems to contradict himself by isolating the issue of the victims' numbers while calling attention to mass killings in other countries, including China.

73 "Kagai no kiroku: Nankin daigyakusatsu 'nikki'" (Records of perpetration: "Diaries" of the Nanjing Massacre), *Shūkan kinyōbi* (10 December 1993): 6–23. They were published later in Ono Kenji et al., compilers, *Nankin daigyakusatsu o kirokushita kōgun heishitachi* (Imperial Army soldiers who recorded the Great Nanjing Massacre) (Tokyo: Ōtsuki Shoten, 1996).

74 Kasahara Tokushi, *Nankin nanminku no hyakunichi* (A hundred days in the Nanjing refugee zone) (Tokyo: Iwanami Shoten, 1995). See also Hora Tomio, *Nankin dai zangyaku jiken shiryō shū* (Sources on the Great Nanjing Atrocity) (Tokyo: Aoki Shoten, 1985); Nakaguchi Kazuki et al., eds., *Nankin jiken Kyōto shidan kankei shiryōshū* (Materials concerning the Kyoto Division in the Nanjing Incident) (Tokyo: Aoki Shoten, 1989).

75 *Asahi shinbun*, 20 October 1993 (evening); 13 May 1994 (evening). For records of some of the court proceedings, see Honda Katsuichi, compiler, *Sabakareta Nankin daigyakusatsu* (The Great Nanjing Massacre on trial) (Tokyo: Banseisha, 1989); National Joint Committee in Support of the Textbook Trials, compilers, *Nankin daigyakusatsu, Chōsen jinmin no*

teikō, 731 Butai (The Great Nanjing Massacre, resistance by the Korean people, Unit 731) (Tokyo: Minshūsha, 1997).

76 For an English-language introduction on their work, see John Dower and John Junkerman, *The Hiroshima Murals* (New York: Kodansha, 1986). See *Asahi shinbun*, 25 April 1996 (Hyōgo).

77 Uchiyama Jirō, " 'Futsū no Nihonjin' ga kokoromita Nankin daigyakusatsu shokuzai no tabi" (The journey of atonement for the Great Nanjing Massacre attempted by ordinary Japanese), *Asahi jā naru* 28, no. 26 (20 June 1986): 22–25; see also *Asahi shinbun*, 15 October 1982; 7 August 1985; 31 March 1986; 27 October 1994; 3 October 1997 (Hiroshima).

78 The figure was given by the assistant director at the memorial. See *Asahi shinbun*, 26 June 1995 (Saitama). See also Duan Yueping, "Qin-Hua Rijun Nanjing Datusha Yunan Tongbao Jinianguan de zhanlan huodong" (Exhibitions at the Nanjing Massacre Memorial) *Kang-Ri zhanzheng yanjiu* (1992): 175–89; Li Haibo, "Unforgettable Atrocity," *Beijing Review* (14–20 August 1995): 22.

79 *Asahi shinbun* is the best source for newspaper reports on such activities.

80 *Asahi shinbun*, 3 August 1997; 7 September 1997.

81 *Sankei shinbun*, 26 April 1996 (evening). Azuma appealed the court decision but lost.

82 *Asahi shinbun*, 31 March 1996 (Western region); 25 April 1996 (Western region); Nicholas D. Kristof, "Today's History Lesson: What Rape of Nanjing?" *New York Times*, 4 July 1996.

83 For an analysis of the political factors behind this failure, see Barbara Wanner, "War Resolution Fails to Settle Japan's Historical 'Debt,' " *Japan Economic Institute Report*, 7 July 1995.

84 Aaron Gerow made this point in an extensive message posted on H-Japan, 20 February 1997.

85 For a comprehensive account of Chinese views of Japan during the 1980s, see Allen S. Whiting, *China Eyes Japan* (Berkeley: University of California Press, 1989). In an epilogue written for the Japanese edition, Whiting brings it to the early 1990s. See *Chūgokujin no Nihon kan*, trans. Okabe Katsumi (Tokyo: Iwanami shoten, 1993), 289–305. For an insightful analysis of Chinese views on issues related to the war with Japan, see Arif Dirlik, " 'Past Experience, If Not Forgotten, Is a Guide to the Future'; or What Is in a Text? The Politics of History in Chinese-Japanese Relations," in *Japan in the World*, ed. Masao Miyoshi and H. D. Harootunian (Durham, NC: Duke University Press, 1993), 29–58.

86 The company in question, Shochiku Fuji, explained that the cut was made because the footage was too graphic for the Japanese. Concern about right-wing interference almost certainly played a role. Suzuki Akira, on the other hand, claimed the cut was justified because it was a Chinese fabrication. See Fukuda Mizuho, " 'Rasutoemperā' no 'Nankin' massatsu" ("Nanjing" erased in *The Last Emperor*), *Asahi jānaru* 30, no. 7 (19 February 1988): 82–87.

87 *Guangming ribao*, 13 August 1982.

88 The figure was given by a curator at the memorial. See *Asahi shinbun*, 26 June 1995 (Saitama). See also Duan Yueping, "Qin-Hua Rijun Nanjing Datusha Yunan Tongbao Jinianguan de zhanlan huodong" (Exhibitions at the Memorial for the Compatriot Victims in the Nanjing Massacre by the Japanese Invading Troops) *Kang-Ri zhanzheng yanjiu* (1992): 175–89; Li Haibo, "Unforgettable Atrocity," *Beijing Review* (14–20 August 1995): 22.

89 Duan Yueping, "Qin-Hua Rijun Nanjing Datusha Yunan Tongbao Jinianguan erqi gongchen quanmian jungong" (Completion of the second phase construction of the Memorial

Hall of the Victims in the Nanjing Massacre of the Japanese Invaders), *Kang-Ri zhanzheng yanjiu* (1998): 237–38.

90 Zhou Erfu, "Nanjing de xianluo" (The fall of Nanjing), *Dangdai* 4 (1985): 198.

91 Xu Zhigeng, *Nanjing datusha* (The Great Nanjing Massacre) (Beijing: Kunlun Chubanshe, 1987). A Taiwanese edition was issued in 1989.

92 *Foreign Broadcast Information Service*, 25 March 1989, 5, and *Dazhong dianying*, March 1989.

93 Y. L. Ting, "Nanjing Massacre: A Dark Page in History," *Beijing Review* (2 September 1985): 20.

94 For a Chinese translation of these Mantetsu surveys, see *Minguo dang'an* (1994).

95 Gao Xingzu, *Rijun qin-Hua baoxing: Nanjing datusha* (Atrocities of the invading Japanese troops: The Great Nanjing Massacre) (Shanghai: Shanghai Renmin Chubanshe, 1985). See also his "Nanjing datusha de shishi burong mosha" (The historical facts of the Great Nanjing Massacre will not be obliterated) *Riben wenti* 16 (1986): 29–38.

96 Committee for the Compilation of Sources on the "Nanjing Massacre" and the Library of Nanjing, *Qin-Hua Rijun Nanjing datusha shiliao* and *Qin-Hua Rijun Nanjing datusha dang'an*; *Qin-Hua Rijun Nanjing datusha shigao* (A Draft history of the Nanjing Massacre by the Japanese troops that invaded China) (Nanjing: Jiangsu Guji Chubanshe, 1987); English rendition is original.

97 Fu Zeng, "Nanjing datusha yu Riben diguozhuyi" (The Great Nanjing Massacre and Japanese imperialism), *Jindaishi yanju* 16 (February 1983): 177.

98 See, for example, the critique by Pan Junfeng in Tanaka Masaaki, *"Nanjing datusha" de xugou* (The fabrication of the "Great Nanjing Massacre") (Beijing: Shijie Zhishi Chubanshe, 1985), 15.

99 Zou Mingde et al., "Nanjing datusha de lishi shishi burong cuangai" (The historical facts of the Great Nanjing Massacre will not allow tampering), *Rishi dang'an* 4 (1982): 88.

100 Li Yunhan, "Youguan 'Nanjing datusha' de zhongwai shiliao pingshu" (A survey of historical materials in China and abroad on the "Great Nanjing Massacre"), in *Kangzhan jianguo shi yantaohui lunwenji* (Proceedings of the Symposium on the War of Resistance and nation-building) (Taibei: Zhongyang Jindaishi Yanjusuo, 1985); Li Enhan, "Rijun Nanjing datusha de tusha ling wenti" (Issues concerning the massacre orders during the Japanese army's great massacre at Nanjing) *Zhongyang yanjuyuan jindaishi jikan* 18 (June 1988); "Ribenjun Nanjing datusha de tusha shumu wenti" (The question of the number murdered by the Japanese troops in the Nanjing Massacre), *Guoli Taiwan shifan daxue lishi xuebao* 18 (June 1990).

101 Qin Xiaoyi, ed., *Rijun zai-Hua baoxing: Nanjing datusha* (Atrocities of the Japanese army in China: The Great Nanjing Massacre) (Taibei: Guomindang Dangshi Weiyuanhui, 1986, 1987).

102 Excerpts from Guo Qi, *Nanjing datusha* (The Great Nanjing Massacre) (Taibei: Zhongwai Tushu Chubanshe, 1979), for instance, were published in the PRC journal *Wanxiang*.

103 *The Rape of Nanjing*, coproduced by China Film Co-Production Corporation and Long Shong Pictures Co., Ltd., of Taiwan.

104 Zhu Chengshan, ed., *Qin-Hua Rijun Nanjing datusha xinchunzhe zhengyanji* (A collection of testimonies by survivors of the Great Nanjing Massacre by the invading Japanese troops) (Nanjing: Nanjing Daxue Chubanshe, 1994); Yuehan Labei (John Rabe), *Labei riji* (The diary of John Rabe) (Nanjing: Jiangsu Renmin Chubanshe, Jiangsu Jiaoyu Chubanshe, 1997). For Chinese reactions to the discovery of Rabe's diary, see *"Labei riji" faxian shimo* (The background of the discovery of the "Rabe Diary") (Nanjing: Qin-Hua Rijun Nanjing

Datusha Yunan Tongpa Jinianguan, 1997). The German publisher, citing the huge potential of the Chinese-language market, demanded U.S. $150,000, a vast sum for Chinese publishers. The final price has not been disclosed.

105 Zhu Chengshan, compiler, *Qin-Hua Rijun Nanjing datusha waiji renshi zhengyanji* (Collected testimonies by foreigners on the Japanese massacre in Nanjing) (Nanjing: Jiangsu renmin chubanshe, 1998).

106 See the article by Yang Qiqiao in *Riben de Zhongguo yimin* (Chinese immigrants in Japan), ed. Chinese Association for the Study of the History of Sino-Japanese Relations (Beijing: Shijie Zhishi Chubanshe, 1987), 340–41.

107 See Sun Zhaiwei, ed., *Nanjing datusha* (The Great Nanjing Massacre) (Beijing: Beijing chubanshe, 1997); Committee for the Compilation of Sources on the "Nanjing Massacre," *Qin-Hua Rijun Nanjing datusha shigao*, 130.

108 Sun, *Nanjing datusha*, 9–10.

109 Sun Zhaiwei, "Nanjing datusha yunan tongpao zhong jiujin you duoshao junren" (How many soldiers were among the compatriot victims in the Great Nanjing Massacre?), *Kang-Ri zhanzheng yanjiu* 26 (April 1997): 8–17.

110 On ideological pitfalls affecting historians in the People's Republic of China, see essays in Albert Feuerwerker, ed., *History in Communist China* (Cambridge, MA: MIT Press, 1968), and Jonathan Unger, ed., *Using the Past to Serve the Present: Historiography and Politics in Contemporary China* (Armonk, NY: M. E. Sharpe, 1993). None of the essays in these two volumes, however, addressed the historiography of the Sino-Japanese War (1937–1945).

111 An example is mentioned in Ian Buruma, *The Wages of Guilt* (New York: Farrar, Straus and Giroux, 1994), 123.

112 Lucian W. Pye, "Memory, Imagination, and National Myth," in Gong, *Remembering and Forgetting*, 26.

113 In early 2000, Chinese hackers reportedly posted incendiary remarks on a number of Japanese government Web sites in protest against a right-wing symposium in Japan calling the Nanjing Massacre the "Greatest Lie of the 20th Century."

114 I address the important issue of individual memories in "Transmitted Experience: Individual Testimonies and Collective Memories of the Nanjing Atrocity," unpublished paper presented at Lund University, April 1999.

115 See Daqing Yang, "The Challenges of the Nanjing Massacre: Reflections on Historical Inquiry," in *The Nanjing Massacre in History and Historiography*, 133–79.

Memories of War and Okinawa

ISHIHARA MASAIE

Translation by Douglas Dreistadt

Background to the Japanese Diet's Resolution on the 50th
Anniversary of the End of World War II

On 9 June 1995, the Japanese Diet hammered out an agreement on the final wording of their Resolution on the 50th Anniversary of the End of World War II. The resolution expressed no acknowledgment of Japan's "war of aggression" and contained no apologies to other countries.

The wording of this resolution is said to have been the result of forceful pressure tactics by the Association of Bereaved Families (ABF) on the Liberal Democratic Party Diet members.[1] This resolution revealed to the world community the narrow, provincial historical consciousness of some sections of the Japanese populace. In a speech two years before this resolution, in August 1993, then Prime Minister Hosokawa stated, "It was a war of aggression. We now admit that the war was a mistake."[2] This was the first time a Japanese prime minister ever admitted that Japan's wartime actions constituted a war of aggression. However, the ABF and other like-minded pressure groups subsequently launched an intense, coordinated campaign to force a retraction of his statement. A few days later, in a speech to the cabinet, Prime Minister Hosokawa did not retract his statement, but, toning down his rhetoric, he avoided the phrase "war of aggression," using instead the phrase "aggressive behavior." The significant difference in the two expressions was not lost on his audience. The phrase "aggressive behavior" (*shinryakuteki kōi*) implies that although the actions of the Japanese military may have appeared "aggressive" to others, they actually were not. It further implies that although unfortunate isolated incidents may have occurred, they were not officially sanctioned. The phrase "war of aggression" (*shinryaku sensō*) connotes officially sanctioned aggression for imperialistic or expansionist reasons. Hosokawa did, however, express his "deep reflection and feelings of apology." Soon thereafter, the *Asahi shinbun* newspaper conducted a public opinion poll and discovered that 76 percent of those polled approved of the prime minister's statements.

However, with the birth of the Murayama coalition government in 1994, the onus of what to do to commemorate the fiftieth anniversary of the end of the war fell on a new administration. An active movement began in the Diet to adopt a statement of "renunciation of war, and an apology for World War II." Incensed, the ABF and its allies organized citizens groups to oppose the "renunciation of war resolution," and has since mounted a national campaign to rationalize Japan's actions in the war. Statements were issued asserting that the Asia-Pacific War was a "war of self-defense to protect Japan and the lives and property of her people," and that it was "a war to free the peoples of Asia from Western colonialism."[3] Statements such as these illustrate the ABF's view of history. They refuse to admit that Japan bears any responsibility whatsoever for the three million Japanese and the twenty million other Asians who died as a result of the war.

Under the influence of its national parent organization, the Okinawan ABF also began to conduct similar activities. But opinion polls in Okinawa have shown that the ABF represent the opinions of only a small minority of the population. In a poll conducted by NHK (the National Broadcasting Agency), residents of Okinawa were asked to consider the Battle of Okinawa in the context of the Asia-Pacific War. Specifically, they were asked if it was "an unavoidable battle necessary for the defense of the fatherland" or "a reckless battle which sacrificed countless Okinawan lives." When the poll was conducted in 1993, 6.2 percent agreed with the former statement, and 87.5 percent with the latter. When the same poll was conducted in 1995, the results were 6.7 percent and 81 percent, respectively.[4] These polls demonstrate that the vast majority of Okinawans totally reject the position of the ABF.

It should also be mentioned here that a Japanese government cabinet meeting gave its approval for a Prime Minister's Address on the 50th Anniversary of the End of the War. In his address, Prime Minister Murayama recognized the "irrefutable historical facts" of "Japan's aggression and colonial rule of neighboring Asian nations."[5] He declared his sincere remorse and issued a clearly stated apology to all of the victims. However, note that the prime minister's statement was issued in the wake of a flood of international criticism over his education minister's statements a few days earlier to the effect that the Japanese government had already gone far enough in its statements about the war. And although Murayama admitted that Japan's prewar national policies were a mistake, later in the news conference he stated that the emperor bore no responsibility for the war. This is in complete contradiction to the historical facts: that the emperor was supreme commander of the three branches of the military, and that the military clique, in close cooperation with the *zaibatsu* financial cliques, promoted a national policy of subjugation and colonial rule of neighboring Asian countries. The peoples of Asia could hardly be expected to be satisfied with this declaration, as it again avoided using the expression "war of aggression" for what clearly was a war of aggression, and made no mention of any of the outstanding issues of individual compensation for the victims.

This essay examines Okinawan memories and popular perceptions of the war historically and in the context of current national politics. It also describes recent efforts to establish Okinawa as a locus for the promotion of world peace. Furthermore, it is not written from the position of a distanced, neutral observer, but from the viewpoint of one who believes that Okinawa, as a result of its culture and history, can make a unique contribution to world peace.

For the first twenty-five years after the war it was virtually impossible to record the testimonies of the survivors of the battle. Due to the incredible horror, cruelty, and shame that they experienced, most people could not bring themselves to talk about it. There was also strong social pressure not to talk about many of the shameful things that happened, such as parents killing their own children, children killing their parents, and civilians cooperating with the Japanese soldiers in killing other civilians who were suspected of spying. In the process of trying to obtain firsthand accounts of people's war experiences, the writer has had continually to find ways to deal with this extreme reluctance to talk about the war. Recently, many people have overcome their reluctance to speak, making it possible to gain a much more accurate picture of what took place. The writer has attempted to consolidate the testimonies collected and, in combination with American and Japanese military histories and historical documents, attain a more comprehensive understanding of the characteristics of the war in Okinawa.

A General Outline of the Special Characteristics of the Battle of Okinawa and the Civilian Fatalities

The Battle of Okinawa was the last great land battle of the Asia-Pacific War. Sporadic aerial bombardment of the Ryukyu archipelago by carrier-based American planes began on 10 October 1944; full-scale bombardment in preparation for the invasion began the following year on 23 March 1945. On 26 March, in a prelude to what was to happen on a much larger scale over the following three months on the main island of Okinawa, the American invasion of the Kerama Islands began, and numerous civilian noncombatants became caught in the crossfire. In the ensuing battle for Okinawa, both the Japanese and American sides suffered heavy casualties, but the number of civilian noncombatant casualties far exceeded the number of military combatant casualties. This high percentage of civilian casualties was characteristic of World War II as a whole, but it was particularly high in Okinawa, making it one of the striking characteristics of the Battle of Okinawa.

Okinawa was the final theater of combat in a war that began initially with the Japanese invasion of Manchuria in 1931, and later developed into a full-scale war of aggression against China in 1937, although there is a mistaken tendency to date the beginning of the war from the Pearl Harbor attack in 1941. Fifteen years of war finally culminated in a confrontation between the Japanese Imperial Army and the Allied military forces in the Battle of Okinawa. The war can justifiably be characterized as a war between the forces of democracy and the forces of totalitarianism.

The mission of the Japanese military in Okinawa also illustrates another important characteristic of the battle. By early 1945, the defeat of Japan was a virtual certainty. The mission of the Imperial Japanese forces in Okinawa was to delay, for even one day or one hour, the invasion of the mainland of Japan in order to secure the strongest possible negotiating position for "preserving the national polity" and "maintaining the emperor system" after the war. To achieve these aims, the Japanese Army adopted what was called the *shukketsu jikyū sakusen* (maximum bloodletting strategy). Including the supply battalions, there were 540,000 American military personnel involved in the Okinawa campaign, compared with a figure of just under 100,000 regular Japanese troops. There is no way the Japanese Army could have won the battle. However, they managed to keep the Allied forces tied down for three months, and in the process extracted a heavy toll of 14,005 American lives. This forced the American military to reconsider how massive the potential loss of life could be in the planned invasion of the Japanese mainland. Although not the only consideration, it can be argued that the extremely heavy American losses in the Battle of Okinawa and the projected casualty figures for an invasion of the mainland constituted the major consideration in the American decision to drop the atomic bomb on Hiroshima.

The Japanese found that their "maximum bloodletting strategy," which made extensive use especially of caves and kamikaze attacks, had worked very well against the Allied forces in Okinawa, and there is every reason to believe that they would have used the same strategy and tactics in Kyushu, which was the next place slated for invasion by the American military. The invasion of Kyushu would most likely have produced heavy casualties to the same degree as had occurred in the Okinawa campaign, but on a much greater scale. James Mac-Gregor Burns reports that during the Battle of Okinawa, President Truman declared to the Joint Chiefs of Staff that he did not want an Okinawa "from one end of Japan to the other." He also states that chairman of the Combined Chiefs of Staff, General George C. Marshall, "considered the use of the powerful new atomic weapon—as many as six bombs—on the Kyushu beaches in a pre-invasion bombardment."[6] The complex factors involved make any guess at the number of potential casualties purely speculative, but based on the conduct of the Okinawa campaign and numerous other factors, Burns conservatively estimates that "total American casualties would have been somewhere between 100,000 and a half a million"[7] for the invasion of Kyushu.

Just before the Battle of Okinawa in February 1945, the former prime minister, Prince Konoe Fumimaro, obtained an audience with the Showa emperor and attempted to persuade him that "the defeat of Japan is inevitable, but even considering that worst case scenario there is yet another matter of even more urgent concern, and that is the possibility of a communist revolution in the wake of Japan's defeat. It is respectfully submitted that Japan should devise a plan to quickly end the war in order to preserve the national polity" (and, by implication, the emperor system). The emperor rebuffed the prince, replying, "First, let us obtain some better results in the next battle."[8]

That next battle was the Battle of Okinawa. And just as the Showa emperor had thought, the Battle of Okinawa brought about all the desired results. It became the final great land battle of the war, and in the end, the emperor system was preserved.[9] But these results were achieved at the cost of tens of thousands of civilian lives—lives that were lost, for example, because, in their efforts to prolong the battle as long as possible, the Japanese Imperial Army used civilians as human shields on the battlefield. Further, as a strategy to keep knowledge of military "secrets" such as battle plans and troop formations, positions, and movements from the enemy, Japanese soldiers were ordered never to surrender. They were told, "You should die before allowing yourself to be taken prisoner." In Okinawa, it was possible for civilians to know about such military secrets, so these orders were extended to include all civilians as well. The military came up with the slogan *Gunkanmin kyōsei kyōshi no ittaika* (Imperial soldiers and civilians live together and die together as one!). Accordingly, civilians were not permitted to surrender under any circumstances. As a result of this policy, civilians died not only because of the relentless bombing of the enemy planes, but also, in various shapes and forms, at the hands of the Imperial Army itself.

In what manner did the civilian victims die during the Battle of Okinawa? How many soldiers of each country were killed? In the process of collecting oral accounts of war experiences, I have attempted to categorize the civilian (and military) fatality figures to present a more complete picture of what took place in the battle. The results are presented in tables 1 and 2.

Table 1. Categories and Types of Civilian Fatalities in the Battle of Okinawa

I. Civilians Who Died in Attacks by the Allied Military Forces
1. Those who died in bombing raids.
2. Those who died due to artillery fire from Allied warships.
3. Those who died from gun and artillery fire of combat troops.
4. Those who died by gasoline, napalm, explosives, or gas while hiding in caves or bunkers (the so-called horse-rider attacks).
5. Those who died in the Buckner Massacre (a massacre that took place in retaliation for the death of General Buckner).
6. Women who died after being raped, both on the battlefield and in the internment camps.
7. Other miscellaneous causes.

II. Civilians Killed by the Japanese Military Forces.
A. Those killed directly by Japanese soldiers [reasons in brackets].
1. Those killed for speaking in Okinawan ["apparent spying"].
2. Those killed for various reasons, such as accidentally wandering too close to Imperial troop positions [suspicion of spying].
3. Those killed for being reluctant to give food to soldiers [lack of cooperation with Imperial soldiers].
4. Those killed for reluctance to give up caves or other hiding places to Imperial soldiers [lack of cooperation with Imperial soldiers].
5. Children and infants killed for crying while hiding in caves or bunkers with Imperial soldiers [to protect military secrets, or to prevent being discovered by the enemy].
6. Those killed for having American surrender instruction leaflets in their possession [anti-Japanese (treasonous) behavior].
7. Those killed for attempting to surrender to American forces [anti-Japanese behavior].
8. Those killed in American internment camps after surrendering. Imperial Army soldiers often attacked American internment camps to prevent those who surrendered from talking [anti-Japanese behavior, spying for the enemy].
9. Those killed for reluctance to transport water, ammunition, or other supplies for the military during bombing raids [lack of cooperation with Imperial soldiers].
10. Those killed for surrendering and subsequently calling out for others to surrender [anti-Japanese behavior, spying].
11. Other miscellaneous circumstances.

Table 1. *Continued*

B. Those killed as a direct result of actions taken by the Japanese military.

1. Deaths due to forced evacuations. For example, death by starvation of people forced to go to areas without any food rations, or death due to malaria of people forced to go into areas known to be infested with malaria.

2. Deaths due to starvation and malnutrition (Japanese soldiers often robbed civilians of all of their food supplies; whole villages were left with nothing to eat).

3. Deaths due to bombing when Imperial soldiers ordered civilians out of caves and other hiding places that they wanted to use.

4. Deaths due to bombing when civilians were forced to leave "strategically sensitive" areas during the intense bombardment later known as the "Typhoon of Steel."

5. Deaths by so-called *jiketsu* (literally self-determination) with Japanese soldiers. Although *jiketsu* is usually translated as "suicide," the actual circumstances cannot accurately be described as suicide. Typically, people would stand in a group and explode a hand grenade.

6. Deaths of people who, at the sight of the horrifying deaths of family members, went insane and ran out onto the battlefield only to be killed by gunfire or bombing.

7. Deaths due to officially sanctioned murder-suicide. Under the slogan "Imperial Soldiers and Civilians Live and Die Together as One!", the Japanese soldiers ordered, coerced, persuaded, or otherwise induced numerous civilians to kill one another. Friends were induced to kill each other, parents were incited to kill their own children, children were deceived into killing their own grandparents, and all this was sanctioned and encouraged. This officially sanctioned murder-suicide later came to be euphemistically called *shūdan jiketsu* (literally, group self-determination). This was not the spontaneous self-sacrifice for the glory of the emperor that the term suggests. It was a calculated military policy conducted for tactical reasons. These actions are perhaps better termed "tactical murder by proxy" (*gunjiteki tasatsu*).

8. Civilians who were killed by other civilians under orders or coercion of the Japanese military. Civilians hiding in caves or bunkers with Japanese soldiers were forced to kill infants and children for crying so they would not be heard and discovered by the enemy.

9. Deaths due to abandonment. When villages were evacuated, people were forced to abandon any relative who was wounded, too sick to walk, elderly, or physically or mentally impaired. Most of those left behind in this manner were killed in the ensuing battle.

10. Other miscellaneous causes.

Table 1. *Continued*

III. Civilians Who Died Due to Other War-Related Causes

1. Deaths by starvation and malnutrition in areas outside the combat zone.
2. Deaths due to poisoning. Numerous people, starving and desperate for food, sometimes ate poisonous plants.
3. Deaths due to lack of medical care. Numerous deaths occurred in noncombat areas because no medical supplies or medical care of any kind was available.
4. Deaths of civilians in American internment camps due to severe malnutrition. At the time of their surrender, many were already too weak to respond to medical treatment.
5. Civilians who killed each other on suspicion of spying. The power of the military war propaganda was so great that some people still considered themselves "loyal Imperial subjects" and killed other civilians because they suspected them of spying for the enemy.
6. Deaths due to fighting over scarce food supplies.
7. Civilians who died at sea in attacks by U.S. submarines. Many schoolchildren died this way in the process of being evacuated to the Japanese mainland.
8. Other miscellaneous causes.

Initially, the civilian casualties were divided into three general categories: those killed by the Allied military, those killed by the Japanese military, and those who died from causes directly related to the war. In the process of collecting data, various patterns and subcategories began to emerge.

There are many people in Okinawa who witnessed or underwent experiences similar to those who died in the battle, but who somehow miraculously survived. The writer has gathered all the information presented in the tables from oral accounts of those who experienced the battle firsthand. The material presented in this paper is based on their firsthand accounts.

Circumstances Surrounding the Collection of Oral Accounts of the War

For those who experienced the war, their memories of it are indelibly etched in their minds, every bit as vivid now, fifty years later, as they were in 1945. Accordingly, these people will carry with them both the physical and the mental scars of the war for the rest of their days.

In the prewar and wartime years, the people of Japan, including Okinawa, were educated to believe that the highest honor one could achieve would be to die for the emperor. The honor and glory of the emperor were held to be of far greater importance than one's own life or the lives of one's family members.

Table 2. Other Casualties of the Battle of Okinawa

Japanese soldiers and support personnel
American soldiers
British soldiers
Korean draftees
Korean "comfort women"
Taiwanese draftees

The status of the emperor can be compared to that of the semidivine status of religious cult leaders. The incessant stream of government propaganda also taught people that the Americans and British were evil, demonic animals. As the war came closer and closer to the Japanese home islands, the government encouraged an almost hysteric effort to eradicate "spies." Anyone who stepped out of line or in any way questioned the validity of the government's propaganda could be accused of spying. During the Battle of Okinawa, even though no Okinawans actually worked as spies, countless people were accused of spying. The paranoia became so intense that there were numerous instances of people killing their own relatives and family members for spying. There are even cases documented where parents killed their own children. Many of the people who committed such acts are still alive, and understandably do not want to talk about this or anything even remotely related to the war. Others also realize how painful the memories can be, and as a result the war has become a taboo subject. Factors such as these often make field research extremely difficult.

After 1945, the United States built many large military bases in Okinawa under its twenty-seven-year postwar Occupation, and Okinawa has played a vital role, both directly and indirectly, in America's wars and Asian Pacific military strategy ever since. Specifically, Okinawa's bases have been vital to American military interests in the Chinese Civil War, the conflict between Taiwan and mainland China, the Korean War, the Vietnam War, and the Gulf War. To the people who lived through the Battle of Okinawa, although one might expect immense relief at having survived the war, the military role Okinawa has since played serves as a constant, painful reminder of their own war experiences.

Even though living outside of the bases, residents are exposed to the dangers of military exercises and maneuvers and the accidents that accompany them. Residents are exposed to other base-related dangers, and some have lost their lives due to problems emanating from the bases. Furthermore, for the past fifty years Okinawans have had to deal with the problem of unexploded bombs left over from the war. It is estimated that it will take another fifty years before that danger can be said to have passed.

There are approximately five thousand dead from the battle still unaccounted for. Forensic teams are periodically sent out to collect bones and to try to identify them. The frequent occurrence of problems like that of unexploded bombs, where entire neighborhoods must be evacuated during the removal of the ordnance, and of such activities as bone collection, in which many people must be mobilized, have created circumstances in which the people are continuously reminded of the war. As much as many people may want to forget, circumstances do not permit.

As can be surmised from the fact that 11 percent of the island is occupied by military bases, many people lost the basis of their livelihood when their land was taken from them. Land that had belonged to Okinawan families for generations was forcibly confiscated after the war for use as military bases. The war had also left Okinawa completely devastated, without any economic base, and entirely dependent on the American military for subsistence. During the American Occupation Okinawans thus had little choice but to work either on the bases or at base-related jobs.

Transformed into military bases, the confiscated land subsequently came to support America's wars in other countries. The fact that the land of their ancestors is being used to support war and killing in other countries is a constant source of anguish for Okinawans. Okinawans work at such jobs as cleaning and loading bombs in airplanes, and so have become accomplices in the deaths of people in other countries who are killed by the bombs. Okinawans, in other words, have been accomplices in all of America's wars of the past fifty years, and there is no end in sight. The legal basis for these circumstances was established on 28 April 1952 with the San Francisco Peace Treaty coming into effect. It is obvious, therefore, that the Japanese government must assume the blame for this situation in which Okinawans are forced to become involved, directly or indirectly, in America's wars. The fact that there are bases in Okinawa also makes Okinawa a target for enemies of America, making it possible for Okinawa to become embroiled in an American war.

The 4 September 1995 incident in which a twelve-year-old Okinawan girl was raped and assaulted by three American servicemen caused all of these sentiments to come to the surface. The Okinawan reaction to this incident has rocked both the Japanese and the American governments, and demands for a review of the U.S.-Japan Security Treaty have brought about talks regarding the future of the bases. The mass protests in the wake of the rape incident must be understood in the context of this situation.

The inception of the first major organized effort to record the accounts of the survivors of the Battle of Okinawa occurred about 1970. Officially organized groups from the prefectural level all the way down to the smallest districts and villages, numerous independently organized groups, and various individuals all became involved in the effort to unearth and record accounts of the war. With little or no training in the collection of oral historical accounts, researchers had to learn their trade by trial and error. Students and ordinary citizens as well as researchers joined in these projects. Much progress has been made, the aim being to record the experiences of every family in every village in as much detail as possible. These firsthand accounts of war experiences, when taken together with the accounts from Japanese and American soldiers as well as other materials and documents, allow us to attain a more comprehensive picture of what happened in the battle.

The war has had an intense and lasting impact on the Okinawan psyche. The mere existence of the military bases serves as a daily reminder of the searing experiences of the war. Add to that the twenty-seven years of undemocratic American military occupation and the seemingly endless series of base-related problems and incidents, such as crimes, fatal accidents, water and noise pollution, live-fire exercises, the discovery of unexploded bombs (from WWII) in residential areas during the construction of houses, and numerous other problems. Further, the wishes of the Okinawan people in these matters have been routinely ignored by the national government. It is within this context that the high degree of public awareness of the war and its effects has developed in Okinawa. People from all sectors of society enthusiastically get involved in projects aimed at educating the younger generation about the war.

The mass media in Okinawa have often taken the lead in research and recording accounts of the war. Books, movies, plays, and video documentaries have played an important role in educating the younger generation about the war. It can be said that the collection of oral histories has become a philosophical and cultural movement in Okinawa, the ultimate purpose being to keep alive in the "public memory" a knowledge of what happened in the war, so that it will never happen again. Accordingly, it may be argued that memories of the war have become an integral part of Okinawan thought and culture. To give one concrete example, teachers at one elementary school asked their pupils to record the war experiences of their grandparents. The teachers subsequently developed the accounts collected by the students into a play, which was then performed in the gymnasium by the teachers and children for the benefit of their parents and grandparents. From inception to the final performance, it took less than two months to produce the play, an extraordinarily short period of time for such a production. This is just one example of how memories of the war have become an integral part of Okinawan thought and culture.

In the process of recording the survivors' war experiences, many things have been learned, and an area of common ground, or consensus, about the war has emerged. One area of agreement is that the Japanese Army did nothing to protect the lives of the citizens of its own country. The military had its own logic which gave priority to itself in all matters concerning its mission, and this resulted in the army's turning against the citizens of its own country.

Another area of consensus is that we can now clearly perceive that this period in Japanese history was a period of aggression against and victimization of other peoples, which led ultimately to our own victimization. If we look only at the accounts of people involved in the Battle of Okinawa, we see Okinawans who had to surrender or be killed by the Americans, or they would be killed by Japanese soldiers who would not allow them to surrender. But this war had been going on for fifteen years by the time the Battle of Okinawa took place, and the battle must therefore be viewed in its historical context. Okinawan soldiers were members of the same Imperial Japanese Army that invaded and occupied Korea, China, and Southeast Asia. Okinawans also participated in Imperial Japan's colonization of Manchuria and Micronesia. Whether or not any Okinawans considered themselves colonial aggressors, from the viewpoint of the people over whom they ruled, they were as much colonial aggressors and exploiters as was any Imperial Army soldier who took land from the local inhabitants. It is also clear that Okinawans later themselves became the victims in the Battle of Okinawa.

The present Japanese government refuses to admit that the war was a war of aggression; it refuses to apologize or express any remorse to other countries. This is reflected by a similar lack of awareness by Okinawans of their complicity in Japan's aggression. But there is still a fundamental difference in attitudes toward the war. Contrast the mainland Japanese attitude toward China to that of the average Okinawan who looked at Okinawa's long history of friendly relations with China and had immense respect for the great cultural influence of China. In Okinawa, China was called *uyafaafuji nu kuni* (the land of our ancestors). With a historical background of trade links with Southeast Asia, the Okinawan soldiers sent to China with the Imperial Army discovered that many customs and other aspects of culture there were similar to their own, and they felt a sense of kinship with the people there. Perhaps this helps account for the relatively rare incidence of accusations against Okinawan soldiers of brutality and cruelty.

It should also be mentioned that Okinawan soldiers were subject to discrimination in the Imperial Army. For example, Okinawans were rarely promoted to higher ranks. At the same time, they were also rarely accused of committing crimes such as the raping of Chinese women, but perhaps it was just that their low military ranks denied them the opportunities. When Japan surrendered in 1945 after fifty years of colonial rule in Taiwan, there was a wave of incidents in which Japanese were seized by their former Taiwanese victims and accused of crimes. But the Taiwanese, who had observed how the Okinawans were discriminated against by the Japanese, felt a sense of kinship with them and did not accuse them of any crimes. Despite these facts, Okinawans did participate in Imperial Japan's aggression in Asia and the Pacific and must take responsibility for their part in it.

In the Battle of Okinawa, two great armies with modern weaponry met on one small island, and the civilian population, caught in between, had no place to run. Civilians became human shields for the Japanese Army, and even when attacked by the enemy, were absolutely forbidden to surrender. Protection of the civilian population had no place in Japanese military strategy. Military operations, strategy, and tactics were given absolute priority. It is clearly evident that no value was placed on the lives of civilians. Okinawans felt much safer in the hands of the victorious enemy soldiers after being captured than they did with the soldiers of their own country. On being captured, the values based on the emperor system, which had been so thoroughly instilled in the people by militarist propaganda over the years, suddenly collapsed.

It is here that a definitive difference in outlook toward the war becomes apparent. Mainland Japanese, who did not experience any ground combat on their own soil, have very different memories of the war. In the Battle of Okinawa, many Okinawans witnessed Japanese troops killing and massacring their own countrymen. Okinawans know that the so-called group suicides, or *shūdan jiketsu* (lit. "group self-determination"), were actually the sanctioned murder of civilians for tactical reasons. Mainland Japanese have romanticized memories of Okinawans who, under the influence of Imperial ideological propaganda, gladly sacrificed their own lives for the glory of the emperor. But very few Okinawans view the situation this way. They blame the Japanese Army for the killings. Okinawans remember these events as atrocities committed by the Japanese Army.

With memories like these, it is easy to understand why Okinawans view the participation of Japan's self-defense forces in UN peace-keeping operations with great alarm, and why there was so much outrage in Okinawa at UN Special Representative Akashi's remark that "Okinawa would be a suitable place to base Japanese peace-keeping troops." The sensitivity of Okinawans to anything that smacks of war-making capability must be viewed in the context of Okinawan memories of the war.

Okinawa as a Locus for the Promotion of World Peace

THE IDEOLOGY OF PEACE IN OKINAWA

The centerpiece of the commemoration of the fiftieth anniversary of the end of the Second World War in Okinawa was the 23 June 1995 unveiling ceremony for a memorial named the Cornerstone of Peace (Heiwa no Ishiji). The characteristic feature of this memorial is that the names of all the people of all nationalities who died in the Battle of Okinawa are engraved on the memorial stones. The names of all Okinawans who were killed anywhere during the entire span of the Asia-Pacific War, from the invasion of Manchuria through the end of the war, are also included. But as for the Battle of Okinawa itself, all people who died there, friend and foe, aggressors and victims, wartime leaders and common people—all 234,123 names are engraved on the memorial stones, divided by nationality and place of birth. The number of names engraved will increase as research proceeds.

This aspect of the Heiwa no Ishiji memorial will undoubtedly establish a historical precedent. We expect the world will notice that this memorial includes the names not only of the soldiers and civilians of the homeland, but also the names of the 14,005 enemy soldiers who died there. People may wonder how this philosophy of peace, tempered by the war experiences of the people of Okinawa, made possible the conception of such a memorial.

Okinawa's historical consciousness has been shaped from the beginning by contacts with China, Korea, and Japan, and later, in the "Golden Age of Trade," the countries of Southeast Asia as well, when men from the tiny Kingdom of Ryukyu traveled without weapons, armed only with words, consideration, and good nature, and maintained peaceful relations with peoples throughout East and Southeast Asia. The Okinawan conception of peace is also reflected in the Declaration of Peace and Opposition to Nuclear Weapons issued by the prefectural government this year. In the spirit of the Okinawan saying Ichariba choodee (Once two men meet, they become brothers), there are strong aspirations that Okinawa can become a place where neighboring countries can meet as equals to build bridges of peace and friendship.

In 1991 I asked my students to write some original mottos for peace. I believe the traditional Okinawan way of thinking about peace is succinctly expressed in a statement written by Arakaki Shōko, one of the sophomore students in that class: "To have 'peace' with injustice is better than to fight a war for justice. But still, I could never resign myself to injustice." I think we can call this the

Figure 1. Heiwa no Ishiji (Cornerstone of Peace). Courtesy of Ryukyu Shimpo and Okinawa Prefectural Government

Figure 2. Crowds at the unveiling ceremony for the Cornerstone of Peace. Courtesy of Ryukyu Shimpo and Okinawa Prefectural Government

Figure 3. Individual names inscribed on the Cornerstone of Peace. Courtesy of Ryukyu Shimpo and Okinawa Prefectural Government

Figure 4. American names on the Cornerstone of Peace. Courtesy of Ryukyu Shimpo and Okinawa Prefectural Government

traditional Okinawan way of thinking. What we now call the "peaceful spirit of Okinawa" insists on a rejection not only of wars of aggression but of all wars, including religious wars, wars of self-defense, and wars for other just causes.

This Okinawan philosophy of peace points to the only way humanity can hope to avoid total destruction in the nuclear age. Without using any weapons, the people of Okinawa finally freed themselves of what was essentially twenty-seven years of a system of American military occupation. This philosophy of peace was put into practice, and it achieved concrete results.

I have designated this traditional way of thinking about peace *hisen no shisō* (the no-war philosophy).

PEACE IN ACTUAL PRACTICE

Allow me to present a brief historical outline of the development of this no-war philosophy. In 1898, the Imperial Japanese Army began drafting Okinawans into the military for the first time. Conscription continued right up until the beginning of the Battle of Okinawa. The conscription office records reveal some interesting information about the character of the Okinawan people. If I may paraphrase the complaints of a Japanese recruiter: "These Okinawans have very little military spirit, they have a weak sense of nationalism, and loyalty to the emperor and to the national polity has not been instilled in them. Furthermore, they lack any concern whatsoever for the fate of the Japanese Empire. If Okinawa were taken over by a foreign country, the people would immediately begin obeying the new rulers, and therefore, they cannot be trusted."[10] These records provide evidence that the peaceful ways of the Okinawan people were not regarded as such, but rather as a weakness of character and as an obstacle to the promotion of the aggressive aims of the Japanese Empire.

After 1945, Okinawa fell under American military occupation. The American military rulers completely denied Okinawans their basic human rights and treated them with contempt. In contrast to the barbaric ways in which they were treated, the Okinawan people responded with dialogue and demonstrations. Misinterpreting the lack of any violent or aggressive response as docility, the American occupiers began to employ more and more repressive policies. Had such repressive policies been carried out in another country, the Americans would surely have been faced with guerrilla warfare, but the Okinawan people did not respond by taking up weapons and fighting. The strongest Okinawan responses were always peaceful measures, primarily strikes and street demonstrations. They persistently demanded restoration of human rights and unconditional removal of all military bases, petitioning both the American military and the Japanese government.

Okinawa was returned to Japan under its Peace Constitution on 15 May 1972.

The American bases remained, but at least the political rights of the people were restored. These circumstances are clearly reflected in the words of the student I quoted above. There was no war against the injustices perpetrated by the American military. People endured the injustice for the sake of a peaceful society. But, on the other hand, people did not resign themselves to their fate. Okinawans vigorously protested their mistreatment with unflagging determination until their political rights were finally restored. After many long years of peaceful struggle for removal of the bases and for restoration of political rights, when reversion was finally realized, then Prime Minister Eisaku Sato was awarded the Nobel Peace Prize for his efforts in bringing about the reversion agreement. Yet very few Japanese today, including Okinawans, even remember that Sato was awarded the Nobel Peace Prize. Looked at in historical perspective, the Nobel Prize should have been awarded to the people of Okinawa, who put their no-war philosophy into practice and who struggled so long, so hard, and so peacefully.

ESTABLISHING OKINAWA AS A LOCUS FOR
THE PROMOTION OF WORLD PEACE
The construction of the Heiwa no Ishiji memorial was inspired by the historical awareness and consciousness of peace of people in Okinawa, and it provides a new perspective that can make a positive contribution to peace in the world.

First, the memorial is designed to elicit contemplation on the war and its consequences. The names of 236,660 people are engraved on the stone surfaces of the memorial (as of June 1997), suggestive of the way the corpses were both heaped up and scattered about the battlefield, thus conveying a strong symbolic message. Accordingly, the sheer number of names engraved on the stones has a strong impact on visitors who have never known the cruelty of war, indirectly conveying the massive amount of bloodshed that took place. The engraving of individual names of all who were killed, friend and enemy, aggressor and victim, wartime leaders and common people, provokes the visitor to imagine the life and death of each person who was killed in the battle, imparting a more subjective, emotional sense of the tragic loss of lives than any amount of statistics could ever do. The names on the stones of this Heiwa no Ishiji memorial enable the visitor to visually grasp the fact that war is not simply a matter of soldiers killing one another: large numbers of civilians, including men, women, children, and the elderly, suffer and are killed as well. Not only is the name of the commander of the Japanese forces engraved here, but so is the name of the American commander and the names of the other 14,004 American soldiers who died. Viewing the seemingly endless number of names engraved there, the visitor comes to realize that to the families and loved ones of each of the people killed, there are no winners or losers, there is only grief. This should serve as a warning to all the contestants in all of the numerous wars and conflicts now occurring around the world.

The names of all the Okinawans who lost their lives as Imperial soldiers in China, the Philippines, Micronesia, and various other parts of the Japanese Empire are also engraved here, as are the names (that so far have been confirmed) of Taiwanese and Korean draftees, and of Koreans who were brought to Okinawa for forced labor and subsequently lost their lives in the battle. The presence of these names reminds the visitor of the history of Japanese aggression. Seeing all of these names here, the postwar generations that have never experienced war are prodded to consider why so many people died here, and why this war happened. Adjacent to this memorial is the Peace Museum, which attempts to answer those questions in comprehensive detail.

Japan must eventually face up to its history of aggression and initiate a direct dialogue between the former aggressors and their descendants, and the victims and their descendants in China, North and South Korea, Taiwan, Southeast Asia, and Micronesia. This memorial can provide the impetus to begin such a dialogue. At the very least, Okinawa can offer a physical space where such a dialogue can take place. This memorial, grounded in the tragic experiences of war, is a concrete manifestation of the Okinawan philosophy of peace, which can provide the venue for dialogue leading to new avenues of peace. This is an age in which the specter of nuclear annihilation still looms on the horizon. Especially because we live in such an age, the establishment and spread of a universal philosophy of peace that enables people to live together in harmony is absolutely essential for human survival. From a global point of view, the significance of the Heiwa no Ishiji memorial lies in its ability to offer international society new values that envision the establishment of peace around the globe in the twenty-first century. The people of Okinawa are now in the process of drawing up concrete plans to make this vision a reality. One example is the establishment of the Okinawa International Institute for World Peace, which will conduct research on war and conflict resolution and invite scholars of peace studies from all over the world for symposiums and conferences. It will also sponsor programs in which children from all over the world can come together for cultural exchanges and learn about the spirit of peace.

Notes

1 The Association of Bereaved Families comprises the families of Japanese soldiers who died in the war. Since its founding, the ABF has been closely allied with the Liberal Democratic Party, the conservative party that ruled Japan for almost the entire postwar era. The ABF has gotten members elected to the Diet on the LDP ticket and has supported the

campaigns of numerous LDP Diet members. The ABF has become one of Japan's most powerful pressure groups, advocating an agenda calling for increased compensation payments to the surviving families and calling for official recognition of the deceased soldiers as honored war dead. They are generally regarded as occupying a position on the far right of the political spectrum.

2 "'Atarashii sengo' no hajimari" (Beginning of the "New postwar era"), *Tokyo shinbun*, 15 August 1993, morning ed., 6.

3 "Kokkai fusen ketsugi: 'kōtai' tsuzukeru jimin" (Diet renunciation of war resolution: The LDP "backs away"), *Asahi shinbun*, 26 May 1995, morning ed., 2.

4 "81% ga Okinawa-sen wa 'mubō'" (81% say the Battle of Okinawa was "reckless"), *Ryūkyū shinpō*, 6 June 1995, morning ed., 1.

5 "Murayama shushō no danwa" (Prime Minister Murayama's statement), *Okinawa taimuzu*, 16 August 1995, morning ed., 3.

6 James MacGregor Burns, "Kyushu, the War-Ending Invasion That Wasn't," *New York Times Weekly Review*, reprinted in *Asahi Evening News*, 18 August 1995, 12.

7 Ibid., 19.

8 Kido Nikki Kenkyūkai, ed., *Kido Kōichi kankei bunsho* (Kido Kōichi documents) (Tokyo: Tokyo Daigaku Shuppankai, 1966), 495.

9 Again, the military objective for the Japanese forces in the Battle of Okinawa was not to win the battle. At this point in the war the Japanese knew they had no chance of winning. The real objective was to make the campaign as devastating and costly to the enemy as possible in order to strengthen Japan's negotiating position. Although realizing that defeat was inevitable, Japan's military leaders were motivated to continue the war in order to bargain for retainment of the emperor system. Abolishing the emperor system would have a devastating impact on the military's power base and their sway over the civilian population. If the Japanese military could make the price of victory high enough, perhaps the Allies would reconsider their demand for unconditional surrender. In the Battle of Okinawa 14,005 Americans were killed. It was reasoned that the possibility of continued combat entailing casualties commensurate with those in Okinawa would make the Allies more conciliatory and willing to accept a conditional surrender in which the emperor system would be retained.

After the Battle of Okinawa, the Allies were forced to rethink their military strategy and tactics. This was the desired result from Tokyo's point of view; the campaign was a success in that sense. Therefore, Okinawa was sacrificed in a gambit to persuade the Allies to accept retention of the emperor system. The Allies wanted to get the Japanese to accept the terms of the Potsdam Declaration without having to continue sustaining the projected heavy combat casualties. Japan demonstrated that it was willing to put up fierce resistance to the extent of sacrificing the entire civilian population just to preserve the emperor system. This fact in itself provided sufficient justification for the Americans to use the atomic bomb.

10 Urasoe Shishi Henshū Iinkai, *Urasoe shishi* (History of Urasoe City) (Urasoe: Urasoe-shi Kyōiku Iinkai, 1984), 5: 299–304.

Images of Islanders in Pacific War Photographs

LAMONT LINDSTROM

Geoffrey White and I have published a couple of books about the effects of World War II on Pacific Islands societies. In a review of one of the books, a photoessay about Pacific Islander war experiences,[1] the U.S. Army's *Stars and Stripes* newspaper noted: "Many Anglo veterans returned home with a poor image of the 'gooks' with their betel-stained teeth, bleached red hair and primitive strength that fitted them to be bearers and stevedores."[2] These images, however, were plastic, under construction, and ultimately partly recast by the war, although *Stars and Stripes* goes on apologetically: "The facts just never got around that these brave, intelligent, skillful and overwhelmingly friendly locals were dedicated fighting men who often helped us make a difference."

Actually, the Allied and Japanese militaries recycled and generated multiple and conflicting images of Pacific Islanders that they deployed for various purposes.[3] A *Pocket Guide to New Guinea and the Solomons*, prepared for American servicemen by the U.S. Army, instructs, "You'd better junk right at the start any ideas you may have about South Sea savages. Here are some of the facts."[4] Long-lived, some of these "facts" continue to inhabit O'Brien's 1991 review: gooks, betel-stained teeth, primitive bearers and stevedores, but also brave, intelligent, skillful, friendly locals who were dedicated fighting men.

Images of the "native" played to the troops in formal and informal training sessions, and they were transmitted to the metropoles in support of narratives by which the warring armies accounted for their presence in the Pacific. The military circulated facts about South Sea savages in its familiarization handbooks and also pictorially. The war generated enormous photographic archives. In these collections today, we can read wartime imagery of the "native" by paying attention to how military photographers posed their subjects. These island images were constructed by war photographers, correspondents, artists, filmmakers, and other commentators on the war. They did so drawing on their own wartime experiences and projects but also on a set of standardized native poses inherited from colonialist photography.

War historians such as John Dower have explored the racist and other rhetorics that the Allies and Japanese used to make sense of themselves in conflict.[5] Standing back in the referential shadows are Pacific Islanders whose homelands were invaded by Japanese and Allied forces alike. These Islanders only occasionally appear and move across the narrative screen, assigned small roles in the larger struggle between the warring camps. They were to enjoy coprosperity; they were victims to be saved from either vicious European colonialism or an evil Japanese empire; they were exotic and primitive jungle dwellers; and they were loyal allies in a good war.

These were roles that Islanders did not always choose for themselves. The Japanese and Allied militaries in the main controlled the scripting and the production of wartime images—at least those that remain available to us in libraries and archives. Multiple and heterogeneous images of Pacific Islanders exist in the photo archives because they once served the military politics of the 1940s. And these stances continue to be recycled by military historians as well as by tourist entrepreneurs in the new Pacific states who hope to convert war memories into dollars.

I analyze, first, a series of "poses" that Islanders take, or are given, in military war photography. I draw these from a collection of several hundred photographs in military, historical, and personal archives in the United States, Australia, Fiji, and Japan. I then discuss uses of photographs of perhaps the best-known Pacific Island war veteran, Jacob Vouza of the Solomon Islands. The regular recycling and rearrangement of Vouza's 1940s images illustrate the course of war memory over the past half century and the several positions that Islanders have assumed within that memory. Just as we can roam through the photo archives seeking news about how military picture-makers imagined Islanders in the 1940s, so can we track the reuse of those photographs to map the changeable, sometimes slippery contours of public war memory.

War Photography

Still photography was the essential medium for reporting and representing the Pacific War, just as, a generation later in the United States, television was in Vietnam. No one knows the exact number of WWII photographs that exist today. The Imperial War Museum in London archives nearly two million negatives. By the end of 1945, U.S. Army Signal Corps photographers alone had sent more than five hundred thousand photographs to military collections in Washington, DC. Photo historian Jorge Lewinski has noted: "From initial erratic coverage by *ad hoc* commissioned photographers, the scale and extent of the documentation had grown until . . . the Second World War was the best covered of any war."[6]

These thousands of photographs freeze in time pictures of certain wartime encounters and events. But claims that photographs reveal the war's reality are easily discounted because we expect these images to be slanted, to come with a politics. "Cameras don't take pictures . . . people take pictures," as Paul Byers wrote once.[7] Susan Sontag's comment about tourist snapshots is also appropriate for war photography: "As photographs give people an imaginary possession of a past that is unreal, they also help people to take possession of space in which they are insecure."[8] The military took pictures of war on purpose. Photographic poses communicate particular stories about fighting, about the self, and about the enemy. Writing in 1947, Clifton Edom applauded the patriotic functions of American military picture snappers: "The cameraman helped fight fifth-column activities on the home front and made us anxious to participate in bond-buying and other patriotic drives. Photographs were used to weld us more firmly to our allies and to widen the gap between us and the foe."[9]

Pacific Islanders played small but important parts in military photographic narratives. The war's thematics of patriotic drives, welding allies, and widening the gap between them and us required that Islanders assume a number of poses. And these photographic poses diversified images of Island men and women. By war's end, the pictures collected in military archives presented multiple and contradictory images. Wartime poses helped subvert earlier facts about South Sea savages. Justification of the war to ourselves and to others eroded the boundary between civilized self and native other. This instability and plurality of native postures also reflected altered colonial realities whose political effect soon became clear in the postwar political struggles of onetime European dependencies.

Wartime Poses

Wartime photographs position the native in a number of key poses. These postures reflect shifting bounds of European self vis-à-vis native other. They compose what might be called a continuum of affinity: Sometimes natives are unlike, and sometimes like, us. (This "us" comprises the photographer and the military and civilian communities he—and sometimes she—served.) Starting at the dissimilar pole of the continuum, these photographic poses move from

> native as exotic savage, to
> native as servant, to
> native as victim, to

native as pupil, to
native as loyal ally, to
native as like us, like the self.

These six common native poses reflect the staging and details of photographs selected from military archives. The war's narrative imperatives pulled imagined natives down along this continuum so that, by war's end, new images of the native as like "us" partly overlaid prewar depictions of the exotic and savage South Pacific Islander.[10] At least this is so for island men. Photographs of women become scarcer as one moves along the continuum, homing in on the male military self. Pictures of savage women and of female servants and victims are not uncommon; but images of native students, allies, and fellow humans are almost entirely masculine.[11]

The plotting of war narratives dictated these native poses as both the Allied and Japanese militaries documented, surveyed, reported, and readied propaganda. But wartime poses also recalled previous traditions of colonial photography, echoing prewar images of native peoples. The military gaze was a variety of the colonial, and the latter had employed photographic technology since the mid-1800s. The invention of photography "at the time of European and American military and economic expansion in Africa, South America, Asia and the Pacific encouraged its use as an organizer of information about new possessions and contributed to the development of a common vocabulary of visual images by which the colonizers chose to understand the colonized."[12] That vocabulary of visual imagery reflected modernist confidence in European racial and progressive technological superiority. Photography itself "represented technological superiority harnessed to the delineation and control of the physical world, whether it be boundary surveys, engineering schemes to exploit natural resources, or the description and classification of the population."[13] Such classification of the colonized—the sorts of poses common among colonial photographers—included native as savage, as child, as vanishing, as sometimes unchanging, but also sometimes improved "by exposure to white civilization."[14]

Military photographers adapted extant colonialist poses for wartime purposes. They, too, frequently pictured Pacific Islanders as savages, servants, victims (especially of progress), or childlike students whose wartime experiences, even if tragic, were ultimately educational and uplifting. As with previous traditions of colonial photography, this imagery was "useful in the reduction of individuals to easily managed and commodifiable 'types.' "[15] But the war in many ways broke open to enlarge and complicate the colonialist photographic archive. Out of its imperatives emerged at least two novel poses for natives—new photographs of Pacific Islanders posed as loyal allies and as kindred humans.

An array of wartime poses clusters about the image of natives as savage—as exotic and unlike the civilized, modern militarized self. "The ready-made stereotype of Islanders as savage, headhunting cannibals" was perhaps the most pervasive prewar image of South Seas natives.[16] In this sort of photograph, the savage in plumes and shells stands juxtaposed to uniformed servicemen (fig. 1). Neatly dressed American officers, hunting wild boar in mountainous island interiors, pose with groups of nearly naked villagers. In weaponry as in clothing, the exotic spear counterposes the civilized tank within the same photographic frame (fig. 2).

Other photographs evoke ancillary images that inhabit Western, racist discourses of savage others. The native is uncivilized. He is ignorant of Western technology and morality. Two Solomon Islanders are depicted carrying their loaded wheelbarrow rather than pushing it (fig. 3). The native is also like a child, and island children were favorite subjects for military photographers (as they were in earlier, colonialist representations of Islanders).[17]

These images of the exotic savage assert cultural and racial distance. The Islander is unlike the military photographer standing behind the camera or the servicemen who share the frame. This human distance is captured in a shot of Americans posing in a "head" hastily constructed as seagoing toilet facilities for men from Tanna Island, recruited to work in military labor corps on Efate Island. The peripheral native toilets overhanging the sea restate photographically the physical distance, and bodily differences, between savage self and military self.

SERVANT

The pose of servant takes the exotic other one step closer to the self. The native may be savage, but he also serves as a domestic servant: the bondsman of civilization. He carries; he waits on table; he acts as personal orderly; he unloads military cargo (fig. 4). Islanders hang Marine laundry up to dry. They carry portly American officers ashore on their shoulders so military boots and cuffs stay dry. They pass the catsup and pour the ice water in mess halls. They scrub white soldierly backs in al fresco bathtubs (fig. 5). It is telling to glance through a handbook on South Seas Pidgin English, prepared for military use by the Linguistic Society of America.[18] Twenty-one percent of the section "Useful Phrases" consists of direct orders and commands. And the longest and most elaborated item in the Pidgin lexicon is a set of useful phrases for "sexual intercourse, have."[19]

These images of domestic service, control, and sexual desire, clearly, reflect the history of Black-White relations within American society. Racial hierarchy

Figure 1. Allied soldiers encounter Konga, a local "chief," in Irian Jaya, March 1944. (Australian War Memorial)

Figure 2. An Australian soldier receives a lesson in native weaponry as an Indonesian soldier and a local man relax, Irian Jaya, March 1944. (Australian War Memorial)

Figure 3. Solomon Islander workers on New Georgia, February 1944. The Navy's release on the photograph noted, "Sailors later taught them the right way." (U.S. National Archives)

Figure 4. Children carry
ashore U.S. Army supplies
on Kiriwina, Papua New
Guinea, July 1943. (U.S.
National Archives)

Figure 5. Munhoe and Otalif
scrub their Australian boss's
back after finishing work
in a field hospital laundry,
Yamil, Papua New Guinea,
July 1945. (Australian War
Memorial)

organized the U.S. military itself, of course, segregated into White and Black units. Black Americans were restricted to service units (e.g., stevedoring and transportation battalions and the like). President Roosevelt, pressured by domestic political interests and the approaching elections of 1944, allowed African Americans into combat only in the final two years of the war. Military photographers situated dark Islanders within the overgrown discourse of American racism, as South Seas versions of Black Americans. Photographically, they sing, they dance, and they smile broadly, white teeth sparkling. Within this frame, Islanders occupy a set of painfully familiar poses, ranging from domestic servant to happy-go-lucky, musical jester.

VICTIMS

Allied war narratives soon looked beyond the immediate wound of Pearl Harbor. The United States was in the war not just to avenge that surprise attack, but to protect democracy in the world. War storytellers cast Pacific Islanders living behind Japanese lines, or in the path of the Japanese advance, as victims. And the Japanese, likewise, portrayed the native as needful of liberation from European colonialist domination.

Military photographers composed shots of island refugees and of Islanders injured by war. Islanders clamber up the sides of military vehicles and vessels, escaping from Japanese occupation and the upheavals of battle (fig. 6). Images of Americans, friendly of course, giving assistance to Islanders were companion pieces to these poses. Wounded and needy natives, particularly, received medical assistance: new limbs, treatment of endemic skin diseases and malaria, injections of modern wonder drugs. One scene, reproduced in several photographs from various Pacific islands, depicts military doctors palpating spleens up and down lines of bare-breasted women who were suspected of having malaria (fig. 7). And in other shots of natives receiving dental care, gap-mouthed boys become the patients of Western agency (fig. 8). Liberated from the Japanese, they are likewise liberated from disease and dental caries by Allied saviors.

APT PUPIL

Images of natives as victim slide smoothly into a related posture of native as pupil. Natives are assaulted by war, but also by modern technology. Along with medical care and other sorts of Western assistance, the war brought real civilization for the first time into the Pacific. Numerous shots of natives suffering this "shock of the new" have a marked playful quality.[20] The Stone Age encounters the Industrial Age. Photographers drolly juxtapose outrigger sailing canoes and seaplanes, dugouts and amphibious vehicles. Natives have their first experiences of the wonders of technology. Motorcycles attract their attention.

Figure 6. U.S. Marines load up local refugees on Saipan, Northern Mariana Islands, June 1944. (U.S. National Archives)

Figure 7. Australian doctor palpates spleens on Koil Island, Papua New Guinea, October 1945. (Australian War Memorial)

Figure 8. Military dentists examine Titus Molirani on Tutuba, Vanuatu, August 1943. (U.S. National Archives)

Phonographs astonish. In one shot of Americans and Islanders listening to recorded music, the white finger points to the future, a wristwatch already ticking on the native wrist (fig. 9). Other photographs play with movie sign-board advertisements, which appear for the first time hung on Pacific Islander backs.

But Islanders are quick studies. The shock of the new passes and natives transform into expert students, guided by military teachers. They sing on military radio to appreciative audiences; they staff the cash registers at roughly constructed post exchanges. They learn skills, such as how to spray D D T to kill mosquito larvae and how to string telephone wire, from military instructors—skills, so war narratives suggest, that will be economically functional in a postwar world of wonderful technology, restored democracy, and new colonial deals (fig. 10).

LOYAL ALLY

Other photographs work to reduce the hierarchy that structures wartime master/servant, savior/victim, and teacher/student relationships. In these shots, the native is no longer the student of the military, but rather an ally. Relationships of allegiance connote at least an implicit equality. The natives join with the Allies in combating a common foe. They make contributions to the war effort. A

Figure 9. Two Solomon Islanders spin records with an American GI, Guadalcanal, August 1943. (U.S. National Archives)

Figure 10. Solomon Islander workers help construct Guadalcanal's first telephone network, June 1943. (U.S. National Archives)

shot from Kiribati (Gilbert Islands) depicts people holding up a mat with the woven logo "Our Present for the War." Photographed Islanders also rescue downed flyers and assist the wounded. The Islander matures into the fuzzy-wuzzy angel, as Australian war poet Bert Beros rhymed:

> And in ways he's like a woman bringing in the sick and hurt,
> Through we curse and call him "Heathen" if he nicks off with our shirt.[21]

A well-known photograph from New Guinea depicts an Islander leading an injured Australian serviceman to hospital. These images invert the pose of native as needy war victim. Here the native, although still fuzzy-wuzzy feminine, leads and is in helpful command.

The natives also volunteer to defeat the Japanese. They join labor corps and defense forces. Pictorially, they line up; they raise their right hands; they make their marks on induction papers. And their allegiance legitimates the Allied presence. The cause is just. The natives join with us rather than with the Japanese. (Needless to say, images of native allies were also common in Japanese productions.) The loyal natives sign up to work to defeat the enemy. They submit to a martial organization of their labor for the good war. Shots from New Caledonia depict Islanders composed into large labor brigades, standing in formation. They willingly shoulder the war's cargo. Islanders unload bicycles, crates, beer, the whole panoply of military cargo from ships and planes.

Loyal natives also sign on to fight the enemy. They take up Allied arms. Military discourse played with popular prewar images of the native as savage warrior. They squint down the barrels of their new rifles. They hit the target bull's-eye (fig. 11). Islanders use their hunting skills to kill the enemy. The loyal native redirects his cannibalistic zest and jungle savvy against a common Japanese foe. (Bert Beros, annotating his poem about an Australian aboriginal soldier, remarked, "To avenge his aboriginal cobber who was killed in the Owen Stanleys, he went naked and stalked the Japanese machine-gun pits, into which he hurled grenades."[22]) Natives also serve photographically as military scouts (fig. 12). They guide Allied troops to Japanese positions along treacherous jungle trails that only they know. The loyal native stands guard over Japanese prisoners, allied with the Americans in victory over Japan.

LIKE US

Images of the native, progressing from exotic savage to loyal ally, increasingly close in upon the self. They question the racial and other boundaries dividing military selves and native others. Although the war did not break down the distinctions separating the civilized West and the savage South Seas,

Figure 11. Papua New Guinean displays his marksmanship with an Owen gun, 1943. (U.S. National Archives)

Figure 12. Papua New Guinean policeman maps out Japanese positions for the U.S. Army, Buna, November 1942. (U.S. National Archives)

photographically these bounds faded and decayed, particularly in playful and sacred moments.

Images of shared effort intimate that the native is like us, or at least somewhat like us. In pictures at least, natives and servicemen work together for joint goals, muscling artillery up a mountainside, unloading PT boats. Poses of shared endeavor and everyday experience connote a common humanity. These shared experiences include having a Coke together, playing checkers, lighting up one another's cigarettes. This last pose is very common in the archives: servicemen and Islanders again and again give each other the courtesy of a light.

Americans also posed themselves learning something from natives, reversing position in the wartime posture of apt pupil. Islanders teach servicemen the crafts of house thatching and weaving. In one shot, Navy Seabees and Islanders from Vanuatu work together plaiting coconut fronds (fig. 13). Photographs capture these likenesses: working together, shirtless and side by side in the sun, the distance between self and other decreases.

Military photographers soon discovered an important religious commonality joining servicemen with natives: the majority of both were Christian.[23] Poses of natives taking communion and servicemen and natives worshipping together also suggest a common humanity (which neatly leaves out the heathen Japanese). Shots of native-built "grass" churches, in which both military personnel and Islanders join in worship, were made throughout the Pacific.

A few photographs capture instances of play counterposed to these sacred moments that invert the equation of common humanity: The natives are like us, but we are also like the natives. This is the penultimate collapse of boundaries and convergence of once disparate identities: the self as other. This creation of an "exotic self" is the antithesis of the alien savage located back at the most distant pole of the continuum of similitude. Soldiers pretend to be natives, balancing large woven baskets on their heads. Both the Japanese and the Americans cross-dressed, ethnically. They played with "the fantasy of otherness as an achievable goal within the self." (I borrow here from Marjorie Garber's analysis of cross-gender dressing.[24]) In one shot, Japanese sailors dress up like natives on Saipan. In another, an American corporal sports a grass skirt on Guadalcanal (fig. 14). The camera captures servicemen going native.

These postures are ironic. These are servicemen at play; their grins signify that they are not real natives. Boundaries between self and other continue to exist and they underlie and permit this photographic irony. But whereas the photograph (noted above) of Americans posing in a makeshift ship's toilet plays with distance, separation, and essential and racial differences between military selves and Tanna Island others, cross-dressing photographs hint at common human affinities.

Figure 13. American Seabee learns how to plait coconut leaf mats, Espiritu Santo, Vanuatu, January 1943. (U.S. National Archives)

Figure 14. Corporal Luigi J. Greasso cross-dresses on Guadalcanal, Solomon Islands, January 1944. (U.S. National Archives)

The narrative demands of the war and the production of photographic poses that served these demands worked to transform the South Seas savage into a partial mirror of the Western self. The war did not extinguish images of the exotic savage, nor did it erode completely boundaries between natives and ourselves. It did, however, enrich and multiply images of the native, who was now reposed to be servant, victim, pupil, ally, and, occasionally, brother human. And in the postwar, postcolonial era in the Pacific, these are the images that continue to haunt war memory.

Recycled Vouza

War narratives require heroes, and not always in uniform. The "Untold Story of Jacob Vouza" continues to get told as part of the larger history of Allied war experiences in the southwest Pacific.[25] Vouza was in the right—or perhaps the wrong—place at the right time, in both battleground and historiography.

The story, roughly, is this. Vouza had served for many years as a policeman for the British Solomon Islands Protectorate. After the outbreak of the war, British Army captain and coastwatcher W. Martin Clemens, once the colonial district officer on Guadalcanal, recruited Vouza as a native spy and guide. Captured by the Japanese who were preparing to attack U.S. forces to recapture Henderson Airfield, Vouza refused to divulge information about Allied positions although tied to a tree, bayoneted, and eventually left for dead. Early in the morning of 21 August 1942, Vouza escaped and made his way through the Japanese forces back to a Marine outpost. There, he reported what he had learned about the Japanese to Allied defenders, who were just then under attack by eight hundred Japanese troops led by Colonel Kiyono Ichiki. Vouza, having been debriefed, collapsed and was driven to a U.S. field hospital, where he received six pints of American blood, convalesced, and eventually recovered. Relying at least partly on Vouza's information, Marines fought off Japanese soldiers trying to cross the Ilu River, killing most of them. Vouza became a media figure and had his photograph taken by several military photographers. He eventually received the Silver Star from the Americans and the George Medal from the British.[26]

Vouza was ripe for position as loyal native ally, and both the Americans and the British soon posed him to this effect. Richard Tregaskis, a U.S. journalist, featured Vouza's heroism and his allegiance to America in his 1943 book, *Guadalcanal Diary.* On the British side, the Central Office of Information in 1946 published *Among Those Present: The Official Story of the Pacific Islands at War Prepared for the Colonial Office.* Vouza occupies several paragraphs in this. The book celebrates him as a first-class scout, an exemplar of "the general fidelity of the

Islanders to the Allied cause."[27] It records Vouza's pledges of loyalty (in his "rather superior brand of pidgin"): "I remember my training in the Police and how they tell me always to be faithful to my King. I think about how naughty I was when I first joined the Police and how much trouble I cause Government. So I tell myself this time I do something good for my King to pay him back for all that trouble. Also I think better me die than Japs take our island because then I know all of us die."[28] Vouza's wounds become part of the master narrative of native loyalty: "a striking disproof of the Axis propaganda claim that the coloured subjects of the Empire have no interest in fighting for its preservation."[29]

Vouza played a larger role, as avatar of native loyalty, in the 1945 book *Vouza and the Solomon Islands* (an American edition was issued in 1948 by Macmillan). This was written by Hector MacQuarrie who, during the First World War, had also offered *How to Live at the Front: Tips for American Soldiers*.[30] Here, Vouza stands in for Solomon Islanders as a whole; his story is their story, a story the Allies— many of them, anyway—wanted told about wartime heroics and ultimate victory in the Pacific. Vouza is also the protagonist of a 1992 military memoir and of a reader issued by the Solomon Islands Pijin Literacy Project.[31]

Vouza photographs along with Vouza stories have reappeared in a variety of settings since the end of the war. Some military histories, in fact, have included only a Vouza photograph with caption—a sidebar to accounts of the more important events of the war, at least from an official military perspective.[32] A half dozen Vouza pictures taken between 1942 and 1945 by military photographers have appeared repeatedly over the years in books about the war in the Solomon Islands. Some publications also offer postwar images of Vouza, taken by latterday pilgrims to his Guadalcanal village. In these, the aging Vouza is almost always portrayed, kitted out for both battle and plaudits, in American military uniform blouse bedecked with his numerous ribbons and medals.[33]

Vouza's war-era photographs preserved in the archives portray him either as shirtless native or as Americanized ally dressed in khaki. He is posed alternately as savage other, as native ally, and as brother soldier. Two Marine Corps photographs, taken apparently in the same photo session on 16 September 1943, place Vouza in one, then the other, of these positions. One shot depicts Vouza dressed in slacks, thick belt, shirt, and tie, his honorary sergeant major stripes on his sleeve, pointing to his battle ribbons (fig. 15). He is in conversation with fellow Sergeant Major Leland L. Chapman of Ludowici, Georgia. In the other photograph, conversation between peers turns into juxtaposition. Vouza has taken off his shirt to turn and face his still clothed American counterpart (fig. 16). The official caption highlights his native oddity and courage: "Vutha [sic], who was tortured and stabbed by the Japs last year when he refused to reveal Marine troop movements, has two vanities; his mop of frizzly reddish-tinged

Figure 15. Vouza, in khakis, points to his battle ribbons and medals, Guadalcanal, Solomon Islands, 16 September 1943. (U.S. National Archives)
Figure 16. Vouza out of uniform, Guadalcanal, Solomon Islands, 16 September 1943 (U.S. National Archives)

Figure 17. Vouza in
U.S. Marine uniform,
Guadalcanal, Solomon
Islands. (U.S. National
Archives)

hair and possum tooth necklace. Right below the necklace and on the stomach can be seen some of the seven scars Vutha bears which were inflicted by a Jap officer with a sword." Uniform and ribbon alternate with possum teeth and that mop of hair.

Both Vouza poses—as frizzly haired savage and as uniformed ally—have been recycled in war narrative. Karig and Purdon and Horton, for example, use a 1943 shot of Vouza standing in a shallow sea grasping the prow of a canoe, shirtless and in ragged lavalava.[34] Other war stories that highlight Vouza as a brave and wily ally instead select one of the uniformed photographs from the archives. Mueller and Richter, for example, both use a shot of Vouza in Marine Corps blouse sporting a Japanese helmet and captured "samarai sword."[35] Vouza looks particularly tough in this shot; the gaze focuses on his strong, white, clenched teeth (fig. 17). Griffith further underlines Vouza's jungle savvy and native martial ferocity by using a crude line drawing of his head and torso with rifle and bandoleer, perhaps derived from this photograph.[36] Those keen teeth, at least, remain the same, although Vouza here has once again lost his shirt.

Depending on the narrative demands of a particular war story, historians can mine both savage and brother-ally Vouzas from the photo archives. In the postcolonial Pacific, it is perhaps no surprise today that stories of wartime loyalty and willing allegiance trump those of alien jungle savagery. The former battlegrounds, now independent South Pacific nations, many of which seek to push economic development a little farther along by cultivating tourism, also are telling war stories of past allegiance and shared suffering and effort to veteran war pilgrims and casual tourists alike (both American and Japanese).

The Solomon Islands, for example, has a small but not insignificant war tourism industry, and veterans groups have cultivated this by marking sites and building memorials of various sorts. Images of Vouza, photographic and otherwise, continue to play within this industry. At the 1992 fiftieth anniversary of the Battle for Guadalcanal, a larger-than-life-size statue of Vouza was unveiled in Honiara, the nation's capital city. But this Vouza—the late Sir Charles Jacob Vouza, Knight of the British Empire—once again loses his shirt. The involvement of veterans organizations in the design of the statue may help explain his bare-chested memorialization in a very dark-colored metal.[37]

These stories of dangerous savage difference and wily native loyalty are built into the World War II photo archives' poses of Islanders as savages, servants, victims, pupils, allies, and fellow humans. Here, Vouza is a shirtless savage; there, Vouza is a uniformed, brave, and clever ally. These archived images remain available for new readings and uses as we look at them again in the twenty-first century. In particular, we might see in them what the contemporary politics of remembering the Pacific War encourages us now to foreground: the once shadowy experiences of women, of gay servicemen, of atomic bomb survivors, of Filipino brigades, of disrupted island peoples, of Jacob Vouza, and of all the other, lowly natives caught up in a multicultural war.

Notes

1   Lamont Lindstrom and Geoffrey M. White, *Island Encounters: Black and White Memories of the Pacific War* (Washington, DC: Smithsonian Institution Press, 1990).

2   Cyril O'Brien, "Island Encounters: Black and White Encounters of the Pacific War," *Stars and Stripes* (10 June 1991).

3   See Hisafumi Saito, "Barefoot Benefactors: A Study of Japanese Views of Melanesians," in *Remembering the Pacific War*, ed. Geoffrey M. White (Honolulu: Center for Pacific Islands Studies, University of Hawai'i, 1991), 207–22; Marty Zelenietz, "Villages without People: A Preliminary Analysis of American Views of Melanesians during World War II as Seen through Popular Histories," in ibid., 187–205. The war also unsettled and transformed Islanders' images of Europeans, Americans, Japanese, and other outsiders; see Geoffrey M. White and Lamont Lindstrom, *The Pacific War: Island Representations of World War Two* (Honolulu: University of Hawai'i Press, 1989). In Vanuatu (then the New Hebrides), for example, fifty thousand American servicemen, many of whom were Black, arrived to establish two large frontline bases. This American presence, which still reverberates today, overshadowed and recast island understandings of the colonial French and British.

Images of Americans continue to circulate locally in Vanuatu in a rich body of oral narrative and song.

4 Special Service Division, Army Service Forces, U.S. Army, *A Pocket Guide to New Guinea and the Solomons* (Washington, DC: War and Navy Departments, 1944), 10.

5 John W. Dower, *War without Mercy: Race and Power in the Pacific War* (New York: Pantheon, 1986).

6 Jorge Lewinski, *The Camera at War: A History of War Photography from 1848 to the Present Day* (New York: Simon and Schuster, 1978), 95.

7 Paul Byers, "Cameras Don't Take Pictures," *Columbia University Forum* 9, no. 1 (1966):27–33.

8 Susan Sontag, *On Photography* (New York: Farrar, Straus and Giroux, 1977), 9.

9 Clifton C. Edom, "Photo-Propaganda: The History of Its Development," *Journalism Quarterly* 24 (1947):238; see also Bernd Hüppauf, "Modernism and the Photographic Representation of War and Destruction," in *Fields of Vision: Essays in Film Studies, Visual Anthropology, and Photography*, ed. Leslie Devereaux and Roger Hillman (Berkeley: University of California Press, 1995), 94–124.

10 My discrimination of these six poses emerges from an analysis of archived photographs, only a few of which can be reproduced here. However, see Lindstrom and White, *Island Encounters*, where the more interesting and significant of our archival selections are reproduced.

11 See Margaret Jolly, "From Point Venus to Bali Ha'i: Eroticism and Exoticism in Representations of the Pacific," in *Sites of Desire, Economies of Pleasure: Sexualities in Asia and the Pacific*, ed. Lenore Manderson and Margaret Jolly (Chicago: University of Chicago Press, 1997), 99–122.

12 Alison Devine Nordström, "Wood Nymphs and Patriots: Depictions of Samoans in *The National Geographic Magazine*," *Visual Sociology* 7, no. 2 (1992):49.

13 Elizabeth Edwards, introduction to *Anthropology and Photography 1860–1920*, ed. Elizabeth Edwards (New Haven: Yale University Press, 1992), 6.

14 Nordström, "Wood Nymphs," 51; see also Catherine A. Lutz and Jane L. Collins, *Reading National Geographic* (Chicago: University of Chicago Press, 1993), 117; Melissa Banta and Curtis M. Hinsley, *From Site to Sight: Anthropology, Photography, and the Power of Imagery* (Cambridge, MA: Peabody Museum Press, 1986), 101.

15 Nordström, "Wood Nymphs," 57.

16 Zelenietz, "Villages without People," 192.

17 See Nicholas Thomas, *Colonialism's Culture: Anthropology, Travel, and Government* (Princeton, NJ: Princeton University Press, 1994); Alison Devine Nordström, "Early Photography in Samoa: Marketing Stereotypes of Paradise," *History of Photography* 15 (winter 1991): 276.

18 Robert Anderson Hall, *Melanesian Pidgin Phrase-book and Vocabulary* (Madison, WI: U.S. Armed Forces Institute, 1943).

19 Ibid., 26.

20 Nordström, "Early Photography," 283.

21 H. "Bert" Beros, *The Fuzzy Wuzzy Angels and Other Verses* (Sydney, Australia: F.H. Johnson Publishing Company, 1944), 96.

22 Ibid., 25.

23 See Ruth Henrich, *South Seas Epic: War and the Church in New Guinea* (London: Society for the

Propagation of the Gospel, 1944); Henry P. Van Dusen, *They Found the Church There: The Armed Forces Discover Christian Missions* (New York: Charles Scribner's Sons, 1945).

24 Marjorie Garber, *Vested Interests: Cross-Dressing and Cultural Anxiety* (New York: Routledge, 1992), 335; for more on the fantasy and mimicry of ethnic cross-dressing, see David Bate, "Photography and the Colonial Vision," *Third Text* 22 (spring 1993):81–91.

25 Don Richter, *Where the Sun Stood Still: The Untold Story of Sir Jacob Vouza and the Guadalcanal Campaign* (Tawe, CA: Toucan Publishing, 1992).

26 See Hector MacQuarrie, *Vouza and the Solomon Islands* (London: V. Gollancz, 1945); Samuel B. Griffith, *The Battle for Guadalcanal* (Toronto: Bantam, 1963), 103–5; Walter Lord, *Lonely Vigil: Coastwatchers of the Solomons* (New York: Viking, 1977); Joseph N. Mueller, *Guadalcanal 1942: The Marines Strike Back* (London: Osprey Publications, 1992), 43–44; Richter, *Where the Sun Stood Still*.

27 Great Britain Colonial Office, *Among Those Present: The Official Story of the Pacific Islands at War* (London: His Majesty's Stationery Office, 1946), 29.

28 Ibid.

29 Ibid., 30.

30 Hector MacQuarrie, *How to Live at the Front: Tips for American Soldiers* (Philadelphia: J.B. Lippincott, 1917).

31 Richter, *Where the Sun Stood Still*; Solomon Islands Pijin Literacy Project, *Stori abaotem Sa Chales Jekop Vouza* (Honiara: Solomon Islands Pijin Literacy Project, 1982).

32 Walter Karig and Eric Purdon, *Battle Report, Pacific War: Middle Phase* (New York: Rinehart and Co., 1947).

33 See Lord, *Lonely Vigil*; William Manchester, *Goodbye, Darkness: A Memoir of the Pacific War* (New York: Dell, 1979); Herbert Christian Merillat, *Guadalcanal Remembered* (New York: Dodd, Mead and Co., 1982).

34 Karig and Purdon, *Battle Report*; D. C. Horton, *Fire over the Islands: The Coast Watchers of the Solomons* (London: Leo Cooper, 1970).

35 Mueller, *Guadalcanal 1942*, 44; Richter, *Where the Sun Stood Still*, 210.

36 Griffith, *The Battle*, 103; see also Richter, *Where the Sun Stood Still*, iii.

37 For two photographs and analysis of Vouza's statue, see Geoffrey M. White, "Remembering Guadalcanal: National Identity and Transnational Memory-Making," *Public Culture* 7 (1995): 529–55.

Imagery and War in Japan: 1995

MORIO WATANABE

Presence and Absence of "War"

Fifty years have elapsed since the demilitarization of Japan in the summer of 1945, yet the majority of present-generation Japanese have lived their entire lives without firsthand knowledge of what war is like. The reality of war has become so detached from their everyday lives that for most young Japanese, popular culture has become the dominant source of learning about wars. During the fiftieth anniversary of the end of the Asia-Pacific War, various orchestrations by the media to commemorate the end of "that previous war" were attempted. Yet the public memories of that war were far from focused and did not engender any sharp images in today's Japan. An editorial in a major newspaper underscored the fact that after fifty years, Japan had not yet resolved the proper name by which to refer to the previous war—testimony to the ambivalent public consciousness in Japan.[1]

Nevertheless, certain images prevailing in the realm of popular culture and the subculture in Japan have criss-crossed with epoch-making social and political incidents that occurred in 1995, most notably the Sarin Incident perpetrated by the religious sect Aum Shinrikyō and the gang rape of a sixth-grade girl by U.S. Marine soldiers in Okinawa.

Before analyzing specific texts, it is necessary to be familiar with events in Japan in 1995 in which these texts were read in context. On 17 January the Hanshin great earthquake, with a magnitude of 7.2, shook Japan. There was extensive television coverage of the destruction that left the Hanshin area with a total of 6,427 dead and of the aftermath of fires that burned down entire communities in Kobe. Although a natural disaster, it reminded many Japanese of the carpet-bombed cities of Japan fifty years earlier.

One pathological aspect of the collective memory of the Asia-Pacific War in Japan is to look back on the war as a natural disaster, perhaps because it allows a psychological absolution of accountability. Meanwhile, we have Asahara Shōkō (born Matsumoto Chizuo), leader of a religious cult called the Aum Shinrikyō, insisting that the Hanshin great earthquake was not a natural disaster but instead was caused by human intervention: that mine weapons were deployed and that "war has already started." On 20 March 1995 five members of Asahara's cult sprayed deadly sarin inside subway trains servicing the government office district, resulting in twelve dead and fifty injured, all of whom were innocent passengers or bystanders. This seemingly quixotic war to save the souls of humankind, since then termed the Tokyo Sarin Incident, lacked a coherent enemy beyond the imaginary "phantom foe." The rape of the twelve-year-old Okinawan girl occurred subsequently.

These series of incidents forced the Japanese to reconsider the "security myth" on which postwar Japan had blindly placed its faith. The Sarin Incident echoed the dark legacy of World War II, because it reminded a few not only of the Japanese Army's chemical warfare experiments in China but also, in an ironical and farcical way, of the recently revealed secret plans of a gas attack on Tokyo by U.S. military forces at the end of World War II.[2] The image of prefectural riot police in battle dress uniform and gas masks breaking into the headquarters of the Aum Shinrikyō near Mt. Fuji was captured on television monitors across Japan, the closest the public got to experiencing a pseudo-war at home in recent years.

Analysis of the Sarin Incident reveals heavy imprints of fifty years of postwar Japanese popular culture on the religious cult, which attracted a number of elite university students. Aum Shinrikyō's obsession with purified clean air (note the irony of how they resorted to spraying poisonous gas) was well-known, and they had installed numerous mechanical devices called "Cosmo Cleaners" in their facilities. The naming of that device was clearly influenced by a cult-status animated film in the seventies called *Uchūsenkan Yamato* (Space Cruiser Yamato) by Matsumoto Reiji. In *Yamato*, the Cosmo Cleaner was designed to rid the Earth of atmospheric radioactivity, whereas the Aum sect claimed their Cosmo Cleaner was capable of neutralizing sarin and mustard gas and filtering out any bacteriological weapons. This cult believed in its leader's prophecy that Armageddon, sparked by conflict between Christian and Buddhist sects leading to World War III, would occur in the year 1997. Accordingly, their thoughts and behaviors were governed by that end-of-the-world framework.

The notion of Armageddon itself has biblical origins, but it gained currency among young people only after Hirai Kazumasa's science fiction novel *Genma taisen* and subsequent animated films became popular in the eighties. Aside from the works previously mentioned, the Aum cult was said to be influenced by various animated works such as *Kidōsenshi Gandamu* (Mobile Suit Gundam,

1981), *Kaze no tani no Naushika* (Nausicaä of the Valley of the Wind, 1984), *Hokuto no ken* (Fist of the North Star, 1986), and *AKIRA* (1988). In this regard, it came as no surprise that much of the cult's discourse seemed to be echoing the eighties' subculture. A critic noted that the Aum's sense of history was completely replaced by those segmented quotations from the eighties' *otaku* (monomania) subculture in Japan.[3] One may add that to talk of Aum Shinrikyō in the context of the eighties subculture itself became a social and intellectual fad in Japan.

August 15 has been a day of deep emotion for older generations in Japan who experienced living through "the" day in 1945. For those who were born later, it is a time of feeling somewhat uneasy pressure from the mass media to extend their imaginations back to the time of the war. August 15, 1995, must have been doubly uncomfortable for many youngsters because it was the fiftieth anniversary of the war and special television programs commemorating the war were lined up for this occasion. Absent from these didactic TV programs, however, were alternative ways in which an individual counts the years. For instance, 1995 was also the centennial anniversary of the Treaty of Shimonoseki that terminated the Sino-Japan War of 1894, from which Japan emerged as an imperialist colonial power in Asia. It was also the forty-fifth anniversary of the start of the Korean War, during which economic activities associated with the war helped lay the foundation for Japan's economic recovery from the devastation wrought by the Asia-Pacific War, benefiting Japan greatly. So, whereas discourse on the "postwar fifty years" dominated the media, these other meaningful historical perspectives were conveniently omitted.

Just as the public's attention from the war and peace agenda was waning, a rape incident occurred on Okinawa, a relatively small island south of the Japanese mainland that accounts for less than 1 percent of Japan's total land area but where 75 percent of all U.S. Forces military bases in Japan are located. Rape incidents are not entirely foreign in places where military bases are located, but this particular incident sparked a storm of protest against the presence of the entire U.S. Forces on Okinawa. Eighty-five thousand people gathered on 21 October to protest the rape incident, with demands that the Japanese government reconsider the Status of Forces Agreement (SOFA) with the United States and ultimately remove U.S. military bases from Okinawa.[4] A stormy campaign was launched by the mass media, eventually resulting in an agreement to return Futenma U.S. Marine Base to Okinawa. Whether the massive protests and tremendous emotional energy expended by the protestors were influenced by the media's portrayal of the victim as symbolic young Japanese girl, or *shōjo*, is unclear.

The image of war in Japan today criss-crosses several dimensions of "realities." Images of the Asia-Pacific War, certainly "constructed" images in themselves, float around, as yet to be appropriated by various and possibly conflicting interest groups. But young people are obtaining their images of war primarily from the compartmentalized fields of the subculture where "virtual reality" and "hyperreality" have long been the norm. This essay analyzes Japanese popular culture texts selected from several genres, encompassing war-simulation novels, *manga* (comics), TV *anime*, animated films, and theatrical films, which were all produced or remembered in the year 1995. Hopefully, they will give a glimpse of what Fredric Jameson calls "the political unconscious" prevailing in contemporary Japanese popular culture.[5]

Hyperreality and Infantilism

The notion of "virtual reality" is being capitalized on by the recent advent of so-called war-simulation novels. They have also been called "if novels," for they portray what might have happened if Japan had acted differently in the Asia-Pacific War. They try to imagine the possibility of a different path taken in history.

The first volume of Aramaki Yoshio's *Deep Blue Fleet* series was published on the last day of 1990. When Aramaki, a former science fiction writer, and his publisher conceived the idea of launching a new series of war-simulation novels, they initially anticipated a readership of about thirty thousand: ten thousand from the so-called military *otaku*, ten thousand from fans of computer simulation games, and another thousand from Aramaki's personal readership.[6] However, the month following its debut, the Gulf War started and sales of Aramaki's book jumped sharply, to the surprise of both the author and the publisher.

The setting for the first volume is a simulated "afterworld" where the Asia-Pacific War is refought by a group of reborn top Japanese leaders possessing knowledge of historical experiences from the war. The reborn character of Admiral Yamamoto Isoroku defeats the U.S. Pacific Fleet in Hawai'i, Hawai'i is declared an independent state, he subsequently forms an alliance with the British and makes peace with the United States. The enemy in this afterworld is Nazi Germany. An element of wishful thinking and repressed desire is evident here. Although it is now inconceivable that Japan could have defeated the entire Pacific Fleet in Hawai'i and made honorable peace with both Great Britain and the United States, it is this kind of imaginary circus that seems to be a necessary come-on to making the Asia-Pacific War worthy of being the focus of simulation game materials and entertainment for young people.

It is the cutting edge of new technology that constitutes the new pieces of the puzzle and is essential to the progression of the narrative. In the case of Aramaki's series, it is the Deep Blue Fleet, a fictional submarine fleet, that makes possible the military advances that lead to the peace treaty with the United States.[7] Aramaki's series eventually acquired an accumulated readership of 3.5 million, a significant number when one normally expects an average readership of ten to twenty thousand in this particular market.

In an in-depth article published in the New York Times in March 1995, Andrew Pollack wrote on this emerging genre, focusing on the Deep Blue Fleet, the most popular series. Commentaries in the Japanese newspapers noted that the report "expressed strong discomfort against the practice of rewriting history at will," and warned about the dangers of such a seemingly pro-war genre.[8] Although Pollack's article appeared well balanced in its attempt to present both views, the Japanese mass media appeared embarrassed and bewildered. It gave a one-sided interpretation of Pollack's article and reacted as if the family's black sheep (Aramaki) had been given the limelight on the world stage, to their discomfiture.

What is interesting is that this sense of apprehension over war-simulation novels is triggered by a foreign media "authority." Understandably, this type of simulation novel is an easy target of so-called progressive media and intellectuals who tend to look on these works as pro-military and potentially capable of endangering the "peace." The tendency of postwar Japanese cultural criticism to classify a piece of work as primarily pro-war or antiwar, second-guessing the author's intention rather than seeking the innate logic of the work, needs to be rectified. One should read Aramaki's text in the context of Japanese socio-cultural dynamism since the end of the war and seek clues as to why it has become so popular now.

Because the authors of this genre do not intend to have their works replace the history textbooks, it appears that one should approach these types of work utilizing a different mind-set. The historical truths of what and when become pieces of a jigsaw puzzle, and the object of the game here is to formulate an entirely different picture using as many pieces of the existing puzzle as possible, while introducing new pieces to make the renewed picture as grand as possible.

Aramaki's Deep Blue Fleet series conforms to an established standard of paperback format called shinsho-novels, each volume having between 200 and 230 pages, light enough to hold comfortably in one hand and read even in the jam-packed commuter trains of Tokyo. Even fifth- and sixth-graders in uniform on their way home can be observed reading Aramaki's book on crowded commuter trains in Tokyo. Subsequently, at bookstores in Tokyo, entire sections are devoted to a vast array of similar type books. A guide book that specializes in so-called what-if novels on war reported that there are 150 titles that deal with World War II, and that the total number of volumes exceeds 250.

The popularity of Aramaki's series does not seem to rest solely on the fact that Japanese military forces in this fictitious otherworld enjoy the victories denied the Imperial forces during World War II. In fact, the author of the *Deep Blue Fleet* is reportedly preparing for Japan's defeat at the end of the series and has commented that "winning constantly decreases the sense of reality and the readers will start feeling it's fake."[9] One of the secrets of his success seems to lie precisely in the way he is able to communicate with the readers and his willingness to construct an imaginary community among them. Taking note of what makes Aramaki's series the most popular of this type of novel, attention is drawn to the unique format he has adopted in the postscript section of each volume.

In the first volume, Aramaki attaches a rather long postscript elaborating on his youthful dream of writing a wartime science fiction adventure, now finally realized. He then invites readers to submit ideas on strategy or tactics that he might adopt in subsequent series. In the second volume, he thanks readers for their letters and acknowledges and apologizes for many elemental mistakes in the first volume that were pointed out by them. In succeeding volumes the author invites readers wishing to take part in his novels as characters to write to him. Readers who actually appeared in Aramaki's book bearing their real names were said to be ecstatic. A "readers' corner" was later established inside the postscript section followed by a *sakusha kinkyō* (author's recent condition) section. These communicative gestures of consideration separate Aramaki's books from the rest. This style was not unique to Aramaki, however, but was established previously in the young women's magazines very popular among self-professed *otome* (innocent girls) in 1910s–1930s Japan.[10] His postscript section seems to act as the nexus of an imaginary community formed by the author and his entire readership.

His average reader is said to be around twenty-five years of age, but even twelve- to fourteen-year-olds now correspond with the publisher and the author. Aramaki infers, from the letters he receives, that many of his readers "have the characteristics of the marginal man or the outsider in their workplace/ school." He declares he is consciously building up a sort of community for these people, where they can feel a sense of belonging.[11]

As the series progresses, the battle scenes are gradually replaced by discourses on world history and philosophy. For instance, five of the seven chapters of a later volume are dominated by an exposition of the author's views on the nation-state, imperialism, military culture, strategic usefulness of ambiguities, and so on. The current state of national affairs is promptly reflected in the book. When Ōe Kenzaburo, Nobel laureate in literature, used the term "ambiguity" in his acceptance speech, Aramaki came up with a new chapter devoted to the "strategic usefulness of the ambiguity." And when Kōbe (Hanshin) was hit by a devastating earthquake, a new chapter discussed natural disaster management. These are just a few examples, but one could infer that Aramaki's main interest lies in exposing his thesis on current world affairs in the framework of the popular war-simulation novel.

Aramaki always includes an annotated bibliography. For instance, in volume fourteen of his *Deep Blue Fleet* series, he lists eleven books and articles, including *Manifesto of the Communist Party* by Marx and Engels, *Socialism* by Paul M. Sweezy, *Rethinking Intellectual History* by Dominick LaCapra, *Cape Cod* by Henry David Thoreau, *The Enigma of Japanese Power* by Karel van Wolferen, and Samuel Huntington's 1993 article "The Clash of Civilizations." Although critics of Aramaki have attributed his popularity to militarism and historical revisionism, his popularity seems mostly based on his willingness and efforts to address the issue of nationhood and construct his version of an "imagined community" where the marginals in real life can find a "home."

Another highly popular *manga* is *Chinmoku no kantai* (The silent service) by Kawaguchi Kaiji. The first volume of this book series was published just after the fall of the Berlin Wall in 1989. The series was completed in 1996 with a total of thirty-two volumes, selling over 27 million copies altogether. It reportedly enjoys a wide readership even among members of Parliament.

The narrative centers on a technologically advanced U.S.-made nuclear submarine secretly ordered by the Japanese government. Funded in its entirety and supported by Japanese engineering, but with concerns over the Japanese "peace" constitution, the submarine is placed under the command of the U.S. Seventh Pacific Fleet. During its maiden voyage, the young captain stages a coup and defects from the U.S. command. Superior capability of the submarine matched with swift maneuvering on the captain's part makes it possible to elude both the U.S. Fleet and the Japanese self-defense forces. The captain astounds both the U.S. and Japanese governments by declaring his renamed ship, the *Yamato*, an independent state. With characters in the story involving politicians and bureaucrats from Japan, the United States, Russia, France, Great Britain, and the United Nations, the story becomes an international political drama, detailing technical information about the current weaponry system of the world.

The sudden popularity of these simulation war series seems to correlate with the dramatic change the world has undergone since the fall of the Berlin Wall. The sudden collapse of the cold war framework that had defined postwar culture since the late 1940s lifted the psychological pall that was hovering over Japan, enabling Japanese to talk about war in the language of computer games. With the constraints of the zero-sum cold war outlook gone, there was initially a fresh air of jubilation that jump-started writers to publish works bearing thoughts seeded in their juvenile dreams. Both Aramaki's and Kawaguchi's works lack a figure of absolute evil (in contrast to Ronald Reagan's reference to "the evil empire" in the mid-eighties), and almost everyone appears to be well-meaning. It is telling that both Aramaki and Kawaguchi chose the submarine as the prime vehicle for their narrative progression, and not the battleship with the connotation of father figure or the carrier that is usually associated with a mother figure. The submarine appropriately fits the image of juvenile vigor and anonymity.

The euphoria of liberation following the fall of the Berlin Wall quickly gave way to the realization in Japan that nothing after all did change, and young people found themselves living the same banal life. Bounded by a constitution that renounces the right of belligerency, war-simulation activities in the form of novels or animation became a hyperreal activity in the postwar Japanese context. Aramaki seems able to capture the hearts of these young people whose sense of reality rests primarily in the technorational, desiring to expand their human network and yet be reoriented by a commander, that is, Aramaki.

The Aum Shinrikyō cult counted among its followers these very same young people who questioned the construction of everyday reality in Japan. They sought extraordinary experiences that would allow them to transcend the banality of everyday life, including physical constraints demanded of one's body. The much publicized picture of cult leader Asahara levitating attracted many young people to the cult who, eager to pursue supernatural ability, started training in practices such as holding one's breath beyond the natural limits of the body.

The reasons they endeavored so much to become "human submarines" and "human aircraft" have not been fully disclosed. We do know that Aum purchased machine guns and a helicopter from Russia and that they had sent some of their members to Russia for military training. In that context, we could speculate as to whether they had any latent hopes of transforming their bodies into supernatural human weapons. What appears twisted is their logic in employing all these weapons (including sarin gas later) toward the "salvation" of humankind.

It may be true that most nations' claims of commencing war for the sake of attaining peace may likewise be a farce, but a religious group attacking by-standers for the sake of attaining salvation seems equally if not more grotesque. It is not surprising to hear believers of Aum Shinrikyō say they were well-meaning and that they acted with good intentions—even while spraying sarin in the subways. Herein lies an element of deception, deep-seated and unrecognized, rooted in a widespread sense of Armageddon, or what has been coined "the end of history." What one might call responsible action lost its collateral in terms of generational perpetuation. And as the Sarin Incident testifies, failure to account for the historicity of the present condition leads to indiscriminate violence.

The nature of the violence exhibited by Aum Shinrikyō was characteristic of the infantile, yet was enabled by cutting-edge technological rationality. This infantile motif of the cult was evident in many ways, including the way they fought the election campaign, where they hopelessly lost. Giant teddy bear–like costumes and free entertainment of songs and dances made headlines in the media, but did not move the electorate. Their utter defeat failed to provide the insight and realization that they might possibly be segmented vis-à-vis the world. After failure in their bid for political representation, they began arming themselves with weapons.

One is tempted to overlap the image of the isolated submarine under the sea with the Aum Shinrikyō cult, who appeared to be secretly preparing to engage in a "war" against the Japanese government. On the surface, both Aramaki's and Kawaguchi's submarines seem to operate in an autistic space. But as their texts indicate, the survival of their ships depends on the network of contacts they made from the iron-enclosed space. So, though Aum Shinrikyō members were highly visible to the public eye, appearing even on TV talk shows, they were in reality living in an identical isolated and autistic space.

At the level of popular culture there still exists a perceived infantilism and/or amorphous libido for violence in today's Japan. To understand the Japanese subculture in the 1980s that emerged concurrently with cults like the Aum Shinrikyō, we need to retrace history further back to the 1970s and the beginning of the postwar era.

Mother and Shōjo

The image of the young girl (shōjo) permeates Japanese popular culture today, in contrast to the time of the Asia-Pacific War, when young Japanese soldiers during critical moments in combat with the enemy anchored their deepest emotions on the image of the mother. The importance of the mother figure is well represented in popular culture such as movies made during that time, for not only were male soldiers at war but young women workers were at home-front military factories. In his second directorial work, Ichiban utsukushiku (The most beautiful, 1944), Akira Kurosawa captures a scene where mother, embodied in a calligraphic form, keeps watch over the heroine while enduring hardship.[12]

On a subcultural level there soon occurred on many fronts a paradigm shift away from the mother's spell. One was the genre of highly popular girls' comic magazines. Until the mid-sixties, the predominant theme in girls' comic magazines remained the mother-daughter relationship.[13] There occurred a gradual movement away from the dominant mother figure in its narrative structure, and by the early seventies the genre had reformulated, shifting its focus to the culture of "cuteness."[14] Mainstream Japanese popular culture itself took on this fad, and cuteness became a marketing tool for almost everything in Japan, from choice of pop music talents to merchandising of everyday items (exemplified by the success of Hello Kitty goods), crossing over even into mainstream gift-giving items.

A study on the development of the Rika-chan doll, the equivalent of the Barbie doll in Japan, showed that the key concept in developing the Rika-chan doll was *kawaisa* (cuteness).[15] Prior to Rika-chan's first appearance in 1967, the image of cuteness had already been disseminated by girls' comic magazines. Unlike Barbie dolls, the producer of the Rika-chan doll did not overlook the creation of Mama-Rika dolls, capitalizing on the strong emotional ties Japanese girls have to their mothers. In the course of subsequent redesigning, Rika-chan's mother's facial and body design underwent several changes. Her adult-like sexual features were de-emphasized so that in the end, she looks just like Rika-chan but with a slightly larger figure, another example of the mother becoming the girl. A unique girl culture (*shōjo bunka*) in postwar Japan thus evolved as a result of interaction among successful merchandising, marketing efforts, and eager young consumers.

Valuation of anything deemed "cute" was further enhanced by the launching of the highly successful Hello Kitty merchandise. Its main character is a cute version of a kitten whose image previously had been utilized in numerous children's products. Lately, even adults have become avid fans, carrying specially designed, cute, kitten-shaped cellular phones, among other items, transforming a fledgling company into a multimillion-dollar business. Another is the chain of Baskin-Robbins ice cream shops. While Baskin-Robbins' attraction to the American consumer may have been its wide selection of flavors, to the Japanese its popularity was due to the "cute" display of a variety of fancy-colored ice cream. As such it became one of the more successful American imports in Japan, coinciding with the year prior to the emperor's visit to Disneyland. When Emperor Hirohito and his wife visited the United States for the first time in 1975, pictures of the emperor taken beside Mickey Mouse in Disneyland flooded the media. Many young people in Japan perceived this as a "cute" photograph, indelibly stamping the image of the "cute" emperor among young girls. This lingered until his death in 1989. Photographs of schoolgirls lining up in front of the Imperial Palace to sign their names while praying for the emperor's recovery from illness became part of the social landscape in late 1988. Questioned about this, their response was that they felt sorry for the emperor.[16] Curiously enough, the etymological root of "cuteness" (kawaii) is associated also with the feeling of "pity" (kawaisō).

If the predominant self-image of postwar Japanese culture is that of the innocuous boy/girl, the question arises as to whether the root of this image lies in the fact that Japan continues to relive the trauma of being publicly referred to as "twelve-year-olds" by the former conqueror and protector, General MacArthur.[17] Was the image of the short and strained Hirohito beside the tall and relaxed MacArthur in the much celebrated picture of September 27, 1945, so piercing that the Japanese internalized the relationship projected in the photo? It certainly is a possibility, although interpretation as to the kind of relationship the photo signifies is open to debate.

Anyone who has seen that photograph cannot help but be impressed by the emperor of Japan appearing subordinate to the American general, which may have been precisely the image that General Douglas MacArthur wanted to project. Some keen observers detect a conjugal relationship in the picture, MacArthur being the husband and Hirohito the wife.[18] Although a close partnership eventually developed between Japan and the United States, looking back at that photograph from the postwar Showa era, there seemed to be little, if any, carnal attraction between them. A more palatable representation for the Japanese would be that of guardian (MacArthur) and innocent boy/girl (Hirohito). The pursuit and popularity of the image of the pure and innocent boy or girl in the realm of popular culture in postwar Japan may be a double image of the pure and innocent Emperor Hirohito, perhaps mirroring the fantasies and desires of Shōwa-era Japanese.

Girls in Battle Dress Uniforms (BDUs)

Kaze no tani no Naushika (Nausicaä of the Valley of the Wind) by Miyazaki Hayao is a grand epic about a young princess' struggle to survive in a gas-poisoned future world inhabited by warring tribes and giant mutant insects. It sets out to explore human ethics in the post-Armageddon world. "In the years that passed since that war, a mutated forest known as the Swamp of Corruption spread on earth. This forest emitted poisonous gas and was home to giant mutant insects. Remaining humans created small countries on the land left untouched by the forest and its poisons"; so goes the narration. Having experienced a catastrophic war of that magnitude, war still dominated people's lives. Nausicaä, the girl protagonist, lives in a small community of five hundred people, surviving at the edge of a toxic forest born out of the ashes of a former metropolis destroyed by years of warfare. Inhabitants of the forest are giant insects resistant to poison gases emitted by fungi.

Geopolitically, Nausicaä's tiny country is no match for the neighboring empires. But members of her community, especially Nausicaä, are gifted with the ability to communicate with nature. Nature in this animated world is not beautiful or sublime. Rather, it is ugly, threatening, and lethal, the abject of industrial civilization. While other survivors of human civilization are threatened by this monstrous nature, only Nausicaä dares communicate with it, discovering the will for salvation of the planet beneath a grotesque outlook. She is not afraid of physical contact with the giant insects called Ohmu. Nausicaä later makes the discovery that the insects protect the toxic forest, which in turn functions to purify the pollution emitted by human beings. Thus, appearance is presented as only a façade and the abject revealed to be sublime. It is easy to understand that in Japan, where the idea of cohabiting with nature has always carried strong appeal, especially for those living in a socially marginal milieu (such as Aum Shinrikyō's Asahara), Nausicaä's message was appealing. Not surprisingly, the animated version was hailed as a seminal work by people concerned with ecological preservation of the planet; they read into the story an ecological message of seeking to come to terms with nature, which humans had destroyed so utterly.

Miyazaki Hayao's fame as a leading Japanese animator was established by the huge success of the 1984 animated film version of the Nausicaä story.[19] But Miyazaki was compelled to continue the unfinished *manga* epic on Nausicaä wrestling with epoch-making changes in the international and global environment in the early 1990s. The *manga* version that extended through fifty-nine episodes further explored the world in which binominal opposition—God vs. Human, Good vs. Evil, Nature vs. Technology—no longer remained valid. Believers of Aum Shinrikyō shared a similar concern over the state of the world but somehow diverted from Miyazaki's position along the way in enacting the Sarin Incident, quite the opposite conclusion from what the *manga* series suggests. It took Miyazaki over ten years to conclude the story, while directing and producing a succession of hit animated films. The final volume of this epic *manga* reached bookstores in January 1995, a few days prior to the Hanshin great earthquake and a few months prior to the Sarin Incident.

The image of the protagonist Nausicaä is a hybrid product of Miyazaki's imagination: Nausicaä as rooted in Greek mythology, and as an insect-loving girl character in a medieval Japanese tale. In retrospect, the image of a petite girl leading warriors in a defensive war against the empire and ferocious nature could have provided alternative imagery of the *shōjo* in Japan, attempting to overcome the autistic social space that the culture of cuteness had brought about. In the nineties, the idea of *shōjo* evolved into *bishōjo* ("aesthetically attractive girl" or simply "beautiful young girl"). The symbolic politics of placing the adjective "beauty" in front of a noun (e.g., *bi-jin* = beautiful person, *bi-nan* = beautiful man, *bi-shōnen* = beautiful boy, etc.) needs to be expounded on separately. For now, suffice it to say that the deluge of discourse on "beautiful personhood" signifies a certain cultural trend in Japanese media in the 1990s.[20]

The animated television series *Sailor Moon* exemplified the *bishōjo* boom in the mid-1990s. Extremely popular among kids and extending its popularity to "boys and girls" in their thirties, this *anime* attracted millions of fans in Japan. The story centers on a seemingly ordinary fourteen-year-old junior high school girl named Tsukino Usagi. She is revealed to possess the supernatural ability to transform herself into Sailor Moon to save "pure and innocent souls" on Earth from the evil forces of the universe. The basic structure of the story bears a resemblance to the Superman series of the 1950s and other double-identity hero action dramas, but the main difference between this and the previous drama is that the protagonist in this series is a young girl. Sailor Moon is a shortcut translation of the original title, *Bishōjo senshi Seirā Moon*, which literally means "beautiful girl warrior Sailor Moon." It contains several interesting elements that constitute the horizon of expectations in contemporary Japanese popular culture. And, as the title indicates, the sailor uniform is an essential part of the play, so we will briefly touch on the dimension of the politics of the costume.

The sailor uniform has been the standard uniform for Japanese schoolgirls for nearly seventy years. People are usually not conscious of its origin, but it goes back to the mid-nineteenth-century British Navy uniforms. The British Navy officially adopted the sailor uniform four years after Commodore Perry's historic visit to Japan in his black fleet. It was soon adopted by the navies of almost all the modern nation-states. We are not certain why this military uniform was adopted as a girl's uniform in Japan, but it was introduced after World War I and spread to the urban centers in the 1920s. It was only after the Asia-Pacific War, however, that it became the standard uniform for schoolgirls throughout Japan.[21] Interestingly, after being defeated at war and under the new "peace constitution," Japan allowed its schoolgirls to wear military uniforms to school.

In contemporary Japan, the sailor uniform has become a fetish for many Japanese men. A CD-ROM version of an illustrated book on sailor uniforms across Japan has even been published, in which minute differences in each of the uniforms are noted and evaluated. It may seem surrealistic to Western observers, but some Japanese men actually purchase and collect used sailor uniforms worn by schoolgirls. If this peculiarity is fetishism, as one might suspect, then the psychology behind this peculiar Japanese male fetish needs to be further examined. Could it be related to the twisted structure of postwar Japanese pacifism? Is it masculine sexual desire associated with the faint memory of militarism beneath the symbol of "pure and innocent" postwar Japanese girls? Granted that it may seem far-fetched to insinuate that the impossible desire of possessing phallic power is reflected in the strange behavior of Japanese males purchasing girls' belongings, I am not aware of any nationality other than the Japanese who have set up businesses trading solely in used sailor uniforms and used underwear—and making a livelihood from it: a phenomenon that may deserve further elaboration.

The second element is the close association of the savior girls with the forces of nature. In congruence with the theme pioneered by *Nausicaä of the Valley of the Wind*, the Sailor Warriors (Sailor Moon, Sailor Venus, Sailor Mars, etc.) mediate the forces of the cosmos. The most famous line Sailor Moon utters when she confronts the enemy is "Tsuki ni kawatte oshioki yo!! [I am gonna punish you on behalf of the Moon!!]." Whereas Japanese feminism started out with references associating women with the Sun, in nineties popular culture the focus is on something "minor": Moon not Sun, and young girls, not women or mother.

Third, the element of transmutation needs to be noted. Ordinary junior high school students are transformed into sailor warriors with a simple incantation ritual. The dazzling process of this transformation constitutes the audiovisual focal point in each episode. In the Superman series, for example, viewers are kept away from witnessing the process of Clark Kent becoming Superman, but viewers in Japan are thrilled to be able to closely observe the process itself.[22]

The transformation from school uniform to military uniform itself is a familiar motif in the social imagery of Japan. As will be discussed in the next section, most popular movies in postwar Japan on the Asia-Pacific War repeatedly portray the "sacrifice of the schoolgirls" and the "sacrifice of the university students" for the sake of the nation. During the war, state-sponsored rituals transformed the school-uniformed students into warriors tasked to defend their homeland. The violence of the war (and even that of the Sailor Warriors) is legitimized by these transformation rituals. In the *Sailor Moon* series, the ethical justification for the violence against cosmic evil, which appears in many shapes and forms, is always the defense of what is "pure and innocent."

Sailor Moon has become a cultural export item; U.S. viewers started receiving the program in September 1995. Minor changes were made in the manufacture of the Sailor Moon dolls, such as decreasing their degree of cuteness and making their hair color more realistic (the Japanese versions have hair dyed yellow, green, blue, brown, purple, and pink) to better suit the American market. The successful commercial marketing of *Sailor Moon* characters poses a definite threat to parents' pocketbooks worldwide.[23] In any case, it is striking to note that the image of the pubertal girl occupies an honorable place as military leader even in contemporary Japanese popular culture, as seen in Nausicaä and Sailor Moon.

Boys and Girls on Screen

The year 1995 marked the centennial anniversary of cinema's public debut, and it merits mention of some of the products of what used to be called the "dream factory." Films commemorating the fiftieth anniversary of the end of the Asia-Pacific War were produced by major Japanese film studios that year. Interestingly, two of the most powerful studios decided to remake renowned "anti-war" stories rooted in historical fact: *Himeyuri no Tō* (Himeyuri Monument) and *Kike Wadatsumi no koe* (Listen to the voices of Wadatsami).

Himeyuri no Tō depicts the ill-fated field hospital nurses corps known as Himeyuri Butai or Star Lily Corps in Okinawa. Its members were local female high school and normal school students between fifteen and nineteen years old and their teachers. Hastily assembled by the Japanese military authorities before their graduation in March 1945, these young girls were thrown into one of the most harshly fought battles of the Asia-Pacific War. Of its 239 members, only 98 survived the battle of Okinawa. Their tragedy was recounted in Ishino Kei-ichirō's novel *Himeyuri no Tō* (1950) with a movie adaptation planned in the same year that was rejected by the Occupation forces.

Director Imai Tadashi realized production of the movie with Mizuki Yōko's film script only after the U.S. Occupation ended in 1952. The film was a huge hit, becoming at that time the most commercially successful movie the Tōei Studio had ever made. More than six million Japanese flocked to see this film, and it was one of the first films looking back at the Asia-Pacific War that touched the heart of the ordinary Japanese. Moreover, it was indeed instrumental in constructing the "national" image of the victimized young maidens whose sincere wish was for "peace."

The terms "national" and "peace" are both problematic in this context, because their denotation historically shifted at the conclusion of the war, and because the "subject of the enunciation" for these terms is ambiguous. First of all, during the Great East Asian War, the national boundary of the Japanese Empire comprised not only Okinawa islands but also the Korean peninsula and Taiwan. Consequently, people living in these areas were national subjects of the Japanese Empire, and some became willing subjects, casting themselves as loyal subjects of the Japanese emperor. No doubt the members of the Himeyuri troop were exemplary national subjects during the war. But by the same token, the comfort women from the Korean peninsula, for example, were acting in a manner expected of loyal national subjects at the time. What separated the subsequent fate of these two groups, one enshrined in "national" memory with adjectives such as purity, suffering, and self-sacrifice, and another forgotten for almost fifty years by the mass media, lies precisely in the redefinition of the word "national" at the end of the Asia-Pacific War.

Another problematic area is the lack of awareness regarding the delicate historical power relationship that mainland Japan exercised over Okinawa. The viewers of the Himeyuri movie, the majority of whom resided in mainland Japan, identified themselves with the tragic plight of the Himeyuri girls. The identification process in the virtual reality environment of a dark movie theater easily led to reinforcing the popular and agreeable view that the Japanese were primarily victims of the war. The fact that the Himeyuri legend, entailing the sacrifice of the pure and innocent maiden as the essential element, originated in mainland Japan and was successfully mass marketed there, spoke of a greater need for mainland Japanese to relate to themselves as pure and innocent victims. The story of Himeyuri became a symbol of civilian tragic suffering in the war, and since then has been regarded as the classic vehicle for carrying out well-intended antiwar messages. Its seductiveness to the Japanese public, however, seems to lie in the fact, above all, that the protagonists are maidens (otome = shōjo) who, through no choice of their own (like Nausicaä and Sailor Moon), fought bravely to defend their <u>home</u>land, whatever meaning this home may signify.

Since the first Himeyuri movie in 1953, the story of the Himeyuri had been made into film four times; 1995's Himeyuri marked the sixth time this popular legend was represented on the screen. This alone is testimony to the degree of emotional depth the story has reached in the hearts of postwar Japanese and that to this day it retains symbolic allure. "To be truthful to the historical facts" were the words director Kamiyama Seijiro spoke of his intention at the latest remake. He also mentioned his desire to recreate the actual feeling of being in the war and on the battlefield. These statements are congruent with the established expectations of this film: to be well-intended and antiwar. What is repressed is a self-reflexive realization that the projection of the film itself is part of the reality-constructing process.

Gotō Kumiko, who personifies the image of bishōjo in mid-1990s Japan, is the star of the latest Himeyuri. The choice of actress is in keeping with the tradition of Himeyuri movies, where the starring role had always been assigned to young actresses—for instance, Yoshinaga Sayuri and Kagawa Kyoko—who were able to project the image of purity and innocence. They used to be called otome (another term for girl, maiden, and virgin, literally meaning "not yet full-blown woman").[24] Today, the term bishōjo has replaced it.

This bishōjo barely lives through the war and dies in a postwar hospital bed. Viewers are led to identify themselves with the beautiful young girl, who is clearly depicted as a victim of the war. Although the producer and the director may not have intended it as such, the underlying structure of the film resembles the grand story of Shōwa-era Japan, that of the pitiful shōjo (the symbolic emperor) surviving the war, wishing for peace, and dying in a hospital bed.

Another film released in the summer of 1995, Kike Wadatsumi no koe is based on a best-selling anthology of notes and letters by young soldiers drafted from their universities who died at war. As the fortunes of Japanese military forces dwindled in 1943, the government began drafting university students, who had been previously exempted. Some of them were mobilized as volunteers for the suicidal kamikaze attacks on enemy fleet. Sensing that the tide was turning against Japan, they reflected on the meaning of their approaching death and left many moving testimonials. A collection of their writings was undertaken after the war and published in 1949 by a committee organized by survivors under the title Kike Wadatsumi no koe. It touched the hearts of many people, and over two million copies have so far been sold. The book has also been translated into many languages; an English translation, Hearken to the Ocean's Voice!, appeared in 1968.

The first adaptation into cinema was in 1950 by director Sekikawa Hideo, in one of the earliest attempts to depict the brutality of the Asia-Pacific War on postwar Japanese screens. On the fiftieth anniversary of the conclusion of the war, director Deme Masanobu stepped up to the challenge of a remake. Whereas the first film exposed the structural violence and lack of humanity inside the Japanese military, director Deme in his 1995 version expanded its horizon by focusing on the common people, the enslaved Koreans, and other Asian peoples whose land had been turned into a battleground.[25] Despite his noble intentions, the film text nevertheless failed to give three-dimensional depth to the characterization of the marginal people. Filipina victims and a Korean "comfort woman" do appear on screen, not insignificant considering their previous unacknowledged status. However, even in the film they are marginalized, having no meaningful reciprocal relationship with the protagonists. Moreover, immoral behaviors during the war are attributed to the "indecent" Japanese soldier, thereby allowing the "pure and innocent" protagonists that the viewer identifies with to retain their moral integrity.

There are some common characteristics we can discern between Kike Wadatsumi no koe and Aramaki Yoshio's war-simulation novels. Both use the narrative device within the text to wander into the historical experience of the Asia-Pacific War, and both profess to embody antiwar sentiment. However, both maintain the morality of the "pure and innocent" Japanese intact from the brutal reality of war, thereby preserving the image of the ideal (Japanese) Self that easily identifies itself with the war victim's viewpoint, masking the memory of actual aggression that the real (Japanese) Self pursued. In this narrative structure, the pain inflicted by the Japanese on other people in Asia does not penetrate into the viewer's/reader's mind. Nonetheless, compared to films such as *Himeyuri no Tō* and *Kike Wadatsumi no koe*, Aramaki's novels seem more candid in acknowledging the futility of properly representing war victims' voices. Aramaki professes that his ideas and thoughts are incomplete and therefore need constant correction and feedback from other people. He bares his own learning process to the readers, an innovation in creating a community readership.

The top box office hit in the summer of 1995, however, was neither *Himeyuri no Tō* nor *Kike Wadatsumi no koe*. It was a crafty animation scripted and produced by Miyazaki Hayao (the same animator who directed *Nausicaä*) titled *Mimi o sumaseba* (Whisper of the heart), a simple love story of a junior high school girl who aspires to become a writer. Rich in the depiction of details of everyday life, it evoked the dreams and anxiety of being a fourteen-year-old *shōjo* in present-day Japan. It became the highest-grossing domestic film of 1995, with distributor revenues of 18.5 billion yen.

Angels and Abjects

A weekly TV *anime* series entitled *Neon Genesis: Evangelion* started on 4 October 1995, and ran for twenty-six weeks (the standard TV *anime* format). In the month prior to its debut the news media had been closely following the odious Okinawa *shōjo* rape incident, so the launching of this animated series initially was not widely noticed except by hardcore *anime* fans, the *otaku*.

The setting is a post-Armageddon world, where fourteen-year-old Shinji is suddenly summoned by the special service agency of the United Nations (NERV), headed by his own estranged father, Gendō Ikari. The agency has been promoting the giant cyborgs called "Evangelion," but the mysterious "enemy," Shito (Angel), comes to attack "the central dogma" hidden inside the basement lounge of NERV. (*Shito* literally means "apostle," but they are called Angels.) Shinji has orders to pilot an Evangelion cyborg and fight the Angel. A battle-wounded girl pilot is on standby lying on a stretcher with an intravenous line in her arm ready to be sent on another mission in case Shinji refuses his father's order. Shinji contains his urge to run away from the daunting task by repeating his signature line, "I shouldn't be escaping, I shouldn't be escaping [Nigecha dameda]." So begins the unusual first episode with this unheroic portrayal of the protagonist.

Neon Genesis: Evangelion is full of mother-child metaphors. As the name Eva implies, Evangelion cyborgs themselves have characteristics of the mother. Pilots of the Evangelion cyborgs are called "children" and are selected from motherless fourteen-year-olds who have been psychologically traumatized. The cockpit is an enclosed capsule that can accommodate only a single pilot, which then is filled with the equivalent of amniotic fluid and inserted into the giant Evangelion. Evangelion cyborgs are connected to NERV with long wires that supply vital power to them and are appropriately named "umbilical cords." So, in terms of Evangelion-NERV relations, NERV becomes mother. Secretly kept at NERV in "the central dogma" is "Adam," from which the Evangelion cyborgs were born. However, what everybody thought of as Adam proves to have been Lilith, the first wife of Adam in the Apocrypha.

As the narrative progressed, word of mouth enticed a wide range of people outside the otaku circle. This rather pedantic anime has become one of the most conspicuous social phenomena of the mid-1990s and is deluged with images and terminology from Christian Orthodoxy, the Apocrypha, and psychoanalysis. The concluding two episodes enraged some of director Anno Hideki's fans who had expected to find all the missing answers to the many enigmas he had installed in the previous episodes. Some fans, on the other hand, marveled at the ingenuity shown by the director in employing a metafictional strategy and not concluding in the conventional manner. Controversy over the last two episodes jammed the network site on the Internet, and soon even major newspapers and literary magazines chimed in to offer comments on this controversy.

To date, there are already over thirty books and well over one hundred articles devoted to interpretation of this anime series.[26] The intense popularity of this anime far exceeded that of 1970s Japanimation such as Space Cruiser Yamato and Mobile Suit Gundam. Revenues from related goods (video, CDs, LDs, plastic models, etc.) exceeded thirty billion yen and continues to rise. The impact of this animation series, including a subsequent film version, seems to be of considerable magnitude when one looks into the future of Japanese popular culture.

In Evangelion director Anno Hideki effectively displays an array of quotations from past Japanese popular cultures, quite appropriate for the fiftieth-anniversary years of the end of the Asia-Pacific War. Even portrayal of the "enemy" is in congruence with past Japanese war films. John Dower once referred to the vague, slippery, and sometimes absent characterization seen in Japanese war films as "phantom foe."[27] The true sense of "enemy" must be analyzed to win a war; the United States had commissioned anthropologist

Ruth Benedict and film director Frank Capra for this purpose during World War II.[28] Japan, on the other hand, confined imagery of the enemy to folklorish representations of monstrous demons, thereby shutting off an investigative avenue for the intellectual mind. When "enemy" becomes an absurdity and is placed above rational representation, the focus becomes redirected internally and competition within the ascribed circle as well as self-discipline become the focal point. Most Japanese war films fall into this category, and postwar girls' comics share the equivalent logic.

The enemy portrayed in Evangelion is a magnified version of the Japanese war films' and postwar popular culture's representation of the enemy. Amorphous in appearance, the Angels (phantom beings) come in various forms: a bird, an insect, an animal, a virus, an inorganic substance, and even a human being. Not only the size, shape, and appearance of the Angel differ each time, but they threaten the very boundary between enemy and ally. The absurdity of the enemy is a reflection of the absurdity of the subject that projects that image. The creator of Evangelion pushes the image to the limit, until the absurdity becomes clear to all. He likewise pursues the image of "pure and innocent" boys and girls, until it becomes obvious to all that the image is always drawn and constructed by someone rather than reflecting reality. Evangelion shares similarities with classic Japanese war films, and yet it gropes to escape the autistic Japanese psychosomatic space that characterizes them. The symbolic significance of this anime in constructing an alternative image of war previously prevalent in Japan cannot be overestimated.

Fourteen signifies the start of adolescence, when boys and girls enter puberty. Girls have developed sexually and are capable of conceiving a child, yet in Japan they are dressed in military-inspired sailor uniforms as if to conceal their sexuality and emphasize their primary attachment to the school system. For some men in Japan, this in itself is a source of eroticism. In Germany during the Third Reich, boys and girls above the age of fourteen were permitted to enter the Hitlerjugend. At the crossroads between childhood and adolescence, fourteen represents vulnerability to borderline characteristics—with the potential of acting both as victim and as aggressor.

Japanese mainstream journalism in the postwar era tended to portray Japan as either victim or aggressor. The prevalence of fourteen-year-old protagonists in the realm of popular culture, especially in sci-fi "war" production, seems to signify uneasiness over the binominal opposition of victim and aggressor when applied to one's self-image. Ambivalence and ambiguity associated with fourteen-year-olds function as potent metaphors for the national self-image in present-day Japan. Just as the commander of the pseudo-family organization NERV needed mediators, represented by fourteen-year-old pilot children, to deliver Evangelion (evangel), there is still a great demand in Japanese popular culture for the mediating power of fourteen-year-olds in luring readers/viewers to the "national" problems facing Japan today.

It may be possible that popular culture's overwhelming concern for the *shōjo* image signifies the aspiration for a new type of individual, able to express herself beyond the subject-object framework of modern European epistemology. Not all of these images point in the same direction, but *Nausicaä* and *Evangelion*, for example, seem to be struggling to offer an alternative model that goes beyond the infertile project of becoming the subject of history. She is neither the subject nor the object, but what in Western epistemology might be called the "abject."[29] In Japanese mythology of the postwar era, she is called *shōjo*, and she occupies that delicate and strategic position.

Interestingly, we can go one step further and contrast this image of the *shōjo* with the individual faces of comfort women across the Pacific. Former maidens of Imperial Japan who were ejected from the consciousness of the postwar era in order to sustain the fantasy of a "pure and innocent" reborn Japan, they are, in the true sense of the word, the *abjects*, cast by the wayside in Japan's march toward postindustrial capitalism. And, painful as it may be, a reconstruction of present-day Japanese identity necessitates walking through this trail littered by the faces of ex-maidens both dead and alive. What lies ahead is hope that this narrow passage created by the image of the *shōjo* can evade appropriation by the movement Asada Akira once called infantile capitalism.[30]

Notes

1 *Yomiuri Shinbun*, editorial, 16 August 1995.

2 Even the *Pacific Stars and Stripes* on 6 August 1995 reported on its front page about this "long-suppressed document" of a planned gas attack on an urban population that "might easily kill 5,000,000 people and injure that many more." After the subway Sarin Incident, the spokesman for the Aum Shinrikyō denied their involvement and instead implicated U.S. military forces for the attack without knowing at that time of the existence of the U.S. document of the secret gas attack plan.

3 Ōtsuka Eiji, "Warera no jidai no Oumu Shinnrikyō" (Aum Shinrikyō, our contemporary) *Shokun!* 27, no. 6 (1995): 53.

4 *Ryukyū shinpō*, 22 October 1995.

5 Fredric Jameson, *The Political Unconscious: Narrative as a Socially Symbolic Act* (Ithaca, NY: Cornell University Press, 1981).

6 Aramaki Yoshio, *Konpeki no Kantai: bekkan* (The Deep Blue Fleet: Extra volume) (Tokyo: Tokuma Shoten, 1993), 187.

7 In 1992, Aramaki initiated another series, *The Fleet Rising Sun*, to cover military campaigns in the Atlantic Ocean, and started publishing a new series of war-simulation novels under a rival publisher to simultaneously progress with the *Deep Blue Fleet* series; the second

series became equally popular. See Aramaki Yoshio, *Kyokujitsu no Kantai* (The Fleet Rising Sun) (Tokyo: Kodansha, 1992–). *Manga* versions of both novels are also being published.

8 See, e.g., *Asahi shinbun*, 14 April 1995. (All translations by author.)

9 Aramaki Yoshio, *Konpeki no Kantai* (Tokyo: Tokuma shoten, 1995), 16: 197–208.

10 See Kawamura Kunimitsu, *Otome no inori* (Prayers of the maiden girls) (Tokyo: Kinokuniya Shoten, 1993).

11 Aramaki Yoshio, *Konpeki no Kantai: Bekkan*, 152, 155–56.

12 Morio Watanabe, *Image Projection at War: Construction and Deconstruction of the Domus through Films on World War II in the U.S. and Japan* (Ph.D. diss., University of Wisconsin, 1992).

13 See Miyadai Shinji, Ishihara Hideki, and Ōtsuka Akiko, *Sabukaruchā shinwa kaitai* (Dismantling myth on subculture) (Tokyo: Parco Shuppankyoku, 1993); Ōtsuka Eiji, *Shōjo minzokugaku* (Girls' folklore) (Tokyo: Kōbunsha, 1989).

14 There are several studies on the emergence of the culture of cuteness in Japan: among others, see Ōtsuka Eiji, *Ribon no furoku to otomechikku no jidai* (Supplements to *Ribon* and the age of *otome*) (Tokyo: Chikuma Shobō, 1995); Masubuchi Sōichi, *Rika-chan no shōjo fushigigaku* (Wonderworld of Rika-chan dolls) (Tokyo: Shinchōsha, 1987); Miyadai Shinji et al., *Sabukarucha shinwa kaitai* (Dismantling myth on subculture) (Tokyo: Parco Shuppankyoku, 1993).

15 Masubuchi Sōichi, *Rika-chan no shōjo fushigigaku.*

16 Ōtsuka Eiji, *Shōjo minzokugaku*, 246–47.

17 MacArthur's comment was made at a hearing conducted by a joint session of the Senate Committee on Armed Services and Foreign Relations, 5 May 1951.

18 Douglas Lummis characterized the picture as a "commemoration of a marriage" in his article, "Genshitekina nikkō no naka de no hinatabokko" (Sunbathing in the atomic light), *Shisō no kagaku*, 17, no. 3 (1981): 16–20. See Katō Norihiro, *Amerika no kage* (Shadow of America) (Tokyo: Kawade Shobō Shinsha, 1985).

19 Not only was *Nausicaä* a huge commercial success, earning 740 million yen in distribution revenues, but it was critically acclaimed, winning the Grand Prize at the Second Japanese Anime Festival, first prize in the Sci-Fi Film Festivals in Europe, and a commendation from the World Wildlife Fund. It was also voted best Japanese film of 1984 by the readers of *Kinema junpō*, the oldest cinema magazine in Japan.

20 See, Inoue Shōichi, *Bijinron* (Tokyo: Liburo Pōto, 1991); Hashimoto Osamu, *Binan e no ressun* (Tokyo: Chūō Kōronsha, 1994); Karasawa Shunichi, *Bishōjo no gyakushū* (Tokyo: Nesuko/Bungei Shunjūsha, 1995); and numerous magazine articles on *bishōjo* and *bishōnonen*. In the world of postwar Japanese literature, the adjective "utsukushii" came into the limelight when Kawabata Yasunari titled his speech "Utsukushii Nihon no watashi" (I of the beautiful Japan) when he received the Nobel Prize in 1968. Ōe Kenzaburo, Nobel laureate in 1994, retitled it "Aimaina Nihon no watashi" (I of the ambiguous Japan). A play on words continued when Okuzaki Kenzō, the subject of the famed documentary film, *Emperor's Army Marches On*, subtitled his book *Aimai de nai Nihon no watashi* (I of the unambiguous Japan).

21 See Inoue Shōichi, "Seirāfuku to gakuseifuku," in *Tsubasano ōkoku* (All Nippon Airways Inflight Magazine), no. 312 (June 1995): 11; Akiyama Masami, *Shōjotachi no Shōwashi* (Girl's Shōwa history) (Tokyo: Shinchōsha, 1992), 36–42.

22 Postwar Japanese popular culture abounds in the hero transformation motif. Interestingly, the successful ones employed the insect motif in the transformation, e.g., *Urutoraman* (Ultra-man) and *Kamen Raidā* (Mask-rider).

23 The *Sailor Moon* series has filtered into the Japanese toy market, and this tie-in with merchandising has already raised $250 million a year. See *Newsweek*, 14 August 1995, 70. The *Sailor Moon* characters are now exported to America, Europe, and Asia.

24 When the subculture took the "cuteness" turn around the mid-1970s, they coined a new word, "otome-tique," to signify the quality of objects and thought that was girlish and cute.

25 See Interview with Deme Masanobu, *Production Notes: Kike, Wadatsumi no koe* (Tokyo: Tōei, 1995).

26 For an anthology of representative articles, see Igarashi Tarō, ed., *Evangelion kairaku gensoku* (Neon Genesis Evangelion pleasure principle) (Tokyo: Daisan Shokan, 1997). For a feminist critique of *Evangelion*, see Kotani Mari, *Seibo Evangelion: A New Millennialist Perspective on the Daughters of Eve* (Tokyo: Magajin Hausu, 1997). Recent worthy additions include Ueno Toshiya, *Kurenai no metaru sūtsu: anime toiu senjō* (Metalsuits, the red: War in animation), Tokyo: Kinokuniya Shoten, 1998; Azuma Hiroki, *Yūbinteki fuantachi* (Postal anxieties) Tokyo: Asahi Shinbunsha, 1999.

27 John Dower, "Japanese Cinema Goes to War," *Japan Society Newsletter* (July 1987): 6.

28 The U.S. war effort during WWII produced works now regarded as classics, such as Ruth Benedict's book *The Chrysanthemum and the Sword* (Boston: Houghton Mifflin, 1946), and Frank Capra's film *Know Your Enemy: Japan* (1945).

29 See Julia Kristeva, *Powers of Horror: An Essay on Abjection* (New York: Columbia University Press, 1982).

30 See Asada Akira, "Infantile Capitalism and Japan's Postmodernism: A Fairy Tale," in *Postmodernism and Japan*, ed. Masao Miyoshi and H. D. Harootunian (Durham, NC: Duke University Press, 1989), 273–78.

2 ≡ POLITICS AND POETICS OF LIBERATION

Deliberating "Liberation Day":

Identity, History, Memory, and War in Guam

VICENTE M. DIAZ

Awakenings

I have memories of a war that took place before I was born. They come from stories told by my parents, who survived the war in the Philippines, and by Chamorro survivors of the Japanese occupation of Guam, where I was born. These stories inhabit my mind and body. In dreams, for instance, I have watched Japanese troops from the rooftop of our home in Kaiser Dededo advance from the corner into our cul-de-sac. Amidst shrieks and screams of neighbors the soldiers approach and storm inside our house below. I do not know what is happening to my family members. I am frozen on the roof, and I begin to pray to God that my family be spared the horrors I have heard about long after the event.

To this day the war rages, even when I wake up with my heart racing and my body and bed drenched. In the transition from sleepytime to this time, when it becomes apparent that this was yet another dream, I grow thankful, and then happy. In the social fold, however, the memories become terrifying once again. For though the stories that shape my identity as an American (Catholic) Pacific Islander help me appreciate what I have today that others didn't have in the past, I am also becoming increasingly aware of the political costs of such memories and the narratives they spin as they bolster American hegemony on this island.

Memories Mediated

Besides its mediation through personal stories and dreams, the memory of "World War II" in Guam is also built on postwar festivities anchored on what is locally called "Liberation Day."[1] Liberation Day is celebrated annually on 21 July, the anniversary of the landing of American military forces in their successful recapture of Guam from the Japanese in 1944. One of the "three biggest holidays celebrated by Chamorros,"[2] Liberation Day has been certified as the official celebration of the war and includes parades, carnivals, beauty contests, raffles, and especially oral accounts of the war in print and electronic media by a steadily decreasing number of survivors.[3]

To further mediate the memories, I want to orchestrate the local interworkings of memory, history, and identity through an official discourse of Liberation Day. This official discourse combines the memories of Chamorro survivors and American soldiers and the political imperatives of a postwar American colonial history and historiography to canonize America's return as one of liberation and to fashion a story of intense Chamorro patriotism and loyalty to the United States. And yet, for unresolved issues such as postwar land condemnations, war reparations, and Guam's neocolonial status, and for the unprecedented economic and social growth and impact on indigenous culture and the land itself, the postwar commemoration of Liberation Day has also begun to feature public challenge and opposition, even through mimicry and sarcasm. It is contested even as it is commemorated. A keynote of this ambivalent discourse is a wartime tune that is readily identified with Liberation Day. Its verses structure the remaining sections:

> "Uncle Sam Please Come Back to Guam"
> Early Monday morning the action came to Guam
> Eighth of December, 1941
> Oh Uncle Sam, Sam, My Dear Uncle Sam
> Won't You Please Come Back to Guam.

Perhaps the most popular song of resistance, "Uncle Sam Please Come Back to Guam" begins with a verse and refrain that invoke the linkages among memory, history, and identity in the island of Guam. In the text, the linkages are explicit, beginning with a recollection of the Japanese invasion and ending with a supplication for America's return that waxes nostalgic. Between the opening and closing lines are the affectionate terms of kinship. Sung under Japanese occupation, the song expresses Chamorro misery with the status quo, harks back to better days, and at the same time, indicates a desire for a shared future with America. When the Japanese learned the meaning of the words to the song, they threatened to kill any Chamorro who sang it. In defiance, the Chamorros would continue to sing the song, either in the vernacular or outside the "earshot of a Japanese."[4]

Chamorro historian Tony Palomo has pondered why "Uncle Sam" was the most popular song during (and after) the occupation. He writes that the song meant "deep love for the values that America was known to espouse," and though at times Palomo feels it was love "*unrequited*," it was "love nonetheless" (emphasis added).[5]

For Pacific War veteran Luther Tom Cook, this (unrequited) love song was more a "Yankee Doodle–type ditty" that reminded him of the "Spirit of the Revolutionary War." He recalled that during the entire occupation the Chamorros "remained true to America. They gained our flag through blood, death and suffering,"[6] a theme echoed by Don Farrell when he wrote that their "deaths and the subtle resistance of the survivors earned for all Guamanians the right to be Americans of the first order."[7]

For the late Chamorro historian "Doc" Pedro C. Sanchez, the song (and the idea?) "Uncle Sam" reflected "the Chamorro way of resistance" that revealed a truth deeper than the survival of a recent war or of mere loyalty to the United States. He also recalled that the song, "like its verses . . . went on and on to the end of the Japanese occupation, much to the despair of the Japanese."[8] Alvin Josephy, then an American war correspondent, also echoed what we might now refer to as the song's (and the people's) "staying power": it went "on and on."[9]

After the Japanese were ousted, the Chamorros would continue to sing the song, but as part of the festivities that make up the annual Liberation Day celebration. If it is a product of and an apparatus for remembering, Liberation Day is also a product of and an apparatus for remembering many different things: it recalls a Chamorro story of intense suffering, of enduring loyalty to the United States, and finally, of intense gratitude and love toward America for returning to "liberate" the Chamorros. But it is also a day opposed, and even appropriated, by Chamorro rights activists who are not so affectionate toward the United States. Liberation Day is a packed term, one that for Cecilia Perez means "different things to different people": "It's a day that touches some people in a very deep and personal way. For others it is simply a day to enjoy a parade, attend a carnival, visit with family and have a day off from work (or school)."[10]

How to unpack that one day? How, and for what reasons and for whose purposes, did the landing of American forces in Guam on 21 July 1944 get remembered and inscribed—indeed canonized—as an act of liberation, of freedom, particularly when there is overwhelming evidence that America's return had more to do with military strategy than some altruistic desire to free the Chamorros from enemy occupation?[11]

American interests on Guam, like the Spanish Catholic ones before, had always been grounded on and ensured by military strategy and presence. America's entire history in the island has always been present in the form of soldiers and teachers whose activities have played a big role in the upkeep of America's sense of itself. An American fiction of itself was inscribed and maintained, fought for and protected in and on places like Guam, and there is perhaps no other local event or discourse that rivals Liberation Day to accomplish that specific act of historical and cultural construction.[12]

Though we can learn much about American desire and anxiety in its imperialism elsewhere,[13] here I choose instead to dwell on the stakes and motives of the Chamorro people, how and why they sang the songs and pledged the pledges they have, especially in the postwar years. How, in particular, do the Chamorro acts of remembering the war write the history of the war, and the contemporary histories of the postwar, and how do these in turn mediate the memories? And what kinds of identities and behavior are permitted or forbidden as a consequence of these textual and social acts of narrativization?

To raise these concerns I turn to three essays by Chamorros who are key participant-observers in and of contemporary Chamorro cultural politics. Robert Underwood and Laura Souder, in their late forties, have historicized and rendered cultural interpretations of Liberation Day, respectively; Ben Blaz, a survivor, wrote an essay that was part of the fiftieth-anniversary celebration. Albeit brief, these three give witness to the historical, cultural, and political significance of Liberation Day for and by Chamorros who are active in the political arena in Guam and in Washington, D.C. As such they provide informed reflections of and for a Chamorro perspective of Liberation Day. Moreover, to the extent that they represent almost an entire generational difference, they also reflect key changes in postwar sentiments on Guam toward the United States. I will elaborate on these and other similarities and differences later. Before proceeding, however, I want to linger for a moment on how the politics of commemoration operate in heavily colonized places like Guam.

The politics of commemoration operate between an official discourse (and increasingly, public opposition to it by a nascent Chamorro political nationalism) and a subaltern memory/history that has its own past and its own guerrilla-like tactics and identity. This contest of official versus subaltern forms can be sensed in the multiple locations and occasions of their remembrances. For example, Guam commemorates the war in the Pacific in annual events but also in everyday rituals. There is, for instance, an annual parade down a one-mile stretch of Marine Drive, the island's thoroughfare, in downtown Agana. Though the parade is an annual celebration—one whose fiesta-like sidelines are often more interesting than the elements on parade—the thoroughfare itself is a daily reminder of Guam's strategic value for Japan and the United States during the war in the Pacific, and its lingering value for America in the postwar years. Named not for aqua life but for the U.S. Marines who played a big role in the "liberation" of Guam in 1944, Marine Drive also connects the U.S. Naval Station in the southwest to Andersen Air Force Base up in the north. As a strategic conduit, and as a civilian thoroughfare, Marine Drive remains a fitting reminder of an ongoing colonial history in which there is mutual but unequal appropriation between colonizer and colonized.

Another form of Chamorro commemoration that doesn't wait for big events such as silver or golden (or even annual) celebrations is the unforgettable memory scarred onto the bodies of Chamorro survivors. For example, late in the final days of the Japanese occupation, Judge Joaquin V. E. Manibusan witnessed the beheading of three Chamorro men. Fifty years later Manibusan breaks his vow of silence: "Although I forced myself to mentally block this memory from my mind, the scars on my legs and on my back are constant reminders every waking moment of my day."[14] The late Beatrice Flores Emsley was another individual who could never forget the war. Emsley was one of the few survivors of an infamous cave massacre, who also survived an attempted decapitation. Like the ones on Judge Manibusan's arms and legs, the scar that traversed the back of Emsley's neck served as a constant occasion for narrating and remembering the traumatic experience.

In rituals of public commemoration, Manibusan's and Emsley's scars and their narratives would become conscripted into official discourses in the postwar years. On the other hand, there are other stories that not only do not support the dominant narratives of liberation, but also do not have the cultural or political capital to trouble them in public, though they circulate in private circuits in the form locally called *chismis* or gossip. Examples of these narratological misfits are gossip about native collaboration with the Japanese, of Chamorro "comfort women" (not a single woman has stepped forward to participate in the war claims presently being made elsewhere in Asia), and finally, of occupation romances.[15] The only anecdote about wartime romances recorded in an oral history book provides a telling example of the contested and layered nature of wartime romance. Here, a necessarily unnamed Chamorro woman chastises her peers who chastise her: "Why is it when I have an affair with a Chamorro, it's perfectly all right. If I have an affair with an American, it's also alright. But now that I'm having an affair with a Japanese, you people look down on me. I have read the Ten Commandments, and the Sixth Commandment said: 'Thou shalt not commit adultery.' Period. It did not say 'Thou shalt not commit adultery with a Japanese!' They are winning the war. So they must be okay. Anyway, should the Americans return, I will have an affair with an American."[16]

These marginalized stories of life at the margins have the potential to disrupt the dominant paradigms but don't because the social and political costs are tremendous and the returns have yet to present themselves. And so they remain not as history but as subaltern memories that continue to reside in private discourse, as well as in the very bodies of many survivors and their offspring.

Absent, these are the very histories (in the sense used by Jameson[17]) whose repression forms the bases for the narrativization of official discourses. Thus the official discourses of history and identity as memorialized in annual commemorations feed off the fragmented experiences of the war in both systematic and unsystematic ways.[18]

Judge Manibusan's and Beatrice Emsley's are only two such memories of trauma that were widespread and commonplace. For the Chamorros of Guam, World War II was a time of great suffering, beginning with Japan's invasion and occupation of the American territory in December 1941, and lasting until America's return with a vengeance in July 1944. During the occupation no families were spared the grief of death, and everybody starved. By the time the Americans began preinvasion bombing and strafing of the island, bewildered and frustrated Japanese soldiers began to round up Chamorros, many of whom were massacred, while most were forced to march to concentration/death camps. The code name for the Guam campaign was "Operation Stevedore," and preinvasion bombardment began on 8 July 1944 as an effort to "soften up" the Japanese defenses for the imminent invasion. Sporadic bombings had in fact begun in late February on Orote Peninsula by American carrier-based planes. Historian Paul Carano called the preliminary attacks "the answer to the Guamanians' prayers . . . [marking] the beginning of the end of the Japanese occupation. . . . The attacks brought real joy to the people of Guam, . . . [But] also ushered in the worst period of Japanese rule."[19] It was at this time, under intense pressure and cut off from their own support systems, that the Japanese began to drop "all pretense of getting along with the natives."[20] This was also the time when the Japanese began moving the people to concentration camps in the interior of the island, a move that has residents, to this day, debating whether the policy was meant to move the people to safer ground or to sentence them to death camps. Whatever the case, this was the beginning of the massive destruction of life and land that has come to be associated with the entire occupation period.

"Uncle Sam Look What You've Done to Us"

> Our lives are in Danger
> You better Come
> And kill all the Japanese
> Right here on Guam

In a 1989 speech to social workers, scholar and activist Laura M. T. Souder took aim at Uncle Sam's colonial legacy in the postwar years by focusing on Chamorro views on Liberation: "Uncle Sam came back with thousands of troops to reclaim 'our land' for democracy. The joys of 'liberation' were sweet. Chamorro survivors of World War II embraced all that was American with overwhelming gratitude and profound respect. Uncle Sam and his men were 'worshipped' as heroes, and rightfully so. No one who lived through the tyranny of Japanese occupation went unscathed. Survival became synonymous with American Military Forces."[21]

The worshipping of the Americans by the Chamorros in the postwar years (at one point, Souder says that the Chamorros regarded the Americans as returning "messiahs") underscores the religiosity of the event, a solemnity and piety of which there was plenty to go around. As his men jumped off the crafts to hit the beach, Major General Roy Geiger of the Third Amphibious Corps delivered a rousing sermon: "The eyes of a nation watch you as you go into battle to liberate this former American bastion from the enemy," he exhorted. "The honor which has been bestowed upon you is a signal one. . . . Make no mistake, it will be a tough, bitter fight against a wily, stubborn foe who will doggedly defend Guam against this invasion." He blessed them: "May the glorious traditions of the Marine Esprit de Corps spur you to victory. . . . You have been honored."[22] Inspired thus, the Marines fought a bloody battle to hit the beach and secure the beachheads. Within a week they had broken the resistance and were chancing upon bedraggled Chamorros who, as Carano has observed earlier, had "been praying for this day." Years later, Carano would reiterate the religiosity of the event, especially the mass martyrdom it effected: it was, he exclaimed, a "glorious event" whose price in lives lost had purchased freedom and later American claims of exclusive rights to the region. Carano points out that America's "honored dead lay in three beautiful military cemeteries,"[23] at least until about 1948, when the bodies were exhumed and repatriated to American soil, a move that offended and disturbed some Chamorros.

As for the living, the soldiers who survived the invasion and subsequent battles, and who would encounter the Chamorros, would be deeply touched for the rest of their lives. In years to come, and climaxing in the fiftieth anniversary called the Golden Salute, scores of veterans of the Guam campaign would return to the island in touching reunions with Chamorros whom they had befriended earlier.

Narratives of freedom were built on encounters between the GI and Chamorro refugees coming out of the bush. The GIs found the Chamorros in a pathetic but bewildered state of euphoria. The Chamorros waved handmade flags they had kept hidden throughout the occupation. Those who did not speak English shouted out any and every English word they knew in utter joy and relief. On the other hand, there was a moment of disappointment on the American side when one group of Marines realized that a bombed-out downtown Agana would cancel any dreams of liberty at shore after months at sea.

According to Souder, the return of the Americans, and the sheer largesse of their material possessions and supplies—the cases of Spam, surplus Jeeps, tents, boots, clothes, and more—activated an indigenous code of indebtedness, obligation, and reciprocity. She explains that Uncle Sam "brought freedom from the Japanese . . . and к-rations like spam, corned beef, cheese, pork and beans . . . medicine, clothes . . . shelters."[24] Elsewhere Souder writes: "Pro-American sentiment on Guam reached its zenith in the years immediately following World War II. A harsh Japanese occupation had predisposed Chamorro survivors to view Uncle Sam's return as somewhat messianic. There was an overwhelming desire to show gratitude. . . . Chamorros were willing to pay whatever price was asked, as our whole cultural ideology rests on principles of reciprocity."[25] Reciprocity meant that the Chamorros became duty-bound to "give the best that they had. And so our people gave precious land and continue to offer their sons and daughters to show their appreciation to Uncle Sam. Obligations being a sacred duty, Chamorros have since been caught in a never-ending cycle of 'paying back.' "[26]

This was a way of life that, she felt, imprisoned the Chamorros in a never-ending relationship of payback that was not reciprocated. How did the Chamorros react to the imbalanced relation? With yet other cultural prescriptions, laments Souder, that only further pacified and further subordinated the Chamorros to the Americans. She cites as an example the proverb Na mesngon hao sa i mesngon mangana (Be tolerant / courageous, for it is the tolerant / courageous that win at the end), which for Souder "helps explain the propensity of Chamorros to not only turn the other cheek but offer their left sides and their right sides and everything in between." Of course, she does not specify to which set of cheeks she is referring. Actually, for Souder, such cultural prescriptions were therapeutic, helping the Chamorros "deal with the increasingly apparent reality that Uncle Sam didn't come back in July 1944 to save the Chamorros, but 'to save face' and to secure a bastion of defense."[27]

Indeed, the idea that the United States had ulterior motives behind its return has not been lost among the Chamorros. In the 1970s former governor Ricardo Bordallo felt that the Chamorros had "already paid dearly by accommodating the U.S. military's huge appetite for land" in Guam.[28] During his terms (1975–1978 and 1983–1986) Bordallo renamed the Liberation Day festivities "Fiestan Guam" to "celebrate Chamorro survival and triumph over hardship, instead of Chamorro indebtedness to the U.S., which liberation implied."[29] America's disregard for the Chamorros was further revealed in other immediate postwar decisions. The bitterness and pain in his voice alludes to an act of betrayal: "I'll *never forget* what my father told me about the Americans," recalls Joe Barcinas. "He said that the Americans didn't return to Guam out of concern for the Chamorros. They truly did not care for us, because after the war, they dug up the bones of their dead that were buried with ours, and sent them back to the States. This action told us that we were not worthy to be buried next to their own, and that we didn't have a common history."[30]

Urelia Francisco, a *manamko* or elder Chamorro, also felt betrayed by the Americans. "It is true," she says, "that the Japanese were cruel and I am so happy that Guam was liberated. . . . But when the U.S. took our land, that was almost worse. Especially since that land was never used even to this day. At least the Japanese let us keep our land."[31] Urelia's son Robert emphasizes the point, and delivers as well an indictment of the United States and its accomplice, the government of Guam, over unjust land takings and condemnations. He asserts: "We are of course thankful that the Americans came over. . . . But the U.S. took advantage of the Chamorros' hospitality and gratitude. Now they are talking about returning the land that was taken after the war back to the Government of Guam. That's not right. They should return it to the original landowners."[32] By invoking the rights of the "original landowners" Robert draws attention not only to the duplicity involved in America's return to liberate the Chamorro (land), but also to the sense of disillusionment that many Chamorros feel toward the local government that has been in existence since 1950. Born after the war, the younger Francisco caps his sentiments with the warning, "God sees this injustice and He *never forgets,*" thereby enjoining certain postwar Chamorro memories with providential vigilance as guarantors of eventual justice against American and local government land takings.[33] These hybridized memories, both Chamorro and providential, constitute a powerful subaltern political consciousness that troubles the official narratives of Liberation Day and its opposition by Chamorro political leaders, even as it does so by utilizing an earlier and perhaps even more politically conservative discourse established by a preceding Spanish colonial heritage on Guam.[34]

In her essays, Souder sought to challenge and politicize her audience's understanding of contemporary Chamorro society. She was especially interested in empowering the Chamorros to be brave and scrutinize "Uncle Sam's motives" even at the risk of facing "God's (other) wrath," the more official articulation of liberation in religious if not providential terms. In an effort to unveil the false deity, Souder held up another image of Uncle Sam and the role of his return to Guam: that of an imperialist power whose story of overseas empire-building began with the overthrow of the Hawaiian monarchy in 1893 and who would later expand its borders to Guam after the Spanish-American War of 1898. She implored her audience to consider Guam's entire relationship with the United States—from 1898 to the present—within the context of war that "has not yet ended": "It was the Spanish-American war that first brought Uncle Sam to our shores. It was World War II that brought him back. Uncle Sam brought Guam into the Korean and Vietnam Wars. Today, we are the unwitting hosts to over 365 nuclear warheads. All this in the name of defense?!" Souder engendered Guam's troubled relationship with the United States thus: "We have become the worst kind of mistress to Uncle Sam. Much like women throughout the world who are 'kept' by possessive, oppressive husbands/lovers." And: "We must be like the 4 year old girl who garnered enough courage to say to her sexually abusive father, 'daddy, I'm not going to let you hurt me with your stick anymore.'"[35] Thus she implored her audience to "put Uncle Sam into focus and recognize him for what he is and what he represents. . . . We must recognize and admit that Uncle Sam is here because of Guam's strategic importance to American defense and not for reasons of love." Souder's final bid continued an ongoing chorus: "We must be courageous enough to rewrite the song:

> Sam, Sam Do Listen and Be Kind
> Look What You've Done to Us."[36]

Red, White(wash), and Blue

> We don't like Sake
> We like Canadian (whiskey)
> We don't like the Japanese
> It's better American

In his article "Red, Whitewash and Blue: Painting over the Chamorro Experience," Chamorro historian, indigenous rights activist, and now U.S. Congressman (!) Robert A. Underwood historicizes Liberation Day as a product of the prewar past under the social sway of U.S. naval rule and a postwar movement for political development.

For Underwood, Liberation Day is the "focal point" of the Chamorro war experience in the postwar years that also relays "a basic image of Chamorro identity as that of the unswerving American patriot."[37] This "rabid patriotism" was shaped by an intensive prewar naval rule that permitted Chamorro identity and peoplehood to be expressed only in terms favorable to America. Moreover, this prewar social engineering by the Americans would be coupled with a postwar political process in which Chamorros (and other American institutions) would stress, if not exaggerate, those terms as a powerful way to ensure "political progress," such as citizenship, self-government, and other desired institutions or benefits considered rightfully earned and receivable. When these were not forthcoming in the 1990s, Underwood, now a U.S. congressman representing Guam, threatened to rename Uncle Sam a "deadbeat uncle."[38]

For Underwood, this obfuscation of Chamorro identity by American terms or symbols—described alternately as an "intertwin[ing]," a "mesh[ing]," a "confusion," a "marriage," or in the metaphor used in the title, a "painting over," specifically, a "whitewashing"—is a problem whose resolution requires a critical process of "separating out" the essential Chamorro experiences from their American signifiers.[39] In this text, as in Souder's, anticolonial historiography and pride in Chamorro peoplehood furnish the critical tools for prying the two apart.

According to Underwood, the Chamorro wartime experience was "the most important phase in the development of this American patriotism." And the focal point of this experience, he continues, is "Liberation Day . . . [the] one day of the year when Chamorros appear to exceed even the limits of reason in their hosannas of praise for the U.S. military."[40]

The "roots" of this Chamorro focus on America were "planted and cultivated by individuals with many motives" and through "long experience under the Navy." This prewar history had the overall effect of providing the means by which Chamorros could articulate or express their experiences. If Chamorro experience was expressed in terms of hyperloyalty to the United States, it was because this was the only political language available to the Chamorros that could be heard and understood by the Americans. Indeed, after surviving a war "not of their own making,"[41] Chamorros would use the terms of patriotism and loyalty to gain what was perceived to be political progress: citizenship and civil government, two cherished institutions for which the Chamorro leadership aspired since the turn of the century, and against which the U.S. naval government took vehement stances.[42]

Aside from the obvious fact that "military governments are not known for encouraging freedom of expression," Underwood also notes that public life under naval rule "always had to include certain patriotic exercises which were obviously calculated to instill an American flavor to Chamorro identity." "It might be argued," he suggests, "that the U.S. Navy deliberately attempted to destroy a sense of peoplehood among the Chamorros." In addition, the Navy passed laws that limited public behavior and expression "within the confines of Navy-interpreted American patriotism." For example, the Navy "forbade the discussion of controversial matters" and even "demanded that citizens [sic] stop dead in their tracks whenever the flag was going up or down."[43]

This past, and the specificities of the immediate and more recent postwar period, says Underwood, would shape how the wartime experience, and the return of the Americans, would be expressed. Reviewing the Liberation Day messages over the ensuing years, Underwood reveals a general pattern. After "dutifully expressing gratitude to the U.S. for extricating Guam's people from an atrocious situation, these messages recount[ed] the hardships endured by the Chamorros. In essence the content of the message (the Chamorro experience) [had to be] be expressed in the symbols made available and easily understood (the Marines and the Stars and Stripes)."[44] Underwood found that such messages usually began "with a word of thanks to the military, a somewhat ponderous explanation of what freedom and democracy mean[t] and invariably include[d] some flag-waving sentimentality. The messages then concentrate[d] on the real content of what [was] being celebrated—the heroic experiences of the Chamorro people." For Underwood, the "heroic experiences of the Chamorro people" during the war were "one of the few things in which they can all take pride. They were placed in a predicament not of their own making, but they met the challenge. They survived the ordeal, and became stronger for it. Within the confines of that pride as a people, there is no mention of the war as a struggle between two great powers trying to exert their dominance over the Pacific and its people."[45]

For Underwood, the heroism of the Chamorro people would become (mis)cast, for lack of a more suitable or appropriate language and symbols and for future political expedience, in terms of hyperloyalty and gratitude to America in the commemoration of the war experience through annual Liberation Day festivities. Chamorros would become identified as more "American than the Americans"[46] and would heap almost irrational praise on the military. These were functions of what he calls the "politicization"[47] of the Chamorro war experience, particularly around the powerful notion of Chamorro loyalty to America. He wrote:

> While the war was laid to rest, the experience was put to other uses. In their search for political rights, the Chamorros hit upon an irrefutable argument for civil government. The Chamorros were patriotic. They survived the ordeal. They proved their loyalty. In fact, the Chamorros not only deserved political rights, the U.S. *owed* it to them. The war experience soon became a hammer to obtain political rights, and subsequently, to obtain federal funds. In order to insure success, the war experience and Liberation Day became expressed with American symbols. . . .
>
> Almost as if they had to prove that they deserved what Americans kept referring to as "inalienable rights," the Chamorros persisted in expressing their experience not as intrinsically heroic, but as being tied to American experience.[48]

This sort of tying of the Chamorro wartime experience to American patriotism was precisely what furnished the ideological idiom of Chamorro leaders such as the late Congressman Antonio B. Won Pat, who personally witnessed the execution of his own family members during the occupation. Throughout his long and distinguished service to the people of Guam and to the U.S. government, Won Pat would use the rhetoric of Chamorro loyalty to the United States to push for equal rights for Guam (something still not achieved) as well as for redirecting benefits and other federal moneys toward the territories. His politicization of the Chamorro wartime experience is exemplified in a speech he delivered in 1981 at the Asian Pacific American Heritage celebration in Washington, D.C. Here he addressed the problem of discrimination in spite of the fact that "American Pacific Islanders have a tradition of patriotism." Won Pat then gave examples of the political and especially economic problems facing the American Pacific islands, but quickly glossed over any tension with what he called "the one thing that will never change": "That is our loyalty to the American Flag. My own island has been a bastion of U.S. military strength for many years. During World War II we on Guam were occupied by Japan and during those horrible years, we remained totally loyal to this nation."[49]

Of course, the only thing that is constant is change, and in spite of this narrative/ideological closure, the late twentieth century has nonetheless witnessed a virtual peeling away of a long and entrenched American influence, whether articulated by American officials or a generation or two of Chamorro political leaders who have seized the language of liberation to secure Chamorro political rights and benefits under the American system. The next generations of Chamorros, represented by activists and intellectuals such as Souder and Underwood, would challenge this rhetoric directly in their concerted push to change Guam's political status through the vehicle of Chamorro self-determination.[50] By 1992 Underwood's trajectory would direct him into the office formerly occupied by Won Pat (and after Won Pat, by Ben Blaz) to become only the third Chamorro delegate to the U.S. House of Representatives in Washington, D.C. since 1972. In his public discourse, Underwood would carry on the tradition established by Won Pat, albeit with a much more self-conscious and critical approach to the rhetoric.[51]

There are other local forms of Chamorro appropriation/contestation of Liberation Day discourse. As part of testimony to a 1994 Federal–Territorial Land Conference sponsored by Congressman Underwood, an entity called "Team Guam" presented its deposition on land issues, entitled "The Next Liberation."[52] Team Guam was a name chosen by Guam leaders to reflect a unified stance among local officials in Guam's effort to negotiate a political status change for Guam. In the previous year under Governor Joseph Ada, the theme for the 1993 Liberation Day festivities was "Commonwealth Is Liberation." In a series of local processes beginning in the late 1960s, local officials began to publicly express their dissatisfaction with Guam's current political status as an "unincorporated territory" of the United States.[53] Although the Chamorros were granted (a limited form of) American citizenship and were given a limited form of self-governance by congressional action in 1950, lingering problems of unresolved land issues and wild and uncontrolled economic and social growth in the island would usher in calls to change Guam's political status.[54] After a series of referenda in the 1970s and 1980s, and not without challenge (and then later support) from Chamorro rights organizations led by Underwood, Souder, and now Guam Senator Hope Alvarez-Cristobal,[55] the interim status of commonwealth was selected and ratified by the island's populace. By 1988 the Commonwealth Act was introduced to Congress by Congressman Ben Blaz, where it has languished since.[56] In 1993 Congressman Underwood reintroduced the act into Congress under the number H.R. 1521, a docket number chosen to memorialize the date of Magellan's arrival and the beginning of the colonization of the Chamorro people. Indeed, the "quest for commonwealth" is another packed site of and for the narrativization of Chamorro and American identity and histories on Guam and is outside of the scope of this paper. It is a historical process that explicitly calls into question an ongoing colonial legacy under the United States and an unresolved issue of the exercise of Chamorro self-determination. The official expression of liberation as commonwealth (as mandated by Governor Ada in 1993) only attenuates the often competing discourses found in the annual Liberation Day celebrations on Guam.[57]

As previously mentioned, opposition in and against Liberation Day celebration was articulated early in the quest for Chamorro self-determination by groups of activists, led by Underwood, Souder, and Alvarez-Cristobal. In 1985, at the height of the heated debate over indigenous rights and political status, the Chamorro rights organization Organization of People for Indigenous Rights (OPI-R) spoke out by asking "Kao Magahet na Manlibri hit?" (Are we truly free).

> I magahet na linibri siempri u fatto gi ya hita kumu gaige i destinu-ta gi kannai-ta. Desde ki ma tutuhon i kinalamten gubetno gi ya Guahan, tay' na i propiu taotao tano'-niha. Est na direcho ma rekoknisa gi palu siha na islan gi uriya-ta, lao yanggen tumacho i taotao put i direcho-na kumu Chamorro, meggai biahi di ma despresia. In hegge na gaige i direcho put i destinon Guahan gi kannai ayu siha i hagasa manman chomma' gi direchon pulitikat guini. Esta ki ma rekoknisa yan ma praktika i direchon Chamorro put estao pulitikat, taya' kabales na linibri. Are We Truly Free?

[True freedom will come to us when our destiny is fully in our hands. Since the beginning of governmental systems of Guahan, the people of the land have never been allowed to decide the fate of their land. This right is recognized in all of the surrounding islands, but when we stand up for our rights as Chamorros, we are frequently derided. We believe that the right of Guam's destiny belongs to those who have been historically denied their political status and rights here. Until the Chamorro right to self-determination on Guahan is recognized and practiced, there is no full freedom.][58]

This outright oppositional consciousness would be articulated even more forcefully in the next generation by Angel Santos, a founder and then spokesperson of the Nacion Chamoru or Chamorro Nation. In 1991 Santos wrote that U.S. return was "reoccupation," not liberation, and that "true freedom for the Chamorro people does not exist on Guam."[59] In the ensuing years, members of the Chamorro Nation would publicly renounce their American citizenship. With American citizenship abandoned as a vehicle for securing political and civil rights and benefits, a new generation of Chamorros reach back to images of a precontact nation that they view as having been suppressed for the past three centuries. With no need for American citizenship, they also dispense with discourses of loyalty and patriotism to the United States. By 1992, 21 July would be celebrated by members of Nacion Chamoru not as Liberation Day but as "Reoccupation Day."[60]

The Chamorro challenge does not always take the form of outright opposition, but sometimes seizes with a vengeance central themes and motifs of an American political identity. Chamorro landowner and real estate agent Tony Artero published this sarcastic advertisement, which refers to Urunao Beach, his clan's landlocked and heavily restricted (by federal and local government statutes) property, as "The Riviera of the Pacific":

> This property is available for rent, but you [need] the key to the Gate from the Federal Government's Fish and Wildlife Service.
>
> As we "Stand ye Guamanians for our land," during this "Golden Salute" in remembrance of those who gave the ultimate sacrifice for freedom in World War II, remember that our government is founded under the principal [sic] of the free enterprise system.
>
> At Urunao Beach, We can: Pay the Taxes; Have our freedom eroded, Private Property Rights Violated; Have our productivity extinguished; Be landlocked and subverted; Accumulate damages for decades.
>
> We cannot: Develop it; Sell it; Lease it; Have Access to it; Just Plain Cannot be economically independent.[61]

In this particular expression of Liberation Day rhetoric, the motif of private property and a system of free enterprise adorn a narrative of betrayal and sarcasm to "celebrate" the Golden Salute. Artero's satirical salute is moved by a deeply entrenched notion of private property rights that, contrary to claims made by local economist John Gilliam in his presentation to the 1994 Federal–Territorial Land Conference, were not traditional features of Chamorro views of land and property.[62]

But when Underwood wrote "Red, Whitewash and Blue" in the 1970s, even the sense of betrayal did not circulate out in the open. Then, Underwood observed the emergence of two generations of postwar Chamorros infused with the rhetoric of Liberation Day and superpatriotism. According to Underwood, this confusion (what Souder would later call a "psyche under siege") could be treated (recall Souder's presentation to the Guam Association of Social Workers) if we disengaged the heroic survival of the Chamorro people from the language of American patriotism. If this could be done, speculated Underwood, we would discover that what "appears to be so widespread . . . may in fact be very shallow."[63]

The Quest Endures

So long with corn beef
With bacon and ham
So long with sandwiches
With juices and ham

In an essay for the fiftieth anniversary of Liberation Day, retired Brigadier General USMC and former U.S. Congressman Ben Blaz plumbed the memories and experiences of survivors to narrate a history of Chamorro struggle for self-determination and freedom. That the staunch Republican would do so in the quintessential American terms of equality under the U.S. Constitution and the American work ethic revealed just how thick the entanglement between Chamorro and American political and cultural consciousness can be, and raised the ante in the contest for meaning over the war experience.

To sense the entanglement, we might contextualize politically the kinship among Blaz, Underwood, and Souder. For starters, Underwood defeated Blaz for the position of delegate to U.S. Congress in 1992. They are rivals, although in 1994 Underwood ran unopposed. Furthermore, Blaz is a half-generation older than Underwood and Souder. Age, in the context of this particular juncture in world history, helps us appreciate one axis of political/ideological difference. As frontline (Chamorro) baby boomers, Underwood and Souder can be seen as products of a generation of men and women who, we might say, finally received the chance to enjoy their own "liberty" after the rigors of the war.

Age marks another particularly packed place in Blaz's narrative: his presence during the occupation and the supposed immediacy of his and other survivors' memories and experiences that function to certify what can and can't be said about the war, and the political and cultural stakes in the discourse about the war. Authorized by age and the supposed immediacy of memory and experience, the narrative salvages notions of freedom and liberty that have recently been contested by a younger generation that includes Underwood and Souder, and Chamorro rights organizations such as OPI-R and Nacion Chamoru. Contrary to what this younger generation of Chamorros assert, the ideas of liberty and freedom are not mere rhetoric. From the experience of war, says Blaz, "We clearly saw and keenly appreciated the basic choices of life, between freedom and bondage; justice and oppression; hope and despair; surviving and perishing."[64] These were not empty, abstract ideas.

Capitalizing on age, experience, and memory, Blaz's narrative makes liberal use of the first-person singular and plural forms when referring to the Japanese occupation. It also permits him to draw qualitative distinctions between that period and the present (the difference being the relative ignorance and absence of good values) as a basis for narrating a story of the past, for commenting on the present, and for envisioning the political future. This narrativization is also highly interested in constructing certain kinds of identities and communities and in providing examples of leadership that will show us how to push forth. "Through the heat and dust and smoke [of the war]," asserts Blaz, "we saw ourselves and what we stood for." To sense the selves he saw and what they stood for, we need to look deeper and wider at how the narrative constructs the basis on which it proceeds.

The essay's authority is reinforced through the ways in which the narrative situates the author and his generation at the outbreak of the war ("My generation was caught between childhood and adulthood") as well as the benefits that that social positioning and that predicament would permit:

> The unexpected and violent interruption of our lives and the common adversity that we shared gave our parents and elders an unusual opportunity to inculcate in us much more vital learning than we could have received in calmer times.
>
> Challenged by the threatening experience of war and pressed to our limits, we learned things about human nature and ourselves that we might never have been able to grasp in peaceful, less demanding, times.[65]

The lessons learned—enabled in the presence of the elders—included cultural prescriptions already noted by Souder and Underwood, prescriptions such as the bid to be "tolerant when conditions were intolerable" and to be "generous where there was so little to give." Indeed, the wartime experience was one that challenged the very survival of the people, an experience that involved "severe deprivation, indignities, and punishment." Blaz recalls that there was "always that pervasive sense of personal insecurity" and that members "of my generation as well as the older generation prefer not to dwell on the scars of those difficult years." And yet, there were also "many pleasant memories," which continue the process of using the period and its lessons as the basis on which to both reach further back to a more distant past and to simultaneously reach forward to the present and to the future. These pleasant but un-innocent moments include "the long hours on a log with our parents sharing their thoughts and experiences with us much like the generations before them had done." Or the groups of neighboring farmers who "pooled their strength to push back the jungle so we could plant; The women caring for the sick, working the gardens preparing food over open fires; the men echoing each other's folksong at twilight as they cut tuba; the labor camps where we realized how we had to protect each other, how we had to care for one another as an island family." In fact, these pleasant memories reconstruct a canon of old Chamorro values and practices, but also begin to canonize those who practiced them. A discourse of heroes and heroines would emerge in the ensuing plot, one that would involve not just rank-and-file Chamorros ("the devout men and women who emerged as our natural leaders and who would always lead us in prayer during our most trying and fearful moments"), but also American soldiers ("the U.S. Marines, the soldiers, the sailors and the Coast Guardsmen who, after hopping from island to island, liberating each one as their own . . . seemed as glad as we were that they had come back to Guam") and the Chamorro men who assisted them ("with equal valor and courage but with even greater pride and determination." These men "demonstrated their loyalty to the United States in the same way they demonstrated their love for the U.S. principles of freedom and democracy: not half-heartedly, but totally and wholeheartedly"). This list would even include certain Japanese soldiers, particularly as they would distinguish themselves from the stereotypical behavior of the enemy: "There was the young Japanese officer who taught me elementary Japanese in exchange for my father teaching him English and who, after getting to know us, innocently asked my father why we were at war." Blaz recalls that this same officer "came to say good-bye . . . as he left to defend against the invasion" and remembers what he called an "indescribably mixed emotion of seeing a new friend leaving to fight those coming to liberate us." Perhaps the mixed emotion is indescribable precisely because of the hold the discourse of liberation enjoyed over the narrativization of the war experience.

Blaz's mediated memory of the war experience was in fact a narrative of an enduring survival of a people and culture, one that would serve as a template on which to recount a more distant past under previous episodes of colonial domination, and that would account for the persistence of colonial rule that still endures, as expressed in the title of his essay: "Chamorros Yearn for Freedom." The story of enduring survival is contained in what Blaz calls the "Chamorro Spirit" that was brought out in and for those Chamorros who experienced firsthand the occupation. "Though only a legend to some," explains Blaz, the Chamorro Spirit "is a living, breathing reality to us; a source of strength that saw us through the worst of times and guides us in all the challenging times ahead." In the war narrative, the Chamorro Spirit is interiorized into what he calls "the inner Guam . . . that the enemy was never privileged to enter." Blaz also describes that Spirit as "the purest product of that cauldron of war, the brightest star in the dark sky of those traumatic times." This Chamorro Spirit, according to Blaz, was "not an abstraction; rather it was demonstrably real during those years and I have drawn inspiration and sustenance from that reality my entire life." Besides being demonstrably real during and after "the war"—Blaz writes that "to this day, whenever we speak of . . . 'the war' we invariably mean World War II" even though Guam has been involved in other wars since—the Chamorro Spirit also preceded the Japanese occupation in earlier histories of colonization. This Spirit, especially as it possessed those who fought for their survival, "has sustained us over the years as a people. In the years since Magellan landed on Guam, our people have been colonized, proselytized, Catholicized, and subsidized. Guam has fallen under Spanish, American, Japanese and again, American rule." In this long history, according to Blaz, the colonizing power never asked the Chamorro people (whom he calls the "Old People") what they as a people wanted. This is the basis of the call for Chamorro Self-Determination.[66] Moreover, the colonizers would employ definitions of social, political and economic progress in their own terms and use their own standards, and, says Blaz, "It was our lot to remain mute to the process . . . and to acquiesce in silence." In time, and "with increased education and opportunities becoming available to the people of Guam," Blaz and others of his generation would realize the disparities embedded in the existing colonial rule and began to question the status quo. "It was," he recalls, "as if we had been born blind and then miraculously had been given sight." New vistas appeared before the Chamorros. For instance, he says, "We had been told for generations that should we join the Navy, we were worthy to serve as servants, as stewards. My generation began to ask: And why not officers? There was no reply." With "accelerating force," says Blaz, "we set out on a quest to achieve our self-determination as a people. . . . Genuine self-determination, if the word is to have any meaning, is a self-help program. If you truly want it, if it truly means anything to you, you must reach out for it and grasp it as your own. That, we have done."

In a final act of memory, Blaz recalls a moment of affection between him and his father sometime after the war, "as I was about to leave Guam after spending a week's leave following my graduation from Notre Dame and my being commissioned a second lieutenant in the U.S. Marines." It is an act of recollection between father and soldier-son that would stage a wider history of social relations between Uncle Sam and the Chamorros. It also redeems a history of colonialism into a proud and heroic story of Chamorro political and cultural survival that runs throughout the narrative. The scene of departure (with other Chamorros who were on their way to basic training) featured the usual crowd of families and well-wishers. As the men headed for the tarmac, Blaz's father grabbed his arm.

> In his eyes was the old fierceness, and despite his failing health, he was the robust and feisty man who had been a boxer and a fighter for equality. To my utter amazement, he said to me, "Since you are now an officer of the United States, Lieutenant, answer me this. Why is it that we are treated as equals only in war but not in peace?"
>
> Still holding my arm, he pulled me to him and said, "You don't have to answer now. Just remember that the quest must endure." My chest was tight as I said, "Yes Sir."
>
> As I finished kissing him good-bye, he whispered, "By the way, you never did return the salute I gave you when you first arrived." I stepped back from him, and standing ramrod straight, I brought my hand to my forehead in a crisp salute but my arm was trembling from the unexpected and affectionate emotion from my Navyman father.

In this particular recollection, a soldier-son is given the blessing of his father, a retired soldier, whose image is one of an old Chamorro fighter whose own patriotism and loyalty to the United States would be restricted by that history of American colonialism and racism toward peoples like the Chamorros. Given this blessing, in these particular terms, Blaz assumes the privileged position of being handed a proverbial torch of freedom and now serves as the new bearer for a long line of Chamorros fighting for their freedom. Thus, he concludes his essay, which was commissioned as part of the Golden Salute, the commemoration of the Golden Anniversary of Liberation Day:

> On this, the 50th anniversary of our liberation, we will be shedding a few tears—of gratitude to our liberators; of remembrance of our brothers and sisters who suffered with us but are unable to join us; and of thanksgiving as we thank Almighty God for all the blessings that have come our way during these golden years.
>
> But after those tears have stopped and have become a precious memory for us all, we must remember that the work begun by the Liberators in 1944 is not yet complete. The people of Guam picked up the torch of freedom passed to them on July 21, 1944. All who call Guam home have worked so hard and so determinedly that the entire world can see the island and its people have come so far from that terrible time of long ago.
>
> But true self-determination and equality still evade our people. Thus, the quest endures.

Play It Again (Uncle) Sam

In 1979, "Doc" Pedro Sanchez noted that "it was easy—and true, of course—to say that loyalty to America kept the Guamanians strong during that occupation." But the truth "went deeper than that," continued Sanchez: "Indeed, that sense of loyalty reflected the inner strength of the people—strength based upon deep religious faith and cultural tradition. It was the kind of ancient strength which helped the Chamorros survive the ages."[67]

Besides revealing historical and cultural depth, Chamorro survival also reveals a great historical and cultural reach, an indigenous (dur)ability to reclaim a space for itself even if it must insinuate itself within the stories of others who have come to the island for their own interests and machinations.[68] And yet, when I remember that the piling up and the scattering of indigenous culture and history and memory occur in and on (and even against) terms established and maintained by American hegemony as manifest in postwar discourses such as Liberation Day on Guam, they suddenly become as frightening as the very realities they were supposed to have liberated us from. These memories of a war that took place before I was born, that continue to preoccupy us in the late twentieth century, are also etched uncomfortably on my mind and body. They are memories of liberation in great need of deliberation.

Notes

Dangkulo na si yu'os maase to Geoff White, Tak Fujitani, and Lisa Yoneyama for inviting me to participate in this project; to Guam Congressman Robert Underwood for encouragement and direction; to Marita Sturken for reading the first draft; to Cecilia C. T. Perez for making her files on Liberation Day available; and finally, to Christine Taitano DeLisle and Nicole Duenas for moral support.

1   The critical task of problematizing memory (and history and identity) should also draw attention to the politics of naming that informs and reflects the remembrance and the historicization of the war in Guam. The war is commonly called World War II, whose chronology begins on 8 December 1941, when Japan invaded and wrested control of Guam from American military forces, and ends in September 1945, when Japan surrendered. The effect of this naming and dating is to demarcate what is hostile and what is not. Laura M. T. Souder reminds us that Guam's entire relationship with the United States is framed by a context of war, and, I should add, a war that also operates through colonialist mappings. See Souder, "Psyche under Siege: Uncle Sam, Look What You've Done to Us," paper presented at the ninth annual conference of the Guam Association of Social Workers, 30 March 1989, 7. Guam's primary significance for the United States lies in its strategic location as a fallback zone for military forces deployed in the "Far East," but also in its location as a buffer zone to protect America's "back door," as the West Coast is commonly described in military discourse. For this, and for a local history of political restlessness, Guam has become classified as an Unincorporated Territory of the United States. See Penelope Bordallo, *A Campaign for Political Rights on Guam, Mariana Islands, 1899–1950* (Master's thesis, University of Hawai'i at Manoa, 1982), and Anne Perez Hattori, "Righting Civil Wrongs: The Guam Congress Walkout of 1949," *Isla: Journal of Micronesian Studies* 3, no. 1 (Rainy season 1995): 1–27. Earlier, Guam was ruled by Spain for over two hundred years until it was seized and secured by the United States following the Spanish-American War in 1898. Whereas the rest of the Micronesian islands were subsequently sold to Germany and then were seized and administered by Japan between 1914 and 1944, only Guam remained a U.S. possession until the period of Japanese occupation. In the "postwar" years, Chamorros have served loyally in American wars and have suffered greatly for the honor, joining other American Pacific Islanders in the dubious ranks of the highest number of men killed per capita in the Korean and Vietnam Wars. Today, in the post–cold war era, the United States still controls about one third of the island's two-hundred-square-mile land mass, and the military presence and interests continue to enjoy a direct and indirect though profound role in Guam's political and social economy.

2   Cecilia Perez, "A Chamorro Retelling of Liberation," *Kinalamten Pulitikat-Siñenten I Chamorro/Issues in Guam's Political Development: The Chamorro Perspective* (Mangilao, Guam: Guam Political Status Education Coordination Commission, 1996).

3   The other two major holidays, of greater antiquity, are Santa Marian Kamalin (in honor of the local manifestation of the Blessed Mother and celebrated annually on 8 December) and All Souls Day (in honor of the *defunto* or deceased, celebrated on 2 November). Title I of the Guam Code Annotated reads, "Liberation Day: (a) Liberation Day is a legal holiday declared in commemoration of the anniversary of the liberation of Guam from the Japanese Occupation on July 21, 1944 and the inauguration of civil government in Guam on July 21, 1950. (b) The Governor is authorized and requested to issue annually a proclamation calling upon the people of Guam to observe Liberation Day by displaying the flag at

their homes or other suitable places, with appropriate ceremonies and festivities expressive of the public sentiment befitting the occasion" (IGCA section 1011, title I. Guam Code Annotated). I am indebted to Cecilia C. T. "Lee" Perez for this and other critical points in her essay on the Chamorro reclamation of Liberation Day, "A Chamorro Retelling of Liberation."

4 Tony Palomo, "Island in Agony: Guam," in *Remembering the Pacific War*, ed. Geoffrey M. White, Honolulu, University of Hawai'i Center for Pacific Islands Studies, Occasional Paper No. 36, 1991, 7. The song "Uncle Sam" was written by the late Tun Pete Rosario, and is reprinted here with permission from his family.

5 Ibid., 143.

6 Quoted in Mike Wennergren, "County Man Is Guest of Guam Government," *Salinas Californian*, 11 July 1984, 17.

7 Don Farrell, *The Pictorial History of Guam: Liberation 1944* (Agana, Guam: Micronesian Publications, 1984), 183. See T. Fujitani's essay in this volume for how this same experience also became a powerful instance for claiming equal rights in the case of Japanese American veterans.

8 Pedro C. Sanchez, *Uncle Sam, Please Come Back to Guam* (Tamuning, Guam: Sanchez Publishing, 1979), 160.

9 Alvin Josephy, *The Long and the Short and the Tall* (New York: Knopf, 1946), 78–79.

10 Perez, "A Chamorro Retelling of Liberation," 72.

11 In *Destiny's Landfall: A History of Guam* (Honolulu: University of Hawai'i Press, 1995), Robert F. Rogers writes, "With regard to American strategic planning, Guam was not invaded just to 'liberate' the island because it was a U.S. territory, despite much propaganda to that effect in the news media." "Although," he concedes, "political considerations played a role in the decision to retake Guam, the major factor was to fulfill U.S. strategic military objectives" (195). On invasion day, Admiral Chester Nimitz, Commander in Chief of the U.S. Forces Pacific and Pacific Ocean Areas, issued Proclamation 1 "to establish the navy's authority on Guam" (178, 195; also see 198–203 for a sense of inter–Armed Services rivalry for control over Guam).

12 A contemporary analogue, from another process in Guam, is a historical and contemporary bid to canonize the Spanish Jesuit Padre Diego Luis de Sanvitores, a seventeenth-century priest who was martyred in the act of Christianizing the Chamorros. Elsewhere I have surveyed the politics of this movement and suggest here that Liberation Day does for Chamorro Americanism what the canonization of Sanvitores attempts to do for Chamorro Catholicism. See Vicente M. Diaz, *Repositioning the Missionary: History, Culture, Power and Religion in Guam* (Honolulu: University of Hawai'i Press, forthcoming).

13 Amy Kaplan and Donald Pease, eds., *Cultures of U.S. Imperialism* (Durham, NC: Duke University Press, 1993).

14 Joaquin V. E. Manibusan, "In Tai, a Day of Terror and Tragedy," in *Liberation: Guam Remembers* (Agana, Guam: Golden Salute Committee, 1994), 36.

15 Although at the time of this writing, Chamorro playwright Peter Onedera is preparing to stage a play about Chamorro views of such comfort women during the Japanese period.

16 Quoted in Tony Palomo, *An Island in Agony* (Agana, Guam: Author, 1984), 88. See also Josephy, *The Long and the Short and the Tall*, 85–86.

17 Fredric Jameson, *The Political Unconscious: Narrative as a Socially Symbolic Act* (Ithaca, NY: Cornell University Press, 1981), 35.

18 Another (potentially) subversive feature of local commemoration derives from a kind of

nonchalance or aloofness to the anniversary of an event that is typically celebrated with religiosity and piety. According to Perez in "A Chamorro Retelling of Liberation," Liberation Day is also little more than a day off from work or school or a day at the beach. This is particularly true for the two or three generations of younger Chamorros for whom the war experience is as much a part of some distant past as the American Civil War or Columbus's circumnavigation of the globe.

19 Paul Carano, "Liberation Day: Prelude to Freedom. Lean Liberty Is Better Than Fat Slavery," *Guam Recorder* 3, no. 3 (July–September 1973): 3. For a recollection of the power of praying in bringing the Americans back, see Remedios Perez, *Guam Past and Present* (Agana, Guam: Government of Guam Department of Education, 1949), 129–37.

20 O. R. Lodge, *The Recapture of Guam* (Washington, DC: U.S. Government Printing Office, 1954), 9.

21 Souder, "Psyche under Siege: Uncle Sam, Look What You've Done to Us," 1.

22 Cited in Farrell, *The Pictorial History of Guam*, 59.

23 Paul Carano, "The Liberation of Guam," *Guam Recorder* 2, nos. 2/3 (April/September 1972), 8.

24 Souder, "Psyche under Siege: Uncle Sam, Look What You've Done to Us," 2.

25 Laura M. T. Souder, "A Tale of Two Anthems," paper presented at the twenty-seventh Pacific Science Congress, Honolulu, Hawai'i, May 1991, 3.

26 Souder, "Psyche under Siege: Uncle Sam, Look What You've Done to Us," 2–3.

27 Ibid., 4.

28 Quoted in Perez, "A Chamorro Retelling of Liberation."

29 Ibid.

30 Personal conversation with author, 1990.

31 Quoted in P. Bassler, "Liberation Is Great, but Time Does Move On," *Pacific Daily News*, *Advertising Supplement* (21 July 1991), 14, 16.

32 Ibid.

33 Ibid. Another Chamorro proverb, *Ti maimaigu Si Yu'os* (God never sleeps), better captures in the vernacular this Chamorro sense of vigilance and warning. It is also a curse.

34 Elsewhere I have studied the ways in which a Chamorro Catholic discourse, through a postwar effort to canonize the seventeenth-century founder of the Catholic faith in Guam and through anti-abortion (pro-life) legislation on Guam, serves to contest both American sovereignty and its local governmental agent, called "GovGuam." See Vicente M. Diaz, "Pious Sites: Chamorro Culture between Spanish Catholicism and American Liberalism," in Kaplan and Pease, *Cultures of U.S. Imperialism*, and *Repositioning the Missionary: History, Culture, Power and Religion in Guam*.

35 Souder, "Psyche under Siege: Uncle Sam, Look What You've Done to Us," 7.

36 Ibid.

37 Robert A. Underwood, "Red, Whitewash and Blue: Painting over the Chamorro Experience," *Islander Magazine* (17 July, 1977): 6.

38 Robert A. Underwood, "Unfunded Mandates," *Congressional Record* 141, no. 8, Proceedings and Debates of the 104th Congress (Washington, DC: U.S. Government Printing Office, January 1995).

39 Underwood, "Red, Whitewash and Blue: Painting over the Chamorro Experience," 6–8.

40 Ibid., 6.

41 Ibid., 6–7.

42 For a study of the prewar and immediate postwar efforts to secure American citizenship

and civil government, see Bordallo, *A Campaign for Political Rights on Guam, Mariana Islands, 1899–1950.* See especially 36–43 for a critical discussion of Chamorro "loyalty" to America.

43 Underwood, "Red, Whitewash and Blue: Painting over the Chamorro Experience," 7.

44 Ibid.

45 Ibid., 6.

46 Ibid., 6.

47 Underwood, personal correspondence, 1995.

48 Underwood, "Red, Whitewash and Blue: Painting over the Chamorro Experience," 8; emphasis added.

49 Antonio Won Pat, speech, Asian Pacific American Heritage Week (May 1981), Papers of Antonio B. Won Pat, Micronesian Area Research Center, Mangilao, Guam.

50 See, for instance, Laura Souder and Robert Underwood, eds., *Chamorro Self-Determination/I Direchon y Taotao* (Agana, Guam: Chamorro Studies Association and Micronesian Area Research Center, 1987), for a compilation of pro-Chamorro perspectives and analyses.

51 Though he has quickly gained a reputation for being an insider and a player, Underwood continues to keep an edge in his presence in Washington, D.C., through a variety of Chamorro antics and tactics. Early in his career he entered into the Congressional Register a fiery speech alleged to have been made by a seventeenth-century Chamorro rebel (Chief Hurao).

52 Team Guam, "The Next Liberation," testimony presented at the Federal–Territorial Land Conference, Agana, Guam, January 1994.

53 Joseph Ada and Leland Bettis, "The Quest for Commonwealth, the Quest for Change," in *Kinalamten Pulitikat-Siñenten I Chamorro/Issues in Guam's Political Development: The Chamorro Perspective* (Mangilao, Guam: Guam Political Status Education Coordination Commission, 1996).

54 For a critical assessment of American colonial policy and immigration to Guam, see Leland Bettis, "Colonial Immigration of Guam," in *A World Perspective in Pacific Islander Migration: Australia, New Zealand and the U.S.A.,* ed. Grant McCall and John Connell (Kensington, NSW: Centre for South Pacific Studies, 1993).

55 Hope Alvarez-Cristobal, "The Organization of Peoples for Indigenous Rights: A Commitment towards Self-Determination," *Pacific Ties* 13, no. 4 (1990): 10–11, 14–15, 17, 21.

56 Robert F. Rogers argues that the bill is snagged because of inflexibility and disunity among Chamorro leadership, including their succumbing to the political pressure of a "small but vocal minority" of Chamorro activists. See Rogers, "Guam's Quest for Political Identity," *Pacific Studies* 12, no. 1 (November 1988): 58. But see Ada and Bettis, "The Quest for Commonwealth, the Quest for Change," for an entirely different perspective. Former Governor Ada chaired the Commission on Self-Determination during his administration from 1987 to 1995, and Leland Bettis continues to serve as the Commission's executive director.

57 The governor's message is in the *PDN Supplement,* 21 July 1993, 13. For an elaboration, see Leland Bettis, "Commonwealth: Our Hope, Our Dream, Our Liberation," *Special Supplement to the Pacific Daily News,* 21 July 1993, 32–33.

58 OPI-R, 1985, 11. In the Chamorro language, the organization's acronym means to speak out, or respond.

59 Angel Santos, "U.S. Return Was Reoccupation, Not Liberation," *Pacific Daily News,* 21 July 1991, 20, 22.

60 Though Santos would later leave the *nacion* and successfully win a seat in the 22nd Guam Legislature, he would abandon neither the indigenous cause nor the fury and militancy with which he has quickly become known.

61 Tony Artero, *Pacific Daily News Liberation Day Supplement*, 21 July 1994, 60.

62 John D. Gilliam, "Tano y Chamorro: A Brief History of Land Tenure of Guam and Suggested Land Reforms," testimony presented at the Federal–Territorial Land Conference, Agana, Guam, January 1994.

63 Underwood, "Red, Whitewash and Blue: Painting over the Chamorro Experience," 8.

64 Ben Blaz, "Chamorros Yearn for Freedom," in *Liberation: Guam Remembers* (Agana, Guam: Golden Salute Committee, 1994), 92. The quotations from Blaz that follow are from this essay.

65 Like Blaz, Tony Palomo was also "caught between childhood and adulthood," and like Blaz, uses that space too for basing his observations of the war in Guam. He writes, "Let me speak about Guam because I was there [at the war] from beginning to end, although I was a bit too young to fight and a bit too old to forget" ("Island in Agony: Guam," 133).

66 Toward the end of his essay, however, Blaz alludes to a broader definition of self-determination when he refers to "all of whom call Guam their home."

67 Sanchez, *Uncle Sam, Please Come Back to Guam*, 160.

68 "Pious Sites: Chamorro Culture between Spanish Catholicism and American Liberalism," and "Simply Chamorro: Tales of Survival and Demise in Guam," *The Contemporary Pacific* 6, no. 2 (spring 1994): 29–58.

Imperial Army Betrayed

CHEN YINGZHEN

When the Sino-Japanese War broke out in 1937, the Japanese colonial government in Taiwan nervously alerted itself to the speech and actions of its Taiwanese subjects, fearing that an oppositional Chinese identity among the Taiwanese
people might prompt support for a Chinese victory. To suppress the emergence
of such an oppositional Chinese motherland consciousness among the Taiwanese, the Japanese colonial authorities reinforced what was called kōminka education, a compulsory educational system to "create imperial subjects," which had
been established to assimilate colonized subjects into the Japanese national empire. The goal of this system, in other words, was to create "loyal subjects of the
Japanese Empire" by depriving the Taiwanese people of their national identity,
pride, culture, language, religion, and customs, and by fostering the emperor-
centered view of national history (kōkoku shikan) that rationalized colonial subordination to Japan. The histories of Taiwan and China, as well as the historical connections between these locations, were written out of the curriculum,
thereby preventing students from recognizing a common Chinese or Taiwanese
historical subjectivity. The persistent de-Sinifying effects of this education exercised considerable influence long after the liberation of Taiwan in 1945.

Within the context of the Sino-Japanese War, the purpose of the kōminka
system is obvious: the Japanese intended to mobilize the combined human and
material resources of Taiwan in their war against China, driving the Taiwanese
people into a tragic war of kindredcide between the Chinese on both sides of the
Taiwan Straits. This paper considers the experiences of eleven Taiwanese men
who confronted these contradictions of colonial subjectivity in Japanese-
occupied Taiwan as soldiers who enlisted into the Japanese Army to fight
against China. In addition to a number of other factors, the soldiers' experiences and their responses to these experiences vary according to whether or not
they were able to return to Taiwan. There is no single representative story.
However, their various stories illustrate vividly the complexity and irony of

Taiwan's postcolonial history: namely, liberation followed by forty years of Guomindang (GMD) martial law that came in the wake of the global celebration of the war that purportedly ended fascism.

To understand the full significance of these individual stories, it is important to first note both the history of the Japanese conscription policy for Taiwanese soldiers and the general history of Taiwan's role in the Sino-Japanese War. In July 1937 Taiwanese troops began to be sent to the battlefield. Initially, they were enlisted as civilian employees in the capacity of interpreters, transporters of materials, agricultural laborers, and other noncombatant-related positions. The Special Volunteer System, whereby Taiwanese men could volunteer for service in the army, was not instituted in Taiwan until 1942. Apparently, this hesitation stemmed from Japanese suspicions about how loyal the Taiwanese would be to the Japanese Empire when fighting in China. Once established, however, even minority peoples in Taiwan were recruited into the Takasago Volunteer Army and fought vigorously in the South Pacific. The Imperial Navy Special Volunteer System was put into practice in July 1943, and a military conscription system finally implemented in 1945.

From 1937 to 1945, more than 207,000 Taiwanese were sent into the Japanese military services: approximately 126,000 as civilian employees and 80,000 as servicemen. Among them, 61,000 were sent to the Philippines and other areas in the South Pacific, and 33,000 to mainland China. War fatalities and those missing in action totaled 50,000. Approximately 2,000 were disabled, 21 were executed as war criminals, and 147 were sentenced to two or three years of imprisonment for war crimes. Presently, the surviving ex-Japanese servicemen and civilian employees are referred to as Taiwanese ex-Japanese soldiers (TEJSs). As a result of the complexity of Taiwan's colonial history, the Chinese civil war, and the cold war formation, these soldiers were denied any postwar reparations by the Japanese government for many years and recently have received only very meager compensation. Because of their wartime past as Japanese soldiers, TEJSs in mainland China have faced many difficulties, especially following the successive ultraleftist movements in the post-1957 years. And the needs of the tens of thousands who survived the war and returned to Taiwan have been neglected by both the Jiang and Li administrations, which, currying favor with Japan, did not want to annoy Japan with demands for postwar compensation due these former soldiers.

For the Nation and the Emperor

Eleven soldiers were interviewed for this project; five now live in different parts of Taiwan and six in Tianjin, Hebei Province, in mainland China. The following are the soldiers' accounts, which I collected on different occasions, of when and why they joined the Japanese Armed Forces. On the one hand, their reasons for enlisting often testify to the effectiveness of kōminka education. On the other hand, their reasons also suggest economic, familial, and local motivations of loyalty to Japan and the emperor. This in turn indicates that the Japanese educational apparatus, however effective, was not entirely successful in producing loyal colonial subjects.

Five of the eleven interviewees claimed that they did not choose to enter the army, but were simply coerced. Wang Qinghuai, now seventy years old, was a farmer at the time of the war. He explained that "in those times there was no way to refuse recruitment." Some, like Xie Yong, seventy-two, who enlisted as "volunteer civilian employees," were actually volunteers in name only. Xie noted, "I was in a vocational high school then. The Japanese military instructor told us that the nation and the emperor needed us." After a short period of training, Xie and some of his classmates became aviation machinists in the Japanese Army. One of the soldiers interviewed, Lin Xinglin, seventy-one, was living in Fukuoka, Japan, at the time of the war, and was recruited into the army while there. He recalled, "Soon they found out that I wasn't Japanese. A Taiwanese was not qualified to be an Imperial soldier of Japan." The result was that Lin was given a position as a civilian employee in a naval base near Fukuoka. "I was young and felt humiliated for not being accepted as an Imperial soldier," said Lin, smiling in reflection, "but my father was happy, because the casualties were lower for civilians than for servicemen."

Two of the interviewees thought that the attractive salary for civilian employees was a far stronger motivation for joining the army than the military's patriotic slogans. For example, Chen Genfa, seventy-five, a truck driver at the time of the war, explained, "They promised 120 yen per month to those who went to Manila. That was twice as much as my monthly income as a truck driver in Taipei." Huang Yongshen, eighty-four, described his experience of joining the army in light of the fact that the salary was a particularly powerful motivation in the later years of the war, when simply getting by became increasingly difficult for the Taiwanese: "A few years before the end of the war, the Japanese wanted me to drive the supply ships between the Japanese-occupied islands of the South Pacific. They said they would pay me handsomely. I was a fisherman and had a family to feed. I was a poor fisherman and knew nothing. I didn't care about the nation or the emperor. I said yes, and a month later they sent me to the Philippines."

Other interviewees did attribute their joining the army primarily to their feelings of patriotism to Japan. Wang Qinghuai was eighteen when he enlisted as a volunteer civilian employee. He decided to work extremely diligently in the hopes that he could become a regular soldier in the Imperial Army when he turned twenty. "Like many young men at that time, I was sort of inflamed by the Japanese spirit," he admitted. Smiling, he continued, "But I wonder who wasn't in those days." Zhou Yichun, seventy-one, was working in the Hygienics Laboratory of the Police Bureau of the Government General when he joined. Now a chop engraver, he pointed out that "it was very unusual for a Taiwanese young man to work in one of the departments of the Government General." He continued with a faint smile, "The position was an honor. You felt you were a step closer to the Japanese than other Taiwanese. Your mind was full of things like the Nation, the New Order of Great East Asia, the Imperial Nation, and the like, you know. I was too young at that time, after all." And Liu Chengqing, seventy-one, who was enrolled in 1944 as a civilian employee soon after his graduation from high school in Japan, boldly admitted during my August 1995 interview in Tianjin, Hebei, that he had felt fully empowered by the "Yamato Spirit," as he was moved by the patriotic songs that thundered every day during the period when he was recruited into service. In 1953, instead of returning to Taiwan, he went to mainland China to seek a new career where, after the Anti-Rightist Movement of 1958, he was labeled a traitor and a spy for Japanese imperialists in socialist China. Liu commented, "Despite all of this, I confess I feel at home speaking Japanese. I always think [about what life would have been like] if I had not left Yokosuka, Japan, for Tianjin forty-two years ago." Liu is now a consultant for a Japanese-owned company in suburban Tianjin. About his job, Liu said, "I taught the Japanese owner how to be strict and pay less to Chinese workers."

War Experiences

The TEJSS' war experiences included important commonalities. Most obviously, they shared the general experience of the war's ending: the sudden landing and attack of the U.S. troops, the total collapse of the Japanese defense, all-out retreat to uninhabited mountain areas, and finally, Japan's surrender on 15 August 1945. Another common experience was the short service time of these soldiers, which was due to the fact that the Army Volunteer System did not begin in Taiwan until April 1942. The Navy Volunteer System only started in July 1943 and colonial Taiwanese were not conscripted until 1945. Moreover, the interviews indicate a further shared experience: that of being enlisted as civilian employees and rarely being assigned to the front lines of battle. This fact, far from being coincidental, reflected the general policy of the Japanese military toward its Taiwanese soldiers. As Wang Qinghuai, a chief cook in two platoons, put it, "The bottom line was that the Japanese did not trust us Taiwanese. We civilian employees were placed in the second or third line as clerks, agriculture experts, civil engineers, machinists, construction workers, drivers, nurses, chemists, and so on." Related to but perhaps more significant than short service time and relative lack of combat experience are shared memories of racial discrimination and atrocities committed by Japanese officers and troops on Chinese soldiers and civilians alike; and, in marked contrast to prevailing conditions of racist cruelty, there were occasional memories of actual friendship between Japanese and Taiwanese soldiers. This section attends to these shared experiences of Japanese racism and violence, and also addresses the not surprising fact that one TEJS reported a desire to desert the Japanese troops and join the Chinese resistance.

A historical fact that has been emphasized by historians of the Sino-Japanese War, but that remains overshadowed by the Jewish Holocaust in many Eurocentric accounts of World War II, is the extent to which Japanese military activity in China neared genocidal proportions. This history was vividly evidenced in the interviews. Huang Yongshen was an eyewitness to a horrific act of violence committed by a Japanese sergeant when Huang's supply ship was dispatched to the island of Hainan to transport munitions. During his stay in Hainan the sergeant requested Huang to accompany him "to find a girl and have some fun." Huang recollected, "I thought he would go to the army comfort girls," but instead, "the sergeant found a girl on the street. He raped her in broad daylight, right before my dumbfounded eyes, right on the street . . ." Huang paused for a cigarette. "And after that, guess what? The sergeant stabbed his bayonet right into the girl's vagina. . . . The sergeant was a demon, I can tell you." The truck driver Chen heard similar stories about such occurrences from other truck drivers. During his interview he recalled a violent incident in a small Filipino village that involved some important documents: "All the men in the village were rounded up, tortured, and then murdered by the Japanese MPs." Chen also remembered American POWs being tortured to death, and a massacre of Chinese peasants: "A Taiwanese civilian employee sent to our island from Guangzhou Bay told me how seven Japanese MPs massacred more than four hundred Chinese peasants in four neighboring villages there. They had sought to avenge the deaths of seven Japanese soldiers by attacking the anti-Japanese peasants." Chen commented, "It is always the common people who suffer most in war."

As some of the TEJSs' statements have already suggested, there was general agreement on the issue of racial discrimination. Most interviewees attested that the Japanese soldiers exhibited a substantial amount of discrimination toward their Taiwanese colleagues. Lu Qinglin, who joined the Japanese Navy in May 1945, described his experience of discrimination: "When they found out I was Taiwanese, they demoted me to civilian employee of the Imperial Air Force." He was then immediately sent to Manchuria, and once in Qiqihar he was assigned to a general affairs office as a clerk, rather than being assigned to a laboratory as would be appropriate for a chemist. "No Taiwanese could work in the lab," he said. "Major Suzuki told me that later."

At the same time, however, not all interviewees felt that discrimination was always intolerably apparent. Laughing, Chen Chunqing put it this way: "Facing the bullets of the enemy, you and the Japanese are equal. Besides, this was war. They needed your absolute loyalty." Chen Genfa similarly offered an anecdote about an experience he had in Manila: "I was in Manila to purchase supplies. A Japanese soldier saw me and called me names. 'Chankoro!' [a derogatory word for Chinese] he shouted." Chen then described how he had stood up and punched the Japanese soldier in the face. Then, "two Japanese M P s came up, and I told them I was there in Manila ready to die for the nation and the emperor, and this son of a bitch calls me Chankoro. The M P s beat up the Japanese soldier right in front of me."

There were even a few isolated instances of humane interaction between Japanese and Taiwanese. Lu Qinglin was only eighteen years old when he was sent to Qiqihar, Manchuria, where he met a Major Suzuki in the general affairs office of the Guandong (Kwantung) Army. Major Suzuki treated Lu as a foster son, caring for Lu by protecting him from the violent discipline of the Japanese Army and providing him with canned foods distributed only to high-ranking Japanese officers. When Lu was transferred to Harbin, the major stocked Lu's baggage with clothing and food and saw him off at the station. The war ended soon after Lu arrived in Harbin, and he was taken with the other troops to Siberia by the Red Army. "One day in the following year, somewhere deep in the frozen wilderness of Siberia, I saw a shabby old man on the platform of a small railway station. It was Major Suzuki." Lu described this moment of reunion as far greater than mere joy. This time, Lu emptied all his pockets to give Major Suzuki the rations, candies, and money that had been supplied by the Red Army. "Major Suzuki took a little of the candy and rations, but insisted on not accepting a dime of mine. 'You are my child,' said Major Suzuki. 'Money is something that a father gives to his child, not the contrary.' That was what Major Suzuki said." They parted that chill autumn in the Siberian wilderness in 1946 and never met again.

On the other side of the spectrum, Chen Chunqing experienced a thorough awakening from the effects of kōminka as a result of his days as a serviceman in the China theater, and became so disillusioned with his own Japanese patriotism that he attempted to desert and join other Taiwanese soldiers who had begun fighting with the Chinese. In 1943, twenty years old and driven by the desire to fight "British and American ghosts and beasts" in support of the construction of the Greater East Asia Co-Prosperity Sphere, he had volunteered to join the Japanese Army. "I was far too young then," Chen said. "I knew nothing. I was only a poor farmer from a remote village in northern Taiwan." Chen was sent to mainland China after one month of training. The peaceful, poverty-ridden, and simple mainland peasants reminded Chen of their counterparts in the poor, remote village that was his own hometown. And Chen was surprised to find that the customs, life, and even religions of mainland China had so much in common with those of Taiwan. "Why should the ideal of the Co-Prosperity Sphere be carried out through plundering, depriving, and killing these peasants?" Chen asked himself. And unanswerable doubts began to spread, little by little, in Chen's restless mind.

These doubts increased when, in early 1944, Chen was transferred to Pukou in Zhejiang and assigned a position as a guard at a concentration camp containing thousands of Chinese slave laborers. He witnessed the harsh labor, hunger, torture, violence, and murder that were part of the daily events of the camp. Then in May of the same year, Chen and twenty other Taiwanese soldiers and civilian employees were sent by train and truck to the northern front in Zhejiang. On the way, they saw corpses in the fields, streets, road sides, and rivers. "Even as a soldier I was shocked to see with my own eyes how China had been ruined by the war," Chen said, "and it was the first time I saw on the walls of the ruins slogans signed by the Taiwanese Anti-Japanese Army that read: 'Down with Japanese Imperialism!'; 'We Shall Win in the Anti-Japanese War!'; and 'We Shall Succeed in Reconstructing the Motherland.' " At the time of his interview Chen stressed how even today he could vividly remember how madly his heart beat on realizing for the first time in his life that Taiwanese soldiers were organizing in mainland China to fight alongside their Chinese compatriots against the Japanese invaders. From that time on Chen aggressively sought out the Taiwan Anti-Japanese Volunteer Army, but unfortunately his efforts were in vain.

That Day, 15 August 1945 . . .

The interviewees described the end of the war as having a significant impact on their sense of national identity. The form this impact took, however, varied in accordance with differing circumstances. Some of the soldiers, for example, did not even know the war had ended until months after the fact due to the remote locations of some of the troops; when they did learn about the Japanese defeat, they sometimes experienced ambivalent feelings, as was the case with Chen Qinglin. Chen was sent back to Taiwan in late autumn 1944 due to a serious illness. In December of the same year, he was again mobilized as a civilian employee and stationed on a remote island in the Philippines. The island, also occupied by U.S. soldiers, underwent an "incredibly strong" attack the third day after Chen's arrival. Chen and a scattering of other Japanese soldiers retreated into the island mountains, where they lived for the next fourteen months. As Chen explained, "As we were deep in the island jungles we did not know that Japan had lost the war until September of 1946." When asked whether or not he had felt happy about the defeat, Chen replied, "Not really." On 12 September 1946, Chen and hundreds of Japanese servicemen left the mountain areas where they had been living, and the U.S. Army took them to a POW concentration camp. With regard to the concentration camp, Chen remarked, "The food was terrible and there wasn't much of it. The labor was intolerable; we worked almost ten hours a day. . . . It wasn't any better than the Japanese concentration camps down there in mainland China." Chen was sent back to Taiwan at the end of 1946.

Other TEJSs also felt ambivalent about the war's ending, Japan's surrender, and China's recovery of Taiwan. Many witnessed extreme reactions to the news by the Japanese servicemen and superior officers. Word of the defeat came to Lu Qinglin on 15 August 1945, while he lay in an army sick ward in Harbin, Manchuria. With the news came rumors of Japanese officers committing suicide. As he recalled, "The Japanese opened up the rations storehouse and ate and drank in enormous amounts as if doomsday were knocking at the door." Liu Chengqing received the news while stationed in Yokosuka, Japan. His superior told him that the Americans had dropped a "super big bomb" on Japan, and that in the name of the Japanese people's survival, the "kind and merciful emperor" had decided to let the war come to an end. He remembered, "I went down the streets of Yokosuka and saw Japanese people kneeling down on the roadsides, crying and wailing."

In addition, some of the soldiers interviewed could not imagine what liberation from Japan and a return to China would mean for Taiwan, given that they themselves had been fighting with Japan in a war against China. Fu Dasheng heard the emperor's "jade voice" announcing the defeat while he was stationed in Changchun, Manchuria (Jilin Province). "Several of the officers killed themselves by harakiri that August 15 night," said Fu, "and a major general blew his head off with a pistol early the next morning." Fu also reported hearing stories about soldiers taking revenge against their superiors for past maltreatment. Some Japanese soldiers told Fu that they believed it was Japan that had lost the war, and the defeat had nothing to do with Taiwanese subjects like Fu. "But I was totally dumbfounded," Fu recalled. "I did not have the slightest idea about what lay ahead for myself and for Taiwan."

One of the interviewees, Chen Genfa, realized with the end of the war that although he was a colonized subject himself, his participation in the war had positioned him as an enemy of the Filipinos and other Southeast Asians in whose countries much of the war had been waged. It was not until 12 September 1945, when his battalion officially surrendered to the U.S. Army, that Chen knew that Imperial Japan had lost its "Holy War." Chen described his experience of the events that followed the surrender: "We Taiwanese civilian employees were sent by train to a concentration camp miles away from the city of Manila. The angry Filipinos threw big stones at our wagons at almost every station where we stopped on the way." Chen remembered that quite a few of the soldiers were injured, and some were even stoned to death. "The American guards were obviously not very serious about stopping those angry shouting Filipinos," Chen noted, "and for the first time, I saw in the furious eyes of the Filipinos, that no matter what, I, a Taiwanese, had been part of the Japanese crimes of war."

The war's ending also enabled the emergence of a Chinese national identity that had been suppressed by the ideological apparatuses of Japanese colonialism, as is suggested by the reminiscences of Zhou Yichun, who, with hundreds of comrades-in-arms, was notified by his lieutenant of the "temporary cessation of fire." This lieutenant told his troops that to assure constant preparedness, they would conduct military exercises in the mountains, miles away from Guangzhou (Guangdong), where they were stationed. Zhou explained, "The lieutenant lied to prevent his army from feeling the sudden shock of news of the defeat." Zhou also recollected that he finally learned the truth about Japan's agreement to an unconditional surrender from leaflets dropped from U.S. planes: "The leaflets stated that Taiwan would be returned to China, and Korea was going to gain independence from Japanese reign. Yesterday, I had striven hard to be a loyal subject of the emperor, and today I discovered something that I remembered my grandfather telling me—that I was a Chinese."

Homecoming

The complexity of Taiwan's postwar situation put the TEJSS in a difficult position: because they had fought against their Chinese compatriots during the war they were not regarded as soldiers of the newly victorious China; however, neither were they simply regarded as Japanese imperial soldiers. They did not share the glory of China's victory, nor were they in a position to mourn the defeat of the great empire of Japan. The following is a brief historical outline of Taiwan's postcolonial period, which sheds some light on the complexity of the TEJSS' predicament in relation to the Japanese, mainland Chinese, and GMD governments.

In 1945, following the Potsdam Declaration and the Cairo Declaration, the newly liberated Taiwan was returned to China. However, in China a civil war between the U.S.-supported GMD and the Chinese Communist Party (CCP) broke out immediately and escalated into a nationwide struggle. In late 1949 the GMD retreated to the island of Taiwan. In June 1950, a few days after the Korean War broke out, the U.S. Seventh Fleet blocked the Taiwan Straits, and the United States reorganized Taiwan as one of its cold war strategic military bases in the so-called Pacific Island Chain. This attempt to contain the People's Republic of China (PRC) and the Soviet Union thus separated Taiwan from China proper. The United States granted the GMD regime international legitimacy by giving Jiang's government diplomatic recognition, preservation of Taiwan's seat on the U.N. Security Council, and military and economic aid. This international legitimacy in turn served as strong justification for legitimizing the GMD's dictatorial internal rule over Taiwan. By strictly adhering to postwar U.S. foreign policy, Japan actually served as an accomplice in separating China and Taiwan, supporting GMD misrule, and demonstrating enmity toward China soon after the end of its fifteen-year war of invasion against China and its fifty years of colonial domination over Taiwan. Postcolonial misrule in Taiwan, moreover, has been twofold. First of all, just as the Occupation authorities in Japan united with former wartime fascist elements against communism after the Korean War, the GMD conducted a cruel purge against the national-democratic tradition in Taiwan, while at the same time absorbing into its power bloc the very Taiwanese landlords, gentry, and bourgeoisie who had collaborated with Japanese rulers during the colonial years. Second, even after the reign of Jiang's martial law came to an end in 1987, the remaining colonial elite, represented by President Li Denghui, emerged into power through the "democratization" of Taiwan—a situation widely praised by Western observers.

The complex and rapidly changing political relations among Taiwan, Japan, China, and the United States allowed the GMD and Japanese governments to refuse to recognize their postwar obligations to these soldiers. Japan, for example, often did not even provide return transportation to Japan or Taiwan and withheld salaries owed to the soldiers. Chen Junqing, seventy-one, acting supervisor of the Association of Taiwanese Ex-Japanese Soldiers, Civilian Employees, and War Bereaved, explained this situation during his interview: "When the war ended with Japan's unconditional surrender, the Taiwanese soldiers and civilian employees in all of the front lines, from places in mainland China to the far reaches of the South Pacific, were simply abandoned and forsaken by the Japanese government." Chen himself had been mobilized as a civilian employee of the Japanese Navy and was sent to Hainan island (Guangdong) in May 1943. He told his own story: "The emperor who had enlisted us did not give any discharge orders when the war ended. We were simply left in the battlefields, jungles, islands, and mountains, and we had to fight for ourselves for our physical survival long after the Japanese troops had been sent back home by American warships."

When the TEJSS were finally able to leave the areas in which they were stationed, they continued to face difficulties whether they returned to China, Japan, or Taiwan. Most returned to Taiwan, but the twists and turns of postwar history resulted in a considerable number of them living in mainland China for more than forty years after the war. Lu Qinglin, for example, had been sent to Manchuria just before the 1945 defeat, and after the war the Soviet Union's Red Army took him deep into Siberia for four years of forced labor. Subsequently, in 1949, Lu was treated as a Japanese soldier and repatriated to Japan. "I was back in Fukui where I had been enlisted for service," Lu said. "A job was very hard to find. At that time, the Japanese people believed that those who were repatriated from Soviet Siberia were dangerous 'Reds.' No one wanted to offer a job to a communist." Lu also described how in 1950 he had written his brother about his situation. "My brother flew to Japan to meet me." Lu's brother, however, insisted that he should not go home, as Taiwan was undergoing a cruel and all-out "Red purge": "My brother told me the stories of the February [28] Incident of 1947, when disappointed Taiwanese rose in revolt against corrupt and oppressive GMD rule. This incident left a bloody scar of mutual suspicion and hostility between the Formosan Chinese and mainlander Chinese." Lu's brother also let him know about the terror that began in 1949. Lu explained: "In Taiwan during that time, a Siberian repatriate was a synonym for communist, and this meant destruction not only for himself but also his family." Therefore, in 1952 when the Japanese economy worsened, Lu decided to go to mainland China: "I was at my wit's end. Besides, Premier Zhou Enlai was then calling for overseas Chinese equipped with skills and technical know-how to return to China for construction of the socialist motherland."

The stories of Fu Dasheng, Lu Qinglin, and Liu Chengqing are similar in their recounting of the events that led them all to settle eventually in Tianjin (Hopei) in the PRC. On their arrival in Tianjin they were warmly welcomed; they were assigned jobs and eventually married. Liu described how this situation changed: "Everything seemed to go well during our first several years in mainland China until 1957, when there was the nationwide Suppressing the Anti-Revolutionaries Movement and the Anti-Rightist Movement of 1958. We TEJSS became targets of attack for almost every political movement from 1957 to 1976, when the Proletarian Cultural Revolution, which aimed at attacking class enemies, revisionists, capitalist roaders, bureaucratism, and corruption inside the Party came to an end." Repeatedly, their records of having served as Japanese civilian employees were investigated and criticized, with most of them being labeled traitors or spies for Japanese imperialism who had been smuggled back into China to subvert the socialist motherland. In the context of the sociopolitical unrest that had been spreading into Eastern socialist states in 1956, Mao Zedong announced his famous 1957 policy—"Let a hundred flowers bloom and let schools of learning contend with one another"—encouraging common people, intellectuals, and noncommunist elements to criticize, to discuss political issues, and to think. However, the criticism and appeals that were leveled against the CCP far exceeded Mao's expectations. In June 1957 the CCP fought back by censuring most of the criticism as anticommunist, antisocialist, and "bourgeois rightist" in nature. The CCP's counterattack developed into a mass antirightist movement; during this time, almost all of the TEJSs in mainland China became targets of antirightist criticism.

Yet those who returned safely to their hometowns in Taiwan were by no means better off. Not surprisingly, the GMD government treated the TEJSs with negligence and prejudice. "It's easy to understand," Wang Qinghuai explained. "Just a few years ago, we TEJSs were part of the Japanese Imperial Army which was invading GMD's China." To make matters more complicated, the Sinophobia of the kōminka propaganda that had proliferated during the war was revived during the February Insurgence of 1947. Reports show that a few war repatriates took part in the Insurgence wearing the uniforms and field service caps of the Japanese Army as they chanted Japanese military songs and marched through the streets, beating up mainlanders they came across. Wang Xiaobo, professor of history at the College of World Journalism and Communication, offers this explanation: "At that moment, these TEJSs were the Imperial Army, fighting the Chinese people again." And after the Insurgence, they were "purged."

In the 1980s the situation of the TEJSs on both sides of the Taiwan Straits began to improve. In mainland China, this change took place after 1979. Regarding this period Fu Dasheng said, "Our [negative] labels were torn off, and no one any longer had the right to point at us and say that we were traitors to our motherland. Some who had been seriously mistreated even won state compensation." The situation of their counterparts in Taiwan also improved after President Li Denghui came to power in 1988. And in May 1993 the Association of Taiwanese Ex-Japanese Soldiers, Civilian Employees, and War Bereaved was inaugurated. Such an organization of Taiwanese ex-Japanese war patriots was unthinkable before 1988, when the iron rule of the Jiang family was in effect. Also, since the early 1990s many TEJSs living in mainland China have returned to their hometowns in Taiwan to visit relatives. Some have remained in Taiwan permanently, but most have returned to Tianjin. On this topic, Lu Qinglin said with a gentle smile, "It is good to have survived and lived through so much, and then finally see my homeland, Taiwan, which has always haunted my dreams."

Among the eleven interviewees, two became members of the CCP. One of them, Xie Yong, now lives in mainland China; the other, Chen Chunqing, still resides in Taiwan.

Some of the events that led Xie to join the Party began with the end of war, when he was serving as a machinist in the Gangshan Air Base. The short-lived euphoria that followed Taiwan's liberation was soon replaced by outrage as a result of the GMD's misgovernment; on his return to Taiwan, Xie found himself one of the young men who gathered regularly to discuss at length Taiwan's deteriorating social conditions and oppressive political situation. When the February 1947 Incident occurred, Xie was one of the members of a storming party that rushed the GMD's military air field in the suburban city of Jiayi. "I did not know that the underground CCP had been watching my activities with great interest," Xie recalled, "and one day in early June 1947, I was led to see Li Madou, then a famous cadet of the underground Party active in the southern spheres of Taiwan." Xie joined the Party that day, a day he stated he would never forget: "Li himself was there to congratulate me."

However, in late 1949 the GMD began its "Red purge," during which time Party organizations all over the island were destroyed. Four thousand alleged communists were shot by firing squads and another six thousand to eight thousand were sentenced to ten to fifteen years of imprisonment. Nearly one hundred were sentenced to life imprisonment. Xie also recalled that "Li Madou was arrested, tortured, and finally shot to death in the early summer of 1951." In December of the same year, Xie fled to mainland China via Hong Kong.

Like Xie Yong, Chen Chunqing returned from the war to discover that the GMD regime's misrule had become intolerable for the local people. On the eve of the February Incident Chen, with his battlefield experience, helped radical students look for ammunition that they believed the Japanese might have left behind in several mountain caves that they had utilized during the war. He thus actively took part in anti-GMD activities. When the Incident was suppressed by armed forced in March 1947, Chen fled Taibei. During his flight he met Chen Wennong. "Chen taught me the ABCs of Marxism and Leninism. He lent me some progressive books and journals to read. That opened my eyes. I read and read with great hunger." Although Chen had loved studying history and geography in primary school, he had been forced to drop out because of poverty. "Reading the books and journals that Chen Wennong lent me made me a new man," he recalled. "I started to understand that the essence of the last war was the contradiction between Japanese and American imperialisms."

Inspired by these readings, Chen Chunqing became a member of the underground Party. He worked diligently in reading circles and to construct a partisan base in Luku, a mountainous area in the northern suburbs of Taibei. In 1953 armed police demolished this base and more than a hundred party cadets and mountain peasants were rounded up; nearly twenty of them were shot to death by firing squad. Chen was one of the very few who managed to escape the mountain base. But this escape ushered in a prolonged period of hiding that lasted until July 1959, when he was finally discovered, arrested, and sentenced to ten years imprisonment. When asked about his thoughts on today's China, Chen, now a cancer patient, replied that it was a great comfort for him to see how China has developed into a modernized society. At the same time, he does not harbor any illusions about the political situation across the Straits, and still worries about at least one thing: "corruption" in regard to mainland China.

A Chill in the Heart

The efforts of the TEJSs in Taiwan to organize and claim reparations from the Japanese government, and the obstacles they have encountered from both the Japanese and Taiwanese governments in these efforts, illustrate the complexity of the histories in which these soldiers formed their national identities. At the same time they also reflect the transnational dimensions of the processes by which each nation has been able to refuse recognition of either the hardships these former soldiers have endured or any national obligations to them. For example, early in 1972 a group of TEJSs in Taiwan failed in their attempt to formally register their organization for claiming war reparations from Japan. Chen Jungqing, now acting supervisor of the Association of Taiwanese Ex-Japanese Soldiers, Civilian Employees, and War Bereaved, explained their lack of success in this early endeavor: "Before 1987, when martial law was in effect, it was absolutely impossible for people to have their own civil organizations." However, he further explained that martial law was not the only reason they had been prevented from receiving official recognition: "The GMD government had good reasons not to be enthusiastic about the interests of those who had fought as Japanese soldiers against China in the last war. Additionally, in 1972 Japan transferred diplomatic recognition from Taibei to Beijing, recognizing Taiwan as part of the PRC; and this compounded difficulties in the negotiation of war reparations between Japan and Taiwan."

The association was finally successfully inaugurated in 1993, with an office on Changsha Street, Taibei. In the office, people like Chen Junqing currently work to collect reparations for unpaid salaries, unliquidated military postal savings, unliquidated military insurance, and indemnity for war casualties and the disabled. So far, however, the Japanese government has agreed to pay no more than 2 million yen per claim. "The money is only enough for a very modest funeral," Chen said. He and most of the TEJSS are especially angry about Japan's insistence on compensating for unpaid salaries, savings, and insurance with only 120 times the original documented amount. "If the unpaid military salary is an average of 1,000 yen, 120 times that is only 120,000 yen," Chen insisted, "and that amounts to only 40,000 NT dollars." Chen noted that forty years ago 1,000 Japanese yen would have enabled one to buy two houses in the most prosperous neighborhoods in Taibei, houses that would be worth more than 10 million NT dollars now. Chen and his fellow TEJSS argue that reasonable compensation is 7,000 times the original amount. "Our calculation is simple," Chen declared. "Currently, a second-class private in the Japanese Self-Defense Force is paid 155,300 yen per month. Forty years ago, we TEJSS were paid 20 yen per month. That is why we think 7,000 times the original amount is just and reasonable."

The Japanese government, however, has not endorsed these calculations and has sternly refused to repay the wartime debts while taking into account the marked increase in the cost of living. This attitude has shocked and hurt most of the Taiwanese ex-Japanese servicemen and civilian employees. Chen Junqing expressed his shock and disappointment at a 1973 trip to Japan, which the TEJSS embarked on to begin reparations negotiations. Chen imagined that he would be warmly received and welcomed by Japanese politicians, veteran superior officers and comrades-in-arms, but this was not the case. Similarly, according to Lin Qiutan, some delegates assumed that they would be accepted as lost loyal subjects of the emperor who had fought bravely in the emperor's army. "But we were absolutely wrong. We pleaded for reparations identical to those the Japanese ex-servicemen enjoyed, because some of us really thought that we had been the Japanese emperor's pious sons rather than Chinese. But almost all Japanese friends frowned at our request. They said we had lost our Japanese nationality at least as early as the signing of the peace treaty between Japan and Taiwan in 1952." Zhou Yichun also expressed his disappointment: "It's our own money. Money we earned with our own sweat and blood. The Japanese should pay the money back because they owe it to us. We are not asking [them to give it to us out of the goodness of their hearts]."

Chen Genfa and Chen Junqing both emphasized their own disappointment at Japanese reactions to their requests. Chen Genfa explained that he had earlier been quite fond of the Japanese. He added that there had been "some stupid reasons" for this, such as the "Yamato Spirit" and kōminka education, which had encouraged him to believe that the Japanese were absolutely trustworthy and honest, had a very strong sense of duty, and could be held accountable for all their promises. "That was why I was so shocked to see all the Japanese people turn their backs on us," he said, "even though we had served as Japanese soldiers, had fought for the Japanese, were killed and disabled for the Japanese people, and had lent our money to the Japanese government in the form of military postal savings." Chen Junqing related his even more moving response to Japanese indifference. Chen has been quite active in claiming unsettled reparations. Utilizing his skill in spoken and written Japanese, he has led delegations to Japan as well as demonstrations protesting Japan's refusal to meet the TEJSS' requests. This ongoing work recently brought him further disappointment: "In November 1993 we staged a demonstration claiming war reparations in Tokyo. With microphones we tried to appeal directly to the Japanese public. But to our astonishment the Japanese people were almost totally indifferent to us. We tried to hand out flyers stating our appeals and requests, but almost no one on the street cared to take and read them. We felt a chill in the heart which we will never forget for the rest of our lives."

It is important to recognize that this disappointment and anger stems from an undeniable affection for Japan. This fact is evidenced in the name of the publication of the Association of Taiwanese Ex-Japanese Soldiers, Civilian Employees, and War Bereaved: *Huangjun tongxun* (Imperial Army Bulletin), whose cover is illustrated with the rising sun pattern of the Japanese national flag. The logo of the association is an imitation of the royal decoration of Japan. Furthermore, some of the TEJSS are fond of wearing the field service caps of the Japanese Army, not only when attending their meetings and participating in demonstration rallies, but also simply for pleasure, while sightseeing in Japan. Along these lines, Wang Qinghuai reflected that once during an association year-end party, he watched an old TEJS, with field service cap on his head, sing Japanese military songs and even the Japanese national anthem: "There were tears in his eyes while he cursed *bakayarō* [damned idiots] at Japan for forsaking these old Taiwanese ex-Japanese soldiers and discriminating against them."

The attitude toward war reparations of the TEJSS in mainland China, however, is quite different. Over the past forty years, they were repeatedly compelled to reflect deeply on this history and their own thoughts and actions in the war. "We heard about what the TEJSS had been doing to claim reparations in Taiwan," said Xie Yong, "but we seldom thought about reparations in money form. What I have been thinking about is how the war that broke out when I was only a high school graduate drastically changed the entire course of my life."

Trauma

The TEJSS' stories vividly express Taiwan's postcolonial trauma as a persisting legacy of the island's contemporary history and politics. For these soldiers, the cultural and political dimensions in which this trauma has exerted its influence have occurred in at least three areas: their own sense of national identity; the cold war–determined exilic condition in which some of them continue to live; and the East Asian cold war formation that allowed both Japan and Taiwan to neglect their responsibilities to these national subjects.

The effect that Taiwan's postcolonial history has had on these soldiers' national identity is a complex one. The TEJSs, having undergone long years of kōminka education and having been deeply affected by this and other Japanese mind control apparatuses, often refuse to identify themselves as Chinese or Taiwanese, and instead continue to claim to be "pious sons of the Emperor Hirohito." Consequently, the cold refusal and negligence of the Japanese government in making war reparations is all the more bitter and heartbreaking for them. In terms of the soldiers' national identities, then, it becomes apparent that Japanese colonization of Taiwan not only deprived the TEJSs of their labor and language, but also cost them their national pride and national identity.

Second, Taiwan's separation from China, a result of the cold war, effectively prevented many TEJSs from returning to their families and relations in Taiwan before the 1990s. When they finally were able to return home, moreover, many of them found that their parents and older relatives had passed away many years earlier. Related to this cold war–determined exile is the fact that the United States and the conservative state of postwar Japan, which preserved complicated connections with wartime fascist elements, entered into an anticommunist alliance. In its status as the most beloved child of the United States, Japan has been able to prudently insist on withholding apologies and compensation for war crimes committed and damage inflicted on Asian peoples. And as another nation whose political allegiances were greatly shaped in the cold war era, Taiwan, both under Jiang and Li, has without the slightest hesitation traded the right to claim TEJS reparations for Japanese political support of Taiwan.

In 1995, as the world and Asia commemorated the fiftieth anniversary of the final victory of the antifascist war, Taiwan remained relatively silent and restrained in criticizing Japanese war crimes in that war, especially in comparison to Korea. Unmet and unrecognized Japanese war responsibilities have left postcolonial Taiwan with a profound spiritual trauma, the complexity of which extends beyond the Taiwan-Japan context and includes uneven and continually changing political and economic relationships with China and the United States. Taiwan's silence on Japanese WWII war crimes, as well as the GMD regime's proximity to the fascism that this war purportedly ended, gain new significance when understood in light of the geopolitical context of the East

Asian cold war formation. Like the war itself, the plight of the Taiwanese ex-Japanese soldiers is one particularly vivid illustration of the ongoing effects of a layered colonial history, effects whose complexity take on a multiplicity of forms, from the WWII "contradiction between Japanese and American imperialisms" to the current post–cold war alignments of East Asian NIC capitalist states.

Korean "Imperial Soldiers": Remembering

Colonialism and Crimes against Allied POWs

UTSUMI AIKO

Translation by Mie Kennedy

Invisible Korean Soldiers

Strangely, the sound of the harmonica brings forth memories of the war, even though I was born in the year the Asia-Pacific War began and have no immediate recollection of it. My home survived the Great Tokyo Air Raid (March 1945) and during the final stages of the war, when up to 90 percent of adult men were recruited by the military, my father stayed home because he was ill from caries. Although my sister died from an illness while at the Ninomiya evacuation site in Kanagawa, I think I suffered the fewest losses among my peers. Yet the war left its mark on our postwar daily life. A family whose home had been burned down and an elderly person with no relatives lived with us in our tiny house. We had to line up to get our rationing of potatoes, and we also traveled to the countryside with knapsacks to get extra food. We felt lucky if we could eat sweet potatoes or some squash.

In those days we often played the harmonica. The harmonica was the only real instrument available for us children. We would hear the harmonica in the streets as well. Wounded soldiers who stood in front of train stations soliciting money played the harmonica while singing sorrowful war songs: "Here in Manchuria hundreds of miles from our honorable country . . ." That tune overlapped with images of the mutilated bodies of soldiers playing harmonicas in the crowd, leaving a deep impression of the war's tragedy.

However, most people passing by ignored these soldiers. Perhaps they were busy putting their own lives back together. Yet how could people be so unresponsive toward these wounded ex-soldiers? Even along the busy Yamanote train line, maybe one or two people per train car would drop money into the cups of begging handicapped or injured soldiers. People pretended not to see them. I remember my father explaining to me the public's indifference and coldheartedness by saying, "It is because those people receive money from the state."

My postwar education never taught me about the organization of the Japanese military system, war songs, or military ranks. But in exchange for not having to learn the militarized patriotism, I also never learned about the history of Japan's "war of invasion" (shinryaku sensō). Thus, although "war" remained in the background of my daily life, I did not know that the Japanese military had recruited soldiers from colonized countries such as Korea and Taiwan. I never imagined that North and South Koreans, whose Japanese nationality had been stripped from them by the Japanese government after the war, were among those wounded soldiers in the streets.

A Growing Doubt

No one taught me that Koreans were conscripted as Japanese military and civilian personnel, and that once the war ended they were considered non-Japanese and thereby lost their ability to receive any kind of compensation from the government. Only after the San Francisco Peace Treaty came into effect on 28 April 1952 did North and South Koreans, dressed in white robes, speak out in the streets about their distressed situation. The laws relating to governmental relief for these ex-soldiers cited "Japanese nationality" as an eligibility requirement. Thus, these formerly colonized people, who lost their status as Japanese nationals as a result of the Treaty, were consequently considered ineligible for military pensions or any other support from the Japanese government. Disabled Koreans who had served in the Japanese military were left in the streets with no government benefits or compensation. Most people did not know any details about the Koreans' situation and most likely shared my father's views. Moreover, most Japanese were not aware that there were Koreans who were treated no differently from the wartime Japanese leader, Tōjō Hideki, and tried as war criminals. Speaking of war criminals usually brings to mind only the leading military and political figures who were tried by the International Military Tribunal for the Far East, otherwise known as the Tokyo War Tribunal. Even in popular films and songs that depicted lower-ranking soldiers who were sentenced as war criminals, Taiwanese and Koreans were not present.

Why did twenty-three Koreans bear the death penalty for Japan's wartime responsibilities? While there were only seven Japanese wartime leaders who were executed as A-Class criminals, there were three times as many B- and

C-Class criminal executions of people from Japan's former colonies. How are we to make sense of that? The emperor, the commander in chief of the military and navy, was not judged to be a war criminal, so why were Koreans sentenced as such? That the emperor was released without trial while Koreans were sentenced as criminals, it seemed to me, revealed a structural problem in accounting for Japan's war responsibility.

I lived in Bandung, Indonesia, from 1975 to 1977. While I was there, a special ceremony took place to recognize three Japanese ex-soldiers as war heroes in Indonesia's struggle for independence. These men had been on duty at a POW camp in Java during the war. After the war, they remained in Indonesia and fought as guerrillas until they were caught and executed by the Dutch Army. One of those men, Yang Ch'i l-sŏng, was a Korean who had been conscripted as a civilian military employee. Although he became an acknowledged hero of Indonesia's independence, there are other Koreans who also fought and died in guerilla warfare for Indonesian independence who have never been recognized.[1]

Four Koreans who had also been civilian military employees responsible for guarding Allied POWs were executed as war criminals at Cipinang prison in Jakarta. Some of their cellmates were later transferred to Sugamo prison in Tokyo; when finally released, they formed a group called the Association for the Mutual Advancement of Korean War Criminals (Kankoku Shusshin Senpansha Dōshinkai). I first learned about this association on a television show titled The Twenty-Fourth Year of B- and C-Class War Criminals (Nijūyonenme no BCkyū senpan) that aired in 1969 (Nihon Television). Directed by Okamoto Aihiko, the show focused on Korean war criminals. I was flipping through channels and saw only the last five minutes or so of the program, but the association's name caught my eye and I visited some of its members after I returned to Japan in 1977.

I met Mun T'ae-bok through the association. Mun had been sentenced to death as a war criminal. He spent several months waiting to die in a prison chamber called P-Hall, from where he could hear the screams of his fellow inmates as they were taken away to be hanged. He received his sentence because he had served as a guard for the Allied POWs who were forced to work on construction of the Burma-Siam Railroad. Later the site became widely known through the popular Hollywood movie Bridge on the River Kwai. Mun may indeed have beaten POWs, but he did not kill anyone, and I wondered why he had been sentenced to death. Brought up in the postwar years with little concept of death, I was overwhelmed by the experiences of Mun and others in the association. I wondered why Koreans who had been colonized by the Japanese were tried in court as Japanese. How and on what grounds did the Allied countries judge Japan's war crimes?

According to the official statistics of the Ministry of Health and Welfare, there were 116,294 Koreans in the military. In addition, there were 126,047 Koreans who, like Mun, were civilian employees in the military and who, though not strictly military personnel, had "sworn an oath and submitted themselves to army or navy duty as employees." Thus, a total of at least 242,341 Koreans served in the Japanese military. This total includes only those whose service can be corroborated officially through various certificates issued by the Ministry of Health and Welfare: for example, certificates of military service, death, and injury. In other words, this is the total of those verified by the War Ministry's incomplete official records, which the Ministry of Health and Welfare inherited after the war's end. However, there are bereaved relatives who have never received death notices and the names of some military and civilian personnel serving in the military were missed altogether by the Ministry of Health and Welfare.

According to *Shinajihen: Daitōa sensōkan rikugun dōin gaikyō* (The China incident: A general history of army mobilization during the Greater East Asia War), a manuscript edited by a staff officer from the Organization and Mobilization Department, General Staff, Ministry of War, 45,000 Koreans were conscripted in each of the years 1944 and 1945. Table 1 gives a breakdown of the positions held by these conscripted Koreans. If we add to this another 35,000 reserves who were called up and 17,200 volunteer soldiers, we can estimate that the number of Korean soldiers totalled 142,200.

The *Zainihon Chōsenjin no gaikyō* (General situation of Koreans in Japan), published by the Public Security Investigation Agency in 1949, states, "Regarding Koreans in the military at the end of the war, there were two lieutenant generals, one major general, and two colonels, under which there were approximately 25 field officers, 200 company officers and probational officers, in addition to 186,980 soldiers, 22,299 sailors and 154,907 army and navy civilian employees" (see Table 2).[2]

Chōsengun gaiyōshi (General history of the Korean Army) indicates that in the category of "Active Soldiers and First Replacement Recruits (Enlisted)," in 1944 there were 51,737 Korean soldiers (including 10,000 in the Navy) in the Korean Army, 3,260 soldiers in the Guandong (Kwantung) Army, and 3 in the Taiwan Army, making a total of 55,000 men.[3] In 1945 there were 41,965 Korean soldiers in the Korean Army and 3,035 in the Guandong Army, making a total of 45,000 for the Army alone. In addition, there were another 10,000 Koreans in the Navy. For these two years, then, the number of Korean soldiers totalled 110,000. If we add the Korean college student volunteers who were mobilized through the so-

Table 1. Korean Soldiers Classified by Branch of Service

Classification	1944	1945
Infantry	29,388	29,780
Cavalry Transport	475	475
Combat Artillery	295	280
Field Artillery	1,890	2,030
Mountain Artillery Troops	1,430	1,500
Medium Artillery	610	645
Engineer	1,477	1,480
Railway Troops	195	200
Air Troops	2,050	1,100
Anti-Aircraft Artillery	4,190	4,000
Transport	2,030	2,060
Shipping Troops	600	700
Air Technician	250	250
Technician	120	120
Heavy Artillery		260
Signal Troops		120
TOTAL	45,000	45,000

Source: *Shinajihen: Daiōa sensōkan rikugun dōin gaishi* (Tokyo: Fuji Shuppan, 1988), 435.

called Extraordinary Enlistment of Special Volunteer Soldiers and the "Special Volunteer Soldiers" who entered the military from 1938, when it first became possible for Korean men to volunteer, the total comes to 130,723 soldiers, as shown in Table 3. (The reader should note that this table does not include civilian military employees.)

Though numerical estimates may vary, the sources indicate that at least 110,000 Koreans were mobilized into the Japanese military as soldiers and sailors. Moreover, there were an additional 120,000 civilian military employees. Furthermore, there were laborers (*gunpu*) who worked for the military but were not counted as formal employees. Clearly, an astonishingly large number of Koreans were mobilized to work for the Japanese military in various capacities.

Roads to the Draft

As the name for the Japanese military indicates, the emperor commanded the Imperial Forces. The first point in the Guntai Naimurei (Military Internal Affairs Ordinance) (effective 1 November 1943) states, "The fundamental principle of the military is to, under the emperor's direct leadership, spread the

Table 2. Figures Related to the Postwar Demobilization of Korean Soldiers and Army Civilian Employees

	Unconfirmed Dead	Confirmed Dead	Possible Survivors	Demobilized	Total
ARMY					
Soldiers	5,660	467	84,381	96,472	186,980
Civilian Employees	1,908	1,084	20,674	46,758	70,424
Subtotal	7,568	1,551	105,055	143,230	257,404

	Dead				Estimate of Previously	
	Before Defeat	After Defeat	Missing	Demobilized	Demobilized	Total
NAVY						
Soldiers	242	8	54	20,843	1,152	22,299
Civilian Employees	6,260	711	117	60,539	16,856	84,483
Subtotal	7,221		171	99,390		106,782
TOTAL	16,340		105,226	242,620		364,186

Source: Compiled from Kōan Chōsachō (Public Security Investigation Agency), *Zainihon Chōsenjin no gaikyō* (Tokyo: Hōmufu Tokubetsu Shinsakyoku, 1949).

foundation of imperial rule and promote the glory of the nation." The second main tenet is: "The spirit of the military command is to unify the hearts of officers and men in sincerity and to guide them, in solidarity, toward the military's fundamental principle."[4]

As the Asia-Pacific War progressed, men mobilized from colonized Korea and Taiwan entered the Imperial Forces. The Military Preparations Section (Heibika) of the Ministry of War calculated that if Koreans and Taiwanese, who were classified as "races outside the mainland" (*gaichi minzoku*), were employed as soldiers, it would be possible to increase army manpower by 200,000 men by 1946 and that in the future 400,000 soldiers could be procured.[5]

Excluding those who entered the Military and Naval Academies as career soldiers, most ordinary Koreans began entering the Japanese military from 3 April 1938, the year after commencement of the Sino-Japanese War. The Special Volunteer Soldier System went into effect that year. *Atarashiki Chōsen* (The new Korea), compiled by the Information Department of the Government-General of Korea, described this system as follows: "The China Incident was

Table 3. Number of Korean Soldiers in the Japanese Military

	Division	Active Soldiers	First Replacement Recruits	Navy Sailors	Total
1938	Extra-ordinary	300	100	—	400
1939	Volunteer	250	350	—	600
1940	Soldiers	900	2,100	—	3,000
1941		1,000	2,000	—	3,000
1942		2,250	2,250	—	4,500
1943		3,200	2,130	—	9,223
	Student Soldiers	3,457	436	—	
Subtotal		11,357	9,366	—	20,723
1944	Conscripts	45,000	—	10,000	55,000
1945		45,000	—	10,000	55,000
Subtotal		90,000		20,000	110,000
TOTAL		101,357	9,366	20,000	130,723

Source: Compiled from "Chōbo jin'in ichiranhyō," *Chōsengun gaiyōshi* (Tokyo: Fuji Shuppan, 1989).

the storm that breathed new life into the Korea that had broken out of its old shell. This storm stirred awake the Japanese consciousness that had been sleeping deep within the hearts of our Korean brethren. It gave fire to the mutual sympathy between Mainlanders and Koreans, a sympathy destined by blood. The ardent wish arose like a surging tide: 'Insofar as we are Japanese, we hope to serve as humble shields [for the nation] as members of the glorious Imperial Forces.' In response to this earnest desire, the Law on Special Volunteer Soldiers from Korea [Chōsen Rikugun Tokubetsu Shiganheirei] went into effect on 3 April 1938, thereby commemorating the auspicious occasion of the Emperor Jimmu Festival."[6]

Rather than following their "consciousness as Japanese" in joining the Imperial Forces, the reality for most Korean voluntary soldiers was most likely that the military provided stable jobs away from their poor farming villages. Yet, the Government-General of Korea promoted the splendor of volunteer soldiers in newspapers and movies and tried to appeal to young men through a variety of techniques. For example, it claimed that soldiers received the best rations, that they were treated with special consideration at local government offices, and that the police respected them. At home, the volunteer soldiers were treated as heroes. Part of this campaign was an anecdote concerning the brave soldier, Superior Private Yi In-sŏk, that was taught in elementary schools:

> Private First Class Yi In-sŏk fought bravely to the end. Although his squad leader shouted, "Private First Class Yi In-sŏk, do not go out. It is dangerous!," he ran with his bayonet held up in order to take on the oncoming enemy. At that instant, he was unfortunately hit by hand grenade fragments and fell to the ground. Sensing the approach of his own end, when a fellow soldier took him by the hands, he recited the words, "Banzai to the emperor," and with that he became the first Volunteer Soldier from the Korean peninsula to die in battle. Later, his squad leader especially noted in his detailed report to the Government-General that, "His death was truly magnificent and, as is befitting a Volunteer Soldier, honorable."
>
> In the meantime, because this was the first such honor for the Korean peninsula, at his hometown of Okch'ŏn where the death notice was received, the county head, chief of police, and other local sympathizers all came to visit the soldier's family, despite the lateness of the hour. They arrived at the house gate, and since there had never been a case like this before, they hesitated for fear of causing grief, but finally summoned up the courage to knock on the door. Representing the group, the county head communicated their news to the family. [Yi In-sŏk's] father Yi Ch'ŏn-jŏn then calmly said, "From the day my son went to the front, I have been prepared for such a day. I am at a loss as to how to thank you for your concerned visit at such an hour." Then the soldier's wife, Yu, carrying her bereaved child of three said without a trace of grief, "I have been honorably prepared for this." The unexpected [response] left the group greatly impressed.[7]

Through such stories and the influence of the police and schoolteachers, the campaign for volunteers proved successful. The number of applicants hoping to enter the training centers for these volunteer soldiers increased and the number of volunteers grew to 84,443 in 1940.

Thus the Japanese military, which had begun its full-blown war against China, attempted to mobilize Korean men for the war effort through the Volunteer Soldier System. The volunteer soldiers were required to be at least seventeen years old and over 160 centimeters in height, and they had to complete six months of training at the Government-General's Volunteer Soldiers' Training Center before entering the military. The training period was shortened to four months in 1941. Because the minimum height for a Japanese to be considered Class A was 155 centimeters (lowered to 152 centimeters in 1942), this meant that the average Korean volunteer soldier was physically superior to his Japanese counterpart.

The Korean Education Ordinance (Chōsen Kyōikurei) was amended at about the same time that the Volunteer Soldier System went into effect. Korean-language classes were abolished and students were forced to recite the three verses of the "Oath as Subjects of the Imperial Nation," beginning with "We will unify our hearts as one and be absolutely loyal to the Emperor." Koreans were also ordered to change their names to Japanese ones. From September 1939 the first day of the month was designated the "Development of Asia Service Day," during which shrine worship and hoisting of the rising-sun flag were enforced. Through such tactics the Korean Government-General promoted the so-called Unity of the Mainland and Korea (Naisen ittai) policy and attempted to transform the Korean people into Japanese imperial subjects, both physically and spiritually.

The road to Japan's defeat began with its crushing defeat at Midway, withdrawal from Guadalcanal, the death of Admiral Yamamoto, and the debacle at Attu Island. On 20 October 1943, the Extraordinary Enlistment of Special Volunteer Soldiers Regulations (Shōwa Jūhachinendo Rikugun Tokubetsu Shiganhei Rinji Saiyō Kisoku, or War Ministry Ordinance No. 48) was promulgated in Korea and went into force. In short, its purpose was to enable the deployment of student soldiers. Of course, the special emphasis on volunteering was only euphemistic and in this sense did not differ from other "volunteer" programs.

Yet such a formalistic volunteer program broke down on 1 March 1943, when the Revision of the Military Service Law (Heiekihō Kaisei, or Law No. 4) made it possible to conscript Korean men beginning on 1 August of that year. One newspaper explained, "Due to the steadily growing desire for the Unity of the Mainland and Korea, the government has responded to our Korean brothers' sincerity by enforcing military conscription in Korea, beginning in 1944. The Cabinet decided at its meeting of the 8th, with no objections, that various preparations for conscription should begin."[8] However, according to an analysis of the War Ministry's Military Preparations Section, "When we consider the difficulties of maintaining military manpower and the related sacrifices that every race [minzoku] must make, the issue of deploying those races living outside the mainland is no longer a topic of discussion but an absolute necessity."[9] This suggests that the real purpose of extending conscription to Korea was to meet the military manpower shortage in replacement recruits and to stem the attrition of the "Yamato Race." The Government-General prepared for over a year to launch military conscription in Korea, and as a result of campaigning and mobilizing its authority, the first conscription examinations (1 April to 20 August 1944) ended "successfully," with some 94.5 percent of those eligible having been examined.

Table 1 shows the various posts to which the conscripted Koreans were sent.

In addition, the previously mentioned *China Incident: A General History of Army Mobilization during the Greater East Asia War* notes: "The distribution of Koreans into the various service branches did not differ from the distribution of common Mainlander soldiers. However, due to their educational level and technical skills, there were very few placed in technical units, and the great majority of those summoned were assigned to regular noncombatant units." It further states, "There are no units made up of only Koreans. The percentage of Koreans is set at no more than twenty percent for front line units, forty percent for rear units, and eighty percent for regular noncombatant units."[10] If these percentages reflect actual practices, there were certain units in which Koreans constituted a majority. Although a civilian employee in the armed forces, Mun T'aebok belonged to a unit made up of about 80 percent Koreans—namely, a unit stationed at a POW camp.

However, the military conscription system, a system that sought to mobilize every last Korean youth, did not produce its intended results. The volunteer soldiers had performed extremely well within the military as the result of having been well trained in the Japanese language and lifestyle. In contrast, there were some young men who entered under the conscription system who did not even know Japanese. And the poor health of the Koreans, brought on by sudden change in their everyday lives, compromised training efforts. There was little solidarity within units, many draftees deserted, and private reprisals against Koreans occurred as well. The situation was described as follows: "Those who were conscripted after September 1944 harbored primarily Korean nationalist feelings and galvanized nationalism. They created a hotbed for incidents compromising military discipline."[11]

Notwithstanding such problems, Korean recruitment into the Japanese military continued until Japan's defeat, resulting in a total of over 110,000 Koreans who supported the Japanese military effort. Furthermore, as I have already explained, according to the Ministry of Health and Welfare over 120,000 Koreans were mobilized as civilian military employees. If we also take mobilized Taiwanese into consideration, it is clear that the Japanese military was in fact a hybrid force of mainland Japanese, Koreans, and Taiwanese.

Japan's Defeat and War Trials

Japan surrendered officially on 2 September 1945. Korean soldiers surrendered as members of the Japanese military and were disarmed accordingly. At the same time, the Allied Forces treated Koreans differently from the mainland Japanese for demobilization and repatriation purposes, and decided to return them to their home country. This reasoning was based on the fact that in accepting the Potsdam Declaration, Japan had renounced its sovereignty over Korea. As *The General History of the Korean Army* notes, "With the Imperial Rescript announcing the war's end in 1945, [Korean soldiers] were no longer subject to the Japanese army and came under the jurisdiction of the Allied Forces, thus resulting in the parting of the ways of Japan and Korea."[12] Likewise, the Detailed Regulations of the Guidelines for Demobilization of the Imperial Army (Teikoku rikugun fukuin yōryō saisoku), issued by the War Ministry on 18 August, immediately after the war's end, states: "The demobilization officer instructs that until further notice soldiers who maintain their family registries in Korea will not be regarded as regular personnel of the relevant units" (Article 10).

Such policies of the Allied Forces met Korean demands. On the eve of defeat, all the discontent and anger that Koreans had until then suppressed came flooding forth, leading to incidents between Korean and Japanese soldiers, as well as resistance against Japanese senior officers everywhere. There were also numerous small-scale rebellions and desertions. Koreans formed anti-Japanese organizations. It has been said that there was a Japanese plan to shoot all Korean civilian military employees stationed at POW camps, along with the POWs under their charge. Documents verifying such an order have not yet been found, but Mun, who was stationed in Thailand, testifies to the truthfulness of this claim. At the very least it is clear that the tension between Koreans and the Japanese military was at such a high pitch that Koreans felt their lives were in serious danger.

After the war, organizations such as the Association for Korean Residents in Thailand (Zaitai Kōraijinkai) and the People's Association for Korean Residents in Indonesia (Zaijawa Chōsen Jinminkai) were formed in Bangkok and Jakarta, respectively. There were so many Koreans in Indonesia that a branch office was created in Semarang. The organizations' leaders were people like Mun, former civilian employees in the military who had been drafted to become POW prison guards. Former comfort women, student soldiers, and civilians also joined. Every morning these organizations put up the Korean flag, sang patriotic songs, studied the Korean language, and waited for the day they might return to Korea. Yet the joy of gaining independence from Japanese rule was shortlived, for one after another, Koreans who had worked at POW camps as civilian employees in the military were imprisoned as war criminal suspects. The Dutch government confined all soldiers and civilian military employees who had worked at POW camps in Indonesia. Fate continued to be against these former prison guards.

The Allied nations came to the mutual agreement that Koreans and Taiwanese should be tried as Japanese in the war trials. Why was such a special agreement made? In the Potsdam Declaration that was accepted by Japan, Article 10 states: "All war criminals, including those who abused our POWs, shall be sentenced severely." During the war, the Allied Forces had repeatedly protested the Japanese government's abuse of POWs. Through neutral countries the Ministry of Foreign Affairs received at least eighty-three such statements of protest and inquiries. Ikeda Tokushin, who worked as a shortwave interceptor in the radio room of the Ministry of Foreign Affairs, claims to have intercepted more protests than he could count.[13] The reason for the persistence of such protests was the Japanese military's real abuse of Allied POWs, which resulted in the deaths of some 27 percent of them.

Of the Japanese POW camps in the so-called Greater East Asian Co-prosperity Sphere, Koreans guarded the camps in Thailand, Malaysia, and Java, and Taiwanese guarded the camp in Borneo. Most of the POWs, who were English, Dutch, and Australian, died while laboring on the construction of airports or railways, such as the Burma-Siam Railroad. The Korean soldiers themselves did not force the POWs to work. They were responsible for seeing after the living conditions of the laboring POWs. However, food and medicine were in desperately short supply, as was clothing. Some POWs even maintained their own agricultural plots for their self-sustenance.

Incidentally, in February 1942 the Japanese military had promised the Allied countries that it would treat POWs according to the guidelines established in the Geneva Conventions. On 18 December 1941, or ten days after the bombing of Pearl Harbor, the United States requested that Japan, which had signed but not ratified the treaty, "apply" the treaty's terms. Both England and Australia made the same request. Foreign Minister Tōgō Shigenori, with the War Ministry's agreement, responded that Japan would "apply *mutatis mutandis (junyō)*" the Geneva Conventions, and the Allied countries took this to mean that Japan would act accordingly. However, the meaning of the term "apply *mutatis mutandis*" later became an important issue. On the one hand, the Allied Forces understood that Japan had agreed to follow the Geneva Convention Treaty. On the other hand, Japan was fighting a total war and did not have the resources to "respect the human dignity and honor" of its POWs, as was stipulated in the Convention. Furthermore, the Japanese military did not in general value the rights and dignity of POWs, as is indicated by the well-known phrase from the "Combatants' Code," announced by War Minister Tōjō Hideki in 1941: it firmly warned, "One must not remain alive to live the shame of a POW."[14]

Moreover, the abject condition of "white" POWs engaged in forced labor was utilized as a propaganda tool to demonstrate Asia's liberation from the long and harsh rule of Western imperialists. The severe working conditions at the construction sites along the Burma-Siam Railroad are well-known, but nearly two-thirds of the POWs building the airport on Haruku Island and almost all of the Australian POWs who marched from Sandakan to Ranau in Northern Borneo died as well. As a result, many POWs were killed.

The POW camps were commanded by officers holding the rank of general or field officer (that is, colonel, lieutenant colonel, or major). Below them were a few company officers (that is, captains and first and second lieutenants). All of these officers' positions were filled by mainland Japanese, while dozens to hundreds of Korean and Taiwanese civilian employees actually ran the camp. The percentage of Korean personnel in these POW camps reached the War Ministry's prescribed limit, as mentioned earlier, of 80 percent for noncombatant units.

Among the Allied nations there were some, such as the Netherlands, that regarded the Japanese POW camps as organized terrorist groups, imprisoned all who worked in them as possible war crimes suspects, and then relied on POWs, other internees, and local residents to expose suspects for trial. Many POWs also filed letters of accusation. The military units that worked on the railways or on airport construction moved frequently from site to site, along with the progress of their projects, so that even when there were individuals within them who had abused POWs, it was difficult to name them. In contrast, the prison guards stayed and moved along with the POWs, wherever they might be assigned. Hence, it was relatively easy to identify them.

After the war, when the POWs were in a position to prosecute those who had been responsible for atrocities, the inevitable targets of their resentment were the civilian military employees whom they had seen on a daily basis and whose names they knew. It was not a matter of concern to them whether or not orders had come from higher-ranking Japanese officials, but rather who had carried out the abuses. Among the Japanese military's war crimes, the abusive treatment of POWs was of utmost concern for the Allied countries, and for the reasons outlined above, the Korean and Taiwanese civilian employees who had served as prison guards were judged to be centrally involved in that crime.

There were twenty-three Koreans and twenty-one Taiwanese among the 984 individuals who were executed for war crimes. And of the 3,419 people sentenced to life or limited imprisonment, 125 were Korean and 147 were Taiwanese. Hence, 7.2 percent of those eventually judged to be war criminals were from countries formerly victimized by the Japanese colonial invasion. Of the 148 Koreans who received sentences (death, life or limited imprisonment), only three were soldiers. It is important to recall here that there was a total of over 110,000 Korean soldiers. Of the remaining 145 Korean war criminals, sixteen were found guilty by the Chinese government for being translators, while the others were civilian employees of the military, such as Mun, who had worked at

POW camps. Furthermore, of the 3,016 Korean men conscripted to work as prison guards, 129 were found guilty of war crimes. These numbers attest to the fact that the Allied nations judged the abuse of POWs with special severity.

It has often been noted that the war trials conducted by the Allied countries were problematic. Phrases such as "victor's justice" and "vengeance trials" perhaps best capture the gist of such criticisms. Yet the important question of why the Allied Forces ignored the issue of Japanese colonialism remains unanswered. The Allied nations presumably did not take up the issue of Japanese colonialism during the International Military Tribunal for the Far East (the Tokyo War Crimes Trial), or at the regional B- and C-Class trials because some of them continued to possess their own colonies and therefore preferred to avoid the subject altogether. Far from interrogating colonialism, they indiscriminately prosecuted as Japanese those from formerly colonized countries. Korean war criminals thus resulted from doubly problematic conditions: namely, the Japanese military policy of deploying young men from colonized countries to guard the POWs, and the Allied Powers' evasion of the colonial issue. The same could be said about the 173 Taiwanese war criminals.

Punished as Japanese, Excluded from Relief as Foreigners

Korean war criminals were executed at the Changi prison in Singapore (ten executions) and the Cipinang prison in Jakarta (four executions). Koreans with life sentences or limited prison terms had been sent to Sugamo prison in Tokyo before the San Francisco Peace Treaty went into effect. Once the Peace Treaty became effective and Japan regained its sovereignty, the Japanese government kept all A- as well as B- and C-Class criminals in its custody, including those who were Korean and Taiwanese. This policy was based on Article 11 of the Peace Treaty, which required the Japanese government to be responsible for enforcing the war crimes sentences.

The warden of Sugamo prison at that time has written that Japanese war criminals had difficulty understanding why they were being detained by their own government. These prisoners became increasingly distressed and an air of desperation ruled the prison. If such was the condition of Japanese war criminals, Korean war criminals must have been in even deeper despair, for they remained in jail despite being stripped of their status as Japanese nationals. Not only did they have no relatives in Japan who might visit and comfort them; their fellow countrymen disdained them as traitors. They were tormented with self-reproach. When the Korean War broke they were greatly concerned about their families but were helpless to do anything and their frustration mounted. Their sense of isolation only grew deeper.

On 14 June 1952 Mun and a number of others, with the assistance of Japanese lawyers, brought a request for their release to court based on the Protection of Personal Liberty Act (Jinshin Hogohō). But on 9 July the Supreme Court rejected their release requests. The court ruled that insofar as Mun and others were Japanese at the time of their sentencing, and insofar as they were detained until the Peace Treaty went into effect, "Japan's obligation to carry out the sentences shall not be affected by a loss or change of their nationality thereafter." Thus their sentences remained valid.

However, while they served their sentences, Mun and the others were excluded from the list of those eligible for government benefits on the grounds that they were no longer Japanese nationals. The Japanese war criminals who were being detained in the same prisons began to receive government benefits, but Mun and other Koreans did not. The Relief Act for the War Injured and Diseased, and for War Bereaved Families and Others (Senshōbyōsha Senbotsusha Izokutō Engohō) that was promulgated on 30 April 1952 and applied retroactively to 1 April, states in the second section of its bylaws: "Those to whom the Family Registration Act (Kosekihō) [of 1947] does not apply shall not come under the provision of this law, for the time being." This effectively excluded Koreans and Taiwanese, including all former civilian military employees and volunteer soldiers who had suffered injuries. This and other laws providing governmental relief to war victims excluded formerly colonial subjects on the grounds of their nationality.

Even in the event that they received provisional releases from prison, Korean war criminals had nowhere to go. They had no jobs and no acquaintances. Because provisional releases restricted where they could reside, they could not return to their homeland. Furthermore, the travel allowance given to prisoners released from Sugamo was not even sufficient for travel beyond Tokyo. To stay in prison was hell, but to come out was also hell. Worse yet, starvation immediately awaited those who were released. Life outside Sugamo prison presented very clear and immediate difficulties. As a result, many refused release from prison, organized sit-in strikes, sent letters of request to the Japanese government, and continued demonstrations before the Diet building. These movements did win "consolation money" from the government equaling the amount paid to Japanese war criminals.

Nevertheless, there has been no drastic reform of the system of laws providing for government relief that has excluded individuals on the basis of nationality. Occasionally the Japanese government has gone through the motions of making efforts, but with little effect. Since the establishment of the 1965 Republic of Korea–Japan Basic Treaty, the Japanese government has refused any further negotiations, claiming that all reparations issues between the Japanese and South Korean governments have been resolved by the treaty. There were North Korean nationals among the war criminals, but the Japanese government has also ignored this difference. To this day, the Japanese government has not paid any compensation nor apologized to those formerly colonized people who have been branded as war criminals and who are held in public contempt for having been "pro-Japanese" traitors.

While Allied policy led to the separation of Korean from Japanese soldiers and repatriation to their country of origin, this also meant that the Japanese government took no responsibility for the demobilization and repatriation of soldiers and civilian military employees from formerly colonized countries. When the Japanese government renounced its colonial rights through acceptance of the Potsdam Declaration, it also abandoned its responsibility to settle issues related to the wartime mobilization of people from the colonies. Thus, while erasing memories of colonialism, the Japanese government launched the postwar era without experiencing the pain or sense of loss that should have accompanied postcolonial normalization and reparations.

Because, in the confusion of the war's aftermath, Korean soldiers were returned directly to their homeland from occupied territories, their wages and other types of military savings remained unpaid. In 1950, the government initiated the payment process by issuing the Ordinance Concerning Special Provisions for Deposits to Pay Liabilities Owed to Foreigners Residing Abroad (Kokugai Kyojū Gaikokujintō ni taisuru Saimu no Benzai no tameni suru Kyōtaku no Tokurei ni kansuru Seirei). Fukuoka prefecture and the Kure Demobilization Department were respectively appointed to settle the Army's and Navy's debts.

Yet it was in fact impossible for those in North Korea, South Korea, and Taiwan to request payment because at that time these countries had no official diplomatic relations with Japan. During the years 1951–1954, these payments were deposited at the Ministry of Justice with the understanding that they would be held there until the establishment of official agreements between Japan and these countries. With respect to South Korea, an agreement in the ROK–Japan Basic Treaty that came into effect in January 1966 deemed all matters regarding claims for various payments to be settled. With this, the issue of wage and savings payments to repatriated Korean soldiers was transferred to the Korean government under the Law Guaranteeing the Rights of Private Claims against Japan (Taeil Min'gwan Ch'ŏnggukwŏn Posangbŏp).

How, then, did the laws treat former Korean soldiers who remained in Japan? During the Allied Occupation of Japan, all payments of military pensions and cash benefits related to repatriation were prohibited, regardless of whether they were to go to Japanese or Koreans. Yet when the Occupation ended with the signing of the San Francisco Peace Treaty, the nationality-based practice of differential treatment emerged. As mentioned earlier, Koreans came to be excluded legally from governmental compensation after Japan's independence. Despite the fact that they were recruited as Japanese, Korean soldiers, civilian military employees, and their families, like Mun and other war criminals of Korean origin, were excluded from various governmental relief programs simply because they were no longer Japanese nationals.

The Unfinished War

In 1991 Chŏng Sang-gŭn filed a suit requesting application of the Governmental Relief Law. He had been conscripted and wounded while serving as a civilian employee of the Navy at Wotje Island in the Marshall Islands. Subsequently, several other suits were filed, including one in November 1991 by the Association for the Mutual Advancement of Korean War Criminals, after over thirty years of activism against an unyielding Japanese government.

However, the Japanese government has consistently taken only minimal steps to deal with this situation. It has applied special measures to individual cases while demanding naturalization, rather than changing the nationality clause. The government has not dealt with the central problem: namely, that Korean soldiers and civilian military employees are categorically excluded from the Governmental Relief Law. Koreans were mobilized for the Japanese war effort as soldiers, sailors, civilian military employees, and military laborers. It would seem only natural that they be compensated in the same way as are Japanese. Yet the Japanese government only reiterates the Japanese nationality requirement. It is also worth noting that Mun and other Koreans did not relinquish their Japanese nationality by choice. Instead, they were unilaterally stripped of it through a single notification from the Japanese government. If the Japanese government today regards these individuals as foreigners, then the morally appropriate action would be to compensate them with all due speed for the pains inflicted by colonizing them and for treating them as "Japanese" in the past. These former "Imperial soldiers" suffered from the Japanese government's pursuit of self-interest; today they struggle to receive compensation from the same government. For those from formerly colonized nations who served as soldiers, sailors, and civilian military employees, the Asia-Pacific Wars are not over.

Addendum

On 13 July 1998, the Tokyo High Court dismissed the November 1991 suit mentioned above, which had been led by Mun T'ae-bok. The plaintiffs were seeking "symbolic monetary compensation" and an apology from the Japanese government. While Chief Justice Ishii Kengo suggested that they had been "disadvantaged" (furieki) in comparison to Japanese and Taiwanese (the latter have received some consolation money) in similar circumstances, he reasoned that the problem requires a legislative solution and rejected their claims. At the same time, he urged the Diet to address this issue.[15] In the seven years since the suit was originally filed, Mun and another former Korean civilian military employee among the plaintiffs has died.[16] As of March 2000, the Liberal Democratic Party was planning to submit bills to the Diet giving limited monetary compensation to non-Japanese former military and civilian personnel in the Japanese military, or their respective bereaved families.[17]

Notes

This is an excerpt from the final chapter of *Chōsenjin "kōgun" heishitachi no sensō* (Korean "imperial" soldiers' wars), *Iwanami bukkuretto, no. 266, Shōgen Shōwashi no danmen* (Tokyo: Iwanami Shoten, 1991), 38–61. The editors wish to thank the author and Iwanami Shoten for permitting us to translate this piece with some minor modifications. Because the original publication was written for a general readership, the author sometimes omits corroborating documentation. Readers interested in further documentation of sources, particularly for the last three sections of this translation, should consult Utsumi's pioneering work, *Chōsenjin BCkyū senpan no kiroku* (A record of Korean B and C class war criminals) (Tokyo: Keisō Shobō, 1982).

1 For more details, see Utsumi Aiko and Murai Yoshinori, *Sekidōka no Chōsenjin hanran* (Korean uprising on the equator) (Tokyo: Keisō Shobō, 1980).

2 Kōan Chōsachō (Public Security Investigation Agency), *Zainihon Chōsenjin no gaikyō* (General Situation of Koreans in Japan) (Tokyo: Hōmufu Tokubetsu Shinsakyoku, 1949), 23.

3 *Chōsengun gaiyōshi* (General history of the Korean Army), (reprinted, Tokyo: Fuji Shuppan, 1989). "Active soldiers" (*gen'ekihei*) refers to those who passed the military examination (the minimum age requirement was originally twenty, but was lowered to nineteen in December 1943) and were inducted into the military. The term of service was two years for the Army and three years for the Navy. In any given year there might be more active soldiers than required and, though still technically active soldiers, the excess were classified as replacement recruits.

It should be noted that the Korean, Guandong, and Taiwan armies were the three Japanese armies based outside of Japan proper, and that their names do not necessarily indicate their racial or ethnic composition.

4 Ōhama Tetsuya and Ozawa Ikurō, eds., *Teikoku rikukaigun jiten* (Encyclopedia for the Imperial Army and Navy), (Tokyo: Dōseisha, 1984), ii.

5 Rikugunshō Heibika, *Daitōa sensō ni tomonau waga jinteki kokuryoku no kentō* (A consideration of our national manpower strength pursuant to the Greater East Asia War), 20 January 1942.

6 Chōsen Sōtokufu Jōhōkyoku, *Atarashiki Chōsen* (The new Korea) (reprinted, Tokyo: Fūtōsha, 1982), 47.

7 Ibid., 48–50.

8 *Asahi shinbun*, 10 May 1942.

9 Rikugunshō, *Daitōa sensō ni tomonau waga jinteki kokuryoku no kentō.*

10 Rikugunshō Sanbō Honbu Hensei Dōinka, *Shinajihen: Daitōa sensōkan rikugun dōin gaikyō* (The China incident: A general history of army mobilization during the Greater East Asia War) (reprinted, Tokyo: Fuji Shuppan, 1988), 436.

11 Ibid., 437.

12 *Chōsengun gaiyōshi*, 81.

13 Personal interview, June 1982.

14 Ōhama and Ozawa, *Teikoku rikukaigun jiten*, 11.

15 *Asahi shinbun*, 14 July 1998.

16 *Asahi shinbun*, 11 July 1998.

17 *Asahi shinbun*, 23 March 2000.

Memory Suppression and Memory Production:

The Japanese Occupation of Singapore

DIANA WONG

To talk of this inheritance, to refer to history, as to refer to translation or memory, is always to speak of the incomplete, the never fully decipherable.
—Iain Chambers, *Migrancy, Culture, Identity*

The year 1995 was of a thousand and one different commemorative ceremonies and memorial statements about the end of the Second World War and its role in the shaping of national and regional destiny in Europe. May 1995 in Europe was dominated by the talk-fest on the war in which "Europe attained a victory over itself" (Mitterand), and similarly, August 1995 would seem to have provided a parallel temporal setting for extensive public commemoration of the historical watershed that the Pacific War represents for Asia.

A more attentive scrutiny of public calendars of events in the Asia-Pacific region, however, reveals subtle—and not so subtle—differences in the way the *Pacific* War was remembered. Indeed, it might even seem as if in Southeast Asia, the war was hardly remembered at all. Certainly, there was nothing to parallel the impressive array of supranational and national ceremonies of commemoration, enacted by the very highest organs and personalities of state, which marked the fiftieth anniversary of the end of the war in Europe, and the impact this had on the private and popular memories of the generation that lived through the war.

Indeed, as Anthony Reid observed in his paper "Remembering and Forgetting the War in Indonesia," there is a puzzling discrepancy between what is known to be the profound sea change that the Japanese era represents in the history of Southeast Asia, and the absence of public commemoration of this fact.[1] Reid contrasts this relation between public memory and social reality to that prevailing in Australia, where the war could not be said to have left an indelible mark, but where there have been tireless rituals of commemorations performed since the fiftieth anniversary of the beginning of the war.

Reid attributes the commemoration frenzy to the impending transformation of memory into history, this being the historical juncture at which the generation of war veterans have a final opportunity to relive their collective past and impart the lessons of their shared experience to the generation for whom all that would be history. It could also be argued that Australia's fascination with the war has to do with the ease with which wars enter the collective imagination and can be shaped into a master narrative of national awakening and identity.[2] This, of course, begs the question of why the historical experience of the veterans of World War II in Southeast Asia has not been fashioned into a historiography of shared national destiny.

The countries involved in the Pacific theater of war, such as the Solomon Islands,[3] present yet another contrast. Here, the fanfare of remembrance resounded with a pomp and ceremony that matched and, in fact, echoed that in the Western capitals of London, Paris, Frankfurt, and Washington. The memory reproduced and represented, however, was cast in the "transnational" text of "loyalty and liberation," against which the dissonant and contending local text of "colonial struggle" was pushed "into full retreat."[4] In the year of global celebration and representation of war memory, local Solomon Island productions of national identity hewn from the collective experience of war remained ineluctably staged by "transnational memory-making."[5] National subjects "colluded" with the "powerful global forces of meaning" to have their official memory scripted for them.[6]

One exception to the pattern of official indifference to, or transnational appropriation of, war memory has been the city-state of Singapore, a key site in the symbolic topography of the Pacific War. As a British colony, Singapore's political identity was inextricably woven into that of British Malaya, and subsequently the independent Federation of Malaysia, until its attainment of full independent political status through its separation from Malaysia in 1965. Whereas Malaysia continued to maintain a distanced silence on the war, with commemorative ceremonies organized by foreign war veterans and their families remaining essentially foreign rituals on local sites, the city-state of Singapore mounted an elaborate program of commemoration, clearly distinct from the commemorative events organized by foreign veteran groups, to etch the collective experience of war into public memory and to derive from this memory production a grand narrative of national beginning and destiny.

The management of the past through the politics of remembering and forgetting in national identity projects has been the subject of much recent academic debate.[7] In this paper, I trace the various attempts by the colonial and postcolonial state in Malaya and Singapore to control memory production and memory suppression with regard to the Japanese Occupation of 1941–1945. Of particular interest is the reinsertion of war memory into public discourse and its place in the national identity project in Singapore.

The Politics of Memory as a Japanese Colonial Practice

As a technique of power, the politics of memory, I would assert, *began* with the conquest of Singapore, the heart of Britain's great trading empire and, in the war of words that preceded the actual fighting, her much-vaunted "impregnable fortress" in the East. Within two days of the triumphal Japanese entry into Singapore, the city was renamed Syonan (Shōnan) "Light of the South." Indeed, the entire mental roadmap of the British colonial city was to be subject to systematic and comprehensive renaming. All traffic signs were reinscribed in the Japanese script. Public buildings such as hospitals and cinema halls, which were sites of mass gatherings as well as points of orientation in the city, were renamed. Businesses had to change the familiar Anglo-Saxon terminology of "company" and "brothers" into Japanese and display their new names accordingly. Monuments erected in memory of the British imperial order, such as the statue of Sir Stamford Raffles, the founder of Singapore, were removed from the public eye, to be replaced by massive and impressive monuments to the new colonial order. The Syonan (Shōnan) Jinja, the memorial dedicated to the Japanese soldiers who died in the Battle for Singapore, was officially unveiled in time for the first anniversary celebration of the fall of Singapore. As repeatedly mentioned in the press, "no traces" of the old Kuala Lumpur or Penang or Singapore, the big cities of the former colony, were to be recognizable in the "New Order." As a contemporary newspaper account noted: "People with no knowledge of Nippon-go, in trying to find their bearings in town, are daily made to realize that they are behind the times, and that they may find themselves contravening regulations as a result of their ignorance."[8]

The Japanese effacement of place-identity was accompanied by the introduction of a new time. In Syonan, the clocks moved forward one and a half hours to follow Tokyo time, and the year 1942 became 2602, the seventeenth year of Shōwa according to the victor's calendar. A new calendar of festivities and commemoration was introduced, beginning with the elaborate celebration of the emperor's birthday on 29 April 1942.[9] This occasion, which always involved a mass gathering of civil servants and schoolchildren in a ceremony that included the reverential bowing to the east, in the direction of the emperor's palace, remained the highlight of the new calendar of festivities. Similar celebrations were held to commemorate the birthday of the Emperor Meiji and the enthronement of Emperor Jimmu, the legendary first emperor of the Japanese people.[10]

Significantly, the calendar of commemorations also highlighted the *local* experience of the war, with "two special days of commemoration for people [*sic*] of Syonan and Malaya:"[11] one was the day Japan declared war against the Allied Powers (8 December) and the other when the British surrendered to the Japanese Army in Singapore (15 February):

> On the former day, with a solemn ceremony, the Gunseikanbu held a big celebration for the commencement of the *Daitōa* [Greater East Asia] War. Newspapers printed statements of military commanders, gunseikan, governors and mayors, sultans and local leaders, each stressing the significance of the war for the liberation of Asia. Also during the ceremony a Japanese official would recite the Imperial Rescript of the Declaration of War reminding people of the *Daitoa* War as a holy war for the establishment of the *Daitōa Kyōeiken* [Greater East Asia Co-Prosperity Sphere]. Reading of the Rescript was regularly observed on the eighth day of every month at schools and offices, as it was done in Japan. Also the fourth day of the month was designated as the day for hosting the *hinomaru* [rising sun flag].[12]

On 15 February 1943, marking the first anniversary of the transformation of Singapore to Syonan-to and the "Rebirth of Malai," a week-long program of activities was instituted, which included the official dedication of the Syonan Jinja, the Japanese memorial at Bukit Batok, a mass drill performed by schoolchildren and government servants, and an athletics rally. In addition, free films (*Light of Asia* and *Battle for Malai*) were screened for the public. Every subsequent 15 February was the occasion for massive celebrations in which "local residents of Syonan and Malaya were reminded by dignitaries of the Japanese military government and local communities of the significance of the day as the occasion for liberation from the yoke of British colonial rule and were urged to rid themselves of vestiges of the Western way of life."[13] The basic vocabulary of all the public ceremonies, which followed a yearly, monthly, and daily rhythm, comprised a mass congregation bowing in the direction of the east, singing in chorus, and engaging in mass light exercise to the accompaniment of catchy music. No one, not even the sultans, were exempted from participation at these civic ceremonies.

Reference has been made in the literature to the impact of the habit of physical violence that characterized the experience of war and Japanese military rule, in contrast to the relative civility of Western colonial domination.[14] Yet the force of the *symbolic* violence expended under Japanese rule is equally noteworthy. The politics of memory it pursued was unrelentingly absolute: all traces of the British past were to be erased from the Japanese present. This radical *renaming* and *retiming* of private and public life was meant to erase the memory of Western colonial rule. Its efficacy is not to be underestimated. The population, stunned by the rapidity of a totally unexpected defeat of the British forces, had no reason to believe in their equally rapid return. Indeed, the spectacular demonstration of Japanese military prowess was underlined by the resolute brutality with which "law and order" was restored in the postinvasion chaos.

In a world "turned upside down,"[15] new spatial and temporal markers of reality possessed remarkable powers of persuasion. Private memories of this past were to lose their spatial and temporal moorings. They were to be submerged in the creation of a hitherto unknown *public* memory. The practice of *commemorations*, through which a public time and a public space are constituted and narrational identity established, was an innovative and constitutive feature of Japanese rule. Once introduced, no subsequent government could afford to do without it.

Contesting Narratives of War

From this vantage point, Reid's observation becomes even more startling. The politics of memory conducted by the Japanese colonial administration appears to have been singularly ineffective. Hardly any traces of the Japanese Occupation can be detected in postwar Malayan public memory or, until very recently, in that of the city-state island of Singapore. The war has not been memorialized; indeed, it would seem that its memory has been deliberately silenced.

During the three years of Japanese rule, 15 February, the day on which the British surrendered Singapore to the Japanese, was inscribed into public memory through lavish commemorative celebrations. An incipient, hitherto nonexistent public memory was built around the way the war began: the narrative of the humiliating rout of the British and the glorious liberation of "Asiatics" from "White" domination. The immediate postwar period in Malaya, however, as T. H. Silcock and Ungku Abdul Aziz note, "can only be understood in terms of the way the war ended."[16]

A triumphant British reconquest of the terrain with the help of communist guerrillas partially trained and armed by the British was to have provided the script for the "liberation" of the country from the cruelties of the Japanese Occupation, as well as the punishment of those who had collaborated with them. The atomic bombs over Hiroshima and Nagasaki, however, which led to the Japanese surrender on 15 August 1945, preempted these plans. Three weeks passed before the British actually landed on the Malay peninsula to accept the official

Japanese surrender in Singapore. The arches of triumph that were erected in the meantime to welcome the "liberators" were meant for those who emerged from the jungle: the guerrillas of the Malayan Communist Party, whose script was that of "colonial struggle."[17]

The memory of war can be narrativised, according to Geoffrey White, as a (transnational) text of *liberation* or as a (local) text of *colonial struggle*. The theme of liberation "depicts World War II . . . as an episode of Japanese invasion and Allied counterinvasion in which harsh, exploitative Japanese occupiers are ousted by American forces working in concert with British and other Allied military. In this context, Solomon Islanders play the role of selfless supporters who put themselves at risk by assisting the Allied war effort as scouts and laborers"[18] Against this *empire-centered* narrative of the loyal native, however, clearly authored by the entrenched colonial authority, was to be found another narrative of liberation, a *nation-centered* one of "colonial (or better, anti-colonial) struggle." This was a script appropriated by several different authors, foremost among whom were the Japanese themselves. Japan was the "Light of Asia," which had unsheathed her sword of righteousness to conduct a Greater East Asian War to liberate Asia from the White colonial yoke. This narrative of Asian liberation from the predatory fangs of Western colonialism constituted an ideological offensive conducted with the same degree of systematic planning and comprehensiveness that had characterized the military conquest of the country. General Yamashita's address to the frightened population as the new master of Syonan called on "the Malayan people to understand the real intention of Nippon and to co-operate with the Nippon Army towards the prompt establishment of the New Order and the Co-Prosperity Sphere." This message was amplified throughout the length and breadth of the country by a group of 150 intellectuals (*bunkajin*) assigned to the 25th Army. According to Yoji Akashi, these men, the first group of whom arrived in Syonan on 17 February 1942, two days after the conquest of Singapore, and the second group a month later, "truly represented the best minds of the day."[19] They crafted a narrative of liberation that did not fail to impress.

Under the colonial regime that had prevailed until the invasion, various Malay royal houses were the nominal rulers of the country. In the wake of the Japanese advance at the beginning of the war, plans for the British retreat called for the inclusion of local royalty. Tungku Abdul Rahman, a politician of royal birth who led the country a decade after the end of the war to independence, "kidnapped" his father, the then sultan, to prevent his "flight" and worked as a district officer under the Japanese administration. Indeed, the local Malay elite, who had been cultivated by the British as the rightful heirs of the country and had been provided limited access to the junior ranks of the colonial administration, as well as the Malay peasantry, responded avidly to the recruitment opportunities into all ranks of the administration, including that of the police and the volunteer army, proffered by the Japanese military.[20] Apart from the evident willingness to serve the new administration, there was some evidence of Malay support for the invading Japanese 25th Army. The left-wing nationalist group of young Malay radicals, the Kesatuan Melayu Muda (KMM), inspired by the Indonesian nationalist movement and dedicated to the attainment of independence through a Greater Indonesia or Melayu Raya, provided intelligence and manpower support to the Japanese intelligence organization, the F Kikan.[21] In short, *the native was not loyal*. This fact caused considerable distress to the forces of colonial restoration. As Naoki Sakai has noted, colonial confidence rests on the presumption of native "love" and colonial administration on native loyalty.[22]

Formed in 1937, the KMM had scripted a narrative of Malayan independence and nationhood (in the larger context of Melayu Raya) even before the landing of Japanese troops on 8 December 1941. A parallel text of liberation was drafted with the establishment of the Indian National Army (INA) in Farrer Park in Singapore on the occasion of the official transfer of the troops of the defeated British Indian Army (estimated at 50,000 men) to the Japanese Army on 17 February 1942, two days after the fall of Singapore. The speech made by Fujiwara, head of the intelligence agency responsible for the collaboration with non-Japanese forces and official representative of the Japanese Army on this occasion, highlighted the theme of Asian liberation. In his memoirs, he writes of this "historic moment": "When I told them of my conviction that the fall of Singapore would provide a historic opportunity for Asian peoples who had suffered under the yoke of British and Dutch colonialism to liberate themselves from bondage, they went into a frenzy. The Park reverberated with such echoes of applause and shouts of joy, that I had to stop my speech until the tumultuous commotion subsided."[23]

For the Indians of Malaya, this act transformed them from "being depressed and uninterested inhabitants of a political backwater . . . [to being] in their own estimation at least, the spearhead of a movement to liberate India."[24] The INA became the military arm of the Indian Independence League, which had been formed in Bangkok in 1941 and which, under the charismatic leadership of Subha Chandra Bose, formed the nucleus of the first Provisional Government of Free India, established in Singapore in October 1943. The bulk of the INA troops comprised deserters from the British Indian Army, although local recruitment occurred through the Indian Independence League branches that were set up in every major town in Malaya. The *Chalo Delhi* (On to Delhi) campaign, supported by massive donations from a community galvanized by the stirring rhetoric of Subha Chandra Bose, culminated in the Battle of Imphal, a mountain pass on the Burmese border to India, where the INA and Japanese troops were defeated in the summer of 1944.[25]

The Malayan Communist Party (MCP) also authored a narrative, which included the twin themes of liberation and colonial struggle, liberation namely from the cruelties of Japanese rule as part of the wider colonial struggle against all forms of foreign domination. Formed on 30 April 1930 in Kuala Pilah,[26] the MCP, even before the outbreak of the war, had called for the establishment of a Malayan People's Republic in its underground propaganda directed against the British.[27] The nucleus of the Malayan People's Anti-Japanese Army (MPAJA), its armed unit, was hastily constituted in early 1942, during the last days of the Japanese invasion, and provided the invading Japanese troops with some of the fiercest resistance it met on its swift sweep down the peninsula.[28] By the end of 1942, eight regiments had been set up, with a full strength of about five thousand combatants by the end of the war in 1945. Throughout the Occupation, it was primarily the guerrillas of the MPAJA who provided armed resistance to the Japanese military and who were to be the partners of the reinvasion army being assembled by the Allied Southeast Asia Command under the leadership of Lord Mountbatten.[29] With the Japanese surrender, arches and banners erected in the large and small towns of the country welcomed the liberators as the men and women of the MPAJA, who emerged from their jungle camps to claim victory over the Japanese. In the three weeks that passed before the British troops returned to reclaim authority over the colony, these guerrillas of the resistance wreaked their own revenge on perceived "collaborators" with the Japanese, among whom were those for whom the Japanese "Occupation" had represented a historical opportunity to craft other narratives of liberation, including the KMM and the Indian Independence League.

Against these multiple scripts of national liberation, the end of the war and the reoccupation of the country by the old colonial power was to be cast as a reconquest and a liberation. The script called for "a campaign in Malaya itself, with British troops landing on the coasts, and supported by guerillas armed and trained to attack from the jungle."[30] The war ended, however, in Japan, which was beaten into submission by the awesome power of the two atomic bombs delivered by American bombers. With the silent surrender and retreat of the remaining Japanese troops into their barracks, it took less time for the guerrillas to emerge from the jungle and be received by the local population as heroes than for the British Army, fighting their way down from Burma, to reach the local shores. The official surrender of the Japanese forces to the Supreme Allied Commander of the Southeast Asia Command, Lord Mountbatten, was staged in Singapore on 12 September, almost a month after the war ended.

British troops returned to a "demoralized" country that it proceeded to demoralize further: "Their corruption, illegal commandeering of property, gun-play against unarmed civilians, and sale of arms to gangsters, undermined in six months a tradition that had taken a century to build. . . . The army of 1945 was the victim of circumstances no less than the army of 1942. But those who understand the roots of British prestige in Malaya appreciate that it was 1945 at least as much as 1942 that undermined the confidence of the public."[31] Under these circumstances, the only conceivable transnational text, the empire-centered narrative of liberation—featuring the heroism of the returning White soldiers and the loyalty of the natives who remained to welcome their masters—was not available for persuasive appropriation. It was not for want of trying. The first official message to the "people of Singapore" by the commander of the land forces upon his belated arrival in Singapore proclaimed the theme of liberation with fanfare:

> On the 12th February 1942, Lord Moyne, Secretary of State for the Colonies, broadcasting to you, said: "I want to send this message to the people of Malaya, Malays, Chinese and British in this hour of stern ordeal. A savage attack has shattered the peace which you have enjoyed for many genera-tions, and has destroyed the fruits of your industry; but there is ranged on our side the whole might of the British Empire and her powerful Allies. Such a struggle must end in our final victory. In spite of grievous reverses we shall break the enemy's power and restore to you your freedom of life." We have returned to make good that promise, and in the name of the Supreme Allied Commander I send you greetings in this hour of your delivery.[32]

The natives, however, had lived through halcyon times and had drawn their own conclusions. In her memoirs, published in 1990, Aisha Akbhar, a Malay woman who was a young teenager when the war broke out, formulated her conclusions thus:

> We were certainly glad that the British had returned to liberate us from the Japanese, but we placed very little weight on their promise to protect us in future. In the past, the British had told us how well defended we were, assuring us that we had no reason to be afraid and then quite suddenly it was all over. The Japanese had taken Singapore with hardly a fight. We felt let down and realized that our gods had feet of clay.
>
> To make matters worse, the only British personnel we saw after the war were the soldiers who acted as poor ambassadors for Britain. We watched the uncouth behavior of the British soldiers with horror. They were often drunk and disorderly, consorting openly with women of the streets. We

were embarrassed for them when they were hauled away by the military police and bundled into trucks and jeeps. They flaunted their bad manners before the shocked eyes of the Asian population, and we winced at the filthy language we heard. Even to us, the new generation of Singaporeans, it was clear that these soldiers did not belong to the same world as their pre-war countrymen. Gone were the charm and dignity we had been taught to expect; the picture of the English gentleman had been shattered."[33]

For their part, the prewar "English gentlemen" who served in the Malayan outpost of the transnational British Empire and who reemerged from three and a half years of impotent captivity to reassume responsibility for the ideological defenses of empire felt plagued by a sense of shame and guilt. Silcock, himself in captivity during the Occupation, captured the mood of the "liberators" as "one of shame for the debacle of 1942, accentuated by the fact that many senior civil servants returning from prison camps had seen nothing of the subsequent course of the war. This feeling was aggravated by a sense of disappointment that events had robbed the British Army of the chance to wipe out the score by a victorious campaign in Malaya."[34] Silcock and Aziz noted further the unsustainability of the preferred text of loyalty: "When, in 1946, a group of ex-internees, in publicly thanking and rewarding a Chinese who had signally helped them in Singapore, referred to his "loyalty," the expression provoked widespread hostility among the Chinese. They felt (no doubt wrongly) that a deliberate attempt was being made to make political capital out of an act of friendship and comradeship against the enemy."[35]

The vocabulary of liberation and nationhood introduced by the Japanese, the KMM, the Indian Independence League, and the MCP, which had seared itself into the popular memory of the war, had undermined the use of this older colonial vocabulary. By the same token, the nation-centered narrative of colonial struggle, which bore the imprint of Japanese and communist thought, was not acceptable to the forces of colonial restoration. What was also no longer sustainable, however, was not to engage in the fabrication of a public text on nationhood at all. The Japanese fostering of public memory and its attendant practices had to be countered.

Given the unsustainability of these two texts, the memory of the war—the memory of British defeat, of "native" disloyalty, as well as of communist resistance—had to be suppressed. The text that came to be adopted was a variation of the "White man's burden": "The propaganda that Britain had defaulted and should return to Malaya in the role of penitent was spread not by Malays but by Englishmen. . . . A sense of loss of prestige presented itself in the more attractive moral guise of an obligation still unfulfilled. But the direction of this obligation was a result of less creditable motives. Feelings were directed toward the Malays, and the Malay sultans in particular, rather than to all the people who had suffered as a result of the loss of Malaya."[36] This memory of the war—namely, "our failure to defend Malaya"[37]—had to be disavowed. The new war that erupted in 1948, the war fought against the communist guerrillas who had emerged from the jungle to claim the fruits of victory over the Japanese and who were now to be forced to return to the jungle from whence they had come, was useful in this respect.[38]

From 1948 to 1956, Malaya became the stage for a second war out of which a British hero emerged: General Templer, the resolute soldier who defeated the guerrillas at their own game. The commanding officer of the Japanese 25th Army, General Yamashita, who had renamed Singapore Syonan-to after its conquest in less than ten weeks, had acquired the adulatory title of the "Tiger of Malaya." It is telling that the authorized biography of General Templer, who was commanding officer of the British troops fighting against the communist insurgency in the country barely five years after General Yamashita was executed as a war criminal, carried the title "Templer, Tiger of Malaya."[39] Notwithstanding the obvious parallel being drawn here to the war waged by the Japanese, I suggest that it was primarily in the ferocity of its *ideological* offensive that this second "jungle war" was comparable to the first. Silcock wrote in 1952, close to the height of the Emergency:

> It is important, especially in view of current attitudes to the emergency, not to exaggerate the heat. Taking Malaya as a whole the danger to a civilian of being killed by a terrorist is hardly significantly greater than the danger of being killed in a road accident. Without details of the numbers subject to risk it is not possible to give an accurate picture of the danger to troops and police, but it is certainly low by any war-time standard, and probably comparable to the hazards of training with live ammunition. "Jungle-bashing" is arduous and unrewarding, and certainly merits being called active service; but I am doubtful whether it is truthful, and even more doubtful whether it is wise, to call it war, except in the sense in which the cold war is war.[40]

Fought ostensibly as a war against a communist takeover of the country, the subtext made a definite identification of the communists with the Chinese. The remnants of the MPAJA, which had borne the brunt of the resistance against the Japanese, became the thinly veiled Chinese "terrorists" of the "Emergency," against whom the interests of the Malays had to be protected. Disavowal was achieved through replay: the forces of liberation and colonial struggle were reinscribed as terrorists from whom the country required deliverance, provided by the superior colonial forces with the help of the loyal natives. A character in *Jungle Green*, a novel about the Emergency that was described by General Templer as "authentic" and officially distributed to the forces in the field, enunciated the "British credo"[41] thus: " 'It seems to me,' he said, 'that either you are a Christian or you are not a Christian, and, whether you like it or not we are. . . . I'll admit it's not our country, but all these niggers who live here look to us to see that the place is decently run. . . . We've got to send these Chinks back to where they came from.' "[42]

This race-centered subtext of the Emergency framed the reading of the Japanese Occupation, to which a direct line of causality was drawn. The predominantly Chinese communist guerrillas, who had fought against the Japanese, were now fighting the Malays and the British. The Japanese Occupation had generated an unfortunate interracial hatred hitherto unknown in this happy country. The war as an anomaly, as an unfortunate hindrance to nationhood because of the communal tensions it incited, became the dominant public narrative of the Japanese Occupation.

The compelling vocabulary of nationhood forged during the war was deployed in the main text of the Emergency as the need to create a Malayan nation to which colonial power could be devolved. In the restorationist narrative that the main text of the Emergency represented, the vocabulary of colonial struggle was replaced by that of colonial *succession*. As noted by Silcock: "People in Malaya . . . know that the Japanese Occupation marked a break in Asia, just as the rising power of the United States has modified the attitude of Europe to Asia as a whole. Yet the Governments in Malaya usually do their best to pretend that our policy remains a continuous whole."[43] Postwar colonial policy had indeed changed, as had postwar colonial discourse. Yet the narrative of nationhood in postcolonial Malaysia came to be crafted as one of continuity and succession. The colonial appropriation of the vocabulary of nationhood and its domestication into a narrative of political succession was effected through the war known as the Emergency, in the course of which *competing* texts of nationhood were successfully silenced.

The Emergency, and not the Japanese Occupation, has come to hold the place of founding myth of the modern Malaysian state. Despite the invariable allusion to World War II as representing a watershed in the history of the country, conventional historiography periodicizes on the basis of prewar and postwar Malaya, with the Japanese Interregnum as an unfortunate anomaly of history. When Singapore became an independent nation-state in 1965, the narrative of nationhood it crafted also made no reference to the past. Public memorialization of the Pacific War had no role to play in the ceremonies of nationhood of either country.

Whereas the narrative of colonial succession and continuity could be sustained by the post-1965 Malaysian state, the newly independent city-state of Singapore felt compelled to disavow more than the episode of the Japanese Occupation in its past; it disavowed its entire (colonial) past. In the words of its then foreign minister, "Until very recently Singapore's past was a matter of supreme indifference for most Singaporeans simply because they believed this island never really had a history worth remembering . . . because all of that history was British colonial history. . . . Patriotism required that we performed some sort of collective lobotomy to wipe out all traces of 146 years of shame."[44] In Kwa Chong Guan's perceptive analysis, this colonial past was not merely "shameful," it had to be *disproved*. For 150 years, colonial historiography had woven a compelling narrative of an organic and indispensable unity between the great entrepôt port of Singapore and its Malay hinterland. In this scheme of things, a politically independent city and nation-state was an anomaly: "Overnight we had to show that our destiny was not linked, much less dependent upon Malaysia. We had to demonstrate that we could stand on our own and survive. We had to either ignore, deny or disprove 150 years of colonial history."[45]

A "collective lobotomy" had to be performed with respect to the past. In 1972, seven short years after the attainment of independence, history as a subject was removed from the primary school syllabus. Generations of schoolchildren were brought up to think that "this island never really had a history worth remembering" until it was reinserted into the school syllabus in the mid-1980s. The construction of national identity had to be undertaken with no recourse to the symbolic resources of the past. The unremitting narrative of survival,[46] which became the national text of collective identity in the first decades of the puny nation-state's political existence, was completely anchored in the present.

From this perspective, 1992 appears to mark the reinsertion of history into Singapore's public culture. On the occasion of the fiftieth anniversary of the Japanese Occupation of Singapore, an extensive program of commemoration was instituted, the highlight of which was an exhibition entitled "Syonan-to." It proved to be the most visited and most successful exhibition ever mounted by the National Museum. The commemorative calendar of events began with the landing of the Japanese troops in Kota Bahru in northern Malaya on 7 December 1941. In addition to the Kota Bahru landing, sites remembered included the Command Center in Fort Canning, the military prison in Changi, and the scene of the British surrender at the Ford factory.

As a follow-up measure, the Ministry of Defense set up a committee to identify World War II sites for the commemorative program due in 1995, the anniversary of the end of the war. Eleven sites were identified, six of which were battle sites, three civilian sites, and two memorial sites, which were sites at which memory had once been erased. One was a monument dedicated to the INA, the other was the Syonan Chureito, the monument to the Japanese war dead. Both had been destroyed by the British on their return to the island. Throughout 1995, the consecutive unfolding of ceremonies marking the dedication of these eleven sites scattered throughout the island and the holding of exhibitions (one at the National Museum on the end of World War II, another encapsulated within the theme of total defense at the Military Institute of the Singapore Armed Forces) and fora at which popular memory of the war could be articulated, made war a remembered theme in the public mind.

This concerted resurrection of the history of the war and the injunction to remember stands in stark contrast to the pro forma activities organized in other capitals in Southeast Asia, with the possible exception of the Philippines, where there has been a tradition of World War II commemoration by individual towns and cities affected by the war and where a commemorative exhibition was mounted by the city of Manila.[47] In Manila as in Singapore, the reservations of the Japanese embassy regarding the representation of the war with Japan was conveyed to the organizers.[48] Clearly, Japanese officialdom has had its own reasons for not wanting the war to be remembered in Southeast Asia.

But the war has never really been forgotten, despite the suppression of public memory of the war for almost fifty years. As oral history and autobiographical accounts suggest, in popular memory, the war was experienced as a profound biographical watershed, through which personal and family histories took a totally new direction.[49] The memory of participation in the Indian Independence League, for example, remained alive in many Indian families, and practices of remembrance were cultivated on a local level. Similarly, Chinese clan associations have commemorated their war dead throughout the years. This "private" interest in the war was one reason for the huge success of the Syonan-to exhibition. That exhibition, which focused on the social memory of everyday life in Syonan-to, was based on artifacts of everyday life, readily forthcoming from rich storehouses of private memory scattered among the inhabitants of the city, somewhat to the surprise of the organizers of the exhibition themselves.[50]

The public focus of Chinese memory of the war has been on the victims of Japanese reprisals against the Chinese population during the period of the Japanese Occupation. One of the earliest actions of the Japanese military after the conquest of Singapore was to conduct a screening operation of the Chinese population in Singapore, with youths taken away for questioning and never returned. Throughout the course of the Occupation, massacres of local communities suspected of supporting the resistance movement continued to occur with unrelenting brutality. Clan associations have set up markers and monuments to such war dead throughout Malaya and Singapore and have remembered the dead as part of the customary rites of remembrance of the Chinese, Qing Ming, and Chong Yang, during which the graves of their ancestors are visited.[51]

In 1962, with the discovery in Singapore of some unidentifiable corpses stemming from this period, a campaign was launched under the leadership of the Singapore Chinese Chamber of Commerce to build a monument to the victims of the war. Six years later, a striking war memorial, in the form of four rising pillars (referred to affectionately by the public as the "four chopsticks"), was erected on land donated by the government in the administrative heart of the city. Since then, the Chinese Chamber of Commerce, on behalf of the Chinese community, has held commemorative rites on 15 February every year at the war memorial. For the occasion, invitations are sent to all embassies, clan associations, and schools in Singapore. In addition, representatives of the different religious groups in Singapore are invited, as well as the veterans association.

The Chinese Chamber of Commerce organized its own program of commemoration to mark the fiftieth anniversary of the end of the war in 1995. The annual ceremony of remembrance was organized on a larger scale, with Brigadier General Lee Hsien Loong, Deputy Prime Minister, as guest of honor, and Brigadier General George Yeo, Minister of Information and the Arts, in attendance. To commemorate the occasion, the Chamber also published a book in Chinese on the anti-Japanese resistance movements, entitled The Price of Peace. In tandem, it would seem, with the military thrust of the official politics of memory, the book identifies war heroes, who are, as noted in the foreword, not merely to be remembered, but also to be emulated.

The Cultural Politics of Singapore's Survival

As has already been alluded to, there has been a strong military thrust in the recent production of war memory in Singapore. The first publication in 1988 of the oral history project on the Japanese Occupation was entitled A Battle to Be Remembered. The latest in the series, published in 1995, is entitled Beyond the Empires and is designed, in the words of the foreword, "to remind future generations of Singaporeans to be vigilant, and not to be complacent about our nation's defence even in peace-time." The themes of vigilance and defenses are indeed central. Less attention, however, is paid to Japanese colonial brutality than to British colonial indifference. In the narrative of the native, the British colonial masters betrayed their loyal natives—and are never to be trusted again. The text of *Beyond the Empires* begins, after a brief preamble, with the following:

> Our colonial masters had always assured us that Singapore would remain an "impregnable fortress" even in the most adverse of circumstances and we believed them. Thus, although the physical reality of the war became greater each day, the idea of a British surrender was still too far-fetched in most of our minds. Surely we could believe the great honorable Winston Churchill when he claimed that the interests of Singapore would be well protected. It was after all unthinkable that the British Empire could be defeated by an Asian power.
>
> It followed that the impossible happened. The British did not look as if they were winning the battle against the Japanese. They did not seem to be quite as prepared as they or as we had believed them to be. We were beginning to lose our previously unwavering faith in the *Great White Man*.[52]

This message was constantly reiterated in the official speeches that were delivered—and reproduced in the local mass media—at the dedication ceremonies of each of the eleven memorial sites held from June to November 1995. A sample is given below from the press report of the speech made on the occasion of the dedication of the plaque to mark the site where the Japanese memorial had once stood: "Dr Ong Chit Chung, MP for Bukit Batok, said in a speech that the surrender of Singapore by the British 'destroyed the myth of the invincibility of the white man' and undermined the legitimacy of the British to rule Singapore. Japanese brutality later spurred Singapore youths to seek independence and determine their own future. The lesson: That 'self-reliance, political will and unwavering commitment are the only ways to ensure the survival of a small country such as Singapore,' he added."[53]

The theme of defense, as this text indicates, is a variation of the narrative of survival that the leadership of the fledgling city-state adopted in the wake of its traumatic expulsion from its natural hinterland. The undertone of desperation often detectable in the stridency of the narration can be attributed to the underlying fear that survival could not possibly be secured in view of the crushing weight of history and geography, the logic of which condemned the project of a Republic of Singapore to a conceptual and political anomaly.[54] Hence the disavowal of history and geography in the earlier narrative of survival.

The resurrection of war memory in the service of this narrative, under the auspices of the Ministry of Defense, has historicized the tale. The lead role of the Ministry of Defense in the restoration of history to official memory in Singapore is surprising only at first glance. Whereas "collective lobotomy" had excised history from all organs of the new city and nation-state, one national institution could not do without it entirely: the military.[55] Military history, without which no esprit de corps could be inculcated, had to be taught to the elite corps of officer cadets into whose hands the defense of the new and fragile nation was entrusted. This military had indeed no history before 1965. It had also never fought a war. The only campaign that could be remembered and analyzed was the Malaya Campaign of the Japanese 25th Army. It became the war all Singapore generals memorized.

As is also evident from the texts, however, the theme of defense is encapsulated in a grander narrative of disenchantment with the West and the quest for national identity, themes that reverberate in other arenas of cultural politics in Singapore.[56] With historicization, the earlier narrative of survival has also acquired a new geography of nationhood. The new topography of war created by the eleven sites of memory represents Singapore as the sole locus of war and not as the final destination in a "Malaya" campaign. This demarcation of national space and its sanctification suggest a national subject reconciled with its geography.

Indeed, I would argue that the reinstatement of history is closely related to a reconceptualization of Singapore's geography. In 1995, fifty years after the end of the war and after thirty years of independent political existence, Singapore's survival as a city-, island-, nation-state no longer appears as an anomaly. The earlier sense of fragility and precariousness of survival has given way to the conviction of success. Brigadier General George Yeo, the minister responsible for the commemoration campaign, has also been instrumental in fashioning a new self-conception of the national subject by reenvisioning the status of city-states and their role in the contemporary regional and global economy. In a speech delivered in May 1995 in Tokyo, he argued: "In the next century, the most relevant unit of economic production, social organization and knowledge generation will be the city or city-region. Nation-states will still exist but an increasing number of policy issues will have to be settled at the city level. This will create new patterns of competition and cooperation in the world, a little like the situation in Europe before the era of nation-states."

The transformative forces of transnationalism have redefined the meaning of geography for Singapore's survival as a nation-state. City-state status is no longer seen as a congenital defect and anomaly, but as *prototypical* of the new global centers or hubs on which hinterlands are built and around which they revolve. This reconceptualization of the national self created a space, indeed induced a necessity, for the identity resources of the past. Whether the recovery of history as a national project can succeed, given the intentional forgetting and the deliberate absences the public narrative of survival exacted, remains to be seen. Private memories, however, survived. With the restoration of a public text on history in Singapore, the terrain has been established for a new politics of memory to unfold.

Conclusion

The fiftieth anniversary of the end of World War II spawned an orgy of commemorations that provided the opportunity for scripting what I would argue to be *empire-centered* and *nation-centered* texts. The narration of the liberation of the loyal native from the yoke of a brutal alien occupation in far-flung theaters of the war is clearly nostalgic of empire, as is the grand narrative of humanity's salvation from the fascist forces of evil, inscribed into every commemorative act in the great capitals of the West. The imperative to remember, however, also permitted specifically local or nation-centered narratives to be articulated. In Europe, it was the narrative of "Europe's victory over itself"; in Australia, it was the memory of a war fought in Asia, and therefore a charter for Australia's being part of Asia. In Singapore, a founding myth to reinvent the present was authored.

Notes

1 Anthony Reid, "Remembering and Forgetting the War in Indonesia," paper presented at the conference on "Memory and the Second World War in International Comparative Perspective," Amsterdam, 1995.

2 John Bodnar, *Remaking America: Public Memory, Commemoration, and Patriotism in the Twentieth Century* (Princeton, NJ: Princeton University Press, 1992).

3 Geoffrey White, "Remembering Guadalcanal: National Identity and Transnational Memory-Making," *Public Culture* 7 (1995): 529–55.

4 Ibid., 531.

5 Ibid., 530

6 Ibid.

7 See the papers collected in John R Gillis, ed., *Commemorations: The Politics of National Identity* (Princeton, NJ: Princeton University Press, 1994); a special issue of *Radical History Review* 56 (spring 1993) on memory and history; a special issue of *Representations* 26 (spring 1989) on memory and countermemory, ed. Natalie Zemon Davis and Randolph Starn; and Rubie S. Watson, ed., *Memory, History and Opposition: Under State Socialism* (Santa Fe, NM: School of American Research Press, 1994).

8 *Shonan Shinbun*, 2 February 1943.

9 Akashi Yoji, "Japanese Cultural Policy in Malaya and Singapore 1942–45," in *Japanese Culture Policies in Southeast Asia during World War II*, ed. Grant K. Goodman (London: Macmillan, 1992).

10 Patricia Lim, "Monuments and Memory: Remembrances of War in Johor," paper pre-

sented at the workshop "War and Memory in Malaysia and Singapore, 1941–1945," Institute of Southeast Asian Studies, Singapore, 1995.

11 Akashi, "Japanese Cultural Policy in Malaya and Singapore 1942–45," 131.

12 Ibid., 132.

13 Ibid.

14 Benedict Anderson, "Japan: The Light of Asia," in *Southeast Asia in World War II: Four Essays*, ed. Joseph Silverstein (New Haven: Yale University Press, 1966).

15 The title of one of the earliest firsthand accounts of life under Japanese Occupation was "Malaya Upside Down." See Kee Onn Chin, *Malaya Upside Down* (Singapore: Jitts, 1946).

16 T. H. Silcock and Ungku Abdul Aziz, "Nationalism in Malaya," in *Asian Nationalism and the West*, ed. William L. Holland (New York: Octagon Books, 1953), 298.

17 These arches were put up by supporters of the communist-inspired guerrillas. Needless to say, their sentiments were not shared by many other segments of the population, for whom the emergence of these "liberators" meant the end of freedom. See Cheah Boon Keng, "Resistance and Social Conflict during and after the Japanese Occupation, 1941–1946," in *Red Star over Malaya* (Singapore: Singapore University Press, 1983).

18 White, "Remembering Guadalcaual: National Identity and Transnational Memory-Making," 531.

19 Akashi, "Japanese Cultural Policy in Malaya and Singapore 1942–45," 119.

20 For accounts of the response of the Malay populace to the Japanese military administration, see Akashi Yoji, "Japanese Military Administration in Malaya: Its Formation and Evolution in Reference to Sultans, the Islamic Religion and the Moslem-Malays, 1941–1945," *Asian Studies*, 7, no. 1 (1969); Abu Talib Ahmad, "The Impact of the Japanese Occupation on the Malay-Muslim Population," in *Malaya and Singapore during the Japanese Occupation*, ed. Paul H. Kratoska, special issue of *Journal of Southeast Asian Studies, Singapore*, Special Publication series, no. 3 (1995); Cheah, "Resistance and Social Conflict during and after the Japanese Occupation, 1941–1946."

21 For an account, see the memoir of the Japanese leader of the F. Kikan, Fujiwara Iwaichi, *F. Kikan: Japanese Army Intelligence Operations in Southeast Asia during World War II*, trans. Akashi Yoji (London: Heinemann Educational Books, 1983).

22 Naoki Sakai, presentation at the conference, "The Politics of Remembering the Asia-Pacific War," East-West Center, Honolulu, 7–9 September 1995.

23 Fujiwara, 185.

24 Silcock and Aziz, "Nationalism in Malaya," 295.

25 For an account of the INA, see Fujiwara, *F. Kikan: Japanese Army Intelligence Operations in Southeast Asia during World War II*, and Joyce Lebra-Chapman, *Jungle Alliance, Japan and the Indian National Army* (Singapore: Donald Moore for Asian Pacific Press, 1971).

26 This date was confirmed by Ho Chi Minh, who attended the founding congress as the Comintern representative. Oral communication with Abdul Rahman Embong.

27 Silcock and Aziz, "Nationalism in Malaya."

28 This account of the MPAJA is based on Cheah, "Resistance and Social Conflict during and after the Japanese Occupation, 1941–1946." For further studies of the MCP and MPAJA, see Gene Z. Hanrahan, *The Communist Struggle in Malaya* (New York: Institute of Pacific Relations, 1954); Hara Fujio, "The Japanese Occupation of Malaya and the Chinese Community," and Akashi Yoji, "The Anti-Japanese Movement in Perak during the Japanese Occupation 1941–45," both in *Journal of Southeast Asian Studies* (1995).

29 It should be noted that armed resistance to the Japanese was also conducted by Koumin-

tang and noncommunist Malay guerrillas. See Wan Hashim Wan Teh, *Perang Dunia Kedua: Peranan Gerila Melayu Force 136* (Kuala Lumpur: Dewan Bahasa Dan Pustaka, 1993).

30 Silcock and Aziz, "Nationalism in Malaya," 298.

31 Ibid., 301.

32 *The Malayan Times*, 7 September 1945.

33 Akbar Aisha, *Aishabee at War: A Very Frank Memoir* (Singapore: Landmark Books, 1990), 229.

34 Silcock and Aziz, "Nationalism in Malaya," 310.

35 Ibid., 294.

36 Ibid., 310.

37 T. H. Silcock, *Towards a Malayan Nation* (Singapore: Eastern Universities Press, 1961), 3.

38 This is not to suggest that the Emergency did not have profound and wide-ranging effects on the development of the country. For accounts of the Emergency, see R. Stubbs, *Hearts and Minds in Guerilla Warfare: The Malayan Emergency 1948–1960* (Singapore: Oxford University Press 1989), and T. N. Harper, "The Colonial Inheritance: State and Society in Malaya, 1945–57" (Ph.D. diss., University of Cambridge, 1991).

39 John Cloake, *Templer, Tiger of Malaya: The Life of Field Marshall Sir Gerald Templer* (London: Harrap, 1985).

40 Silcock, *Towards a Malayan Nation*, 44.

41 Victor Purcell, *Malaya, Communist or Free?* (Stanford: Stanford University Press, 1954), 17.

42 Quoted in ibid., 17.

43 Silcock, *Towards a Malayan Nation*, 48.

44 Rajaratnam, quoted in Kwa Chong Guan, "Remembering Ourselves," paper presented at the conference "Our Place in Time," Singapore, 18–20 September 1994, 5.

45 Kwa, "Remembering Ourselves," 5.

46 See Chan Heng Chee, *Singapore: The Politics of Survival, 1965–1967* (Singapore: Oxford University Press, 1971); Geraldine Heng and Janadas Devan, "State Fatherhood: The Politics of Nationalism, Sexuality, and Race in Singapore," in *Nationalisms and Sexualities*, ed. Andrew Parker, Mary Russo, Doris Sommer, and Patricia Yaeger (New York: Routledge, 1992).

47 Oral communication, Dr. Rico Jose, University of the Philippines.

48 Oral communication, Kwa Chong Guan and Lim Hou Seng, for Singapore; Dr. Rico Jose for Manila.

49 See Patricia Lim, "Memoirs of War in Malaya," in *Malaya and Singapore during the Japanese Occupation*, ed. Paul H. Kratoska, special issue of *Journal of Southeast Asian Studies*, Special Publications Series, No. 3 (1995).

50 Oral communication, Kwa Chong Guan, chairman of 1992 Heritage Day Working Committee.

51 Lim, "Monuments and Memory: Remembrances of War in Johor."

52 Cindy Chou, *Beyond the Empires: Memories Untold* (Singapore: National Heritage Board, 1995), 1; italics in the original.

53 *Straits Times*, 10 July 1995.

54 Compare the remark made recently by Fang Chuang Pi, otherwise known as the Plen, a leading member of the MCP, that Singapore is a "freak." In *Straits Times*, 22 July 1997.

55 I owe this insight, as well as the following account of the teaching of history in the Singapore military, to Kwa Chong Guan.

56 Chua Beng Huat, "Culture, Multiracialism and National Identity in Sinapore," Department of Sociology Working Papers 125, National University of Singapore, 1995; Kwok

Kian Woon, "Beyond Cultural Defensiveness and Cultural Triumphalism: Globalization and the Critique of Western Forms of Modernity," paper presented at conference "Globalization: Local Challenges and Responses," Universiti Sains Penang, Penang, 19–21 January 1995; and C.J. W.-L. Wee, "Staging the New Asia: Singapore's Dick Lee, Pop Music and a Counter-modernity," *Public Culture* 8 (1996).

Go for Broke, the Movie: Japanese American Soldiers

in U.S. National, Military, and Racial Discourses

T. FUJITANI

It was because he was Japanese and, at the same time, had to prove to the world that he was not Japanese that the turmoil was in his soul and urged him to enlist.
—John Okada, No-no Boy[1]

The Most Remembered, Almost Forgotten Soldiers

It is often said of the Japanese American soldiers who served during the Second World War that they are the forgotten heroes of that great conflict. In fact, over the past half century this point has been made so often that it might now be more accurate to say that they are probably the most remembered, almost forgotten heroes of the war. To be sure, not all who live in the United States today have heard about the military exploits of the 100th Infantry Battalion or the 442nd Regimental Combat Team, the two nearly all-Nisei segregated units that made up, as the legend goes, the most highly decorated group of soldiers in U.S. history. Still less known are the thousands of Japanese Americans who joined the war effort in the Pacific as translators and interpreters. Yet there can be no doubt that the stories of Japanese American military heroism, especially as juxtaposed to the discrimination they experienced, has in the past half century achieved a specific and now for the most part unproblematized location in the dominant U.S. memory. This is especially true on the West Coast and in Hawai'i. Moreover, the absence of Japanese American WWII valor in the memories of some Americans, coupled with the force of ongoing anti-Japanese and anti-Asian sentiments throughout U.S. society, continue to push Japanese American veterans, their children, and their admirers toward more retellings and commemorations of Nisei heroism. Reunions and celebrations of Japanese American WWII veterans continue to be held throughout the country; highways in California have recently been named for the 100th, the 442nd, and for Japanese Americans who served in military intelligence; in 1998, Hasbro, the toymaker, added a 442nd Americans of Japanese Descent Combat Soldier to its G.I. Joe Classic Collection; and the Japanese American National Museum in Los Angeles recently featured an exhibit on Japanese Americans in the military.[2]

In the 1990s, mainstream narratives of the war, whether voiced by leaders in government or carried in the popular media, fairly routinely at least mention Japanese American internment and military service. On 3 August 1995, for example, CBS aired a two-hour program on the Pacific War called *Victory in the Pacific*. Narrated by Dan Rather and none other than General H. Norman Schwartzkopf of Gulf War fame, this program carried a fairly predictable and conservative (meaning American Legion–type) story of the war. Its premise was that the war had begun with Pearl Harbor—never mind the Western and U.S. imperialism and colonialism that had brought the U.S. Navy to Pearl Harbor and the Pacific in the first place—and had been brought to a close with the dropping of the atomic bombs. Yet even this decidedly unreflexive interpretation of the war with Japan also covered, however inadequately, the internment, allowing several Japanese Americans to speak about their suffering. It also mentioned that some thirty-three thousand "Americans of Japanese descent" had fought with exemplary valor for America in Europe and had served as translators and interrogators in the Pacific.

During the fiftieth-anniversary commemorations of Pearl Harbor, no less a figure than President George Bush narrativized these Japanese American experiences into his commemoration speeches. The *New York Times* reported that, "as he did at every place he spoke, the President lauded the Japanese-Americans who fought in the American armed forces during the war and expressed regrets to those interned 'innocent victims who committed no offense.' " "This ground," he said in one of his speeches in Honolulu, "embraces many American veterans whose love of country was put to the test unfairly by our own authorities. These and other natural born American citizens faced wartime internment and they committed no crime. They were sent to internment camps simply because their ancestors were Japanese."[3]

Moreover, newspapers and popular magazines routinely carried descriptions of the internment and Japanese American military service. *Life*, for example, in its Collector's Edition commemorating Pearl Harbor, devoted one of its major sections to a pictorial essay on "Life behind Barbed Wire," and it showed a photograph of a young soldier and his parents in Manzanar. "Of the more than 25,000 Japanese-Americans who volunteered for duty," said the caption, "4,000 came from the camps, including this soldier saying goodbye to his parents."

Elsewhere in the same issue, Senator Daniel Inouye from Hawai'i, who lost an arm fighting in Europe, recounted his experiences following the Pearl Harbor attack. He spoke of joining the 442nd, of the extraordinary valor of Japanese Americans and of his mainlander comrades, "90 percent" of whom had "volunteered while in internment camps."[4] Clearly, the tragic story of Japanese Americans who supposedly fought and died for freedom even while experiencing its opposite has achieved a degree of respectability in mainstream memories of the war.

The unique non-White prominence in public discourse and representation of Japanese American soldiers cannot be explained by their heroism and sacrifices alone. We ought not to imagine that the objective weight of their achievements and their enormous sacrifices were such irrepressible forces in themselves, that they could not but compel their fellow (White) Americans to overcome racism and to respect Japanese Americans. This is perhaps what many Japanese American veterans would like to believe, and it is a narrative that, as I argue more fully below, fits neatly into postwar racial and national ideology. Certainly, we know that African Americans as well as other minorities within the United States proper and its colonies have similarly demonstrated many times in modern history, including during the Pacific War, what would be regarded as military heroism and sacrifice. To take only the case of Filipino soldiers, some 90 percent of the Allied forces that took their last stand against the Japanese on the Bataan peninsula were Filipinos and of the 7,000 to 10,000 men who died in the Bataan death march, only about 600 were not. Shortly after the Bataan surrender the valor of Filipinos became widely known within the United States proper, and in February of 1942 the First and Second Filipino Infantry Regiments were formed so that Filipinos residing in the United States could join the war effort. Yet in 1946 Congress refused to fulfill FDR's promise to the 100,000 Filipino soldiers who had fought with U.S. troops that they would be allowed U.S. citizenship and veterans' benefits. Instead, it was not until 1990 that Congress granted citizenship rights to surviving veterans, and as of this writing they still do not receive full veterans' benefits.[5]

It is not my desire to minimize or even to assess Japanese American military heroism as a social fact. Certainly, by current commonsensical standards of military heroism in the United States, the feats of Nisei soldiers were incredible. As the usual litany goes, the 100th Infantry Battalion and the 442nd Regimental Combat Team together earned 9,486 Purple Hearts, 18,143 individual decorations for bravery, and 7 Presidential Unit Citations[6]—an amazing feat indeed when one considers that the total number of Japanese American men who served in the military has been estimated at about 33,000, including several thousand who were not part of these units.[7] Nor do I wish to trivialize the experiences of these individuals and their families or to insist that they should have refused military service in protest against racism.

Instead, my purpose is to critique the ways in which Japanese American soldiers have been narrativized into dominant yet contradictory U.S. discourses concerning race, nationalism, and war. It should become evident that one consequence of the dominant modes through which memories about Japanese American soldiers have been recuperated has been to occlude enduring, yet also changing structures of racism in the postwar years, and to reinforce narratives that proclaim the strength of universal values—most importantly, freedom, equality, and progress—within the particularity of the recent U.S. past, and despite the weight of contradictory evidence.

In reconsidering the belief that military heroism earned Japanese Americans their equal rights as U.S. citizens, we need to be attentive to the fact that the celebratory memory of Japanese Americans in the military and the current status of Japanese Americans as a "model minority" are products of the negotiations between nationalism and racism in the late wartime and postwar years, not of racism's disappearance or of linear progress. Moreover, postwar memories of Japanese Americans as well as their/our current status within U.S. society cannot be separated from the international political order under U.S. hegemony that gave the nation of Japan a unique location in the global community as the United States' capitalist and "almost, but not quite White" younger sibling. Japan came to be positioned in a way that was in some important respects homological to the new location of Japanese Americans in a reracialized postwar U.S. society.

Disavowing Racism

In an essay on the reciprocal relations of racism and nationalism, Etienne Balibar has observed that at least insofar as the "already constituted national states" are concerned, "the discourses of race and nation are never very far apart, if only in the form of disavowal."[8] Borrowing from this insight on the mutually constitutive associations between racism and nationalism, I want to especially highlight the last clause in the quote, namely, that which draws our attention to the propensity of modern nation-states, including the United States, to deny that they condone racial discrimination even as they continually reproduce it in close alliance with nationalism. For the purposes of this essay, we can begin by noting that the success of U.S. nationalism, especially during the war years and onward, rested precisely on the official disavowal of racism. Without it the racialized people making up the nation could not be mobilized for war or the protection of national interests as more broadly construed by the ruling elite. Oddly enough, or perhaps precisely because of the undeniability of anti-Japanese racism during the Second World War, from the time of their concentration camp internment up to the present day, Japanese Americans have served as one of the primary sites on which to claim steady progress in the national renunciation of racism.

It is often noted that during the war years many barriers to social and political mobility for Asians who were not Japanese rapidly diminished. In particular, Chinese, Filipinos, and Asian Indians living in the United States tended to be identified with their countries of origin and became beneficiaries of the fact that these countries were U.S. allies. Most important, in late 1943 Congress rescinded the anti-Chinese exclusionary laws and granted Chinese the right to become naturalized as citizens—a right that until then had been available only to aliens considered to be White or African American. Just after the war, in 1946, Filipinos and Asian Indians also became eligible to apply for naturalization.[9] In contrast, it is said that Japanese Americans experienced worsening racism and ultimately internment because they were obviously identified with the enemy.

This view is no doubt accurate in some respects, especially insofar as it explains Japanese American internment. Yet it also obscures the fact that many of the very men who directed the racist policy leading to incarceration were just as assiduous in denying that they harbored any racist feelings at all against Japanese Americans. This ought not to be understood as duplicity at the individual level, where morally defective individual leaders spoke of racial equality even while they secretly held and acted on their deep-seated racism. The contradiction was more systemic, part of a regime of duplicity that appears to be at the heart of most nation-states. It corresponds to what has been called the "doubletalk" of colonial and postcolonial regimes, wherein the promise of acceptance or assimilation has coexisted with discourses and practices of separation and unassimilability.[10] The systematic disavowal of racism coupled with its ongoing reproduction lies at the heart of the treatment of Japanese Americans during the war and an analysis of it helps to explain the mechanisms of a more "liberalized" postwar racism. In this sense, the 1952 McCarren-Walter Act, which finally allowed the naturalization of Japanese, was not a simple reversal of the earlier racist policy that had targeted those identified with an enemy nation. It was the culmination of the wartime drive, evidenced in the new possibility of Asian naturalization, to disavow racism in the interest of mobilizing ever greater numbers of people toward nationalism, even from ethnically or racially distrusted and even despised groups.

Thus I am in agreement with Cynthia H. Enloe, who long ago argued that most states in modern nation-states, including the U.S. state, have conscripted ethnic military personnel in times of extraordinary manpower need despite retaining a clear ethnic hierarchy.[11] However, I am also insisting that the recruitment and even conscription of minoritized soldiers during moments of national crisis demonstrates in a more general way the possibility of national inclusion for all, even as racial hierarchies are reproduced. The primary impetus for this inclusion is that in modern nation-states and especially conditions of total war, national security depends not simply on more soldiers but on the loyalty and active participation of all the people, civilian and military. This loyalty and active participation can be won only through demonstrations of the promise and evidence of equality and inclusiveness.

It was in fact none other than President Franklin D. Roosevelt who declared the following and now famous words (at least to Japanese Americans who experienced the war) on 1 February 1943, just less than a year after having himself fully sanctioned the mass incarceration of approximately 120,000 Japanese Americans through Executive Order 9066: "No loyal citizen of the United States should be denied the democratic right to exercise the responsibilities of his citizenship, regardless of his ancestry. The principle on which this country was founded and by which it has always been governed is that Americanism is a matter of the mind and heart; Americanism is not, and never was, a matter of race or ancestry. A good American is one who is loyal to this country and to our creed of liberty and democracy." This statement approved the formation of the segregated Nisei combat team, the 442nd, and coincides with the official shift from a government policy of simple segregation and confinement of Japanese Americans to reintegration of those considered "loyal" back into White America.[12] It exemplifies, in other words, the reemphasis in U.S. nationalism of the promise of acceptance and set the stage for the remarkable transformation of Japanese Americans in general, and especially Japanese American citizen-soldiers, from the obvious symbol of racial discrimination into a living representation of America's denunciation of racism. In this situation there could be nothing better to both mask the virulence and violence of racial discrimination and to mobilize the racially, economically, and socially marginalized into a national cause, than to construct, somehow, Japanese Americans into military heroes. They became, in other words, the prototype for the "model minority," an appellation that became popularized from the mid-1960s.

The exploits of these Japanese American soldiers have received and continue to receive great public attention because they can be easily subsumed into a teleological narrative of progress that celebrates America, "right or wrong." The Japanese American soldiers became part of a grand story, nearly biblical in form, whose premise is that all events in U.S. history have been steps on the road to the realization of a glorious end that was in fact already foretold at the nation's beginning. In this narrative, the end of national history is prefigured in its origins, the Constitution, where liberty and equality are guaranteed. All the past is then made to contribute to the grand narrative in such a way that every moment between the beginning and the end, including anomalies such as institutional racism, can be reinscribed as minor aberrations on the path to the promised land. The problem with this narrative, of course, is that realization of the promise may be forever deferred or shifted onto different groups.

In the war's last years, Japanese American citizen-soldiers were rapidly experiencing inclusion into this grand narrative. The media lauded Nisei soldier heroics and began to represent them as above all "normal" Americans. A Hearst newsreel segment titled "Japanese-Yank Troops Join U.S. Army in France," for example, showed individual faces of Nisei soldiers and noted that they were "Americans of Japanese parentage fresh from the U.S." The footage showed that these soldiers faced wartime difficulties that were basically no different from those that confronted (White) Americans. Thus the narrator noted that for these soldiers fighting in France, "How to speak French is their first problem." He does not mention the concentration camps or racism. Instead we see a handful of mostly Japanese faces poring over what appears to be a textbook with the title French. These are, the newsreel informs us, "loyal Japanese Americans." What we are seeing are "signal corps films of U.S. born Japanese fighting in the cause of freedom."[13] Ronald Reagan—incidentally, a man who sometimes seems to believe that he took part in combat during the war because of the movie roles he played—also noted while a participant in a 1945 award ceremony for a Japanese American hero, "America stands unique in the world, the only country not founded on race, but on a way—an ideal. Not in spire of, but because of our polyglot background, we have had all the strength in the world. That is the American way."[14]

While U.S. troops were still fighting the war against Japan, the War Relocation Authority, in collaboration with the War Department, issued a pamphlet called Nisei in Uniform.[15] It cited Roosevelt to proclaim, once again, that Americanism rested not on race, but on spirit: "Every race and nation from which our population has been drawn is represented among the young Americans who are fighting side by side to overthrow the Axis powers." This was true of Germans fighting the Nazis, of Italians waging war on the Italian Axis forces, and of course of "men whose parents came from Japan [who] are showing that devotion to America and gallantry in action are not determined by the slant of the eyes or the color of the skin." The text certainly told of the Japanese American evacuation from the West Coast, but the emphasis lay elsewhere. Photographs showed Nisei soldiers involved in activities that one might expect of any soldier: engaging in military exercises, fighting in combat, searching for mines, standing guard, and so on. Above all, the Japanese American soldier appeared as a recognizable likeness of the White soldier. "American soldiers with Japanese faces," read one caption, inadvertently revealing that Americanness was indeed associated with Whiteness, "Edwin Iino, Saburo Ikuta, and Robert Yonemitsu were all born and raised in California where they were educated in American schools. They have never visited Japan." The individuals pictured were in most respects unremarkable from what one might have expected of their White counterparts: a former bantam-weight boxing champion, a star on a wrestling team, graduates of the University of Washington or the University of Utah, a minister of a Congregational Church, and the brother of a stage dancer. They liked mail call, they went sightseeing, their pastimes were no different from those of other Americans, their brides wore wedding gowns and they cut wedding cakes at their marriages, and they enjoyed Christmas packages from home. Nisei WACs were also mimetic of their White counterparts. Nisei soldiers were heroic and, like other fighting men, they suffered severe injuries and often dismemberment. Yoshinao Omiya of Honolulu, for example, "fought bravely until both eyes were blown out by a land mine." Race did not conflict with Americanness, so it seemed, as long as signs of cultural difference disappeared.

Frank Capra's infamous propaganda film *Know Your Enemy—Japan* is perhaps one of the most blatant examples of the duplicity of U.S. nationalist discourse.[16] Surprisingly, it begins not with a general statement about the "Japs" over there, but with praise for Japanese Americans and particularly the Nisei soldier. The film informed its audience that the children of Japanese immigrants to America were citizens and that not only had they been educated in American schools and not only did they speak "our" language, but "a great many of them share our love of freedom and our willingness to die for it," including and most especially the Nisei soldiers in Europe. This film, the statement concluded, was not about Japanese Americans. Instead, it told "the story of Japs in Japan to whom the words liberty and freedom are still without meaning." Thus what mattered was not racial type, but national citizenship. Yet at the same time, the film repeatedly blurred the distinction between the "Jap" over there and the "Jap" over here. It showed fishermen off the coast of California and warned that they were part of the same family of treacherous Japanese people. And it cautioned Americans to beware of "Jap" spies in their midst: shopkeepers, barbers, and flower shop owners, all working for Tokyo. Thus, while in the Rooseveltian fashion disavowing race as a standard of Americanism, it yet warned of the particular dangers that inhered in those perceived as racially different.

Among the most celebrated moments in (White) America's recognition of the Nisei soldier was President Truman's awarding of a presidential citation to the 442nd on the White House lawn in July 1946. After marching down Constitution Avenue, the men of the 442nd listened to Truman's speech explaining the significance of their accomplishments. Like others, he began by placing himself in the Rooseveltian mode of disavowal: "I believe it was my predecessor who said that Americanism is not a matter of race or creed, it is a matter of the heart." He congratulated the Nisei soldiers for their contributions to the nation and to the world and then noted, "You fought not only the enemy, but you fought prejudice, and you have won." Yet the speech also made it clear that the accomplishments of the Nisei soldiers would always be overwritten by the teleological narrative of American progress. "Keep up that fight," he exhorted, "and we continue to win—to make this great Republic stand for just what the Constitution says it stands for: the welfare of all the people all the time."[17]

The emphasis on the grand narrative is even more powerfully in evidence in Hearst newsreel footage of the ceremony.[18] In it we see the Japanese American troops marching in formation, but these men are not clearly individualized, and in fact appear not so different from the "Jap" soldiers in the Capra film who were described as just like so many "photographic prints off the same negative." The newsreel ceremonial is about the Nisei in only a distantly secondary way, for it is Truman standing in for America whose gaze, face, and speech dominate the proceedings. He is the only person marked as an individual and his are the only words that we hear. The president is there to validate the Nisei, but in his recognition of them he affirms that their victories should be read only as victories for America. When he declares that the Nisei have made the Republic "stand for just what the Constitution says it stands for," he is insisting that all heroisms are always already foreordained by the Constitution. He guards against any slippage of meaning that might throw the grand narrative of progress under suspicion.

Go for Broke

The 1951 movie Go for Broke marked a new moment in memorializing the Nisei soldier and configuring him in relation to the reciprocal yet contradictory discourses of nation and race.[19] Pamphlets, newspaper and magazine articles, and celebratory newsreel footage had already created a public image of the Japanese American fighting men, but Go for Broke was a Hollywood movie starring one of the industry's leading actors, Van Johnson, and it circulated images of the Nisei soldier-citizen that had not been previously possible. Its premiere took place in Washington, D.C., and millions saw the movie. The film's director and screenwriter was Robert Pirosh, an Army combat veteran who had earlier won an Academy Award for the film Battleground. Dore Schary produced the movie.

Schary, it seems, had originally contemplated making a film about the identity of an unknown soldier in the Tomb of the Unknowns, which would have suggested that this soldier might have been from any ethnic background.[20] And in an eerie conflation of life inside and outside of the movies, all the men playing soldiers in the 442nd were actually veterans of that unit, except for the actor who played the important role of Tommy.

There are at least two central narratives that run through *Go for Broke*. The first and most obvious is the story of the Nisei soldiers' achievements—from training in Camp Shelby, Mississippi, to combat in Europe—as they battle both racism within American society and the national enemy. The film does not hide that many Nisei soldiers from the mainland have families in camps. A soldier sends a package of gifts to his loved ones who are suffering under miserable camp conditions, and Nisei mainlanders on the warfront await letters from loved ones back home, in camp. The highlights of Nisei glory include victories in Italy and France, the capture of enemy officers who cannot comprehend the appearance of their captors—"What kind of troops are these, Chinese?"—and the 442nd's famous rescue of the all-Texas battalion, the "Lost Battalion," in France.

However, it is the other story that dominates the film and subsumes the 442nd's heroism. This is the odyssey of Lieutenant Grayson (played by Van Johnson), who begins his spiritual journey as a man who despises the "Jap" soldiers that he must lead, but who in the course of the film comes to disavow that racism. When Grayson initially reports to Camp Shelby he immediately requests a transfer out. He denies that his reason for doing so is that the men under his command will be "Japs," but the movie makes it clear that this is indeed the problem. Two officers in succession lecture Grayson, explaining that the Japanese Americans are loyal citizens. A colonel castigates Grayson: "They're not Japs; they're Japanese Americans, Nisei; or as they call themselves, Buddhaheads; all kinds of Buddhaheads, Lieutenant. . . . They're all American citizens and they're all volunteers, remember that." But Grayson is not convinced. He is repulsed by the culture of the Hawaiian "Japs," by their ukulele playing, singing, and hula dancing. Finally, he experiences a moment of relief when he learns that his platoon sergeant will be Sergeant O'Hara. But as it turns out, the sergeant's full name is Takashi Ohara.

On his way to the battlefront in Europe, Grayson reads his orders. They tell him that the Italian leaders are trying to convince their people that Americans are racist, but that in truth "racial prejudice is abhorrent to our American concept of democracy." He pauses to reflect on his own negative feelings toward his men, but he is as yet unrepentant and still looks forward to transferring out. "A guy gets in to fight the Japs and winds up fightin' with them," he says. Following the Nisei soldiers' exploits in battle, however, Grayson is gradually won over. When he meets an old friend named Culley from the Texas Division, he is offended and angered by this man's racist attitude toward the Nisei. They're not "Japs," he tells his old friend, and he gets into a fistfight to defend those whom he had not long ago despised himself. Soon Culley too becomes an admirer of the Nisei, especially after he is rescued by them, and shouts the 442nd slogan, "Go for Broke." Racism has been overcome.

Grayson's and Culley's renunciations of racism are clearly allegories of America's overcoming of it. America's disavowal is foretold at the movie's beginning with the famous quote from Roosevelt—that Americanism is a "matter of mind and heart" and not of "race or ancestry"—and the possibility of interpreting both Nisei heroics and the White men's disavowal as anything but the realization of America's promise is foreclosed by the film's ending. The film concludes with the Nisei soldiers' triumphal return to the United States, followed by newsreel footage of the previously described ceremonial in which Truman confers the presidential citation on them. Certainly, the men of the 442nd are much more individualized in the movie than in earlier newsreels and Truman is less of a presence, for instead of Truman's face we see a succession of blurred faces of the individual heroes of the 442nd. Yet, as the film comes to a final close, the Nisei soldiers drop from sight. The camera pulls away to reveal anonymous soldiers marching down the Pennsylvania Avenue processional route. The White House looms sublimely over the capital. The End.

Despite similarities with earlier representations of the Nisei soldiers—most importantly, the overwriting of the teleological narrative onto the story of the Nisei valor—there are some significant departures that link the film more directly to the later "model minority" discourse. Most important, unlike earlier representations of the soldiers, there is a greater tolerance for both individual and cultural difference. There is much in the film that today's moderate liberal multiculturalists would probably applaud. However shallowly developed, these are real, not stereotyped Japanese American people, and there is a recognition that these men have a culture that is different from but quite as respectable as that of (White) Americans. They have their own pastimes, like playing the ukulele, singing, and dancing hula, that even Lieutenant Grayson comes, in time, to appreciate. They use their own "pidgin English," and sometimes even speak in Japanese. They call themselves "Buddhaheads" and the officers "haoles," but this does not interfere with their work as American soldiers. A Nisei soldier lies wounded in the attempt to rescue the Lost Battalion. A White Catholic chaplain sees him holding rosaries and wonders why he has not seen him in Catholic services. The reason why, the soldier responds, is that these rosaries are different; he is a Buddhist. But religious difference is not problematic and the chaplain leaves with a gesture of tolerance: "I'll be here if you want me."

Indeed, cultural difference is sometimes represented as an asset in the war effort. At one point, Grayson and Culley are separated from the U.S. troops and when they hear the 442nd's soldiers at a distance they must, without approaching and risking being shot at, identify themselves with the password. But Grayson does not know the new password, so he shouts out the only Japanese that he has learned, *bakatare* (damned idiot). The Nisei soldiers conclude that he must be one of them and stop firing their rifles. In effect, Grayson and Culley are saved by a White American's multicultural literacy. In another episode, the Germans have captured a field telephone and are calling into headquarters in English. They pretend to be a part of the 442nd so as to sabotage the efforts of the U.S. troops. But a quick-witted Nisei minding the headquarter's phone suspects that something is amiss, so he begins to speak to the German in Japanese. He assumes that if the man on the other end is really a part of the 442nd he should be able to understand and respond. The German has no idea what is being said to him and can only keep repeating that his name is Sergeant Sugimoto. A White officer at headquarters commends the Nisei soldier for his resourcefulness and the soldier responds, "Thank you, sir, it's just that good old Yankee knowhow."

The cultural or ethnic differences evoked in the film are not critical ones that could upset the unspoken but assumed racial hierarchy. In the film as in life, the officers are all White, with one low-ranking exception. One of the Nisei men is seemingly always grumbling about racism, but none is unruly. There is, moreover, an overall emasculinization of the Nisei soldiers that serves to domesticate them in such a way as to safely position them in the existing racial hierarchy. U.S. propaganda such as *Know Your Enemy* had only a few years earlier created an almost superhuman image of the "Jap" soldier. It was said that although physically small, averaging "five-foot three inches and one hundred and seventeen pounds," "Jap" soldiers were tough and hardened, fantastic soldiers who would "just as soon go over a mountain as around it." And fear of the yellow men living in the United States was often expressed as a fear of their sexual insatiability.[21]

Go for Broke helped harness these menacing images of Japanese American male physicality and sexuality. Most pertinent is an odd subplot of the film involving Tommy. Tommy is the smallest of the small soldiers. When Grayson first sees him he is wearing a uniform that is grossly oversized. Tommy is nearly childlike in his personality as well as his physical size. He confesses in tears one day that he wants to fight against the Japanese because both his parents were killed at Pearl Harbor. He has no parents, no girlfriend, and he longs to but never receives letters. One day while in combat he finds a baby pig, which he decides to adopt. Only a little earlier, we have seen Grayson listening to records, kissing, and drinking wine with a beautiful local Italian woman, but the closest Tommy gets to the erotic is in his adventures with the pig.

As the film proceeds the baby pig gets bigger. A local Italian peasant says he would like to buy Tommy's pig so that he can mate it with his female pig. This is the first intimation we have that Tommy's pig has a sex, and as the pig turns his hindquarters toward us, we can see that he is indeed a male. "*Bambinos, amore,*" the Italian implores, but Tommy misunderstands and thinks the Italian and his family want to buy his pig to eat. The Italian peasant's children assure him, "No eat, no eat." Tommy finally gets the point, smiles, but protests that the pig is too young. He will grow bigger, the peasant responds. Yet Tommy refuses the offer and appears disturbed by even the thought of such a union.

Soon the men of the 442nd ship out from Italy on their way to France, and Tommy smuggles the pig aboard. But we can see that the pig is growing quite large and is rambunctious as well. Tommy can barely hide the squirming pig in his duffle bag. In France, Tommy must ask a poor peasant family to care for the pig while he himself goes off to combat. Later, Tommy returns for his pig and rewards the peasant with two packs of cigarettes. The peasant is grateful, but disappointed, for his large family, which includes several children, has very little to eat. Tommy looks down at the pig, but decides not to offer it as food to the French family. But as he walks away he sees the Frenchman's wife cradling a small infant, while looking nearly lifeless herself. Tommy returns to the Frenchman's barn and comes out alone. His flirtation with the sexual ends. The fat pig is presumably eaten. Tommy's desexualization is one condition for postwar acceptance of Japanese Americans into (White) America. There is some irony in this, as the masculinist discourse of military heroism has been one element mobilized by Japanese American men to recuperate their self-esteem. Moreover, there has been a great price paid in terms of the status of Japanese American women, because one consequence of the discourse of the male Japanese American soldier as citizen has been the figuring of Japanese American women as citizens of a secondary rank.

"Model Minority" and the Cold War

Go for Broke was part of the postwar transition to a discourse on the nation and racialized peoples within it that countenanced cultural difference as long as it did not upset the top of the racial hierarchy. As we have seen, earlier representations of Japanese Americans as soldiers and citizens tended to erase difference as the condition for acceptance in (White) America. *Go for Broke* and the discourse on the "model minority" that followed it is to be contrasted with this radically assimilationist view—a view that had been held by leading figures in the internment administration such as Dillon S. Myer as well as by liberal citizens who were not officials—where cultural differences, described as dangerously "nationalistic," would eventually be erased altogether as racial minorities blended into communities throughout the (White) nation.[22] *Go for Broke* was part of a new pattern of representations and discourses in which values considered to be traditional in Asian societies were celebrated as conducive to Americanism.

As others have already pointed out, the heyday of the "model minority" discourse took place in the mid-1960s, when Chinese Americans, and even more so Japanese Americans, came to be represented as the examples toward which all Americans, including even Whites, should aspire. At that time articles such as the sociologist William Petersen's "Success Story, Japanese-American Style" and "Success Story of One Minority Group in U.S." began to appear in the mainstream media.[23] These articles made a connection between what were perceived to be traditional Asian values and achievement in education and employment. Respect for authority, love of learning, a work ethic, and so on were supposed to be the secrets of Asian American success. Moreover, to focus more specifically on Japanese Americans and military heroism, Petersen argued that unlike what he called the "problem minorities," Japanese Americans had practically overcome racial discrimination and succeeded as citizens in American society "by their own almost totally unaided effort." And he cited their military record against the backdrop of internment as evidence of Japanese American efforts and abilities to transcend extreme prejudice on the way to becoming model citizens. While he noted that some Japanese Americans had understandably refused to serve, "most accepted as their lot the overwhelming odds against them and bet their lives, determined to win even in a crooked game."[24]

Many activists and scholars have already pointed out the utility of this logic in the 1960s for conservative denials of the debilitating effects of racism. Following the rise of the Civil Rights Movement, Black militancy, urban uprisings, and a move toward greater state intervention in race relations, the model minority success story could be mobilized to delegitimate the demands of other minorities for more aggressive measures to achieve social justice. In other words, it could be argued that Asian Americans and especially Japanese Americans had succeeded through their own efforts despite racial prejudice and that other minorities should do the same. Ultimately, minorities who failed had only themselves to blame for their miserable circumstances.

Yet, the minor explosion into the public arena of a discourse on Japanese

Americans as the model minority must also look beyond the domestic scene. The prominence of Japanese Americans as the "almost but not quite White" minority coincides in both logic and historical timing with the construction of a discourse on Japan as the honorary White nation. As early as the end of the Asia-Pacific War, Japan was seen as a potential ally for the United States in East Asia against the Soviet threat, and this forced a fundamental transformation of popular images about Japan and the Japanese people. Particularly in the cold war years, images of Japan underwent a miraculous metamorphosis, from a backward nation peopled by an insectlike or herdlike population, to the United States' most reliable, friendly, and democratic ally (although racism and stereotypes obviously continued to exist in latent and sometimes blatant form).[25] As the democratic, capitalist, and "almost but not quite White" nation, "Japan" came to be deployed as the new model for aspiring peoples of color throughout the world.

This reconstitution of Japan and the Japanese people found scholarly support in social science theorizing. Modernization theory as applied to Japan began toward the end of the 1950s and reached the height of its popularity in the 1960s and early 1970s, in other words, precisely at the moment when the model minority discourse achieved its first explicit articulation.[26] In effect, modernization theory remade Japan into what I would call the "global model minority." Japan, it was argued, had waited a long time to modernize. The roots of its ability to modernize, which primarily meant to industrialize and to become an economic superpower, had already existed in Japan centuries ago in the Tokugawa period. Among the most influential of such works was that of the sociologist Robert N. Bellah, who found in the religious beliefs and practices of seemingly all Japanese people in the Tokugawa period Japanese analogues to Max Weber's famous Protestant ethic.[27] In other words, it was as if the Japanese people, possessed of an ethic of hard work and frugality, had already been desiring to be the Same as (White) Americans and Western Europeans even before the arrival of the West. The related message to the rest of the non-Western (non-White) world, however, was that they had only themselves and their culture or lack of culture to blame for their backwardness or lack of development. They were not possessed of the attributes, particularly the positive traditional values of the Japanese global model minority, and should aspire to be like them. In addition, it was often argued that the other nations of the non-Western world should be patient. It had taken a long time for Japan to modernize and it would take a long time for other nations to develop as well.[28]

The locations of Japan in the world and Japanese Americans in U.S. society were both homological and mutually reinforcing, with the direct influence of modernization theory on the production of the domestic model minority discourse especially evident. Petersen, for example, set up the terms of his problematic by asking why Japanese Americans, in contrast to "Negroes, Indians, Mexicans, Chinese and Filipinos," had been able to overcome "color prejudice." The Japanese immigrant group had been like every White ethnic immigrant group, each of which had within a generation or two taken "advantage of the public schools, the free labor market and America's political democracy; it climbed out of the slums, took on better-paying occupations and acquired social respect and dignity."[29] Why, he asked rhetorically, had the Japanese been the sole non-White minority group to successfully emulate the White minorities? For the answer, Petersen turned to the work of social scientists of Japan such as Bellah. The secret to Japanese American success, it seemed, was to be found in the quality of the culture that the Japanese immigrants had brought with them from Japan. As Petersen put it: "The issei who came to America were catapulted out of a homeland undergoing rapid change—Meiji Japan, which remains the one country of Asia to have achieved modernization. We can learn from such a work as Robert Bellah's 'Tokugawa Religion' that diligence in work, combined with simple frugality, had an almost religious imperative, similar to what has been called 'the Protestant ethic' in Western culture." Moreover, like Bellah's functionalist interpretation of the Japanese version of the Protestant ethic, Petersen praised Japanese American values not for their explicit surface features—it mattered little, for example, whether Japanese Americans were Christian or Buddhist—but for their utility in providing the motive force for Japanese American success.[30]

Again, to make this point, Petersen used the negative example of "Negroes." The inability of the "Negroes" to overcome racism, he said, could be explained not by their distance from "American culture," but rather by their alienation from African culture. "Negroes," he maintained, are the "minority most thoroughly imbedded in American culture, with the least meaningful ties to an overseas fatherland." Therefore, the "Negro" has "no refuge when the United States rejects him. Placed at the bottom of this country's scale, he finds it difficult to salvage his ego by measuring his worth in another currency." In contrast, the Japanese "could climb over the highest barriers our racists were able to fashion in part because of their meaningful links with an alien culture."[31] In other words, according to Petersen, the inability of African Americans to succeed in American society was the direct result of the inadequacy of their culture, whereas the success of Japanese Americans was due precisely to the fact that they were not alienated from their cultural legacy. This is a far cry from the earlier radical assimilationist model for Japanese American disappearance into White America. It marks the postwar and cold war racialization of U.S. society where Japanese Americans and some other Asian Americans became the "almost but not quite White" model minority, whereas "Negroes" and other racial minorities were represented as incompetent citizens because their cultures could not function similarly.

I have made this rather long excursion into modernization theory and its linkages to the production of global and domestic model minorities to further advance the thesis that the prominence of Japanese American military heroism in mainstream discourse cannot be explained by the sheer force of heroism alone. Instead, domestic and global conditions colluded to secure the hegemony of the White, capitalist, and liberal domestic powers through the construction of global and domestic model minorities. In the end, the prominence of Japanese American military valor in postwar U.S. war memory must be seen as having been enabled, at least in part, by the postwar and cold war position of Japan.

Overcompensation and Hyperidentification

Thus far, I have tried to explain the prominence of Japanese Americans in U.S. military and national discourse from the point of view of the reracialization of postwar U.S. society and the world order under U.S. hegemony. I want to take a different tack now, that of examining the subjective drive within a large group of Japanese Americans that would cause them to actively participate in the production and reproduction of discourses that in fact serve to maintain both U.S. nationalism and racial hierarchy. The main text I take up is the autobiography of Mike Moses Masaoka. Although Masaoka has been vilified by Asian American activists who have objected to his overidentification with White America, there is no doubt that as the Japanese American Citizens League's first executive secretary and as probably the most well-known Japanese American lobbyist in Washington during the past sixty or so years, he has been, as a recent publication put it, "arguably the most famous and most influential Japanese American of his time."[32] Moreover, Masaoka's case is particularly compelling in examining Japanese Americans within U.S. national, racial, and military discourses because he was one of the community's strongest advocates for admitting Japanese Americans into the military during the war years, supposedly the first Nisei to volunteer for the 442nd, and a long-term proponent of Japanese American assimilation. Furthermore, Masaoka served as the special consultant for the film Go for Broke.[33] He was, so to speak, the film's primary native informant.

This is not to say that Masaoka's was the only possible response to the contradictory discourses of U.S. nationalism and racism. Hundreds of men from the ten concentration camps refused to ignore the logical incommensurability of the nationalist discourse that disavowed racism and the racist discourses and practices that put Japanese Americans in the camps: 315 Japanese American men were convicted of draft evasion and most spent around two years in prison. Their reasoning, as Frank Emi, one of the draft resistance leaders, has succinctly put it, was that "if we were citizens what the hell were we and our families doing in these concentration camps without semblance of due process. If we were not citizens, the draft does not apply to us."[34] Likewise, Tamotsu Shibutani has given us an account of how one group of Japanese American men, far from exhibiting exemplary heroism in military service, became so thoroughly demoralized by discrimination and their inability to live up to the high expectations placed on them, that they came to form "one of the more disorderly units in United States history." According to Shibutani, Company K became an object of scorn to many, including many Nisei veterans; it was commonly identified as a "fuck-up outfit."[35]

Moreover, long ago in her classic history of the concentration camps, Michi Weglyn concluded that those "patriots who roundly cheered the development [of allowing Nisei enlistment in the military] were vastly outnumbered, and in centers where feelings ran high, those who volunteered did so secretly, fleeing the camps in the dead of the night." In the end, although the recruitment effort was a spectacular success in Hawai'i, where there had been no wholesale internment, it was a dismal failure on the mainland. According to an internal official history of the Office of the Provost Marshal General, although a quota of 3,000 Japanese American volunteers had been set for the mainland, fewer than 1,500 eventually volunteered. Almost two months after the announcement of Japanese American eligibility, only 1,253 out of 23,606 eligible male citizens had enlisted, so that "it became clear by the end of March [1943] that the recruiting drive had failed because the evacuees resented what they considered to be unjust treatment at the hands of the War Department and other government agencies."[36]

That even second-generation Japanese Americans such as Joseph Kurihara, who had never lived in Japan, sometimes adopted a pro-Japan stance as a result of racism and the internment experience has long been known (though the memory has usually been suppressed).[37] At the Tule Lake camp, where those considered to be "disloyal" as a result of their responses to the infamous loyalty questions of 1943 had been moved, a "Japanese" cultural and political renaissance took place. Whatever their individual reasons might have been, it has been estimated that some eight thousand people of Japanese descent—a number that includes Issei, Nisei, and Kibei (Nisei who had been educated partly or wholly in Japan, who subsequently returned to the United States)—left the United States for Japan during or immediately after the war years.[38] New research has begun to recover the experiences of perhaps thousands of Japanese in Hawai'i and the mainland United States who not only failed to serve in the

U.S. military, but who chose to emigrate to Manchuria as part of the Japanese imperial project; it is clear that in the face of racism, other Japanese Americans sometimes rejected the claims of U.S. nationalism by actively utilizing their skills to promote Japanese expansionism on the Asian continent.[39]

Finally, for many the demand for a total and exclusive commitment to either U.S. or Japanese nationalism led to confusion and finally resignation to particular courses of action to which even they themselves were not fully devoted. The case of the thousands of men and women who renounced their U.S. citizenship under severe duress is relevant here. It is clear that many who renounced did so because they feared the reprisals of pro-Japan elements in the camps or, conversely, because they believed that if considered "loyal Americans" they might be released into racist and violent communities outside the camps. Others gave in to parental pressure to show loyalty to Japan, acted out of fear that relatives abroad would be persecuted by the Japanese government if they did not demonstrate their disloyalty to the United States, or for other reasons having little to do with absolute devotion to any nation.[40] In short, Japanese Americans reacted to the war in a variety of ways and Mike Masaoka's hyperidentification with "America" represents only one possibility within a range of choices that were made. Nevertheless, it is worth examining a response such as Masaoka's because it is the one that has occupied the dominant position in both mainstream and Japanese American memories of the war. Moreover, his writings suggest why even those in highly disprivileged locations within racist nations might desire to identify with those very collectivities.

They Call Me Moses Masaoka reveals the splitting effects of the duplicitous discourses of nationalism and racism on the racialized subject-citizen that results in an extreme identification with the Nation. As is probably the case in all modern nation-states, the message generated by U.S. nationalism and racism has been *duplex*, as in the language of electronics, where two messages can be sent simultaneously in opposite directions through the same wire. On the one hand, it promises equality, freedom, and opportunity for all, while on the other hand maintaining a strict hierarchy of differences whereby all subjects are evaluated on a standardized basis of qualifications or distinctions and are compelled toward normalization. Some of these qualifications can be acquired, such as through educational achievement, correction of social behavior (acquiring civility in a general way, speaking properly, keeping clean, not eating smelly foods, and so on), or through exceptional military service. But others are presumed to be inherent and therefore cannot be easily overcome by individual effort, such as with perceived race, ethnicity, or gender. The latter "deficiencies" can only be compensated for by extraordinary efforts in attaining the former qualifications. This is the structure, reduced to its bare essentials, of modern nationalist and racist discourses that compel many members of minoritized groups toward extreme demonstrations of "love" for the national community. In other words, overcompensation or hyperidentification is one reasonable response to the contradictory ways in which national subjects are interpellated as both equal and as less than equal. For the purposes of this paper, it can be said that this is the mechanism that drove many Japanese Americans toward military heroism and death.

Frantz Fanon noted long ago that "to speak is to exist absolutely for the Other."[41] Speaking appears as an obsession in Masaoka's life and autobiography. Throughout the autobiography Masaoka repeatedly refers to his extraordinary ability to speak as the (White) Other.[42] He writes proudly of his enormous successes as an award-winning member of debating teams, of his superb qualifications as a spokesman for Japanese American and American interests, and he seems to have had just as much pride in his inability to speak Japanese. However, as much as he sought recognition from the Other as the (White) Other, his anxiety intensified as that Other throughout his life reminded him that he was precisely other than White. Yet this appears only to have generated an even greater desire for recognition as the Same.

Masaoka himself tells a tragic and pathetic story of his own desire to speak as the (White) Other, coupled with the Other's unwillingness to recognize him as such. He prefaces the story of his own discovery of oratory with reflections on the racism that he experienced as a Japanese. He remembered that at the movies, for example, the Nisei were forced to sit in the "topmost seats in the balcony—then known as nigger heaven—along with the blacks." Yet despite the discrimination that he and other Japanese faced, he participated in typical schoolboy activities and through them became infatuated with public speaking: "I had always been articulate. Sometimes I was contentious. The thought of standing before an audience and speaking was both exciting and frightening. Oratory at that time in Salt Lake City, when radio was just beginning to come in, was a major youth activity. . . . A good speaker was looked up to, like a football or basketball star."[43]

After a self-professed illustrious high school career as a debater, Masaoka entered the University of Utah and joined the university forensics team. Despite the Depression and the burdens of working his way through college, he writes of happy days on the debating team, of his successes and what he took to be full acceptance by other squad members. He liked rubbing shoulders with these young men of the university social elite and describes them as later becoming enormously successful in business or politics: "Traveling to various parts of the Intermountain West to debate, we shared dreams and hopes of the future. All my teammates had excellent minds and were stimulating company. Despite the differences in backgrounds, I was fully accepted. In fact, I might have been considered their leader. I was welcome in their homes and became acquainted with their girls" (41). Speaking seemed to offer an avenue to becoming the Other, as well as to share the company of what he describes as the possessions ("their girls") of these young White elite men.

Yet, as the narrative proceeds, we soon learn that the moment of Masaoka's greatest speaking triumph in youth also presented him with a devastating reminder that White America would usually choose to recognize him as anything but White. The incident occurred in 1936 at the National Invitational Tournament in Denver, "the biggest challenge we (the University debate team) had faced." Masaoka came away from the challenge with the highest honors, yet the leading newspaper in the Intermountain West carried an incredible editorial, a portion of which is well worth citing at some length:

> This Republic is a land of liberty, democracy, and equal opportunity. . . . In an oratorical contest held recently in Denver, a young Japanese student of the University of Utah carried off the honors as the most effective speaker at the conference. . . .
>
> When an alien of Asiatic parentage is able to master the intricacies and absurdities of our orthography and to overcome lingual handicaps in pronunciation and articulation, to acquire an ability to think, to arrange his ideas in logical sequence, and to express them clearly and forcefully, there is no excuse for failure among American students. . . .
>
> Boys and girls with inherited aptitude, with mental and physical adaptation transmitted by successive generations of ancestors, with the incalculable advantage of always having heard the tongue in which they plead every cause from infancy to age, have little excuse to complain and fail in competition. (42–43)

In other words, the *Salt Lake Tribune* had simply assumed that Masaoka was nonnative, and when the editorial concluded by saying that his extraordinary performance "should also remind the world that neither race, nor creed, nor color constitute a bar to advancement here when merit asserts itself," it also showed Masaoka that being of the other race, creed, or color is in fact automatic grounds for assuming that one must certainly exist outside the Nation. "No matter what we do to demonstrate our Americanism, no matter how many generations we have been in the United States, many see our nonwhite faces as evidence of alien status" (42).

Yet this episode led not to Masaoka's abandonment of the desire for acceptance, but to an even greater vigilance over the (non-White) Other within, including that Other within that would speak as other than White. Although he does not mention it in his autobiography, it is known that in April 1942 he advised Milton Eisenhower, then director of the War Relocation Authority, that a central part of its policy of turning Japanese in the camps into Americans would be to correct their habits and speech. "Special stress should be laid on the enunciation and pronunciation of words," he implored, "so that awkward and 'Oriental' sounds will be eliminated."[44]

The American dream of steady progress toward the end of racism had an even hallucinatory effect on Masaoka. In his 1940 statement, "The Japanese-American Creed," written down, as he put it, "in one furious writing session" and then publicly circulated and even finding its way into the *Congressional Record*, Masaoka simply pretended to be living the American dream. Stating his pride in being an "American citizen of Japanese ancestry," he began a chorus of praises for all that America had given him, including "liberties and opportunities such as no individual enjoys in this world today." Moreover, he wrote that "She," the woman America, had "permitted me to build a home, to earn a livelihood, to worship, think, speak, and act as I please—as a free man equal to every other man." Yet, as Masaoka later reflected, some of what he had written was completely falsified. In fact, "I was barely earning a livelihood, and certainly I was in no position to build a home. But I had hopes, I was looking into the far future, I wrote in all sincerity; and never have I had occasion to change my mind about the meaning of America."[45] The American dream would be deferred, but he would act as if he lived it.

More broadly, Masaoka demonstrates in his autobiography what can perhaps best be described as an obsessional neurosis in which he must constantly locate the national/racial/cultural source of every attribute of his personality, as well as of other Japanese Americans around him. The Japanese side of the binary is not necessarily entirely negative, and therefore the split between the (White) Other and the (non-White) Other within does not have quite the rigid Manichean quality of the colonial subjectivity described by Fanon. Rather, it dovetails with what I earlier described as the logic of modernization theory and the "model minority" ideal, where the unique quality of the non-White nation/race/culture is allowed to exist insofar as it does not upset the dominant position of the White nation/race/culture and in fact assists the subject in becoming the (White) Other.[46] Thus, Masaoka writes that he learned the virtue of fortitude and patience from the Japanese side of his upbringing: "The Japanese have a word for that: *gaman*. It means to hang tough, endure, stick it out. That is what my parents did, and by example that is what they taught their family. . . . but I learned more than the virtue of enduring. I learned to fight for my rights. That was the American part of my heritage."[47] In his estimation, his wife, Etsu, sister of Congressman Norman Mineta, also had this split and hierarchized identity:

"Although she is American through and through, she combines her American strength, initiative, and independence with the finest qualities of Japanese womanhood, which are loyalty, dependability, compassion, and thoughtfulness" (368). And so on. Above all, Masaoka needs constant reassurance that despite his numerous experiences of (White) American racism, his vigilant subordination of the (non-White) Other within has been and continues to be justified.

The account of his first trip to Japan in 1952 is in effect a story in which he reassures himself that despite the existence of a Japanese side to his character and upbringing, he is at heart a (White) American. He revels in the fact that Japanese recognize him not as Japanese, but as American. In an amusing if pathetic story of his meeting with Prime Minister Yoshida Shigeru, he recounts how, not having a good grasp of the formal Japanese spoken language, he called the prime minister *ojisan*. For those who understand standard and formal Japanese, this would obviously be far too informal a way of addressing any senior male in a position of authority, let alone a man in such a high position. It would be the equivalent of an adult on formal business calling the U.S. president Uncle Bill, or perhaps something even less appropriate. But Masaoka writes that all adult men in the community of his childhood were called *ojisan*, and that was the term that came to him. The prime minister's aides were shocked, but Masaoka happily recalls how Yoshida himself simply told him, "You have taught us that Nisei are Americans. Certainly you are not Japanese" (262).

Later, Masaoka visits his father's birthplace, Hiroshima, and discovers numerous relatives, "simple folk, bronzed by the sun, their hands cracked by hard labor, uncomfortable in their best clothing" (265). Then he visits the family burial plot outside of town, a place of bamboo groves, thatched roofs, and ancient tombstones where he could feel the "presence of unknown ancestors." And "somewhere one of the season's last cicadas sang its raucous song." But this nostalgia for cultural/racial/national roots does not last long, for "Etsu looked at me and I looked at her, and we shared the same thought without speaking: Here, but for the grace of God, go I. More than ever I was grateful that my father had had the courage to seek a better life in the land called America, despite all its faults and shortcomings" (266).

Military service became the most effective method by which to compensate for the (White) Other's recognition of Masaoka as anything but White. Though the autobiography is again silent on this point, it is known that as a last-ditch effort to demonstrate Japanese American loyalty and to thereby avert an internment policy, Masaoka recommended that Nisei volunteers should be allowed to form a "suicide battalion." Not only would Nisei join such a squad, the U.S. government could keep the parents of these Nisei volunteers as hostages as an even greater guarantee of loyalty.[48] Moreover, as he states explicitly in the auto-biography, Masaoka welcomed the opportunity to compensate for his race with Japanese American blood: "Unfair as this discriminatory action [of internment] was, our national leaders laid down another condition: since we were untested as Americans, only in blood could we demonstrate loyalty to our country in its hour of peril." Masaoka and his four brothers all took up the challenge; one brother was killed in action and another returned home severely disabled. But Masaoka was far from bitter about America, for he emphasized that through this sacrifice in blood, he, his brothers, and his fellow Japanese American soldiers overcame racial prejudice and proved their "right to share the American dream."[49]

It has surely been of great comfort for many Americans—from FDR and Truman to Ronald Reagan and George Bush, to mention just a few named in this paper—to imagine and then remember that Nisei wartime heroism stemmed from an irrepressible love of country. The Japanese Americans loved their country so much, so the story goes, that they were able to look beyond the discrimination they experienced and in time overcame racism to realize the promised land that was already foretold in the nation's origins. Nisei heroism in this warmed-over, romanticized, and hallucinatory explanation was a way to demonstrate a natural and unproblematic love. Yet I would argue that for many (if not all) Nisei, the rate of casualties being so high as to suggest a near fanaticism (the 100th had the nickname "Purple Heart Battalion") can better be explained as stemming at least in part from the paranoia that grew out of the contradictions I have been describing—in other words, out of the fear of exclusion or nonacceptance that operated precisely because of the promise of inclusion. Japanese American heroism certainly does not sound so glorious when put in these terms. Yet, especially in our present moment, when anti-immigrant and racist sentiments are yet again on the rise even as racial discrimination is consistently disavowed, we are compelled to place the undeniably enduring though changing structures of racism and nationalism in the United States under more realistic scrutiny.

Notes

I have received the generous assistance of many people in the course of writing this chapter, and I would like especially to thank the following for their extraordinarily insightful comments and encouragement: Michael Bernstein, David Gutierrez, Yuji Ichioka, George Lipsitz, Lisa Lowe, Lisa Rofel, Geoff White, and Lisa Yoneyama.

1 John Okada, *No-no Boy* (reprint; Seattle: University of Washington Press, 1979), 121. The quotation describes a character in the novel, Kenji, who is a disabled WWII veteran.

2 Takashi Fujitani, "National Narratives and Minority Politics: The Japanese American National Museum's War Stories," *Museum Anthropology* 21, no. 1 (spring 1997): 99–112; and "G.I. Joe® Salutes the WWII Soldiers of the 442nd," *Pacific Citizen* 3–16 July, 1998.

3 *New York Times*, 8 December 1991; Bush speech on *From Hawaii to the Holocaust: A Shared Moment in History*, executive producer, Judy Weightman, The Hawai'i Holocaust Project, 1993.

4 *Pearl Harbor*, Collector's Edition of *Life* (fall 1991).

5 Ronald Takaki, *Strangers from a Different Shore* (Boston: Little, Brown, 1989), 357–63; Theo Gonzalves, 'We Hold a Neatly Folded Hope': Filipino Veterans of World War II on Citizenship and Political Obligation," *amerasia journal* 21, no. 3 (winter 1995–1996): 155–74; Leslie Bernstein, "Unhealed Wounds: Filipino Soldiers from WWII Are Still Fighting to Win Full Veterans Benefits," *Los Angeles Times*, 7 July 1995; and "Filipino Veterans Equity Bill Seeks Benefit Restoration," *Pacific Citizen*, 3–16 October 1997.

6 See, for example, Lyn Crost, *Honor by Fire* (Novato, CA: Presidio Press, 1994), 311–15; Chester Tanaka, *Go for Broke* (Richmond, CA: Go For Broke, Inc., 1982), 1.

7 Masayo Duus, *Unlikely Liberators: The Men of the 100th and 442nd*, trans. Peter Duus (Honolulu: University of Hawai'i Press, 1987), 231.

8 Etienne Balibar, "Racism and Nationalism," in Etienne Balibar and Immanuel Wallerstein, *Race, Nation, Class*, trans. Chris Turner (London: Verso, 1991), 37.

9 For example, Suchen Chan, *Asian Americans* (Boston: Twayne Publishers, 1991), 121–42.

10 Chungmoo Choi, "The Discourse of Decolonization and Popular Memory: South Korea," *positions* 1 (1993): 77–102. Interestingly, one Filipino soldier in the First Filipino Infantry Regiment, a segregated unit in the U.S. Armed Forces that had been established in February 1942, made a similar observation about the United States during the war years. Commenting on the contradiction between the promise of acceptance into American society provided by the possibility of serving in the military and ongoing racism, Manuel Buaken spoke of some towns in California as "this land of double-talk" (quoted in Takaki, *Strangers from a Different Shore*, 361).

11 Cynthia H. Enloe, *Ethnic Soldiers: State Security in Divided Societies* (Athens: University of Georgia Press, 1980).

12 The convergence of the formation of the 442nd with the policy for reintegration into life outside the camps is covered in Commission on Wartime Relocation and Internment of Civilians, *Personal Justice Denied* (Washington, DC: U.S. Government Printing Office, 1982), 185–212; for the Roosevelt quote, 191. The possibility of utilizing interned Japanese Americans to meet wartime labor shortages also no doubt contributed to the official shift toward a policy of reintegration. See, for example, Michi Weglyn, *Years of Infamy: The Untold Story of America's Concentration Camps* (New York: William Morrow, 1976), 93–102. Furthermore, the U.S. government used Nisei soldiers as a global propaganda tool to demonstrate to the world that its war was not a racist war to preserve White imperialism and privilege in Asia (see T. Fujitani, "Raishawaa no kairai tennōsei kōsō" [Reischauer's plan for a puppet regime emperor system], *Sekai* 672 [March 2000]: 137–46).

13 Hearst newsreel footage, "Japanese-American troops," UCLA Film and TV Archive (ca. 1944).

14 Quoted in Mike Masaoka with Bill Hosokawa, *They Call Me Moses Masaoka* (New York: William Morrow, 1987), 178. On Reagan's experiencing of the movies as the hyperreal, see Michael Paul Rogin, *Ronald Reagan, the Movie and Other Episodes in Political Demonology* (Berkeley: University of California Press, 1987).

15 U.S. Department of the Interior, War Relocation Authority, in collaboration with the War Department, *Nisei in Uniform* (1945), unpaginated.

16 *Know Your Enemy—Japan*, directed by Frank Capra, U.S. Army Pictoral Service, Signal Corps, 1945.

17 *New York Times*, 16 July 1946. Truman's speech is almost always cited in Nisei soldier commemoratives.

18 Hearst newsreel footage, "Japanese-American troops," UCLA Film and TV Archive (ca. 16 July 1946).

19 *Go for Broke*, produced by Dore Schary, directed by Robert Pirosh, MGM, 1951.

20 This is according to Masaoka, *They Call Me Moses Masaoka*, 216.

21 On the latter point, see Dennis Ogawa, *From Japs to Japanese: An Evolution of Japanese-American Stereotypes* (Berkeley: McCutchan Corporation, 1971), 14–16.

22 Richard Drinnon, *Keeper of Concentration Camps: Dillon S. Myer and American Racism* (Berkeley: University of California Press, 1987). One of the most well-known private citizens to proffer such a radically assimilationist view was the photographer Ansel Adams, who in his *Born Free and Equal* (New York: U.S. Camera, 1944), declared that minorities such as Japanese Americans could "protect themselves" by "scatter[ing] throughout the country—to avoid concentration in nationalistic groups in towns and rural areas" (36). Under this logic, he argued that the forced evacuation of Japanese Americans and their subsequent dispersal into mainstream American society could actually aid in the national project of rejecting racism, of treating all as equal individuals regardless of their "race, color, or religion."

23 William Petersen, "Success Story, Japanese-American Style," *New York Times Magazine*, 9 January 1966; "Success Story of One Minority Group in U.S.," *U.S. News and World Report*, 26 December 1966. For critiques of the "model minority" discourse, see, for example, Bob H. Suzuki, "Education and the Socialization of Asian Americans: A Revisionist Analysis of the 'Model Minority' Thesis," in *Asian Americans: Social and Psychological Perspectives*, ed. Russell Endo, Stanley Sue, and Nathaniel N. Wagner (Palo Alto, CA: Science and Behavior Books, Inc., 1980), 2:155–75; and Keith Osajima, "Asian Americans as the Model Minority: An Analysis of the Popular Press Image in the 1960s and 1980s," in *Reflections on Shattered Windows*, ed. Gary Y. Okihiro et al. (Pullman: Washington State University Press, 1988). Petersen later expanded his views in the book *Japanese Americans: Oppression and Success* (New York: Random House, 1971).

24 Petersen, "Success Story, Japanese-American Style," 36.

25 For prewar and wartime U.S. images of Japan, see John Dower, *War without Mercy* (New York: Pantheon, 1986).

26 For example, the six volumes in the most ambitious publication project of the modernization theorists were published by Princeton University Press between 1965 and 1971 in the series "Studies in the Modernization of Japan."

27 Robert N. Bellah, *Tokugawa Religion: The Values of Pre-Industrial Japan* (Glencoe, IL: Free Press, 1957).

28 I have written in more detail on modernization theory in "*Minshūshi* as Critique of Orientalist Knowledges," *positions* 6, no. 2 (fall 1998): 303–22.

29 Petersen, "Success Story, Japanese-American Style," 40.

30 Ibid., 41

31 Ibid., 43

32 Brian Niiya, ed., *Japanese American History: An A-to-Z Reference from 1868 to the Present* (New York: Facts On File, Inc., 1993), 226.

33 Masaoka, *They Call Me Moses Masaoka*, 216.

34 Frank Emi, "Resistance: The Heart Mountain Fair Play Committee's Fight for Justice," *amerasia journal* 17, no. 1 (1991): 49. With regard to the ongoing division within the Japanese American community concerning the legitimacy of Nisei draft resistance during the war, see Susan Moffat, "Draft Rift Lingers 50 Years Later," *Los Angeles Times*, 12 March 1993. On 5 February 1995 the Pacific Southwest District of the Japanese American Citizens League voted, but after much "heated debate," to issue a formal apology to the draft resisters for the JACL's past unwillingness to recognize the legitimacy of their resistance (*Pacific Citizen*, 17 March–6 April 1995). The issue of draft resistance is an important and complex one that I cannot treat adequately here. I simply note that although I believe draft resistance was legitimate by practically any criteria, the Japanese American discourse on it today tends to reinforce the nationalist narrative that deems the Japanese American experience to have been an aberration.

35 Tamotsu Shibutani, *The Derelicts of Company K* (Berkeley: University of California Press, 1978), vii, 3.

36 Michi Nishiura Weglyn, *Years of Infamy: The Untold Story of America's Concentration Camps*, updated ed. (Seattle: University of Washington Press, 1996), 136. Office of the Provost Marshal General, "World War II: A Brief History" (ca. November 1945), 259, RG319, Records of the Army Staff, Records of the Office of the Assistant Chief of Staff, G-2 (Intelligence), Historical Studies and Related Records of G-2 Components, 1918–1959, Box 31, Miscellaneous Files, National Archives. The effort to recruit WACs was also a "complete failure": out of a quota of 500 volunteers only 142 had volunteered by the end of October 1945 (263). I thank Yuji Ichioka for his generosity in making this report available to me. The conclusions I have reached are, of course, my own.

37 See the biographical notes on Joseph Yoshisuke Kurihara in Dorothy Swaine Thomas and Richard S. Nishimoto, *The Spoilage* (Berkeley: University of California Press, 1946), 363–70, which includes excerpts from Kurihara's own manuscripts. By his own account and the records of informants, Kurihara was a Hawai'i-born Nisei and WWI veteran who was staunchly pro-American prior to the Second World War. However, he became pro-Japanese as a result of his belief that the United States had betrayed him. He is well-known as one of the leaders of the famous Manzanar uprising of December 1942 and also as among the first to renounce his U.S. citizenship.

38 Donald E. Collins, *Native American Aliens: Disloyalty and the Renunciation of Citizenship by Japanese Americans during World War II* (Westport, CT: Greenwood, 1985), 120–21.

39 For an important recent attempt to reconsider the question of Japanese American "loyalty," see the articles in Yuji Ichioka, guest ed., *Beyond National Boundaries: The Complexity of Japanese-American History*, special issue of *amerasia journal* 23, no. 3 (winter 1997–1998). In particular, John Stephan's "Hijacked by Utopia: American Nikkei in Manchuria" (1–42) discusses the allure of Manchuria for Japanese Americans who faced racism in Hawai'i and the Americas; and Yuji Ichioka's "The Meaning of Loyalty: The Case of Kazumaro Buddy Uno" (45–71) is a case study of a journalist in California, a one-time supporter of the assimilationist Japanese American Citizens League, who ultimately responded to U.S. racism by writing propaganda for the Japanese expansionist regime. For the Tule Lake renaissance, see Weglyn, *Years of Infamy*, 229–48. I am not suggesting that opting for

Japanese nationalism and imperialism was a better choice than celebrating American nationalism. At this historical juncture it seems most appropriate to critique the totalizing and exclusionary demands of both Japanese and U.S. nationalism.

40 Weglyn, *Years of Infamy*, 229–65; Collins, *Native American Aliens*. John Okada's *No-no Boy* is a moving fictional account of the nearly impossible situation that many Nisei found themselves in during the war, as well as a powerful interrogation of the legitimacy of both U.S. and Japanese nationalism. Okada actually served in the U.S. Army during the war but wrote sympathetically from the perspective of a young man who refused military service. This refusal stemmed not so much out of loyalty to Japan, but out of an inability to resolve the contradictory and arbitrary demands of Japanese and U.S. nationalism, as well as out of reaction to U.S. racism.

41 Frantz Fanon, *Black Skin, White Masks*, trans. Charles Lam Markmann (New York: Grove Press, 1967), 17.

42 Conversely, Sansei in many communities, including the community in which I grew up, often mimicked the speech of the (Black) Other as a tactic of disidentification with Whites.

43 Masaoka, *They Call Me Moses Masaoka*, 31.

44 Reproduced in Frank Chin, "Come All Ye Asian American Writers of the Real and the Fake," in *The Big Aiiieeeee*, ed. Jeffrey Paul Chan et al. (New York: Meridian, 1991), 59. Though I can agree with several of Chin's observations in the article in which this document is reproduced, and although he has done us a valuable favor in making important documents such as this one available, the article as a whole is fundamentally flawed and extremely offensive. His simplistic dichotimization of the "real" and the "fake" in Asian American writers and his arrogation of the right to determine authenticity to himself, as well as his masculinist rhetoric, are particularly appalling. His treatment of Masaoka and other "fakes" also tends toward personalized attacks rather than critical analyses of the ways in which Asian American writers have historically been interpellated in complex ways by the structures of U.S. racism and nationalism.

45 Masaoka, *They Call Me Moses Masaoka*, 50.

46 Fanon writes in *Wretched of the Earth*, trans. Constance Farrington (New York: Grove Press, 1968): "Because it is a systematic negation of the other person and a furious determination to deny the other person all the attributes of humanity, colonialism forces the person it dominates to ask themselves the question constantly: 'In reality, who am I?'" (250). Though different, the obsessive questioning and need to order self is quite similar.

47 Masaoka, *They Call Me Moses Masaoka*, 22.

48 Duus, *Unlikely Liberators*, 52–53.

49 Masaoka, *They Call Me Moses Masaoka*, 22–23.

Moving History: The Pearl Harbor Film(s)

GEOFFREY M. WHITE

For mainstream America, World War II remains largely the "good war." But elements such as compensation for interned Japanese Americans and the controversy surrounding the Smithsonian's ill-fated *Enola Gay* exhibit suggest that America's nostalgic war memories are beginning to fray around the edges. One of the mainstays of the canonical American narrative of World War II as the good war has been the story of Pearl Harbor, a story that locates the historical and moral origins of the Pacific War in a single, defining moment.[1] From that moment onward, the call to "Remember Pearl Harbor!" has continued to work as an interpretive frame for postwar memory.[2]

The sacred center of Pearl Harbor memory for the American imaginary is the USS *Arizona* Memorial, a national historic landmark and shrine built in 1962 over the sunken battleship.[3] Managed by the National Park Service and the U.S. Navy, the memorial is a location for national ceremonies of remembrance, for military enlistments and visitations, and for international tourism by more than a million and a half visitors each year. At the Visitor Center visitors find a museum, film, and interpretation from Park Service Rangers and Pearl Harbor veterans. The most consistent mode of representation in this milieu is a twenty-three-minute documentary film shown to everyone who wishes to board a boat to view the memorial.[4]

This paper takes advantage of the production of a new memorial film in 1991–1992 to examine national history "in the making." In comparing the old and new films, the paper plots a brief history of memory, mapping both continuities and transformations in Pearl Harbor narrative. The comparison reveals that certain features of Pearl Harbor history are remarkably robust through time. Despite the intent of the producers to make an entirely new film without reference to the one being replaced, the two films exhibit remarkable similarities. I interpret these parallels as evidence for the force of both narrative and politics as constraints on film-mediated national history.[5] By examining not only the text of the film but also the discussions and negotiations that produced it, I locate the film in a field of social relations of interest and power that include federal Park Service personnel, veterans, public historians, and filmmakers, all of whom turned out to have quite different stakes in Pearl Harbor history and its representations.

Those involved in making the film recognized the contested nature of their topic. In a memo written in response to cost overruns and delays encountered in finishing the project, the film's producer explained, "We are all doing a very difficult thing. We are making a major motion picture to be shown at the most controversial site the National Park Service manages. This site generates more letters to Congressmen and Park Service executives than any other site in America."[6] The contentious nature of official Pearl Harbor narrative framed the project from the beginning. As I show here, textual meanings were discussed and debated in ways that reveal official history-making to be more fluid, contested, and internally fractured than usually attributed to government-sponsored history. That being the case, what does it mean to speak of *official* history, or of a dominant or hegemonic national narrative? This paper argues that the Pearl Harbor film does not so much tell a single story as it mediates diverse readings among multiple publics. And yet the film itself does shape public understanding and sentiment, particularly in terms of what is seen as official history. By tracing the process through which a new Pearl Harbor narrative was scripted, critiqued, and finally institutionalized in film, it is possible to identify cultural and political forces that converge in national memory-making.

Historical Angst: Revisioning the Nation

Pearl Harbor is both past and present: symbol of national history and site of present-day military activity. Hence, the *Arizona* Memorial is inevitably surrounded by a certain amount of anxious monitoring and regulation—by ordinary citizens, by mass media, and by government and military agencies charged with managing the site. These anxieties are compounded by the fact that the memorial functions in multiple ways: as a sacred site of burial, as a location for military visits and ceremonies, and as a tourist destination. Concerns about the need to protect the integrity of the memorial are reflected in Park Service efforts to counter any "Disneyland effects" and in periodic comments by visitors objecting to the intrusion of "revisionist" histories deemed too sympathetic to the Japanese.[7]

Controversy regarding representations of history at the memorial came to a head in the year leading up to the fiftieth anniversary in 1991. Media interest in those controversies included an article in the *Wall Street Journal*, a nationally syndicated column by Thomas Sowell, and coverage on National Public Radio and the McNeil/Lehrer television program aired 6 December. In several respects, the pattern of criticism that emerged during this time resembled the Smithsonian controversy that would erupt three years later. As in the Smithsonian case, the most vocal critics were veterans and veterans groups, although their views were widely shared and repeated in the media. Their concerns centered on perceived attempts to dilute the nation's war history so as not to offend the Japanese, whether as allies and trade partners or as tourists coming to Hawai'i. At both the *Arizona* Memorial and the Smithsonian, representations of the war in markedly national spaces became an occasion for debate over competing claims to historical truth and authenticity.[8]

The memorial was built in 1961–1962, just after Hawai'i had become a state and as mass tourism was beginning to take off with the advent of commercial air travel. Managed by the National Park Service in cooperation with the U.S. Navy (and located within the bounds of today's Pearl Harbor Naval Base), the memorial is now the most frequently visited tourist destination in Hawai'i. In 1980 as Hawai'i's tourism industry entered a period of phenomenal growth, a visitor center was added with a small museum, gift shop, and two theaters for showing a documentary film before the visit to the memorial itself.

Although management of the memorial is closely regulated by the Park Service, many "official" voices speak there. Park rangers, veteran volunteers, and Navy personnel all participate in the active interpretation of Pearl Harbor history in a variety of ways, including theater talks, boatride narrations, lectures, museum displays, and simply answering questions. As visitors wait their turn to view the film and take the boatride to the memorial, they may ponder the museum displays, browse in the bookstore, or wander the grounds of the Visitor Center to view interpretive signs and vistas of today's Pearl Harbor.[9]

The most elaborate means of representing Pearl Harbor history at the Visitor Center is the documentary film. A visit to the memorial itself, with its wall of names of the 1,177 crew who lost their lives on the *Arizona*, is a moving but silent experience. In contrast, the film presents the story of the attack in an expanded, visual narrative. Even though only twenty-three minutes long, it weaves together historical photography, newsreel footage, and recent film of the memorial into a coherent narrative that moves chronologically through causes, details, aftermath, and, finally, to the present. Like the memorial, the film acquires a kind of sacred significance as an object that is unique to this site. It can be seen only at the memorial, it is not for sale as video, and it is not otherwise promoted or commercialized. When shown at the Visitor Center, there are no titles or credits of any kind. It is film documentary of a pure type, with the hand of the makers rendered invisible. Once people are settled in their seats (the theater has a capacity of about 150), a park ranger or veteran volunteer gives a few instructions and interpretive remarks, the lights go down, and the film rolls with the opening sequence.

The park rangers who manage the memorial and interpret its history for visitors recognize the narrative authority of the film. To quote from a memo written by the memorial's superintendent, "The film is our central interpretative tool. While . . . not our only interpretative tool, it is the only one that all visitors to the Memorial see. It must also be understood that it is the only interpretative element that all visitors experience that has an opportunity to present a consistent viewpoint. Ranger talks and survivor talks do not, by their very nature, provide for this consistency."[10]

In 1990 the Park Service managers decided to replace the film that had shown continuously since 1980. There were several reasons why. First, working copies of the 1980 film were wearing out and the original master had been lost (it was subsequently located). More important, there were a number of concerns about the content of the film—expressed by ordinary citizens as well as by the Park Service. Furthermore, the fiftieth anniversary in 1991 was deemed an ideal time to release a new, updated film. Probing the motives behind the making of a new Pearl Harbor film, the politics of its production, and the diverse reactions that it has evoked reveals a number of tensions and ironies in the process of official history-making.

Just as multiple and often conflicting interpretations of Pearl Harbor intermingle at the memorial, so there were numerous, sometimes contradictory motivations for making a new film. Although there were technical problems with the original film, the most powerful incentives for change came from public criticism of the film's content, voiced by various constituencies. I will mention two countervailing lines of criticism.

First of all, in the context of 1980s economic globalization, the original film had become the focus for generalized fears that the nation's history was being diluted to appease Japanese interests. This echoes veterans' criticisms of the Smithsonian *Enola Gay* exhibit. Second, the Park Service staff who manage the memorial, particularly the historical and curatorial staff most directly concerned with the content of interpretive exhibits, felt that the film had too many inaccuracies, too much "Hollywood" footage, and set a tone that was too aggressive for the kind of atmosphere appropriate to a memorial experience. Thus, the 1980 film, which had been produced by the U.S. Navy, was seen by some as too soft on the enemy and by others as too militaristic.

On the evening of 6 December 1991, the day before the fiftieth anniversary of the attack, the McNeil/Lehrer television program featured a brief extract from the 1980 film and noted that some survivors returning for the anniversary were unhappy with it. Although the vast majority of visitors to the memorial were leaving positive remarks about the film and their experience generally, some had reacted negatively, even to the extent of writing letters of complaint to congressional representatives or local newspapers. Foreshadowing the Smithsonian controversy, this criticism perceived a creeping revisionism that was distorting history in deference to Japanese sensitivities.

Interestingly, many of the letters of concern sent to congressional offices came from people who had neither visited the memorial nor seen the film but had read something about it written by someone else, who in turn may not actually have been there. One of the many publications on Pearl Harbor released during this period that provoked public reaction from people who had not been to the memorial was a book devoted to the theme of national "betrayal" at the highest levels of government. The book's authors captured the essence of these suspicions in their criticism of the memorial's 1980 film: "Presumably to assuage the modern consciences and the economics of Japanese tourism and business interests in Hawai'i, the film has been carefully sanitized so as to play down the treacherous nature of the attack that morning, which was made while diplomatic negotiations were still in progress. . . . Revisionist history is commonplace in communist countries, but it is bizarre to find it so grotesquely displayed in one of America's great shrines."[11]

This book, and the above passage in particular, inspired a letter-writing campaign by the organization American Ex-Prisoners of War. The organization circulated a memorandum quoting from this book to all chapter commanders asking that members write their lawmakers in Washington with the signed declaration, "I hereby protest the desecration of our national shrine, the USS *Arizona*." Among the specific points mentioned as examples of "historical revisionism" were assertions that the Park Service tour and film referred to Admiral Yamamoto as a brilliant strategist and implied that Japan was forced to attack Pearl Harbor. These complaints included the assertion that "Yamamoto's destruction of the fleet at Pearl Harbor is gloated over and applauded by Japanese tourists." When a journalist later queried the memorial's superintendent, Donald Magee, as to whether anyone had ever seen Japanese tourists applauding their victory at Pearl Harbor, Magee assured the journalist that he had checked with the projectionist and others who had worked there since 1980 and no one had ever heard of such a response.[12]

In the course of discussing the 1980 film, the superintendent gave me a copy of the script on which he had highlighted the most criticized lines—lines mentioned by the Ex-Prisoners of War group and others as well. These lines concerned two main points: reference to the Japanese attack as brilliant, and rationalization of the attack as justified from the Japanese point of view. As for the first point, the opening portion of the film shows the Navy ships at anchor in Pearl Harbor and states that they would "become the object of one of the most brilliantly planned and executed naval attacks in history." Later in the script, the commander of the Japanese fleet is referred to as "the brilliant strategist, Admiral Isoroku Yamamoto." The other lines in the script that Magee highlighted describe events leading up to the attack, labeling the United States an isolationist nation and saying that "Japan was being squeezed, cut off from oil, money frozen in the United States. Nearing economic ruin but still negotiating with America, Japan felt that her back was to the wall."

The Ex-Prisoners of War memorandum assumed that the Park Service was responsible for "sanitizing" the film and the interpretive program at the memorial and demanded that the U.S. Navy take over operation of the tours. Even though they were wrong about this (it was in fact the Navy that produced the film), they were getting at certain real tensions over interpretations of the events called Pearl Harbor. From the point of view of the park superintendent and historians, the original film had not inappropriately rationalized the Japanese attack. When I asked the superintendent about criticisms of the 1980 film, he said, "We've gotten all these complaints about how our old film justifies the attack on Pearl Harbor by the Japanese, which it didn't do really. I didn't see that."[13] Thus, although the Park Service concerns about the old film were quite different from those voiced by veterans' groups, veterans' criticisms provided additional incentive to make a new film.

What concerns were motivating the Park Service to make a new film? First of all, they felt that the old film emphasized "cold war" themes of military strength and preparedness and hence created an aggressive mood inconsistent with the somber tone appropriate to a memorial. Second, they were concerned about the film's historical accuracy and authenticity. They wished to eliminate staged footage and include only historical photographs and film.

The park rangers and volunteers who work daily at the memorial see the film in the larger context of a visit to a cemetery or tomb. Historical interpretation is linked with the personal experience of visiting a shrine and remembering the dead. As part of an embodied *practice* of remembrance, the film is a prelude to personally viewing the sunken ship and contemplating the shrine room's wall of names. Hence the memorial staff were concerned to set a serious tone of reflection that would counter any hint of the "Disneyland effect" that comes with people on vacation visiting a tourist site—which is, for many visitors, the way *they* define the situation as one part of a vacation in Hawai'i. In discussing the intent of the new film, nearly everyone involved in the project made this point.

The person charged with drafting the initial storyline and acting as liaison with the film company was the memorial's museum curator, Bob Chenoweth. When interviewed about the film prior to its completion, he put it this way:

> [The original film didn't] give the visitor a very good sense of what it was they were actually going out [to] see. By that I mean that it didn't set much of a tone for the fact that people were going out to a cemetery; that this was in fact not only a sunken ship out in the harbor. It's a place where nearly twelve hundred people lost their lives in an instant. There should be a certain amount of respect and reverence and reflection that occurred when people went out there. And it's always been a criticism in the park that you have a number of visitors that would go out there and not have that sense of understanding that this was, that they were walking into a cemetery. . . . And I think this is very important for people who come out to the memorial with, if there are survivors, or World War II veterans or something like that, this is very important for their lives; and to have kids running around or . . . visitors hooting and screaming and, you know, carrying on. It was clear that the message wasn't being transmitted.[14]

The producer, Lance Bird, echoed these sentiments when he talked about the importance of the film for setting the proper context for visiting the memorial, for giving it an appropriate emotional meaning: "The overridingly important thing about this film was that it prepare people for the emotional experience of being at Pearl Harbor. Because people sometimes literally show up there with coolers of beer thinking they are going to a Disneyland kind of experience, a tourist attraction. You know, sort of goofy stuff and then they are shocked of course when they walk in the front door and see what is going on there."[15]

For the Park Service historians at the memorial, the problems had less to do with the "economics of Japanese tourism and business interests in Hawai'i" than with the film's promotion of cold war attitudes toward military strength, specifically, naval power. In Superintendent Magee's view, the 1980 film concentrated too much on the lesson of military preparedness and not enough on remembrance of those who died on 7 December. After his views were written up in a feature article in Smithsonian magazine on the eve of the Pearl Harbor fiftieth anniversary,[16] Magee received several letters of concern. One of them, written by Joseph DeSanctis, complained: "The Park Service planned (at press time) to produce a new film for the visitors center, and that 'one point that [the film] won't make is that eternal preparedness is the lesson of Pearl Harbor.' I have not been to Pearl Harbor yet, and certainly hope to visit. But if Mr. Zinsser is correct in his characterization of the lessons of your new visitor's film, then I must raise strong objections. . . . No, the Arizona matters because it demonstrates so clearly the danger of not being prepared."[17] To this the Superintendent replied: "We do not disagree with the motto, 'Be Prepared' or 'Keep America Alert,' however, as a Memorial we believe that our focus should be on remembering the sacrifices made on December 7, 1941. During the years of WWII the slogan 'Remember Pearl Harbor' motivated an entire population to support the war effort. However, as the years go by there are fewer and fewer who do remember Pearl Harbor. . . . It is, therefore our duty and mission to tell the Pearl Harbor story through the new film, exhibits, and talks by both park rangers and seven Pearl Harbor survivors who generously volunteer their time and effort."[18]

The park historian, Daniel Martinez, was more direct. When interviewed for a newspaper story about the change of films, he stated flatly that the Navy film "was very much a product of a Cold War mind-set."[19] When the admiral in command of the Pearl Harbor Naval Base read these comments, he called the memorial superintendent and objected to this attribution of a cold war mentality to the Navy.[20] The admiral's call is indicative of the closely watched environment in which Pearl Harbor history is represented at the memorial. The disagreement itself indexes wider differences between U.S. Navy interests in the memorial and the National Park Service's view of its role in preserving and interpreting national history—differences manifest in contrasts between the two films.

Park Service historian Martinez and museum curator Chenoweth also felt that the 1980 film failed to take advantage of the extensive amount of historical photography that had become available since the original film was made. In particular, they objected to the indiscriminate mixing of historical film with Hollywood footage from the original propaganda film *December 7th* produced in 1943 to fuel the war effort.[21] As public historians, they emphasized the need to utilize historical and archival materials to represent the attack as fully and accurately as possible. The memorial staff were laying claim to a professional commitment to objectivity. As Chenoweth put it, "The original film was created by the Navy in 1979 and 1980 and was based on information, accurate or inaccurate, that was at hand at the time. [It] is a film that, obviously, since it was made by the Navy, reflects the Navy's point of view. In some ways it is very objective. In other ways there are historical inaccuracies and in some cases . . . the interpretation is not exactly in line with what we know to be accurate today."[22]

The range of concerns analyzed above contributed to the Park Service's decision to make a new film—a long and (as it turned out) expensive process. Funding came primarily from the *Arizona* Memorial's Museum Association and proceeds from the Visitor Center and gift shop. Indeed, given the differing motives brought to this project by the various parties involved, the task of scripting a new narrative proved to be more complicated and contentious than anyone predicted. A project originally estimated to take six months with perhaps three or four script revisions ended up taking two years and seventeen scripts. A closer look at the scripting process—at who got to speak about Pearl Harbor history on this occasion, their concerns, and the influence their voices had on the crafting of the film—offers a glimpse into the interests and institutions that shape national memory.

The Politics of Production

The first step for the Park Service and the Museum Association was to select a production company. Two companies were already making films for the fiftieth anniversary, and both were approached. One, the American Studies Film Center in New York, stood out because of its reputation for making good American history documentary films. The overall project, then, was undertaken as a contract between two parties: the film company and the National Park Service (or, more precisely, the memorial's Museum Association as funder).

Each party brought in a wider circle of individuals and organizations to review scripts and preliminary rough cuts of the film. Roughly thirty individuals evaluated and commented on the film. Filmmaker Lance Bird said that he had "never worked with that many people in an oversight relationship. . . . There were so many people who had a stake in this thing turning out well, [and] they emerged as the movie got going."[23] Perhaps because this film is shown at a site that is first and foremost a memorial and then a museum and historic landmark, the process of oversight and consultation placed veterans groups, especially Pearl Harbor survivors, in a privileged position of review and comment. These constituencies were represented at both the national level and in the memorial itself, where Pearl Harbor veterans work as volunteers and serve on the board of the Museum Association.

Wide consultation resulted in a slower and more expensive process than anyone had anticipated. But it also worked to head off the kind of adversarial posture taken by veterans groups challenging the *Enola Gay* exhibit at the Smithsonian's Air and Space Museum three years later. Although clear differences of historical vision emerged among the various parties consulting on the film, these did not lead to the kind of suspicion and alienation that erupt in media confrontation (although the memorial is no stranger to such media exposure, as demonstrated during the weeks leading up to the fiftieth anniversary of Pearl Harbor).[24]

The oversight process also provided a mechanism for validating the film as one acceptable to those most often regarded as guardians of national war memory: veterans, in this case World War II veterans. Specifically, the chief historian of the Park Service formed a review committee composed of representatives of the U.S. Navy and veterans groups, most notably the Pearl Harbor Survivors Association and two Medal of Honor winners.[25] Though useful as a way of fending off critics concerned with the subversion of patriotic values at the memorial, the high-level involvement of veterans and military authorities inevitably highlighted differing visions of the film and its message. Distinct differences emerged between the memorial staff and the film company on the one hand, and between the memorial staff and national advisors on the other.

One of the broad points of difference between the approach of the Park Service staff at the memorial and that of both the film company and the national military and veteran advisors concerned the use of personal stories and perspectives, as opposed to a more generalized narrative voice. The superintendent, historian, and curator at the memorial envisioned a film that would tell the story in terms of the larger sweep of history, supported by maximal use of historic photographs and film shot on 7 December. In contrast, both the film company and the military/veteran advisors wished to take a more personal approach and tell the story through the experience of particular individuals, such as those recognized for acts of heroism. The latter technique, that of telling the big story through a series of smaller, human stories, is essentially the literary device used by the most-read book about Pearl Harbor, *Day of Infamy* by Walter Lord. In a style reminiscent of John Hersey's *Hiroshima*, Lord's book begins and ends within the frame of a single day, 7 December 1941, telling the story of the attack through personal experiences of the bombing.

Because the American Studies Film Center was already engaged in producing a longer film about Pearl Harbor for broadcast on public television during the fiftieth anniversary, they had accumulated a great deal of oral historical testimony from Pearl Harbor survivors and others. They were anxious to use this material in producing the shorter film for the memorial. Yet, when they sent their first rough cut for review by the memorial's staff and the Museum Association, it was greeted with some disturbance as so far from the desired result as to require starting over. Among the problems discussed were the absence of a coherent historical story line, the use of Hollywood footage, and the mixing of multiple voices in the narration.

One aspect of this first cut that was regarded as particularly problematic was a segment narrated in the voice of a Japanese woman commenting on the rise of Japanese militarism in Japan. Whereas this met the park historians' desire to put the attack in a larger context, it was out of line with other expectations. As the film producer recalled the process, as more and more people reviewed the film, opinion swayed against devoting so much time to "the Japanese side of it":

"They thought the key historical points were being left out to give the time to the Japanese side of it."[26]

More generally, Park Service staff felt that the film company had failed to include enough information and to put it in the form of a consistent, chronological narrative. Mixing together a variety of voices and genres without a guiding story line did not achieve the kind of documentary portrayal they desired. In a letter to his superior in the Park Service Administration, Superintendent Magee wrote specifically of the difficulty of including "personal perspectives" in the film script, and the value of the film as a special type of interpretive tool:

> While it has always been considered important to provide a personal perspective to the telling of the story it has never been considered the primary view point from which the story would be told. This is done in ranger and survivor talks, and in books available through the bookstore. The early scripts, while attempting to present the Pearl Harbor story from a "personal" point of view, failed to tell the story accurately not only in the narrative but in the use of visual images. These early scripts and the "rough cut" viewed by AMMA [USS *Arizona* Memorial Museum Association] and park staff lacked a clear voice in telling the story; the same survivor voice describing Army and Navy activities. It was a good experiment, but obviously it didn't work for us. . . . It was our feeling that a straight forward telling of the events surrounding the attack would best serve the interpretative needs of the park. In support of this we feel that telling the story from a personal point of view has the tendency to exclude everyone else.[27]

Magee would soon be hearing calls for greater inclusion of the "personal voice" from other quarters, specifically from military and veteran representatives being consulted by the Park Service's chief historian in Washington, Edwin Bearss (himself a Marine veteran of the Pacific War). In addition to consulting with officials within the Park Service, Bearss distributed a copy of the script to officials in the Navy and the Park Service and to representatives of the major national veterans organizations and certain high-profile Pearl Harbor survivors. These included an assistant secretary of the Navy, director of the Naval Historical Center, and representatives of the American Legion, the American Ex-Prisoners of War, and the Pearl Harbor Survivors Association, as well as Medal of Honor recipient Captain Donald Ross and author Walter Lord.

On 20 April 1992, Bearss convened a "blue-ribbon panel" of individuals from these organizations to review the initial rough cut of the film. On the same day, they received a copy of a revised script produced by memorial curator Chenoweth. Their "major concern" about the revised script, as expressed by Bearss in a letter to Superintendent Magee, was that it conveyed an "overemphasis on death and suffering as opposed to heroism." The "recommended redress" suggested by this group was for the script to include more references to "acts by Medal of Honor winners and others."[28] This recommendation was followed up with a more forceful letter saying, "The reference to those heroes of December 7 (Ross, Finn, Hill, Dorie Miller, Welsh, and Taylor) that were indicated in our review of the last draft must be included. If cuts are to be made, they should be made elsewhere. These figures represent the common fighting men. If Kimmel, Short, Nagumo, and Yamamoto are to be mentioned by name, these men deserve mention."[29] Realizing that it would be difficult to effect changes in the film at this late date, Bearss added a note of authority to these recommendations: "We must insist on those changes and the following additions that reflect the thorough consensus of all members of our blue-ribbon panel and the desire of [NPS] Deputy Assistant Secretary Salisbury to be responsive to the comments of veterans and veterans organizations."[30] The insistence here reflects the emotive power of heroes as embodiments of a kind of personalized national sentiment. But despite this, the insistence of veterans and veterans organizations on this point did not in the end produce changes in the final script.

Magee, through the NPS director of the Western Region, responded that the film was not long enough to include references to individual heroic acts. The film already had an integrity of its own, guided more closely by the vision of the memorial staff and of a uniform documentary voice. At the end of the long process of production, the Park Service succeeded in implementing its vision of a new, authoritative film that would utilize historic film footage to tell the story of Pearl Harbor in a consistent and encompassing voice. The new film premiered on 2 December 1992 to generally laudatory reviews. Initial reactions indicated that the film somehow managed to meet the producers' stated goal of navigating between the poles of "Japan-bashing" and "justification."

Two Films/One Narrative

In comparing the two films, I argue that, despite significant differences between them, both the 1980 Navy film and the 1992 Park Service film represent variants of a common national mythohistory. There are many factors that predispose the two films toward narrative similarity. In addition to the constancies of institutional context, both were produced within the same film genre (documentary history), and both had to be about the same length (the new film came in slightly longer, at twenty-three minutes). Yet the people responsible for making the 1992 film saw their task as creating an entirely new film, as deliberately crafting something original without reference to the film it replaced.[31]

Although the two films do contrast in many ways (and some are taken up below), they are remarkably alike in narrative structure. Given that the film-makers set out, deliberately, to make a new film that would not borrow from the previous one, and that most of the public discussion of the new film focused on *differences* between the 1992 film and its 1980 predecessor, reviewing their similarities can reveal some of the workings of narrative schemata and relations of power.

First, both the 1980 film and the 1992 film tell the story of Pearl Harbor within the same basic time frame. Both begin by focusing on the *Arizona* and the names of the dead crew. The 1980 film takes the viewer underwater and whispers the names of crew who died as the camera runs along the length of an encrusted anchor chain. The new film achieves a similar effect (but less dramatic) by scanning the names of the crew etched into the marble wall of the shrine room. Each film frames the story by referencing the dead memorialized at the site. Both then ask, How did this happen? and shift to a historical chronology. It is in the episodic structure and visual imagery that the films' similarities emerge.

These can be analyzed as a sequence of five episodic chunks: (1) *historical prelude* to the attack; (2) scene setting, establishing Hawai'i as a site of tropical pleasure and *innocence*; (3) the *bombing* itself, depicted by burning and exploding ships; (4) followed, most importantly, by *recovery*, in which the nation unifies to win the war, beginning with the rebuilding of ships; and, finally, (5) an overtly *moral* sequence that spells out implications of the attack for the present.

HISTORICAL PRELUDE

The opening portions of both films provide historical background for the attack, reviewing the collision of Japanese and American colonial interests in the Asia-Pacific region. Interestingly, it is this aspect of the films that differs the most from the 1944 film *December 7th*, which contains no historical context whatsoever, but simply begins with the scene-setting devices that appear in the second phase of the two memorial films. Significantly, this is the portion of the memorial film that has attracted the greatest criticism. Critics cite this as suggesting that the Japanese were "forced" into war. That has the effect of rendering the bombing *reasonable* and therefore dilutes the interpretation of the bombing as an immoral "sneak attack," a phrase that has been the signature phrase of Pearl Harbor since the war itself, and has remained replete with connotations about the devious nature of the Japanese character.

The new film avoids reference to Japanese brilliance in planning and executing the attack. But it does present the same political and economic pressures on Japan described in the first film—the kind of contextualization that attracted criticism as rationalizing the Japanese attack (see fig. 1). The script for this section of the new film reads as follows:

Figure 1. Shanghai Power Company. Both films include a historical prelude about conflicting colonial interests in Asia. (NPS orientation film, 1992)

> President Franklin Roosevelt demanded an end to Japanese aggression. To back up his demands, he stopped all sales of American oil to Japan. Oil: the lifeblood of the Japanese war machine.
>
> Committed to the conquest of Asia, Japan could not meet American demands without great humiliation. The hard-line military leaders had forced Japan into a position from which there was no exit but war.[32]

The memorial's curator, Chenoweth, who drafted an initial historical chronology for the script, was intent on supplying this kind of content. Yet, as he put it, "almost all of that ended up being cut out" because "no matter how you tell the story, it's a favorable story from the Japanese point of view. . . . any nation state makes those kinds of decision all the time. But anytime you talk about that in the context of Pearl Harbor, people in the United States are going to criticize you for sympathizing with Japan. And that's not at all what I was trying to do."[33]

HAWAIIAN INNOCENCE

Each film then shifts to Hawai'i on the eve of the attack. The Hawai'i in these films is a serene tropical paradise where U.S. military forces relax in touristic complacency (see fig. 2). Palm trees, beaches, hotels, and "hula girls"

Figure 2. Hawai'i as tropical playground. (NPS orientation film, 1992)

accompanied by Hawaiian ukulele and big band music are the context for the U.S. military in Hawai'i (see fig. 3). Ordinary American boys at play, unaware of the death and destruction about to rain down on them, give little indication that the base was a well-armed military and colonial outpost in the middle of the Pacific. These scenes maximize the contrast between naïve serenity and the lethal attack to follow—contrasts that amplify the presumed treachery of the bombing and give the Pearl Harbor story much of its dramatic tension.

Stereotypic images of Hawai'i as a holiday paradise were already well established in American popular culture even before the war. Recall that the 1944 propaganda film *December 7th* dispenses with any historical background and begins with just this kind of scene setting. By the 1980s, when the first film began showing at the memorial, these icons of Hawai'i as a tropical paradise had become the stock-in-trade of Hawai'i's tourism promoters. Indeed, most of the tourist visitors seeing the films at the memorial would already have encountered such images of Hawai'i in the hotels, restaurants, and entertainment spots of contemporary Honolulu.

ATTACK/DEATH

With the prelude to the attack established in terms of both the rise of an expansionist Japanese militarism and the innocence of American military in

Figure 3. Hawai'i embodied. (NPS orientation film, 1992)

Hawai'i, both films then narrate the details of the surprise attack, with a similar litany of mistakes and breakdowns in U.S. preparedness and warning systems. The footage devoted to the attack itself reaches its climax with views of exploding and burning ships, although avoiding any of the grisly details of bodies torn apart and disfigured (see fig. 4). The narration displaces the horror of violent death with metaphors of "falling" and "resting." The death toll is carefully enumerated in terms of the number of American dead as well as ship losses.

RECOVERY

After the climactic explosions and thick smoke billowing from sunken battleships, both films shift from the confusion of attack and destruction to the marching band rhythms of unification and recovery, including the organizational feats of engineering and shipyard construction aimed at salvaging ships. Where the 1980 Navy film features the work of salvaging and redeploying ships damaged in the attack, the new film concentrates on the patriotic response of American citizens to the call to "Remember Pearl Harbor" (see fig. 5). This is done with newsreel shots of Roosevelt's famous "date that will live in infamy" speech to Congress, of hometown parades marching to the tune of the wartime song "Let's Remember Pearl Harbor," and of young recruits lining up to enlist. The shots of inductees with shaved heads collecting their military-issue cloth-

Figure 4. Images of exploding and burning battleships became emblematic of the Pearl Harbor attack. (NPS orientation film, 1992)

ing is an essentially timeless image of individuals being turned into national citizens, embodying the process of national unification (see fig. 6). Newsreel strains of the popular song "Let's Remember Pearl Harbor" may easily evoke sentiments of empathy and identification from Americans in the audience who are themselves about to become participants in the ongoing legacy of remembrance. The activity of recovery and shipbuilding at Pearl Harbor presages American victory in the Pacific. Both films conclude their narrative histories of the war with reference to the ensuing chain of island battles that led to the Japanese surrender.

But it is in the images and narration used to represent the subsequent course of the war that differences in moral and emotional tone between these films emerge most distinctly. The 1980 Navy film continues its war history with a listing of famous battle sites marking the string of Allied victories across the Pacific: "Coral Sea, Midway, Guadalcanal, the Gilberts, Marshall Islands, New Guinea, Marianas, the Philippines, Iwo Jima, Okinawa, Japan" (not, interestingly, Hiroshima or Nagasaki). This steady, decisive recitation of names is accompanied by triumphant martial music, scenes of ships in combat, and reference to the wartime accomplishment of building the "greatest armada the world had ever seen."

Figure 5. Recovery and recruitment. (NPS orientation film, 1992)
Figure 6. America embodied. (NPS orientation film, 1992)

Figure 7. Grim-faced Marine on a beach in the Pacific. (NPS orientation film, 1992)

In contrast to the coda of military triumph and strength, the new film presents the subsequent course of the war in a more somber tone of melancholy. The film refers to the hard-fought American victories in the Pacific, but accompanies these with quite different visual and auditory images. Instead of battleships firing off powerful salvos and clips of Marines storming the beach in island invasions, the new film includes wounded Marines on stretchers and a close-up of a young Marine looking anxiously at the camera while taking cover in the sand (see fig. 7). These contrasts signal a broader difference in the moral work attempted by each film, such that the new film transforms the triumphant feelings of victory with a more mournful reflection of losses inflicted by war.

The 1992 film's theme of suffering and loss is accentuated by the female voice of the narrator, actress Stockard Channing. This shift in gendered voice is perhaps the single most distinctive contrast between the new film and the one it replaced. Certainly it is the most commonly noted difference reported by viewers who have seen both films. The military subject matter would seem to call for male narration, as in the 1980 Navy film. In fact, the first choice for a narrator for the new film was Robert Mitchum, well-known for his work in war movies. However, when he was unavailable, producer Lance Bird began to think of the film's voice as that of a woman. He said he imagined the narrator as, perhaps, the wife of a Navy survivor, someone who had a close connection to the story. Bird thought specifically of Channing and ultimately was able to enlist her for the job. Her voice carries a deep, lilting quality that conveys a sense of historical inevitability and sadness about Pearl Harbor and the ensuing course of the war. The broader significance of this regendering of voice is suggested in recent work on Civil War narratives by historian Drew Gilpin Faust, who has noted differential reactions to the outbreak of war by Confederate men and women, with men speaking of "courage and glory" and women fearing "war's approaching harvest of death."[34]

MORAL

The greatest differences between these two films come at the end, when each offers self-conscious reflection about the meaning and purpose of remembrance. Both films do this by shifting tense and voice and returning the viewer to the present with shots of the *Arizona* Memorial. The new film devotes more time to contemporary reflection by showing scenes from memorial services held at the Visitor Center, before closing with the memorial at sunset.

As noted earlier, the memorial's superintendent felt that the 1980 film's theme of military preparedness created an aggressive mood inappropriate for a visit to the memorial. It is not surprising, however, that a film produced by the U.S. Navy would frame the lesson of Pearl Harbor in terms of military strength. Such a lesson has clear implications for the importance of maintaining today's Navy as a dominant power in the Pacific. The 1980 film was explicit about this: "If we forget December 7, 1941; if we forget over 1,000 men still entombed aboard the USS *Arizona*; if we forget that a nation unprepared will sacrifice her finest men and women, then we would forget what America stands for and that is why we must remember Pearl Harbor. Homeport still for one of the world's most powerful Naval forces, the United States Pacific Fleet."[35]

The 1992 film concludes quite differently, deleting direct references to military preparedness and strength and calling for a more generalized remembrance, marked by sentiments of mourning and grief. Recall that this moral-emotional tone was criticized by the panel of military and veteran advisors, who felt the script should include more references to the actions of decorated heroes. That panel asked that the final lines of the script referring to grief and mourning be deleted. Although some changes were made, this portion of the script remained largely intact. As it now stands, the film concludes with the following thoughts about the meaning and purpose of remembrance:

> How shall we remember them, those who died?
> Mourn the dead.

Remember the battle.
Understand the tragedy.
Honor the memory.

Let our grief for the men of the *Arizona* be for all those
whose futures were taken from them on December 7th, 1941.

Here they will never be forgotten.[36]

The contrast between these lines and the concluding reflections on the 1980 film, amplified by differences in the sound and visual imagery between the two films, accounts for much of the shift in mood reported by people who have seen both films. Coming as they do at the end of the films, as a kind of moral coda, they each use quite different linguistic and rhetorical means to engage their audience. Thus, the 1980 film concludes in the voice of a distinctly American, national "we" ("If we forget that a nation unprepared will sacrifice her finest men and women . . . then we would forget what America stands for"). In contrast, the 1992 film utilizes a more ambiguous "we," appropriate, perhaps, to the increasingly international and global audience of the memorial in the 1990s ("How shall we remember them, those who died? . . . Let our grief for the men of the *Arizona* be for all those whose futures were taken from them"). And, just as pronominal usage signals a different sense of public, so the rhetorical styles of these endings are markedly different, with the 1980 film employing a certain if-then logic typical of persuasive argument, and the 1992 film ending in a question-response format more like a religious discourse. The latter's list of directives—"Mourn the dead," "Remember the battle," and so forth—are uttered in the rhythmical cadence of biblical statements, involving the audience in the performative activity of remembering.[37]

When the new film was first released, the memorial superintendent and others talked about the differences between the two films in a language of emotion. Interviewed by Honolulu newspapers when the new film first showed in December 1992, Superintendent Magee said, "Visitors now come out of it [the film] as somber as they could be. . . . They used to come out a lot more aggressive. We wanted to impress upon them that this thing is more than a pile of concrete; it's a tomb."[38] These comments are echoed by park rangers and volunteers who escort visitors in and out of the theaters and report a consistently teary-eyed audience leaving the film. They are also reflected in the results of a survey of impressions formed by American visitors to the memorial. In 1994 we asked two hundred visitors to characterize their feelings in response to the film. The dominant emotions were sadness and pride, with anger expressed less often, but concentrated among older citizens.[39]

There is an important ambiguity in the way the film answers its question, "How shall we remember them, those who died?" When the memorial's historian Martinez commented on an earlier version of this paper, he underlined this question and the line that follows ("Mourn the dead") and added a marginal note: "This line was purposeful so that it represented the U.S. & Japan." Martinez and others in the scripting process saw this passage as widening the moral sphere of remembrance. As the narrator continues, the widening becomes more explicit: "Let our grief for the men of the *Arizona* be for all those whose futures were taken from them on December 7th, 1941." The inclusive impulse here is also evident in the film's earlier reference to the losses of the Pacific War, described as millions of "soldiers and civilians" who "would suffer and sacrifice before the war's end." The visual images here move from American Marines on stretchers to piles of helmets of war dead, including some that are recognizably Japanese.

When the film then moves to the present, it changes focus from the objects of memorialization (those who died at Pearl Harbor) to the subjects who memorialize. As it does so it shows a distinctly international cast participating in annual memorial services, thus further expanding the relevant public for Pearl Harbor remembrance. At a point in the script where liner notes call for "Japanese and American mourners," the film portrays Japanese Buddhist priests at one of the memorial's annual ceremonies:

> Every year on December 7th special ceremonies of remembrance are held here at the Visitors' Center.
>
> The dead are mourned; the heroes are remembered. People from all over the world honor young men they never knew, whose lives were cut short on December 7th, 1941.

Given the intense concern in many quarters to bound the memorial as a sacred national space, this phrasing represents a remarkable move toward greater inclusiveness. As already indicated, the filmmakers were well aware of the multiple audiences for the film and the difficulties in satisfying multiple points of view. In his memo responding to problems in completing the film, producer Lance Bird pointed to the size and complexity of the film's international public (although referring to other of America's allies in the war and avoiding reference to the Japanese tourist audience for the film): "One of the things that made this a difficult assignment is that we were all making a film here for the whole Nation. . . . And one could say for the World. We are making a film that over 10 million people will see, both Americans and foreign visitors. Some of these foreign visitors were also threatened by the Japanese attack on Pearl Harbor."[40]

While the realities of global tourism and a world audience presented one context for the filmmakers' thinking, national cultural politics provided another. From the outset the producers were particularly conscious of the diversity of American attitudes toward Japan, ranging from antagonistic to sympathetic. In his memo reflecting on delays and difficulties in completing the film, Bird characterized one of the challenges of the project as somehow navigating between the shoals of a polarized public: "From the beginning one of our goals was to make a film that could not be accused of 'Japan bashing' nor could it be attacked by Pearl Harbor survivors who might feel that the film was trying to justify the attack."[41] Magee echoed these sentiments when he stated that he hoped the new film, with its use of actual historical footage, would both "better inform visitors" and "appease veterans groups."

In fact, the local newspaper story on the new film was titled "New December 7 Film Debuts at *Arizona*" and subtitled "The Old One Was Criticized as Being Soft on the Enemy." Given the similarity of the new film's narration of historical context to the old, together with the more inclusive voice of the new film, it is somewhat surprising that the new film would be characterized as less "soft on the enemy" and "appeasing veterans groups." It may be that the removal of wording that had been specifically marked as contentious (such as "Japan felt her back was to the wall" and references to Yamamoto as brilliant) was sufficient for these purposes. Whatever the reasons for its reception, these public comments reflect the general cognizance that veterans are a primary constituency for the memorial and its film, a cognizance that shapes the context within which representations of Pearl Harbor history are produced at the memorial.

One index of the multiple publics that intersect at the memorial and their diverse interpretations of Pearl Harbor history comes in the form of written comments left behind by visitors. People who wish to leave comments about their experience at the memorial may fill out comment sheets made available by the Park Service. The film is one of the most common subjects of these comment sheets, revealing a wide latitude in responses, particularly to its depiction of Japan. Consider the following comments written by four different individuals. Two are upset that the film is pro-Japanese and two say that it is anti-Japanese and xenophobic.

> The new movie takes away from the impact that really happened & the new pro-Japanese segment (i.e., they were provoked) is not an issue that should be represented at Pearl Harbor and is a matter of personal interpretation as to whether they were provoked or not. I apologize for the writing but I am

very emotional about this & the new movie should have been left on the cutting room floor. I will not see it again, however, I will return to throw flowers into the water in honor. (Comment sheet, 17 February 1993)

Film sugar coats Japanese starting the war in the Pacific. Almost says the U.S. forced them into it, which is pure B.S. Film should be changed. (Comment sheet, 28 June 1994)

It is too bad that the U.S. Government (Park Service) chooses, through its film and Ranger presentations, to exacerbate an already strained relationship between Americans and Japanese. I sincerely feel that this racist, xenophobic presentation needs to be historically grounded and made to be balanced, i.e., how many people died at Hiroshima and Nagasaki as a result of our bombing. (Comment sheet, 13 February 1993)

The film . . . portrays the Japanese as all evil incarnate. The film isolated the P.H. attack incorrectly. It is impossible to remove it from the rest of the events of WWII—namely the bombings of Hiroshima and Nagasaki. The film needs to reflect the events and sentiments of the entire war and of all the U.S. citizens—Asian American included. Also, how is it that nothing was mentioned in detail or in any length about the impact on the local Hawaiian who were the inhabitants of the island? (Comment sheet, 27 June 1994)

The apparent contradictions among these comments highlight deep disparities in historical perspective. In part, these are associated with generational differences, although distinct social and historical sensibilities might be mapped across differences of gender, ethnicity, locale, and other facets of identity that entail contrastive forms of cultural memory. Just as the war generation draws on personal experience and 1940s-era memories to interpret the film, so others, such as native Hawaiians and Americans of Japanese ancestry, find meaning and emotion in relation to their own narratives of social history.

Conclusion

Substantial continuities between Pearl Harbor films made at different points in time suggest that a kind of mythic history is operating from one epoch to another in the postwar period. Yet, at the same time, dominant moral and emotional meanings of Pearl Harbor can now be seen shifting away from wartime feelings of outrage toward a more generalized sense of loss and grief associated with war in a global perspective. In this paper I have suggested that the context for this shift is the ongoing expansion of the memorial's publics in local, national, and international spheres of interest. In addition to these effects of globalization and audience expansion, conflicts over the representation of Pearl Harbor also reflect ongoing local struggles to redefine Hawai'i as a certain kind of social and national space. In this regard, most of the effects of the film are to be found in absences and silences: silences about colonial history that first established Pearl Harbor as a military base, about the indigenous population (cast, perhaps, as a hula girl in fig. 3), and about the local Japanese population, referred to only briefly in the film's scene-setting moves. It is these complicated contexts for Pearl Harbor memory that are explicitly cited in the last letter of complaint quoted earlier.

Examining the process of film scripting exposes some of the conflicts and anxieties that underlie dominant representations of history, showing official, state-sponsored history to be more fluid, contested, and ultimately ambiguous than normally assumed. This is not to say there is no dominant model in national representations of Pearl Harbor, only that such models are neither monolithic nor static, and are themselves entangled in conflicting interests.

On the one hand, the representation of Pearl Harbor history at such a highly institutionalized and sacred site as the USS *Arizona* Memorial achieves a remarkable degree of fixity and continuity—a continuity that follows from the constraints of both narrative and power. However, variability in everything from the motives for making a new film to perspectives on the script and reactions to the finished product indicate that the Pearl Harbor films, like cultural forms in general, are susceptible to a range of interpretations.

In the United States, official national histories of war are produced in a multitude of ways: by military units, at historic sites, in war museums, and in textbooks.[42] During the period of World War II fiftieth anniversaries, the Department of Defense organized scores of commemorative activities, projects, and exhibitions through its World War II 50th Anniversary Committee.[43] The National Archives, the Smithsonian Institution, the National Park Service, and many military bases and museums were also active in sponsoring World War II exhibits and activities during the anniversary period. The *Arizona* Memorial, however, occupies a more complex public space than most of these. Operated by the National Park Service in cooperation with the U.S. Navy for a national and international audience of over a million and a half visitors annually, the memorial necessarily combines multiple functions for multiple publics. Whereas the memorial offers the U.S. Navy and other military personnel a site for enlistment ceremonies and memorial rites of various kinds, it is also a public historic landmark that, like other national parks, is devoted to historic preservation and public history.

In discussing both the aesthetics and the politics of producing a new film for the *Arizona* Memorial, I have attempted to trace connections between the memorial as a certain kind of cultural institution and the representational practices that create Pearl Harbor history there. The National Park Service historians at the memorial see the mission of public history as representing the past in terms that are, as much as possible, "balanced and accurate" for a broad national, and even international, public. But the films discussed here are embedded in the context of memorializing, and so must also work, pragmatically, to tell a certain kind of story appropriate to "remembrance" and its emotions. Conflicts over history and representation evoked by the production of a new film mark these multiple purposes and audiences.

This more inclusive history is more often expressed in the depersonalized voice of documentary history than in the personal voice of national heroes. In the words of Donald Magee, "The National Park Service does two things very well. . . . We preserve history and we teach history. We don't take sides at Civil War battlefields or at any other sites where controversial decisions were made, like the Custer battlefield, and here at Pearl Harbor we don't condemn the Japanese."[44] However, according to conservative commentators such as Thomas Sowell, "balanced and accurate" has no place in a national shrine, which ought to be a place dedicated to displaying and teaching *patriotic* history. Caught in this tension between a vision of the memorial as a space devoted to promoting a specifically national memory heightened by the events and emotions of war, and one that sees it as a historic site devoted to reevaluating history and advancing public education for global audiences, the memorial and its film become sites of contestation where ambiguities and anxieties of the nation play themselves out in the vicissitudes of historical representation.

Notes

I have benefited substantially from discussions with Takashi Fujitani and Lisa Yoneyama, and other participants in the 1995 East-West Center Conference. I am also indebted to numerous people for assistance with ongoing research on Pearl Harbor memory. The Wenner-Gren Foundation for Anthropological Research supported nine months of fieldwork at the USS *Arizona* Memorial, carried out with Marjorie Kelly during 1994. Lance Bird generously offered detailed and perceptive comments on an earlier version of this paper. Tani Barlow, LeeRay Costa, Jane Desmond, Mike Forman, and Marsha Kinder also gave helpful readings. I have learned much from the work of others who have written about the *Arizona* Memorial, especially Edward Linenthal, Patricia Masters, Michael Slackman, and Phyllis Turnbull. Turnbull is author of "Remembering Pearl Harbor: The Semiotics of the *Arizona* Memorial," in *Challenging Boundaries: Global Flows, Territorial Identities*, ed. Hayward Alker Jr. and Michael Shapiro [Minneapolis: University of Minnesota Press, 1996]: 407–33.) Finally, I want to thank the Pearl Harbor veterans and members of the National Park Service at the *Arizona* Memorial who have provided advice and support for this research, particularly Daniel Martinez, Bob Chenoweth, Gary Beito, and Superintendents Donald Magee and Kathy Billings.

1 Throughout the recent period of fiftieth anniversaries, for example, veterans, news commentators, and politicians repeatedly invoked Pearl Harbor as an antidote to ambivalence associated with such events as the firebombings of Japanese cities and, especially, the debates about the atomic bombings of Hiroshima and Nagasaki.

2 The meaning of "Remember Pearl Harbor!" as a vengeful call for retribution began to change immediately with the Japanese surrender in 1945 and the creation of a postwar alliance between the United States and Japan (perhaps more immediately for official policy than for popular sentiment). Subsequently, books such as Walter Lord's *Day of Infamy* and films such as the 1970 Hollywood epic *Tora! Tora! Tora!* have kept Pearl Harbor alive in postwar American memory, if in new and transformed ways. During the Korean and Vietnam Wars, political speeches frequently referenced Pearl Harbor as a reminder of the need for military strength, but often without specific reference to Japan. With the end of the cold war, economic globalization, increasing trade friction with Japan, and the intensification of America's own "culture wars," Pearl Harbor would again be a topic of interest and controversy. This interest came to a head in 1991 when fiftieth-anniversary ceremonies staged in Honolulu attracted more media attention than the Iraq War, as gauged by the number of reporters registered with military coordinators. See Roger Dingman, "Reflections on Pearl Harbor Anniversaries Past," *Journal of American–East Asian Relations* 3, no. 3 (1994): 279–93; Geoffrey White, "Mythic History and National Memory: The Pearl Harbor Anniversary," *Culture and Psychology* 3, no. 1 (1997): 63–88.

3 Edward T. Linenthal, *Sacred Ground: Americans and Their Battlegrounds*, rev. ed. (Urbana: University of Illinois Press, 1993); Michael Slackman, *Remembering Pearl Harbor: The Story of the USS Arizona Memorial* (Honolulu: Arizona Memorial Museum Association, 1986).

4 To briefly underscore the significance of the films shown at the Visitor Center, consider the scope of their reach. Since 1980, when the Visitor Center opened, the number of people who have been to the memorial and seen one of the films shown there exceeds 18 million—the majority Americans, but also millions of tourists from all over the world. See Patricia Masters, "Another Way of Seeing: Pearl Harbor as Memory," paper read at East-West Center Conference on Cultural Identities and National Histories, Honolulu, 1992, for a discussion of Japanese visitors to the Pearl Harbor memorial.

5 As Hayden White has argued, the forms and structures of narrative emplotment exert a powerful influence on historical understanding. See White, "Storytelling: Historical and Ideological," in *Centuries' Ends, Narrative Means*, ed. Robert Newman (Stanford: Stanford University Press, 1996). This point is even more compelling when history is represented in film, a medium that relies on distinctive storytelling practices to hold audience attention. See also Robert A. Rosenstone, ed., *Revisioning History: Film and the Construction of a New Past* (Princeton, NJ: Princeton University Press, 1995); Hayden White, "AHR Forum: Historiography and Historiophoty," *American Historical Review* 93, no. 5 (1988): 193; and Bill Nichols, *Blurred Boundaries: Questions of Meaning of Contemporary Culture* (Bloomington: University of Indiana Press, 1994).

6 Memorandum from L. Bird to G. Beito, 2 October 1992, files of the USS Arizona Memorial Museum Association.

7 Marjorie Kelly, "Enshrining History: The Visitor Experience at Pearl Harbor's USS Arizona Memorial," *Museum Anthropology* 20, no. 3 (1996): 45–57; Linenthal, *Sacred Ground*.

8   See Geoffrey White, "Museum, Memorial, Shrine: National Narrative in National Spaces," *Museum Anthropology* 21, no. 1 (1997).

9   Today's Pearl Harbor is home to the largest Navy base and nuclear submarine facility in the Pacific. In gazing on the site of historic events that drew the United States into World War II, visitors standing on the lawn of the Visitor Center looking across the harbor take in a panorama of modern weaponry and naval power that must signify, for some, the moral of military preparedness long associated with the story of Pearl Harbor.

10 Superintendent to Regional Director, Western Region, 28 January 1992, p. 2.

11 James Rusbridger and Eric Nave, *Betrayal at Pearl Harbor: How Churchill Lured Roosevelt into WWII* (New York: Summit Books, 1991).

12 Linenthal, *Sacred Ground*, 235–36.

13 Donald Magee, interview with the author, 24 February 1994, tape 94-5A; files of the author.

14 Robert Chenoweth, interview with the author, 30 September 1992; files of the author.

15 Lance Bird, interview with M. Kelly, 14 April 1994, tape 94-8B; files of the author.

16 William Knowlton Zinsser, *American Places: A Writer's Pilgrimage to 15 of This Country's Most Visited and Cherished Sites* (New York: HarperCollins, 1992), 200.

17 Letter from DeSanctis to Magee, 25 February 1994; Superintendent's files, USS *Arizona* Memorial.

18 Letter from Magee to DeSanctis, 3 March 1994; Superintendent's files, USS *Arizona* Memorial.

19 Quoted in Burl Burlingame, "New Dec. 7 Film Debuts at Arizona," *Honolulu Star Bulletin*, 3 December 1992, A-10.

20 Daniel Martinez, personal communication, 1994.

21 *December 7th*, shot by Gregg Toland and produced by John Ford, was the first major film about the Pearl Harbor attack. Made by order of the Department of War for the express purpose of stirring the nation to fight, this thirty-four minute film was a potent instrument in the U.S. arsenal of emotional war weapons and was the recipient of the 1943 Academy Award for best documentary. See Geoffrey M. White and Jane Yi, "*December 7th*: Race and Nation in Wartime Documentary," in *Classic Whiteness: Race and the Hollywood Studio System*, ed. Daniel Bernardi (Minneapolis: University of Minnesota Press, forthcoming); James M. Skinner, "*December 7*: Filmic Myth Masquerading as Historical Fact," *Journal of Military History* 55 (October 1991): 507–16. Like most Hollywood features produced during the war, it had the aim of building morale and instilling a will to fight. See Clayton R. Koppes and Gregory D. Black, *Hollywood Goes to War: How Politics, Profits and Propaganda Shaped World War II Movies* (Berkeley: University of California Press, 1987).

22 Robert Chenoweth, interview with the author, 30 September 1992; files of the author.

23 Letter to the author, 18 October 1995.

24 See Linenthal, *Sacred Ground*; White, "National Memory."

25 See Magee to DeSanctis, 3 March 1994; Superintendent's files, USS *Arizona* Memorial.

26 Lance Bird, interview with M. Kelly, 14 April 1994; tape 94-5A; files of the author.

27 Memorandum from Magee to Western Region Regional Director, NPS, 28 January 1992, regarding "status of USS *Arizona* Memorial Film Script," files of the author.

28 Memorandum from NPS Chief Historian Edwin Bearss to USS *Arizona* Memorial Superintendent Donald Magee, 5 May 1992; Superintendent's files, USS *Arizona* Memorial.

29 Ibid.

30 Ibid.

31 When I sent the producer, Lance Bird, an earlier draft of this paper, he asserted that calling their project a "remaking" of the previous film was inappropriate: "The creative team's view was that we were in no way 'remaking' the existing film. In fact we were consciously trying to make a film that would stand in sharp contrast to the existing film; that effort extended from the look of our film to its tone and the words heard on its sound track. . . . We never studied the earlier film (in fact, I've only seen it about three times). No shots were consciously taken from it and no narration was taken from it" (Letter to the author, 18 October 1995).

32 Lance Bird and Tom Johnson, USS *Arizona* Memorial orientation film script, 1992; files of the superintendent, USS *Arizona* Memorial, 5. Cf. National Park Service, 1980 Navy film, typescript; files of the superintendent, USS *Arizona* Memorial.

33 Robert Chenoweth, interview with the author, 30 September 1992.

34 Drew Gilpin Faust, "The Civil War's 'Riddle of Death,' " *Chronicle of Higher Education* (February 1997): A6.

35 1980 Navy film, 8.

36 USS *Arizona* Memorial orientation film script, 1992, 16.

37 I am indebted to Marsha Kinder for this point.

38 Quoted in Burlingame, "New Dec. 7 Film Debuts at *Arizona*," A-1.

39 In this survey we posed a set of questions to 198 American visitors, including a question asking people to characterize their reactions to the film in terms of several emotion categories (sad, angry, proud, surprised, disgusted, bored). Nearly everyone indicated some degree of sadness and pride (with two-thirds saying they felt "very" sad or "very" proud). One-fourth of the people responding indicated that the film made them "very" angry, and over half said they felt "somewhat" angry. See White, "Mythic History and National Memory."

40 Memorandum from L. Bird to G. Beito, 2 October 1992, p. 2; files of the USS *Arizona* Memorial Museum Association.

41 Ibid.

42 Catherine Lutz and Lesley Bartlett, *Making Soldiers in the Public Schools: An Analysis of the Army JROTC Curriculum* (Philadelphia: American Friends Service Committee, n.d.).

43 Geoffrey White, "Remembering Guadalcanal: National Identity and Transnational Memory-Making," *Public Culture* 7 (1995): 529–55.

44 Quoted in Zinsser, *American Places*, 82.

3 ≡ ATONEMENT, HEALING, AND

UNEXPECTED ALLIANCES

"Trapped in History" on the Way to Utopia:

East Asia's "Great War" Fifty Years Later

ARIF DIRLIK

"Past experience, if not forgotten, is a guide to the future." This line concludes the century-long history on exhibit at the Anti-Japanese War Memorial Museum at Lugouqiao outside of Beijing. It was spoken by Zhou Enlai on the occasion of the Zhou-Tanaka Communiqué in 1972, which "normalized" relations between China and Japan. It was repeated frequently in the 1980s by Chinese critics of attempted textbook revisions in Japan, which sought to clean up Japan's image as aggressor during World War II.[1]

Fifty years after World War II ended in East Asia with Japan's formal surrender on 15 August 1945 (East Asian time), memories of the "past experience" to which Zhou Enlai referred have faded into the past, or persist only as hearsay for new generations in East Asia. The forces that structure the experiences of these new generations emanate from a global situation that differs vastly not only from the world of 1945, but even from the world that 1945 created, which has been relegated to the past by the radical changes of the past decade. What meaning could the war have in the present, except as another marker in that accumulation of markers that goes by the name of "history," safely distant from the present in its irrelevance—and an aberrant marker at that, viewed from the vantage point of a present that has supposedly overcome its historical legacy? The Chinese historian Liu Danian has referred to those who "find it difficult to understand why some should advocate the study of an event [the anti-Japanese War] that is more than forty years in the past . . . [because] human beings live not by history, but by productive labor, by the constant creation of new environmental conditions."[2]

Under the circumstances, can there by any significance to recalling memories of the war on this fiftieth anniversary of its conclusion other than as just another historical ritual? Worse, could such recollection serve anything but a negative, divisive purpose under circumstances of newfound unity in East Asia? Is insistence on memories of "past experience" in this "post-historical" age anything but a sign of being "trapped in history," in the words of that "end of history" hack, Francis Fukuyama?[3]

I address these questions in my discussion below. I do believe that there is good reason to recall memories of the "past experience" to which Zhou Enlai referred. The question is what experiences, and how to recall them? Commemorations, even if they are inspired by the past, take the present as their goal. This also shapes what we remember of the past, and what we forget. Critical remembering, I argue, needs to account for the diversity of experience in the East Asian war, diversity not at the level of states but at the level of the people at large, that resists appropriation of what the war was about by a nationalist teleology. Such critical remembering is essential also to reaffirming the historicity of the present against efforts to erase it by a utopianism of capital, which is plausible only to the extent that it can suppress (by relegating to the past) contemporary problems that are its very products. The past remembered, rather than being passé, may be a source of critical insights into the present. These concerns call into question, finally, the date chosen for the commemoration, the surrender of Japan on 15 August 1945. If the present commemoration is to open up questions about the present that ritual reenactment might conceal, it is also necessary to look beyond the event being commemorated to the history before and after, the history it was to produce as well as the history of which it was the product.

World War/Worldwide War

Memory does not rest long on the airwaves of 15 August 1945 before it is launched irresistably toward other dates, different places: 6 August 1945, when the first A-bomb was dropped on Hiroshima with devastating results that guaranteed the surrender (a second bomb dropped on Nagasaki three days later should not be forgotten, even if Hiroshima has captured symbolic significance); 16 June 1945, when the first nuclear bomb was exploded at Alamogordo, New Mexico; 7 December 1941, when Japanese forces attacked Pearl Harbor, inaugurating the war with the United States; December 1937, when Japanese troops massacred tens of thousands of hapless Chinese soldiers and civilians in Nanjing; 7 July 1937, when Japanese forces at Lugouqiao outside of Beijing inaugurated the war with China; 18 September 1931, when the Japanese military began its conquest of China's northeastern provinces; 22 August 1910, when Korea was formally annexed to Japan as a colony; 4 February 1899, when the United States began the conquest of the Philippines (to be annexed as a colony two years later); 7 July 1898, when the United States annexed Hawai'i; April 1895, when by the Treaty of Shimonoseki Japan annexed Taiwan and occupied Korea; 1884, when France, having defeated China in a naval skirmish, consolidated its hold on Vietnam; 1842, when the Treaty of Nanjing, concluding the Opium War between Great Britain and China, set the stage for the emergence of a new political order in East and Southeast Asia.

Memory does not stop here. Other memories might land at different times in different places. The point here is that 15 August 1945 recalls not just the end of a war, but a whole series of events, wars, and processes of which that war was a culmination. I for one would not care to assign a definitive origin to the war. Nor do I imply by the chronology of memory causes and effects, let alone an inevitability. The accumulation of events does point to an emergent structure in which the United States and Japan, having risen to power status simultaneously in the second half of the nineteenth century, confronted each other across and within the Pacific. The confrontation shaped the histories of others as well—of China, Korea, Vietnam. But each experienced the structuring differently, if only because the war began at different places at different times.

The date 15 August 1945 recalls the future as well. The day has the decisiveness of an end-marker for Japan alone, even if the *Mainichi shimbun* marked it by observing "that history offered examples of superior races regenerating themselves after setbacks."[4] For others, wars were beginning before the war had ended. Already on 9 August 1945, stating that the Anti-Japanese Resistance War was over for all practical purposes, Mao Zedong in China called for preparation for the civil war to come.[5] In Vietnam, where the Japanese defeat inspired hopes for liberation from colonialism, the Viet Minh Central Committee on 16 August 1945 called for a general insurrection in the cause of national liberation.[6] Korea was liberated from half a century of colonialism, only to be divided when, in Washington on the night of 10–11 August, policymakers drew a line across the 38th parallel to separate the zone of U.S. occupation from that of the Soviet Union.[7]

This is not to say that 15 August 1945 was not an important day, but only that the war did not end on that day. From a battleground between the United States and Japan, East Asia on 15 August turned into a battle zone between the United States and the Soviet Union, which was to set the stage for the postwar (dis)order. Within five years, this new confrontation would justify the Korean War, which was brought to a standstill by the armistice of 1953. With the Communist Party having gone through civil war and achieved victory, as Mao had predicted, the People's Republic of China established in 1949 was at war with the United States in late 1950, this time on the battlefields of Korea. Vietnam would be at war for another thirty years, first against the French, who returned to recolonize it after Japan's defeat, and from 1964 on against the

United States, until the latter conceded defeat in 1975. The United States, needless to say, was at war in Asia throughout these years.

World War II! The very term invokes a discrete historical event, with a beginning and an end. So long as it lasted, the war was a World War; the wars before and after are separated out from it as local wars of one kind or another. War did indeed become worldwide for a while, touching nearly every corner of the earth, drawing within its compass numerous national histories, transforming the globe. It ushered colonialism out of history by draining the power of colonialists to subjugate others. An earlier multiplicity of world powers was reduced to two powers, the United States and the Soviet Union, whose confrontation would shape the world for the next four decades. In the capitalist world, it left the United States alone as a world power, to remake the world in its own image.

It is not playing trivial word games, however, to distinguish the war as a worldwide war from a world war. Spatially speaking, there is no difference between the world war and the worldwide war. But the distinction makes an enormous difference temporally—by abolishing the convenient distinction between world war and local wars. For a while, local wars may have been incorporated into a world war, to reappear as local wars after its conclusion. But for the people involved, the relationship was the reverse: it was the world war that was to become for a while part of the local war that carried for them the utmost significance. For the Chinese, World War II has always been first and foremost the Anti-Japanese Resistance War, with its origins predating World War II as seen from Europe or the United States. For Korea and Vietnam, the war was part of a long struggle for national liberation from colonialism, beginning long before World War II and continuing long after its conclusion. Even for the Japanese, the war was more the Pacific War, rather than World War II.

Different historical contexts endow the war with different temporalities and, therefore, different historical meanings, which have been the source of much misunderstanding. In these different contexts, enemies and friends appeared differently. Liu Danian writes that "China's total victory over Japanese militarism after eight years of war transformed the hundred year old rules of the game."[8] His reference is not just to Japan, but to the whole history of imperialism in China since the Opium War that deprived the Chinese people of their "self-confidence." To the Vietnamese, viewing the war from the perspective of the struggle for national liberation, France, Japan, and the United States represented successive colonial powers in a history of struggle against outside domination. To Koreans, for whom memories of the war are inseparable from the continuing realities of national division, it was not just Japan that was the oppressor, but also the Soviet Union and the United States, who partitioned the country, prolonging the struggle for unity and liberation. Jon Halliday and

Bruce Cumings have written that "the Korean problem is what we would now call a 'North-South' or 'Third World' problem, a conflict over how best to overcome the debilities of colonial rule and comparative backwardness. In the Cold War milieu of the time, however, it was always seen by Americans as an East-West problem."[9] Part of the reason might be, I would suggest, the predominant part that World War II plays in American consciousness, magnifying the struggle of the forces of good against the forces of evil. Americans have difficulty grasping that in different histories they may appear differently, that they are not always viewed as the saviors of Asian societies from the evils of Japanese imperialism or the Soviet Union.[10]

Viewing the war from the perspective of East/Southeast Asian societies brings to the foreground two other questions. If the United States viewed the war and its outcome as an "East-West" problem, it was not alone in this regard, as Asians too, in the course of a century of subjugation at the hands of Western powers, had become aware of the racial/cultural divides that had justified their subjugation, and sought now to reassert their "Asianness" against Euro-American hegemony. Pan-Asian consciousness, Stephen Hay has argued, was as untenable as the Euro-American Orientalist view of an Asian civilizational essence, because its promoters projected on Asia what they took to be the essences of their own societies.[11] Nevertheless, evidence of colonialism (as well as discrimination against Asian immigrants in the United States) brought a Pan-Asianist dimension into nationalist ideologies in the course of national liberation struggles. Tagore, a foremost Pan-Asianist, finally abandoned his Pan-Asianism in the face of Japanese imperialism, but not all Asians did. In the words of John Dower:

> The allied struggle against Japan exposed the racist underpinnings of the European and American colonial structure. Japan did not invade independent countries in southern Asia. It invaded colonial outposts which the Westerners had dominated for generations, taking absolutely for granted their racial and cultural superiority over their Asian subjects. Japan's belated emergence as a dominant power in Asia, culminating in the devastating "advance south" of 1941–1942, challenged not just the Western presence but the entire mystique of white supremacism on which centuries of European and American expansion had rested. This was clear to all from an early date: to the Japanese; to the imperiled European and American colonials; and, not the least, to the politically, economically, and culturally subjugated peoples of Asia.

Japan's Pan-Asiatic slogans played upon these sentiments, and the favorable response of many Asians to the initial Japanese victories against the

Americans, British and Dutch intensified Western presentiments of an all-out race war in Asia.[12]

Pan-Asianism complicates the understanding of nationalism in Asia. It is important to recall that many in China and Korea, as well as in Southeast and South Asia, collaborated with Japanese rule. To the victors, collaborators were traitors to the national cause. But unless we seek to understand Pan-Asianism as part of nationalist ideologies in Asia, there is much about the national histories that we are likely to miss. Of this, more later.

The other question is the question of "people's war." The perspective of national liberation struggles in East and Southeast Asia also underlines the significance of revolutionary social movements, especially prominent in China, Korea, and Vietnam. Nationalism, divorced from the larger masses of people already by the mid-1920s, had lost its credibility in the anticolonial struggles, enhancing the appeal of social revolutionary solutions to national problems.[13] Both during the war and in the struggles that ensued, "people's wars" led by the communists were to play the central part in national liberation. The threat of communism had been part of the repertoire of Japanese imperialist ideology. It is not surprising but ironic that once Japan was defeated, the United States assumed the burden for suppressing "communism" in all of these societies, which, not surprisingly, also made the United States the enemy of national liberation.

Global Capitalism and Memory

The date 15 August 1945 recalls not just the end of the war but, viewed from the perspectives of the societies in East Asia, the beginning of the end of a history of colonialism and imperialism and the national liberation struggles that came to a head during the war years. National liberation struggles brought to the fore the importance of bringing the people into politics. They also sought to reassert national-popular cultures against colonialisms that had denied them racial/ cultural equality. In some cases, national regeneration was seen as part of a regeneration of Asia after centuries of European domination. The latter was crucial to Japanese imperial propaganda, which fell on receptive ears in some sections of Asian societies.

It was not until the mid-1970s that the last of these national liberation struggles came to a conclusion. If we view national divisions, primarily in China and Korea, as part of the legacy of colonialism, however, that history has still not ended. But how relevant is it to the present?

In terms of power, the great transformation brought about by the war was the emergence of the United States to supremacy in Asia and the Pacific. In 1900, on the occasion of the U.S. conquest of the Philippines, Senator Albert Beveridge proclaimed: "The Pacific is our ocean. . . . And the Pacific is the ocean of the commerce of the future. Most future wars will be conflicts for commerce. The power that rules the Pacific, therefore, is the power that rules the world. And . . . that power is and will forever be the American republic."[14]

Senator Beveridge's prophecy has come about, perhaps more prophetically than he might have wished. By the end of the war, the Pacific had indeed become an American Lake. And the United States, in its confrontation with the Soviet Union (represented in East Asia by China and North Korea), proceeded to shape East Asia and the Pacific. During the seven-year Occupation of Japan, Japan was remade in the American image, the success of which was evident by the 1960s.[15] During these years, U.S. economic and political policy also brought about a linkage between the Japanese economy and the economies of Japan's former colonies, South Korea and Taiwan.[16]

The United States, ironically, succeeded too well. Led by Japan in the 1970s and followed by Taiwan and South Korea in the 1980s, East Asian economies achieved a successful development that would challenge U.S. economic hegemony as well as spearhead the development of a new phase of capitalism. Others, namely the societies of Southeast Asia, have followed suit. By the mid-1980s, the power of an emergent Global Capitalism was such that it led to a full-scale retreat in communist societies as well. By the late 1980s, the communist societies of Eastern Europe and the Soviet Union had fallen apart. In the meantime, the "reopening" of China beginning in the 1970s was to culminate in nearly total accommodation of capitalism after 1992. Under the guise of developing a "socialism with Chinese characteristics," the communist leadership in China has transformed the country into a new haven for global capital. The only "dark" spot that remains on capital's map of East Asia is North Korea. Judging by recent U.S. efforts to create frictions in North Korea, it is possible that this "dark" spot also affords opportunities of counteracting through political/military means the declining American influence in East Asian societies. But the buyout of North Korea is also in the offing.

U.S. decline must not be exaggerated. Aside from political and military power, the enormous U.S. market continues to dynamize the economic growth of East Asian societies, now including China.[17] Besides, since corporate "re-engineering" and economic/political downsizing got under way in the mid-1980s, U.S. transnationals have once again assumed leadership in corporate efficiency. The decline is not of their power, but of the living conditions of the majority of U.S. population, which continues to see its standard of living imperiled as corporations give priority to corporate over public citizenship. Due to its enormous military power, the United States is also able to retain its role as overseer of the new order of capital. The decline is a decline from earlier years, but it is by no means absolute. The recent economic "meltdowns" in East and Southeast Asia have shown once again how much the "miracle" economies of the world remain dependent on the United States.

The emergence of Global Capitalism, accompanied by the fall of communism, has given renewed power and credibility to the utopia of capital that is captured in Fukuyama's "end of history" thesis. But the vision is not Fukuyama's alone, or restricted to conservatives; its most fervent advocates are the "New Dealers" of Global Capitalism, currently ensconced in the White House, and New Age liberals. Peace and prosperity through the market and the transnational corporation is in the United States today the ideological underpinning of corporate capitalism. It has taken by storm the ideology of educational institutions, which are busy remaking the "multiversity" of yesteryear into the "global university" of the 1990s. One university president writes that "there are . . . strong impulses to world citizenship for higher education, as common trading areas demonstrate their ability to provide a better life for their citizens, and as economic and political entities are more tightly knit through multinational corporations."[18]

There is no need to rehearse at length here what Global Capitalism has wrought. Transnational corporations have become the locations of global spaces par excellence. As they have globalized, they have created both a "transnational capitalist class," consisting of not only the managers of capital but all the professional groups crucial to its operations, as well as a transnational culture that now advertises itself as "multiculturalism." These new social and ideological formations provide new opportunities for globalism to replace the nation-states that earlier served as sources of conflict globally. It is not that the nation-state or politics has disappeared, but they have increasingly shed the social obligations they had assumed in an earlier period to reassume the "proper" role of overseeing the smooth operations of capital. The World Trade Organization that is the imminent promise of the most recent GATT agreement will be the organizational embodiment of the new age of Global Capital.

Globalization is not just economic, but political and social as well. So-called diasporic populations, nourished by transnational flows of different kinds of labor, create "flexible citizenship" (in Aihwa Ong's words) that bind nations together—even if they also contribute to the increasing prominence of ethnicity and race in contemporary social and political formations. Nongovernmental organizations bring together people from different places in joint social action, even if they also serve purposes of political influence and domination. Contradictory, incoherent, and chaotic may be the world of globalization, but it is a different world nevertheless.

What is at issue here is that the world of World War II, and even of the remnant national liberation struggles of two decades ago, seems from the contemporary perspective to belong in another age. With peace and prosperity breaking out all over the world in the wake of the motions of capital, is it an act of unwarranted pessimism, or even bad faith—or, as Fukuyama would have it, entrapment in history—to recall that previous age, which can serve only to undermine the promise of the present? Will not forgetfulness better serve the cause of human happiness?

There may be a case to be made for "forgetfulness," especially on the part of those who are the beneficiaries of Global Capitalism. The beneficiaries are not only the powerful. They include also the victims of the colonialism of an earlier day, who have benefited from the openness that is also an undeniable product of the reconfiguration of politics and culture globally. The Pacific historian Klaus Neumann writes, "These days, Papua New Guineans . . . do not appear overtly interested in being told about the horrors of colonialism, as such accounts belittle today's descendants of yesterday's victims."[19] Adult Aboriginal students in Australia complain about the classroom emphasis on White oppression, because it "seems designed to call forth in them responses of hostility and racism . . . which they believe causes a crisis of identity."[20] Forgetfulness may find different expression among those of different classes or other social groupings, but it is not bound to any one group in society. But it is not therefore any the less problematic—because it risks erasing not just a past that refuses to vanish, but also the evidence of the present that points not to utopia but to disaster. The utopia of globalization is just that, a utopia. The dissonances of the present, on the other hand, are not just remnants of a bygone day, but the very products of Global Capitalism that endow with new meaning even that which may be a leftover from the past.

I focus on a few issues here, bypassing such obvious contemporary phenomena as murderous ethnic conflict, which has replaced regulated conflict between nations, and such "intangibles" of everyday life as loss of a sense of place, insecurity, cultural uncertainty, and the reduction of human beings to units of consumption. First, does Global Capitalism indeed promise universal prosperity? The evidence is hardly in, and what is available suggests something different. Projections indicate that only a small portion of the world's population is likely to benefit from the prosperity of Global Capitalism; for the rest, the only compensation for the destruction of inherited ways of life will be marginalization in the new economy. For those who benefit from the new economy, the benefit inevitably comes at somebody else's expense: for every Chinese who benefits from the new global economy, someone else somewhere suffers a loss. This could be viewed as a redistribution of wealth globally, to take something away from those who have long had it to hand over to those who were long deprived, but it is not so simple. What shapes the redistribution is not any goals of human welfare, but corporate profit, which renders any redistribution to occur quite fickle: what the corporation gives today it takes away tomorrow when it moves its operations to more profitable (read: cheaper labor/no controls) locations, leaving in its wake the destruction of the old without anything to replace it. So far, the redistribution of wealth has been mainly from the poor to the rich, from working people to the owners of capital. Where there is such redistribution across national boundaries, those who suffer unaccustomed deprivation, as for example working people in the United States, direct their frustration not at the operations of capital, but at those who are victims themselves: "foreigners" who seem to be stealing jobs from the natives. Evidence of this is the proposition passed in California recently that would revengefully deprive of services illegal immigrants, who were dislodged from their lives by the same capital that undermines the livelihood of Californians by moving its operations to China or the Philippines or wherever.

Second, although a globalized capitalism has indeed created common bonds among people economically and culturally, it also, ironically, has exacerbated older divisions. The newfound economic power of Asian societies has also empowered the reassertion of native ideologies, long suppressed by diffidence to Euro-America. The idea of "Asianness" itself has been revived, as Asian societies have become conscious of themselves as the "dynamoes" of the new Global Capitalism. But this is a different "Asianness" than that of Gandhi, Tagore, Sun Zhongshan, or Mao Zedong. Rather than the spiritual homeland to the world, the new Asia is celebrated as the location for material wealth. In the hands of a Lee Kuan Yew, "Asianness" serves as a weapon with which to counter arguments for democracy, and an earlier spiritual enrichment of the world turns into the advocacy of social control and engineering—all in the name of wealth. As the prime minister of Malaysia said in an interview published in *Third World Resurgence* in August 1993, few care about democracy so long as a high annual growth rate can be sustained. Though the challenge to Eurocentrism in the name of Asian cultures promises greater cultural equality than before, the reverse side is the use of "culture" to justify oppression at home, as in the case of China and South Korea. There is obviously much in these arguments that is appealing to managers of capital, who have made the likes of Lee Kuan Yew into heroes of the contemporary world. In early 1995, U.S. Secretary of State Warren Christopher came in for abuse not just from the Chinese government but from American businessmen in China for his mission to promote human rights in that country.[21]

The instability of Global Capitalism, however, is barely disguised by the ideology of globalization, as was evidenced by the responses to the economic "meltdown" of these Asian economic "miracles" in late 1997. Overnight, the much touted Asian values supposedly responsible for rapid development in East and Southeast Asia turned into liabilities, as the sources of corruption and "crony capitalism" that accounted for the meltdown. On the other side, the same Malaysian Prime Minister Mahathir Mohamad was quick to revive the language of colonialism and nationalism as he muttered warnings about the possible recolonization of Malaysia by Euro-American transnationals ready to take advantage of the crisis.

Stephen Hay, in his analysis of Pan-Asianism, was wrong about portraying Pan-Asianism as a passing phenomenon of a certain stage of modernization, but quite right in his observation that Pan-Asianism represented the projection on Asia of perceived national values. If Pan-Asianism appears today as a means to challenge Euro-American values, it barely conceals conflicts among Asian nations over whose values are to be representative of Asia. "Asia," a song composed for the Pan-Asian games in Beijing in 1991, having sung praises of Asia as home to the longest rivers and the highest mountains in the world, proceeds to identify China as the location of the highest of the high and longest of the long. The song is symbolic of the competition within Asia. Different Asian societies claim Islam, Confucianism, or Hinduism these days as the ideological source of their success in development. "Greater China," encompassing the People's Republic, Taiwan, Hong Kong, and Singapore, claims for itself a greater developmental power than Japan. Meanwhile, Koreans and Japanese are locked in controversy over claims to priority in the origins of "national" civilizations. And in all of these societies, a "cultural nationalism" that essentializes national traditions as the source of developmental success ironically has accompanied economic internationalization, as if an essentialized national culture were the only defense against the erosion of native values by incorporation into Global Capitalism, which is also much in evidence. But the result is to strengthen right-wing claims on the nation and increase the possibility of conflict.[22]

And, sure enough, prognostications of conflict have not been long in coming. Once the Soviet threat appeared to be subsiding, conflict could be projected on the Pacific, as in the prolific literature of the 1980s in the United States devoted to "the coming war with Japan," which in the 1990s (with the economic depression in Japan and the rise of China) has turned its attention to "the coming war with China." The most dramatic example in the United States was provided by the publication in 1993 of an article by the influential political scientist Samuel Huntington, entitled "The Clash of Civilizations?"[23]

Arguing that the great division among humankind was cultural, Huntington predicted that "the clash of civilizations will dominate global politics" in the future, with the age-old clash between Christianity and Islam as a priority, but East Asia not far behind. But the clash need not be between Euro-American and other civilizations. A special issue of *Newsweek* in 1993 was devoted to the possibility of conflict "between a resurgent China and Japan.[24]

Against the naïve faith in the utopia of Global Capitalism, finally, let me briefly cite here two scenarios for disaster that recently have been outlined by *Business Week*, a periodical that is otherwise devoted to the promotion of capital. Perhaps not surprisingly, both scenarios focus on East Asia. They also have much to say about the actual workings, rather than the utopian aspirations, of contemporary capitalism:

> China breakup: Chinese provinces gain increasing autonomy as Beijing's authority erodes. Key provinces reject Beijing's tax levies and statist controls, triggering a chain of secessions supported by local army commanders. The political crisis brakes China's economic growth and disrupts agriculture, causing widespread unemployment and food riots. Fighting erupts among provinces, some armed with nuclear weapons. Fearful of spreading conflict, neighboring countries hunker down and capital flees, putting an end to Asia's boom.[25]

> From tiny Haiti to giant China, environmental stresses and depletion are becoming acute. So thick is the smog over Benxi, a city of one million in northeastern China, that the city doesn't appear on satellite maps. In Tianjin, wells are draining groundwater so fast that the city is sinking 2.5 meters per year. Across China, soil erosion and urban sprawl are shrinking farmland in a country with 14 million new mouths to feed every year.
>
> To boost income and head off discontent, Beijing's aging hierarchs believe they have only one choice: Go for growth, and worry about the environment later. But with roughly 1.2 billion people living on a limited resource base, swift environmental deterioration could put a sharp brake on growth. If China runs into an environmental wall, the shocks could reverberate around the world.[26]

Neither the pillage of the environment nor the pillage of the people is a specifically Chinese or Third World problem, but one would hardly expect *Business Week* to go so far as to lay them at the feet of Global Capitalism, which feeds off a fetishism of development and a reification of corporate greed that has now become worldwide. The admission of the possibility of disaster by a mouthpiece of capital is sobering enough, and could be held up as an example before many an academic apologist for "globalization." On the other hand, the prognostication of disaster overlooks that for many, the disaster does not lie in the future but is all around us, if we are only willing to see it. The recent massacres in Chiapas, Mexico, confirm the Zapatista diagnosis that the Fourth World War has already begun.[27] Whereas in Pentagon perspective the immediate conflicts looming on the contemporary horizon may be "brush wars," that perspective overlooks that to the people in the brush, a brush war is a holocaust.

The conditions under which the battles of the past were fought may belong in the past. But the past lives on in the formative effect it has had on present-day structures, and it is always available for appropriation even in a vastly different world. The question is how it is appropriated. Where World War II is concerned, memories of the past serve to promote nationalism that, weakened in organization by developments in capitalism, finds in the realm of culture and past existence a means both to perpetuate and to preserve a contemporary status quo that is very much in jeopardy. Harry Harootunian has observed that it was in the 1960s when some Japanese, increasingly conscious of the material power of Japan, began to question the prevailing image of World War II Japan as victimizer, suggesting that Japan perhaps had been the victim. The erasure of memories of the war would serve well the new economic "coprosperity sphere" that was already in formation. Perhaps it would also help erase memories of the shame of occupation. In either case, the leadership in Japan directly contributed to efforts to revise memories of the war. The responses to that effort in other East Asian societies were equally based on nationalist considerations. The calligraphy that Nie Rongzhen contributed to the first issue of the periodical *KangRi zhanzheng yanjiu* stated: "Research the history of the Anti-Japanese Resistance War to promote patriotic education" (*Yanjiu KangRi zhanzheng shi, jiaqiang aiguo zhuyide jiaoyu*). Liu Danian and others were to add frequently in the 1980s that memories of the war were also important to "upholding the four principles" by showing the important part the Communist Party had played during the war.

Though these nationalist appropriations of the war may be justifiable for different reasons in different societies, are they the only legacy of the war? In the concluding lines of his *War without Mercy*, Dower observes that "to return to that terrible conflict of four decades ago is . . . inevitable and essential—and fraught with peril. It can teach us many things, but can also fan the fires of contemporary anger and self-righteousness."[28] Anyone who doubts his words may be reminded of the U.S. Postal Service's aborted intention to commemorate the end of the war with a postage stamp showing a mushroom cloud. Such are the pitfalls of nationalist memories. But the nationalist consciousness is mediated by a longer history of Orientalism. The United States confronts Asian nations not just as nations, but as *Asian* nations, who do not share in a common notion of humans and human rights. Where World War II is concerned, "Asiatic" memories are marked by a recalcitrance that obstructs recognition of the sins of war. In Asia, even Nazis turn into good Nazis as angels of mercy.

There is, however, a different way to remember the war: not as a war among nations, but as a war in which many fought against structures of oppression. Memories of national liberation struggles, which were not just struggles for the nation but also struggles against oppression at home, may be especially important at a time when there is a tendency to erase awareness of oppression by a utopianism of capital. It is not fashionable these days to speak of oppression, but a utopia that sweeps that problem under the rug is not much of a utopia— besides being an instrument of oppression rather than of liberation. Unfortunately, even those who fought the wars of liberation earlier, in line with class interests or dreams of nationalist power, seem to have forgotten that aspect of their struggles.

The date 15 August 1945 is too intimately connected with national victories or defeats to bring out this aspect of memory. There is, however, another date that pushes to the surface the full horror of the war for all concerned. In 1964, in response to the Chinese explosion of a nuclear bomb, Kenzaburo Oe wrote:

> In such a time as this, I want to remember, and keep on remembering, the thoughts of the people of Hiroshima—the first people and the first place to experience full force the world's worst destructive capability. Hiroshima is like a nakedly exposed wound inflicted on all mankind. Like all wounds, this one also poses two potential outcomes: the hope of human recovery, and the danger of fatal corruption. Unless we persevere in remembering the Hiroshima experience, especially the thoughts of those who underwent that unprecedented experience, the faint signs of recovery emerging from this place and people will begin to decay and real degeneration will set in.[29]

With Oe's injunction in mind, I would like to supplement this essay with brief summaries of two other ways of remembering, one historical, the other fictional. I choose the case of comfort women not because it has made headlines, but because it illustrates the "transnationality" of oppression. The Oda account, on the other hand, is important not only for demonstrating the complexity in the constitution of the "enemy" over there, but more importantly for bringing the war back "home." It is fiction because it is based on fictional characters and ends with a fictional revenge, but it is based as much on experience (if not on written documentation) as any work of history.

War, Oppression, and Human Unity

In April 1993, an aging, silver-haired woman from the Anhui countryside entered the Korean Embassy in Beijing.[30] The sight of the Republic of Korea flag outside the Embassy, followed by familiar sounds from which she had been long cut off, proved to be too much for her. She broke down in tears. Thus begins the story of the Korean "comfort woman," Li Tianying.

In Li's story is intertwined the histories of Korea, Japan, and China during World War II. She was born Cheng-Gae Hua on 28 April 1925 in Gyeng Shang-do in southeastern Korea, into a poor rural family. When she was seven years old, her mother was killed due to a beating she suffered by a Japanese supervisor at the fish-processing factory where she worked. Her father's illness forced the family into debt to a local pharmacy. Li, then nine years old, was obliged to work to pay off the debt. Unbearable treatment at the pharmacy led to escape. With her father and elder brother, Li ended up in Pusan, where she found a job with a family doing household work. She was around twelve when she last saw her father and elder brother.

One day in 1939, to escape the sexual advances of one of the sons of the household, Li escaped. On the Pusan docks where she wandered she was gagged and blindfolded by several youths. Next thing she knew, she was on a Japanese Army transport train, along with several other women. When the train finally stopped, she was in Harbin.

Her life as a comfort woman began with a rape and a beating shortly after her arrival in Harbin. She and the other women at the "comfort station" discovered quickly that the consequence of resistance to rape was torture. She recalls vividly still an experience at the station in the Andong Bridge region of Harbin, when eight young Chinese girls, in punishment for resistance, had their "feet tied up, kerosene poured over them, and burned." From then on, she, like the others, knew that their only option was to endure their fate.

In 1940, when the comfort station was in Zaozhuang (Shandong), Li made her first attempt at escape. An elderly Chinese man who did chores at the station helped her out by opening a hole in the wall, provided her with a change of clothing and little money—and a new name, Li Tianying. In her gratitude, Li would keep that name for the rest of her life.

Li was able to run into the mountains, where she met another escapee. But they were soon caught by the Japanese, and Li was severely punished for her escape. Back in the station, she followed the troops to Shijiazhuang and, in 1941, to Linben in Shanxi, where she would spend the next four years. By that time, the women were joined by Japanese Army prostitutes brought to Shanxi from Hong Kong.

In 1944, when the Japanese Army in Linben was under attack from the Chinese troops of Yan Xishan, Li managed to escape once again, this time with the help of a Chinese woman. With help from other Chinese, she ended up with troops from Yan Xishan's army, which she was to serve as a nurse for the duration of the war. Shortly after Japan's surrender, these troops were captured by a communist army under Deng Xiaoping's command. Li continued with the communist army as a nurse.

During the lull in the Chinese civil war in 1946, Koreans in China were given the opportunity for repatriation. The communist hospital in which Li worked provided her with fifty Chinese dollars and a letter of introduction to return to Korea under Kim Il-sung. Outfitted in communist uniform, complete with a Mao badge, she was apprehended by Guomindang troops as a communist spy. The scars on her body testified to her innocence, however, and she was sent to an army vehicle repair shop to work as a mechanic.

In Zhengzhou (Henan) with the Guomindang armies, Li met Dai Yonggui, a soldier from a peasant family. They were married. At the beginning of 1949, when the Guomindang troops were finally defeated by the communists, the couple returned to Dai's village in Shucheng township. That is where the victorious revolution found them. Land redistribution had provided them with a little bit of land. Though no one in the village knew about Li's past, or that she was even Korean, her inability to bear children because of her scars brought on her the disdain of her husband's family. Unable to bear her husband's disloyalty, Li was divorced in 1955.

In the meantime, in the revolutionary campaigns of the early 1950s, she was arbitrarily labeled with the "crime" of leading an "unhealthy way of life," which landed her in a rehabilitation center. A woman official at the rehabilitation center was able to find out about Li's past, but Li's good behavior gained her her freedom within two years. Because she had nowhere to go, she remained at the rehabilitation center as a farm technician. In 1964, she met and married Guan Chaoxin, who had been sent to work at the same farm after rehabilitation. In 1965, the two moved to Guan's village. No one, including her husband, knew about Li's past, except the authorities.

The Cultural Revolution years witnessed new pressures. Because of the weakness of her body, Li suffered from discrimination at the hands of village authorities. Her sterility once again brought discrimination from her relatives. In her poverty, she was unable to get the operations she needed. She left the village for a while to work on a dam construction project, but suffering the same kind of maltreatment, she returned to Kangmiao village, to endure discrimination and coldness from her husband.

It was a Korean film popular in China in 1971, *A Girl Who Sells Flowers*, that was to bring to Li an unexpected happiness. A young Chinese man, Li Shaolin, who saw the movie was deeply touched by the film, which reminded him of his own misfortunes as an orphan. Hearing that there was an elderly Korean woman living in the countryside all alone and with no one to take care of her, he went looking for her. She needed a son, and he a mother. They adopted one another. Li Shaolin's affection for his newfound mother was such that even after he found out, in 1972, about her past, he was not changed; if anything, his affection for her got stronger. The two of them, twenty years later, showed up at the Korean Embassy in Beijing.

On Li's body is inscribed the history of war and revolution in East Asia. It was not just the Japanese Army that abused her, but also poverty and discrimination, from childhood in Korea to old age in China. Though the horror of "comfort stations" may be an episode from the past, what do we make of the thousands of new bodies on which another history is being inscribed in our day—this time by the market-driven forces of the flourishing "tourist industries" of Asia?

THE BOMB

Hiroshima, in Oda's "novel," is "like a nakedly exposed wound inflicted on all mankind."[31] The story he tells is a story of "fatal corruption." It also offers hope of "human recovery" and redemption.

It is impossible to summarize this allegory on discrimination and human destruction. Oda takes the bomb away from Hiroshima to make it into a symbol of universal human destruction. He does this in two ways, first by placing the destruction in two locations: Hiroshima and White Sands in New Mexico, where the bomb was born. The first victims of the bomb were not in Hiroshima but in the United States, especially among the Native Americans on whose sacred lands the first bomb was tested on 16 June 1945. They, and others who were used in the test or in digging up uranium mines, were the first ones to be irradiated. Their wounds have yet to heal.

The second is the way in which Oda peoples his novel. There is no story line to the novel, just stories of many kinds of people, victimized and victimizers, whom war and discrimination throws together in White Sands and Hiroshima. The flash in Hiroshima on 6 August is seen through the blindfolded eyes of Joe, a captured American airman from New Mexico, known back home as "the runner" because he loved to run across the desert. Aside from the ordinary inhabitants, Hiroshima on that day was the gathering place for Keiji, a Japanese teenager from Osaka, who suffered discrimination for his physical weakness at the hands of his burly country cousins; for Eul Sun, the Korean woman who, with her husband, had been driven to Hiroshima out of poverty in Korea; for Tommy Nakata, *kibei* Japanese American teenager, sent to Japan by his parents, who had suffered discrimination in his birthplace for being a "Jap" and now suffers discrimination in his ancestral land for being an "American spy," but who has come to believe that "Japan has to win. . . . If we don't win, we'll all become 'Japs.' "

Discrimination in the novel is not the cause of the war, the translator tells us in the preface, but war and discrimination are part of an overall structure of oppression that corrupts everyone. If the story Oda tells does not have a clear narrative line, its emplotment follows the Hopi myth of creation and the Four Worlds, which is worth quoting at some length as it is told in the novel. The teller of the myth is Chuck Paweki, "the first Indian Olympic medal winner" from a displaced tribe committed to peace, who wishes to pass on tribal knowledge to his nephew, Ron Muchuck, another "runner":

> "In the First World, in the beginning, the different languages did not cause them any trouble. No matter how much they multiplied, they all felt for each other as one. They could understand each other without language. It was the same for birds and animals as for humans. This was because they all felt and shared the blessings of their mother earth, and because they revered their father, Taiowa.
>
> "But in time, some began to lose their reverence for Taiowa. They forgot the blessings of their mother earth. There appeared the Mochni bird, the Talker. He flew around, talking about the differences between peoples— about the differences in their languages, about their different skin colors, and of course about the differences between people and animals.
>
> "Then the animals began to stay away from men, and men began to separate themselves from each other. Differences in color, differences in language, those who remembered why the Creator made the world and those who didn't . . . differences bred differences, and conflict began to spread until it was terrible.
>
> "Still, there were some who continued to revere their Creator. There were some among every race, speaking every language. Sotuknang told them: 'I have talked with my uncle, Taiowa, and I have come to a decision: I will destroy this world, and I will make a new one, where mankind can start all over again. You have been chosen for that purpose.'
>
> " 'Make haste,' Sotuknang said. 'Your *kopavi*, the gateway in your head that connects you with your Creator, will show you your destination . . .'
>
> "In the end the believers all came together in one place. The color of

their skin was different, and they spoke different languages, but they were one because their *kopavi* had shown each of them the cloud and the star and had guided them there. . . .

"Sotuknang led them to the hill of the Ant People. He ordered the Ant People to make a hole at the top and commanded the believers to go inside. 'You will be safe here. You must stay while I destroy the world around you. While you are here, learn about the way of life of the Ant People. They work hard. During the summer they store provisions for the winter. When it is hot outside, it is cool inside here, and when it is cold outside, it is warm inside. They lead a very harmonious life.'

"With the humans safely inside with the Ant People, Sotuknang rained fire on the earth until it was destroyed. . . . Air, earth and water became a flaming ball. Nothing on the face of the earth was spared, only the chosen ones hiding in its bowels. That was the end of the First World."

So it was with the Second and Third Worlds. Now it is the Fourth. Ron wonders:

"I wonder if this world will be destroyed by Sotuknang too. Maybe it will become a big ball of fire."

Chuck nodded. "Perhaps. People always seem to want to fight." Ron realized he was referring to the war—the one that had just started with the Japs, and the one in Europe that was still going on. "Taiowa must be angry." (38–40)

Unity comes in the end, in the radiation treatment ward where, once again, many different kinds of people are together, dying, "where there are no names, no male or female, no old, young, and even no human." All the names are interchangeable, and all the differences of color are buried beneath "blood, soot and mud." Ron is there, irradiated at the "hole of the Ant People," ground zero for the test bomb. To Ron now, everyone is his Uncle Chuck, who has disappeared.

"What country did you come from in the last world, Ron? Were you an Indian?"
"Mm, that's right, Chuck."
"Were you a Chink, Ron?"
"Mm, that's right, Chuck."
"Were you a Jap, Ron?"
"Mm, that's right, Chuck."
"Were you a nigger, Ron?"
"Mm, that's right, Chuck."
"Were you a white?"
"Mm, that's right, Chuck."

"Were you a man, Ron?"

"Mm, that's right, Laura."

"Were you a woman, Ron?"

"Mm, that's right, Laura." (191)

The novel ends with an attack by the dead on the White House, where the president (also the "Commander of the United States Forces") is meeting with the emperor of Japan ("the Jap boss," whose name begins with an H: "I tried to say it, but it came out as *Hiroshima*"). The attack is commanded by a Marine hero, killer of gooks from Korea to Vietnam and a veteran of the troops tested at ground zero. He is accompanied by a Black man and the Indian gook Ron. Their mission: to dump on the "killers" on the White House lawn a boxful of dirt from ground zero, so that "the killers will be killed . . . and the order of the world will change from the bottom."

The final expression of hope comes, as does the plot, from a Hopi prophecy in *The Book of the Hopi* by Frank Waters: "It is only materialistic people who seek to make shelters. Those who are at peace in their hearts already are in the great shelter of life. There is no shelter for evil. Those who take no part in the making of world division by ideology are ready to resume life in another world, be they of the Black, White, Red or Yellow Race. They are all one, brothers."

While a student in the United States, Oda was mistaken for a Navajo while drinking at a bar near a Hopi reservation. To the Whites, the Japanese Americans in his novel, as well as the other Asians, are interchangeable with Native Americans: they are all "gooks." His own experience may have inspired the emplotment of the novel in terms of a Hopi myth, but what is relevant is the timeless message he discovers in the history of a people who have not yet been totally corrupted by the social, political, and technological alienations of a modern society, and whose continued subjection to "radioactive colonialism" is a reminder of a legacy of radioactive pollution that imperils us all, even after the immediate danger of the bomb has subsided. The wounds caused by the bomb are inseparable from the wounds of humankind's alienation from nature and from its own "species-being," to use Karl Marx's term. We are "trapped" in history so long as that alienation persists. And so we must remember the war, and all the other wars that are hidden within it, if we are to have any hope of overcoming the way we have made the world—and ourselves within it.

The Endless War

One of the anonymous readers of this volume commented that the present essay "reads as an odd collection of bits and pieces that don't seem to hold together very well." The point is well taken, but off the mark. The essay is intended not just in content but in form to convey the disjointedness of memories of World War II against narrative coherence that inevitably ends up with narrative closure on how the war is to be remembered. The way I view them, commemorations should provide occasions for reflecting on the present and the ways in which different reflections on the present enter into the ways in which we remember the past. The "bits and pieces" could be multiplied indefinitely, not to diminish the importance of World War II as historical event, but to demonstrate its significance by showing the many ways it touched the lives of so many drawn into it, the multiplicity of the experiences of war, and how those experiences show the way to a fecund critical appreciation of the present. I have chosen a few "bits and pieces" that seem to me to be of relevance for the present. Other essays in this volume offer others. As the editors point out in their introduction, the volume is intended not to celebrate nor to condemn, but to recall as many experiences as are possible within the limits of a mere volume, which at best may illustrate the variety of experiences of such a momentous event without any claim to comprehensiveness—as narrative coherence often implies—and the hegemonic claims that are often the result of pretension to omniscience. War may even liberate!

As liminally destructive events, wars especially lend themselves to such hegemony. And they are often used on commemorative occasions to consolidate social and political structures based on inequality and domination that are responsible in the first place for making warfare into a condition of human existence. One of the most interesting—and devastating—consequences of the place assigned to warfare in history is to silence opposition to the existing order of things and to compel participation in the rendering of war into the inevitable condition of human existence. It is, needless to say, the structure of domination that shapes the way the "enemy" is thought, and the way the experience of war enters history. In his recently published account of peasant participation in the Chinese revolution, Ralph Thaxton writes: that

> Peasants [of North China] did not assign the same importance to the definitive historical event that shaped the political identity of many of the ccp [Chinese Communist Party] leaders who formed the revolutionary Hebei-Shandong-Henan border area government during wwii: the Japanese invasion and the War of Resistance. To be sure, the War of Resistance was important to many village people; but for the great majority its significance paled in comparison to the remembrances of a war against the police instrument of Kuomintang fiscal order. This latter war preceded, intersected with, and persisted beyond the ccp-led War of Resistance

and, in many ways, posed a greater challenge to the permanency of peasant life and culture.[32]

Peasants, of course, do not determine the content of commemorative occasions, except possibly in their own villages and when they rise up against the existing order of things.

There may be two lessons here. First, that wars are a diversion from the oppression and exploitation that for most people are the conditions of everyday life, who more often than not have to participate in wars that are not of their own making. Second, wars in historiography serve to cover those very relations as they are rendered into the heritage of whole societies, rather than those who are responsible for and make warfare.

The confounding of the structural causes of war with the experience of war of the rank and file who are dragged into it has played an important part in the controversies surrounding the commemoration of World War Ii in 1995. The cultural circumstances surrounding the commemoration have had the unfortunate consequence of trivializing those controversies into issues of "political correctness," for which both proponents and opponents must bear some responsibility. The mythmaking activities of the proponents do not require much comment within the context of this volume. More important is to recognize that the critique of such mythmaking—the critique of power, in other words—must take care not to erase the experiences of those who, dragged into war, nevertheless experienced it not as an abstraction or exercise in social criticism, but as a matter of life and death. The burden of memory surely lies more heavily on the living than on the dead. And it is important that their memories not be erased as other memories are exhumed from a buried past. If it is to avoid falling into the same exclusionary mentality of the White patriarchal nationalism that it would repudiate, critique must be tempered by a recognition that White male soldiers also die and suffer pain, and perhaps seek in commemorations not just the celebration of power, but some explanation for the suffering they have experienced. The relationship between nationalism and a postcolonial cosmopolitanism is not a zero-sum relationship. Recognition of its complexity ought to serve instead to bring forth the diversity of memory that is suppressed in a historiography that is bound to servitude under changing configurations of power.

Notes

1 For a discussion of these criticisms, see Arif Dirlik, " 'Past Experience, if Not Forgotten, Is a Guide to the Future'; or, What Is in a Text? The Politics of History in Chinese-Japanese

Relations," in *Japan in the World*, ed. Masao Miyoshi and Harry Harootunian (Durham, NC: Duke University Press, 1993), 49–78.

2 Liu Danian, "Zuo shenme, zenme zuo-Zai Zhongguo kangRi zhanzheng shixue hui chengli dahui shangde jianghua" (What to do, and how to do it: Talk at the founding meeting of the Chinese Anti-Japanese War Historical Society), *KangRi zhanzheng yanjiu* (Anti-Japanese War Research) 1(1991): 3.

3 Quoted in "Land Mines on the Road to Utopia," *21st Century Capitalism*, special issue of *Business Week* (18 November 1994): 137.

4 Quoted in John Dower, *War without Mercy: Race and Power in the Pacific War* (New York: Pantheon Books, 1986), 301.

5 Mao Zedong, "The Situation and Our Policy after the Victory in the War of Resistance against Japan," in *Selected Works* (Peking: Foreign Languages Press, 1975), 4:11–26.

6 Bernard B. Fall, ed., "Appeal for General Insurrection," in *Ho Chi Minh on Revolution: Selected Writings, 1920–66* (New York: Frederick A. Praeger, 1967), 139–40.

7 Bruce Cumings, *The Origins of the Korean War: Liberation and the Emergence of Separate Regimes, 1945–1947* (Princeton, NJ: Princeton University Press, 1981), 120.

8 Liu, "Zuo shenme," 7.

9 Jon Halliday and Bruce Cumings, *Korea: The Unknown War* (New York: Pantheon, 1988), 27.

10 For a recent example of such total miscomprehension, see James A. Matray, "Diplomatic History as a Political Weapon: An Assessment of Anti-Americanism in South Korea Today," *The SHAFR* (Society for Historians of American Foreign Relations) *Newsletter* (1989). Matray was recruited by the USIA to counteract the influence on Korean intellectuals of Bruce Cumings's *The Origins of the Korean War*. It does not seem to have occurred to the USIA or Matray (a Korea specialist) that Cumings's work may have been appealing for good historical reason, but then, they cannot seem to imagine as history anything other than their version of it.

11 Stephen N. Hay, *Asian Ideas of East and West: Tagore and His Critics in Japan, China, and India* (Cambridge, MA: Harvard University Press, 1970).

12 Dower, *War without Mercy*, 5–6.

13 For discussions of Korea and Vietnam, see Michael E. Robinson, *Cultural Nationalism in Colonial Korea, 1920–1925* (Seattle: University of Washington Press, 1988), and Hue-Tam Ho Tai, *Radicalism and the Origins of the Vietnamese Revolution* (Cambridge, MA: Harvard University Press, 1992). For the social revolutionary movement in Korea following the war, see Cumings, *Origins of the Korean War*.

14 Senator Alfred J. Beveridge, "Our Philippine Policy," in *The Philippines Reader*, ed. Daniel B. Schirmer and Stephen Rosskamm Shalom (Boston: South End Press, 1987), 24.

15 Harry D. Harootunian, "America's Japan/Japan's Japan," in *Japan in the World*, ed. Masao Miyoshi and Harry Harootunian (Durham, NC: Duke University Press, 1993), 197–221.

16 Bruce Cumings, "The Origins and Development of the Northeast Asian Political Economy: Industrial Sectors, Product Cycles, and Political Consequences," *International Organization* 38, no. 1 (winter 1984): 1–40.

17 Meredith Woo-Cumings, "Market Dependency in U.S.–East Asian Relations," in *What Is in a Rim? Critical Perspectives on the Pacific Region Idea*, ed. Arif Dirlik (Boulder, CO: Westview Press, 1993), 135–57.

18 Nannerl O. Keohane (president of Duke University), "Higher Education in the 21st Cen-

tury: The Global University," *Global Perspective: Newsletter of the Center for International Studies at Duke University* 7, no. 1 (fall 1994): 1.

19 Klaus Neumann, " 'In Order to Win Their Friendship': Renegotiating First Contact," *The Contemporary Pacific* 6, no.1 (spring 1994): 122.

20 Deirdre Jordan, "Aboriginal Identity: Uses of the Past, Problems for the Future," in *Past and Present: The Construction of Aboriginality,* ed. Jeremy R. Beckett (Canberra: Aboriginal Studies Press, 1994), 119.

21 For an excellent analysis of Lee Kuan Yew's ideological formations, see Ien Ang and Jon Stratton, "The Singapore Way of Multiculturalism: Western Concepts/Asian Cultures," paper presented in the public lecture series on Multiculturalism in a Global Context, East-West Center, Honolulu, 4 August 1994.

22 For further discussion, see Arif Dirlik, "Confucius in the Borderlands: Global Capitalism and the Reinvention of Confucianism," *boundary* 2, 22.3 (November): 228–73; Harumi Befu, ed., *Cultural Nationalism in East Asia* (Berkeley: Center for Chinese Studies, 1993); and Kosaku Yoshino, *Cultural Nationalism in Contemporary Japan: A Sociological Inquiry* (London: Routledge, 1992). These works all demonstrate, though they do not necessarily enunciate, the close connection between incorporation in Global Capitalism and the revival of cultural essentialisms.

23 Samuel P. Huntington, "The Clash of Civilizations?" *Foreign Affairs* 72, no. 3 (summer 1993):22–49.

24 "Japan vs. China: The Great Asian Power Struggle Has Begun," *Newsweek,* international ed. (15 November 1993):12–25.

25 "Land Mines on the Road to Utopia," 137.

26 Ibid., 140.

27 Subcommandant Marcos, "Why We Are Fighting: The Fourth World War Has Begun," *Le Monde Diplomatique* (August–September 1997). Marcos assumes, needless to say, that the very "hot" cold war was the Third World War.

28 Dower, *War without Mercy,* 317.

29 Kenzaburo Oe, *Hiroshima Notes,* ed. David L. Swain, trans. Toshi Yonezawa (Tokyo: YMCA Press, 1981), 90.

30 This brief account is based on Sun Young Park, "Hanguo weian fu zai Zhongguo" (A Korean "comfort woman" in China) manuscript, 1993. Ms. Park, then a Ph.D. candidate in history at Nanjing University, interviewed Li Tianying in 1993. Her account has been published in Chinese, Japanese, and Korean. This account is based on the ms. that she has shared with me, for which I am grateful.

31 Makoto Oda, *The Bomb: A Novel,* trans. D. H. Whittaker (Tokyo: Kodansha International, 1990); originally published in Japanese as *Hiroshima.*

32 Ralph A. Thaxton Jr., *Salt of the Earth: The Political Origins of Peasant Protest and Communist Revolution in China* (Berkeley: University of California Press, 1997), xv.

For Transformative Knowledge

and Postnationalist Public Spheres:

The Smithsonian *Enola Gay* Controversy

LISA YONEYAMA

There is no document of civilization which is not at the same time a document of barbarism. And just as such a document is not free of barbarism, barbarism taints also the manner in which it was transmitted from one owner to another.
—Walter Benjamin, *Illuminations*

The exhibition by the Smithsonian National Air and Space Museum (NASM) of the *Enola Gay*, which commemorated the fiftieth anniversary of the end of the Second World War, set off a heated controversy concerning national ideologies, the collective memory of self-victimization, and contestations over historical knowledge. This essay explores the ways in which the Smithsonian debate was fought out primarily in the U.S. public media and in congressional hearings about history and memory. By examining some of the central narratives that constituted the debate, this essay investigates the following questions.

The first half of the essay focuses on the various predicaments in the attempts to produce a nation's public history and memory. What does it mean, and is it at all possible, to produce a single and definitive public history and memory shared commonly and objectively by a nation? Production of any overarching narratives about the past inevitably incites various contestations and struggles over historical truths. Inseparable from this process, therefore, is the question regarding the limits of a mode of argumentation that relies on the force of factual authenticity and objectivity. The essay cautions against the pitfalls of making too hasty a distinction, as was often the case during the controversy, between the commemorative desire that is thought to derive from one's personal experience and the claims for objective truths of historical knowledge.

The second half of this essay is devoted to illuminating what might be best described as the transnational warping of political positions in the Smithsonian debates. The Smithsonian controversy exhibited the tension common in any official memory making today, namely, the negotiations between the process by which various transnational and discordant factors participate in the generation of a nation-state's dominant historical consciousness and the process wherein such transnational movements in the production of collective memory have been constantly censored.[1] Even while reminding us of the tenacity of national imaginings and proving that nation-states can still lay powerful claim to a possessive relation with a single, uniform historical consciousness, the debates showed that disparities in historical awareness concerning the Asia-Pacific War and the two atom bombings do not necessarily originate in national differences. What appears to be a conflict limited to one national public sphere is in fact constituted by factors that cross the boundaries of a nation's official remembering. Through critiquing the problems of selective amnesia produced by a type of remembering that assumes an isomorphic relationship between a nation and a single coherent and consistent historical consciousness, this essay also proposes an alternative historiography, one that posits postnationalist public spheres in the production of historical knowledge.

The essay furthermore attempts to situate the Smithsonian debates within the larger context of the conditions of knowledge that circumscribe those of us who work in U.S. academic circles in the 1990s. It reflects on the claims made by House Speaker Newt Gingrich, talk-show host Rush Limbaugh, and others that the Smithsonian controversy ended with an American victory over "anti-American radicals" and cultural elites, who conspired to promote "political correctness."[2] How are we to locate such claims on our intellectual mapping of the U.S. academy? And what sorts of historical subjects do these claims attempt to interpellate?

Historical Facts, Commemoration, and Critical Knowledge

The Smithsonian *Enola Gay* controversy—or the "Smithsonian atom bomb exhibit debates," as the Japanese-language news media more precisely named it—concluded with a major departure from the comprehensive exhibit originally planned by the museum. During more than a year of negotiations between the public and the NASM curatorial staff, the scripts were rewritten a number of times, and in the end, all of the following were eliminated: the details of debates among U.S. political leaders, scholars, and military commanders over the decision to use the atom bombs; a great number of photographs and descriptions concerning Japan's military invasions and colonial atrocities committed in East

Asia, Southeast Asia, and the Pacific Islands; photographs showing physical and human damage in Hiroshima and Nagasaki; and general observations about the subsequent development of the atomic age and nuclear weapons proliferation.[3]

Let us begin by examining two strikingly similar, yet contrasting, statements in the U.S. news media. A *Los Angeles Times* editorial titled "Wrong Place for Anti-Nuclear Message: Smithsonian Scotches *Enola Gay* Exhibit amid a Controversy That Shouldn't Have Happened" (1 February 1995) indicated that the *Enola Gay* dispute was "one of those historical arguments in which the factual context is often obscured by ideological presuppositions." While admitting the significance of warning against the destructive force of the atomic bombs and questioning the subsequent nuclear arms race, it concluded that "a Smithsonian exhibit that rightfully should have been primarily dedicated to commemorating the end of World War II and honoring those who fought to defeat Nazism and Japanese militarism clearly was not that place." Contrast this remark with a *New York Times* editorial, "Hijacking History" (30 January 1995). Cautioning against yielding to the political pressure of conservative Congress members and veterans, the editorial argued that "historians and museums of history need to be insulated from any attempt to make history conform to a narrow ideological or political interest."

These two statements remind us of the ways in which, as sociologist John B. Thompson puts it, the term *ideological* always precludes references to the self and is summoned only when used to condemn and discount others.[4] They also epitomize the way in which the notion of factual neutrality, despite the prominence of veterans' claims for experiential authority as witnesses, has served as the governing and most persuasive source for legitimacy across nearly the entire discursive terrain of the disputes between those who supported and those who attacked the exhibit plans prepared by the NASM curators. In their heated exchanges, both the historians and journalists who tried to save the comprehensive version of the exhibit and those who in the end succeeded in altering the exhibit so as to honor the plane's mission relied on the power of facticity to substantiate their credibility. Almost all who participated in the controversy emphasized that their positions were grounded in historical facts, thereby underscoring their objectivity and/or neutrality, while simultaneously denouncing their opponents as blinded by personal judgments, political bias, and emotional investment.

On the one hand, the so-called revisionist historians who defended the curators' plans sought to refute their opponents by emphasizing the academic authenticity of the prepared texts. For instance, Kai Bird, perhaps one of the most vocal and active historians to denounce the politicians' violation of curatorial and academic freedom, argued that the controversy stemmed from the "inaccurate but understandable belief of the veterans that the atomic bomb saved their lives from being sacrificed."[5] Still others defended the exhibit plan by differentiating the concepts "commemorative history" and "public history." Edward T. Linenthal, a professor of religion and American culture who served on the advisory committee for the original exhibit planning, promoted such a distinction in his efforts to counter the politicians' and veterans' interventions.[6]

In his testimony of 18 May 1995 at one of the public hearings that were convened before the U.S. Senate Committee on Rules and Administration to investigate the controversy over the Smithsonian's exhibition plans, Linenthal argued, "There is tension between the commemorative voice and the historical voice, which seeks to discern motives, understand actions, and discuss consequences that were impossible to analyze during the event itself. . . . It is a voice that to some can feel detached, even when those who speak out of this voice view their work as a way to deepen our understanding of an event."[7] When the newly appointed Smithsonian secretary I. Michael Heyman announced to the press the cancellation of the display of the ground-level effects of the bombs and the radical scaling down of the exhibit as a whole, he too signaled that the controversy originated in "a basic error in attempting to couple a *historical treatment* of the use of atomic weapons with the 50th anniversary *commemoration* of the end of the war" (my emphasis).[8] The Smithsonian staff's defenders, though of course in various ways, argued that the controversy stemmed from the clash between the academic attempt to produce a comprehensive and objective public history and the desire of those who witnessed the event to celebrate their—and, by imaginary extension, the nation's—honorable past.

Such characterizations, however, provoked vehement rebuttals from many veterans and conservative journalists and historians. Earlier, Martin Harwit, the director of the NASM who was eventually forced to resign as a result of the controversy, had portrayed the dispute as a conflict between a historical view that "appeals to our national self-image" and another historical perspective that is "more analytical, critical in its acceptance of facts and concerned with historical context."[9] A *Washington Post* editorial titled "Context and the *Enola Gay*" (14 August 1994) reacted sharply to this depiction of the debate. The editorial criticized Harwit in no uncertain terms, charging that although he and others were quick to dismiss their critics' take on the *Enola Gay* exhibit as one that lacked "intellectual sophistication," the problem in fact lay in the "curatorial inability to perceive that political opinions are embedded in the exhibit or to identify them as such—opinions—rather than as universal, 'objective' assumptions all thinking people must necessarily share." The editorial also attributed the source of the problem to what the editors perceived as a growing postmodern relativism in the academy, an issue to which I will return. To counter the charges that they were simply being subjective and not academic, those who attacked the NASM curators tried to demonstrate the objective and analytical nature of their criticisms by listing the publications they relied on to construct their arguments.[10]

With respect to this endless exchange of facts, during the 18 May 1995 Senate committee hearing, Linenthal expressed the distress and frustration shared by many of the museum's staff. He pointed out that despite the immediate and substantial changes made to the exhibit plans in response to the criticisms of veterans and the historian of the Office of the Secretary of Defense (who at one point reportedly approved of the revised comprehensive version of the prepared text), the media's and the Air Force Association's attacks continued to intensify. At the same time, the museum staff was forced to negotiate with those who criticized the omission of photographs of the human devastation caused by nuclear weapons. Linenthal summarized the process as follows:

> As script after script deleted material about historical controversies regarding the decision to drop the bomb, added photographs of mushroom clouds and structural damage, and removed most photographs of dead Japanese, historians and peace activists met with museum officials to argue for what they believe should be restored or newly incorporated. The scripts were a kind of Rorschach test. People were concerned with different questions, paid attention to different "facts," and interpreted the same facts differently. In the end, everyone believed their history had been "stolen," resulting either in a "revisionist" exhibit or in one showing a disregard for the complexity and irony of history.[11]

Linenthal's observation that the two opposing camps were talking past each other and that both sides grounded their legitimacy on a selective use of historical facts and events unwittingly puts into relief a number of issues inherent in the politics of knowledge in general. Most important, his remark suggests that there are limits to a mode of argument that relies solely on positive factual accounts as a means of accessing the power to be represented in a public sphere. Accordingly, this problematizes the idea that habitually presupposes— as in Secretary Heyman's inaugural remark "Let the object speak for itself"[12]— that positive historical knowledge can automatically render a shared and unified history.

It is not my intention to undermine the work of professional historians who strive to identify through positivist methods multiple sets of competing, contingent, and often indeterminate factors that have worked to produce a single historical event such as President Truman's executive order to use the two atomic bombs. Throughout the entire course of rewriting the master historical narrative concerning the use of the atomic bombs, it has become increasingly evident that one cannot overemphasize the critical significance of uncovering and examining documents and records or the instrumental power that resides in the presentation of "facts." The findings of the so-called revisionist historians have played a pivotal role in putting the naturalized image of the past into critical perspective, however gradually.[13] In relativizing the ruling historical narrative by calling attention to particular "facts," historians have certainly disturbed our common sense, offering vital moments of suspicion about received knowledge. Moreover, as historian Barton Bernstein has emphasized, the very awareness of the fact that knowledge has been deliberately suppressed or withheld from the public further generates a critical consciousness of the government's censorship and the general ways in which the world is made known to us.[14]

What needs to be interrogated is not so much the historians' administering of facts as such, but rather the simplistic distinction between "history" and "memory," or "public history" and "commemorative desire." These binaries frequently figured in the discourses of both those who defended and those who attempted to sabotage the exhibit. Despite their instrumental value for rhetorical purposes, such oppositions cannot be posited a priori. History, like commemorative rituals, can always be mediated by the desire to speak in voices of and for the dead, to honor victims and martyrs, and to memorialize past events.

Furthermore, the clear distinction between a "commemorative exhibit" that is created out of empathy and the subjective judgment of those who hold shared communal ties to the remembered event, and a "public history" fashioned out of the analytical and detached examination of a historical incident assumes the possibility of attaining a transcendent and universal position from which a subject can observe the past. Such an understanding may also lead to the categorical dismissal of testimonial voices as personal, conjectural, and mystified, subordinating them too hastily to the knowledge produced by institutionalized expertise. The consequence of such a dismissal leads to a situation Dominick LaCapra observed in the German *Historikerstriet* over European memory and the history of Nazism. In his commentary on historians' texts on everyday life under the Nazi regime, LaCapra argues that the "overly simple oppositions between history and 'mythical memory' or between dry reconstruction of facts and ritualization" not only may serve as a psychological defense mechanism that disavows traumatic experiences but also may encourage the repressed to return, as a supplement, in a reified, uncritically valorized state. He proposes instead that we recognize, in addition to the scientific inquiry of historical accuracy, significance in identifying the ritualized aspects of psychological transference that shape any historical representation. For the ways in which the subject positions of scholars/rememberers are cathected to the objects of their inquiry/remembering determine the degree to which the processeses of working through (*Durcharbeitung*) historical trauma can be attained or evaded.[15]

To draw an analogy in the Smithsonian debates, attempts to avert attacks by claiming that the opponents of the original plan were infatuated with their personal memories and that they lacked the intellectual authenticity of scientific history inadvertently prompted the return of what was repressed in such a counterfeit distinction between history and memory, reifying the originality and genuineness of the experiential truths advocated by many who witnessed the war. To be sure, in a given situation of amnesic hegemony, a singular witness account, as a reconstructed memory of a firsthand experience, can restore a heretofore suppressed past, although not in its originary form. It can thus initiate the demystification of officialized historical knowledge. There are countless examples of such workings in various kinds of subaltern historiography.

The Smithsonian debate was not really about facts, nor was it about which side represented the facts more accurately. Rather, it centered around questions about for whom, for what objectives, and for whose community the event needed to be remembered. The difference between the two camps did not reside in whether one side distorted the facts more than the other, although there were indeed a number of instances in which conservative politicians and veterans deliberately refused to acknowledge the existence of certain information and records, thus precluding a more comprehensive view of the event. On the one hand, many veterans, members of the Air Force Association, conservative politicians, and intellectuals desired to commemorate the important mission that led America to victory. They strove to memorialize the martyrs of their sacred war and to remember the atomic bombings through the mediation of the cold war paradigm, which justified the use of military power to achieve and maintain the doctrine of Pax Americana. On the other hand, those who planned the canceled exhibit aspired to remember the millions of victims of the war, including those who were killed before and by *Enola Gay*'s mission, those who have continued to suffer from radiation effects, and those who might in the future become victimized by yet another nuclear catastrophe.

It is imperative for us to reconsider in this particular light the significance of Harwit's choice of words when he described the curators' perspective as being "more analytical, critical in its acceptance of facts." The originally planned exhibit narrative was conditioned by a specifically "critical" perspective on our naturalized view of history, while it also warned of the present global condition in which we find ourselves thoroughly contaminated by nuclear weaponry. The prepared text was comprehensive and analytical, and thus objective at the level of cognitive knowledge, in its explication, for instance, of the processes that led to the decision to use the bombs. It was, however, no less perspectival than the opponents' narrative in that aesthetic and moral factors came into play in the construction of knowledge.[16]

In sum, the *Enola Gay* debate exhibited the predicament within the liberal understanding of the public sphere and its history, an understanding that uncritically presumes the possibility for plural yet harmonious commemoration.[17] It reminds us that, contrary to the ideal of a national public sphere that operates as an open forum in which plural voices freely enter into dialogues and negotiate with each other, certain voices that insist on representation are in reality capable of drawing disproportionate authority and power from the structural positions they occupy within existing social, economic, and political arrangements, and not only from experiential truths or factual authenticity. Likewise, we need to attend perhaps even more urgently to the controversy's unintended consequences. What is represented in a nation's public sphere in such places as the Smithsonian is rendered less susceptible to questioning as to whether it, too, might be partial. It becomes difficult to see that what is deemed to be the commonly shared historical truth is as factional and relatively constructed as what has not been represented in the public space. Given the reality in which their representation of history was in the end disallowed at the museum, there is a risk in even acknowledging that Harwit's and the other curators' position was grounded in critical perspectives.

This was especially true when conservative politicians and veterans repeatedly criticized the "presentism" and "historical relativism" of the prepared text. They argued that one cannot apply the Vietnam War generation's 1990s sensitivity to reconstruct the history of the 1940s.[18] Similarly, in a testimony that I discuss below in more detail, retired U.S. Air Force Major General Charles W. Sweeney, a member of the *Enola Gay*'s crew and the commander of the Nagasaki mission, alleged that the revisionists' intrusion into even this very patriotic site was caused by "the advancing erosion of our history, of our collective memory."[19] What is remarkable in this statement is that while it betrays the intimate association between a nation's history and the memory possessed by a specific collectivity, at the same time it authorizes the historicist position by grounding the speaker's perspective on experiential truths, thereby castigating the "presentist" view of history as an inauthentic construction. In their study on the production and consumption of colonial Williamsburg, Eric Gable, Richard Handler, and Anna Lawson succinctly summarize the danger I am describing here: "A relativizing rhetoric—in this case, an explicit recognition of historical 'presentism'—seems easier to apply to the cultures and histories of minorities than to those of the mainstream."[20]

Incidentally, there is yet another problematic aspect of Sweeney's evoking the term "memory" while simultaneously insinuating the subordination of his personal experience as a soldier and a witness to a formal and publicized "history." His statement reflects the perception that the position occupied by many veterans and political conservatives such as he is, as it were, being minoritized within present U.S. society, when in fact it was the veterans and conservatives and not the museum curators or revisionist historians who succeed in mobilizing the massive support of legislators.

The Smithsonian controversy thus eloquently demonstrates that one cannot effectively seek proper representation in a national public sphere solely by claiming to possess universal knowledge that is grounded on factual authenticity. To subscribe to the distinction between factual history and imaginary commemoration—an opposition enabled by simple trust in the power of facticity—is problematic precisely because it can prove debilitating when trying to prevail over those who adhere to diametrically opposed understandings of history. Moreover, as observed in the Smithsonian dispute, to rationalize the demand for representation in the public sphere by grounding one's legitimacy on factual authenticity alone may unwittingly help perpetuate the myth that the subaltern history is more partial, conjectural, and constructed than mainstream history. The recovery and accumulation of knowledge about the past—what Walter Benjamin called the "additive" method of universal history—do not themselves automatically produce new knowledge and perceptions. What matters is not how much we know about the past but rather through what structural access, and under what personal, social, and historical conditions, we come to an awareness of it.

There is still another important difference between the discursive strategies pursued by those who supported the prepared exhibit script and by those who disparaged it. In the following, I discuss the negotiations between, on the one hand, the desire to defend the imaginary border of one nation's memory and its boundary of empathy and, on the other hand, the endeavors to challenge the naturalized narratives of the past that were premised on the shared collectivity of remembering subjects and of the remembered.

Transnational Warps and Nationalist Memories

The dissension centering on historical understandings about whether it was necessary and justifiable for the United States to use atom bombs against two Japanese cities has often been conflated, in both Japanese- and English-language contexts, with the national distinction between Japan and the United States. It is even typical for an individual researcher's opinion to be understood as emblematically representing an entire nation's viewpoint, or indicating what is often referred to as the "U.S.-Japan gap."[21] The tendency to regard disparities in perceptions of the destruction at Hiroshima and Nagasaki as corresponding isomorphically to national differences has governed the popular discourse on the Smithsonian controversy as well. For the offended veterans and others in the United States, to hold compassionate sentiments toward the ground-level suffering caused by the Enola Gay's mission was often regarded as a position influenced by the "Japanese" viewpoint. Likewise, in the Japanese-language news reports, as the expression "[the differing] atom-bomb perceptions between the Japanese and American nations" (nichibei ryōkokukan no genbakukan) illustrates,[22] the clash of opinions in the Smithsonian controversy continued to be represented and understood within national frameworks.

Yet it is also true that the reporting of the Smithsonian debates simultaneously revealed that the national boundaries of collective memories have constantly been infiltrated.[23] Evidence of such transnational penetration and the national censoring of memory processes can be found in the language and activities of both those who supported the initial Smithsonian plans and those who opposed them. Several NASM staff members visited Hiroshima and Nagasaki at an early planning stage. By borrowing artifacts from the two cities, the curators sought to add a ground-level perspective to the pilot's-eye view of the atomic explosions. Such aerial images had thus far dominated national imaginings. The curators also hoped to complicate that historical moment so as to remember it not solely as the war's last act but simultaneously as the inaugural event in the subsequent nuclear age. However, for conservative politicians, journalists, intellectuals, veterans, and others who opposed the display of photographs depicting what they saw as "Japanese" victimization, the Smithsonian curators' contact with the former enemy was nothing less than a treacherous, "un-American" move. Herman G. Harrington, chairman of the American Legion's National Internal Affairs Commission, for instance, angrily denounced what he saw as the museum curators' willingness to "conform to the Japanese perspective" when they attempted to borrow artifacts from Hiroshima and Nagasaki.[24]

At the same time, while some tried to limit the Smithsonian debate to the U.S. national context,[25] those who opposed the exhibit frequently cited Japan to construct their argument. They attempted to justify their demands to eliminate artifacts and photographs that showed the effects of the atom bombs on humans by calling attention to present Japanese amnesia about the nation's past conduct, both before and during the war. They warned that unless one elaborated the "historical contexts" leading to the bombs' use, displays of the Hiroshima and Nagasaki destructions would only contribute to the historical understanding they saw as still prevalent in Japan, namely, that the Japanese were solely victims of the war and not the perpetrators of war atrocities and colonial aggression.

Major General Sweeney's testimony before the U.S. Senate Committee on Rules and Administration illustrates the case well. In identifying what he felt were problems with the prepared text by referring to the situation in Japan, Sweeney argued that knowing the "facts" and understanding the historical context allowed one to appreciate the necessity of President Truman's decision to drop the bombs. He recounted Japan's invasion of China and mainland Asia for the purpose of building the Greater East Asia Co-Prosperity Sphere and the numerous instances of plundering, torture, and massacres that took place throughout the area, beginning with Nanjing. He further noted the "sneak" attack on Pearl Harbor, together with the loss of American servicemen in Saipan, Iwo Jima, and Okinawa. Furthermore, he emphasized that Japan had not surrendered despite the commencement of air raids on Japan's major cities.

Continuing in his testimony, Sweeney asked why conflicts occurred concerning the bombs' necessity despite the unanimous view that the atomic bomb strategy had ended the war. He answered this question in the following way:

> Fifty years after their defeat, Japanese officials have the temerity to claim they were the victims. That Hiroshima and Nagasaki were the equivalent of the Holocaust.
>
> And believe it or not, there are actually some American academics who support this analogy, thus aiding and giving comfort to a 50-year attempt by the Japanese to rewrite their own history, and ours in the process.
>
> There is an entire generation of Japanese who do not know the full extent of their country's conduct during World war [sic] II.
>
> This explains why they do not comprehend why they must apologize.

He then cited such matters as the so-called comfort women issue and the medical experiments on Allied POWs as reasons for the Japanese refusal to apologize properly. He concluded, "In a perverse inversion, by forgetting our own history, we contribute to the Japanese amnesia, to the detriment of both our nations."[26] Sweeney thus tried to link American appreciation of the historical context for the atomic bombings to the lack of Japanese reflection on the past.

In this transnational citation of Japan's historical amnesia, Sweeney argued that remembering only Japanese victimization in Hiroshima and Nagasaki occludes the fact that the war's lasting almost fifteen years and Japan's colonial expansion that began at the turn of the century were acts of aggression. This statement is remarkable in that its reasoning employs the same arguments that many critics in Japan have routinely used in their efforts to contend with the cluster of deeply rooted issues that have contributed to Japan's historical amnesia. These include the Ministry of Education's textbook approval system, which had until recently censored overt criticisms of Japan's military aggression and colonial policies; the repeated refusal of politicians to fully acknowledge the magnitude of the destruction caused by Japan; and the insufficiency of the government's undertakings in dealing with its postwar and postcolonial responsibilities. In other words, there has been reflection among progressive citizens of Japan, including survivors in Hiroshima and Nagasaki, who recognize that remembering a historical event only in terms of unprecedented self-victimization may serve to mystify other national conditions in the past and present. The Japanese citizen's counteramnesic practices have been underpinned by the conviction that to secure the memories of Japan's prewar and wartime imperialism and military aggression in school textbooks and other public apparatuses that produce national history is inseparably linked to the pursuit of peace, human rights, and other democratic ideals of a civil society. Moreover, many construe the act of remembering Japan's military and colonial pasts as leading also to critically reflecting on Japan's postwar neocolonial economic dominance in the region.[27]

In the Japanese political and social context, those who have long questioned their country's insufficiency of remorse for its invasions and the suffering it inflicted on the people of Asia and the Pacific have until very recently identified primarily with the left or with progressives. They have also been challenging the historical view that for the past fifty years has supported the claims of members of the Japanese Association for the War Bereaved and conservative political leaders and intellectuals that colonial aggression and military expansion were justifiable. According to that understanding of history, establishing the Greater East Asia Co-Prosperity Sphere and waging the Greater East Asian War were acts of self-defense against and emancipation from the encroaching Western superpowers, and they did not have the invasion of neighboring Asian countries as their original objective. It is as if U.S. conservative interest groups, politicians, and intellectuals who attacked the Smithsonian staff took up the claims of progressives in Japan, "warping" the discourse to meet different political ends. The contradiction I am trying to identify here can be summarized as follows: As a result of its transference into a different national public sphere, the discourse has come to be used in support of a political position that was originally unintended or irrelevant. In other words, there appears to have been a binational warping of political positions.

This warping, moreover, has a number of troubling effects. Above all, transferring a critical political position from one context to another for the purpose of justifying views guided by nationalist interests makes invisible various ongoing practices that try to critically intervene and challenge the present transnational and statist global ordering. (I will return to this point in conclusion.) At the same time, such warps obscure the fact that the questions of historical amnesia are not some other country's problem but very much our own and that they need to be addressed as questions common to many modern nation-states and the formation of capitalism.

Indeed, despite its antipodal appearance, the selective amnesia that Sweeney identified in Japan in many respects parallels that found in the United States. This is evident in some of the presumptions concerning the U.S. role in Asia and the Pacific that are constitutive not only of Sweeney's own testimony but also of many other arguments deployed to attack the planned exhibit. For instance, although it interrogated Japan's colonial invasions, Sweeney's narrative totally omitted any mention of the United States' imperial expansion into the Asia Pacific region, its capitalist incentive for securing markets in China, and other related issues. It condemned the Japanese military's attack on Pearl Harbor but ignored the questions of how in the first place Hawai'i had come to be a U.S. territory and why a U.S. naval base existed there. Those who opposed displays of atomic bomb victims tended to share an arbitrary and selective amnesia about their own country's history of colonial and military aggression.

Moreover, Sweeney's testimony summarizes the widely shared conviction that because we must properly tutor the Japanese to have a correct view of history, we as Americans ought to possess unadulterated historical knowledge. Sweeney's lengthy testimony further included a perspective on postbomb history that maintained that it was precisely because his country used the atomic weapons when it did that the Japanese people were enabled to receive various benefits in the postwar years. He alluded, for instance, to the view that the atomic bombings saved Japanese lives and rescued the Japanese people from the control of military fanatics; that they deterred a Soviet occupation and prevented Japan from becoming communist or experiencing territorial division; and that they created the conditions for Japan's subsequent democratic reforms and incredibly swift economic recovery. Furthermore, according to Sweeney's view of history, his own country's nuclear armament and military policy provided postwar Japan with a shield against the Soviet and Chinese threats while facilitating Japan's economic development. In short, such presumptions call on the Japanese to be grateful for the United States' "benevolent" and timely use of the atom bombs.[28]

It may also be worth noting that the paternalistic presumptions and understandings of history that inform Sweeney's and others' arguments are strikingly similar to those of Japanese conservatives who continue to insist that Japanese colonialism, despite—as they never fail to add—the "unfortunate" and regrettable outcome, contributed to the modernization and postwar economic development of Asian countries that had formerly been under Western colonial rule. Although it cannot be described fully in this limited space, there are also parallels in that Sweeney and the others, like their Japanese counterparts, characterize their compatriots unidimensionally as victims, thereby obscuring the history of U.S. imperialism and other acts of aggression against various parts of Asia and the Pacific.

The attacks on the NASM staff continued despite the fact that the curators, from a very early stage in the negotiations, agreed to incorporate what were often called the absent "historical contexts" into their exhibit narratives. The angry attacks by members of the American Legion, the Air Force Association, Congress, and a number of journalists and intellectuals concerning what they saw as the NASM curators' "un-American" and insulting attitude toward the glorious accomplishments of former political leaders and soldiers did not subside until all the displays of Japanese casualties were removed and Director Harwit was forced to resign. According to the 14 August 1994 *Washington Post* editorial cited earlier, the museum's critics charged that the planned exhibit would "build sympathy for the Japanese" by portraying the *Enola Gay* mission as causing "death, radiation sickness, despair and the beginning of nuclear terror."[29] Tom Crouch, the chairman of the NASM Aeronautics Department, who was central in designing the prepared exhibit, astutely observed that what continued to upset the critics was not so much how the story about the ground-level destruction was presented as the fact that the "whole story" was told.[30]

Let us briefly observe what happened at the other end of the binational warping. In the first draft of the plan for the Smithsonian exhibit, one phrase indicated that the United States fought the war in the Pacific in a way that was fundamentally different from the way it waged war against Germany and Italy. The draft stated that Americans had fought the war against the Japanese as a "war of vengeance. For most Japanese, it was a war to defend their unique culture against Western imperialism."[31] This phrase appeared in the script as an ironic summary of Japanese officials' gross justification for atrocities committed during the war, including the civilian massacre in Nanjing, the abuse against POWs, and the biological experiments on living human beings.[32] Again, curators revised the phrase at a very early stage of the negotiations. Yet critics continued to cite it out of context and to condemn the museum staff for suggesting that the United States was the victimizer and Japan the victim.

Historian Martin Sherwin was one of those who called for the need to contextualize this phrase, particularly for a Japanese-speaking audience.[33] Sherwin's intervention was an especially important one, for even while placing

Japanese aggression within the broader historical context of the Western impe-rialist expansion into Asia and other parts of the world that preceded it, he also prevented this historicization from being appropriated by ultranationalists and conservatives in Japan, who continue to justify Japanese military and colonial aggression as acts of "self-defense." In other words, Sherwin's cautionary remarks to a Japanese audience sought to deter yet another warping of critical discourses by obstructing the dovetailing of the U.S. revisionist historians' progressive position with that of the Japanese conservatives.

The binational warping of political positions, in short, is an effect that results from the ways in which national framings of historical narratives deflect our analyses away from phenomena such as capitalist economic expansion, na-tionalism, and military domination that exist in common across national bor-ders. The narrating of history premised on the self-contained unit of the nation-state is also a condition that allows the victimization of one segment of a society to stand for the victimization of the entire national collectivity. Furthermore, insofar as such national assumptions remain unquestioned, it will not be possi-ble to recognize that during most of the twentieth century, the conservative elite in the United States (which has sought, for instance, to obstruct "nonpatriotic" activities) and the conservative forces in Japan (which continue to suppress critical activities, including opposition to the emperor system) are in many respects complicit with each other in their capitalist and nationalist desires.

Conclusion

The 19 February 1995 issue of the *San Diego Union Tribune* devoted an entire page to introducing opposing perspectives on the *Enola Gay* controversy. An expan-sive black-and-white aerial photograph of Hiroshima, taken approximately one month after the bombing, occupies most of the page. The details of the city are vague. Two rivers run dark, one at the bottom, another at the center of the photo, while broad white avenues extend toward the hazy hills in the distance. Except for the sparse remains of a few European-style buildings, the entire city appears to have been burned down and is in ashes. Here again, as in the Smithsonian exhibit, the damage suffered by civilians is obscured. Yet, precisely because one cannot see the Asian faces or alien street scenes, the newspaper photograph serves to detemporalize and dislocate the image of the ruined city from any specific historical moment and place. In other words, it could be argued that the photograph suggests the stark reality of nuclear proliferation in this world, when such devastation can occur anywhere and anytime beyond Hiroshima 1945.

Yet how many people actually followed the concrete details of the controversy in the newspapers and other media? Most likely, museum visitors were not fully exposed to all of the debates surrounding the exhibits they saw. They may have been indifferent to the discussions about the decision making that led to the use of the two atomic bombs, or to the disputes about whether the museum's curatorial freedom was violated by legislative intervention. Nor can we assume that those who visited the NASM to view the commemorative exhibit were concerned about nuclear issues in general. As one woman remarked in a CNN interview, what was perhaps most attractive and thrilling about visiting the exhibit was the possibility of access to a genuine historical artifact, that is, the ability to come close to the aura of factual authenticity. This is precisely why it is highly regrettable that no objects from the ground level—such as a mutilated lunch box, a photo of a disfigured horse, a melted iron bar, a bloodstained school uniform, or a specimen of a deformed fetus—were displayed. Perhaps even more than the exhibit's proponents, those who opposed the plans for displays on Hiroshima and Nagasaki were fully aware of the unsettling meanings that such artifacts could generate in viewers' minds.

In closing, it should be emphasized that the museum curators' attempt to create an exhibit that would encourage a rethinking of the nation's dominant understanding of Hiroshima and Nagasaki, as well as of other nuclear-related issues, was inextricably linked to the ways that developments in the social and human sciences had led to the interrogation of various accepted ideas and categories. The attack against the curators' attitude—which Harwit had called "more analytical, critical in its acceptance of facts"—must be understood in relation to various reactions against the increasing ambiguity of the post–cold war milieu and the accompanying broader reorganization of knowledge.

When war veterans and others, including Sweeney, vehemently criticized the curators, they were particularly disturbed by the script's suggestion that there were elements of U.S. aggression and imperialism even in what had been considered the most just and sacred of American wars. In the Senate testimony described above, Sweeney lashed out at his foes, saying that to remember the Japanese not just as villains but also as victims of the U.S. atom bombings was an "assault on our language and history by the elimination of accurate and descriptive words." It was, he said, equivalent to saying "Up is Down, Slavery is Freedom, Aggression is Peace." In contrast, fifty years ago, "the threat was clear, the enemy well defined."[34]

This disillusionment demonstrates that the conservatives' intervention in the Smithsonian's exhibit plans was not unrelated to the recent barrage of attacks against certain critical scholarship in the social and human sciences. This critical scholarship—which has included Marxism and critical theories, feminist theories, postcolonial and ethnic studies, queer theories, and cultural studies, to name a few—has played a crucial role in the rethinking and complicating of reified concepts, routinized and institutionalized processes, the taken-for-granted, and essentialized categories. Critical scholarship has endeavored to question the transparency of accepted meanings. It asks, to take the concrete example of Sweeney, whether what we have assumed to be the progress of civilization (read "up") might instead connote a regression toward barbarism (read "down"), as critical theorists would argue; whether what has been uncritically acclaimed as increasing freedom from the old regime might in fact entail our enslavement to an oppressive society of self-surveillance and control (read "slavery is freedom"), as Michel Foucault would have it; or whether what has been unproblematically promoted as the means to achieve peace might be inseparable from tools of aggression (read "aggression is peace"), as the Smithsonian curators tried to show.

Newt Gingrich, in his gross debasement of the popular, announced "victory" in the Smithsonian controversy by arguing that "the Enola Gay fight was a fight, in effect, over the reassertion by most Americans that they're sick and tired of being told by some cultural elite that they ought to be ashamed of their history."[35] Yet this statement should not be taken literally as a simple celebration of the victory of patriotism. Rather, it may best be understood as an exulting over the successful defense of the stability of the language with which the nation's history is written against the infiltration of critical and reflexive knowledge. Perhaps this also explains why the conservative elites concluded that the controversy had ended in a victory over "political correctness."[36] In other words, the Smithsonian debate ended in the defeat of those who sought critical rethinking, as well as the defeat of those who questioned the self-evident, the natural, and the inevitable, and the victory of those who felt threatened by obfuscation of the contours of conventional knowledge. In this sense, the controversy centering on the Smithsonian ought to be understood as but one symptom of larger battles that are raging within the social and human sciences.

In closing, I would like to suggest an alternative to such conventional attitudes toward history and knowledge and to the warping of political positions. In the Name of the Emperor, a documentary on the Nanjing Massacre made by two Asian American directors, Christine Choy and Nancy Tong, offers us an important example of how historical memories can be made urgently relevant to the questioning of current global situations and may even render new alliances of critical discourses across nationality, ethnicity, class, and generation.

The documentary is composed primarily of historical film footage of and interviews concerning the Japanese Army's atrocities in Nanjing. The film manages both to reconstruct conditions at that historical moment and to interrogate the processes through which forgetfulness about the Nanjing Massacre has been produced in Japan. It questions, in particular, the fact that the film footage it contains was not used as evidence in the Tokyo War Crimes Trial and that this footage had been buried and deliberately forgotten for so long. It shows that the trial was inadequate because it failed to consider the emperor's war responsibility even though it had been the United States' and Japan's insistence on resolving the matter of the emperor system that had prolonged the war and resulted in the unnecessary and catastrophic loss of lives. Moreover, the film suggests that the trial was premised on a Eurocentric historical worldview and that it interrogated only Japan's crimes against the former Western colonial powers rather than the violence committed against the common people of Asia and the Pacific. In addition, the documentary touched on the recent apology demands of women formerly enslaved sexually by Japanese military. It furthermore implicates the United States by showing that its cold war policy led to the long-term postwar suppression of movements within Asian countries that had tried to expose the facts about war damages and colonial rule, including such movements in immediate postwar Japan.

While making each country and government absolutely accountable for its conduct, the directors at the same time refuse to represent the nation as a noncontradictory and undivided subject with containable boundaries. Concerning the crimes committed by the Japanese military on the Asian and Pacific peoples, the documentary relentlessly reminds its viewers that the conservative critics of Japan and the United States were in fact accomplices in promoting forgetfulness. By criticizing the transnational complicity between conservative and anticommunist elements in Japan and the United States, it produces a historical narrative that refuses to allow critical discourses to be subsumed by a single national position. Even as the documentary makes it absolutely clear that the Japanese Army committed atrocities against those identified as Chinese, it deploys one person's testimony to emphasize that the experiencing of the atrocities was at the same time inflected by class differences, for the wealthy had greater resources with which to escape the city. It thereby prevents the memories of the Nanjing Massacre from being subsumed under an imagined and singular national collectivity. While condemning the Japanese government's decades-long underemphasis of the massacre, the two directors do not fail to describe activism by which Japanese progressive historians have interrogated for many years the statist occlusion of Japan's wartime atrocities. The documentary also points out that concerning the issue of historical memory there has been a long accumulation of activism that involves feminists, labor activists, and other progressive critics in Korea, Japan, and Asian American communities. In this way, and contrary to the narratives exemplified by Sweeney's testimony, Choy and Tong succeed in illuminating what the discursive warping I described above has made invisible—namely, the transnational alliances that are not compatible with the U.S. or other nationalist and corporate concerns.

The representation of history in Choy and Tong's documentary may be understood as an effective example of a postnationalist historiography, or what historian Miriam Silverberg has termed an "associative history" in her call for an examination of racial politics in prewar and wartime Japan.[37] To be sure, insofar as a nation-state exists as an institutional entity and its apparatuses of knowledge continue to produce their own distinct historical knowledge, its temporal and spatial specificities must be taken into account. Yet, it is also important not to confuse historically produced institutional distinctiveness with the ideological effects of corporate and other forms of nationalism. With regard to the histories of Hiroshima and Nagasaki, how one understands the two atom bombings is a question that concerns not only those who reside in Japan and the United States. Rather, it is a question that inevitably involves several tens of thousands of atom bomb victims who reside in North and South Korea; millions of people throughout Asia and the Pacific region who were victimized and affected by Japan's war of aggression, as well as by European, Japanese, U.S., and Chinese imperialist expansion, both before and after the war; and those who became diasporas as a result of colonial and military histories of violence, who now reside as the racially minoritized in Japan, the United States, and other parts of the world.

Perhaps one of the most valuable outcomes of the Smithsonian debates was that they generated a sense of urgency for the necessity of fashioning postnationalist public spheres in which diverse historical understandings can overlap in multiple ways and be shared coalitionally. The crafting of such spaces will at the same time help us establish a position from which it is possible to discern those crucial elements that have been excluded in the process of constituting a nation-state's dominant way of collective remembering. To secure a position critical of the paradigm that has long confined our memory work to the boundaries of nationality and nationhood will also keep us from reverting to patriotic appeals when trying to legitimate our arguments, as some historians involved in the Smithsonian debates inadvertently did in countering the accusation that their activities were "un-American."[38] Finally, such a coalescing of denationalized, discrepant historical memories will in turn broaden the scope of our historical inquiries and the questions we ask of our pasts and future.

Notes

This essay was originally prepared for the conference "The Politics of Remembering the Asia-Pacific War" at the East-West Center, Honolulu, 7–9 September 1995. An earlier, abridged version of the essay was published in Japanese as "Ekkyo suru sensō no kioku: Sumisonian genbakuten ronsō o yomu," *Sekai*, no. 614 (October 1995): 173–83. A slightly different version appeared earlier in English as "Critical Warps: Facticity, Transformative Knowledge, and Postnationalist Criticism in the Smithsonian *Enola Gay* Controversy," *positions* 5, no. 3 (winter 1997): 5–29. The research was supported by an Academic Senate Research Grant from the University of California, San Diego.

Over the past years, I have had a number of occasions to present versions of this essay at different conferences and symposia. I wish to thank the many people who gave me useful feedback on these occasions. The essay especially benefited from comments by the following individuals: Chungmoo Choi, Tak Fujitani, Yoshiye Funahashi, Richard Handler, Yeong-hae Jung, Takeshiro Kurisu, Masao Miyoshi, Minoru Ōmuta, Michael Schudson, Takumi Usui, and Geoffrey White. I thank Eric Cazdyn, who worked as my research assistant, and Shun'ichi Matsubayashi, Kenji Ōhara, and Keisaburō Toyonaga for their generous efforts in collecting valuable and often difficult to acquire materials, including local newspaper, magazine, and journal articles, transcripts from TV news programs and interviews, and the first and final versions of the canceled Smithsonian script. I am especially thankful to Geoffrey White for sharing records of Senate committee hearings as well as other transcripts obtained through the Internet.

1   Geoffrey White has observed that the Smithsonian controversy was rooted in the inability to negotiate national and extranational ways of remembering what was in essence an international event: the war. He writes, "The particular difficulties for this exhibit in navigating between opposed calls for critical history and patriotic history stem from the fact that it was dealing with an intensely international subject in an intensely national site." See White, "Memory Wars: The Politics of Remembering the Asia/Pacific War," *AsiaPacific Issues*, no. 21 (July 1995): 1–8. White's earlier analysis of Guadalcanal's fiftieth-anniversary commemorative events alerted me to the transnational aspect of memory-making processes; see "Remembering Guadalcanal: National Identity and Transnational Memory-Making," *Public Culture* 7 (spring 1995): 529–55.

2   See Mike Wallace, "The Battle of the *Enola Gay*," *Radical Historian Newsletter*, no. 72 (May 1995): 1–12, 22–32, for a succinct overview of the entire controversy and the quote from Rush Limbaugh.

3   Two important collaborative projects were produced in response to the legislators' censoring of national history. See "Remembering the Bomb: The Fiftieth Anniversary in the United States and Japan," special issue of *Bulletin of Concerned Asian Scholars* 27, no. 2 (April–June 1995), and the articles collected in "Hiroshima in History and Memory: A Symposium," special issue of *Diplomatic History* 19, no. 2 (spring 1995). For readers of Japanese, historian Daizaburō Yui has succinctly summarized the entire course of events and the problems with the dominant historical understanding in the United States about the use of atom bombs. Yui's book also examines the U.S.-Japan gap in perceptions of the Pacific War, the Korean War, and the Vietnam War. See Daizaburō Yui, *Nichibei sensōkan no sōkoku: Masatsu no shinsō shinri* (Antagonisms in U.S.-Japan views on war: Deep psychology of conflicts) (Tokyo: Iwanami Shoten, 1995).

4   See John B. Thompson, *Studies in the Theory of Ideology* (Berkeley: University of California Press, 1984), 1.

5   Kai Bird, "A Humiliating Smithsonian Retreat from the Facts of Hiroshima," *International Herald Tribune*, 12 October 1994.

6 See Michael King, "Revisiting the *Enola Gay*," *Post-Crescent* (Appleton, WI), 20 November 1994.

7 U.S. Senate Committee on Rules and Administration, *Hearing: The Smithsonian Institution Management Guidelines for the Future*, 104th Cong., 1st sess., 11 and 18 May 1995, 48.

8 Quoted in Eugene L. Meyer and Jacqueline Trescott, "Smithsonian Scuttles Exhibit," *Washington Post*, 31 January 1995.

9 Martin Harwit, "The *Enola Gay*: A Nation's, and a Museum's, Dilemma," *Washington Post*, 7 August 1994.

10 See the statement of Herman G. Harrington in U.S. Senate, *Hearing: The Smithsonian Institution Management Guidelines*, 20–27.

11 U.S. Senate, *Hearing: The Smithsonian Institution Management Guidelines*, 49. The Rorschach test image also appears in Gaddis Smith, "Hiroshima: The Rorschach Test of the American Psyche," *Los Angeles Times*, 30 July 1995.

12 Quoted in "*Enola Gay* Exhibit Remains Unsettled," *San Diego Union Tribune*, 12 March 1995.

13 The most important of the earlier seminal works by revisionist historians include Gar Alperovitz, *Atomic Diplomacy: Hiroshima and Potsdam* (New York: Simon and Schuster, 1965); Martin J. Sherwin, *A World Destroyed: The Atomic Bomb and the Grand Alliance* (New York: Knopf, 1975); and Barton Bernstein, "Atomic Diplomacy and the Cold War," in *The Atomic Bomb: The Critical Issues*, ed. Barton Bernstein (Boston: Little, Brown, 1976), 129–35. The argument that Truman was aware in early July of Japan's likely surrender appeared in Gar Alperovitz, "*Enola Gay*: A New Consensus . . . ," *Washington Post*, 4 February 1995. In his more recent *Decision to Use the Atomic Bomb and the Architecture of an American Myth* (New York: Knopf, 1995). Alperovitz rearticulates the revisionist view and juxtaposes it, in great detail, to the ways the mainstream U.S. understanding about the bomb's use was manufactured. For the official manipulation of the estimated American casualties and deaths, see Barton Bernstein, "Understanding the Atomic Bomb and the Japanese Surrender: Missed Opportunities, Little-Known Near Disasters, and Modern Memory," *Diplomatic History* 19, no. 2 (spring 1995): 227–73. For a summary of the historians' new consensus, see J. Samuel Walker, "History, Collective Memory, and the Decision to Use the Bomb," *Diplomatic History* 19, no. 2 (spring 1995): 319–28.

14 This point was made by Bernstein in his remarks at the conference "Hoping for the Worst: The Planning, Experience, and Consequences of Mass Warfare, 1930–1950," University of California, Berkeley, November 1995.

15 Dominick LaCapra, "Representing the Holocaust: Reflections on the Historians' Debate," in *Probing the Limits of Representation: Nazism and the "Final Solution*," ed. Saul Friedlander (Cambridge, MA: Harvard University Press, 1992), 108–27; see 122 for quote. For an earlier discussion of the difficulties and possibilities in the act of confronting the past, see Theodor W. Adorno, "What Does Coming to Terms with the Past Mean?" in *Bitburg in Moral and Political Perspective*, ed. Geoffrey H. Hartman (Bloomington: Indiana University Press, 1986), 114–29. See also Eric L. Santner, "History beyond the Pleasure Principle: Some Thoughts on the Representation of Trauma," in Friedlander, *Probing the Limits*, 143–54. Santner links LaCapra's discussion on "working through" to his conceptualization of the possibility of redemption through the proper form of "mourning" loss. Santner also points out that the German inability to mourn emerges as what he calls "narrative fetish," which serves as yet another repression of the repressed, in a manner similar to the "acting

out" of historians that LaCapra observes. See also Eric L. Santner, *Stranded Objects: Mourning, Memory, and Film in Postwar Germany* (Ithaca, NY: Cornell University Press, 1990).

16 See Hayden White, "The Value of Narrativity in the Representation of Reality," and "Narrativization of Real Events," in *On Narrative*, ed. W. J. T. Mitchell (Chicago: University of Chicago Press, 1981), 1–23, 249–54. In understanding the hegemonic tendency to misappropriate arguments that take into account the aesthetic and moral dimensions of the construction of knowledge, I find especially insightful Peter Novick's historical accounts of how the question of objectivity has been transfigured, primarily in the U.S. academic sphere since the beginning of the twentieth century. Novick writes that, given post–World War II conditions in which the empiricism/objectivism of social science has been a vital source of ideological and intellectual legitimation in the U.S. academy, it is no surprise that critiques of constructionist arguments are still often articulated as attacks against "anti-American" ideals. See Novick, *That Noble Dream: The "Objectivity Question" and the American Historical Profession* (New York: Cambridge University Press, 1988).

17 Pin-hui Liao urges us to extend our rethinking of the Habermasian utopian presumption of a single, unitary public sphere to historical consciousness and memories. Following the critiques of Nancy Fraser and others, Liao underscores the significance of modifying the liberal public-sphere notion with respect to the postcolonial condition in Taiwan, where multiple layers of modern experiences and historical identities coexist. See Liao, "Rewriting Taiwanese National History: The February 28 Incident As Spectacle," *Public Culture* 5 (winter 1993): 281–96.

18 Among numerous examples of this reasoning, see especially Edwin M. Yoder Jr., ". . . Or Hiroshima Cult?" *Washington Post*, 4 February 1995.

19 U.S. Senate Committee, *Hearing: The Smithsonian Institution Management Guidelines*, 11.

20 Eric Gable, Richard Handler, and Anna Lawson, "On the Uses of Relativism: Fact, Conjecture, and Black and White Histories at Colonial Williamsburg," *American Ethnologist* 19, no. 4 (1992): 792. I am especially thankful to Richard Handler for pushing me to think through the conflation of history and memory in Sweeney's testimony.

21 When a Harvard professor stated at the United Nations Hiroshima Disarmament Conference that he believed the use of the atom bombs helped hasten the war's end and saved both American and Japanese lives—which indeed is the dominant view shared by most people in the United States—*Asahi shinbun* reported the contention his statement elicited with the headline " 'Nuclear Consciousness,' Japan-U.S. Gap" (11 December 1992).

22 *Chugoku shinbun*, 30 September 1994.

23 In the Japanese-language media the controversy has offered opportunities for people in Japan to rethink such a simple nationalized perspective on history. Detailed reports on the controversy's background explained that the criticisms of the sympathetic portrayals of Japanese casualties in the prepared texts were not generated solely by World War II veterans but had been fostered by a series of recent conservative turns in U.S. society, including a patriotic reemphasis in history education, anti-immigrant sentiments exemplified by the passing of Proposition 187 in California, intensifying antiabortion terrorism, and attacks on affirmative action. Practically every major newspaper reported on the intense negotiations between the museum staff and their advisors on the one hand, and representatives of the American Legion, the Air Force Association, and conservative historians and journalists on the other. The newspapers and journals published their own interviews with individuals who protested publicly against Congress's intervention in curatorial research and intellectual engagements. Later in the year, when American Uni-

versity in Washington held a public symposium and opened its own exhibits on Hiroshima and Nagasaki, both the visual and print media very quickly introduced the exhibits' contents, along with accounts of the counterexhibit on the Rape of Nanjing that was organized by protesting Chinese Americans. Unlike conventional arguments over nuclear matters, the fact that the various debates concerning the Smithsonian exhibit were publicized as a "controversy" *within* American society contributed to debunking the popular understanding that the United States upholds a single unified view about Hiroshima, Nagasaki, and related issues. See *Asahi shinbun*, 15 June 1995, for one of the most detailed articles that dealt with the overall social and political environment in the United States.

24 U.S. Senate Committee, *Hearing: The Smithsonian Institution Management Guidelines*, 24.

25 For instance, the spokesperson for the Air Force Association, Jack Giese, described the Smithsonian controversy as "an internal American debate with an American institution that wasn't doing their job." See Nigel Holloway, "Museum Peace: U.S. Curators Seek Truce over the Plane That Atom-Bombed Hiroshima," *Far Eastern Economic Review* (2 February 1995): 32.

26 U.S. Senate Committee, *Hearing: The Smithsonian Institution Management Guidelines*, 11.

27 Elsewhere I have discussed at length the counteramnes(t)ic—namely, unforgetful and unforgiving—practices in postwar Hiroshima, as well as the intimate link present in Japan among the politics of representing the country's war of aggression, memories of colonialism, and the testimonial practices of the atom bomb survivors. See *Hiroshima Traces: Time, Space, and the Dialectics of Memory* (Berkeley: University of California Press, 1999).

28 For a statement that most succinctly reveals the understandings of history and U.S.–East Asia relations described here, see James R. Van de Velde, "*Enola Gay* Saved Lives, Period," *Washington Post*, 10 February 1995. The Smithsonian controversy also demonstrated that some of the cold war perceptions that justified the use of the atomic bombs and the subsequent nuclear buildup are still strongly upheld by many in the United States. See, for example, Thomas Sowell, "The Right to Infiltrate," *Forbes* (13 March 1995): 74. It should be further noted that the view held by Sweeney, Van de Velde, and others need not necessarily be identified as a national (i.e., an American) one, for such a historical awareness is also widely found among citizens of Japan and other Asian nations. The irony, of course, is that such justifications for the bombs' use are premised on an argument that the prepared text's opponents have themselves been refuting. This cold war historical narrative in fact unwittingly appropriates the factual grounds used by so-called revisionist historians to argue that the atomic bombs were unnecessary from a strictly military point of view, that is, the argument that the decision to drop the bombs was necessary not for the purpose of bringing the war to a rapid close but rather for containing the Soviets in the postwar settlement.

29 "Context and the *Enola Gay*," *Washington Post*, 14 August 1994. See also Richard Serrano, "Smithsonian Says It Erred, Scraps Exhibit on A-Bomb," *Los Angeles Times*, 31 January 1995, for William M. Detweiler's comment in which he noted "the museum curators' attempt to depict the Japanese as victims and Americans as coldhearted avengers."

30 Hugh Sidey, "War and Remembrance," *Time*, 23 May 1994. Crouch had been explaining to the public that survivors' testimonies and displays of articles that demonstrate the ground-level effects of the bombs made up the planned exhibit's "emotional center." It would have included photographs of mutilated women and children and audiovisual tapes of survivors' testimonies. Throughout the controversy, the museum curators' critics problematized the proposed exhibit for placing the emotional center on the destruction

caused by the atomic bombing. See also James Risen, "War of Words," Los Angeles Times, 19 December 1994; and "War of Words: What Museum Couldn't Say," New York Times, 5 February 1995. Journalists such as Air Force Magazine editor John Correll expressed their disgust at the fact that the museum curators' script would have included more photographs of Japanese casualties than of American soldiers. See "The Mission That Ended the War," Washington Post, 14 August 1994. That the number of Chinese killed by the Japanese military far exceeded either American or Japanese casualties was the least of their concerns.

31 Holloway, "Museum Peace," 32.

32 National Air and Space Museum, "The Crossroads: The End of World War II, the Atomic Bomb, and the Origins of the Cold War, First Script," National Air and Space Museum, Washington, D.C., 1994, mimeograph, 5.

33 Martin Sherwin, "Hiroshima gojūnen, rekishi to kioku no seijigaku" (Hiroshima fifty years, politics of history and memory), Kokusai bunka kaikan kaihō 6, no. 4 (October 1995): 8.

34 U.S. Senate Committee, Hearing: The Smithsonian Institution Management Guidelines, 12.

35 Gingrich's speech is quoted in Stephen Budiansky et al., "A Museum in Crisis: The Smithsonian Heads into Rough Times after the Enola Gay Debacle," U.S. News and World Report (13 February 1995): 73–74.

36 For characterizations of the NASM curators' effort to include multiple dimensions of the two atom bombs' use as stemming from the sensitivities of "political correctness" and of the 1960s Vietnam War generation, see, above all, Sowell, "The Right to Infiltrate," 74; the testimony of Evan S. Baker, president of the Navy League of the United States, in U.S. Senate Committee, Hearing: The Smithsonian Institution Management Guidelines, 11 May 1995; and Risen, "War of Words." William M. Detweiler, who was one of the first to openly attack the NASM staff, drew a connection between the Smithsonian controversy and the National Standards for U.S. History, through which "students will learn more about the politically correct people, places and events." See "Assault on American Values," Washington Post, 11 February 1995.

37 Miriam Silverberg, "Remembering Pearl Harbor, Forgetting Charlie Chaplin, and the Case of the Disappearing Western Woman: A Picture Story," positions 1, no. 1 (spring 1993): 24–76.

38 Kai Bird, for instance, argued that the Smithsonian script did not assault "the patriotism of World War II veterans. But neither should one question the patriotism of scholars who labor in the archives at the difficult task of peeling away layers of historical truth." See his "Humiliating Smithsonian Retreat." Martin Sherwin also responded to the press: "I'm appalled that Congress has come into this with an official history over the debate, leaving no room for informed debate. In my view, this cancellation undermines the democratic process for which these veterans fought in World War II" (quoted in Karen De Witt, "U.S. Exhibit on Bomber Is in Jeopardy," New York Times, 28 January 1995). It is unclear from this quote whether Sherwin himself is equating the democratic process with the particular U.S. constitutional process. But when read against the larger context of Detweiler's and others' accusation that the NASM staff and their supporters lack American patriotism, it produces precisely such an effect.

"Frantic to Join . . . the Japanese Army":

Black Soldiers and Civilians Confront the

Asia-Pacific War

GEORGE LIPSITZ

I began to feel a terrified pity for the white children of these white people, who had been sent, by their parents, to Korea, though their parents did not know why. Neither did their parents know why these miserable, incontestably inferior, rice-eating gooks refused to come to heel, and would not be saved. But I knew why. I came from a long line of miserable, incontestably inferior, rice-eating, chicken-stealing, hog-swilling niggers— who had acquired these skills in their flight from bondage—who still refused to come to heel, and who would not be saved.
—James Baldwin, *The Devil Finds Work*

In his celebrated autobiography, Malcolm X explains how he escaped the draft in 1943 during World War II. At a time when "the only three things in the world that scared me" were "jail, a job, and the Army," the Harlem street hustler devised a plan to fool his foes. Aware that military intelligence units stationed "black spies in civilian clothes" in African American neighborhoods to watch for subversive activity, Malcolm (then named Malcolm Little) started "noising around" Harlem bars and street corners ten days before his scheduled preinduction physical exam. He let it be known that he was "frantic to join . . . the Japanese Army."

Just in case the military found his dramatic displays of disloyalty insufficient, Malcolm informed a psychiatrist at his physical exam that he was eager to enter the military. "I want to get sent down South," he asserted. "Organize them nigger soldiers, you dig? Steal us some guns, and kill crackers!" Not surprisingly, the Selective Service judged Malcolm Little mentally disqualified for military service, sending him home with a 4-F deferment on 25 October 1943.[1]

The distinguished historian John Hope Franklin secured a similar result for himself by very different means. Swept up in the patriotic fervor that followed the bombing of Pearl Harbor, Franklin genuinely *was* frantic to join . . . the U.S. Navy. He saw an advertisement indicating that the Navy needed skilled office workers who could type, take shorthand, and run business machines. At that point in his life, Franklin had six years of experience at secretarial work, had won three gold medals in typing, had taken an accounting course in high school, knew shorthand, and had a Ph.D. in history from Harvard University. The Navy recruiter told him that he was lacking one credential: color. They could not hire him because he was Black.

Franklin then directed his efforts toward securing a position with the Department of War, then assembling a staff of historians. But here again, color mattered. The Department hired several White historians who had not obtained advanced degrees, but never responded in any way to Franklin's application. When he went for his preinduction physical exam, a White doctor refused to let Franklin enter his office and made him wait for a blood test on a bench at the end of a hall near the fire escape until Franklin's protests got him admitted to the physician's office.[2]

Years later, Franklin recalled that these experiences changed his attitude toward the war. They convinced him that "the United States, however much it was devoted to protecting the freedoms and rights of Europeans, had no respect for me, no interest in my well-being, and not even a desire to utilize my services." Franklin came to the conclusion that "the United States did not need me and did not deserve me. Consequently, I spent the remainder of the war years successfully and with malice aforethought outwitting my draft board and the entire Selective Service establishment."[3] Instead of serving in the military, Franklin devoted his time to teaching, scholarship, and activism aimed at undermining the system of White supremacy.

Although they started out with very different intentions, Malcolm X and John Hope Franklin both ended up avoiding military service during World War II. Their actions were hardly typical; an overwhelming majority of Americans, and even an overwhelming majority of African Americans, who were eligible for the draft accepted induction and served effectively. Black draft resisters accounted for fewer than 5 percent of the 12,343 conscientious objection cases processed by the Justice Department, and more than one million Black men and women served in the armed forces during the war.[4] But the conflicts with the Selective Service System experienced by Malcolm X and Franklin bring into sharp relief the potentially explosive racial contradictions facing the United States during the war.

Franklin and Malcolm X expressed more than individual ingenuity and personal pique in their resistance to the draft. They articulated and acted on a suspicion about the relationship between World War II and White supremacy widely held in their community: about the shortcomings of democracy in the United States, about the racialized nature of the war, about the potential power of non-White nations around the globe, and about the viability and desirability of covert and overt resistance to racism. Although they expressed a decidedly minority view about the draft itself in their own communities during the war, they touched on shared social perceptions that gained majority approval in the postwar period. The emergence of Malcolm X in the postwar period as a Black nationalist leader who connected antiracist struggles in the United States with anti-imperialist efforts around the globe, Martin Luther King Jr.'s role as the leading opponent of the U.S. war in Vietnam as well as the leader of civil rights and poor people's movements, and the actions of a generation of young people in the 1960s who used the research of scholars including Franklin to fashion their own understanding of their obligations to the nation at home and abroad all testify to the generative nature of wartime tensions and conflict.

Most important, the strategic maneuvering that Franklin and Malcolm X deployed in their struggles with the Selective Service System highlights the volatile instabilities sedimented within seemingly stable narratives of nation and race. Malcolm X initially presented himself as an admirer of America's enemies and as an active agent of subversion simply so he could stay on the streets and pursue his own pleasures as a petty criminal. Yet, his eventual imprisonment for crimes committed on the streets led him to a religious conversion and political awakening that made him an actual opponent of U.S. foreign policy, turning his wartime charade into an important part of his life's work. Franklin initially approached the government as a superpatriot eager to enlist in the American war effort, but the racism directed at him by the government led him to evade military service and embark on a lifetime of oppositional intellectual work and activism. In this essay, I hope to show how the affiliations and antagonisms made possible by a historically specific confluence of race and nation in the period from the 1940s through the 1970s offer important frames for understanding the current historical moment in which unexpected affiliations and antagonisms based on gender now play the role that fell to race in the World War II and postwar era.

By feigning a desire to join the Japanese Army and by announcing his interest in shooting southern segregationists, Malcolm X drew on ideas and practices with deep roots in his own life and in the politics of his community. His threat to join the Japanese Army in particular carried weight because it played on the paranoia of White supremacy by posing the possibility of a transnational alliance among people of color. In the process, it brought to the surface the inescapably racist realities behind the seemingly color-blind national narrative of the United States and its aims in the war.[5] The element of internationalism that informed Malcolm X's efforts to evade the draft had deep roots in his individual history and in the collective consciousness of African Americans.

Historically, the prospect of escape to Indian territory, Canada, or Mexico and the assistance offered by European abolitionists made slaves and free Blacks sensitive to international realities in the antebellum period. Robin D. G. Kelley's research on Black communists in Alabama in the 1930s indicates that charges of being instigated by "outside agitators" influenced by Russia had little effect on the descendants of slaves who had been freed from bondage in part by an invading army from the north.[6] But the Japanese were not just any outsiders to African Americans in the 1940s; they were people of color with their own independent nation, a force capable of challenging Euro-American imperialism on its own terms, and possible allies against the oppressive power of White supremacy.

Paul Gilroy and others have written eloquently about a "Black Atlantic"— about the importance of Africa and Europe as influences on the Black freedom struggle in North America. But there has been a "Black Pacific" as well. Images of Asia and experiences with Asians and Asian Americans have played an important role in enabling Black people to complicate the simple Black-White binaries that do so much to shape the contours of economic, cultural, and social life in the United States.[7] In addition, it is not only elite intellectuals who have had an international imagination; working people whose labor in a global capitalist economy brought them into contact with other cultures have often inflected their own organizations and institutions with international imagery and identification.

The African American encounter with Japan has been especially fraught with contradictions. In their zeal to identify with a "non-White" nation whose successes might rebuke Eurocentric claims about White supremacy, Blacks have often overlooked, condoned, and even embraced elements of Japanese fascism and imperialism. Within the United States, Japanese agents sometimes succeeded in promoting the crudest kinds of racial essentialism and male chauvinism among Black nationalist groups. But as Laura Mulvey argues, "It cannot be easy to move from oppression and its mythologies to resistance in history; a detour through a no-man's land or threshold area of counter-myth and symbolisation is necessary."[8] The African American engagement with the existence of Japan has provided precisely that kind of detour through a symbolic terrain sufficiently complex to allow an oppressed racial minority in North America to think of itself instead as part of a global majority of non-White peoples. In addition, as Malcolm X's performance at his preinduction physical demonstrated, imaginary alliances and identifications with Japan could also create maneuvering room for dealing with immediate and pressing practical problems.

African American affinities with Asia have emanated from strategic needs, from the utility of enlisting allies, learning from families of resemblance, and escaping the categories of Black and White as they have developed historically in North America. These affinities do not evidence any innate or essential characteristics attributable to race or skin color; on the contrary, they demonstrate the distinctly social and historical nature of racial formation. Neither rooted in biology nor inherited from history, racial identity is a culturally constructed entity always in flux. During World War II, the racialized nature of the Pacific War, the racist ideals of Nazi Germany, the enduring legacy of White supremacy, segregation, colonialism, and conquest in the United States, as well as antiracist activism at home and abroad generated contradictions and conflicts that radically refigured race relations in the United States and around the world.

Global politics and domestic economic imperatives have shaped relations between Asian Americans and African Americans from the start. White planters and industrialists in the nineteenth-century United States favored the importation of Asian laborers as a means of simultaneously driving down the wages of poor Whites and gaining even greater domination over slaves and free Blacks. As immigrants ineligible for naturalized citizenship according to the terms of the 1790 Immigration and Naturalization Act and as a racialized group relegated largely to low-wage laboring jobs, Asian Americans could offer little resistance to employer exploitation and political domination. White workers in California and elsewhere often took the lead in demanding exclusion of Asian immigrants from the U.S. labor market, but many manufacturers and entrepreneurs also came to view Asian immigrants as actual or potential competitors and consequently came to favor exclusion.[9] The U.S. Congress passed the first of several acts excluding Asians from immigrating in 1882, shortly after the Compromise of 1877 guaranteed the subjugation of southern Blacks and therefore eliminated the need for employers to use another group of racialized immigrants as competitors with African American laborers. Significantly, one of the important voices raised against the act in congressional debates was that of Senator Blanche K. Bruce of Mississippi, the only African American in the Senate.[10]

Contradictions between domestic racism and the imperial ambitions of the United States came into sharp relief as early as 1899, during the Filipino insurrection against occupying U.S. troops in the aftermath of what North Americans call the Spanish-American War. African American soldiers from the 24th Infantry Regiment could not help but notice that White Americans used many of the same epithets to describe Filipinos that they used to describe them, including "niggers," "black devils," and "gugus."[11] One Black enlisted man in the regiment felt that the rebellion he was sent to suppress emanated from the fact that "the Filipinos resent being treated as inferior," which he believed "set an example to the American Negro" that should be emulated. Similarly, the regiment's Sgt. Major John Calloway informed a Filipino friend that he was "constantly haunted by the feeling of how wrong morally . . . Americans are in the present affair with you."[12]

Filipinos fighting under the command of Emilio Aguinaldo made appeals to Black troops on the basis of "racial" solidarity, offering posts as commissioned officers in the rebel army to those who switched sides. Most remained loyal to the U.S. cause, but Corporal David Fagen deserted the 24th Regiment's I Company on 17 November 1899 to become an officer in the guerrilla army. He married a Filipina and served the insurrectionists with distinction, engaging U.S. units effectively and escaping time after time. Fearing that his example might encourage others to follow suit, U.S. officers offered extensive rewards and expended enormous energy in efforts to capture or kill Fagen. On 5 December 1901, U.S. officials announced that a native hunter had produced "a slightly decomposed head of a negro" and personal effects that indicated the skull belonged to Fagen. Although this may have been a ruse on Fagen's part to cease further searches for him, the gradually weakening position of the rebels made further resistance impossible, and one way or the other, Fagen disappeared from the combat theater. But his example loomed large in the minds of military and diplomatic officials, especially when contemplating military activity against non-White populations.[13] Nearly five hundred African American soldiers elected to remain in the Philippines at the conclusion of the conflict, and Filipino civilians later related stories about Fagen and about the Black soldiers who refused to crush the Moro Rebellion in 1914 to Black U.S. soldiers stationed in their country during World War II.[14]

Just as some Black soldiers from the 24th Infantry Regiment viewed the Filipino independence struggle as a battle with special relevance to their own fight against White supremacy, individuals and groups in Japan took an interest in Marcus Garvey's Universal Negro Improvement Association around the time of World War I. Charles Zampty, a native of Trinidad and a leader of the Garvey movement in Detroit for more than fifty years, originally learned about the UNIA by reading Garvey's newspaper, *Negro World*, which he obtained from Japanese sailors in Panama while he worked at the Panama Canal.[15] As early as 1918 Garvey warned that "the next war will be between the Negroes and the whites unless our demands for justice are recognized," adding, "with Japan to fight with us, we can win such a war."[16]

Other African American intellectuals also looked to Japan for inspiration. Shortly after the war between Russia and Japan, Booker T. Washington pointed to Japanese nationalism as a model for African American development.[17] W. E. B. Du Bois included the "yellow-brown East" among the "darker world" poised to resist "white Europe," in his novel *Dark Princess: A Romance*, where Du Bois fantasized about an alliance linking an Asian Indian princess, a Japanese nobleman, and an African American intellectual.[18] In his 1935 classic study, *Black Reconstruction in America*, Du Bois counted U.S. support for colonialism and imperialism in Asia, Africa, and Latin America as one of the enduring consequences of the concessions to the South required to suppress African Americans in the years after the Civil War. "Imperialism, the exploitation of colored labor throughout the world, thrives upon the approval of the United States, and the United States gives that approval because of the South," he argued. Warning that war would result from the reactionary stance imposed on the United States by its commitment to White supremacy, Du Bois reminded his readers, "The South is not interested in freedom for dark India. It has no sympathy with the oppressed of Africa or of Asia."[19]

At times, Black grassroots organizations recognized families of resemblance between their status and that of other racialized minorities. In San Francisco in the early years of the twentieth century, Black community groups and newspapers opposed efforts to send Japanese American children to segregated schools because they recognized the demeaning nature of segregation from their own experiences. In addition, in their public mobilizations, they pointed repeatedly to the ways in which opposition to immigration from Japan manifested more than a generalized fear of foreigners, but rather the racist prejudices of White Americans.[20]

Malcolm X's Garveyite father and West Indian mother encouraged him to be internationalist in his thinking, to look to Africa, to the Caribbean, and beyond, to render the hegemonic White supremacy of North America relative, contingent, and provisional. This tradition affected Malcolm X directly, but it also shaped the broader contours of relations between African Americans and people of Asian origin. In 1921, members of Garvey's UNIA and Japanese immigrants in Seattle joined forces in an attempt to create a Colored People's Union open to all people "except the whites or Teutonic races."[21] In New York, a young Vietnamese merchant seaman regularly attended UNIA meetings and became friends with Garvey himself in the early 1920s. Years later he would apply the lessons he learned about nationalism from Garvey when he took on the identity "Ho Chi Minh" and led his country's resistance against Japanese, French, and U.S. control.[22]

Forty members of the Garvey movement in Detroit converted to Islam between 1920 and 1923, largely as a result of the efforts of an Ahmadiyah mission from India. Elijah Muhammad, then Elijah Poole, associated with Garveyites in Detroit during the 1930s before founding the Nation of Islam, which Malcolm Little would later join while in prison during the late 1940s. The Nation of Islam went beyond Garvey's pan-Africanism to include (at least symbolically) all "Asiatic" (non-White) people in the same religion.[23]

During the 1930s, a Japanese national using the names Naka Nakane and Satokata Takahishi (sometimes spelled Satokata Takahashi) organized African Americans, Filipinos, West Indians, and East Indians into self-help groups, including the Society for the Development of Our Own, the Ethiopian Intelligence Sons and Daughters of Science, and the Outward Movement of America.[24] Born in Japan in 1875, Nakane married an English woman and migrated to Canada. He presented himself as a major in the Japanese Army and a member of a secret fraternal order known as the Black Dragon Society. Nakane promised financial aid and military assistance to African Americans in Detroit if they joined in "a war against the white race."[25]

Deported in 1934, Nakane moved to Canada and continued to run Development of Our Own through his African American second wife, Pearl Sherrod. When he tried to reenter the United States in 1939, federal officials indicted him for illegal entry and attempting to bribe an immigration officer. The FBI charged in 1939 that Nakane had been an influential presence within the Nation of Islam, that he spoke as a guest at NOI temples in Chicago and Detroit, and that his thinking played a major role in shaping Elijah Muhammad's attitudes toward the Japanese government. As proof, the FBI offered a copy of a speech that they claimed had been "saved" by an agent since 1933, in which Muhammad predicted "the Japanese will slaughter the white man."[26]

The Pacific Movement of the Eastern World, founded in Chicago and St. Louis in 1932, advocated the unification of non-White people under the leadership of the Empire of Japan. Led by Ashima Takis, who also used the names Policarpio Manansala, Mimo de Guzman, and Itake Koo (among other pseudonyms), the group expressed its ideology of racial unity in the colors of its banners: black, yellow, and brown.[27] The PMEW implied that it had the backing of the Japanese government in offering free transportation, land, houses, farm animals, and crop seed to the first three million American Blacks willing to repatriate to Africa.[28] Although Marcus Garvey warned his followers against the PMEW, Takis frequently represented himself as an ally and even agent of the Garvey movement, and his group enjoyed considerable allegiance among Garveyites in the Midwest, especially in Gary, Indiana, and East St. Louis, Illinois.[29] Madame M. L. T. De Mena of the UNIA defied Garvey's prohibitions and arranged speaking engagements for Takis and Chinese associate Moy Liang before Black Nationalist audiences.[30] "The Japanese are colored people, like you," Takis told African American audiences, adding pointedly, "the white governments do not give the negro any consideration."[31] In 1940, Takis told one African American group that war would soon break out between the United States and Japan, and that they would receive rifles from Japan to help them mount an insurrection in the Midwest while Japanese troops attacked the West Cost.[32] In the 1930s, the leader of the Peace Movement of Ethiopia, Mittie Maud Lena Gordon, had asked newly elected President Franklin Roosevelt to help finance Black repatriation to Africa. After the Japanese attack on Pearl Harbor, Gordon described 7 December 1941 as the day when "one billion black people struck for freedom."[33]

Thus, Malcolm X's presentation of himself in 1943 as pro-Japanese and anti-White supremacist picked up on elements of his own personal history as well as on significant currents of thought and action among Black nationalists. He also exploited well-founded fears among government officials. Some recognized that the pathology of White supremacy posed special problems for the nation as it sought to fashion national unity in a war against German and Japanese fascism. White racism in the United States undermined arguments behind U.S. participation in the war and made it harder to distinguish the Allies from the Axis. Racial segregation in industry and in the Army kept qualified fighters and factory workers from positions where they were sorely needed, while the racialized nature of the war in Asia threatened to open up old wounds on the home front. Most important, asking African American, Asian American, Mexican American, and Native American soldiers to fight for freedoms overseas that they did not enjoy at home presented powerful political, ideological, and logistical problems. But other government officials worried more about conspiratorial collaboration between African Americans and agents of the Japanese government.

As far back as the 1920s, the Department of Justice and agents from military intelligence had expressed fears of a Japanese-Black alliance. One report alleged, "The Japanese Associations subscribe to radical negro literature. In California a negro organization, formed in September, 1920, issued resolutions declaring that negros would not, in case of the exclusion of Japanese, take their place; a prominent negro was liberally paid to spread propaganda for the Japanese; and various negro religious and social bodies were approached in many ways." The report continued to claim, "It is the determined purpose of Japan to amalgamate the entire colored races of the world against the Nordic or white race, with Japan at the head of the coalition, for the purpose of wrestling away the supremacy of the white race and placing such supremacy in the colored peoples under the dominion of Japan."[34]

Similar fears haunted policymakers during World War II. Secretary of War Henry L. Stimson attributed Black demands for equality during the conflict to agitation by Japanese agents and communists. Stimson recognized no legitimate grievances among African Americans, but instead interpreted their demands for jobs in industry and positions in combat as evidence of Japanese-initiated efforts to interfere with mobilization for national defense. In the same vein, the Department of State warned against Japanese infiltration of Black protest groups such as A. Philip Randolph's March on Washington Movement as part of an effort "to direct the Negro Minority in a subversive effort against the United States."[35]

Southern journalist and racial "moderate" Virginius Dabney feared African American identification with the Japanese war effort because, "like the natives of Malaya and Burma, the American Negroes are sometimes imbued with the notion that a victory for the yellow race over the white race might also be a victory for them."[36] These predictions could become self-fulfilling prophesies; by showing how frightened they were by the prospect of alliances between African Americans and people of color elsewhere in the world, anxious Whites called attention to a potential resource for Black freedom struggles that would eventually come to full flower in the 1960s in the form of opposition to the Vietnam War by the Student Nonviolent Coordinating Committee and the Southern Christian Leadership Conference and expressions of solidarity with anti-imperialist struggles in Asia, Africa, and Latin America by more radical groups.

Even though extensive surveillance and infiltration of Japanese American and African American organizations by intelligence agents conclusively found little reason to fear any significant systematic disloyalty or subversion, once the war started government officials moved swiftly and decisively against Black nationalist draft resisters and organizations suspected of sympathy with Japanese war aims. F. H. Hammurabi, leader of World Wide Friends of Africa (also known as the House of Knowledge), was indicted in 1942 for delivering speeches praising Japan and for showing his audiences films of the Japanese attack on Pearl Harbor.[37]

Federal agents placed Ashima Takis under surveillance because of the PMEW's efforts to persuade Black nationalists in New York to ready "the dark-skinned races for armed uprisings should Japanese forces invade United States soil."[38] He received a three-year prison sentence for cashing a fraudulent money order some years earlier and served as a star witness in a federal prosecution of St. Louis area members of the PMEW.[39] Followers reported that Takis spoke German, French, and Spanish, that his English was perfect in private conversation but heavily accented in public speeches, and that he enjoyed success as a faith healer in Black neighborhoods.[40] Robert A. Hill describes Takis as a Japanese who masqueraded as a Filipino under the pseudonym Policarpio Manansala, while Ernest V. Allen represents him as a Filipino who masqueraded as a Japanese national under the pseudonym Ashima Takis and as a Filipino as Mimo de Guzman and Policarpio Manansala.

Prosecutors also brought charges of sedition and inciting draft resistance against leaders of the Peace Movement of Ethiopia and the Nation of Islam. Federal agents arrested Elijah Muhammad in May 1942, and a federal judge sentenced him to a five-year prison term at the Federal Correction Institute in Milan, Michigan. FBI agents raided the Chicago Temple of the NOI in September 1942, tearing "the place apart trying to find weapons hidden there since they believed we were connected with the Japanese," one suspect later recalled. The agents found no weapons or documents linking the group to the Japanese government, but those arrested all served three years in prison for draft evasion.[41]

Although he later joined the Nation of Islam where he fashioned an impassioned and precise critique of the connections linking U.S. imperialism overseas and anti-Black racism at home, we have no reason to doubt the representation Malcolm X provides in his autobiography that in 1943 his conscious motivations entailed little more than a desire to avoid "jail, a job, and the Army."[42] But he could not have failed to notice that the war against Japan gave him leverage that he would not have had otherwise. In that respect, his vision corresponded to that of millions of other African Americans.

Immediately after the Japanese attack on Pearl Harbor, Robert L. Vann, editor and publisher of one of the nation's most important Black newspapers, the *Pittsburgh Courier*, called on the president and Congress "to declare war on Japan and against racial prejudice in our country."[43] This campaign for "double victory" had actually started before the war commenced, when A. Philip Randolph used the threat of a mass march on Washington in June 1941 to extract Executive Order 8802 from President Roosevelt mandating fair hiring in defense industries. James Boggs, then a Black auto worker in Detroit, later recalled, "Negroes did not give credit for this order to Roosevelt and the American government. Far from it. Recognizing that America and its allies had their backs to the wall in their struggle with Hitler and Tojo, Negroes said that Hitler and Tojo, by creating the war which made the Americans give them jobs in the industry, had done more for them in four years than Uncle Sam had done in 300 years."[44]

Yet, even in the midst of a war against a common enemy, White Americans held onto their historic hatreds and prejudices. At the Packard Main factory in Detroit, White war workers protesting desegregation of the assembly line announced that it would be preferable to lose the war than have to "work beside a nigger on the assembly line."[45] John L. De Witt of the 4th Army Western

Defense Command in San Francisco complained to the Army's chief of classification when badly needed reinforcements that he had requested turned out to be African American soldiers. "You're filling too many colored troops up on the West Coast," De Witt warned. "There will be a great deal of public reaction out here due to the Jap situation. They feel they've got enough black skinned people around them as it is, Filipinos and Japanese. . . . I'd rather have a white regiment."[46]

Black workers had to wage unrelenting struggles to secure and keep high-paying posts in defense industries on the home front, while African American military personnel served under White officers in a largely segregated military whose high command did its best to keep Black troops out of combat so that they could not claim the fruits of victory over fascism.[47] On the other hand, to promote enthusiasm for the war among African Americans, the military also publicized the heroism of individual Black combatants like Dorie Miller, a steward on the battleship *West Virginia*, which was among those vessels attacked at Pearl Harbor on 7 December 1941. According to the Navy, Miller was stationed on the bridge of the *West Virginia* near its commanding officer at the time of the enemy attack. Miller reportedly dragged the ship's wounded captain from an exposed spot on the bridge, and then manned a machine gun, shooting down two enemy planes, despite never having been formally trained on the weapon. Twelve weeks after the incident, the Navy bowed to pressure from African American organizations and decorated Miller, awarding him the Navy Cross.[48] Skeptics have subsequently raised doubts about whether Miller could have actually accomplished the feats for which he was decorated, but his fame made his fate an issue among African Americans regardless. They noted that he received no transfer to a combat position, as would have been consistent with Navy policy at the time, but remained limited to serving food and drink to White officers on the escort carrier *Liscombe Bay*, where he died when that ship sank on 24 November 1943.[49]

Black soldiers sought positions in combat, but found themselves relegated to roles as garrison troops at Efate in the New Hebrides, at Guadalcanal in the southern Solomons, and at Banika in the Russells group. But Black soldiers from the First Battalion of the 24th Infantry Regiment (which had been David Fagen's unit in the Philippines) and members of the all-Black Ninety-third Division eventually served with White soldiers in combat in March 1945 at Bougainville.[50] More than a million Black men and women served in the Armed Forces during the war, more than half of them serving overseas in Europe or the Pacific.

Despite clear evidence of African American loyalty to the Allied effort, counterintelligence officers made Black people special targets of surveillance, investigation, and harassment. Naval intelligence officials in Hawai'i ranked "Negroes" second only to "Japanese" people as primary suspects of subversion.[51] The FBI issued a wildly inflated estimate of more than one hundred thousand African American members of pro-Japanese organizations (perhaps counting those who escaped the draft in the way Malcolm X did).[52] Yet, while mass subversion by Blacks was largely a figment of J. Edgar Hoover's always active imagination, the racialized nature of U.S. policy and propaganda in relation to the Japanese did elicit strong responses from African Americans.

In Lonely Crusade, a postwar roman à clef based on his own wartime experiences as an African American assembly line worker, Chester Himes narrates the complicated relationship between Japan and his lead character, Lee Gordon. When Navy training exercises make him think for a moment that a Japanese invasion is in progress, Gordon exults, "They're here! Oh, God-dammit, they're coming! Come on, you little bad bastards! Come on and take this city." Himes's narration explains, "In his excitement he expressed a secret admiration for Japan that had been slowly mounting in him over the months of his futile search for work. It was as if he reached the conviction that if Americans did not want him the Japanese did. He wanted them to come so he could join them and lead them on to victory; even though he himself knew that this was only the wishful yearning of the disinherited."[53]

The Office of War Information conducted a confidential survey of African Americans in 1942. Eighteen percent of the respondents indicated that they expected their own personal conditions to improve if Japan invaded the United States; 31 percent reported that their circumstances would remain the same; 26 percent had no opinion or refused to answer.[54] The OWI concluded that only 25 percent of African Americans supported the war effort wholeheartedly and that 15 percent had "pro-Japanese" inclinations," yet a careful study of letters to the editor and editorials in the Black press also determined that most African Americans neither supported nor condemned Japan.[55]

Detroit journalist Gordon Hancock accused White government officials of "colorphobia" in their close surveillance of Japanese expansion in the Far East while virtually ignoring what Hancock saw as "the manifestly greater dangers posed by German actions in Europe."[56] Chester Himes worked his reaction to the Japanese internment into another mid-forties novel, If He Hollers Let Him Go, by having his narrator, Bob Jones, identify the roots of rage against White supremacy: "Maybe it wasn't until I'd seen them send the Japanese away that I'd noticed it. Little Riki Oyana singing 'God Bless America' and going to Santa Anita with his parents the next day. It was taking a man up by the roots and locking him up without a chance. Without a trial. Without a charge. Without even giving him a chance to say one word. It was thinking about if they ever did that to me, Robert Jones, Mrs. Jones's dark son, that started me to getting scared."[57]

Gloster Current, NAACP director of branches, noted how these countersubversive measures taken against Japanese Americans raised special concern in the Black community. When the government announced its plans to incarcerate more than 110,000 law-abiding Japanese Americans, Current observed, "Many a Negro throughout the country felt a sense of apprehension always experienced in the face of oppression: Today them, tomorrow us. For once the precedent had been established of dealing with persons on the basis of race or creed, none of us could consider ourselves safe from future 'security' measures."[58] This sense of interethnic solidarity among aggrieved racial groups was one of the main products of the World War II experience and one of its most important enduring legacies in the postwar period.

Before the war, African Americans and Japanese Americans lived in close proximity to one another in many western cities. On Jackson Street in Seattle, Japanese restaurants and Black barber shops catered to customers from both races as well as to customers of Filipino, Chinese, and Mexican ancestry. White-owned hotels, restaurants, and motion picture theaters denied service to Black customers, but Japanese American entrepreneurs welcomed them.[59] In Los Angeles, African Americans and Japanese Americans shared several areas of the city, notably the neighborhood bounded by Silver Lake, Sunset, and Alvarado, the section near Vermont, Fountain, and Lucille, and the streets near Arlington, Jefferson, and Western. People in these neighborhoods shared experiences with discrimination as well; because of the "subversive" and "heterogeneous" nature of their communities, the Home Owners Loan Corporation Secret City Survey Files designated the property of homeowners in each of these districts as undesirable for federal loan support.[60]

Less than a week after the attack on Pearl Harbor, Seattle's Black-owned and -edited newspaper, *Northwest Enterprise*, opposed plans to evacuate Japanese Americans from the West Coast. "Don't lose your head and commit crimes in the name of patriotism," a front-page editorial cautioned. Addressing African American readers in terms they well understood, the newspaper reminded its readers, "The same mob spirit which would single them [Japanese Americans] out for slaughter has trailed you through the forest to string you up at some crossroad."[61]

Personal relationships between Japanese Americans and members of other racialized groups motivated some responses to the internment at the individual level. Chicano playwright Luiz Valdez remembers that the incarceration of Japanese Americans brought a temporary moment of prosperity to his family in

Delano when the U.S. Army made his father manager of a farm previously run by Japanese Americans. Yet, prosperity had its price. The Japanese American farmer who lived on the land refused to go to the camps, and instead hanged himself in the kitchen of the house that Valdez and his family inhabited for the duration of the war. The playwright remembers being afraid to enter the kitchen late at night, and recalls that during one evening of telling ghost stories he and his cousins thought they could see the farmer's body hanging from a lamp. After the war, the Valdez family returned to the fields and life as impoverished farm workers.[62]

At the Manzanar Relocation Center in 1944, authorities discovered that one of the Japanese Americans incarcerated in their camp was actually Mexican American. Ralph Lazo decided to present himself as a Japanese American at the time of the internment in order to stay with his high school friends. "My Japanese-American friends at Belmont High School were ordered to evacuate the West Coast, so I decided to go with them," Lazo explained. "Who can say I haven't got Japanese blood in me? Who knows what kind of blood runs in their veins?" When embarrassed relocation officials ordered his release from Manzanar, Lazo enlisted in the Army.[63] One African American in Seattle drove a Japanese American family to the train scheduled to take them to a relocation center, and stood by them until it was time to get on board. An interpreter overheard the Black man tell a Japanese American woman in the group, "You know that if there's ever anything I can do for you, whether it be something big or small, I'm here to do it."[64] In the San Francisco Bay Area, the chair of the Alameda County Branch of the NAACP's Legal Committee wrote to the organization's national spokesperson, Walter White, in July 1942 to protest the "inhumane treatment of Japanese evacuees, and the simultaneously eased restrictions against white enemy aliens."[65] Frank Crosswaith of the Negro Labor Committee criticized the Supreme Court's decision to uphold curfews on Japanese Americans on the West Coast as evidence of "the spread of Hitler's despicable doctrine of racism."[66] When New York's usually liberal Mayor Fiorello La Guardia objected to the placement of relocated Japanese Americans in that city in 1944, Roy Wilkins, editor of the NAACP's The Crisis, joined with George Schuyler, then assistant editor of the Pittsburgh Courier, Fred Hoshiyama of the Japanese American Citizens League, and socialist Norman Thomas in addressing a mass protest rally. Although Cheryl Greenberg is absolutely correct in arguing that the NAACP responded too timidly and too parochially to the internment—the organization opportunistically attempted to take advantage of the internment by seeking to secure positions for Blacks as replacement workers for Japanese American farm hands in California's agricultural fields—she also demonstrates that the organization did more than most other civil rights or ethnic groups in defending Japanese Americans. Especially in California, the NAACP offered aid to returned evacuees and supplied them with extensive legal assistance.[67]

In 1945, Charles Jackson condemned attacks in California against Japanese Americans returning from the internment camps in an editorial in *The Militant*, the organ of the Socialist Workers Party. Jackson urged his fellow Blacks to "go to bat for a Japanese-American just as quickly as we would for another Negro. These people are obviously being denied their full citizenship rights just as we are. They are pictured in the capitalist press as toothsome, 'brown-bellied bastards,' and are described by the capitalist commentators as 'half-man and half beast.' This vicious type of prejudice indoctrination is familiar to every Negro."[68]

The kind of interethnic identification between people with similar but not identical experiences with racism that characterizes Jackson's response to the assaults on Japanese Americans played an important part in reconfiguring racial politics during World War II. Members of racialized "minority" groups frequently found themselves compared to one another. For example, military officials and political leaders in California favored a plan to move urban Japanese Americans to farm work in rural areas because they hoped that such a move would prevent the influx of "a lot of Negroes and Mexicans" into the farming regions.[69] At the Poston internment camp, a staff person complained that many of the facility's officials knew little about Japanese Americans but "almost automatically transferred attitudes held about Negroes to the evacuees."[70]

When deployed in combat and support roles, African American service personnel often confronted that fear so characteristic of colonial officials everywhere, that contact between native peoples and armed troops of their own race might "contaminate" the population. For example, when large numbers of Black U.S. troops arrived in Trinidad, British colonial officials on that island protested that the "self-assurance" of the troops would spread to the islanders and make them uncontrollable. The U.S. Department of State agreed with the British officials and consequently ordered the troops replaced by Puerto Ricans who spoke mostly Spanish and so constituted less of a threat to the Black Anglophone population.[71]

The Puerto Rican presence in Hawai'i seemed to play a different role in race relations there. Thirty thousand African American sailors, soldiers, and war workers came to Hawai'i during the war, and they discovered that according to the standards of the Hawai'i census, people of African origin were classified as Puerto Rican—and therefore "Caucasian"—to distinguish them from native and

Asian inhabitants of the islands.[72] Thus, by moving to Hawai'i, Blacks could become White. In addition, native Hawaiians often displayed sympathy for Blacks in unexpected ways. One bus driver tried to help African Americans defeat their White tormentors when racial fights broke out on his vehicle. He kept the rear doors closed if Blacks were winning, and then opened the doors to let them slip away when the fights ended. As a Black war worker recalled, "There was what you would call an empathy from the local people as to what the black people had endured. They sort of, I guess, sympathized with us to a degree."[73]

Nonetheless, service in Hawai'i hardly insulated Blacks from White racism. During the war, brothels in Honolulu's Hotel Street district refused admission to African Americans or Hawaiians of color because White servicemen and war workers from the mainland objected to their presence.[74] Constantly warned against associating with Black men, local women sometimes viewed the African American presence on their islands with fear. One Chinese Hawaiian wrote, "I am very scared of these Negro soldiers here in Honolulu. They make my skin shrivel and my self afraid to go near them."[75]

Communities of color found their fates intertwined during the war; it was not possible for them to isolate themselves from one another. When large numbers of African American workers from the South moved to war production centers on the West Coast, city officials, realtors, and military authorities saw to it that they found housing in the sections of Seattle, San Francisco, and Los Angeles that had been left vacant by the Japanese American internment rather than in White neighborhoods.[76] At the same time, some Mexican Americans felt more vulnerable to racist attacks after the relocation of Japanese Americans. "In Los Angeles, where fantasy is a way of life," argued liberal journalist Carey Mc-Williams, "it was a foregone conclusion that the Mexicans would be substituted as the major scapegoat group once the Japanese were removed."[77] After mobs of White sailors attacked Mexican American youths wearing zoot suits in June 1943, the Los Angeles Times printed a caricature of Japanese Premier Tojo riding on horseback and wearing a zoot suit.[78]

A 1942 Gallup poll discovered that "American" respondents held slightly more favorable opinions of Mexicans than of Japanese people, but Los Angeles County Sheriff's Department Lieutenant Edward Duran Ayers demonstrated the opposite. He made use of many popular stereotypes and slurs in grand jury testimony, where he paradoxically contrasted "violence-prone" Mexicans with "law-abiding" Chinese and Japanese populations, of course not explaining why 110,000 law-abiding Japanese Americans has been shipped off to internment camps. Even more contradictorily, Ayers "explained" the propensity toward violence that he discerned among Mexicans as a result of the "oriental" background of their pre-Columbian ancestors, which left them with the "oriental" characteristic of "total disregard for human life."[79]

While racialized groups retained their separate (and sometimes antagonistic) interests and identities, pan-ethnic antiracist coalitions emerged on occasion in support of Japanese Americans as well. Representatives of African American, Filipino, and Korean community groups met with delegates from sixteen federal, state, and local agencies at the Palace Hotel in San Francisco in January 1945 to establish the Pacific Coast Fair Play Committee. They agreed that "any attempt to make capital for their own racial groups at the expense of the Japanese would be sawing off the limbs on which they themselves sat."[80] Sometimes, identification could come from a perception of common problems. In the novel Lonely Crusade, Chester Himes has his Black protagonist learn about the ways in which Black, Mexican, and Asian American residents share similar experiences with White racism when he reads a newspaper that reports on "a white woman in a shipyard" who "accused a Negro worker of raping her," on a group of White sailors who "had stripped a Mexican lad of his zoot suit on Main Street before a host of male and female onlookers," and about a "Chinese girl" who had been "mistaken for Japanese" and "slapped on a crowded streetcar by a white mother whose son had been killed in the Pacific."[81]

By the end of the war, race had become a decidedly visible and clearly contested element in all areas of American life. The humiliation and indignity imposed on the Japanese during their incarceration left lasting scars, demonstrating once again how state policy marked Asian Americans as permanently foreign in a manner quite dissimilar to every other immigrant group.[82] Japanese Americans not only lost years of their lives and millions of dollars in property that went mostly to Whites during the war, but they suffered a systematic assault on their culture by incarceration and surveillance policies aimed at wiping out the key conduits of Japanese culture in America.[83] In addition, a wave of violent attacks against Japanese American persons and property swept the West Coast toward the end of World War II, and the leniency shown to the perpetrators by law enforcement officials and juries portended permanent second-class status for Americans of Japanese ancestry.[84]

Yet, Japanese Americans also secured some victories in the postwar period as well. In 1948, California voters rejected efforts to institutionalize and extend the state's anti-Japanese Alien Land Law by an overwhelming vote of 59 percent against and only 41 percent in favor. The 1952 McCarren–Walter Immigration Act reversed the ban on non-Whites becoming naturalized citizens that had been on the books since 1790, even though the national origins quotas in the act still displayed strong prejudice against immigrants from Asia. Large-scale migration by African Americans and Mexican Americans seeking work in war industries changed the composition of the region's non-White population during the war. California's Black population increased from 124,000 to 462,000 during the war; the population of Seattle quadrupled between 1941 and 1945 as African Americans replaced Japanese Americans as the city's largest minority group.[85] In some ways, increased hatred against Blacks and Mexicans eased some of the pressures against Japanese Americans. For example, Roger Daniels points out that the same voters who rejected the 1948 Alien Land Law Referendum in California also voted overwhelmingly against a Fair Employment Practices measure aimed mainly at prohibiting job discrimination against African American and Mexican American workers.[86]

For African Americans, the Pacific War helped produce a new militancy. Struggles to secure high-paying jobs in defense industries and positions on the front lines in combat led logically to postwar activism that ranged from massive campaigns for voting rights in the South to access to jobs and housing in the North. A. Philip Randolph organized resistance to the draft among African Americans in the postwar period until President Truman capitulated and ordered the desegregation of the military in 1948. But the war did more than incubate a certain amount of militancy; it taught lasting lessons about the inescapably racialized nature of power and politics in the United States.

African Americans responded with mixed emotions to the lessons they had been taught about White racism by their wartime experiences. In a postwar rumination, James Baldwin recalled, "The treatment accorded the Negro during the Second World War marks, for me, a turning point in the Negro's relation to America. To put it briefly, and somewhat too simply, a certain hope died, a certain respect for white Americans faded."[87] John Hope Franklin felt some of those same feelings. "Obviously I was pleased with the outcome of the war," he later recalled, "but I was not pleased with certain policies pursued by our government. I wish that the government could have been less hypocritical, and more honest about its war aims. I wish that it could have won—and I believe it could have—without the blatant racism that poisoned the entire effort; without its concentration camps for our Japanese citizens, which smacked too much of Hitlerism; and without the use of the atomic bomb."[88] A Black soldier stationed in the Philippines, Nelson Peery, drew a parallel between the postwar fate of African Americans and the destiny of the Filipino people he had come to know during his time in the service: "I knew. No one had to tell me. I knew that America was going to beat us back into line when we got home. The Negro troops got a taste of racial equality in foreign lands. As they came home, that had to be beaten and lynched and terrorized out of them before they would go back to building levees and picking cotton. I could see no reason to expect that the Filipinos, also referred to as 'niggers,' were going to get any better treatment. It was the reason I felt such a deep sense of unity with, and loyalty to, the islands and their people."[89] In a book published immediately after the surrender of Japan, Walter White observed, "World War II has given to the Negro a sense of kinship with other colored—and also oppressed—peoples of the world. Where he has not thought or informed himself on the racial angles of colonial policy and master-race theories, he senses that the struggle of the Negro in the United States is part and parcel of the struggle against imperialism and exploitation in India, China, Burma, South Africa, the Philippines, Malaya, the West Indies, and South America."[90]

The postwar period also served as a crucible for antiracist thought and action among members of other aggrieved racial groups. Chicano scholar and author Americo Paredes served as a Pacific staff correspondent and editor for the U.S. military's newspaper *Stars and Stripes* during the war. He entered Japan with the U.S. Occupation forces and after meeting and marrying a Japanese national, he remained in that country after the war to report on the trials of Japanese leaders charged with atrocities. The kinds of racial insults directed against the accused by the military reminded Paredes of things he had heard said about Chicanos back home in South Texas, and in that context he felt an affinity for the accused. Paredes went on to work as a journalist in Korea and China during the postwar years, and his student and biographer Jose Limon notes that Paredes "developed an attachment to these Asian peoples and a conviction that racism had played a key role in the extension of American military power in that part of the world. This conviction was reinforced when he and his wife decided to return to the United States and encountered racist immigration quotas for Japanese designed to discourage marriages such as his."[91]

Malcolm X certainly embraced a similar sense of anti-imperialism and internationalism after he converted to Islam in a Massachusetts prison in the late 1940s. When the Korean War broke out he wrote a letter from prison (which he knew would be read by that institution's censors as well as by outside intelligence agents) explaining, "I have always been a Communist. I have tried to enlist in the Japanese Army last war, now they will never draft or accept me in the U.S. Army."[92] Paroled in 1953, he secured employment moving truck frames and cleaning up after welders at the Gar Wood factory. FBI agents visited him at work demanding to know why he had not registered for the draft. He pretended that he did not know that ex-convicts had to register and the FBI apparently believed him. His draft board in Plymouth, Michigan, denied his request for status as a conscientious objector, but judged him "disqualified for military service" because of an alleged "asocial personality with paranoid trends."[93]

Black encounters with Asia became increasingly important between 1940 and

1975, as the United States went to war in Japan, the Philippines, Korea, China, Vietnam, Laos, and Cambodia. These U.S. wars in Asia have played an important role in reconfiguring race relations in North America. They have augmented racist tendencies to conflate Asian Americans with the nation's external enemies, as evidenced most clearly by hate crimes against people of Asian origin in the wake of the war in Vietnam and the emergence of economic competition between Asian and North American industries.[94] But U.S. wars in Asia have also repeatedly raised the kinds of contradictions faced by communities of color during World War II. For example, Gerald Horne and Mary L. Dudziak have shown how the Supreme Court's 1954 decision in *Brown v. Board of Education* responded in part to the imperatives of the cold war and the ways in which desegregation made it difficult for the United States to present itself as the defender of freedom to emerging nations in Asia, Africa, and Latin America.

In addition, U.S. wars in Asia and their costs to communities of color generated new critiques of their nation's domestic and foreign policies.[95] Amiri Baraka argues that the Korean conflict created many of the preconditions for the modern-day civil rights movement, and indeed many Korean War veterans including James Foreman and Bobby Seale played prominent roles in African American protest groups during the 1950s and 1960s.[96] Ivory Perry, a prominent community activist in St. Louis, always credited his service at Camp Gifu, Japan, and in combat in Korea as the crucible for his own subsequent activism. For Perry, meeting Japanese and Korean citizens who seemed to him refreshingly nonracist compared to the White Americans he had known helped him see that White supremacy was a primarily historical national phenomenon and not human nature. In addition, the contrast between the freedoms he was sent overseas to defend and the freedoms he could not realize at home made him more determined than ever to bring about changes in his own country. As he remembers thinking on his return to the United States from the war, "I shouldn't have been in Korea in the first place because those Korean people they haven't ever did anything to Ivory Perry. I'm over there trying to kill them for something that I don't know what I'm shooting for. I said my fight is here in America."[97]

When Muhammad Ali (whose conversion to Islam involved the direct intervention and assistance of Malcolm X) refused to fight in the Vietnam War because "I ain't got no quarrel with them Viet Cong," his celebrated case not only established that anti-imperialist and internationalist thinking had a broad base of support among African Americans, it also played a major role in publicizing, legitimating, and proselytizing for an antiwar movement that was interracial in many significant ways.[98] As Edward Escobar, Carlos Muñoz, and George Mariscal have shown, the Chicano Moratorium in Los Angeles in 1970 demonstrated mass opposition to the war among Mexican Americans, but it also played a crucial role in building the Chicano movement itself.[99] Antiwar protest among Chicanos held particular significance because it required them to oppose the official positions of important institutions in the community, including the Catholic Church, trade unions, and veterans groups.[100]

Just as U.S. wars in Asia brought to the surface the racial contradictions facing African Americans and Mexican Americans, antiracist movements among Blacks and Chicanos also helped Asian Americans address their unresolved grievances in respect to White supremacy in the United States. During the Vietnam War, militant Asian American political and cultural groups emerged as important participants in interethnic "Third World" coalitions. African American examples played an important role in guiding these groups. Rie Aoyama, a Japanese American activist from Seattle, explains, "We had no role models for finding identity. We followed what blacks did. Within the whole Asian American identity, part of the black identity came with it. Usually when you say Asian American, you are going to have some aspect of black experience too."[101] Nancy Matsuda similarly attributes her politicization to her recognition while in high school of the parallels between Asian Americans and Blacks: "I realized how blacks were an oppressed people, and I saw how Asians were oppressed too. So for me, it was a complete turn around from wanting to be associated with the whites to wanting to be associated with the blacks, or just a minority."[102] In 1968, Toru Sakahara, a Japanese American attorney and community leader in Seattle, organized a discussion group that brought representatives of the Black Panther Party to dialogue with members of the Japanese American Citizens League and Jackson Street business owners whose property had been damaged during a civil insurrection in that city.[103]

Thus, we can see that the racialized nature of the Pacific War has had enduring consequences for race relations in the United States. It exacerbated the antagonisms and alienations of race, while at the same time instigating unexpected alliances and affinities across communities of color. Yet, it is important to understand that fights between men of different races often involved competition for power over women or over access to them. The prophetic currents of African American and interethnic antiracist activity during World War II addressed important issues about race, nation, and class, but they did precious little to promote an understanding, analysis, or strategy about the ways in which hierarchies of gender initiated, legitimated, and sustained social inequalities and injustices.

The Black nationalist organizations that identified with Japan and other "non-White" nations during the 1920s and 1930s also advocated a rather consistent subordination of women to men. In some of these groups, women did attain visibility as organizers and activists: government agents shadowed Mittie

Maud Lena Gordon because of her work as head of the Peace Movement of Ethiopia, and they put Madame M. L. T. De Mena under surveillance because of her public association with Ashima Takis. Pearl Sherrod took over Satakota Takahishi's newspaper column in local papers after he was deported, and she served as well as nominal leader of the Development of Our Own. Takahishi himself spoke out forthrightly for women's rights, condemning the "peculiar ideas prevailing among a certain group of men, that the women should not hold any office in an organization, nor even have a voice at the meetings."[104] Counseling respect between men and women, Takahishi reminded his followers that a woman held the post of international supervisor in his organization. That woman, however, did most of her speaking to White audiences that Takahishi refused to address. In addition, he demonstrated his "respect" for women by having an affair with a young female follower while Pearl Sherrod Takahishi ran his organization for him. This development led Sherrod to report her husband to the Immigration and Naturalization Service herself when he tried to return to the United States in 1939.[105]

The White servicemen who attacked Mexican American youths in Los Angeles in the 1943 "zoot suit riots" justified their actions as a defense of White women from the predatory attentions of non-White "hoodlums." At the same time, many Mexican American youths saw the zoot suiters as heroic defenders of Mexican women from advances by White men. In an article about the riots for the NAACP journal *The Crisis*, Chester Himes compared the sailors to storm troopers, dismissing them as uniformed Klansmen. But he portrayed the riots as primarily a fight about access to women. Condemning the "inexplicable" and "incomprehensible" ego that allows "southern white men" to believe that they are entitled to sex "with any dark skinned woman on earth," Himes explained that Mexican American and Black youths objected to White men dating women of their races because "they, the mexican and negro boys, cannot go out in Hollywood and pick up white girls."[106]

Himes analyzed the ways the war in the Pacific emboldened White men about approaching women of color. He recounted an incident that he witnessed on a streetcar when three White sailors on leave from the "Pacific skirmishes" began talking loudly about "how they had whipped the Japs." Himes noted sarcastically, "It seems always to give a white man a wonderful feeling when he whips a Jap." One sailor boasted about his prowess in combat, and then bragged, "Boy, did those native gals go fuh us." Looking around the streetcar, one of them announced that a White man could get any woman he wanted, in a clear attempt to intimidate two "Mexican" youths in the company of an attractive girl. Himes complained that African American and Mexican American men could not protest remarks like these made to their wives and sweethearts by

White men, and even worse, that unescorted Black women would "get a purely commercial proposition from every third unescorted white man or group of white men."[107] Although he fashioned a sensitive and perceptive critique of how official sanction for the attacks on zoot suiters replicated the rule by riot that dominated the lives of Blacks in the South, Himes never identified the role played by gender in constructing racial identities or the ways in which desires for equality based on equal male privileges over women undermined the egalitarian principles and hopes that he saluted elsewhere.

Part of the prejudice directed at Black soldiers originated from White servicemen who warned the women they met about the dangers of being molested and raped by Black men. A Japanese American woman in Hawai'i noticed how her views had been channeled in that direction one day after she shared an uneventful bus ride with four African American servicemen. Surprised that they had not accosted her, she wrote to a friend, "Gee, I was very frightened . . . Funny isn't it how I am about them. One would be that way after hearing lots of nasty things about them."[108] On the home front and overseas, battles between Black and White war workers, service personnel, and civilians stemmed from struggles over sex—over "rumors of rape, competition for dates, and symbolic and real violations of the privileges of white masculinity."[109]

In his important analysis of government distribution of "pin-up" photos among U.S. servicemen during World War II, Robert Westbrook shows how the maintenance of White male prerogatives and privileges involved much more than the regressive thinking or selfish behavior of individuals. Westbrook makes a persuasive case that the entire war effort had to be presented as a defense of middle-class male norms in order to solve some difficult ideological problems raised by the government's need for popular sacrifice. Westbrook explains that liberal capitalist states have difficulty providing compelling reasons for their citizens to go to war. Based on promises of protecting private property and personal happiness, how can the liberal capitalist state ask its subjects to surrender property, happiness, liberty, and life in the name of public goals?

In the United States during World War II, the answer came from couching public obligations as private interests, by stressing military service as the defense of families, children, lovers, friends, and an amorphously defined but clearly commodity-driven "American Way of Life." Just as wartime advertisers' promises about the postwar period featured full refrigerators rather than the four freedoms, just as Hollywood films presented soldiers sacrificing themselves for apple pie, the Brooklyn Dodgers, and the girl they left behind rather than for the fight against fascism, the U.S. government chose to supply its fighting men with pictures of Betty Grable in a swimsuit as an icon of the private world of personal pleasure that would be restored to them when the war was won. Grable's identity as a blonde, White, wholesome, middle-class, and married beauty made her an appropriate icon for fitting the war effort firmly within the conventions, history, aspirations, and imagery of middle-class European American life and culture.[110] Consequently, when White men engaged in racist violence against soldiers and civilians of color, they acted on an understanding of their privileges and prerogatives that the government and other important institutions in their society had encouraged.

After World War II, American economic expansion and military engagement in Asia led to a new stage of racial formation. The same propagandists who deployed alarmist images of violated White women as the reason to resist "yellow feet" on American soil during the war, now fashioned fables of romantic love between White U.S. servicemen and Asian women as allegories of empire.[111] In his perceptive analysis of race as the "political unconscious" of American cinema, Nick Browne shows how World War II occasioned a displacement of some of the U.S. film industry's traditional images of African Americans onto Asia. In films such as The Teahouse of the August Moon (1956) and Sayonara (1957), the American presence in Asia becomes naturalized by a grid of sexual relations in which White males have general access to all women, White women are prohibited from sex with non-White men, non-White men have access to non-White women only, and non-White women submit to both non-White and White men. Consequently, in Browne's formulation, the social world created by the complicated intersections of race, gender, nation, and class attendant on the U.S. presence in Asia relies on a unified "gender-racial-economic system built as much on what it prohibits as what it permits."[112] This use of gendered imagery to make unequal social relations seem natural and therefore necessary endures today as a particularly poisonous legacy of the Asia-Pacific War, especially at a time when so much of the project of transnational capital depends on the low-wage labor of exploited Asian women workers.

During World War II, African Americans used Asia as a source of inspiration and emulation, as a site whose racial signifiers complicated the binary Black-White divisions of the United States. They exposed the inescapably international past and present of U.S. race relations, and they forged intercultural communications and contacts to allow for the emergence of antiracist coalitions and consciousness. Liberal narratives about multiculturalism and cultural pluralism to the contrary, race relations in the United States have always involved more than one outcast group at a time acting in an atomized fashion against a homogeneous "White" center. Interethnic identifications and alliances have been powerful weapons against White supremacy. All racial identities are relational; communities of color are mutually constitutive of one another, not just competitive and/or cooperative.

The history of interethnic antiracist coalitions among even ostensibly essentialist and separatist Black nationalist groups points toward potentially effective strategies for the present. Yet to abstract race from the other social relations in which it is embedded would be to seriously misread the nature of racial formation and the social construction of identities. As Susan Jeffords argues, "The complex intersections between all of the manifestations of dominance in patriarchal structures will vary according to historical moments and location, and must be specified in each situation in order to be adequately understood and challenged."[113]

In our own time, when the rapid mobility across the globe of capital, commodities, images, ideas, products, and people creates fundamentally new anxieties about identities connected to nation, race, class, and gender, the enduring relevance of transnational interracial identifications and alliances prefigured during World War II should be manifestly evident. Race is as important as ever; people are dying every day all around the world because of national narratives with racist preconditions. But at a time when women make up so much of the emerging low-wage world workforce, when patriarchal narratives continue to command the allegiance of killers for so many causes, it is also evident that the same imagination and ingenuity that allowed for unlikely coalitions across continents in the past on the issue of race must now also include a fully theorized understanding of gender as it intersects with identities based on narratives of nation, race, and class.

Notes

Versions of this essay appeared previously in Lisa Lowe and David Lloyd, eds., *The Politics of Culture in the Shadow of Capital* (Durham, NC: Duke University Press, 1997), and in George Lipsitz, *The Possessive Investment in Whiteness: How White People Profit from Identity Politics* (Philadelphia: Temple University Press, 1998).

1 Malcolm X and Alex Haley, *The Autobiography of Malcolm X* (New York: Grove Press, 1965), 104–5, 106. Robin D. G. Kelley's adroit analysis of this incident in his splendid and indispensable book *Race Rebels* directed my attention to the significance of Malcolm's story. See *Race Rebels: Culture, Politics, and the Black Working Class* (New York: Free Press, 1994), 171. FBI Surveillance File on Malcolm X, 30 November 1954, quoted in Ferruccio Gambino, "Malcolm X, Laborer: From the Wilderness of the American Empire to Cultural Self-Identification," paper presented at the Colloque 1984 de L'Association Française D'etudes Americaines Dourdan, 25–27 Mai 1984, 17; manuscript in the author's possession.

2 John Hope Franklin, "Their War and Mine," *Journal of American History* (September 1990): 576–77.

3 Ibid., 578.

4 Brenda Gayle Plummer, *Rising Wind: Black Americans and U.S. Foreign Affairs, 1935–1960* (Chapel Hill: University of North Carolina Press, 1996), 74–75. Plummer's comprehen-

sive, persuasive, and fascinating book makes a major contribution to rethinking the roles of race and nation in the U.S. past and present.

5 On the African American trickster tradition, see George P. Rawick, *From Sundown to Sunup* (Westport, CT: Greenwood, 1972), 98. For the definitive analysis of the racialized nature of the Pacific War, see John Dower, *War without Mercy: Race and Power in the Pacific War* (New York: Pantheon, 1986).

6 Robin D. G. Kelley, *Hammer and Hoe* (Chapel Hill: University of North Carolina Press, 1991).

7 Paul Gilroy, *Black Atlantic* (Cambridge, MA: Harvard University Press, 1994); Joseph E. Holloway, ed., *Africanisms in American Culture* (Bloomington: Indiana University Press, 1991); George Lipsitz, *Dangerous Crossroads* (New York: Verso, 1994).

8 Laura Mulvey, "Myth, Narrative, and Historical Experience," *History Workshop* (spring 1987): 3–19.

9 Gary Okihiro, *Margins and Mainstreams: Asians in American History and Culture* (Seattle: University of Washington Press, 1994), 44, 45; Daniel Rosenberg, "The IWW and Organization of Asian Workers in Early Twentieth Century America," *Labor History* 36, no. 1 (winter 1995): 77–87; Richard White, *It's Your Misfortune and None of My Own* (Tulsa: University of Oklahoma Press, 1991).

10 On exclusion acts, see Lisa Lowe, *Immigrant Acts: On Asian American Cultural Politics* (Durham, NC: Duke University Press, 1996), 180–81. On the importation of Asian immigrant labor, Reconstruction, and exclusion, see Okihiro, *Margins and Mainstreams*, 46–48.

11 Michael C. Robinson and Frank N. Schubert, "David Fagen: An Afro-American Rebel in the Philippines, 1899–1901," *Pacific Historical Review* 64, no. 1 (February 1975): 71.

12 Quoted in ibid., 72.

13 Ibid., 75, 81–82.

14 Nelson Peery, *Black Fire: The Making of an American Revolutionary* (New York: New Press, 1994), 277–78.

15 Tony Martin, *The Pan-African Connection: From Slavery to Garvey and Beyond* (Dover, MA: Majority Press, 1983), 64.

16 Quoted in Ernest V. Allen, "When Japan Was 'Champion of the Darker Races': Satokata Takahishi and the Flowering of Black Messianic Nationalism," *The Black Scholar* 24, no. 1 (1995): 29.

17 See ibid.

18 Michiko Hase, "Race, Status, and Culture in Trans-Pacific Perspective: African American Professionals in Japan," presentation at the American Studies Association meetings, Nashville, Tennessee, 28 October 1994, 9–10; manuscript in author's possession; W. E. B. Du Bois, *Dark Princess* (Jackson: Banner Books, University Press of Mississippi, 1995). See also Gilroy, *Black Atlantic*.

19 W. E. B. Du Bois, *Black Reconstruction in America* (1935; Simon and Schuster, 1995), 706, 704.

20 David J. Hellwig, "Afro-American Reactions to the Japanese and the Anti-Japanese Movement, 1906–1924," *Phylon* 37, no. 1 (1977): 94–96.

21 Quintard Taylor, "Blacks and Asians in a White City: Japanese Americans and African Americans in Seattle, 1890–1940," *Western Historical Quarterly* 23, no. 4 (November 1991): 426.

22 Karl Evanzz, *The Judas Factor: The Plot to Kill Malcolm X* (New York: Thunder's Mouth, 1992), 22.

23 E. U. Essien-Udom, *Black Nationalism: A Search for Identity in America* (Chicago: University of Chicago Press, 1962), 44–45, 74–75; Tony Martin, *Race First: The Ideological and Organizational Struggles of Marcus Garvey and the Universal Negro Improvement Association* (Westport, CT: Greenwood Press, 1976), 74–77; Humphrey J. Fischer, *Ahmadiyah* (Oxford: Oxford University Press, 1963); Gambino, "Malcolm X, Laborer," 25–26.

24 Dominic J. Capeci Jr., *Race Relations in Wartime Detroit: The Sojourner Truth Housing Controversy of 1942* (Philadelphia: Temple University Press, 1984), 53; Evanzz, *The Judas Factor*, 24, 138; Dower, *War without Mercy*, 174

25 Capeci, *Race Relations in Wartime Detroit*, 53.

26 The record of the FBI in counterintelligence is such that any document they release should be met with suspicion. Yet, even if fabricated, this document at the very least shows the anxiety felt at high levels of government about the possibility of African Americans feeling allegiance to Japan because it was a non-White country. See Evanzz, *The Judas Factor*, 138.

27 Ernest Allen Jr., "Waiting for Tojo: The Pro-Japan Vigil of Black Missourians," *Gateway Heritage* 15, no. 2 (fall 1994): 19, 26.

28 Robert A. Hill, ed., *The Marcus Garvey and UNIA Papers* (Berkeley: University of California Press, 1983), 596; Bob Kumamoto, "The Search for Spies: American Counterintelligence and the Japanese American Community, 1931–1942," *Amerasia Journal* 6, no. 2 (1979): 50.

29 Hill, *The Marcus Garvey and UNIA Papers*, 506–507.

30 Ernest V. Allen, "When Japan Was 'Champion of the Darker Races,'" 37.

31 Hill, *The Marcus Garvey and UNIA Papers*, 506.

32 Ibid., 507.

33 Ernest V. Allen, "When Japan Was 'Champion of the Darker Races,'" 25.

34 Gary Y. Okihiro, *Cane Fires: The Anti-Japanese Movement in Hawaii, 1865–1945* (Philadelphia: Temple University Press, 1991), 116–17.

35 Kumamoto, "The Search for Spies," 54.

36 Stimson and Dabney quoted in Dower, *War without Mercy*, 173–74.

37 Ernest V. Allen, "When Japan Was 'Champion of the Darker Races,'" 37.

38 Capeci, *Race Relations in Wartime Detroit*, 54.

39 Ernest Allen Jr., "Waiting for Tojo," 27, 28.

40 Ibid., 19.

41 Essien-Udom, *Black Nationalism*, 48–49, 67.

42 Malcolm X and Haley, *The Autobiography*, 107.

43 Beth Bailey and David Farber, *The First Strange Place: Race and Sex in World War II Hawaii* (Baltimore: Johns Hopkins University Press, 1992), 133.

44 James Boggs, *The American Revolution: Pages from a Negro Worker's Notebook* (New York: Monthly Review Press, 1963), 79. I thank Suzanne Smith for calling my attention to this quote.

45 Walter White and Thurgood Marshall, *What Caused the Detroit Riot? An Analysis by Walter White and Thurgood Marshall* (New York: National Association for the Advancement of Colored People, 1943), 15.

46 Quoted in Roger Daniels, *Concentration Camps USA: Japanese Americans and World War II* (New York: Holt, Rinehart, and Winston, 1971), 36.

47 George Lipsitz, *Rainbow at Midnight: Labor and Culture in the 1940s* (Urbana: University of Illinois Press, 1994), 73–83; Bernard C. Nalty, *Strength for the Fight: A History of Black Americans in the Military* (New York: Free Press, 1986), 143–203.

48 Dennis Denmark Nelson, "The Integration of the Negro into the United States Navy, 1776–1947" (M.A. thesis, Department of Sociology, Howard University, 1948), 28–29; Otto Lindenmeyer, *Black & Brave: The Black Soldier in America* (New York: McGraw-Hill, 1970), 88; Robert Ewell Greene, *Black Defenders of America, 1775–1973* (Chicago: Johnson Publishing Company, 1974), 202.

49 Nalty, *Strength for the Fight*, 186

50 Ibid., 166, 169.

51 Bailey and Farber, *The First Strange Place*, 159.

52 Cheryl Greenberg, "Black and Jewish Responses to Japanese Internment," *Journal of American Ethnic History* 14, no. 2 (winter 1995): 22.

53 Chester Himes, *Lonely Crusade* (New York: Thunder's Mouth Press, 1986), 46.

54 Ernest V. Allen, "When Japan Was 'Champion of the Darker Races,'" 37.

55 Dower, *War without Mercy*, 174.

56 Capeci, *Race Relations in Wartime Detroit*, 53.

57 Chester Himes, *If He Hollers Let Him Go* (New York: Thunder's Mouth Press, 1986), 3.

58 Quoted in Greenberg, "Black and Jewish Responses to Japanese Internment," 19–20.

59 Taylor, "Blacks and Asians in a White City," 408, 413.

60 Records of the Federal Home Loan Bank Board of the Home Owners Loan Corporation, records group 195, Los Angeles City Survey File, box 74, areas D-50, D-33, D-30.

61 Quoted in Taylor, "Blacks and Asians in a White City," 425.

62 Luis Valdez, *Envisioning California*, Sacramento, Center for California Studies, Keynote Address Publication Series, publication no. 3, 1995, 7.

63 Quoted in Beatrice Griffith, *American Me* (Cambridge, MA: Houghton-Mifflin, 1948), 321.

64 Quoted in Taylor, "Blacks and Asians in a White City," 424.

65 Quoted in Greenberg, "Black and Jewish Responses to Japanese Internment," 15.

66 Quoted in ibid., 18.

67 Ibid., 16, 18, 19.

68 Charles Jackson, "Plight of Japanese Americans," *Militant* (10 March 1945), reprinted in C. L. R. James, George Breitman, Edgar Keemer, and others, *Fighting Racism in World War II* (New York: Monad Press, 1980), 342.

69 Daniels, *Concentration Camps USA*, 59.

70 Ibid., 105.

71 Nalty, *Strength for the Fight*, 167.

72 Bailey and Farber, *The First Strange Place*, 139.

73 Quoted in ibid., 161.

74 Ibid., 103.

75 Quoted in ibid., 162.

76 Daniels, *Concentration Camps USA*, 163.

77 Quoted in Mauricio Mazon, *The Zoot-Suit Riots: The Psychology of Symbolic Annihilation* (Austin: University of Texas Press, 1984), 19.

78 Ibid., 52. On the "zoot suit riots," see Lipsitz, *Rainbow at Midnight*, 83–86.

79 Quoted in Mazon, *The Zoot-Suit Riots*, 23.

80 Daniels, *Concentration Camps USA*, 158.

81 Himes, *Lonely Crusade*, 207.

82 I thank Lisa Lowe for reminding me of the ways in which anti-Asian racism entails this rendering of Asian Americans as "permanently foreign."

83 Kumamoto, "The Search for Spies," 66–68.

84 Daniels, *Concentration Camps USA*, 159, 168.

85 Ibid., 162; Taylor, "Blacks and Asians in a White City," 428.

86 Daniels, *Concentration Camps USA*, 170. See also Kevin Allen Leonard, " 'Is That What We Fought For?' Japanese Americans and Racism in California: The Impact of World War II," *Western Historical Quarterly* 21, no. 4 (November 1990): 480.

87 James Baldwin, *The Fire Next Time* (New York: Dial, 1963), 63.

88 Franklin, "Their War and Mine," 579.

89 Peery, *Black Fire*, 200.

90 Quoted in Dower, *War without Mercy*, 177–78.

91 Jose Limon, *Dancing with the Devil: Society and Cultural Poetics in Mexican-American South Texas* (Madison: University of Wisconsin Press, 1994), 78.

92 Quoted in Gambino, "Malcolm X, Laborer," 18.

93 Ibid., 19.

94 Yen Le Espiritu, *Asian American Panethnicity* (Philadelphia: Temple University Press, 1992).

95 Mary L. Dudziak, "Desegregation as Cold War Imperative," in *Critical Race Theory*, ed. Richard Delgado (Philadelphia: Temple University Press, 1995), 110–21; Gerald Horne, *The Fire This Time: The Watts Uprising and the 1960s* (Charlottesville: University of Virginia Press, 1995).

96 Amiri Baraka (LeRoi Jones), *Blues People* (New York: Random House, 1963).

97 Quoted in George Lipsitz, *A Life in the Struggle: Ivory Perry and the Culture of Opposition* (Philadelphia: Temple University Press, 1995), 63.

98 Thomas R. Hietala, "Muhammad Ali and the Age of Bare Knuckle Politics," in *Muhammad Ali: The People's Champ*, ed. Elliott J. Gorn (Urbana: University of Illinois Press, 1995), 138; John Hope Franklin, *From Slavery to Freedom: A History of Negro Americans*, 4th ed. (New York: Knopf, 1974), 474.

99 Edward Escobar, "The Dialectics of Repression: The Los Angeles Police Department and the Chicano Movement, 1968–1971," *Journal of American History* 74, no. 4 (March 1993): 1483–1504; Carlos Muñoz, *Youth, Identity, Power: The Chicano Movement* (London: Verso, 1989).

100 George Mariscal, " 'Chale Con La Draft': Chicano Antiwar Writings," *Viet Nam Generation* 6, nos. 3–4 (1995): 130.

101 Quoted in Yasuko I. Takezawa, *Breaking the Silence: Redress and Japanese American Ethnicity* (Ithaca, NY: Cornell University Press, 1995), 147.

102 Quoted in ibid., 148–49. See also David Gutierrez, *Walls and Mirrors* (Berkeley: University of California Press, 1995), for a discussion of how the Chicano movement grew from a similar desire to identify with Blacks rather than with Whites.

103 Quintard Taylor, *The Forging of a Black Community: Seattle's Central District from 1870 through the Civil Rights Era* (Seattle: University of Washington Press, 1994), 225–26.

104 Quoted in Ernest V. Allen, "When Japan Was 'Champion of the Darker Races,' " 33, 25, 37.

105 Ibid., 33, 36.

106 Chester B. Himes, "Zoot Riots Are Race Riots," *The Crisis* (July 1943): 200.

107 Ibid., 200, 201.

108 Quoted in Bailey and Farber, *The First Strange Place*, 162.

109 Lipsitz, *Rainbow at Midnight*, 81–86.

110 Robert B. Westbrook, " 'I Want a Girl Just Like the Girl That Married Harry James': American Women and the Problem of Political Obligation in World War II," *American Quarterly* 24, no. 4 (December 1990): 587–614.

111 See Nick Browne's very significant "Race: The Political Unconscious of American Film," *East-West Journal* 6, no. 1 (1992): 9.

112 Ibid.

113 Susan Jeffords, *The Remasculinization of America: Gender and the Vietnam War* (Bloomington: Indiana University Press, 1989), 180.

Colonialism and Atom Bombs:

About Survivors of Hiroshima Living in Korea

TOYONAGA KEISABURŌ

Translation by Eric Cazdyn and Lisa Yoneyama

EDITORS' NOTE: Before presenting the following paper in Hawaiʻi, Toyonaga Kei-saburō began with an apology for the Japanese military attack on Pearl Harbor on 7 December 1941. One participant, whose primary intellectual interest has been to de-construct "Japan" and its national discourses, raised the question of why Toyonaga, who was nine years old at the time of the attack and who, along with his family, had been victims of both the United States and Japan, had to "apologize" for Japan's past deeds. Yet, as Norma Field has written with great sensitivity, the act of offering an apology demands complex analysis.[1] In the following, Toyonaga recounts his experiences as an atomic bomb victim as well as a Japanese activist who demands governmental repara-tions for Korean survivors who have been triply victimized by Japanese colonialism, U.S. atomic attacks, and alienation from South Korean society. His narrative shows us how the problems of "the nuclear age" need to be addressed in their connections to various other social issues and in global terms. Moreover, the various legal battles he describes mean more than simply redressing past injustices. Rather, they are fought because of the urgent need to transform present arrangements in ethnic relations, historical knowl-edge, the neocolonial environment, and proliferating nuclearism. To be sure, direct responsibility for the two nuclear atrocities lies with the U.S. government. Yet, Toyo-naga's story urges us to think through the complex ways in which apologies are de-manded in political, judicial, and moral terms.

Over fifty years have passed since the attacks of the atomic bombs on Hiro-shima and Nagasaki. As a Japanese *hibakusha* (i.e., a survivor of a nuclear bomb and/or radiation exposure), I anticipate with great hope the day when nuclear weapons will be extinct and lasting world peace will become a reality. The fact remains, however, that those voices exclaiming, "No More Hiroshimas!" and "No More Nagasakis!" are not taken as seriously as they deserve to be.

For Americans, the story generally goes like this: *Japan attacked Pearl Harbor, and Japan was preparing for all-out war on the Japanese archipelago. Were it not for the bombs, many lives would have been lost. It was also the quickest way to end the war.* For many living in those Asian countries that were formerly occupied by Japan, the story goes like this: *The use of the bombs put an end to the aggression and colonialism waged against Japan's neighbors. It was the quickest way to free Asia.* And for many in Japan, the story goes like this: *America dropped the bombs to gain control over postwar negotiations and for absolute dominance in the cold war era. As Japanese, we must pledge never to repeat this act of inhumanity elsewhere in the world.*

Why are there such contrasting views between those inside and outside Japan regarding the use of the two bombs? One reason may be because the disastrous consequences of the nuclear destruction are insufficiently known beyond Japan. The U.S. policy of suppressing and controlling information about the serious human and environmental damages caused by nuclear explosions has been primarily responsible for such worldwide ignorance. Yet, as we approach the end of the twentieth century, movements to protest the inhumanity and wretchedness of atomic warfare appear to have been revitalized. Some of these activities gained visibility when the U.S. government suspended the Smithsonian's exhibit on the ground-level effects of the atomic attack, and others gained momentum when France and China continued their nuclear weapons tests. Still other grassroots antinuclear campaigns became active in response to India's and Pakistan's entry into the devastating nuclear arms race.

This is indeed a critical moment for protests. The experiences of Hiroshima and Nagasaki need to be heard even more urgently to create a global consensus regarding the bomb's atrociousness and the imminent threat of a global nuclear disaster. However, there are other crucial factors that prevent the voices from Hiroshima and Nagasaki from being heard in earnest: namely, that Japan has neither properly accepted moral responsibility for the war nor provided full reparations to those who suffered from Japanese colonial rule.

The nuclear bombs used against Hiroshima and Nagasaki affected not only Japanese but also tens of thousands of Korean residents, Chinese, some Southeast Asian foreign-exchange students, and prisoners from the nations of the Allied forces who were detained near the bomb sites. Many of the Korean victims returned to their home country after liberation. But because of the general lack of knowledge about the bombs' atrocious consequences and the lingering effects of radiation, many were forced to endure harsh conditions of discrimination and alienation even on returning to their home country. The Japanese government and those in the peace and antinuclear movements have long neglected the plight of Korean victims who returned to Korea. When considering the historical records, it is undoubtedly clear that Japan was an aggressor toward Asia.

As for myself, whenever speaking to young audiences about my own experiences as a *hibakusha*, I find it crucial to address the problems of the nuclear age from such a perspective. In other words, it is important to speak about the atrocities and victimization experienced in Hiroshima and Nagasaki through historical reflections on Japanese military and colonial aggression, while at the same time considering the problems encountered by victims of wars in general, nuclear attacks, nuclear experiments, and nuclear power plant accidents throughout the world. For all those *hibakusha* who have passed on before me, and for all those suffering in hospitals today, I will continue to discuss Hiroshima from such a point of view.

An Atomic Bomb Experience

On 6 August 1945, I was nine years old. I lived near a military installation in Onaga, a community currently known as Yamane, in Hiroshima City. On the morning of 6 August, I was in Sakamaki, a town located more than eight kilometers away from Hiroshima City. I was on my way to see the doctor about an ear infection. At around 8:15, when the bomb was dropped, I was walking in the middle of the town. Suddenly, I heard a thundering sound. Dust blew all around and I hid behind a house. I hurried back to the station and waited for the train bound for Hiroshima station. As I waited I saw mushroom clouds rising above Hiroshima Bay. I clearly saw the demonic faces of our enemies, Roosevelt and Churchill, looking down on me. After a long wait the train finally arrived. I got on board, but the train did not reach Hiroshima. I then got off the train just outside Hiroshima, at a station near where my grandparents lived.

The first thing I wanted to do was to go and search for my family. But because Hiroshima burned more intensely and the sky was redder than on any previous night after an air raid, I was forced to stay at my grandparents' house. At that time my family consisted of my mother, my little brother, and myself. My father passed away in 1942, and since then my mother had been raising her two sons alone. On that day, my mother took my three-year-old younger brother to join other members of our neighborhood association to build bomb shelters. They were located not far from the bomb's epicenter.

Along with my grandparents and my cousin, who was then in grammar school, I spent the following two days walking around the city in search of my mother and brother. At last, on 8 August, I found them taking refuge at a mountain crematorium in Onaga. Mother's face was completely burnt and swollen beyond recognition. My little brother, in contrast, was not hurt at all. If not for my brother, I could not have identified her. My mother must have instinctively protected my brother with her own body at the moment of the bomb's explosion. Of the 150 residents of the neighborhood community, my brother was one of only two who did not bear any apparent injuries from the bomb.

The destruction was total. There was no medicine. My mother applied slices of raw vegetables to treat the burns on her face and her left arm. Although my three-year-old brother did not show a single scar at the time of the bomb blast, he gradually fell ill. He soon took on the symptoms of what we know today as acute radiation sickness; he developed severe diarrhea, rapid weight loss, bleeding flecks, and bulging eyes. Nevertheless, our fate turned out to be quite good. After receiving generous care from my grandparents, aunt, and other relatives, by the end of the year my mother and brother were slowly able to recover and support themselves. Considering that all three of us are still alive, we must regard ourselves as some of the most fortunate among those victimized by the atomic bomb.

In 1971 I visited South Korea with several other schoolteachers. It was a period when we were becoming increasingly aware of the need for special education for ethnic and other minority students. The primary purpose of the visit was to obtain some ideas about education in Korea. During the trip I became more concretely aware of the difficult life circumstances of the atomic bomb victims living there. On 15 August, the anniversary date to commemorate Korea's liberation and independence, I visited the Korean Atomic Bomb Victims Relief Association (Hanguk Wŏnp'ok P'ihaeja Wŏnho Hyŏpoe, or Kankoku Genbaku Higaisha Engo Kyōkai, which was renamed in 1977 Kankoku Genbaku Higaisha Kyōkai; hereafter, Relief Association) in Seoul. There I met Sŏ Sŏk-u and other members of the association and learned of how the atomic bomb victims living in Korea have been forsaken by both the Korean and Japanese (not to mention American) governments. After I returned from Korea, I looked for ways I might help them. I also applied for a Hibakusha Health Certificate for the first time in my life. As I explain below, the certificate legally identifies me as a hibakusha. Until then, I had not particularly considered myself as such. I thus regard my certificate as a gift from Korean hibakusha. In December of the same year the Citizens Relief Council for Korean Atomic Bomb Victims (Kankoku no Genbaku Higaisha o Kyūen suru Shimin no Kai; hereafter, Citizens Council) was inaugurated in Japan. And I immediately acted in kind by establishing a branch office in Hiroshima.

The Citizens Council supports not only Korean *hibakusha* living in Korea, but all bomb victims who live outside Japan, for instance, in China, the United States, and Brazil. Most recently, the council has been urging equal application of the Hibakusha Relief Law to all *hibakusha*, regardless of whether they reside in Japan. The council has also been involved in special efforts to rectify another problem concerning a great number of Korean atom bomb victims, namely, the matter of compensation for unpaid work to those who were mobilized as laborers under Japanese colonialism.

There are significant differences between the conditions of Korean atomic bomb victims residing in Korea and those in Japan. After returning to Korea, the bomb victims were abandoned and given no formal or informal relief for a long period of time. In Japan, with the 1957 passage of the Atomic Bomb Medical Assistance Law (Genshibakudan Hibakusha ni taisuru Iryō nado ni kansuru Hōritsu, or Genbaku Iryō Hō), the Japanese residents who were acknowledged legally as *hibakusha* were issued Hibakusha Health Certificates (Hibakusha Kenkō Techō) and became entitled to free health examinations and medical treatment. Yet in many cases, the bomb destroyed not only the health of *hibakusha* but also their entire livelihoods. Radiation's late effects also began to affect the aging *hibakusha*. Responding to the survivors' demands for more general assistance, including various kinds of social welfare, the Atomic Bomb Special Measure Law (Genbaku Tokubetsu Sochi Hō) was passed in 1968. Together with the Medical Assistance Law, it systematized medical care and social welfare for all *hibakusha* residing in Japan.

In 1994 these two laws were combined in the Hibakusha Assistance Law (Hibakusha Engo Hō). To be sure, the Hibakusha Assistance Law is far from ideal. It does not respond to the demands of many bomb victims that the state officially acknowledge its responsibility for the disaster. Moreover, the law does not clarify responsibilities for reparations. Yet, despite the insufficiency of these laws, *hibakusha* of all nationalities residing in Japan have received support in various forms.

In contrast, those living outside Japan, including bomb victims in Korea, have been entirely excluded from all provisions. It is important to remember that many *hibakusha* in Korea were forcibly brought to Japan near the war's end, during the total manpower mobilization effort. As a result of Japan's colonial policies, many Koreans also emigrated to Japan to seek better economic opportunities, only to find prisonlike working conditions and finally to be bombed in Hiroshima and Nagasaki. After national liberation, many of the survivors returned to Korea. Despite the suffering they endured from the lingering effects of the bomb as well as the discrimination they faced in Korea, many hibakusha began requesting reparations only in the late 1960s. Although they brought a lawsuit against the Japanese government and sent a representative to Japan, the Japanese government has continually refused requests for reparations.

Korean hibakusha were oppressed three times over: by Japan's colonial rule, by the atomic assaults, and by fifty years of abandonment in their home society. As these victims age, the postbomb torment of illness and financial burdens have become more intense. The chances of receiving assistance in a timely manner are also decreasing. I believe it is our duty as Japanese to demand that the Japanese government no longer deprive these Korean bomb victims of their basic human rights and dignity and that they be granted both a good-faith apology and urgently needed reparations.

In May 1995 the Relief Association requested that the Japanese government and Diet accept fundamental responsibility for Japanese aggression and colonial rule. It also demanded that at the very minimum the Japanese government grant Korean victims the same medical care and health relief received by bomb victims living in Japan. In short, the association requested that money and reparations should be granted under the assumption that Korean victims had been living in Japan throughout the postwar years. This amount was estimated to be approximately $2.3 billion, a calculation based on a request for reparations made in 1987 by the association. At the same time, the Relief Association requested equal application of the Hibakusha Assistance Law to those residing outside Japan.

Chŏng Sang-sŏk, the association's chairperson, has said, "We are making these demands in order to have our human rights restored and we must resolutely pursue these reparation demands until our very deaths." As Japanese, we must do everything to press this issue before these people die. The fact is, however, that many Japanese are ignorant of the situation. This is because the Japanese education system does not offer sufficient knowledge about the war, the bomb, and the history of Japanese colonialism in Korea. To be sure, we do have the so-called Peace Pedagogy, a program in which we teach about the role Japan played as victimizer during the war, as well as about the plight of Japanese atomic bomb victims. Along with this instruction about Japan's aggression, I insist on inclusion of materials regarding the conditions of atomic bomb victims outside Japan. Without a comprehensive pedagogy on the war and colonialism, antiwar and antinuclear ideals will not flourish.

The Movement of the Korean Atomic Bomb Victims

The conclusion of the ROK–Japan Basic Treaty in 1965, which assumed official settlement of the war and colonial reparations issues, betrayed many of the

Korean hibakusha's hopes. The Korean bomb victims felt ignored by both the Korean and Japanese governments. Yet, with the growth of media activities during the early 1960s, the link between the survivors' health problems and the effects of the nuclear bomb became more widely known in Korea. Inquiries and investigations made by friends of hibakusha also helped spread knowledge concerning the connections between the two.

In July 1967 the Relief Association was formed and it began to demand reparations from both the Korean and Japanese governments. From the beginning of the Korean War in 1950 until the Vietnam War in 1965, Korean society had been in perpetual chaos and the problems regarding the atomic bomb had been widely ignored. The victims had to confront a terribly unsympathetic environment. Though their organizing was not necessarily extremely efficient, their courage was truly praiseworthy. Beginning with 800 members, by 1973 there were seven branches organized throughout the country and 9,362 were registered with the association. However, though experiencing steady growth, the association had little success with regard to achieving its demands. The organization's numerous demands on the Japanese government would always meet the same response: that the issue has been settled by the ROK–Japan Basic Treaty.

In December 1970 a bomb victim by the name of Sŏn Chin-du was arrested when entering Japan without documentation. "I came to Japan because Korea does not have proper medical facilities to treat atomic bomb illnesses," Sŏn explained through the media. He went on to complain, "Since the condition of my body was caused by Japan, it has the responsibility to provide medical treatment." Sŏn then applied for a Hibakusha Health Certificate, which would enable him to receive free medical treatment. But the Fukuoka prefectural authorities and the Ministry of Health and Welfare rejected his request, arguing that the Medical Assistance Law is meant to promote the welfare of local communities and should thus provide services only to those who have intimate ties with (i.e., are residents of) those communities. In October 1972 Sŏn filed suit against Fukuoka Prefecture and the Ministry of Health and Welfare. He demanded that a Hibakusha Health Certificate be issued to him on the grounds that the Japanese government owed responsibilities to Koreans who became victims of the atomic bombs as a result of Japanese colonial policies.

On 30 March 1974 the Fukuoka District Court delivered its verdict. It ruled that the Medical Assistance Law should be regarded as one of the many laws assisting war victims. It held that the law's application should not be restricted to members of Japanese society and that it should be applied to all hibakusha, regardless of residency. On 30 March 1978, following several appeals, the Supreme Court ultimately supported the initial District Court ruling and determined that the Medical Assistance Law was intended as humanistic legislation and that it should be applied to all hibakusha regardless of their nationality or residency. Moreover, it noted that the law should also be regarded as a form of state reparation for atom bomb victims.

Through Sŏn's legal cases it became clear that hibakusha in Korea are urgently in need of medical and other types of relief. In 1979 the ruling parties of Japan and Korea (the Liberal Democratic Party and Republican Party, respectively) mutually agreed to send Korean doctors to Japan to receive medical training; dispatch Japanese doctors to Korea to provide medical services; and cover the cost of up to sixty hibakusha residing in Korea annually for stays of from two to six months in Japan to receive medical treatment. However, the Relief Association found these provisions insufficient and demanded that a hospital devoted especially to the treatment of atomic bomb illnesses be built in Korea. It also called for legislation establishing a governmental reparations program for hibakusha and their second- and third-generation offspring living in Korea.

Despite the association's demands and the agreement made between the two governments, the only provision to be realized was that which offered assistance for treatment visits to Japan. Between 1980 and 1986, 226 survivors of the Hiroshima bombing and 123 of the Nagasaki bombing traveled to Japan and received free medical treatment under the Medical Assistance Law. While the Japanese and Korean governments considered this specialized care as an end in itself, the Relief Association regarded it as only a first step and continued its struggle for more aid. Moreover, in response to the $2.3 billion demanded by the association in 1987, the Japanese government in 1990 offered basic relief of only $40 million. For the bomb victims in Korea, the very small sum of money led to nothing more than another bitter disappointment. To rectify the situation, the Citizens Council is currently working toward the following goals: full reparations from the Japanese government for the bomb victims living in Korea; cooperation with and full support to Korean hibakusha; and acknowledgment from industrial corporations who took advantage of Korean forced laborers during the war of their legal responsibilities and immediate reparations to these former laborers.

Korean Hibakusha and the Hiroshima Mitsubishi Heavy Industry

We do not yet fully know the details of the plight of Korean atomic bomb victims. Both the Korean and Japanese governments have failed to fully investigate the history and current situations of hibakusha in Korea. Yet it is clear that there was an extremely large number of Koreans bombed in Hiroshima.

Hiroshima formerly flourished as a center of military industry and culture. It was home to rows of munitions factories that produced weapons for the war of invasion. Hiroshima Mitsubishi Heavy Industry was one such company. After Japan formally colonized Korea in 1910, Hiroshima attracted many Koreans looking for employment. Many of these immigrants were farmers deprived of their land by the colonial government's Land Survey Project of 1910–1919. Especially after Japan launched its total war against China in 1937, the number of Koreans living in Hiroshima increased very rapidly, expanding by some 265 percent (from about 30,000 to 80,000) between 1939 and 1944 due to the growing need for labor at the munitions factories. The figure is about 1.5 times higher than the growth rate of the Korean population throughout the Japanese mainland (approximately 960,000 to 1,930,000). In 1944 approximately 2,800 Korean laborers are estimated to have been forcibly brought to Mitsubishi Heavy Industry's two production sites in Hiroshima: Hiroshima Machinery Factory (Mitsubishi Jūkōgyō Hiroshima Kikai Seisakusho) and Mitsubishi Hiroshima Shipyard (Hiroshima Zōsenjo).

The Japanese government gathered Koreans of working age mostly from Korea's southern provinces, focusing primarily on the area around Kyŏnggi province. Many of them were tenant farmers living under harsh conditions. Many former workers have testified that at the time of their recruitment they were told by Hiroshima Mitsubishi that their compulsory period of employment would be one to two years and that not only would wages be better than for other jobs available in Korea, but the work would also be safer. They were also told that Mitsubishi would remit half their pay to their families back in Korea. But in general they were not informed of either the exact amount of their wages or details concerning the nature of their work. Once they began working, they netted about 25 yen per month, with additional compensation for night shifts. Many believed that the reason their wages were so meager was because half their earnings were being sent to their families in Korea.

The morning of 6 August 1945 was just like any other for the detained workers. The Mitsubishi factory was located about four to five kilometers from the hypocenter. First came the violent flash, then the explosion, and then the factory and dormitory buildings collapsed. Many of the workers were thrown in the air by the force of the blast. They suffered serious head injuries and broken limbs; many were hit by flying roof slates and shards of glass. At about 10 in the morning large drops of black rain started to fall.

After the bombing, the factory stopped all operations and abandoned its supervision. After national liberation on 15 August, the workers were able to return to their families in Korea. Yet, without money and still suffering from the effects of the bomb, they had little choice but to earn the boat fare of about 20 to

40 yen by taking up day labor at construction sites and farms. By September many of them were able to return to Korea, but on unlicensed boats.

Fukagawa Munetoshi, a *hibakusha* poet who once worked for Hiroshima Mitsubishi, has described the company's irresponsible actions at the close of the war in his book *Atom-Bombed Korean Workers Who Died at Sea: Requiem over the Strait (Umi ni kieta hibaku Chōsenjin chōyōkō: chinkon no kaikyō)*. Mitsubishi neither offered sufficient postbomb care for its workers nor assisted them in returning to Korea. In July 1945 Fukagawa was appointed to serve as the supervisor for all Korean workers living at Mitsubishi West Dormitory. There he had nightly conversations with the workers and listened to their anguish and grievances. Apparently he then became one of the Japanese most trusted by the workers. Fukagawa recalls that by October 1945 several families contacted Mitsubishi inquiring as to why the laborers had not been returned to Korea. Mitsubishi, however, did not respond to their inquiries. Fukagawa speculates in his book that some must have died during the trip back due to the effects of the bomb. Having made it to the boats, the laborers must have been horrified to discover that they would then have to battle typhoon storms on the trip back to Korea. Those with the good fortune to make it back to their families alive then faced the wretched living conditions that their families were forced to endure, for Mitsubishi had not fulfilled its initial promise of remitting 50 percent of each worker's salary to his family.

Fukagawa was the first to formally take up with Hiroshima Mitsubishi the issue of Korean forced laborers and their unpaid salaries. Following the end of the war, Fukagawa was also living a desolate life, for he too had been affected by the bomb and felt hopelessly uncertain about the future. On 21 October Mitsubishi finally fired Fukagawa along with hundreds of other employees. With the outbreak of the Korean War in 1950, Fukagawa lost all contact with his acquaintances who had returned to Korea. It was during those years that he began experimenting with literature. Along with the *hibakusha* poet Tōge Sankichi and others, Fukagawa became active in the antiwar and peace literary movement.

In July 1973 Fukagawa began his own investigations into the lives and whereabouts of the former Korean forced laborers who had presumably returned to Korea. He was particularly concerned about the 246 laborers with whom he had last parted company at Hiroshima station on 15 August 1945. Through witnesses in southwestern Japan, Fukagawa discovered that many of these former workers had died near the Iki and Tsushima islands while on their sea journey back to Korea. At least one boat was sunk by a severe typhoon that hit the area immediately after the war.

On 20 November 1973 Fukagawa took his first trip to Pusan, Korea, to continue his investigations. There he confirmed that the Mitsubishi workers he had befriended had indeed been lost at sea. Not one of the 246 had returned. Fukagawa subsequently made several visits and together with No Chang-su and the latter's younger brother, he eventually located thirty bereaved families.

In April 1974 the families of the deceased forced laborers in Korea formed the Association for Families of the Deceased Korean Atom Bomb Victims, Japan Hiroshima Mitsubishi Heavy Industry (Nihon Hiroshima Mitsubishi Jūkōgyō Kankokujin Hibakusha Chinbotsu Izoku Kai; hereafter, the Association for Families of the Deceased Victims). Encouraged by this development, Korean survivors of the Mitsubishi factory formed the Hiroshima Mitsubishi Factory's Forcibly Mobilized Korean Laborers Collective (Kankokujin Genbaku Higai Mitsubishi Chōyōsha Dōshikai; hereafter, the Korean Laborers Collective). Two hundred former laborers have been identified by this organization. Responding to the formation of these two groups in Korea, in 1976 Fukagawa and other concerned citizens established a support organization in Japan. In 1981 this organization adopted the name Association for Korean Atom Bombed Mitsubishi Forced Laborers, Families of the Deceased, Missing Returnees, and Postwar Issues (Kankoku no Mitsubishi Chōyōkō Hibakusha/Ikazoku/Kikoku Sōnansha/Sengo Mondai Taisaku Kai). Fukagawa and others thus took on a mediating role and began to convey the demands of the two Korean groups to Hiroshima Mitsubishi.

Negotiating with Hiroshima Mitsubishi and the Hiroshima Justice Bureau

Since the mid-1970s the Association for the Families of the Deceased Victims and the Korean Laborers Collective, assisted by Fukagawa and his group in Japan, have continued negotiations with Mitsubishi. It has been a tough battle, for during these years the issues of forced labor mobilization and corporate responsibilities for war and colonial efforts have not received wide public attention.

During the 1990 negotiations a Japanese Ministry of Foreign Affairs official publicly asserted that the agreements contained in the 1965 Japan–Korea Basic Treaty had settled all state-to-state reparations issues, and that reparations sought from private corporations such as Mitsubishi should be dealt with at the individual level. Mitsubishi has also maintained that the Basic Treaty concluded all reparations issues.

As for the unpaid salaries, however, in 1974 Mitsubishi officially stated that as of 7 September 1946 it had "deposited" (kyōtaku) with the Hiroshima Justice

Bureau payments in the amount of 170,849 yen and 66 sen due to 1,950 workers, together with relevant documentation. Under pressure from the Allied Forces Occupation authorities, the Japanese government had ordered Mitsubishi to entrust all related records to the Justice Bureau. A number of other companies that had mobilized workers from occupied territories during the total war period had similarly "deposited" such records concerning their workers with their local Justice Bureaus. Although the disclosure of such documents would open up the possibility of receiving various reparations for wartime forced labor, many documents were lost or burned during the war. It was therefore fortunate but also extremely ironic to discover that Mitsubishi's documents were preserved in Hiroshima, the city that had experienced nearly total atomic destruction.

Fukagawa immediately requested that he be allowed to view the list of "deposits," but was denied. Later, in 1992, a Japanese lawyer's group sent the Justice Bureau a request to view the document on behalf of three members of the Korean Laborers Collective. However, they too were rebuffed on the grounds that the list could be shown only to individuals whose names appeared on it. According to the Bureau, this verification was needed because the names appearing on the "deposits" list were Japanese. Of course, the irony here is that it had been the Japanese government in the first place that had forced Koreans to adopt Japanese surnames during the Name Changing Campaign (sōshi kaimei) of the colonial period.

Our grassroots movements for wartime and colonial reparations also grew to involve those mobilized and then bombed in Nagasaki. In July 1992 Kim Sun-gil, a former worker in the Nagasaki Mitsubishi factory, filed suit against both the Japanese government and Mitsubishi. He demanded reparations for being forcibly mobilized and for the consequent damages he had suffered from the atomic bomb. Encouraged by Kim's legal struggles, the Korean Laborers Collective and its support groups in Japan also became more active in our pursuit to clarify the issue of unpaid salaries.

Pak Ch'ang-hwan is one of the three members of the Korean Laborers Collective who in 1992 applied to the Hiroshima Justice Bureau in 1992 for clearance to view the "deposits" list submitted by Mitsubishi. Pak is also president of the Kiho Branch of the Korean Atomic Bomb Victims Relief Association. When he requested permission to view materials relevant to his case at the Hiroshima Justice Bureau, he was rejected on the grounds that he could not prove that he was in fact the same individual as the one named on the document, Minamoto Shōkan. As a result, Pak was forced to go through painstaking efforts to produce the documents necessary to prove his identity. These included, for instance, a copy of his family registry during the colonial period, which showed that his Korean family name had been crossed out and written over with the Japanese surname Minamoto.

Despite such efforts, the Justice Bureau continued to reject his applications. At one point it argued that it was necessary for Pak to prove that within his entire province only his family had adopted the particular Japanese surname Minamoto. We were all outraged. Not only did the Justice Bureau show no remorse for Japan's colonial past, it made Pak suffer for its improper handling of records that were produced by the colonial administration.

On 1 February 1995, after having submitted various documents and paying a number of visits to the Justice Bureau, Pak was finally allowed to view his records. This was the first time that the Japanese government had ever granted access to such official documents. Following Pak, ten other individuals were also permitted to view the "deposits" list and confirm their names and the amount of their unpaid salaries. Pak's case was a great success on the part of our collective movement, and it has also stimulated subsequent movements to demand reparations.

Paralleling the movements in Hiroshima, Mitsubishi's corporate responsibility for its involvement in utilizing forced colonial labor has also been confirmed through different channels, namely, local social insurance offices and the Ministry of Health and Welfare. Until the late 1980s, both the Korean Laborers Collective and the Families of the Deceased Victims Association had struggled independently to demand reparations for forced labor. But since then, various groups in Asian countries began requesting that the Japanese government consider further reparations for various kinds of damages that had not been dealt with during governmental negotiations in the early postwar years. In the course of the new activism, it was revealed that all the mobilized Korean workers had been forced to participate in the government-sponsored Welfare Security Program (Kōsei nenkin hoken) through mandatory deductions of their salaries, and that individual workers' records of their premium payments had been permanently stored at local social insurance offices. The records of paid insurance premiums have so far served as the most crucial evidence that individuals demanding reparations had worked for Japanese companies. It was also discovered that the former workers were entitled further to special reimbursements upon their dismissal from the companies.

In Nagasaki, Kim Sun-gil confirmed his name on the identifying document and demanded reimbursement of his payments. The Ministry of Health and Welfare and the social insurance offices first rejected Kim's request, with the reasoning that the period of eligibility for such an action had expired. However, after several rounds of negotiations Kim succeeded in securing reimbursement from the Ministry of Health and Welfare. On 29 October 1996 he received the entire amount owed to him, 35 yen. The Ministry made no adjustments to account for currency value changes or interest that would have accrued. The entire process of Kim's struggles became the topic of an award-winning documentary made by Nagasaki Broadcasting Corporation. In 1994 Pak and three others followed Kim's lead. By April 1995 the certification of fifty-three laborers had been achieved, and Pak and his colleagues donated the money they received from the social insurance offices to the Hiroshima Red Cross/Atom Bomb Hospital.

In hindsight, it is clear that during the course of our movement we had two options: either to discontinue responding to the Justice Bureau's unreasonable demands and challenge its abusive attitude, or to continue to pursue our quest for full access to the records by submitting all required materials. In the end, we chose the latter option. However, this choice placed a tremendous burden on Pak. In fact, a victim of Japanese colonialism was further victimized in the course of condemning his aggressor. Most regrettably, none of us realized that Pak's health was deteriorating rapidly during this long process. The day before Pak was to visit the Bureau to finally access the records, he experienced heart failure and had to be hospitalized. Two Japanese lawyers and I went in his stead and viewed the list deposited by Mitsubishi for the first time in postwar history.

To be sure, the Justice Bureau warned that although Pak's right to access his documents had been confirmed, this did not imply that he would also be entitled to receive any unpaid salary. However, as the two lawyers who supported our cases stated at the press conference, the Justice Bureau's sudden change in posture in granting us access to the list was no doubt the result of the pressures placed on it by grassroots movements. In 1997 Shin Nihon Seitetsu agreed to pay approximately $174,000 to the families of former Korean mobilized workers who were killed in the atomic attack. The plaintiffs withdrew their case against the company but continue to fight legal battles against the Japanese government. Cases such as these provide us with great encouragement and hope.

Ongoing Struggles

Thus far, during the course of various trials and court hearings, the Japanese government has consistently insisted that even if the state was politically responsible for forced mobilization, it cannot be held legally liable for damages because the action occurred under the prewar constitution and a different body politic. It also maintains that the postwar Governmental Reparation Law (Kokka Baishōhō) cannot be applied retroactively to the period prior to its enactment.

Mitsubishi has also insisted that the present company is an entirely different corporate organization. To be sure, Mitsubishi's official history includes references to its entire development over the past hundred years. Yet, it maintains that the prewar Mitsubishi was a different legal entity. Moreover, it argues that the company was not directly involved in demobilization efforts. A separate company called Ryōjū became responsible for dissolving the Mitsubishi zaibatsu under the Allied Forces Occupation. Ryōjū exists to this day and maintains an office inside Mitsubishi's main building in Tokyo. We therefore filed a suit against Ryōjū as well, although some expressed concern that filing a suit against Ryōjū might be considered an endorsement of Mitsubishi's argument concerning itself as a corporation distinct from its prewar and wartime incarnation.

Currently we are waging legal battles at local courts in Hiroshima, Nagasaki, and Osaka, all in coalition with each other. We primarily focus on three areas in these ongoing lawsuits. We demand the payment of unpaid salaries. We demand clarification of the illegality of forced mobilization and acknowledgment of Mitsubishi's unlawful conduct, including its use of violence and discrimination against Korean workers, as well as full reparations for these acts. Finally, we demand relief and compensation for victims of the atomic bomb residing outside Japan. What distinguishes our cases against Mitsubishi in Hiroshima and Nagasaki from other cases demanding war and colonial reparations is the additional suffering resulting from the atomic bombs.

As of 1998 there are forty-one plaintiffs involved in various suits in Hiroshima. There they have testified to the coercive nature of mobilization by Mitsubishi, the unfulfilled promise to send 50 percent of salaries to families in Korea, discrimination in the workplace and dormitories, the atomic bomb attack, Mitsubishi's failure to properly demobilize workers, and the loss of land and other means of production resulting from mobilization. The suit in Nagasaki involved Kim Sun-gil; however, he passed away suddenly on 20 February 1997 and his suit has now been succeeded by his two bereaved sons and his supporters.

In Korea, antiwar and antinuclear movements have had difficulty developing due to the tensions aroused by U.S. cold war policy. Japan has therefore been home to both antinuclear and antiwar movements in the postwar years. However, the Japanese government and Japanese society remain indifferent to the abandoned bomb victims living abroad. As I mentioned earlier, there is no stipulation regarding nationality in the Hibakusha Relief Law and it is therefore applied to Koreans living in Japan. However, the Japanese government maintains that the law ceases to be applicable should a hibakusha move outside of Japanese territory. Thus far the Citizens Council has worked around this regulation by raising funds to bring *hibakusha* living abroad to Japan. Yet even more than to provide aid to Japanese atomic bomb victims like myself, I believe that we must work even harder to offer aid to victims residing in places other than Japan. The ongoing suit in Osaka focuses primarily on efforts to rectify the contradictions in the Hibakusha Relief Law's application.

I believe that responsibility for the long-term abandonment of the atomic bomb victims in Korea and elsewhere rests primarily with the Japanese government. In the 1952 San Francisco Peace Treaty the Japanese government relinquished every right to demand reparations from the United States. Later in 1963, five Japanese *hibakusha* and their families filed a lawsuit against the Japanese government. They argued that the government was obligated to provide governmental compensation to *hibakusha* because by signing the San Francisco Treaty it had disallowed the Japanese people from demanding reparations from the United States, despite the fact that use of two atomic weapons was a violation of international law. Ultimately the Tokyo District Court ruled that the plaintiffs do not have the right to demand individual reparations from the Japanese government, even though it acknowledged that use of atomic weapons violated international law. Here, both the Japanese government and the Court denied the Japanese government's responsibility to provide compensation. They reasoned that the government's signing of the San Francisco Treaty did not preclude the right of individual Japanese people to demand reparations from the United States. In contrast, the Japanese government has insisted that individuals who were formerly victimized by Japan cannot demand reparations from it because their individual right to do so had been dissolved by the ROK– Japan Basic Treaty and other similar postwar agreements. In this regard the 1963 atom bomb trial's affirmation of the right of one nation's citizens to demand compensation from another government, despite any treaties that might have been entered into by the two relevant governments, seems to hold important implications for the ongoing trials.

Finally, I believe that current legal inadequacies and contradictions also indicate a lack of remorse for past Japanese military and colonial aggression. Moreover, even though fifty years have elapsed since the war's end, racial discrimination against Koreans living in Japan continues. For these reasons as well it is imperative that we continue to pressure the Japanese government to live up to its responsibilities. We must take matters into our own hands to fight for the Korean victims, and the Japanese government should follow us in doing so. The two bombed cities, Hiroshima and Nagasaki, must uphold an unambiguous policy regarding these matters. Indeed, we must cry out for peace throughout the world.

Notes

Since Toyonaga first presented this paper in 1995 there have been a number of important developments. With the author's permission we have incorporated new information into this essay based on the following materials: Mitsubishi Hiroshima/Moto Chōyōkō Hibakusha Saiban o Shien suru Kai, *Mitsubishi wa mibarai chingin o shiharae!* (Mitsubishi ought to pay the unpaid wages!) (Hiroshima: Mitsubishi Hiroshima/Moto Chōyōkō Hibakusha Saiban o Shien suru Kai, 1996); Matsuda Motoji and Ichiba Junko, "Naigaijin fubyōdō no keifu: Nihon no hibakusha gyōsei to Kankokujin hibakusha" (Genealogy of unequal treatment of residents and nonresidents: Japan's *hibakusha* administration and South Korean *hibakusha*). *Sekai jinken mondai kenkyū sentā kenkyū kiyō* (World human rights issues study center research bulletin), no. 2 (March 1997): 145–65; *Hayaku kyūen o!* (Hurry relief!) nos. 102, 103, and 104 (March, July, September 1998); and an interview with Motoji Matsuda on 12 October 1998 at Kyoto University. The late effects of radiation are still underinvestigated. But for a good recent summary of findings, the author recommends Kusano Nobuko, compiler, *Atomic Bomb Injuries*, rev. ed. (Tokyo: Tsukiji Shokan, 1995).

1 Norma Field, "War and Apology: Japan, Asia, the Fiftieth, and After," *positions* 5, no. 1 (spring 1997): 1–49.

The Politics of War Memories toward Healing

CHUNGMOO CHOI

Pain is the very condition of a move towards no-pain, without, at the same time, obviating the need for the operation of sympathy.
—Rajeswari Sunder Rajan, *Real and Imagined Women*

The Violence of Gendered Silence

There is a grotesque but fantastic scene in the short story "The Island of Silence" (1987) written by South Korean Yi Wŏn-gyu. The narrative is about an uninhabited island off the west coast of Korea. On a tranquil sunny day, a frail old mother and her middle-aged son visit the island in search of the son's father, who disappeared during the Korean War almost forty years earlier. Until their visit, the raging waters surrounding the island permitted no one entrance. However, as the boat that carries the mother and son nears the island the sympathetic water subsides its rage and opens the way. There, in a valley hidden from external view, the two find scores of perfectly sun-dried white skeletons lying on rocky, black terrain under the clear blue sky. For forty years, the skeletons have been waiting there for their stories to be told and their rage and resentment to be appeased. These skeletons in their corporeality were denied dissension in the postcolonial ideological war and shared the fate of thousands of others: banishment into absolute silence. The skeletons lying on this abandoned island silently attest to Korea's violent past and the repression thereof. The mother and son offer a ritual on the spot to appease the souls of the dead and bring back one skeleton for a proper burial. They have no way of knowing the identity of the skeleton, but theirs is a symbolic gesture to heal the wounds of thousands of others whose violent stories have been silenced.

Modern Korean history is the history of violence. Not properly healed, this violence has left a deep scar on the psyche of the Korean people and a bleeding wound in the everyday lives of the surviving victims. The case of the comfort women provides a prime example of such a wound. In this essay, I explore the politics of war memories toward healing, especially healing the wound of the comfort women.

Since three Korean women filed suit in December 1991 against the Japanese government for the atrocities its military afflicted on women in Asia, many women who have revealed their humiliating past have been suspended between public and private realms, hope and despair, while subjected to public scrutiny and even insults. Many others who have not come forward still live in fear of exposure and social stigma. Among the women who did step forward to let the world know about the war crimes, several have already passed away.

During these seven years, public efforts and activist movements to rectify this historical wrongdoing have been commendable. Various international and national women's organizations and NGOs have been involved in this movement to educate the public and to seek reparation for the victims. Although a few upper-echelon officials of the Japanese government have issued apologies, the work of paying reparations has been deferred to a private fund administered by a private organization, the Asian Women's Peace Foundation. This has created major controversy and painful division among the activists, comfort women, and policymakers of the victims' countries.[1] This fund is considered "sympathy money" privately raised from charitable individuals and organizations rather than official compensation that the Japanese government pays in accepting its wrongdoing against the women. In January 1997, one week prior to the visit of the Japanese minister of Foreign Affairs, the Foundation delivered promissory notes to a few Korean comfort women who agreed to receive the private fund. A few activist groups in South Korea protested that this was the Foundation's attempt to divide the victims and the activists, and tried to penalize these women by petitioning the South Korean government to stop its monthly living cost assistance payment, which the women had received since 1993. At the fountainhead of this controversy is the question of honor. The comfort women discourse maintains that only a proper apology from and reparation by the Japanese government will restore the victims' honor. The logic of this symbolic economics categorizes the privately raised money as "sympathy money" that would disgrace the victims once again by relegating them to the position of charity recipients. It is in this discursive context that some women who decided to accept money from the Foundation were severely criticized. On 21 April 1998, in the midst of unprecedented economic crisis, the Kim Dae Jung government of South Korea decided not to seek reparation from the Japanese government and instead offered $27,900 to each of 152 women who identified themselves as former comfort women.[2]

The South Korean government's decision to now pay the women stems from the humanitarian and practical consideration that these women are old and in dire financial need. The decision appears to stand against the formidably unsympathetic position of the Japanese government. There is no need for material compensation after the death of these women, and one may suspect that the Japanese government is waiting for the women to die so that it will not have to pay up. Yet the South Korean government's decision is more a political gesture to smooth its diplomatic relationship with Japan, especially in these tense economic times in Asia, than a recognition of these women's struggles. Furthermore, the decision signals the shift of the South Korean government's focus of the comfort women issue from reparation and war responsibility to morality. As if in response, on 27 April 1998 Yamaguchi District Court in southern Japan ruled that the Japanese government must pay $2,272 to three former comfort women from South Korea.[3] The Japanese government spokesperson, Muraoka Kanezō, called this court ruling regrettable, because it stood against the official position of the Japanese government. Notwithstanding all the political implications, the Japanese court ruling and the South Korean government's decision to pay the victims are certainly encouraging signs to the victims themselves. By freeing us of the need to take immediate action for the women's material economic status, these decisions offer us opportunities to further our thinking on the questions of war memories and the colonial past in Asia.

As we can see, the comfort women are caught in conflicting national agendas, which suppress the women's own subjectivity and often their basic material needs. Furthermore, these women's tragedy serves as a powerful instrument for Japan's former colonies to display their historical wounds and express anger toward their former colonial master for the imperial atrocities it committed. The comfort women's first small victory at the Yamaguchi Court notwithstanding, many questions still remain. How can the nominal amount of $2,272 restore the women's honor and undo the damage that was done to them at such a young age? More important, how does the global-level publicity, the local and international activism help the women and the nations in whose discourses they are caught to heal the wound that continues to bleed? Is any apology justly quantifiable to undo the wrongdoing or restore the lost opportunity of life? Is it not necessary to reformulate our question of "how much apology (or how much reparation) is enough,"[4] and redirect our energy by asking how to heal the wound? Such a strategic reformulation of the question may serve a further purpose of easing repressed antagonism between Japan and other Asian countries, especially when the Japanese government maintains a position of silent denial. The discourse and practice of healing may also intervene in the drive for masculinization in these countries under the name of anticolonial nationalism, a drive that generates self-destructive oppression within and beyond the respective national borders.

As signified by the body metaphor of this historical tragedy, the women's corporeal experiences lie at the core of the comfort women issue. The pain has registered on their bodies and memories: of repeated rape and the pain it causes; the pain from sessions of beating, torture, and mutilation that were frequently inflicted on their bodies; the dreadful weekly injection of Arsphenamine, which induces violent vomiting; the hunger; the rampant abuse of opium to ease both the bodily and ontological pain, and the painful seizures of its withdrawal. The list continues. As Elaine Scarry points out in *The Body in Pain*, one of the problematics of bodily pain is that it has no object outside the boundaries of the body. Scarry argues that because of the objectless nature of bodily pain, the capacity to experience physical pain, though primal to human experience, differs from other bodily and psychic events that have objective references. It is precisely the absence of reference that prevents this pain from being rendered in language.[5] In the discourse of comfort women, the memories of corporal pain that are inscribed in the women's bodies cannot be articulated in the present tense. Without language to represent it, the women's bodily pain is instead drowned in a magnified sense of national shame—particularly because their bodily experiences intersect with the discourse of anticolonial nationalism. As I have discussed elsewhere, anticolonial nationalism in Korea, as in most other former colonies, has been unmistakably gendered to privilege national masculinity.[6] The agenda of such gendered nationalism is to feminize the subjugated nation and thereby place it in the subordinate power position. It follows, then, that the teleological goal of such a struggle often envisions the remasculinization of the nation. Precisely because the bodily experience of the comfort women is that of sexual violation, the comfort women issue directly assaults the masculine desire of the Korean nation to overcome the symbolic emasculation that Japanese colonialism has left on the Korean male psyche.

Out of this desire emerges the need to redress the comfort women issue exclusively at the metaphoric level, which separates women's bodies from their experiences. It need not be emphasized that the Confucian patriarchal ideology that has objectified women as the property of men accounts for the initial erasure of women's subjectivity. Beyond the existing Confucian patriarchal ideology, anticolonial nationalism once again elides women's subjectivity. That is because anticolonial nationalism as a discourse of symbolic remasculinization represses women's subjectivity while it underscores their bodies. This enables nationalist discourse to remetaphorize and reequate the nation with women's bodies. From these perspectives it is not difficult to see why the comfort women movement with its anticolonial nationalist agenda chose to adopt the national-ist remetaphorization of women's bodies as signifiers of the violated nation. And this is precisely why the comfort women movement in South Korea by-passes the question of individual agency and subjectivity, and instead constructs the women solely as innocent virgins whose bodies have been violated. The nationalistic undertones of the comfort women discourse thus centralizes the national shame and the symbolic economics thereof, inducing collective am-nesia about the pain of these women. Indian feminist Lata Mani critiques the colonial discourse of sati, in which women who commit sati are not "subjects" or even "objects" but rather the ground of the discourse.[7] In a similar way, the comfort women discourse displaces the women's subjectivity, which is grounded on pain, and constructs the women only as symbols of national shame. As such, the primacy of the discourse on comfort women attends not to the welfare of women's subjectivity but to the national agenda of overcoming colonial emasculation.

This may explain why the comfort women discourse and movement in South Korea fail to address the issues of modern-day comfort women: the sex workers around the U.S. military bases. One of the major contentions regarding the comfort women is the Japanese government's involvement in the operation and management of the comfort station. Although the historical circumstances under which the Korean sex workers become involved in international prostitu-tion vary, the U.S. military prostitutes in South Korea are equally controlled by the U.S. and South Korean governments.[8] The military prostitutes are fre-quently subjected to violence and even murder, while the Status of Forces Agreement (SOFA) has protected the perpetrators from Korean law until re-cently. However, the issues of these sex workers fall on deaf ears among the comfort women activists. This may be due to Koreans' projection of melan-cholia, the mourning of Korean national subjectivity coupled with the sense of castration brought about by continued colonization. This sense of castration deepened and became increasingly problematic to the Korean patriarchy, which considered Korea masculine (near the center of the Sinocentric world order) and Japan feminine (at its edge). Drawing on Freud, we can conjecture that for South Korea, identifying with the Super Ego or the United States in all its display of hypermasculine military and capitalistic power, was a way of over-coming the shame of colonial emasculation. The comfort women discourse as a masculine nationalist discourse, then, cannot but avoid the issue of present-day military prostitution because it is an accomplice to the Oedipal process of masculinization.

Seen from this perspective, the current comfort women discourse, which aims to liberate women from the presence of pain, cannot adequately address the larger issue of military prostitution. That is because it is grounded not on women's subjectivity but on the constructed image of the women whose purity has been violated by the colonizing forces. In this way, the language of the Oedipally driven nationalistic discourse further disfranchises the women, allowing them very little power and denying them hope for truly meaningful expression. As the South Korean activists' petition to discontinue the governmental subsidy to comfort women that I described above signifies, the comfort women discourse, which should be used to express the women's painful experiences, could be oppressive in the name of the nation. The elision of the national discourse with women's bodies at the expense of female subjectivity confirms the assumptions of French feminist Hélène Cixous. Cixous maintains that official language is essentially male dominated as it is by a grammar of hierarchy, which is built into the linguistic order. Therefore, official language is inadequate to express women's experiences. From this position she calls for a language that would subvert and disrupt the masculine linguistic order.[9] Grounded on the masculinist nationalist language, the comfort women discourse is inadequate to articulate the physical and psychic problems of comfort women. The comfort women discourse that would heal these wounds, which are present in the lives of real women, not just metaphorized symbols of national subjugation, then requires an effective intervention.

One of the main causes of these women's wounds is not simply their lack of a subversive language but an absolute lack of language itself. For fifty years these women have been kept in forced silence. What is necessary to begin the healing process for them is what activist poet and critic Adrienne Rich calls women's "speaking silence." In her work, Rich pays attention to the ways in which women of color and colonial and working-class writers bring silence and speechlessness into their narratives. Through this process of breaking silence, the unnamed and misnamed in the received history can be recovered. Though agreeing with Cixous's distrust in official language, Rich sees the healing power of language.[10] For these women to speak their fifty years of silence, it is necessary for us to separate their subjectivity, grounded in pain, from the anticolonialist discourse that has represented them. That subjectivity should take into account the women's corporal and ontological experience of/in pain. We might turn to Rajeswari Sunder Rajan's suggestion for efficacious intervention into mystifying sati. Furthering Lata Mani's critique of sati discourse, Sunder Rajan points to its inefficacy as an interventive measure that excludes the women's pain of/in burning.[11] The politics of the comfort women discourse, as I have argued, has undergone a path similar to that of sati discourse in its construction of the women as signifiers of a victimized nation with no consideration of the women's subjectivity. Acknowledging the comfort women's subjectivity grounded on pain is essential for them to speak the gendered silence and to heal the wound that bleeds in ever-present memory.

Pain and Voice

In this vein I would like to examine three documentary films that may offer some useful insights into the ways in which women speak silence: 50 Years of Silence, made by Ned Lander for Australian SBS Television in 1994, and The Murmuring (1995) and Habitual Sadness (1997), both made by South Korean feminist filmmaker Byun Young-joo (Pyŏn Yŏng-ju). 50 Years of Silence is the story of a Dutch woman, Jan Ruff-O'Herne, who was drafted to provide sex to the Japanese officers in Indonesia and who is now living in Australia. The Murmuring depicts the lives of Korean comfort women: eight women who live in the Sharing House, a Buddhist-run refuge home in South Korea, and three who live working-class existences in Wuhan, China. Habitual Sadness is the sequel to The Murmuring, which tells the story of the women at the Sharing House two years later. In the Sharing House, eight women share not only their war memories but also present-day events, including participation in the weekly Wednesday Rally that occurs before the Japanese Embassy in Seoul, a practice that began in 1992.

Let us begin by meeting the women in The Murmuring. The interviews of the eight women in the Sharing House and the three women in Wuhan attest to the present tense of the women's pain in their daily lives, not only in their psyches but in their bodies as well. Most of the women complain about their illnesses and pains. Tears roll down Ha Kun-ja's wrinkled cheeks as she speaks for the first time of being raped at the age of sixteen by the Japanese Army doctor "who was older than my father" and the acute pain that the rape left on her body ("After that, it hurt so much I couldn't even go to pee"). She talks of the first rape of fifty years ago as if it happened yesterday. Her memories are vivid and her emotions fresh. When Hong Kang-rim speaks of how the Army doctor mutilated her vagina so that her body could receive a greater number of soldiers, the seventy-five-year-old woman trembles in fear and hatred. Her voice cracks, her teeth are clenched, and her speech is halting. We can clearly see that these women have rarely had opportunities to release their pent-up anger and resentment. Instead, they continue to relive their past in the present. The interviews with the three women in Wuhan are particularly striking because these women had been doubly silenced in the place where they were forced to survive: first in the Japanese language and then in the Chinese language. The third comfort woman in Wuhan is the oldest among the three but has lost her Korean language ability. While her Chinese daughter speaks of her mother's memories in terms only of pain, the mother sits next to the daughter and sobs. Fifty years have taken away not only her youth and dignity, but the woman's speech as well. To help ease the trauma of the women who had been deprived of opportunities of schooling, a feminist artist volunteered to give them art lessons. By 1995, when The Murmuring was completed, a few women at the Sharing House had begun painting. They began telling their stories visually in lieu of language and literacy.[12]

Compared to The Murmuring, which is filled with women fighting their resentment and lamenting their ruined lives, 50 Years of Silence in a way celebrates a woman who has managed to overcome her tragic past. 50 Years of Silence opens with an elegant, well-preserved Jan Ruff-O'Herne riding a bike to her upper-middle-class suburban house, a stark contrast to the state of the ailing Korean comfort women. 50 Years of Silence includes numerous clips from home movies and still photos that capture the prosperous and happy days of Ruff-O'Herne's extended Dutch family in colonized Indonesia before the war. When the war broke out, Ruff-O'Herne, a college graduate, was preparing to become a Catholic nun and teacher. Her dream to pursue a religious profession was shattered when her priest advised against it on hearing her confession of the violation of her body. Instead, she married a British soldier who came to Indonesia with the Armed Forces and she had her reproductive organs surgically reconstructed in order to bear children. After some years living in England, Ruff-O'Herne's family immigrated to Australia and has had a comfortable life there. Now her grown daughter, a professional painter, accompanies her to the international hearings of the comfort women.

The position of Jan Ruff-O'Herne is a world apart from that of Korean comfort women. She was part of a European colonial power that did not necessarily hold Japan in high esteem. In fact, the Japanese military acknowledged the power differentials based on race and treated Dutch women differently from the indigenous women. According to Ruff-O'Herne, when she resisted the Japanese officers' demands by cutting her hair she was threatened with removal to the thatched hut where indigenous girls were detained to serve the ordinary soldiers. Korean women, unlike Dutch women, were girls from the colony who were doubly subjugated both by the colonial power and by the desire of their own men to maintain a code of patriarchal masculinity.[13] In addition to the racial cum power differences, the enormous difference between Ruff-O'Herne and the Korean comfort women may not be unrelated to the politics of war memories in how these memories are structured and/or articulated. What may have contributed to the differences in the women's subject positions is the way in which the memories have been articulated or not allowed to be articulated. The scene that shows Ruff-O'Herne's poised and articulate testimony at the hearing in Tokyo cuts to the testimonial footage of Korean comfort woman Kim

Hak-sun, one of the three women who filed a suit in 1991. On screen Kim's emotion appears very raw and her anger still fresh.[14] Dramatic gesticulation in place of literary fluency accompanies Kim's angered and often halting speech. It is apparent that she has not had an opportunity to sort through her experiences in her own terms. Instead, she has acquired the official rhetoric of the comfort women discourse in Korea and articulates her experience in that language. Unfortunately, Kim's language is confined to the rhetoric of anticolonial nationalism of the South Korean comfort women discourse, which silences individual women's painful experiences. While Ruff-O'Herne candidly speaks of the impact of the repeated rape on her sexual life, no Korean comfort woman ever mentions any aspect of her sexuality. Instead, their language on the subject of sexuality is predominantly that of shame. It is once again evident that the anticolonial nationalist discourse, which completely desexualizes the comfort women issue, has made a great impact on the formation of the comfort women's subjectivity. During the interviews and the testimonial speech, Ruff-O'Herne protests that "comfort women" is a misnomer. She strongly objects to the use of the term and defines the women as "Japanese war rape victims." It is apparent that even in silence Ruff-O'Herne has had an opportunity to critically analyze and situate the nature of her personal tragedy in a historical context. Despite her tragic past, she has established a certain emotional distance and made peace with her life. In contrast, the lives of the Korean comfort women remain suspended and wandering in the unresolved past.

Seeing these differences, one cannot but wonder how Jan Ruff-O'Herne's speaking silence came about. She had not spoken about her past in public until the case of the three Korean comfort women reached the Australian media. The title of the film, *50 Years of Silence*, refers only to the silence in the public arena. Although Ruff-O'Herne and her mother never discussed what happened at the comfort station, she had told her sisters after they pledged secrecy. Ruff-O'Herne says she also discussed the matter in intimate detail with her then fiancé. In her own words, her husband had been supportive of her all his life, even when she herself could not enjoy sexual intercourse due to the memory of repeated rape. Indeed, it was her husband who reported the sexual slavery of Dutch women to the Allied authorities and helped her undergo reconstructive surgery after their marriage. Since she told her daughters of her tragedy, one daughter has produced numerous paintings that are based on her mother's stories of sexual slavery. In addition, she has written a detailed log of what happened at the comfort station in preparation for telling the story at some future time. It is obvious from the film that Ruff-O'Herne not only shared the nightmarish war memories with her close family members, who, in return, supported her, but also that the painful memories have been kept alive and relived in artistic and literary articulation. One can imagine the mother and daughter spending many hours re-membering and analyzing the darkest moments of the mother's past. Through this process of "speaking silence," Jan Ruff-O'Herne has found a language and voice of her own. All in all, her traumatic past has had relatively little impact on her life conditions. Indeed, the celebratory cinematic images of her surrounded by a large number of extended family members attest to her dignified and blessed life. In other words, although war memories haunt the life of Ruff-O'Herne, they do not govern her life with the kind of intensity that seems to grip the Korean comfort women.

What is instructive in the case of Jan Ruff-O'Herne is the process of her "speaking silence" in the private sphere, which seems to have contributed to easing the pain. One may imagine ways of channeling this strategy of nonofficial speaking silence into a more public space of far-reaching and constructive results. So far, the energy of the comfort women movement has concentrated on the balance in symbolic economics that would restore the honor of comfort women as dignified human beings. Activists demand that the Japanese government offer reparation and proper apology. In other words, the key to restore the women's honor remains in the hands of the Japanese government. Under the circumstances, the victims continue to be kept in the position of passive recipients of honor. Although the Japanese government is undoubtedly responsible for restoring justice and rectifying historical wrongs, we also need to pursue a way of bringing the women themselves to center stage in an effort to heal their wounds by transforming their own subjectivities.

It is noteworthy that a few Korean comfort women have attempted to speak their silence in the nonofficial public sphere by becoming shamans. In the absence of "official" ways of healing their wounds, these women have appropriated culturally available healing devices. The workings of shamanic ritual offer useful insights into the ways of making the privatized way of speaking silence a possibility for collective healing. Shamanism in Korea has long been marginalized outside the dominant organized religions. Consequently, the practitioners of shamanism and participants in the rituals are almost exclusively women. Shamanic ritual often is the site where oppressed women bring their resentment and grudges to public attention. The Korean notion of han, the pent-up resentment that can bring destruction into human relationships, stems from a situation where such repressed emotion is not allowed to emerge. Simply put, when the oppressed people are not allowed to speak their silence, their pent-up energy explodes into something destructive. Shamanic ritual often facilitates an occasion where oppressed people, especially women, find opportunities to sublimate han. In the context of the ritual, the participating women analyze the etiological source of the problems and together reach a resolution. What is often described of ritual's efficacy in the ethnographical literature as symbolic transformation is not a change in actual situation but a transformation of the perception of reality. In other words, what the shaman and her clients achieve is the transformation of their subjectivity, which contributes to the healing of their wounds.[15] This transformation takes place by way of locating the source of the problem within the culturally constructed map of social reality. Furthermore, in the course of clarifying and articulating the problem, the women are allowed and encouraged to speak the silenced and repressed issues. The ritual provides a culturally constructed religious language with which to articulate the problems. Culturally, the shamans are believed to have undergone a lengthy bout of symbolic illness, through which experience they acquire the ability to see others' suffering. As a seer and healer, the shaman facilitates a forum where women can share their experience of suffering. During the ritual, women often speak on forbidden and repressed subjects such as sexuality rather freely in the pretext of fantastic religious imagination. In that sense, shamanic ritual offers an alternative space for women who are confined in the normative boundary of Confucian patriarchy.

It is in this cultural context that Japanese artist-activist Tomiyama Taeko's painting The Night of the Festival of Garungan, (1986)—one of two oil paintings collectively titled Memory of the Sea—imagines a way of healing the emotional and physical wounds of war.[16] In The Night of the Festival of Garungan Tomiyama depicts a Korean shaman's spiritual journey to the South Pacific in search of the dead comfort women. The shaman encounters there the remains of a sunken Japanese Navy ship that was carrying both soldiers and comfort women. Tomiyama sees through the shaman's eyes that death at the bottom of the sea has not been consummated. Using the Korean shamanic imagination, Tomiyama depicts most of the dead bodies not yet cleansed. The corpses at the bottom of the sea are still wearing flesh, which signifies that the souls of the dead have not been liberated from the memories of the suffering body. Like zombies, the war victims are still living in death. There, at the bottom of the ocean, the shaman makes a food offering. Tomiyama borrows visual images of the Indonesian Garungan festival, the festival of offering food to appease the dead. The ritual in the painting anticipates the liberation of the souls from the memories. As such, the shaman in the middle of the painting starts collecting emancipated skeletons by her side. By doing so, the shaman in Memory of the Sea makes the presence of pain recede into the permanent past. In other words, Tomiyama's painting is an attempt not only to recuperate the horrible war memories but also to liberate the souls of the victims from that memory. In this way, the painting itself is performing the healing ritual of cleansing and liberating.

Figure 1. Tomiyama Taeko, *Memory of the Sea*. Oil on canvas. (Used by permission of the artist)

The film *Habitual Sadness* suggests a similar possibility. *Habitual Sadness* was made at the request of the comfort women themselves. As a sequel to *The Murmuring*, the film captures the everyday lives of the eight women at the Sharing House with no specific purpose other than the camera and the filmmaking crew witnessing the last days of Kang Tŏk-kyŏng, who was then dying of cancer and eventually died in January 1997. In her last days, Kang became known for her paintings that vividly recuperate memories of the comfort women and articulate their *han*. Initially, Korean feminists criticized *Habitual Sadness* for its lack of political agenda and clear cinematic direction.[17] However, if we consider feminist documentary filmmaking as cultural activism rather than cultural representation, the making of Habitual Sadness has elicited an effect similar to that of any successful shamanic ritual. The women in Habitual Sadness do not characterize their lives with a sense of shame, as they did three years earlier when they were interviewed for The Murmuring. Instead, they express a healthy pursuit of self-reliance rather than an acceptance of helpless passivity. They articulate their sexuality, albeit in the form of songs and jokes. The women also express their cherished dreams, even with a clear knowledge of their near impossibility. They articulate their desire to educate the world of the wrongdoing of the Japanese government with commitment rather than raw bitterness. In the sequel, the women have gained humor and laughter and a resolute sense of independence. The Murmuring brims over with the dangerous and uncontrollable memories told by women whose war wounds and memories have been neglected for half a century; in a way, the title of the film is a misnomer. The dominating voice of the film is more the wailing of suffering women than murmuring, although the passivity of the women is much pronounced. The title Habitual Sadness is another misnomer, for the women in this film are no longer passive, nor do they dwell in habitual sadness. The eight women in Habitual Sadness demonstrate that their collective sharing of war memories free from the official language has made them assertive and active. They have been healing their wounds through the years of speaking their silence verbally and visually to the camera (and its crew) and among themselves. They have found the power of language through which their subjectivity has been transformed. This is what gives them strength and dignity. In other words, it is neither an apology nor compensation money but the power of language that has allowed the women to speak fifty years of silence and helped to heal their wounds.

Fifty years after the end of the Pacific War, silencing and denying its horrors remain the dominant mode of operation in Japan as well as in other Asian countries. Silencing impregnates violence. It prevents war survivors from healing, and instead leaves their individual wounds and the collective national wound open and bleeding. The merit of a nationalistic approach is that it addresses the rectification of historical wrongdoings. However, this approach does not heal the psychic and subjective wounds but deepens them when not properly executed. As I have demonstrated above, the healing power of language(s) outside the circuit of hierarchical masculine language can be useful not just for the healing of comfort women or women at the margin, but for all those whose psyches have been damaged by war and silenced war memories. The question then is how to open up and facilitate such a space so they can speak the pain of war memories and their subjectivity grounded on pain transformed.

Notes

1 On the issue of private foundations, see Chungmoo Choi, "Guest Editor's Introduction," in *Comfort Women: Colonialism, War, and Sex*, special issue of *positions* 5, no. 1 (spring 1997).

2 "Kagŭi, wianbu 49ŏgwŏn chiwŏn ŭigyŏl" (Cabinet decided to pay 49 billion wŏn to the comfort women), *Hanguk Ilbo* (Korea Times), 21 April 1998.

3 "Japan Ordered to Compensate 3 Sex Slaves," *Los Angeles Times*, 28 April 1998.

4 See Norma Field, "War and Apology: Japan, Asia, the Fiftieth, and After," in *Comfort Women: Colonialism, War, and Sex*, special issue of *positions* 5, no. 1 (spring 1997): 1–49.

5 Elaine Scarry, *The Body in Pain* (Oxford: Oxford University Press, 1985).

6 For general discussion, see Elaine H. Kim and Chungmoo Choi, eds., *Dangerous Women: Gender and Nationalism in Korea* (New York: Routledge, 1998).

7 Lata Mani, "Contentious Traditions," in *Recasting Women*, ed. Kumkum Sangari and Sudesh Vaid (New Brunswick, NJ: Rutgers University Press, 1990), 152.

8 Katharine H. S. Moon, "Prostitute Bodies and Gendered States in U.S.-Korea Relations," in *Dangerous Women*, ed. Kim and Choi, 141–74.

9 Hélène Cixous, "The Laugh of the Medusa," in *New French Feminisms*, ed. Elaine Marks and Isabelle de Courtivron (New York: Schocken Books, 1981), 256.

10 See Jane Hoogestraat, " 'Unnamable by Choice': Multivalent Silences in Adrienne Rich's *Time's Power*," on *Violence, Silence, and Anger: Women's Writing as Transgression*, ed. Dierdre Lashgari (Charlottesville: University Press of Virginia, 1995), 25–37.

11 Rajeswari Sunder Rajan, "The Subject of Sati," in *Real and Imagined Women* (London: Routledge, 1993), 15–39.

12 Among these paintings, several by Kim Sun-dŏk and Kang Tŏk-kyŏng are introduced in *positions* 5, no. 1 (spring 1995): 277–78.

13 I discuss this issue in more detail in "Nationalism and Construction of Gender in Korea," in *Dangerous Women*, ed. Kim and Choi, 9–31.

14 In the scene, Jan Ruff-O'Herne, a well-preserved, elegant woman, calmly testifies on the atrocities of the Japanese military and her own sexual problems, a deep imprint that the fear of repeated rape at the comfort station had left on her psyche. Poised, well-coifed, and in elegant blue business suit, Ruff-O'Herne reads the prepared statement, followed by Kim Hak-sun in traditional Korean white dress, who wails and shouts her accusation of the brutality of sex slavery and her shame. The striking difference between the two consecutive scenes almost confirms the Orientalistic construction of virile and rational West versus irrational and feminized Orient, especially when Kim's speech/wail is not translated or subtitled. This untranslated wail could give the English-speaking audience an impression of an unintelligible, primitive cry of an Asian woman. The contrast between the modern and tradition is also signified in the two women's respective dress. The mise-en-scène and theatricality of the testimony scenes may not be an intended construction on the part of the filmmaker. If it is, it is not the major concern of this essay. I would rather address the question of the presentation of self of these two women. What historical factors may have allowed such dramatic differences, and what does that mean for the politics of the comfort women movement?

15 Chungmoo Choi, "The Artistry of the Shamans and the Ritual Aesthetics in Korea," *Journal of Ritual Studies* 3, no. 2 (summer 1989): 235–49.

16 Tomiyama Taeko, "Silenced by History," in *Chonggun wianburŭl wihan chinhongok* (Requiem for the military comfort women), ed. Yi Kwan-hun (Seoul: Tonga Gallery, 1995). For a

further discussion of Tomiyama's work, see Rebecca Jennison, " 'Postcolonial' Feminist Locations: The Art of Tomiyama Taeko and Shimada Yoshiko," *U.S.-Japan Women's Journal*, no. 12 (1997): 84–108.

17 Kim Soyoung and Kim Eun-shil, "Conversation," in *Najŭn moksori II chejak notŭ* (*Habitual Sadness* production notes), ed. Boim (Seoul: Boim, 1997).

≡ Bibliography

Abu, Talib Ahmad. "The Impact of the Japanese Occupation on the Malay-Muslim Population." In *Malaya and Singapore during the Japanese Occupation*, ed. Paul H. Kratoska. Special issue of *Journal of Southeast Asian Studies*, Singapore, Special Publication Series, no. 3 (1995).

Ada, Joseph, and Leland Bettis. "The Quest for Commonwealth, the Quest for Change." In *Kinalamten Pulitikat—Siñenten I Chamorro/Issues in Guam's Political Development: The Chamorro Perspective.* Mangilao, Guam: Guam Political Status Education Coordination Commission, 1996.

Adams, Ansel. *Born Free and Equal.* New York: U.S. Camera, 1944.

Adams, Michael C. C. *The Best War Ever: America and World War II.* Baltimore: Johns Hopkins University Press, 1994.

Adorno, Theodor W. "What Does Coming to Terms with the Past Mean?" In *Bitburg in Moral and Political Perspective*, ed. Geoffrey H. Hartman. Bloomington: Indiana University Press, 1986.

Aisha, Akbhar. *Aishabee at War: A Very Frank Memoir.* Singapore: Landmark Books Pte Ltd., 1990.

Akashi, Yoji. "The Anti-Japanese Movement in Perak during the Japanese Occupation 1941–45." In *Malaya and Singapore during the Japanese Occupation*, ed. Paul H. Kratoska. Special issue of *Journal of Southeast Asian Studies*, Singapore, Special Publication Series, no. 3 (1995).

——. "Japanese Cultural Policy in Malaya and Singapore 1942–45." In *Japanese Culture Policies in Southeast Asia during World War II*, ed. Grant K. Goodman. London: Macmillan, 1992.

——. "Japanese Military Administration in Malaya: Its Formation and Evolution in Reference to Sultans, the Islamic Religion and the Moslem-Malays, 1941–1945." *Asian Studies* 7, no. 1 (1969).

Akiyama Masami. *Shōjotachi no Shōwashi* (Girls' Shōwa history). Tokyo: Shinchōsha, 1992.

Allen, Ernest V. "When Japan Was 'Champion of the Darker Races': Satokata Takahashi and the Flowering of Black Messianic Nationalism." *The Black Scholar* 24, no. 1 (1995): 29–37.

——. "Waiting for Tojo: The Pro-Japan Vigil of Black Missourians." *Gateway Heritage* 15, no. 2 (fall 1994): 16–33.

Alperovitz, Gar. *The Decision to Use the Atomic Bomb and the Architecture of an American Myth.* New York: Knopf, 1995.

———. *Atomic Diplomacy: Hiroshima and Potsdam.* New York: Simon and Schuster, 1965.

Alvarez-Cristobal, Hope. "The Organization of Peoples for Indigenous Rights: A Commitment towards Self-Determination." *Pacific Ties* 13, no. 4 (1990): 10–11, 14–15, 17, 21.

Anderson, Benedict. "Japan: The Light of Asia." In *Southeast Asia in World War II: Four Essays,* ed. Josef Silverstein. New Haven: Yale University Press, 1966.

Ang, Ien, and Jon Stratton. "The Singapore Way in Multiculturalism: Western Concepts/Asian Cultures." Paper presented in the public lecture series on "Multiculturalism in a Global Context," East-West Center, Honolulu, 4 August 1994.

Antze, Paul, and Michael Lambek, eds. *Tense Past: Cultural Essays in Trauma and Memory.* New York: Routledge, 1996.

Aramaki Yoshio. *Konpeki no Kantai* (The Deep Blue Fleet). Vols. 1–20. Tokyo: Tokuma Shoten, 1990–1996.

———. *Kyokujitsu no kantai* (The fleet Rising Sun). Vols. 1–16. Tokyo: Kodansha, 1992–1996.

Asada, Akira. "Infantile Capitalism and Japan's Postmodernism: A Fairy Tale." In *Postmodernism and Japan,* ed. Masao Miyoshi and H. D. Harootunian. Durham, NC: Duke University Press, 1989.

Asahi Shinbun. *Asahi shinbun midashi dēta bēsu* (*Asahi shinbun* headlines database). Tokyo: Asahi Shinbunsha, 1995.

Asan Beach Guide. Agana, Guam: War in the Pacific National Historical Park and Arizona Memorial Museum Association, 1994.

Azuma Hiroki. *Yūbinteki fuantachi* (Postal anxieties). Tokyo: Asahi Shinbunsha, 1999.

Azuma Shirō. *Waga Nankin puratūn* (Our Nankin platoon). Tokyo: Aoki Shoten, 1987.

Bailey, Beth, and David Farber. *The First Strange Place: Race and Sex in World War II Hawai'i.* Baltimore: Johns Hopkins University Press, 1993.

Baldwin, James. *The Devil Finds Work.* New York: Dell, 1976.

———. *The Fire Next Time.* New York: Dial, 1963.

Balibar, Etienne, and Immanuel Wallerstein. "Racism and Nationalism." In *Race, Nation, Class,* trans. Chris Turner. London: Verso, 1991.

Banta, Melissa, and Curtis M. Hinsley. *From Site to Sight: Anthropology, Photography, and the Power of Imagery.* Cambridge, MA: Peabody Museum Press, 1986.

Baraka, Amiri (LeRoi Jones). *Blues People.* New York: Random House, 1963.

Barnouw, Eric. "Hiroshima-Nagasaki, August 1945." In *Transmission,* ed. Peter D'Agostino and David Tafler. Thousand Oaks, CA: Sage, 1995.

Basinger, Jeanine. *The World War II Combat Film.* New York: Columbia University Press, 1986.

Bate, David. "Photography and the Colonial Vision." *Third Text* 22 (spring 1993): 81–91.

Befu, Harumi, ed. *Cultural Nationalism in East Asia.* Berkeley, CA: Institute of East Asian Studies, University of California, 1993.

Bellah, Robert N. *Tokugawa Religion: The Values of Pre-Industrial Japan.* Glencoe, IL: Free Press, 1957.

Benedict, Ruth. *The Chrysanthemum and the Sword.* Boston: Houghton Mifflin, 1946.

Benjamin, Walter. "Theses on the Philosophy of History." In *Illuminations*, ed. Hannah Arendt, trans. Harry Zohn. New York: Schocken Books, 1969.

Berlant, Lauren. *The Anatomy of National Fantasy.* Chicago: University of Chicago Press, 1991.

Bernstein, Barton. "Understanding the Atomic Bomb and the Japanese Surrender: Missed Opportunities, Little-Known Near Disasters, and Modern Memory," *Diplomatic History* 19, no. 2 (spring 1995).

——, ed. *The Atomic Bomb: The Critical Issues.* Boston: Little, Brown, 1976.

Beros, H. "Bert." *The Fuzzy Wuzzy Angels and Other Verses.* Sydney: F. H. Johnston Publishing Company, 1944.

Bettis, Leland. "Colonial Immigration of Guam." In *A World Perspective in Pacific Islander Migration: Australia, New Zealand and the U.S.A.*, ed. Grant McCall and John Connell. Kensington, NSW: Centre for South Pacific Studies, 1993.

Beveridge, Senator Alfred J. "Our Philippine Policy." In *The Philippines Reader*, ed. Daniel B. Schirmer and Stephen Rosskam Shalom. Boston: South End Press, 1997.

Blaz, Ben. "Chamorros Yearn for Freedom." In *Liberation: Guam Remembers.* Agana, Guam: Golden Salute Committee, 1994.

Bodnar, John. *Remaking America: Public Memory, Commemoration, and Patriotism in the Twentieth Century.* Princeton, NJ: Princeton University Press, 1992.

Boggs, James. *The American Revolution: Pages from a Negro Worker's Notebook.* New York: Monthly Review Press, 1963.

Bordallo, Penelope. "A Campaign for Political Rights on Guam, Mariana Islands, 1899–1950." Master's thesis, University of Hawai'i at Manoa, 1982.

Boyarin, Jonathan. *Storm from Paradise: The Politics of Jewish Memory.* Minneapolis: University of Minnesota Press, 1992.

——, ed. *Remapping Memory: The Politics of TimeSpace.* Minneapolis: University of Minnesota Press, 1994.

"Breakthrough Books." *Lingua Franca* (March–April 1995): 16–17.

Browne, Nick. "Race: The Political Unconscious of American Film." *East-West Journal* 6, no. 1 (1992): 5–16.

Bruner, Jerome. *Acts of Meaning.* Cambridge, MA: Harvard University Press, 1990.

Buruma, Ian. *The Wages of Guilt: Memories of War in Germany and Japan.* New York: Farrar, Straus and Giroux, 1994.

Byers, Paul. "Cameras Don't Take Pictures." *Columbia University Forum* 9, no. 1 (1966): 27–33.

Capeci, Dominic J., Jr. *Race Relations in Wartime Detroit: The Sojourner Truth Housing Controversy of 1942.* Philadelphia: Temple University Press, 1984.

Carano, Paul. "Liberation Day: Prelude to Freedom. Lean Liberty Is Better Than Fat Slavery." *Guam Recorder* 3, no. 3 (July–September 1973): 3–9.

——. "The Liberation of Guam." *Guam Recorder* 2, nos. 2–3 (April–September 1972): 2–8.

Carucci, Laurence M. "The Source of the Force in Marshallese Cosmology." In *The Pacific Theater: Island Representations of World War II*, ed. G. M. White and L. Lindstrom. Honolulu: University of Hawai'i Press, 1989.

Chambers, Iain. *Migrancy, Culture, Identity.* London: Routledge, 1994.

Chan, Heng Chee. *Singapore: The Politics of Survival, 1965–1967.* Singapore: Oxford University Press, 1971.

Chan, Suchen. *Asian Americans.* Boston: Twayne Publishers, 1991.

Cheah, Boon Kheng. "Resistance and Social Conflict during and after the Japanese Occupation, 1941–1946." In *Red Star over Malaya.* Singapore: Singapore University Press, 1983.

Chin, Frank. "Come All Ye Asian American Writers of the Real and the Fake." In *The Big Aiieeeee,* ed. Jeffrey Paul Chan et al. New York: Meridian, 1991.

Chin, Kee Onn. *Malaya Upside Down.* Singapore: Jitts, 1946.

China Institute, compiler. *Chūgoku nenkan 1970* (China yearbook 1970). Tokyo: Taishūdō, 1970.

Chinese Association for the Study of the History of the Sino-Japanese Relations. *Riben de Zhongguo yimin* (Chinese immigrants in Japan). Beijing: Shijei Zhishi Chubanshe, 1987.

Choi, Chungmoo. "Nationalism and Construction of Gender in Korea." In *Dangerous Women: Gender and Korean Nationalism,* ed. Elaine H. Kim and Chungmoo Choi. New York: Routledge, 1998.

——. "Guest Editor's Introduction." *positions* 5, no. 1 (spring 1997): v–xiv.

——. "The Discourse of Decolonization and Popular Memory: South Korea." *positions* 1, no. 1 (spring 1993): 77–102.

——. "The Artistry of the Shamans and the Ritual Aesthetics in Korea." *Journal of Ritual Studies* 3, no. 2 (summer 1989): 235–49.

——, ed. *The Comfort Women: Colonialism, War and Sex.* Special issue of *positions* 5, no. 1 (1997).

Chōsen Sōtokufu Jōhōka. *Atarashiki Chōsen* (The new Korea). Reprint ed. Tokyo: Fūtōsha, 1982.

Chōsengun gaiyōshi. Reprint ed. Tokyo: Fuji Shuppan, 1989.

Chou, Cindy. *Beyond the Empires: Memories Untold.* Singapore: National Heritage Board, 1995.

Chua, Beng Huat. "Culture, Multiracialism and National Identity in Singapore." *Department of Sociology Working Papers* 125. Singapore: National University of Singapore, 1995.

Cixous, Hélène. "The Laugh of the Medusa." In *New French Feminisms,* ed. Elaine Marks and Isabelle de Courtivron. New York: Schocken Books, 1981.

Cloake, John. *Templer, Tiger of Malaya: The Life of Field Marshal Sir Gerald Templer.* London: Harrap, 1985.

Collins, Donald E. *Native American Aliens: Disloyalty and the Renunciation of Citizenship by Japanese Americans during World War II.* Westport, CT: Greenwood, 1985.

Commission on Wartime Relocation and Internment of Civilians. *Personal Justice Denied.* Washington, DC: U.S. Government Printing Office, 1982.

Committee for the Compilation of Sources on the "Nanjing Massacre." *Qin-Hua Rijun Nanjing datusha shigao* (A draft history of the Nanjing Massacre by the Japanese troops that invaded China). Nanjing: Jiangsu Guji Chubanshe, 1987. English rendition in original.

Committee for the Compilation of Sources on the "Nanjing Massacre" and the Library of Nanjing. *Qin-Hua Rijun Nanjing datusha dang'an* (Archival documents relating to the horrible Massacre by Japanese troops in Nanjing in December 1937). Nanjing: Jiangsu Guji Chubanshe, 1987. English rendition in original.

——. *Qin-Hua Rijun Nanjing datusha shiliao* (Source materials relating to the horrible massacre committed by the Japanese troops in Nanjing in December 1937). Nanjing: Jiangsu Guji Chubanshe, 1985. English rendition in original.

Coser, Lewis A., ed. *Maurice Halbwachs on Collective Memory.* Chicago: University of Chicago Press, 1992.

Costello, John. *The Pacific War.* New York: Quill, 1982.

Crost, Lyn. *Honor by Fire.* Novato, CA: Presidio Press, 1994.

Cumings, Bruce. "The Origins and Development of the Northeast Asian Political Economy: Industrial Sectors, Product Cycles, and Political Consequences." *International Organization* 38, no. 1 (winter 1984): 1–40.

——. *The Origins of the Korean War: Liberation and the Emergence of Separate Regimes.* Princeton, NJ: Princeton University Press, 1981.

Daniels, Roger. *Concentration Camps USA: Japanese Americans and World War II.* New York: Holt, Rinehart, and Winston, 1971.

Davis, Natalie Zemon, and Randolph Starn, eds. Special issue of *Memory and Counter-Memory. Representations* 26 (spring 1989).

Deme Masanobu. *Production Notes: Kike, Wadatsumi no koe* (Production notes: Listen to the voices of Wadatsumi). Tokyo: Tōei, 1995.

Diaz, Vicente M. *Repositioning the Missionary: History, Culture, Power and Religion in Guam.* Honolulu: University of Hawai'i Press, forthcoming.

——. "Simply Chamorro: Tales of Survival and Demise in Guam." *The Contemporary Pacific* 6, no. 2 (spring 1994): 29–58.

——. "Pious Sites: Chamorro Culture between Spanish Catholicism and American Liberalism." In *Cultures of U.S. Imperialism,* ed. Amy Kaplan and Donald Pease. Durham, NC: Duke University Press, 1993.

Diller, Elizabeth, and Ricardo Scofidio. *Back to the Front: Tourisms of War.* Princeton, NJ: Princeton Architectural Press, 1994.

Dingman, Roger. "Reflections on Pearl Harbor Anniversaries Past." *Journal of American–East Asian Relations* 3, no. 3 (1994): 279–93.

Dirlik, Arif. "Confucius in the Borderlands: Global Capitalism and the Reinvention of Confucianism." *boundary* 22, no. 3 (fall 1995): 229–73.

——. "'Past Experience, If Not Forgotten, Is a Guide to the Future'; or What Is in a Text? The Politics of History in Chinese-Japanese Relations." In *Japan in the World,* ed. Masao Miyoshi and Harry Harootunian. Durham, NC: Duke University Press, 1993.

Dower, John. "Japanese Cinema Goes to War." *Japan Society Newsletter* (1987).

——. *War without Mercy: Race and Power in the Pacific War.* New York: Pantheon Books, 1986.

Dower, John, and John Junkerman. *The Hiroshima Murals.* New York: Kodansha, 1986.

Drinnon, Richard. *Keeper of Concentration Camps: Dillon S. Myer and American Racism.* Berkeley: University of California Press, 1987.

Duan Yueping. "Qin-Hua Rijun Nanjing Datusha Yunan Tongbao Jinianguan de zhanlan huodong" (Exhibitions at the Nanjing Massacre Memorial). *Kang-Ri zhanzheng yanjiu* (1992): 175–89.

Du Bois, W. E. B. *Black Reconstruction in America*. New York: Simon and Schuster, 1995.

——. *Dark Princess*. Jackson: University Press of Mississippi, 1995.

Dudziak, Mary. "Desegregation as Cold War Imperative." In *Critical Race Theory*, ed. Richard Delgado. Philadelphia: Temple University Press, 1995.

Duus, Masayo. *Unlikely Liberators: The Men of the 100th and 442nd*, trans. Peter Duus. Honolulu: University of Hawai'i Press, 1987.

Duus, Peter. "Japan's Wartime Empire: Problems and Issues." In *The Japanese Wartime Empire, 1931–1945*, ed. Peter Duus et al. Princeton, NJ: Princeton University Press, 1996.

Edom, Clifton C. "Photo-Propaganda: The History of Its Development." *Journalism Quarterly* 24 (1947): 221–26, 238.

Edwards, Elizabeth. Introduction to *Anthropology and Photography 1860–1920*, ed. Elizabeth Edwards. New Haven: Yale University Press, 1992.

Emi, Frank. "Resistance: The Heart Mountain Fair Play Committee's Fight for Justice." *amerasia journal* 17, no. 1 (1991): 49.

Enloe, Cynthia H. *The Morning After: Sexual Politics at the End of the Cold War*. Berkeley: University of California Press, 1993.

——. *Ethnic Soldiers: State Security in Divided Societies*. Athens: University of Georgia Press, 1980.

Escobar, Edward. "The Dialectics of Repression: The Los Angeles Police Department and the Chicano Movement, 1968–1971." *Journal of American History* 74, no. 4 (March 1993): 1483–504.

Espiritu, Yen Le. *Asian American Panethnicity*. Philadelphia: Temple University Press, 1992.

Essien-Udom, E. U. *Black Nationalism: A Search for Identity in America*. Chicago: University of Chicago Press, 1962.

Evanzz, Karl. *The Judas Factor: The Plot to Kill Malcolm X*. New York: Thunder's Mouth, 1992.

Falgout, Suzanne, Lin Poyer, and Laurence M. Carucci. " 'The Greatest Hardship': Micronesian Memories of World War II." *Isla: A Journal of Micronesian Studies* 3, no. 2 (1995): 203–22.

Fanon, Frantz. *Wretched of the Earth*. Trans. Constance Farrington. New York: Grove Press, 1968.

——. *Black Skin, White Masks*. Trans. Charles Lam Markmann. New York: Grove Press, 1967.

Farrell, Don. *The Pictorial History of Guam: Liberation 1944*. Agana, Guam: Micronesian Publications, 1984.

Faust, Drew Gilpin. "The Civil War's 'Riddle of Death.' " *Chronicle of Higher Education* (February 1997): A6.

Ferguson, Kathy E., and Phyllis Turnbull. "Narratives of History, Nature, and Death at the National Memorial Cemetery of the Pacific." *Frontiers* 16, nos. 2–3 (1996): 1–23.

Feuerwerker, Albert, ed. *History in Communist China*. Cambridge, MA: MIT Press, 1968.

Field, Norma. "War and Apology: Japan, Asia, the Fiftieth, and After." *positions* 4, no. 1 (spring 1997): 1–49.

——. *In the Realm of a Dying Emperor: Japan at Century's End.* 1991; New York: Vintage Books, 1993.

Fifi'i, Jonathan. "World War II and the Origins of Maasina Rule." In *The Big Death: Solomon Islanders Remember World War II,* ed. G. M. White et al. Suva, Fiji: Institute of Pacific Studies, 1988.

Fischer, Humphrey J. *Ahmadiyah.* Oxford: Oxford University Press, 1963.

Franklin, John Hope. "Their War and Mine." *Journal of American History* 77, no. 3 (September 1990): 576–78.

——. *From Slavery to Freedom: A History of Negro Americans.* New York: Knopf, 1974.

Fu Zeng. "Nanjing datusha yu Riben diguozhuyi" (The Great Nanjing Massacre and Japanese imperialism). *Jindaishi yanju* 16 (February 1983).

Fujioka Nobukatsu. *Ojoku no kingendaishi: ima kokufuku no toki* (A disgraceful modern and contemporary history: Now is the time to overcome it). Tokyo: Tokuma Shoten, 1996.

Fujitani, T. "Raishawaa no kairai tennōsei kōsō" (Reischauer's plan for a puppet regime emperor system), *Sekai* 672 (March 2000): 137–46.

——. "Minshūshi as Critique of Orientalist Knowledges." *positions* 6, no. 2 (fall 1998): 303–22.

——. "National Narratives and Minority Politics: The Japanese American National Museum's War Stories," *Museum Anthropology* 21, no. 1 (spring 1997): 99–112.

——. *Splendid Monarchy: Power and Pageantry in Modern Japan.* Berkeley: University of California Press, 1996.

Fujiwara Akira. *Nankin dai gyakusatsu* (The Great Nanjing Massacre). Tokyo: Iwanami Shoten. 1985.

Fujiwara, Iwaichi. *F. Kikan: Japanese Army Intelligence Operations in Southeast Asia during World War II.* Trans. Akashi Yoji. London: Heinemann Educational Books, 1983.

Fukagawa Munetoshi. *Umi ni kieta hibaku Chōsenjin chōyōkō: chinkon no kaikyō* (Atom-bombed Korean workers who died at sea: Requiem over the strait). 1974; Osaka: Akashi Shoten, 1992.

Fukuda Mizuho. " 'Rasuto emperā' no 'Nankin' massatsu" ("Nanking" erased in the "Last Emperor"). *Asahi jānaru* 30, no. 7 (19 February 1988): 82–87.

Fussell, Paul. *Wartime: Understanding and Behavior in the Second World War.* New York: Oxford University Press, 1989.

——. *The Great War and Modern Memory.* Oxford: Oxford University Press, 1975.

Gable, Eric, Richard Handler, and Anna Lawson. "On the Uses of Relativism: Fact, Conjecture, and Black and White Histories at Colonial Williamsburg." *American Ethnologist* 19, no. 4 (1992): 791–805.

Gao Xingzu. "Nanjing datusha de shishi burong mosha" (The historical facts of the Great Nanjing Massacre will not be obliterated). *Riben wenti* 6 (1986): 29–38.

——. *Rijun qin-Hua baoxing: Nanjing datusha* (Atrocities of the invading Japanese troops: The Great Nanjing Massacre). Shanghai: Shanghai Renmin Chubanshe, 1985.

Garber, Marjorie. *Vested Interests: Cross-Dressing and Cultural Anxiety.* New York: Routledge, 1992.

Gilliam, John D. "Tano y Chamorro: A Brief History of Land Tenure of Guam and Suggested Land Reforms." Testimony presented at the Federal–Territorial Land Conference, Agana, Guam, January 1994.

Gillis, John R., ed. *Commemorations: The Politics of National Identity.* Princeton, NJ: Princeton University Press, 1994.

Gilroy, Paul. *The Black Atlantic.* Cambridge, MA: Harvard University Press, 1994.

Gong, Gerrit W., ed. *Remembering and Forgetting: The Legacy of War and Peace in East Asia.* Washington, DC: Center for Strategic and International Studies, 1996.

Gonzalves, Theo. " 'We Hold a Neatly Folded Hope': Filipino Veterans of World War II on Citizenship and Political Obligation." *amerasia journal* 21, no. 3 (winter 1995–1996): 155–74.

Great Britain, Colonial Office. *Among Those Present: The Official Story of the Pacific Islands at War.* London: His Majesty's Stationery Office, 1946.

Greenberg, Cheryl. "Black and Jewish Responses to Japanese Internment." *Journal of American Ethnic History* 14, no. 2 (winter 1995): 3–37.

Greene, Robert Ewell. *Black Defenders of America, 1775–1973.* Chicago: Johnson Publishing Company, 1974.

Griffith, Beatrice. *American Me.* Cambridge, MA: Houghton Mifflin, 1948.

Griffith, Samuel B. *The Battle for Guadalcanal.* Toronto: Bantam Books, 1963.

Guam Code Annotated. IGCA section 1011, title I. Agana, Guam, 1998.

"Guam: Operations of the 77th Division, 21 July–10 August 1944." Bulletin, American Forces in Action series, Historical Division, War Department, Washington, DC, 1946.

Guam: War in the Pacific. Agana, Guam: Government Printing Office, 1994.

Guo Qi. *Nanjing datusha* (The Great Nanjing Massacre). Taibei: Zhongwai Tushu Chubanshe, 1979.

Guo Shijie. *Rikou qin-Hua baoxing* (Atrocities of the Japanese invasion of China). Beijing: Lianhe Chubanshe, 1951.

Gutierrez, David. *Walls and Mirrors.* Berkeley: University of California Press, 1995.

Haley, Alex, and Malcolm X. *The Autobiography of Malcolm X.* New York: Grove Press, 1965.

Hall, Robert Anderson. *Melanesian Pidgin Phrase-book and Vocabulary.* Madison: U.S. Armed Forces Institute, 1943.

Halliday, Jon, and Bruce Cumings. *Korea: The Unknown War.* New York: Pantheon Books, 1988.

Handler, Richard. *Nationalism and the Politics of Culture in Quebec.* Madison: University of Wisconsin Press, 1988.

Hanrahan, Gene Z. *The Communist Struggle in Malaya.* New York: Institute of Pacific Relations, 1954.

Hara, Fujio. "The Japanese Occupation of Malaya and the Chinese Community." In *Malaya and Singapore during the Japanese Occupation,* ed. Paul H. Kratoska. Special issue of *Journal of Southeast Asian Studies,* Singapore (1995).

Harootunian, Harry D. "America's Japan/Japan's Japan." In *Japan in the World,* ed. Masao Miyoshi and Harry Harootunian. Durham, NC: Duke University Press, 1993.

Harper, T. N. "The Colonial Inheritance: State and Society in Malaya, 1945–57." Ph.D. diss., University of Cambridge, 1991.

Hase, Michiko. "Race, Status, and Culture in Trans-Pacific Perspective: African American Professionals in Japan." Paper presented at the annual meeting of the American Studies Association, Nashville, Tennessee, 28 October 1994.

Hata Ikuhiko. "Ronsō shi kara mita Nankin gyakusatsu jiken" (The Nanjing Massacre as seen from the history of the controversy). *Seiron* 198 (February 1989): 234–35.

———. *Nankin jiken: "gyakusatsu" no kōzō* (The Nanjing incident: Structure of the "Massacre"). Tokyo: Chūō Kōronsha, 1986.

Hata Kensuke. "Horyo no chi ni mamireta Byakko Butai" (The White Tiger Unit besmeared in captives' blood). *Nihon shūhō* (25 February 1957): 13–15.

Hata Shunroku. "Nankin no gyakusatsu wa tashikani okonawareta ka" (Did the atrocities in Nanjing really happen?). *Maru* (Special issue on the military history of the "Great Army") (15 December 1956): 166–68.

Hattori, Anne Perez. "Righting Civil Wrongs: The Guam Congress Walkout of 1949." *Isla: Journal of Micronesian Studies* 3, no. 1 (Rainy season 1995): 1–27.

Hay, Stephen N. *Asian Ideas of East and West: Tagore and His Critics in Japan, China, and India.* Cambridge, MA: Harvard University Press, 1970.

Heiferman, Marvin. "One Nation, Chiseled in Pictures." In "Lee Friedlander: American Monuments." *The Archive* 25 (1989).

Hein, Laura, and Mark Selden, eds. *Living with the Bomb: American and Japanese Cultural Conflicts in the Nuclear Age.* New York: M.E. Sharpe, 1997.

Hellwig, Daniel J. "Afro-American Reactions to the Japanese and the Anti-Japanese Movement, 1906–1924." *Phylon* 37, no. 1 (1977): 93–104.

Heng, Geraldine, and Janadas Devan. "State Fatherhood: The Politics of Nationalism, Sexuality, and Race in Singapore." In *Nationalisms and Sexualities*, ed. Andrew Parker, Mary Russo, Doris Sommer, and Patricia Yaeger. New York: Routledge, 1992.

Henrich, Ruth. *South Sea Epic: War and the Church in New Guinea.* London: Society for the Propagation of the Gospel, 1944.

Hietala, Thomas R. "Muhammad Ali and the Age of Bare Knuckle Politics." In *Muhammad Ali: The People's Champ*, ed. Elliott J. Gorn. Urbana: University of Illinois Press, 1995.

Higa, Karin M., ed. *The View from Within: Japanese American Art from the Internment Camps, 1942–1945.* Seattle: University of Washington Press, 1992.

Higuchi, Wakako. "War Reparations in Micronesia and Japan's Responsibility." Unpublished paper, Micronesian Area Research Center, University of Guam, 1994.

Hijiya-Kirschnereit, Irmela. "Hana to gyakusatsu: Nankin jiken to Mishima Yukio no 'botan' " (Flowers and the massacre: The Nanjing Incident and "Peonies" by Mishima Yukio). *Gunzō* 52, no. 8 (August 1997): 154–59.

———. " 'Nanking' in Japanese Literature." *DIJ Newsletter* (October 1997): 1.

Hill, Robert A., ed. *The Marcus Garvey and UNIA Papers.* Berkeley: University of California Press, 1983.

Himes, Chester. *If He Hollers Let Him Go.* New York: Thunder's Mouth Press, 1986.

———. *Lonely Crusade.* New York: Thunder's Mouth Press, 1986.

———. "Zoot Riots Are Race Riots." *The Crisis* (July 1943): 200–222.

Hirsch, Marianne. *Family Frames: Photography, Narrative, and Postmemory.* Cambridge, MA: Harvard University Press, 1997.

Ho Chi Minh. "Appeal for General Insurrection." In *Ho Chi Minh on Revolution: Selected Writings, 1920–66*, ed. Bernard B. Fall. New York: Frederick A. Prager, 1967.

Hobsbawm, Eric, and Terence Ranger, eds. *The Invention of Tradition.* Cambridge, England: Cambridge University Press, 1983.

Hogan, Michael J. *Hiroshima in History and Memory.* Cambridge, England: Cambridge University Press, 1996.

Holloway, Joseph E. *Africanisms in American Culture.* Bloomington: Indiana University Press, 1991.

Honda Katsuichi. *Nankin e no michi* (The road to Nanjing). Tokyo: Asahi Shinbunsha, 1987.

——. *Chūgoku no Nihon gun* (The Japanese Army in China). Tokyo: Sōjusha, 1972.

——. *Korosu gawa no ronri* (The logic of the killers). Tokyo: Suzusawa Shoten, 1972.

——. *Chūgoku no tabi* (The journey in China). Tokyo: Asahi Shinbunsha, 1971.

——, compiler. *Sabakareta Nankin daigyakusatsu* (The great Nanjing Massacre on trial). Tokyo: Banseisha, 1989.

Hoogestraat, Jane. " 'Unnamable by Choice': Multivalent Silences in Adrienne Rich's *Time's Power.*" In *Violence, Silence, and Anger: Women's Writing as Transgression*, ed., Deidre Lashgari. Charlottesville: University Press of Virginia, 1995.

Hora Tomio. *Nankin dai zangyaku jiken shiryō shū* (Sources on the Great Nanjing Atrocity). Tokyo: Aoki Shoten, 1985.

——. *Nankin daigyakusatsu: "maboroshi"-ka kōsaku hihan* (The Nanjing Massacre: Repudiation of the "illusionization"). Tokyo: Gendaishi Shuppankai, 1975.

——. *Nankin jiken* (The Nanjing Incident). Tokyo: Shin Jinbutsu Ōraisha, 1972.

——. *Kindai senshi no nazo* (Puzzles in modern military history). Tokyo: Jinbutsu Ōraisha, 1967.

——. compiler. *Nit-Chūsensō shi shiryō 8, 9: Nankin jiken* (Sources of the history of the Sino-Japanese War 8 and 9: The Nanjing Incident II). Tokyo: Katetsu Shoten, 1973.

Hora Tomio, Fujiwara Akira, and Honda Katsuichi, eds. *Nankin jiken no genba e* (To the scene of the Nanjing Incident). Tokyo: Asahi Shinbunsha, 1988.

——, eds. *Nankin jiken o kangaeru* (Reflections on the Nanjing Incident). Tokyo: Otsuki Shoten, 1987.

Horton, D. C. *Fire over the Islands: The Coast Watchers of the Solomons.* London: Leo Cooper, 1970.

Huntington, Samuel P. "The Clash of Civilizations." *Foreign Affairs* 72, no. 3 (summer 1993): 22–49.

Hüppauf, Bernd. "Modernism and the Photographic Representation of War and Destruction." In *Fields of Vision: Essays in Film Studies, Visual Anthropology, and Photography*, ed. Leslie Devereaux and Roger Hillman. Berkeley: University of California Press, 1995.

Huyssen, Andreas. *Twilight Memories.* New York: Routledge, 1995.

Ichioka, Yuji. "The Meaning of Loyalty: The Case of Kazumaro Buddy Uno." *amerasia journal* 23, no. 3 (winter 1997–1998): 45–71.

———, ed. *Beyond National Boundaries: The Complexity of Japanese-American History.* Special issue of *amerasia journal* 23, no. 3 (winter 1997–1998).

Ienaga Saburō. "*Misshitsu*" *kentei no kiroku* (Records of authorization behind "closed doors"). Tokyo: Meicho Kankōkai, 1993.

Igarashi Tarō, ed. *Evangelion kairaku gensoku* (Evangelion pleasure principle). (Tokyo: Daisan Shokan, 1997).

Imai Masatake. "Nankin jōnai no tairyō satsujin" (Massive killings inside Nanjing City). *Tokushū bungei shunjū* (5 December 1956): 154–58.

Ishijima Noriyuki. "Nankin jiken o meguru aratana ronsōten" (New issues of contention concerning the Nanjing Incident). Reprinted in *Chūgoku kankei ronsetsu shiryō* (Collected essays on China), part 4, vol. 2 (1986).

Ishikawa Tatsuzō. "Ikiteiru heitai" (The living soldiers). *Chūō kōron (rinji zōkan) Gekidō no shōwa bungaku* (November 1997): 274–350.

Itakura Yoshiaki. "Matsui Iwane nikki no kaizan ni tsuite" (On tampering with the diary of Matsui Iwane). *Bungei shunjū* (January 1986): 192–94.

———. "Matsui Iwane taishō 'jinchū nikki' no kaizan no kai" (Suspicions of tampering with the "field diary" of General Matsui Iwane). *Rekishi to jinbutsu* 15 (winter 1985): 318–31.

"Iwayuru 'Nankin jiken' ni kansuru jōhō teikyō no onegai" (A request for information concerning the so-called "Nanjing Incident"). *Kaikō* 395 (November 1983): 35–37.

Jackson, Charles. "Plight of Japanese Americans." *Militant* 10 (March 1945). Reprinted in *Fighting Racism in World War II*, ed. C. L. R. James et al. New York: Monad Press, 1980.

Jameson, Fredric. *The Political Unconscious: Narrative as a Socially Symbolic Act.* Ithaca, NY: Cornell University Press, 1981.

"Japan vs. China: The Great Asian Power Struggle Has Begun." *Newsweek*, international ed. (15 November 1993): 12–25.

Jeffords, Susan. *The Remasculinization of America: Gender and the Vietnam War.* Bloomington: Indiana University Press, 1989.

Jennison, Rebecca, " 'Postcolonial' Feminist Locations: The Art of Tomiyama Taeko and Shimada Yoshiko." *U.S.-Japan Women's Journal*, no. 12 (1997): 84–108.

Johnson, Chalmers. " 'Go-banken-sama, GO HOME!' " *Bulletin of the Atomic Scientists* (July–August 1996): 22–29.

———. "The Patterns of Japanese Relations with China, 1952–1982." *Pacific Affairs* 59 (fall 1986): 402–20.

Joint Committee of Returnees from China, compiler. *Sankō* (Three all's). Tokyo: Kōbunsha, 1957.

Jolly, Margaret. "From Point Venus to Bali Ha'i: Eroticism and Exoticism in Representations of the Pacific." In *Sites of Desire, Economies of Pleasure: Sexualities in Asia and the Pacific*, ed. Lenore Manderson and Margaret Jolly. Chicago: Chicago University Press, 1997.

Jordan, Deirdre. "Aboriginal Identity: Uses of the Past, Problems for the Future." In *Past and Present: The Construction of Aboriginality*, ed. Jeremy R. Beckett. Canberra: Aboriginal Studies Press, 1994.

Josephy, Alvin. *The Long and the Short and the Tall.* New York: Knopf, 1946.

Kaikōsha. *Nankin senshi* (A history of the Nanjing battle). 3 vols. 1989; Tokyo: Kaikōsha, 1993.

Kammen, Michael. *The Mystic Chords of Memory: The Transformation of Tradition in American Culture*. New York: Knopf, 1991.

Kang Chae-ŏn and Kim Tong-hun. *Zainichi Kankoku/Chōsenjin: rekishi to tenbō* (South and North Korean residents in Japan: History and prospects). Tokyo: Rōdō Keizaisha, 1989.

Kaplan, Amy, and Donald Pease, eds. *Cultures of U.S. Imperialism*. Durham, NC: Duke University Press, 1994.

Karasawa Shunichi. *Bishōjo no gyakushu*. Tokyo: Nesuko/Bungei Shunjūsha, 1995.

Karig, Walter, and Eric Purdon. *Battle Report, Pacific War: Middle Phase*. New York: Rinehart and Co., 1947.

Kasahara Tokushi. *Nankin nanminku no hyakunichi* (A hundred days in the Nanjing refugee zone). Tokyo: Iwanani Shoten, 1995.

Kasza, Gregory J. *The State and the Mass Media in Japan, 1918–1945*. Berkeley: University of California Press, 1988.

Katō Norihiro. *Amerika no kage* (Shadow of America). Tokyo: Kawade Shobō Shinsha, 1985.

Katokawa Kōtarō. "Shōgen ni yoru Nankin senshi: sono sōkatsu teki kōsatsu" (The history of the battle of Nanjing: An overall examination). *Kaikō* 411 (March 1985): 9–18.

Kawamura Kunimitsu. *Otome no inori* (Prayers of the maiden girls). Tokyo: Kinokuniya Shoten, 1993).

Kelley, Robin. *Race Rebels: Culture, Politics, and the Black Working Class*. New York: Free Press, 1994.

———. *Hammer and Hoe*. Chapel Hill: University North Carolina Press, 1991.

Kelly, John. "Diaspora and World War, Blood and Nation in Fiji and Hawai'i." *Public Culture* 7, no. 3 (1995): 475–97.

Kelly, Marjorie. "Enshrining History: The Visitor Experience at Pearl Harbor's USS *Arizona* Memorial." *Museum Anthropology* 20, no. 3 (1996): 45–57.

Keohane, Nannerl. "Higher Education in the 21st Century: The Global University." *Global Perspective: Newsletter of the Center for International Studies at Duke University* 7, no. 1 (fall 1994): 1–3.

Kido Nikki Kenkyūkai, ed. *Kido Kōichi kankei bunsho* (Kido Kōichi documents). Tokyo: Tokyo Daigaku Shuppan Kai, 1966.

Kim, Elaine H., and Chungmoo Choi, eds. *Dangerous Women: Gender and Korean Nationalism*. New York: Routledge, 1998.

Kim, Hyun Sook. "History and Memory: The 'Comfort Women' Controversy." *positions* 5, no. 1 (spring 1997): 73–106.

Kim Souyoung and Kim Eun-Shil. "Conversation." In *Najŭn moksori II chejaknotŭ* (Habitual Sadness production notes), ed. Boim. Seoul: Boim, 1997.

Kimijima Kazuhiko and Inoue Hisashi. "Nankin daigyakusatsu hyōka ni kansuru saikin no dōkō" (Recent developments concerning the evaluations of the Great Nanjing Massacre). *Rekishi hyōron* 433 (April 1986).

Kimura Kuninori. "Kaisetsu: Nakajima Kesago chūjō to Nankin jiken" (An explanation of Lieutenant General Nakajima Kesago and the Nanjing Incident). *Zōkan rekishi to jinbutsu* (1984): 260–61.

Kinjō Seitoku and Takara Kurayoshi. *Iha Fuyu*. Tokyo: Shimizu Shoin, 1972.

Kōan Chōsachō. *Zainihon Chōsenjin no gaikyō* (The general condition of Zainichi Koreans). Tokyo: Hōmufu Tokubetsu Shinsakyoku, 1949.

Kobayashi Yoshinori. *Sensōron* (On war). Tokyo: Gentōsha, 1998.

Koppes, Clayton R., and Gregory D. Black. *Hollywood Goes to War: How Politics, Profits and Propaganda Shaped World War II Movies*. Berkeley: University of California Press, 1987.

Kotani Mari. *Seibo Evangelion: A New Millennialist Perspective on the Daughters of Eve*. Tokyo: Magajin Hausu, 1997.

Kramer, Jane. "Letter from Germany: The Politics of Memory." *New Yorker* (14 August 1995).

Kumamoto, Bob. "The Search for Spies: American Counterintelligence and the Japanese American Community, 1931–1942." *amerasia journal* 6, no. 2 (1979): 45–75.

Kusano Nobuko, compiler. *Atomic Bomb Injuries*. Rev. ed. Tokyo: Tsukiji Shokan, 1995.

Kwa, Chong Guan. "Remembering Ourselves." Paper presented at the conference "Our Place in Time," Singapore, 18–20 September 1994.

Kwok, Kian Woon. "Beyond Cultural Defensiveness and Cultural Triumphalism: Globalization and the Critique of Western Forms of Modernity." Paper presented at the conference "Globalization: Local Challenges and Responses," Universiti Sains Penang, Penang, 19–21 January 1995.

La Capra, Dominick. "Representing the Holocaust: Reflections on the Historians' Debate." In *Probing the Limits of Representation: Nazism and the "Final Solution,"* ed. Saul Friedlander. Cambridge, MA: Harvard University Press, 1992.

Laenui, Poka. *Hawaiian Sovereignty and Pearl Harbor History*. Honolulu: East-West Center, 1992.

Lal, Brij. "For King and Country: A Talk on the Pacific War in Fiji." In *Remembering the Pacific War*, ed. G. M. White. Honolulu, University of Hawai'i Center for Pacific Islands Studies Occasional Paper No. 36, 1991.

"Land Mines on the Road to Utopia." *Business Week* (18 November 1994): 136–40.

Langer, Lawrence. *Holocaust Testimonies: The Ruins of Memory*. New Haven: Yale University Press, 1991.

Lebra-Chapman, Joyce. *Jungle Alliance: Japan and the Indian National Army*. Singapore: Donald Moore for Asian Pacific Press, 1971.

Leonard, Kevin Allen. " 'Is This What We Fought For?' Japanese Americans and Racism in California: The Impact of World War II." *Western Historical Quarterly* 21, no. 4 (November 1990): 463–82.

Lewinski, Jorge. *The Camera at War: A History of War Photography from 1848 to the Present Day*. New York: Simon and Schuster, 1978.

Li Enhan. "Ribenjun Nanjing datusha de tusha shumu wenti" (The question of the number murdered by the Japanese troops in the Nanjing Massacre). *Guoli Taiwan shifan daxue lishi xuebao* 18 (June 1990).

——. "Rijun Nanjing datusha de tusha ling wenti" (Issues concerning the massacre orders during the Japanese army's great massacre at Nanjing). *Zhongyang yanjuyuan jindaishi jikan* 18 (June 1988).

Li, Haibo. "Unforgettable Atrocity." *Beijing Review* (14–20 August 1995).

Li Yunhan. "Youguan 'Nanjing datusha' de Zhongwai shiliao pingshu" (A survey of historical materials in China and abroad on the "Great Nanjing Massacre"). In *Kangzhan jianguo shi yantaohui lunwenji* (Proceedings of the Symposium on the War of Resistance and nation-building). Taibei: Zhongyang Jindaishi Yanjusuo, 1985.

Liao, Ping-hui. "Rewriting Taiwanese National History: The February 28 Incident as Spectacle." *Public Culture* 5 (1993): 281–96.

Lim, Patricia. "Memories of War in Malaya." In *Malaya and Singapore during the Japanese Occupation*, ed. Paul H. Kratoska. Special issue of *Journal of Southeast Asian Studies, Singapore*, Special Publication Series no. 3 (1995).

———. "Monuments and Memory: Remembrances of War in Johor." Paper presented at the workshop "War and Memory in Malaysia and Singapore, 1941–1945," Institute of Southeast Asian Studies, Singapore, 1995.

Limon, Jose. *Dancing with the Devil: Society and Cultural Poetics in Mexican-American South Texas*. Madison: University of Wisconsin Press, 1994.

Lindenmeyer, Otto. *Black and Brave: The Black Soldier in America*. New York: McGraw Hill, 1970.

Lindstrom, Lamont, and Geoffrey M. White. *Island Encounters: Black and White Memories of the Pacific War*. Washington, DC: Smithsonian Institution Press, 1990.

Linenthal, Edward T. *Sacred Ground: Americans and Their Battlegrounds*. Rev. ed. Urbana: University of Illinois Press, 1993.

Linenthal, Edward T., and Tom Engelhardt, eds. *History Wars: The "Enola Gay" and Other Battles for the American Past*. New York: Henry Holt, 1996.

Lipsitz, George. *A Life in the Struggle: Ivory Perry and the Culture of Opposition*. Philadelphia: Temple University Press, 1995.

———. *Dangerous Crossroads*. New York: Verso, 1994.

———. *Rainbow at Midnight: Labor and Culture in the 1940s*. Urbana: University of Illinois Press, 1994.

Liu Danian. "Zuoshenme, zenme zuo—Zai Zhongguo kangRi zhanzheng shixue hui chengli dahui shangde jianghua" (What to do, and how to do it: Talk at the founding meeting of the Chinese Anti-Japanese War Historical Society). *KangRi zhanzheng yanjiu* 1 (1991): 3–15.

Liu Liangmo. "Kuai ba gaoyang bianchen tie de duiwu" (Let's quietly turn lambs into troops of iron). *Kangzhan sanri kan* 58 (29 June 1938): 5–6.

Lodge, O. R. *The Recapture of Guam*. Washington, DC: U.S. Government Printing Office, 1954.

Lord, Walter. *Lonely Vigil: Coastwatchers of the Solomons*. New York: Viking Press, 1977.

Lowe, Lisa. *Immigrant Acts: On Asian American Cultural Politics*. Durham, NC: Duke University Press, 1996.

Lummis, Douglas: "Genshiteki na nikkō no naka de no hinatabokko" (Sunbathing in the atomic light). *Shisō no kagaku* 7, no. 3 (1981): 16–20.

Lutz, Catherine, and Lesley Bartlett. *Making Soldiers in the Public Schools: An Analysis of the Army JROTC Curriculum*. Philadelphia: American Friends Service Committee, n.d.

Lutz, Catherine A., and Jane L. Collins. *Reading National Geographic*. Chicago: University of Chicago Press, 1993.

MacQuarrie, Hector. *Vouza and the Solomon Islands.* London: V. Gollancz, 1945.

———. *How to Live at the Front: Tips for American Soldiers.* Philadelphia: J. B. Lippincott, 1917.

Manchester, William. *Goodbye, Darkness: A Memoir of the Pacific War.* New York: Dell, 1979.

Mani, Lata. "Contentious Traditions." In *Recasting Women: Essays in Indian Colonial History,* ed. Kumkum Sangari and Sudesh Vaid. New Brunswick, NJ: Rutgers University Press, 1990.

Manibusan, Joaquin V. E. "In Tai, a Day of Terror and Tragedy." In *Liberation: Guam Remembers.* Agana, Guam: Golden Salute Committee, 1994.

Mao Zedong. "The Situation and Our Policy after the Victory in the War of Resistance against Japan." In *Selected Works,* vol. 4. Peking: Foreign Languages Press, 1975.

Mariscal, George. " 'Chale Con La Draft': Chicano Antiwar Writings." *Viet Nam Generation* 6, nos. 3–4 (1995): 126–31.

———, ed. *Aztlan and Viet Nam: Chicano and Chicana Experiences of the War.* Berkeley: University of California Press, 1999.

Marling, Karal Ann, and John Wetenhall. *Iwo Jima: Monuments, Memories, and the American Hero.* Cambridge, MA: Harvard University Press, 1991.

Martin, Tony. *The Pan-African Connection: From Slavery to Garvey and Beyond.* Dover, MA: Majority Press, 1983.

———. *Race First: The Ideological and Organizational Struggles of Marcus Garvey and the Universal Negro Improvement Association.* Westport, CT: Greenwood Press, 1976.

Masaoka, Mike. *They Call Me Moses Masaoka.* New York: William Morrow, 1987.

Masters, Patricia. "Another Way of Seeing: Pearl Harbor as Memory." Paper presented at East-West Center conference on Cultural Identities and National Histories, Honolulu, 1992.

Masubuchi Sōichi. *Rika-chan no shōjo fushigigaku* (Wonderworld of Rika-chan dolls). Tokyo: Shinchōsha, 1987.

Matray, James A. "Diplomatic History as a Political Weapon: An Assessment of Anti-Americanism in South Korea Today." *The SHAFR (Society for Historians of American Foreign Relations) Newsletter* (1989).

Matsuda Motoji and Ichiba Junko. "Naigaijin fubyōdō no keifu: Nihon no hibakusha gyōsei to Kankokujin hibakusha" (Genealogy of unequal treatment of residents and nonresidents: Japan's *hibaku* administration and South Korean *hibakusha*). *Sekai jinken mondai kenkyū sentā kenkyū kiyō* (World human rights issues study center research bulletin), no. 2 (March 1997): 145–65.

Matsumoto Shigeharu. "Tsuini Nankin senryō, sono jitsuzō" (Finally the occupation of Nanjing and its real image). *Ekonomisuto* (21 May 1985): 82–87.

———. *Shanhai jidai* (The Shanghai era). Tokyo: Chūō Kōronsha, 1975.

Mazon, Mauricio. *The Zoot-Suit Riots: The Psychology of Symbolic Annihilation.* Austin: University of Texas Press, 1984.

Mei Ruao. "Guanyu Gu Shoufu, Songjing Shigeng he Nanjing datusha shijian" (On Tani Hisao, Matsui Iwane, and the Great Nanjing Massacre Incident). *Wenshi ziliao xuanji* 22 (1961): 16–36.

Merillat, Herbert Christian. *Guadalcanal Remembered.* New York: Dodd, Mead, 1982.

Mitsubishi Hiroshima/Moto Chōyōkō Hibakusha Saiban o Shien suru Kai. *Mitsubishi wa mibarai chingin o shiharae!* (Mitsubishi ought to pay the unpaid wages!) Hiroshima: Mitsubishi Hiroshima/Moto Chōyōkō Hibakusha Saiban o Shien suru Kai, 1996.

Miyadai Shinji, Hideki Ishihara, and Akiko Otsuka. *Sabukaruchā shinwa kaitai* (Dismantling myth on subculture). Tokyo: Parco Shuppankyoku, 1993.

Miyazaki Kiyotaka. *Gunpō kaigi* (Military courts). Tokyo: Fuji Shobō, 1953.

Moon, Katherine H. S. "Prostitute Bodies and Gendered State in U.S.–Korea Relations." In *Dangerous Women*, ed. Elaine H. Kim and Chungmoo Choi. New York: Routledge, 1998.

Mosse, George L. *Fallen Soldiers: Reshaping the Memory of the World Wars*. New York: Oxford University Press, 1980.

Mueller, Joseph N. *Guadalcanal 1942: The Marines Strike Back*. London: Osprey Publications, 1992.

Mulvey, Laura. "Myth, Narrative, and Historical Experience." *History Workshop* (spring 1987): 3–19.

Muñoz, Carlos. *Youth, Identity, Power: The Chicano Movement*. London: Verso, 1989.

Nakaguchi Kazuki et al., eds. *Nankin jiken Kyōto shidan kankei shiryōshū* (Materials concerning the Kyoto Division in the Nanjing Incident). Tokyo: Aoki Shoten, 1989.

Nalty, Bernard. *Strength for the Fight: A History of Black Americans in the Military*. New York: Free Press, 1986.

Nanjing University History Department. *Riben diguozhuyi zai Nanjing de datusha* (The Great Nanjing Massacre of the Japanese imperialism). Nanjing: Nanjing University History Department, 1979.

Nash, Gary B., Charlotte Crabtree, and Ross E. Dunn. *History on Trial: Culture Wars and the Teaching of the Past*. New York: Knopf, 1997.

National Joint Committee in Support of the Textbook Trials. *Nankin daigyakusatsu, Chōsen jinmin no teikō, 731 Butai* (The Great Nanjing Massacre, resistance by the Korean people, Unit 731). Tokyo: Minshūsha, 1997.

——. *Ienaga kyōkasho saiban jūnenshi* (A ten-year history of the Ienaga textbook trials). Tokyo: Sōtosha, 1977.

Nelson, Dennis Denmark. "The Integration of the Negro into the United States Navy, 1776–1947." Master's thesis, Howard University, 1948.

Nelson, Hank. "*Taim Bilong Pait*: The Impact of the Second World War on Papua New Guinea." In *Southeast Asia under Japanese Occupation*, ed. A. W. McCoy. New Haven: Yale University Southeast Asia Studies, 1980.

Nero, Karen L. "Time of Famine, Time of Transformation: Hell in the Pacific, Palau." In *The Pacific Theater: Island Representations of World War II*, ed. G. M. White and L. Lindstrom. Honolulu: University of Hawai'i Press, 1989.

Neumann, Klaus. " 'In Order to Win Their Friendship': Renegotiating First Contact." *The Contemporary Pacific* 6, no. 1 (spring 1994): 111–45.

NHK Broadcasting Public Opinion Research Institute. *Zusetsu sengo yoron shi* (An illustrated history of postwar public opinion). 2d ed. Tokyo: Nihon Hosō Shuppan Kyōkai, 1982.

Nichols, Bill. *Blurred Boundaries: Questions of Meaning of Contemporary Culture*. Bloomington: University of Indiana Press, 1994.

Niijima Atsuyoshi. "Rittai kōsei Nankin daigyakusatsu" (The Great Nanjing Massacre in three dimensions). Shinhyō (May 1971): 48–57.

Niiya, Brian, ed. Japanese American History: An A-to-Z Reference from 1868 to the Present. New York: Facts on File, Inc., 1993.

Nora, Pierre. "Between Memory and History: Les Lieux de Mémoire." Representations 26 (spring 1989): 7–25.

Nordström, Alison Devine. "Wood Nymphs and Patriots: Depictions of Samoans in The National Geographic Magazine." Visual Sociology 7, no. 2 (1992): 49–59.

——. "Early Photography in Samoa: Marketing Stereotypes of Paradise." History of Photography 15 (1991): 272–86.

Novick, Peter. That Noble Dream: The "Objectivity Question" and the American Historical Profession. New York: Cambridge University Press, 1988.

O'Brien, Cyril. "Island Encounters: Black and White Encounters of the Pacific War." Stars and Stripes (10 June 1991).

Oda Makoto. The Bomb: A Novel. Trans. D. H. Whittaker. Tokyo: Kodansha International, 1990. Originally published in Japanese as Hiroshima.

Oe, Kenzaburo. Hiroshima Notes. Ed. David L. Swain. Trans. Toshi Yonezawa. Tokyo: YMCA Press, 1981.

Ogawa, Dennis. From Japs to Japanese: An Evolution of Japanese-American Stereotypes. Berkeley: McCutchan Corporation, 1971.

Okada, John. No-no Boy. Seattle: University of Washington Press, 1979.

Okihiro, Gary. Margins and Mainstreams: Asians in American History and Culture. Seattle: University of Washington Press, 1994.

——. Cane Fires: The Anti-Japanese Movement in Hawai'i, 1865–1945. Philadelphia: Temple University Press, 1991.

Okinawa Heiwa Nettowāku, ed. Shin aruku/miru/kangaeru Okinawa (Walking/seeing/ thinking Okinawa: New edition). Naha, Okinawa: Okinawa Jiji Shuppan, 1997.

Ono Kenji et al., compilers. Nankin daigyakusatsu o kirokushita kōgun heishitachi (Imperial Army soldiers who reordered the Great Nanjing Massacre). Tokyo: Ōtsuki Shoten, 1996.

Osajima, Keith. "Asian Americans as the Model Minority: An Analysis of the Popular Press Image in the 1960s and 1980s." In Reflections on Shattered Windows, ed. Gary Y. Okihiro et al. Pullman: Washington State University Press, 1988.

Ōtsuka Eiji. "Warera no jidai no Oumu shinrikyō" (Aum Shirikyō, our contemporary). Shokun! 27, no. 6 (1995).

——. Shōjo minzokugaku (Girls' folklore). Tokyo: Kōbunsha, 1989.

Palomo, Tony. "Island in Agony: Guam." In Remembering the Pacific War, ed. Geoffrey M. White. Occasional Paper 36. Honolulu, University of Hawai'i Center for Pacific Islands Studies, 1991.

——. An Island in Agony. Agana, Guam: Published by the author, 1984.

Park Sun Young, "Hanguo weian fu zai Zhongguo" (A Korean "comfort woman" in China). Unpublished manuscript, 1993.

Peattie, Mark R. Nan'yo: The Rise and Fall of the Japanese in Micronesia, 1885–1945. Honolulu: University of Hawai'i Press, 1988.

Peery, Nelson. *Black Fire: The Making of an American Revolutionary*. New York: New Press, 1994.

Perez, Cecilia. "A Chamorro Retelling of Liberation." In *Kinalamten Pulitikat—Siñenten I Chamorro/Issues in Guam's Political Development: The Chamorro Perspective*. Mangilao, Guam: Guam Political Status Education Coordination Commission, 1996.

Perez, Remedios. *Guam Past and Present*. Agana, Guam: Government of Guam, Department of Education, 1949.

Petersen, William. *Japanese Americans: Oppression and Success*. New York: Random House, 1971.

Plummer, Brenda Gayle. *Rising Wind: Black Americans and U.S. Foreign Affairs, 1935–1960*. Chapel Hill: University of North Carolina Press, 1996.

Pritchard, John, and Sonia Magbanua Zaide, compilers. *The Tokyo War Crimes Trial*. 27 vols. New York: Garland Publishing, 1987.

Purcell, Victor. *Malaya, Communist or Free?* Stanford, CA: Stanford University Press, 1954.

Qin Xiaoyi, ed. *Rijun zai-Hua baoxing: Nanjing datusha* (Atrocities of the Japanese army in China: The Great Nanjing Massacre). Taibei: Guomindang Danshi Weiyuanhui, 1986, 1987.

Qin-Hua Rijun Nanjing Datusha Yunan Tongpa Jinianguan. *"Labei riji" faxian shimo* (The background of the discovery of the "Rabe Diary"). Nanjing: Qin-Hua Rijun Nanjing Datusha Yunan Tongpa Jinianguan, 1997.

Rabe, John (Yuehan Labei). *Labei riji* (The diary of John Rabe). Nanjing: Jiangsu Remin Chubanshe and Jiangsu Jiaoyu Chubanshe, 1997.

Radical History Review 56 (spring 1993). Special issue on *Memory and History*.

Rawick, George P. *From Sundown to Sunup*. Westport, CT: Greenwood Press, 1972.

Reid, Anthony. "Remembering and Forgetting the War in Indonesia." Paper presented at the conference "Memory and the Second World War in International Comparative Perspective," Amsterdam, 1995.

Remembering the Bomb: The Fiftieth Anniversary in the United States and Japan. Special issue of *Bulletin of Concerned Asian Scholars* 27, no. 2 (April–June 1995).

Richter, Don. *Where the Sun Stood Still: The Untold Story of Sir Jacob Vouza and the Guadalcanal Campaign*. Tawe, CA: Toucan Publishing, 1992.

Rikugunshō Sanbō Honbu Hensei Dōinka. *Shinajihen: daitōa sensōkan rikugun dōin gaikyō* (The China incident: A general history of army mobilization during the Greater East Asian War). Reprint ed. Tokyo: Fuji Shuppan, 1988.

Robinson, Michael E. *Cultural Nationalism in Colonial Korea, 1920–1925*. Seattle: University of Washington Press, 1988.

Robinson, Michael, and Frank N. Schubert. "David Fagen: An Afro-American Rebel in the Philippines, 1899–1901." *Pacific Historical Review* 64, no. 1 (February 1975): 69–83.

Roeder, George H., Jr. *The Censored War: American Visual Experience during World War II*. New Haven: Yale University Press, 1993.

Rogers, Robert F. *Destiny's Landfall: A History of Guam*. Honolulu: University of Hawai'i Press, 1995.

——. "Guam's Quest for Political Identity." *Pacific Studies* 12, no. 1 (November 1988): 49–70.

Rogin, Michael Paul. *Ronald Reagan, the Movie and Other Episodes in Political Demonology.* Berkeley: University of California Press, 1987.

Rosenberg, Daniel. "The IWW and Organization of Asian Workers in Early Twentieth Century America." *Labor History* 36, no. 1 (winter 1995): 77–87.

Rosenstone, Robert A., ed. *Revisioning History: Film and the Construction of a New Past.* Princeton, NJ: Princeton University Press, 1995.

Rusbridger, James, and Eric Nave. *Betrayal at Pearl Harbor: How Churchill Lured Roosevelt into WWII.* New York: Summit Books, 1991.

Saito, Hisafumi. "Barefoot Benefactors: A Study of Japanese Views of Melanesians." In *Remembering the Pacific War,* ed. Geoffrey M. White. Honolulu: Center for Pacific Islands Studies, University of Hawai'i, 1991.

Sanchez, Pedro C. *Uncle Sam, Please Come Back to Guam.* Tamuning, Guam: Sanchez Publishing, 1979.

Santner, Eric L. "History beyond the Pleasure Principle: Some Thoughts on the Representation of Trauma." In *Probing the Limits of Representation: Nazism and the "Final Solution,"* ed. Saul Friedlander. Cambridge, MA: Harvard University Press, 1992.

——. *Stranded Objects: Mourning, Memory, and Film in Postwar Germany.* Ithaca, NY: Cornell University Press, 1990.

Santos, Angel. "U.S. Return Was Reoccupation, Not Liberation." *Pacific Daily News* (21 July 1991): 20, 22.

SCAP Civil Information Section. *Shinsō hako: Taiheiyō sensō no seiji, gaikō, rikukaisen no shinsō* (The truth box: The truth about the politics, diplomacy, land and battles of the Pacific War). Tokyo: Kozumo Shuppansa, 1946.

Scarry, Elaine. *The Body in Pain: The Making and Unmaking of the World.* Oxford: Oxford University Press, 1985.

Scott, Joan W. "The Evidence of Experience." *Critical Inquiry* 17, no. 4 (summer 1991): 737–97.

Sherwin, Martin J. *A World Destroyed: The Atomic Bomb and the Grand Alliance.* New York: Knopf, 1975.

Shibutani, Tamotsu. *The Derelicts of Company K.* Berkeley: University of California Press, 1978.

Shimada Katsumi. "Nankin kōryakusen to gyakusatsu jiken" (The attack on Nanjing and the massacre incident). *Tokushū jinbutsu ōrai* (June 1956): 106–11.

Shimono Ikkaku and Gotō Kōsaku. *Nankin sakusen no shinsō: (Kumamoto) Dai-6-shidan senki* (The truth about the Nanjing battle: Battle records of the Sixth Division). Tokyo: Tokyo Jōhōsha, 1966.

Silcock, T. H. *Towards a Malayan Nation.* Singapore: Eastern Universities Press, 1961.

Silcock, T. H., and Ungku Abdul Aziz. "Nationalism in Malaya." In *Asian Nationalism and the West,* ed. William L. Holland. New York: Octagon Books, 1953.

Silverberg, Miriam. "Remembering Pearl Harbor, Forgetting Charlie Chaplin, and the Case of the Disappearing Western Woman: A Picture Story," *positions* 1, no. 1 (1993): 24–76.

Skinner, James M. "*December 7:* Filmic Myth Masquerading as Historical Fact." *Journal of Military History* 55 (October 1991): 507–16.

Slackman, Michael. *Remembering Pearl Harbor: The Story of the USS Arizona Memorial.* Honolulu: Arizona Memorial Museum Association, 1986.

Snow, Edgar. *The Battle for Asia.* New York: Random House, 1941.

Sŏ Kyŏng-shik. *Kōminka seisaku kara shimon ōnatsu made: zainichi Chōsenjin no "Shōwashi"* (From the imperial subjectification policy to fingerprinting: A "Shōwa history" of Korean residents in Japan). Tokyo: Iwanami Shoten, 1989.

Solomon Islands Pijin Literacy Project. *Stori abaotem Sa Chales Jekop Vouza.* Honiara: Solomon Islands Pijin Literacy Project, 1982.

Sone Kazuo. *Shiki Nankin gyakusatsu* (A personal account of the Nanjing Massacre). Tokyo: Sairyūsha, 1984.

Sontag, Susan. *On Photography.* New York: Farrar, Straus and Giroux, 1977.

Souder, Laura M. T. "A Tale of Two Anthems." Paper presented at the twenty-seventh Pacific Science Congress, Honolulu, Hawai'i, May 1991.

——. "Psyche under Siege: Uncle Sam, Look What You've Done to Us." Paper presented at the ninth annual conference of the Guam Association of Social Workers, Agana, Guam, 30 March 1989.

Souder, Laura M. T., and Robert Underwood. *Chamorro Self-Determination/I Direchon y Taotao.* Agana, Guam: Chamorro Studies Association and Micronesian Area Research Center, 1987.

Special Service Division, Army Service Forces, United States Army. *A Pocket Guide to New Guinea and the Solomons.* Washington, DC: War and Navy Departments, 1944.

Stephan, John. "Hijacked by Utopia: American Nikkei in Manchuria." *amerasia journal* 23, no. 3 (winter 1997–1998):1–42.

Stubbs, R. *Hearts and Minds in Guerilla Warfare: The Malayan Emergency 1948–1960.* Singapore: Oxford University Press, 1989.

Sturdevant, Saundra Pollock, and Brenda Stoltzfus, eds. *Let the Good Times Roll: Prostitution and the U.S. Military in Asia.* New York: The New Press, 1992.

Subcommandant Marcos. "Why We Are Fighting: The Fourth World War Has Begun." *Le Monde Diplomatique* (August–September 1997).

Sun Zhaiwei, ed. *Nanjing datusha* (The Great Nanjing Massacre). Beijing: Beijing Chubanshe, 1997.

——. "Nanjing datusha yunan tongpao zhong jiujin you duoshao junren" (How many soldiers were among the compatriot victims in the Great Nanjing Massacre?). *Kang-Ri zhanzheng yanjiu* 26 (April 1997): 8–17.

Sunder Rajan, Rajeswari. *Real and Imagined Women.* London: Routledge, 1993.

Suzuki Akira. "*Nankin daigyakusatsu*" *no maboroshi* (The illusion of the "Great Nanjing Massacre"). Tokyo: Bungei Shunjūsha, 1973.

Suzuki, Bob H. "Education and the Socialization of Asian Americans: A Revisionist Analysis of the 'Model Minority' Thesis." In *Asian Americans: Social and Psychological Perspectives*, vol. 2, ed. Russell Endo, Stanley Sue, and Nathaniel N. Wagner. Palo Alto, CA: Science and Behavior Books, Inc., 1980.

Swedenburg, Ted. *Memories of Revolt: The 1936–1993 Rebellion and the Palestinian National Past.* Minneapolis: University of Minnesota Press, 1995.

Tai, Hue-Tam Ho. *Radicalism and the Origins of the Vietnamese Revolution.* Cambridge, MA: Harvard University Press, 1992.

Takaki, Ronald. *Strangers from a Different Shore: A History of Asian Americans*. New York: Penguin, 1989.

Takezawa, Yasuko I. *Breaking the Silence: Redress and Japanese American Ethnicity*. Ithaca, NY: Cornell University Press, 1995.

Tanaka, Chester. *Go for Broke*. Richmond, CA: Go For Broke, Inc., 1982.

Tanaka Masaaki. *Nankin jiken no sōkatsu* (A summary of the Nanjing Incident). Tokyo: Kenkosha, 1987.

——. *Matsui Iwane taishō no jinchū nisshi* (The field diary of General Matsui Iwane). Tokyo: Fuyō Shobō, 1985.

——. " 'Nankin daigyakusatsu kinenkan' ni monomōsu" (Objections to the "Memorial Hall to the Great Nanjing Massacre"). *Seiron* 160 (December 1985).

——. *"Nanjing datusha" de xugou* (The fabrication of the "Great Nanjing Massacre"). Beijing: Shijie Zhishi Chubanshe, 1985.

Tawara Yoshifumi, *Kenshō 15-nen sensō to chū kō rekishi kyōkasho* (An examination of the Fifteen Years' War in middle and high school textbooks). Tokyo: Gakushū no Tomosha, 1994.

——. "Kyōkasho no 'Nankin jiken' kijutsu wa dō kawatta ka" (How did the textbook coverage of the "Nanjing Incident" change?). Paper distributed at an international symposium on the sixtieth anniversary of the Nanjing Massacre, Tokyo, 13 December 1988.

Taylor, Quintard. *The Forging of a Black Community: Seattle's Central District from 1870 through the Civil Rights Era*. Seattle: University of Washington Press, 1994.

——. "Blacks and Asians in a White City: Japanese Americans and African Americans in Seattle, 1890–1940." *Western Historical Quarterly* 23, no. 4 (November 1991): 401–30.

Team Guam. "The Next Liberation." Testimony presented at the Federal–Territorial Land Conference, Agana, Guam, January 1994.

Thaxton, Ralph A. *Salt of the Earth: The Political Origins of Peasant Protest and Communist Revolution in China*. Berkeley: University of California Press, 1997.

Thomas, Dorothy Swaine, and Richard S. Nishimoto. *The Spoilage*. Berkeley: University of California Press, 1946.

Thomas, Nicholas. *Colonialism's Culture: Anthropology, Travel, and Government*. Princeton, NJ: Princeton University Press, 1994.

Thompson, John B. *Studies in the Theory of Ideology*. Berkeley: University of California Press, 1984.

Timperley, H. J. *Japanese Terror in China*. New York: Modern Age Books, 1938.

——. *Wairen mudu zhong zhi Rijun baoxing* (Atrocities of the Japanese troops as witnessed by foreigners). Hankou: Guomin Chubanshe, 1938).

Ting, Y. L. "Nanjing Massacre: A Dark Page in History." *Beijing Review* (2 September 1985).

Tomiyama Taeko. "Silenced by History." In *Chonggun wianburŭl wihan chinhongok* (Requiem for the military comfort women), ed. Yi Kwan-hun. Seoul: Tonga Gallery, 1995.

Tregaskis, Richard. *Guadalcanal Diary*. New York: Random House, 1945.

Turnbull, Phyllis. "Remembering Pearl Harbor: The Semiotics of the *Arizona* Memorial." In *Challenging Boundaries: Global Flows, Territorial Identities*, ed. Hayward Alker Jr. and Michael Shapiro. Minneapolis: University of Minnesota Press, 1996.

Uchiyama Jirō. " 'Futsū no Nihonjin' ga kokoromita Nankin daigyakusatsu shokuzai no tabi" (The journey of atonement for the Great Nanjing Massacre attempted by ordinary Japanese). *Asahi jānaru* 28, no. 26 (20 June 1986): 22–25.

Ueno Toshiya. *Kurenai no metaru sūtsu: anime to iu senjō* (Metal Suits, the red: War in animation). Tokyo: Kinokuniya Shoten, 1998.

Underwood, Robert A. "Unfunded Mandates." *Congressional Record* 141, no. 8 (January 1995). Proceedings and Debates of the 104th Congress. Washington, DC: U.S. Government Printing Office, 1995.

——. "Red, Whitewash and Blue: Painting over the Chamorro Experience." *Islander Magazine, Pacific Daily News* (17 July 1977): 6–8.

Unemoto Masami, et al. " 'Nankin gyakusatsu' sankasha no shōgen" (The testimony of participants in the "Nanjing Massacre"). *Bungei shunjū* (December 1984): 232.

Unger, Jonathan, ed. *Using the Past to Serve the Present: Historiography and Politics in Contemporary China*. Armonk, NY: M.E. Sharpe, 1993.

Utsumi Aiko. *Chōsenjin ⟨kōgun⟩heishitachi no sensō* (Korean "imperial" soldiers' wars). Tokyo: Iwanami Shoten, 1991.

——. *Chōsenjin BCkyū senpan no kiroku* (A record of Korean B and C class war criminals). Tokyo: Keisō Shobō, 1982.

Utsumi Aiko and Murai Yoshinori. *Sekidōka no Chōsenjin hanran* (Korean rebellion under the equator). Tokyo: Keisō Shobō, 1980.

Valdez, Luis. *Envisioning California*. Sacramento Center for California Studies Keynote Address Publication Series, no. 3, 1995.

Van Dusen, Henry P. *They Found the Church There: The Armed Forces Discover Christian Missions.* New York: Charles Scribner's Sons, 1945.

Walker, J. Samuel. "History, Collective Memory, and the Decision to Use the Bomb." *Diplomatic History* 19, no. 2 (spring 1995).

Wallace, Mike. "The Battle of the Enola Gay." *Radical Historian Newsletter* 72 (May 1995): 1–12, 22–32.

Wan Hashim Wan Teh. *Perang Dunia Kedua. Peranan Gerila Melayu Force 136* (World War II: The role of the Malay guerrillas in force 136). Kuala Lumpur: Dewan Bahasa Dan Pustaka, 1993.

Watanabe, Morio. "Image Projection at War: Construction and Deconstruction of the Domus through Films on World War II in the U.S. and Japan." Ph.D. diss., University of Wisconsin, 1992.

Watson, Rubie S., ed. *Memory, History and Opposition under State Socialism.* Santa Fe, NM: School of American Research Press, 1994.

Wee, C. J. W.-L. "Staging the New Asia: Singapore's Dick Lee, Pop Music and a Countermodernity." *Public Culture* 8, no. 3 (1996).

Weglyn, Michi Nishiura. *Years of Infamy: The Untold Story of America's Concentration Camps.* Updated ed. Seattle: University of Washington Press, 1996.

Weinberg, Gerhard L. *A World at Arms: A Global History of World War II.* Cambridge, England: Cambridge University Press, 1994.

Wennergren, Mike. "County Man Is Guest of Guam Government." *Salinas Californian* (11 July 1984): 17.

Wertsch, James V., Pablo del Rio, and Amelia Alvarez, eds. *Sociocultural Studies of Mind.* New York: Cambridge University Press, 1995.

Westbrook, Robert. " 'I Want a Girl Just Like the Girl That Married Harry James': American Women and the Problem of Political Obligation in World War II." *American Quarterly* 24, no. 4 (December 1990): 587–614.

White, Geoffrey M. "Museum, Memorial, Shrine: National Narrative in National Spaces." *Museum Anthropology* 21, no. 1 (1997).

——. "Mythic History and National Memory: The Pearl Harbor Anniversary." *Culture and Psychology* 3, no. 1 (1997): 63–88.

——. "Remembering Guadalcanal: National Identity and Transnational Memory-Making." *Public Culture* 7 (1995): 529–55.

White, Geoffrey M., and Lamont Lindstrom. *The Pacific Theater: Island Representations of World War II.* Honolulu: University of Hawai'i Press, 1989.

White, Geoffrey M., and Jane Yi. "*December 7th*: Race and Nation in Wartime Documentary." In *Classic Whiteness: Race and the Hollywood Studio System,* ed. Daniel Bernardi. Minneapolis: University of Minnesota Press, in press.

White, Hayden. "Storytelling: Historical and Ideological." In *Centuries' Ends, Narrative Means,* ed. Robert Newman. Stanford: Stanford University Press, 1996.

——. "AHR Forum: Historiography and Historiophoty." *American Historical Review* 93, no. 5 (1988): 1193.

——. "Narrativization of Real Events." In *On Narrative,* ed. W. J. T. Mitchell. 1980; Chicago: University of Chicago Press, 1981.

——. "The Value of Narrativity in the Representation of Reality." In *On Narrative,* ed. W. J. T. Mitchell. 1980; Chicago: University of Chicago Press, 1981.

White, Richard. *It's Your Misfortune and None of My Own.* Tulsa: University of Oklahoma Press, 1991.

White, Walter, and Thurgood Marshall. *What Caused the Detroit Riot? An Analysis by Walter White and Thurgood Marshall.* New York: National Association for the Advancement of Colored People, 1943.

Whiting, Allen S. *China Eyes Japan.* Berkeley: University of California Press, 1989.

Winter, Jay. *Sites of Memory, Sites of Mourning: The Great War in European Cultural History.* New York: Cambridge University Press, 1995.

Won Pat, Antonio B. Speech, Asian Pacific American Heritage Week (May 1981). Papers of Antonio B. Won Pat, Micronesian Area Research Center, Mangilao, Guam.

Woo-Cumings, Meredith. "Market Dependency in U.S.–East Asian Relations." In *What Is in a Rim? Critical Perspectives on the Pacific Region Idea,* ed. Arif Dirlik. Boulder, CO: Westview Press, 1993.

Wright, Peter, and John Armor. *Manzanar.* New York: Times Books, 1988.

Xu Zhigeng. *Nanjing datusha* (The Great Nanjing Massacre). Beijing: Kunlun Chubanshe, 1987.

Yamamoto Shichihei. *Watashi no naka no Nihongun* (The Japanese army that I knew). 1975; Tokyo: Bungei Shunjūsha, 1983.

Yamamoto Takeshi. *Ichi heishi no jūgun kiroku* (A record of one soldier's time at the front). Tokyo: Yasuda Shoten, 1985.

Yang, Daqing. "The Challenges of the Nanjing Massacre: Reflections on Historical Inquiry." In *The Nanjing Massacre in History and Historiography*, ed. Joshua A. Fogel. Berkeley: University of California Press, 2000.

Yi Wŏn-gyu. *Ch'immuk ŭi sŏm*. Seoul: Hyŏnamsa, 1988.

Yoneyama, Lisa. *Hiroshima Traces: Time, Space, and the Dialectics of Memory*. Berkeley: University of California Press, 1999.

——. "Memory Matters: Hiroshima's Korean Atomic Bomb Memorial and the Politics of Ethnicity." *Public Culture* 7 (spring 1995): 499–527.

Yoshida Yutaka. *Nihonjin no sensō kan: sengoshi no naka no henyō* (Japanese views of the war: Transformations in postwar history). Tokyo: Iwanami Shoten, 1995.

——. *Tennō no guntai to Nankin jiken* (The emperor's army and the Nanjing Incident). Tokyo: Aoki Shoten, 1986.

Yoshino Kosaku. *Cultural Nationalism in Contemporary Japan: A Sociological Inquiry*. London: Routledge, 1992.

Young, James E. *The Texture of Memory: Holocaust Memorials and Meaning*. New Haven: Yale University Press, 1993.

Yui Daizaburō. *Nichibei sensōkan no sōkoku: masatsu no shinsō shinri* (Antagonisms in U.S.-Japan views on war: Deep psychology of conflicts). Tokyo: Iwanami Shoten, 1995.

Zelenietz, Marty. "Villages without People: A Preliminary Analysis of American Views of Melanesians during World War II as Seen through Popular Histories." In *Remembering the Pacific War*, ed. Geoffrey M. White. Honolulu: Center for Pacific Islands Studies, University of Hawai'i, 1991.

Zhou Erfu. "Nanjing de xianluo" (The fall of Nanjing). *Dangdai* 4 (1985).

Zhu Chengshan, ed. *Qin-Hua Rijun Nanjing datusha xinchunzhe zhengyanji* (A collection of testimonies by survivors of the Great Nanjing Massacre by the invading Japanese troops). Nanjing: Nanjing Daxue Chubanshe, 1994.

Zhu Chengshan, compiler. *Qin-Hua Rijun Nanjing datusha waiji renshi zhengyanji* (Collected testimonies by foreigners on the Japanese massacre in Nanjing). Nanjing: Jiangsu Renmin Chubanshe, 1998.

"Zhuiyi Rikou Nanjing datusha" (Recollections of the Great Nanjing Massacre committed by the Japanese invaders). *Xinhua yuebao* 3 (1951): 988–91.

Zinsser, William Knowlton. *American Places: A Writer's Pilgrimage to 15 of This Country's Most Visited and Cherished Sites*. New York: HarperCollins, 1992.

Zou Mingde et al. "Nanjing datusha de lishi shishi burong cuangai" (The historical facts of the Great Nanjing Massacre will not allow tampering). *Lishi dang'an* 4 (1982).

≡ Filmography

Bird, Lance. Untitled. USS *Arizona* Memorial orientation film, Honolulu, HI: National Park Service, film, 23 min., 1992.

Bird, Lance. *Pearl Harbor: Surprise and Remembrance*. Santa Monica, CA: Direct Cinema Ltd, video, 88 min. 1991.

Byun, Young-joo (Pyŏn, Yŏng-ju). *The Murmuring*. Seoul: Docu-Factory VISTA, 1995.

Byun, Young-joo (Pyŏn, Yŏng-ju). *Habitual Sadness*. Seoul: Docu-Factory VISTA, 1997.

Capra, Frank. *Know Your Enemy: Japan*. U.S. Army Pictorial Service, Signal Corps, 1945.

Choy, Christine, and Nancy Tong. *In the Name of the Emperor*. New York: Film News Now Foundation, videocassette, 51 min., 1996.

Fleischer, Richard, Toshio Masuda, and Kinji Fukasaku. *Tora! Tora! Tora!* Twentieth-Century Fox, film, 143 min., 1970.

Ford, John, and Gregg Toland. *December 7th*. U.S. Navy, film, 37 min./83 min., 1943.

Hearst newsreel footage. "Japanese-American troops." UCLA Film and TV Archive, ca. 1944.

Lander, Ned, with Carol Ruff. *50 Years of Silence*. Australia: SBS Television, 1994.

Nakamura, Robert. *Something Strong Within*. Los Angeles: Japanese National Museum, 1994.

Okasaki, Steven. *Unfinished Business: The Japanese American Internment Cases*. San Francisco: Mouchette Films, 58 min., 1984.

Pirosh, Robert. *Go for Broke*. MGM, 1951.

Sturges, John. *Bad Day at Black Rock*. 1954.

Tajiri, Rea. *History and Memory*. Brooklyn, NY: Akiko Productions, videocassette, 33 min., 1991.

≡ Index

(Page references in italics indicate photographs.)

Absence of memory, 18; images and, 34–37; in Pearl Harbor films, 291. *See also* Forgetting/forgetfulness

Ada, Joseph, 168

Adams, Ansel, 38, 264 n.22

Adolescent protagonists: in Japanese popular culture, 148–49

Affirmation of the Great East Asia War, An (Hayashi), 57

African Americans: affinities with Asians and Asian Americans, 350–55, 368, 371; and Asian Americans in U.S. labor market, 351; attitudes about the war surveyed, 359; Black nationalist groups, 350, 352–57, 368–69, 372; in defense industry, 355–58, 364–65; draft resistance of, 348–49, 356, 357, 365–67; and engagement with Japan, 350–51, 353; and identification with other people of color, 351–52, 365–66; Japanese interest in Black nationalism, 352, 354–55; job discrimination against, 355–58, 365; William Petersen on inability to overcome racism by, 254–55; postwar activism by, 348, 349, 365, 367–68; pro-Japanese sentiment among, 354–55, 359; responses to Japanese American internment, 360–62, 364, 365; solidarity with Japanese Americans, 353, 360–62; U.S. government fears of subversive activity by, 355–57, 358–59, 368–69, 374 n.26

African American soldiers, 111, 114, 126 n.3, 348, 356; and Filipino insurrection, 351–52; in Hawai'i, 362–63, 370; at Pearl Harbor, 358; prejudice against, 348, 357–58, 370

African American women: in sexual hierarchy, 369–72

Aguinaldo, Emilio, 352

Air Force Association, 327, 329, 336

Aisha, Akbhar, 226–27

Akashi Yasushi, 99

AKIRA (film), 131

Ali, Muhammad, 367

Alien Land Law (California), 364, 365

Allen, Ernest V., 357

Alperovitz, Gar, 343 n.13

Alvarez-Cristobal, Hope, 168

Ambiguity. *See Utsukushii*

American Ex-Prisoners of War, 271–72

American Legion, 332, 336

American POWs, 185

American Studies Film Center, 275, 276

America's Concentration Camps (museum exhibit), 37

Amnesia: historical, 333–34, 335, 339–40. *See also* Forgetting/forgetfulness; Memory

Among Those Present: The Official Story of the Pacific Islands at War Prepared for the Colonial Office, 122–23

Hiroshima (Hersey), 276
Hiroshima Justice Bureau, 388–90, 391
Hiroshima Mitsubishi, 385–88; ongoing reparations negotiations, 388–91
Hiroshima Mitsubishi Factory's Forcibly Mobilized Korean Laborers Collective, 388–90
Hiroshima/Nagasaki bombings, 131, 222, 300, 330, 365, 378–79; Battle of Okinawa and, 90, 106 n.9; contrasting views of, 379; as Holocaust analogue, 333; images of, 34–36, 40; in Oda novel, 315–18; Ōe on experience of, 312; recollections of, 188, 380–81, 386; transnational disparities in views of, 331–37, 341; U.S. justifications of, 36, 333, 335, 345 n.28, 379. See also Atomic bomb victims; Enola Gay exhibit controversy
Hirota Kōki, 79 n.15
Hirsch, Marianne, 42–43
Historical amnesia, 333–34, 335, 339–40. See also Forgetting/forgetfulness
Historical artifacts: of Japanese American internment, 37, 43–44; potency of, 338
History: commemorative practices and, 17–18; critiques/subaltern views, 3–6, 21–23, 320, 324; facticity and, 20, 325–28, 331; historian's role, 78; marginalized memories in, 4; memory/history opposition, 34, 328–29; opposition of public and commemorative history, 326, 331; postnationalist historiography, 341; power of public representation, 330; public, and competing views of historical truth, 323; reenactment of, 45–46; relationship to memory, 33–34. See also Official war/liberation narratives
History and Memory (film), 18, 34, 37–38, 40, 41, 42, 43, 44, 45, 46, 48.
Ho Chi Minh, 353
Hokuto no ken (film), 131
Holidays: Japanese-established, in Sin-gapore, 220–21, 222. See also Liberation Day (Guam)
Holocaust Museum, 46
Honda Katsuichi, 59, 60, 61, 64, 66, 83n. 65
Hong Kang-rim, 401
Hoover, J. Edgar, 359
Hopi creation myth: in The Bomb (Oda), 316–17, 318
Hora Tomio, 58, 60, 61, 64, 68, 83n. 65
Horne, Gerald, 367
Hoshiyama, Fred, 361
Hosokawa Morihiro, 87, 88
Hotta Yoshie, 56
House of Knowledge, 356
Huang Yongshen, 183, 185
Huntington, Samuel, 309–10
Huyssen, Andreas, 35

Ichiban utsukushiku (film), 137
Ienaga Saburō, 57, 61, 63, 66
If He Hollers Let Him Go (Himes), 359–60
"If novels": Japanese, 22, 132–36, 145–46
Ikeda Tokushin, 210
Illusion of the Nanjing Massacre, The (Suzuki), 60–61
Images: American image icons of Asia-Pacific War, 35–36, 40; of Japanese American internment, 36, 38–40; relationship with memory, 34–37. See also Films; Photography and photographs
Imai Tadashi, 143
Immigrants: and U.S. anti-immigrant sentiment, 308, 351
Immigration and Naturalization Act (1790), 351
Immigration policy, U.S., 243, 351, 364
Imperialism. See Colonialism
Imperial War Museum (London), 108
Imphal, battle of, 224–25
India, 8, 224–25, 379; sati discourse, 399, 400
Indian Independence League, 224, 225, 231

Nagasaki Atomic Bomb Museum, 68

Nagasaki bombing. *See* Hiroshima/Nagasaki bombings

Nagasaki Flag Incident, 55

Nakajima Kesago, 65

Nakane, Naka (a.k.a. Satakota Takahishi), 354, 369

Nakasone Yasuhiro, 69

Name Changing Campaign, 389

Nanjing Incident, The (Hora), 60

Nanjing Incident Investigation and Research Group, 64, 66

Nanjing Massacre, 7, 50–78, 300; Chinese characterizations of Japanese debate over, 62; Chinese memories of, 7, 51, 69, 73; Chinese publications and films about, 72–73, 74; Chinese report of 1960, 55–56; compensation sought for survivors, 67; contemporary accounts of, 51–53; contemporary Chinese reactions to, 52; documentary film on, 7, 339–41; estimates of victim numbers, 53, 56–59, 63, 66, 68, 72, 75; eyewitness accounts of Japanese participants, 65, 68; Japanese debate over, 50, 51, 60–68, 76–78; Japanese denials of, 22–23, 60–61, 64–69, 73; Japanese publications on, 50–51, 60–61, 64–66; in Japanese textbooks, 63; memorialization in Japan, 67; memorials, 50, 51, 67, 69, 70, 71, 72, 74–75; nomenclature to describe, 78 n.1; and postwar anti-American sentiment in China, 54; postwar Chinese accounts and views of, 54–56; postwar Japanese accounts and views of, 56–61; significance in China today of, 50, 76; Taiwanese views of, 74; war crimes trials over, 53, 56, 57, 68, 73, 79 n.15

Nanjing, Treaty of, 301

Naoki Sakai, 224

Narrative coherence: vs. multiplicity of experience, 319

National Association for the Advancement of Colored People (NAACP), 360, 361–62, 369

National Endowment for the Humanities (NEH), 24

National identity: and commemorative practices, 17–18; development in Singapore, 230–35; and ethnic identity, in national war narratives, 9; in the Pacific Islands, 10; Taiwanese soldiers and, 189, 197

Nationalism: anticolonial in Korea, 397–401; appropriations of official war narratives, 311; Black nationalist groups, 350, 352–57, 368–69, 372; "cultural nationalism" and Asian economic success, 309

Nationalist China, 54, 76; and investigations of Nanjing Massacre, 53

Nationalist discourse: Korean, and comfort women, 8, 397–401; and racism, 242, 243; U.S., and racism, 242–47, 257–58; war memories in, 7–8. *See also* Official war/liberation narratives

National liberation struggles, 302–4, 312

National Memorial Cemetery of the Pacific (Punchbowl Cemetery), 6–7

National symbolic, 47

Nation-centered (vs. empire-centered) war/liberation narratives, 219, 223, 227, 235. *See also* Official war/liberation narratives

Nation of Islam, 353–54, 357

Nation-states: vs. city-states, 234; impacts of globalization on, 306

Native Americans: and atomic bomb, 315; in Oda novel *The Bomb*, 315–18

Native loyalty: as foundation of colonialism, 224; in official war/liberation narratives, 10–11

Natives, in wartime photographs, 10, 11, 109–22; as loyal allies, 116, 118, 119, 123; as pupils, 114, 116, 117; as savages, 111, 112; as servants, 111, 113, 114; as victims, 114, 115, 116; Jacob Vouza, 108, 122–26, 124, 125

Outward Movement of America, 354
Ōya Sōichi, 58

Pacific Coast Fair Play Committee, 364
Pacific Islanders: Allied and Japanese
    views of, 107, 108; religious com-
    monality with Allied servicemen, 120;
    Jacob Vouza, 108, 122–26, 124, 125; in
    wartime photographs, 109–22, 112–
    13, 115–17, 119, 121
Pacific Islands, 9–10, 20
Pacific Movement of the Eastern World
    (PMEW), 354–57
Pacific War, The (Costello), 6
Pain: inarticulability of, 398, 400
Pak Ch'ang-hwan, 389–90, 391
Pakistan, 379
Palau: Japanese tourism/investment in,
    22
Palomo, Tony, 156–57, 180 n.65
Pan-Asianism, 303–4, 308, 309
Papua New Guinea, 10, 113, 115, 119, 307
Paredes, Americo, 366
Peace Movement of Ethiopia, 355, 357,
    369
Peace Museum (Okinawa), 105
Peace Pedagogy (Japan), 383
Pearl Harbor attack, 6, 7, 9, 300; African
    American heroism in, 358; alternate
    views of, 355; commemorations of,
    22, 240; Japanese context for, in Pearl
    Harbor films, 271, 276, 279–80; mur-
    ders of Asian Americans following, 49
    n.11; "Remember Pearl Harbor!" slo-
    gan, 267, 274, 282–83, 293 n.2. See
    also Pearl Harbor films
Pearl Harbor films, 9, 267–92; cold war
    themes in, 273–74; criticisms of 1980
    film, 268–75; female narration in 1992
    film, 285–86; 1980 and 1992 films
    compared, 278–87; objections to con-
    textualization of attack, 271, 276, 279–
    80, 289–90; personal experiences as
    storytelling device, 276–77; produc-
    tion of 1992 film, 275–78; responses

to 1992 film, 287, 289–90, 295 n.39;
    stills from, 280–87
Pearl Harbor survivors: and Arizona
    Memorial films, 275–78
Pearl Harbor Survivors Association, 276
Peery, Nelson, 365
People's Association for Korean Resi-
    dents in Indonesia, 209
People's Daily (newspaper), 62
People's Republic of China: cultural
    nationalism in, 309; economic growth
    in, 305; government protests against
    Japanese textbook revisions, 62; gov-
    ernment role in views of Nanjing Mas-
    sacre, 75–76; and Korean War, 301;
    mass killings cited by Japanese writ-
    ers, 60, 68, 83 n.72; nuclear weapons
    testing by, 312, 379; official narrative
    of Anti-Japanese Resistance War, 55;
    oppression in, 308; postwar treatment
    of Taiwanese soldiers, 191–92; and
    relations with Japan, 55–62, 67, 69,
    194, 299; and relations with U.S., 54;
    U.S. worries about, 310; views and
    memorialization of Nanjing Massacre,
    54–56, 69–76
Perez, Cecilia, 157
Perry, Ivory, 367
Personal experience: in Pearl Harbor nar-
    ratives, 276–77. See also Survivors;
    Veterans
Petersen, William, 252, 254–55
Philippines: anticolonial struggles, 351–
    52; commemorative activities, 231;
    U.S. conquest/annexation, 300, 305,
    351–52
Photography and photographs, 107–9;
    colonial, 110, 111; Hirohito at Disney-
    land, 138; Hirohito with MacArthur,
    139; Iwo Jima flag raising, 35–36, 40,
    48 n.3; of Japanese American intern-
    ment, 38, 240–41; and Japanese war
    photography, 118; of native women,
    110; Pacific Islanders in wartime pho-
    tographs, 112–13, 115–17, 119, 121;

Reid, Anthony, 8, 218–19, 222
Religion: Chamorro people, 177 n.12; shamanism among Korean comfort women, 404–5; shared religion of Pacific Islanders and Allied servicemen, 120. *See also* Aum Shinrikyō cult
"Remember Pearl Harbor!" slogan, 267, 274, 282–83, 293 n.2
Reparations: atomic bomb victims, 383–85, 388–93; Korean comfort women, 396–97; Korean ex-Japanese soldiers, 200, 212–16; Korean forced laborers, 388–91; Taiwanese ex-Japanese soldiers, 194–96, 213, 215
Representation: as basis of memory, 35; public, force of, 330
Representation technologies: influences on memory, 19–20. *See also* Images
Republic of Korea-Japan Basic Treaty, 213, 214, 383–84, 388, 393
Republican Party (South Korea), 385
Revisionism: in Japan, 23, 57–64, 66, 69, 299, 311, 334; pro-Japanese, outside Japan, 22, 270, 271
Rich, Adrienne, 400
Rika-chan doll, 138
Road to Nanjing (Honda), 64
Ro Chang-su, 388
Rogers, Robert F., 177 n.11, 179 n.56
Roosevelt, Franklin D., 36, 114, 241, 244, 262, 280, 355, 357
Ruff-O'Herne, Jan, 401–4, 408 n.14
Russia: Aum Shinrikyō ties with, 136. *See also* Soviet Union
Ryōjū, 392
Ryukyu, Kingdom of, 100. *See also* Okinawa

Sailor Moon (television series), 141–43
Sailor uniforms: in Japan, 141–42, 148
Saipan, photographs, 115
Sakahara, Toru, 368
Sakurauchi, Yoshio, 22–23
Salt Lake Tribune, 259

Sanchez, "Doc" Pedro C., 157, 175
San Diego Union Tribune, 337
Sands of Iwo Jima (film), 36, 40
San Francisco Peace Treaty, 12, 96, 200, 212, 214, 393
Sankei shinbun (newspaper), 64
Sansei: impacts of internment on, 42–43, 46–48. *See also* Japanese Americans; Japanese American soldiers
Santner, Eric L., 343 n.15
Santos, Angel, 169, 180 n.60
Sarin Incident, 22, 129, 130–31, 136–37, 149 n.2
Sati discourse, 399, 400
Sato Eisaku, 104
Sayonara (film), 371
Scarry, Elaine, 398
Schary, Dore, 247–48
Schnock, Frieder, 46–47
Schudson, Michael, 3
Schuyler, George, 361
Scott, Joan, 18
Seale, Bobby, 367
Seattle, 360, 363, 365, 368
Sekikawa Hideo, 145
Self-determination (*jiketsu*), 93; Chamorro efforts for political, 167, 168, 173–75, 179 n.56
Sensōron (Kobayashi), 23
Sexual access: and race, 369–72
Sexual assaults: by Japanese soldiers, 185; by U.S. military personnel, 13, 96, 129, 131
Sexuality: comfort women's ability to speak about, 403, 405
Sex workers: U.S. military bases, 399–400
Shamanism: among Korean comfort women, 404–5
Sherrod, Pearl, 354, 369
Sherwin, Martin, 336–37, 346n. 38
Shibutani, Tamotsu, 256
Shih, Shumei, 25
Shimonoseki, Treaty of, 131, 300–301
Shin Nihon Seitetsu, 391

Syonan Jinja memorial (Singapore), 220, 221

Tagore, Rabindranath, 303, 308
Taiwan, 14–15, 143; GMD government, 14, 182, 189–94; Japanese colonization, 181, 197, 300–301; kōinka educational system, 181, 183, 197; postcolonial trauma in, 196–98; postwar economic development, 305; postwar political developments, 189–93; postwar relations with Japan, 182, 194, 197, 214; views of Nanjing Massacre, 74; war crimes accusations against Japanese, 99
Taiwanese Anti-Japanese Army, 187
Taiwanese soldiers, in Japanese Imperial Army, 14, 181–96, 204; accounts of enlistment, 182–84; exclusion from benefits and reparations claims, 194–96, 213, 215; feelings about Japanese defeat/surrender, 187–89; and national identity, 189, 197; postwar membership in CCP, 193–94; postwar treatment of, 182, 190–92; as POW camp employees, 210; war crimes trials, 182, 209, 212; wartime experiences, 184–87
Tajiri, Rea, 18, 34, 37–38, 40, 42, 43, 46
Takahishi, Satokata (Naka Nakane), 354, 369
Takis, Ashima, 354–55, 356–57, 369
Tanaka Kakuei, 59
Tanaka Masaaki, 64–66, 83 n.65
Tani Hisao, 53
Teahouse of the August Moon, The (film), 371
Team Guam, 167–68
Television: Japanese animated programs, 141–43, 146–49; role in American conception of Vietnam War, 19
Templer, Gerald, 228, 229
Textbook revision debates, Japan, 23, 57, 61–64, 66, 69, 299, 334
Thailand, 209, 210
Thaxton, Ralph, 319–20

They Call Me Moses Masaoka (Masaoka), 255, 257–62
"Third World" coalitions, 368
Third World Resurgence, 308
Thirty Seconds over Tokyo (film), 36
Thomas, Norman, 361
Thompson, John B., 325
Timperley, H. J., 51–52, 60, 61
Tōge Sankichi, 387
Tōgō Shigenori, 210
Tōjō Hideki, 23, 200, 210, 363
Tokyo: U.S. gas attack plans, 130, 149 n.2
Tokyo Sarin Incident, 22, 129, 130–31, 136–37, 149 n.2
Tokyo War Tribunal, 200; Nanjing Massacre, 53, 57, 68, 73, 79 n.15, 340. See also War crimes trials
Toland, Gregg, 294 n.21
Tomiyama Taeko, 405
Tong, Nancy, 7, 339–41
Tonga, 9
Tourism: Hawai'i, 269, 271, 281; and international audiences for memorials, 22, 271, 288–89; Solomon Islands, 126; Vietnam, 22
Toyonaga Keisaburō, 24, 25, 378, 380–81
Transformation motifs: in Japanese popular culture, 142, 150 n.22
Transnational capitalism. See Global capitalism; Globalization
Transnational war/liberation narratives, 219, 223, 226
Treaty of Peace and Friendship, 62, 69
Tregaskis, Richard, 122
Trinidad, 362
Truman, Harry, 36, 90–91, 246–47, 262, 365
Truth Box, The (radio program), 52–53
Tule Lake internment camp, 256
Tungku Abdul Rahman, 223
24th Infantry Regiment (U.S. Army), 352, 358
Twenty-Fourth Year of B- and C-Class War Criminals, The (television program), 201

graphic portrayals of natives as, 114, 115, 116. *See also* Survivors

Victory in the Pacific (television program), 240

Viet Minh Central Committee, 301

Vietnam, 22, 301, 302

Vietnam Veterans Memorial, 46

Vietnam War, 12, 59, 95, 164, 176 n.1, 301–2; and anti-Asian sentiment in the U.S., 367; development of memorial sites in Vietnam, 22; opposition to, 349, 356, 367–68; television's role in, 19

Vouza, Jacob, 108, 122–26

Vouza and the Solomon Islands (MacQuarrie), 123

Wang Qinghuai, 183–84, 184–85, 192, 196

Wang Xiaobo, 192

War crimes trials, 200–201; abuse of Allied POWs, 209–13; Nanjing Massacre, 53, 56, 57, 68, 73, 79 n.15; Taiwanese and Korean soldiers, 182, 200–201, 209–13

War narratives, U.S., 303; images' impacts on, 35–36; Japanese American internment as disruption of, 47; Japanese American soldiers in, 239–47; mainstream version, 6–7, 47, 267; military service as defense of white male prerogatives, 370–71; modes of production, 291; Pearl Harbor, 290–91

War photography. *See* Photography and photographs

War of Resistance. *See* Anti-Japanese Resistance War

War simulation novels: Japanese, 22, 132–36, 145–46

Wartime romances, 159

War without Mercy (Dower), 311

Washington, Booker T., 353

Washington Post: on *Enola Gay* exhibit, 326–27, 336

Watanabe, Morio, 22

Watanabe Shōichi, 64

Waters, Frank, 318

Weber, Max, 253

Wednesday Rally, 401

Weglyn, Michi, 256

Weinberg, Gerhard, 3

Welfare Security Program (Japan), 390

"What if" novels: Japanese, 22, 132–36, 145–46

What War Means: Japanese Terror in China (Timperley), 51–52, 60, 61

White, Geoffrey, 223, 342 n.1

White, Walter, 361, 366

White supremacism, 367, 371; and colonialism in East Asia and elsewhere, 303–4, 353; and U.S. participation in the war, 349–50, 355. *See also* Racism

Wilkins, Roy, 361

Women: intersections of U.S. race and gender hierarchies, 368–72; native, in wartime photographs, 110; sexual assaults against, 13, 96, 129, 131, 185; U.S. government distribution of pin-up photos, 370–71; U.S. military sex workers, 399–400. *See also* Comfort women; Gender

Wong, Diana, 8

Won Pat, Antonio B., 167

World Trade Organization (WTO), 306

"World" war: local perspectives on, 3, 302–3, 311

World War I: redistribution of German colonies in the Pacific, 9–10

World War II 50th Anniversary Committee, 19–20, 291

World Wide Friends of Africa, 356

Wu Ziniu, 73

Xie Yong, 183, 193, 196

Xinhua Yuebao (periodical), 54

Yamamoto Isoroku, 207, 271, 272

Yamamoto Shichihei, 61

Yamashita Tomoyuki, 223, 228

☰ CONTRIBUTORS

CHEN YINGZHEN is a writer working in Taipei. He is the chief editor of the journal *Ren chian* (Human) and is a honorary member of the Chinese Academy of Social Sciences. His publications include *Chen Yingzhen xiaoshuoji* (Collected stories) and *Chen Yingzhen zuopinji* (Collected writings).

CHUNGMOO CHOI teaches cultural theories, anthropology, colonialism and postcoloniality, feminism of color, and Korean literature at the University of California, Irvine. She is the author of the forthcoming book *Frost in May: Decolonization and Culture in South Korea*, coeditor of *Dangerous Women: Gender and Korean Nationalism*, and editor of a special issue of *positions: east asia cultures critique* on *The Comfort Women: Colonialism, War, and Sex*.

VICENTE M. DIAZ is a Pohnpeian-Filipino born and raised on Guam and educated in Hawai'i and California. He is Associate Professor of Pacific History and Chair of the graduate program in Micronesian Studies at the University of Guam. He is the author of the forthcoming book *Repositioning the Missionary: History, Culture, Power, and Religion in Guam*.

ARIF DIRLIK is Professor of History at Duke University. His most recent publications include *The Postcolonial Aura: Third World Criticism in the Age of Global Capitalism; After the Revolution: Waking to Global Capitalism; What Is in a Rim? Critical Perspectives on the Pacific Region Idea;* and *Chinese on the American Frontier*.

T. FUJITANI teaches modern Japanese history at the University of California, San Diego. He is the author of *Splendid Monarchy: Power and Pageantry in Modern Japan* and articles dealing with historiography, nationalism, militarism, and colonialism.

ISHIHARA MASAIE teaches in the Sociology Department of Okinawa International University. He has published numerous collections of oral histories and interviews on Okinawan experiences, including of the war. He is centrally involved in various peace-related projects in Okinawa, such as planning a peace museum and international peace studies institute.

LAMONT LINDSTROM is Professor of Anthropology at the University of Tulsa. He is the author of *Knowledge and Power in a South Pacific Society* and editor of volumes on cultural policy, war ethnohistory, and traditional drug use in the Pacific.

GEORGE LIPSITZ teaches in the Department of Ethnic Studies at the University of California, San Diego. His recent works include *Dangerous Crossroads, Rainbow at Midnight, Sidewalks of St. Louis, Time Passages*, and *Possessive Investment of Whiteness*.

MARITA STURKEN teaches at the Annenberg School of Communication, University of Southern California. She is the author of *Tangled Memories: The Vietnam War, the AIDS Epidemic, and the Politics of Remembering*.

TOYONAGA KEISABURŌ is President of the Citizens Relief Council for Korean Atomic Bomb Victims (Kankoku no Genbaku Higaisha o Kyūen suru Shimin no Kai), Hiroshima Branch. He is also a member of the *hibakusha* storytelling association, Hiroshima o Kataru Kai.

UTSUMI AIKO teaches peace studies and the history of Japanese colonialism and militarism in Asia and the Pacific at Keisen University. She has been centrally involved in numerous postwar reparations movements and lawsuits. Some of her recent works include *Jawa/Orandajin shōnen yokuryūsho* (The Japanese military's internee camps for Dutch youth in Java during WWII) and *Taimen Tetsudō to Nihon no sensō sekinin* (The Thai-Burma railroad and Japan's war responsibility).

MORIO WATANABE teaches comparative cultures and political science at Kyushu International University. His recent publications include, "Seisaku kettei katei ni okeru gekiteki dōin: Beikoku taigai enjo hōan kettei katei no gensetsu bunseki" (Theatrical factors in the U.S. foreign aid policy decision-making processes: A discourse analysis) (*Kyōyō kenkyū*, 3, no. 3, March 1997) and " 'Dōbutsuen' no shōchō seijigakuteki shosō" (*Gendai Shisō* 24, no. 4, April 1996).

GEOFFREY M. WHITE is Professor of Anthropology at the University of Hawai'i and Senior Fellow at the East-West Center. His publications include *Identity through History: Living Stories in a Solomon Islands Society; Island Encounters: Black and White Memories of the Pacific War* (with Lamont Lindstrom); and *The Pacific Theater: Island Representations of World War II* (coedited with Lamont Lindstrom).

DIANA WONG is Associate Fellow, Institute of Malaysian and International Studies, National University of Malaysia. She is the author of *Peasants in the Making: Malaysia's Green Revolution* and coeditor of *War and Memory in Malaysia and Singapore*.

DAQING YANG teaches modern Japanese history at George Washington University. He is completing a book on telecommunications networks and Japanese empire building in the early twentieth century and has written several articles on the Nanjing Massacre.

LISA YONEYAMA teaches cultural studies and Japanese studies at the University of California, San Diego. She is the author of *Hiroshima Traces: Time, Space, and the Dialectics of Memory* and has published articles on multiculturalism, minority writings, and cultural studies.

Library of Congress Cataloging-in-Publication Data

Perilous memories : the Asia-Pacific War(s) / edited by T. Fujitani, Geoffrey M. White, Lisa Yoneyama.

p. cm.

Includes bibliographical references and indexes.

ISBN 0-8223-2532-2 (cloth : alk. paper) — ISBN 0-8223-2564-0 (paper : alk. paper)

1. Sino-Japanese Conflict, 1937–1945. 2. Sino-Japanese Conflict, 1937–1945—Personal narratives. 3. World War, 1939–1945. 4. World War, 1939–1945—Personal narratives. I. Fujitani, Takashi. II. White, Geoffrey M. (Geoffrey Miles). III. Yoneyama, Lisa.

DS777.53 P44 2001

940.53—dc21   2001-027441